The Study of
International Relations

THE CENTURY
POLITICAL SCIENCE SERIES
Edited by FREDERIC A. OGG

The Study of International Relations

Quincy Wright

UNIVERSITY OF CHICAGO

New York: APPLETON-CENTURY-CROFTS, Inc.

To

L. L. W.

PREFACE

SINCE WORLD WAR I there has been an increasing number of college courses offered in "International Relations," and many textbooks have appeared under that name. Many universities have instituted committees or departments which recommend for degrees in the field, and several professorships in international relations have been established. A number of writers have undertaken to analyze academic offerings in this field in the United States, Great Britain, and elsewhere; and conferences have discussed the teaching of international relations, the scope and methods of the subject, and the appropriate courses for undergraduates, graduates, and professionals in the field. There have been learned societies and journals devoted to international relations and the world is spending over one hundred million dollars a year in supporting official organizations whose purpose is to regulate or improve international relations.

With all this activity there might seem to be little doubt that international relations exists. Yet there is some doubt on this point or, at least, on the sense in which it exists.

Since 1931 the University of Chicago has had an interdepartmental committee which organizes curricula for students in international relations and recommends for the master's and doctor's degree. It has recognized a number of sub-fields, relevant to international relations, from which candidates select four for examinations and one for specialization. These include general fields such as International Law and Organization, Diplomacy and Diplomatic History, International Economics, Psychology of International Relations, Political Geography, Communications and Colonial Policy, and regional fields such as North America, Latin America, Europe, British Commonwealth, Slavic countries, Middle East, South Asia, and Far East. The courses in these fields are given under the auspices of various Departments of the University—Political Science, Economics, History, Geography, Sociology, Psychology, and Anthropology—and the Committee on International Relations has included members of most of these Departments.

From time to time students have complained that while the courses recommended usually had more or less relevance to what might be called international relations, they were not quite sure what that subject was. It seemed to branch out in various directions and the ends of the branches often seemed quite unrelated to one another. Furthermore, the courses seemed, sometimes, to rest upon different assumptions and to reach divergent conclusions, leaving the student in confusion. To obviate this difficulty, the Committee employed two devices. First, it instituted a "core-field," including courses in international law, international politics, international economics, American diplomacy, and world resources, which all students were expected to take and which, it was hoped, would indicate the heart of international relations and provide a common background for all who did advanced work in the field. Second, it established an advanced course in the "Study of International Relations" that would attempt a further integration of the field of international relations among students who had done more or less specialized work in several of the sub-fields into which international relations is divided.

I have given this course since 1947 and the present volume includes its subject matter. It continues an analysis of the disciplines relevant to international relations set forth in my *Study of War* (1942) and was assisted by the enterprise of the New York Council on Foreign Relations in bringing together regional conferences of teachers of international relations in 1946. These conferences threw light upon the actual state of academic instruction in the field at that time as well as the evaluation of the relevant courses by those giving them. The results of these discussions were brought together by Professor, now President, Grayson Kirk of Columbia University in a small volume entitled *The Study of International Relations in American Colleges and Universities.*

Even earlier the series of meetings of teachers of International law and related subjects sponsored by the Carnegie Endowment for International Peace dealt with the study of international relations, and the Institute of Intellectual Co-operation under the League of Nations in 1930, sponsored a continuing International Studies Conference, which stimulated Sir Alfred Zimmern, S. H. Bailey, James T. Shotwell, and others to explore the scope and methods of the study of international relations. The International Studies Conference of 1938 at Prague dealt particularly with the study and teaching of international relations and the results were reported in a volume edited by Sir Alfred Zimmern. UNESCO continued the work of the International Institute of Intellectual Co-operation and the International Studies Conference. The latter organization had a meeting at Windsor in 1950 on the University Teaching of International Relations, the results of which were reported in a volume edited by Geoffrey L. Goodwin. UNESCO has developed other projects for improving and stimulating academic study of the United Nations and international relations generally. Its Conference on the Teaching of the Social Sciences in September, 1952, brought forth a valuable study by C. A. Manning on the teaching of international relations.

I have received considerable inspiration from the series of volumes resulting from the Conferences on Science, Philosophy, and Religion, held at Columbia every year. Men from widely separated disciplines have here conferred on basic problems of international relations, illustrating the diversity of approaches and the difficulty of devising a common meeting ground. I have also profited greatly from discussion with colleagues at the University of Chicago and from the comments of students in my courses. I particularly value the comments of Professor Frederick S. Dunn of the Center of International Studies, at Princeton University, who read the entire manuscript.

These discussions have made me aware of the danger that I will be misunderstood in the effort to analyze the large and controversial field of international relations by using terms which are laden with popular connotations. This is particularly true of the terms *history, art, science,* and *philosophy.* Each of these terms has many meanings, but I have attempted to use them consistently as I have defined them. My usage of the term *international politics* has also been criticized. Some would prefer to use it to include the whole of "international relations," and to subordinate this field to that of "political science." While it is true that in American colleges and universities political science departments usually provide much of the instruction bearing upon international problems, yet it is also true that the co-operation of other social science departments—economics, sociology, anthropology, psychology, geography and history—has been found necessary as the study of international relations has developed. This suggests that if the term *international politics* were used in the comprehensive sense it would be necessary to find another term to distinguish those aspects of the subject dealt with in political science departments. Furthermore, it seems to me that both popular and scholarly usage justifies the more restricted meaning of the term *international politics.*

International relations is today a discipline in process of formation. The subject with which this developing discipline deals is in process of rapid change. Wise judgment upon the direction and rapidity of that change and upon the relative importance of the factors involved may be assisted by development of the discipline. By education in such a discipline the public may be guided to a clearer understanding of the complexities of the situation, to a more mature comprehension of the purposes of over simplified interpretations continually offered, and to a capacity to choose the better values. The leaders may be assisted in their task of perceiving possible alternatives of action in a given situation and of committing themselves to that alternative most likely to realize those values.

Whether viewed as a discipline or as a condition, international relations needs thought and ordering in the atomic age. It is hoped that this volume may contribute to that end.

QUINCY WRIGHT

University of Chicago

CONTENTS

PART IV

THEORETICAL ANALYSES OF INTERNATIONAL RELATIONS

PART V

TOWARD A UNIFIED DISCIPLINE OF INTERNATIONAL RELATIONS

PART
I

The Meaning of
International Relations

CHAPTER
1

The Meaning of
International Relations

THE WORD *international* appears to have been first used by Jeremy
Bentham (2) in the latter part of the eighteenth century, although its
Latin equivalent *intergentes* was used by Richard Zouche (12) a century
earlier. These men used the word to define the branch of law which had
been called the law of nations or *jus gentium,* a term of Roman law referring to the principles applied by a Roman official—the *praetor pere-
grinus*—in cases involving aliens. The concept, therefore, was that of a
universal law applicable to persons irrespective of nationality, discovered,
however, by observing similarities of practice rather than by reasoning
from generally accepted principles, as was the case with the *jus naturale*
or natural law. As the concept of sovereignty developed in the sixteenth
century and came to be applied to geographically defined societies known
as nations in the seventeenth century, it was seen that the Roman law
concept of *jus gentium* did not adequately express the developing law
between sovereign nations. Consequently, the term *international* served
a genuine need in defining the official relations between sovereigns. Perhaps the word *interstate* would have been more accurate because in
political science the state came to be the term applied to such societies.

There were relations between nations other than official, legal, and
diplomatic relations. Trade and finance developed international economic
relations sometimes official and sometimes unofficial. Activities of missionaries; travel of students, teachers, and tourists; migrations of peoples;
and the development of the press, radio, and films developed international
cultural relations mostly unofficial, but sometimes supervised or even con-

3

ducted by governments. Private and public organizations representing groups within, or governments of, many nations were formed, especially since the mid-nineteenth century. Their activities in all aspects of human interest—communication, transportation, commerce, finance, agriculture, labor, health, sports, science, philosophy, education, arbitration, disarmament, peace—established innumerable international social relations and gave birth to the word *internationalism* to suggest both the fact of the increase of international relations of all kinds and the interest of many people in such an increase. The word *internationalism* has been preferred by modern writers because, without denying the existence and autonomy of nations, it recognizes them as parts of a larger whole. It excludes both the excessive standardization and integration of mankind implied by the words *imperialism* and *cosmopolitanism* and the militant insistence upon sovereignty implied by the words *nationalism* and *isolationism* (3, 7, 9, 11).

The development of internationalism, however, gives rise to two questions: (1) Is it only the nations that are related? (2) Is there a universal community of which numerous groups or even individuals are members?

The words *nation, state, government,* and *people* are sometimes used interchangeably, but each has a distinct connotation. The word *nation* suggests a considerable group of people, united by common culture, values, standards, and political aspirations, usually occupying a definite territory, but not always, as witness the Jewish nation during the Diaspora, and usually enjoying legal sovereignty, but not always, as witness the Scotch nation within Great Britain or the Bohemian nation within the Habsburg Empire.

The word *state* has a legal flavor. It is a term of art in political science referring to political groups that enjoy legal sovereignty, but it is also commonly applied to nonsovereign political groups as the states of the United States or the states of India before independence. A state in the modern sense implies a population occupying a definite territory, subject to a government which other states recognize as having some legal status. The population may be a nation, but not necessarily so, as in the case of such multinational states as the Habsburg, British, and Russian Empires before World War I.

The word *government* refers to the organization which makes and enforces the law of the state, decides and carries out its policy, and conducts its official relations. In absolutisms, the government and the state merge in one man, but in democracies, the state is the entire people legally organized while the government is only that small portion of the people for the time being constituting and operating its organization.

The word *people* has biological and geographical implications with cultural and social overtones making it similar to the word *nation,* but without the element of self-consciousness. Anthropologists use the word *people* as a term of art to designate primitive groups that exhibit a considerable degree of biological, cultural, and often linguistic uniformity and occupy a defined territory even though not politically or socially organized as a group. Use of the word *people* suggests some type of similarity—racial, geographic, cultural, linguistic, political, or social—among the individuals who compose it, but without definite specification of a particular type of similarity. The United States Constitution was said to have been made by "we the people of the United States" while the United Nations Charter was said to have been made by "we the peoples of the United Nations," thus suggesting that it was easier to think of all the individuals of the United States as a "people" than to think of all the individuals of the world as a single "people." There was, however, a vigorous debate during the San Francisco Conference in which some urged that the word *people* be used in the singular in the Preamble of the Charter.

It is clear that international relations is intended to include not only relations between nations, but also relations between states, governments, and peoples. It does, however, ordinarily refer only to relations between nations, states, governments, and peoples which are *sovereign*. That term, however, presents new difficulties. The word is not static. There are entities like Massachusetts, Geneva, Bavaria, Hyderabad, the six nations of the Iroquois, Tunis, Algeria, and Scotland, which once were, but are no longer, entirely sovereign. And there are entities like Israel, Egypt, Ukraine, Iceland, Ireland, Pakistan, Jordan, Burma, Philippine Islands, Canada, Indochina, and Korea, which have recently become, or are in process of becoming sovereign, or have certain aspects of sovereignty. Clearly international relations includes relations between many entities of uncertain sovereignty. As a subject of study it is not limited by the legal formalism which alone could at any moment precisely define what entities are sovereign and what are not.

It may be suggested that international relations, even if it abandoned the qualification of *sovereign* for the entities which it relates, must insist on the qualifications *political* and *territorial*. It is said to be concerned only with the relations among *political* communities occupying definite *territories*. The relations of Virginia and Pennsylvania may be international relations (certainly they were during the Battle of Gettysburg), but the relations of the United Mine Workers of America and coal mining companies seem not to be, even though both are large groups exercising considerable power imperfectly controlled by the laws of the United States to which both are nominally subject. But doubt arises whether even this limitation is always applicable. The United Nations makes agreements with the Specialized Agencies. The International Labor Organization has dealt with the World Federation of Trade Unions. UNESCO deals with numerous international, cultural, educational, and scientific organizations which are unofficial. Many *nongovernmental organizations* have a recognized status in relation to the United Nations. To the sociologist the difference between the co-operation, competition, bargaining, and fighting of industrial groups is in the same class as the co-operation, competition, bargaining, and fighting of states (4). Thus, for purposes of scientific treatment, it seems that international relations includes the relations of all groups exercising some degree of independent power or initiative. While it may be that the central interest in international relations today is the relation between sovereign nations, in the Middle Ages the central interest was in the relations of Pope and Emperor and in antiquity in the relations between cities.

Of the future one speaks with diffidence. Relations between great regions—the Atlantic community, the Soviet bloc, the Commonwealth—each composed of many nations, many states, many governments, and many peoples may be important. Perhaps the relations between universal parties—Communists, Democrats, Catholics, Moslems, Zionists—will be of increasing importance, or relations between universal organizations of labor, of agriculture, and of commerce. As once, in the United States, relations of North, South, and West were of major significance, so today relations of agriculture, labor, and capital are of equal or of greater importance. It has been said that the growth of national parties crossing sectional lines and the development of rivalries among them, superseding in importance sectional rivalries, accounts for the survival of the United States (8).

We must, therefore, answer our first question negatively. It is not only the nations which *international relations* seeks to relate. Varied types of groups—nations, states, governments, peoples, regions, alliances, confederations, international organizations, even industrial organizations, cultural organizations, religious organizations—must be dealt with in the study of international relations, if the treatment is to be realistic.

With this wide concept of the subject, we come to our second question. Should not our subject be renamed *world affairs*, or perhaps *cosmopolitanism*, with such divisions as *world economy*, *world politics*, *world culture*, *world organization*, and *world law*? Is not the subject matter of *international relations* really the history, organization, law, economy, culture, and processes of the world community? Should we not conceive of the human race as a community which, while divided into numerous geographic, functional, cultural, racial, political, economic, and other subgroups, is becoming integrated into a society with the progress of technology and the growth of population bringing the members of all subgroups into closer and closer contact with one another?

The adjective *world* certainly rivals the adjective *international* in textbooks and treatises on the subject. It suffers, however, from the objection that there are *international relations* which are not *world relations* as for instance Anglo-American relations, Latin American relations, relations among the Arab countries, and so forth. Until recently *international rela-*

tions generally concerned diplomatic or military relations between two states. The word *world* also fails to indicate the dominant problems dealt with in the subject, that is, the relations between the major groups. The phenomena of national, regional, functional, and political groups in rivalry with one another is likely to dominate the life of mankind even if the world shrinks much more than it has today, and even if the national sovereign state becomes less important. The divergencies of interest and policy inherent in climatic and geographical differences, varied resources, differences of culture and political tradition, assure that mankind will not in any foreseeable future be reduced to a uniform mass.

Cosmopolitanism, envisaged as an ideal by the Stoics of Rome and the Deists of the Enlightenment, failed to take adequate account of the factors making for a differentiation of mankind into groups with different objectives and often in opposition to one another. For this reason, as has been noted, modern writers like Jeremy Bentham, Nicholas Murray Butler, Sir Alfred Zimmern, and Inazo Nitobe have preferred the word *international*.

While recognizing that the term *international relations* is too narrow—perhaps *relations between powerful groups* would be technically better—it seems advisable to accept predominant usage. The term *international relations* will therefore be used as the subject of study, dividing it into such special studies as *international politics, international law, international organization, international economics, international education, international ethics,* and the *psychology and sociology of international relations*. The term will, however, also be used to include such studies as world history, political geography, political demography and technology which have a *world* rather than an *international* orientation. These studies are clearly fundamental to the understanding of *international relations*.

Before leaving the subject of terminology, reference should be made to the frequent use of the adjective *foreign* in preference to either *world* or *international* relations. Foreign relations, foreign affairs, foreign policy, foreign trade, are words of common discourse. Clearly the adjective *foreign* implies the point of view of one nation and thus is hardly suitable for use in a discipline or study designed to be of universal validity and understanding. The use of the word, however, raises the question whether a discipline of *international relations* is possible. It has been suggested that the conditions, material and ideological, of each nation are so peculiar that the *foreign relations* of each country must be studied as a unique discipline. As the American lawyer studies American law and can learn little useful to his professional activity from the study of French or Japanese law, so it is said that the American statesman or citizen should confine his study to *American foreign relations*. However, there are general disciplines of *jurisprudence, comparative law,* and *sociology of law,* useful to lawyers of all countries. The thesis is accepted in this book, as it has been in general practice, that general disciplines exist in the field of *international relations* (1, 5, 6, 10). These disciplines have proved useful to statesmen and citizens of all countries and their synthesis is at least conceivable.

We will, therefore, accept the term *international relations* to designate the relations between groups of major importance in the life of the world at any period of history, and particularly relations among territorially organized nation states which today are of such importance. We will also use the term to designate the studies or disciplines describing, explaining, evaluating, or assisting in the conduct of those relations.

REFERENCES

1. BAILEY, S. H., *International Studies in Modern Education* (London, Oxford University Press, 1938).
2. BENTHAM, Jeremy, *Introduction to the Principles of Morals and Legislation* (London, 1789).
3. BUTLER, Nicholas Murray, *The International Mind* (New York, Scribner, 1913).
4. JACKSON, Elmore, *Meeting of Minds, A Way to Peace Through Mediation* (New York, McGraw-Hill, 1952).
5. KIRK, Grayson, *The Study of International Relations* (New York, Council on Foreign Relations, 1947).
6. MANNING, C. A. W., *The University Teaching of Social Sciences: International Relations* (Paris, UNESCO, 1954).
7. NITOBE, Inazo, "Development of International Co-operation," *Lectures on Japan* (Chicago, University of Chicago Press, 1938).
8. TURNER, Frederick Jackson, "American Sectionalism and World Organization," *American Historical Review*, Vol. 48 (April, 1942), pp. 545 ff.
9. WRIGHT, Quincy, "Specialization and Universal Values in General International Organization," in *Approaches to Group Understanding*, Sixth Symposium on Science, Philosophy, and Religion (New York, Harper, 1946), Ch. 20.
10. ZIMMERN, Sir Alfred, ed., *University Teaching of International Relations*, Eleventh International Studies Conference (Paris, International Institute of Intellectual Co-operation, 1939).
11. ———, "The Development of the International Mind," *Problems of Peace* (London, Geneva Institute of International Studies, 1925), Lecture 1.
12. ZOUCHE, Richard, *An Exposition of Fecial Law and Procedure, or of Law Between Nations, and Questions Concerning the Same* (1650), trans. by J. L. Brierly (Washington, Carnegie Institution, 1911).

CHAPTER
2

International Relations
as a Condition

INTERNATIONAL RELATIONS refers both to the facts of international life and to the exposition of those facts. Similarly, history is used to refer to what actually happened and to what Herodotus, Thucydides, or Ranke wrote about those happenings. In one sense it is said that George Washington made history; in the other sense that Francis Parkman wrote history. The same ambiguity exists in most terms of social science. International relations as a fact or condition is a phase of *reality*. As an exposition or description it ought to be a phase of *truth* (9).

In the field of international relations, as indeed in other fields of politics and social action, the words *reality* and *truth* are often used as terms of propaganda rather than of exposition. Inferences drawn from certain scandalous incidents or unflattering assumptions about human nature are said to be the *truth* about some phase of international relations because the speaker wants to influence the listener's opinion. A pessimistic or skeptical point of view is said to be *realistic* because the speaker wants to emphasize its importance or to protect himself against the charge of wishful thinking. In this sense realism has been contrasted with idealism especially in the international field (10).

Plato and the medieval *realists* applied the word *reality* to abstract forms, ideas or universals, while the concrete things one saw or felt were only shadows in the cave or imperfect approximations of *reality*. The *real* circle was the perfect circle as geometrically defined but never completely *realized* by any circle one might observe. God, the creator of all things and values, was the ultimate *reality*, while man and the world

9

were mere *creatures,* which imperfectly *realized* his will. The medieval *nominalists* and seventeenth-century scientists on the other hand applied the word *reality* to concrete observations, and considered universals merely names for classes or groups. To them the maple tree in the front yard was a *real* tree while the idea of a tree was simply the name for a convenient classification bringing together things that resemble one another in some way. To them Tom, Dick, and Harry were *real* while a group or society or nation composed of numerous individuals was merely an idea or ideal which might be more or less *realized* in the behavior of these individuals (7). In this sense some modern *realists* in the field of international relations discount the traditional formalisms of state sovereignty and international law, and direct attention to the actual processes of decision-making and policy-making in particular governments (2).

Descartes, Berkeley, and the modern *idealists,* like the medieval mystics, considered introspection the road to reality. What I think or feel or otherwise experience I know more certainly than anything else. The external universe may be merely an hallucination, a projection of my thoughts and feelings, and wishes. I can never know whether it *really* exists. On the other hand, Francis Bacon took a "common sense" view of reality. He assumed that it was what sensory experience disclosed when freed from the distorting influence of prejudice and desire, the idols of the cave, theatre, market place, and tribe. Reality to him was what exists apart from any observer or manipulator (1). Like the Platonists he regarded reality as outside the observer, but unlike them he thought it concrete rather than abstract, to be discovered by sensory experience rather than by conceptual reasoning. Kant and later critics have, however, insisted that even sensory experience is selective and classificatory. The *ding an sich* escapes both sensory observation and conceptual analysis (4).

Hegel tried to transcend the skepticism of Kant's analysis by identifying reality with the historical process of continuous building and becoming, a conception developed in the activism of Nietzsche and Bergson, harking back to the Heracleitian emphasis upon change and motion as the only reality, in contrast to the insistence by Parmenides and the Eleatics that only permanence and rest are real (7).

In the political field, guidance of action by Machiavellian self-oriented expediency has been called *realistic* as has its opposite. Grotius thought it realistic to act in accord with principles of reason flowing from the nature of the international society (5, 10).

Since the word *reality* has been employed to designate both the most abstract and the most concrete, the most subjective and the most objective, the most active and the most passive, the most self-interested and the most disinterested, it conveys little information to designate something as *real* unless the speaker's philosophy is known.

I will begin by using the word, as I believe it is commonly used by modern scientists, to designate existence in time and space apart from any observer, assuming without argument that time and space are characteristics of a world which exists apart from any observer. In this sense, reality can for purposes of social studies be conveniently divided into four classes: (1) the actual, what is or was, (2) the probable, what may be or is likely to be, (3) the possible, what can be, and (4) the desirable, what should be. The first three of these classes of reality are clear enough. They constitute the kinds of reality which it is respectively the object of the historian, the scientist, and the practitioner to discover. They occupy respectively the realms of certainty, of probability, and of possibility. They were respectively recognized by the philosopher Charles Sanders Peirce as "actual facts," "the rule to which future events have a tendency to conform" and "positive, qualitative possibilities" (6). It should be observed, however, that the modern tendency is to treat reality relativistically and to beware of dogmatism, especially about the future, a tendency illustrated by Peirce's use of the word *tendency* in dealing with the future. Even in regard to the past and present, while it would usually be agreed that certain events either occurred or did not occur at a designated time and place, the historian or judge will be careful to note that our capacity to say so is relative to the available evidence and the evidence seldom does more than establish the fact "beyond reasonable doubt." In regard to the future, modern science hesitates to accept the theory of determinism. There is uncertainty, resulting not only from the scientist's ignorance, but also, in all probability, from the nature of the universe. The best verified scientific generalization depends either on the statistical stability of large numbers or on the organizational stability of complex equilibria and must be qualified by a margin of probable error because the numbers dealt with are finite or the equilibria involved are subject to contingencies (8). Science can only state probabilities or tendencies, but what will probably be or what tends to be, are forms of reality.

In regard to possibilities, contingency is of the essence. The artist, practitioner, inventor, and statesman seek to create possibilities of being or becoming beyond the competence of science to predict. What is possible under conditions which may arise is, however, a form of reality even though those conditions have never occurred in the past and application of scientific method discloses that their probability in the future is slight. The field of the possible includes the exploration of values (what should be) and demands (what shall be), some of which may be on the edge of the impossible, as well as the creation or invention of new values, and of conditions and combinations to realize them (9).

In the field of human affairs, where the numbers dealt with are small and the contingencies involved in organizational equilibria are great, scientific method operates with large margins of error, but possibilities discovered by creative imagination are an especially important aspect of reality. The exposition of such possibilities may operate on human minds, and may thus influence their own *realization* (9).

What ought to be is often characterized as the *ideal*, antithetic to *what is* characterized as the *real*. Even jurists characterize the law as what is and criticize amateurs who assume that the law is what ought to be. However, in social affairs, the desirable cannot be altogether excluded from reality. In fact jural law, at least in a democratic society, may be defined as the effort of the society to make what, in public opinion, ought to be, into what is, through the application of legal sanctions. While the law exists apart from the ethical opinion of any one individual, it does usually incorporate in its rules, principles, and standards, the ethical opinions generally accepted in the community, and also, in proportion as its sanctions are effective, it describes actual behavior within the society. Furthermore, as Durkheim has pointed out, some acceptance of a value system and some attribution of values by a culture give an objective reality to values in the sense that they function in the society (3).

What should be is the form of reality most frequently in the consciousness of the philosopher. He is aware that man is not an automaton but a creator, realizing his aims, purposes, intentions, aspirations, ideals, in short converting what *really* ought to be into what *really* is. He is concerned with the validity of ends and goals in the sense of their logical consistency, their desirability and their realizability. Philosophic reality unites the desirable with the feasible, what ought to be with what can be. Behind him stand the historian, warning him that some of his purposes have never been realized, and the scientist warning him that some are highly improbable, but in front of him stands the creator, the reformer, and the saint telling him that the law can be passed; the business can succeed; the airplane can fly; the war can be won; the candidate can be elected; the patient can be cured; the world can be stabilized; the good, the true, and the beautiful can be realized. Philosophic conclusions establishing the logical consistency of preferred values with one another and with what is known about nature and human nature cannot be denied the title of *reality*.

Reality therefore emerges from the abstract as well as the concrete, from the subjective as well as from the objective, from invention as well as from understanding, from desire as well as from observation. It is a phenomenon of mind as well as of matter and is certain to be distorted by confinement to any particular theory.

These forms of reality are not distinct. They merge into one another in thought as well as in action. I was once thinking about these relations as I walked through a Vermont woodland where abandoned roads could be traced around ledges and hillocks until they disappeared in a mass of brambles only to emerge again in a cluster of maples or at a crossroad.

I thought how the pioneers considered the various possible paths to a sugar bush, a cleared pasture, or a connecting highway, directed by the inexorable conditions of contour, ledge, and ravine. Having chosen the general direction and appraised the possibilities, they applied axe and saw to clear the path, thus increasing the probability that subsequent wayfarers would traverse the same path. A surveyor plotting the area could predict where traffic would probably move. Thus the goals of philosophy become the probabilities of science through the decisions and actions of the practitioners, and the historians, following after, could explain how it happened to be what it became, recreating each step as seen by the people at the time. The process is continuous.

Surveys permit a new generation to discern other exploitable resources and other possible routes. Some much-travelled roads are abandoned in favor of others as engineers expand the realm of the possible by the use of blasting equipment and bulldozers. The probable course of travel then becomes very different from what it was.

The mind functioning in the brain with its complex of paths of nervous energy is like the pioneer in the forest. Philosophies and religions establish goals of thought relating desire and experience. Possible paths to these goals are discovered, marked, and cleared by the collation of evidence, the repetition of rituals, and the organization of ideas, thus becoming the most probable routes of human thought. Dogmatic systems seek to preserve them by censorship but invention and exploration is difficult to prevent, particularly when advancing practice and science have created new possibilities. What is now possible, becomes what is desirable, that becomes increasingly probable, and eventually what actually is, and then what was, as new possibilities emerge.

In society the arts of technology, education, politics, and poetry continually broaden the realm of the possible, permit the philosophers to explore new values, and require the social scientists to redefine the realm of the probable, while the historians, with new evidence and new modes of interpretation are continually able to recreate the past more accurately showing just how the artists, philosophers, and scientists thought and behaved, and why they thought and acted as they did.

What is the reality of international relations? According to many writers it is *power politics*. States exist, they wish to continue to exist, and they can rely only upon power to avoid conquest by their neighbors. Consequently, the struggle of each to be more powerful in itself or with its allies than any probable enemy or any combination of enemies is the heart of the matter. Policies may have special aspects but fundamentally the struggle for power as the requisite for continued existence is the policy to be expected of states as well as the policy which they have been observed to follow in the past.

The importance of this interpretation as a generalized description of the situation of the present and of the past few centuries cannot be denied, but what of the future?

Social scientists analyze the changing conditions of the world. They observe inventions and new technologies shrinking the world in respect to the speed and abundance of communication and the vulnerability of peoples to sudden attack and possible elimination. They observe populations increasing in size and mobility and ideas creating new aspirations and revolutionary dissatisfactions. They observe processes of decision-making seeking to adopt action to these conditions, and resulting in changes—social, political, and economic—proceeding more rapidly than ever before. Viewing long spans of history during which systems of power politics have risen and disappeared in past civilizations, they suggest trends and probabilities that may alter the basis of international relations in the future.

Political and social philosophers envisage even wider horizons. Arguing from fundamental human needs and desires, aware of the great variety of human organizations and relations developed among primitive and historic peoples, conversant with the influence which reason can have upon custom, they suggest new forms of international or world organization and new ways of conducting international relations to realize higher values.

In the meantime, the diplomats, the legislators, and the executives of national governments; the officials of the United Nations; and the citizens of the great and small nations on both sides of the iron curtain, somewhat influenced by a few persons who consider themselves citizens of the world, are each devising laws and pursuing or supporting policies asserted to lead to a world different from that which led to two world wars. Unfortunately these visions of the future world often differ from one another. Many axemen are cutting paths through the forest in different directions. Some may be possible, some may lead to impossible cliffs, and some may emerge on unwanted marshes. The trees felled to clear one may block another and all cannot be traversed at the same time. It is difficult to say which will probably be most travelled, especially when some of the axes are directed, not toward the trees, but toward other woodsmen. The disparity between efforts to realize what ought to be and to defend what is in a world of power politics underlines the difficulty of describing the *reality* of international relations. Each of the disciplines with which we will be concerned describes it somewhat differently.

REFERENCES

1. CONANT, James B., *Science and Common Sense* (New Haven, Yale University Press, 1951).
2. DUNN, Frederick S., "The Present Course of International Relations Research," *World Politics,* Vol. 5 (October, 1949), pp. 80 ff.

3. DURKHEIM, Emile, *Elementary Forms of the Religious Life* (London, Allen and Unwin, 1915).

4. HAYEK, F. A., *The Sensory Order* (Chicago, University of Chicago Press, 1952).

5. HERZ, John H., *Political Realism and Political Idealism, A Study in Theories and Realities* (Chicago, University of Chicago Press, 1951).

6. PEIRCE, Charles Sanders, *Collected Papers* (Cambridge, Harvard University Press, 1931), Vol. 1, paragraphs 23 ff.

7. RUSSELL, Bertrand, *A History of Western Philosophy* (New York, Simon and Schuster, 1945).

8. SCHROEDINGER, Erwin, *What Is Life?* (Cambridge, Cambridge University Press, 1946).

9. WRIGHT, Quincy, *A Study of War* (Chicago, University of Chicago Press, 1942), Chs. 3, 16, 38, Appds. 25.

10. ———, "Realism and Idealism in International Politics," *World Politics*, Vol. 5 (October, 1952), pp. 116 ff.

CHAPTER
3

International Relations
as a Discipline

As A DISCIPLINE, expounded in classrooms, written in textbooks, or developed in learned journals, dissertations, monographs, and treatises, international relations should tell the truth about the subject.

The word *truth* is obviously no less ambiguous than the word *reality*. The theologian's conception of what it takes to prove a proposition true obviously differs from that of the scientist. The truths which the business man or politician accept as guides for action differ from either, and the truth which the closeted historian seeks to wrest from ancient documents or the harassed juryman seeks to discover by disentangling evidence from the rhetoric presented at a trial are again something different.

I will assume that truth is a body of propositions or a combination of symbols which express reality. Since there are several types of reality there are also several types of truth. Semanticists have usefully classified propositions as informative, evaluative, incitive, and formulative (9). Informative propositions are intended to establish the occurrence or characteristics of something and they may be more or less *convincing*. They deal with the actual and figure especially in history and science. Evaluative propositions are intended to convey the attitude or opinion of the speaker or writer and they may do so more or less *effectively*. They deal with the desirable and figure in philosophy and literature. Incitive propositions are intended to influence the behavior of the listener or reader and they may be more or less *persuasive*. They deal with the possible and figure in religious, political, and business propaganda. Formulative propositions are intended to relate ideas or concepts to one another and they

16

may do so more or less *correctly*. They deal with the probable and figure especially in logical and mathematical treatments of science and philosophy (7, 11). This classification suggests that if the truth of a proposition is equated to its adequacy in fulfilling its intention, there are several varieties of truth and that each variety of truth is relative rather than absolute. One does not say that a proposition is true or false, but that it is more or less true, more or less adequate to its purpose (2a).

If one agrees that the qualities in a statement of being convincing, of being effective, of being persuasive, and of being correct are all forms of being true, one has to admit that there are different kinds of truth. A propaganda statement may be judged untrue because it does not convince the reader of its accuracy in reporting facts. Yet it may be true in the sense that it persuades the persons to whom it is addressed to do what the speaker wanted them to, whether to buy a new brand of breakfast food, to sign a contract, or to vote for a favored candidate. A philosophical system or a work of art may be effective in communicating to the reader or observer the values or the state of mind intended. Yet the premises of the philosophical system may be unprovable and the work of art may not represent anything that ever did or could exist.

These different types of truth vary in their degree of certainty. Formulating statements may often be designated without dissent among experts as correct or incorrect, either logically, or grammatically, and logicians usually reserve the term *true* for correct statements (7), often identifying convincing, persuasive, and effective statements, not with the true, but with the real, the good, and the beautiful. It is often difficult to obtain unanimity in designating informative statements as convincing or unconvincing (2). These two types of truth are, however, more susceptible of treatment as absolutes, than are evaluative or incitive statements. Scientists and historians often refuse to apply the true-false category to the latter types of statement and common usage tends to support them though the standard dictionary defines truth as "conformity to fact, standard, ideal, duty, profession, and so forth." This definition indicates that in the fields of religion, philosophy, and practical affairs, truth often refers to the effectiveness or persuasiveness of propositions. In this sense, truth is obviously relative. A philosophic or religious *truth* accepted by one person will not be accepted by another. A political *truth* which induces action from some will leave others cold or even hostile.

Recognition of the objective relativity of truth is not incompatible with recognition of a practical expediency in social life of treating certain propositions "as if" absolutely true (12). Commitment by every member of a group to the absolute truth of certain propositions may be the best means for assuring the satisfaction of certain expectations and the realization of certain group purposes. Whether such commitments have actually had this result, in some circumstances, has been a matter of controversy.

Is an academy desirable to define once and for all the *true* meaning of words and the *correct* rules of grammar, or should these meanings and rules be permitted to change with usage? Is it desirable that churches assert certain dogmatic *truths,* or that states assert certain self-evident *truths,* or should religious and political doctrines be permitted to change with new conditions, new experience, and new insights? It may be that social order and progress will profit under certain conditions by general faith in absolutes and under other conditions by general understanding that no statements are absolutely true though they differ in their degree of probability. As Comte suggested, civilization may tend to move from a metaphysical to a scientific basis. But in any case it seems probable that if absolute truths exist, they do so in the order of certain societies or universes of discourse, not in the order of nature.

The opinion generally held in some societies, that unquestioning belief in some *absolute* values and principles is socially useful, probably accounts for the anomaly that preachers and politicians, whose truths are by nature relative, often assert that they are absolute, while scientists and historians whose truths sometimes approach absolute verification, usually acknowledge that they are only relative and subject to continuous revision as knowledge advances. While much of modern industrial society depends on the reliability of the technology based on scientific truths, it usually makes little difference what the average man thinks about those truths, consequently there is no social urge to declare their absoluteness (14).

Philosophers have recognized the diversity of types of truth. Descartes distinguished between rational demonstration from self-evident premises which could yield absolute truth, and sufficient reason for practical action which could be expressed only as relative truth. "In relation to practice," he wrote, "it is sometimes necessary to adopt, as if above doubt, opinions which we discern to be highly uncertain" (4). Kant made the same point in distinguishing pure and practical reason, although he proposed for the latter a categorical imperative to be treated as if absolutely true. Justice Holmes, urging toleration for diverse opinions, pointed out that every day we risk our lives on uncertain predictions (6, 11).

This distinction between the relatively certain and the relatively uncertain types of truth suggests a classification of propositions into those that tend to be believed because they are true in the sense of being convincing or correct, and those that are true because their presentation is so effective and persuasive that they are generally believed. The first or objective type of truth deals with reality in the sense of the actual and the probable. Its uncertainty flows largely from the nature of things. The distortions of human observation and human reasoning can be in considerable measure eliminated by the application of scientific method. The latter or subjective type of truth deals with reality in the sense of the possible and the desirable. Its uncertainty flows from the differences in human reactions consequent upon the infinite variety in the heredity, early experience, education, and cultural, professional, and social environment of different people (13). This distinction has been developed by such semanticists as Cassirer and Langer in pointing out that *discursive* statements are capable of being refuted by other statements, while *nondiscursive* statements, such as those in lyrics, are not (5, 8). The distinction has also been made between semantic and logical truth on the one hand and expressive and pragmatic truth on the other, according as *truth* means that the proposition is adequate with respect to its subject matter and its symbolic structure or that it is adequate with respect to the writer and the reader (9).

Propositions which concern the behavior of the heavenly bodies, insusceptible of human manipulation, or the inferences to be drawn from abstract definitions or relations within a logical system, accepted as absolute in the discourse, are the type of objective truth, though modern historians of science emphasize the relativity even of this kind of truth (1). The sciences and mathematics of the Greeks, Arabians, and men of the Enlightenment arose from dealing with this kind of material. The desire of men for absolute certainty has, however, led to the ascription of this kind of truth to propositions in the fields of social value and action not susceptible to that kind of treatment. Eighteenth-century rationalism was guilty of this error.

Anthropological studies indicate that the values among different social groups vary greatly. The opinions prevailing in the group concern in part the principles which should be accepted or the policies which should be pursued to realize the values accepted by the group, and in part the facts of nature or of human nature which support these values. Gunnar Myrdal (10), in studying the racial problem in the United States, discovered that in the South the accepted value system in considerable degree depended upon general belief in a distinction between the races. Ethical principles and social policy were based upon this evaluative distinction. Policies or philosophies deduced from the assumption of white predominance were effective. There was also a body of beliefs drawn from reported observations or traditions which were thought to demonstrate white superiority. These beliefs were welcome to the whites because they persuaded people to accept the basic value system. There was a will to believe and so they were believed. The established value system in a society, which when appealed to is likely to persuade a member of the society of the validity of an argument, and the body of social habits which are effective in supporting these values constitute in the society a body of opinion so widely accepted that within the society it is treated as truth. For a member of the society it is truth. While such *truth* can be criticized from outside societies with different values and different beliefs, internal criticism is difficult. It may even be dangerous. The more the society is isolated from external contacts, the more such opinions become *truth* within the society. Opinions universally accepted by the human race as a whole would remain truth for mankind however erroneous they might seem to invaders from another world (13).

Subjective truth which everyone accepts has all the practical effects of objective truth. The truths of faith and the truths of science resemble one another in social consequences however much they differ in the methods of demonstration, and it appears that even this difference is only relative. It is, however, important in the social sciences to recognize this distinction. Propositions which no competent investigator can help but believe are very different from propositions which everyone believes because they have never been questioned. Both kinds of truth exist, but their confusion may be unfortunate. The problems of international relations usually concern the divergence of the subjective truths accepted by different societies and regarded by each to be objective truth.

In a recent discussion concerning the advisability of requiring loyalty investigations of candidates for scientific fellowships, a distinguished scientist said science must question everything. Nothing must be taken for granted. The questioning type of mind which might question traditional values was necessary, he thought, if science was to advance. The congressional advocate of loyalty investigations said: "Why should not this scientific virtue be applied in loyalty investigations? Why should civil servants and recipients of federal grants have their loyalty taken for granted? Why should loyalty not be investigated in every case?" The scientist did not have a ready answer, but he might have answered: "Experience has shown that the general invasion of privacy and the mutual suspicion involved in secret police operations necessary for such investigations would destroy the basis for a democratic society. The expectation of freedom is no less important for such a society than the expectation of loyalty. These values are, like all values, relative, and neither must be wholly sacrificed for the other. From the point of view of such a society, to investigate nature is a virtue, but to investigate the members of the society is a vice. To extend the scientific method into challenging the fundamental values of a society may destroy the society. A society implies some unquestioned beliefs among its members as well as a belief that some things should be continually questioned."

Galileo was tried by the Inquisition for disclosing his observation that the earth moved around the sun. Prudently he recanted but was said to have observed *sotto voce* that it moved anyway. The Inquisition was attempting to extend the method of faith (insistence on belief by the faithful without scientific evidence) into a field which was not directly related to the value system of the church. The result may have been more detrimental to the church than to science, though it convinced Descartes that he had better go slowly in publishing his scientific conclusions (4).

Reflection on these efforts to universalize the methods either of science or of faith suggests that both varieties of truth are important, but each should be applied in its proper sphere. This is perhaps not unlike the conclusions reached by Aquinas as to the roles of faith and reason, although modern science would somewhat alter the line which he placed between the aspects of life susceptible to one or the other treatment. It also resembles the conclusions of some modern scientists distinguishing the fields of science and of the humanities, although some scientists would not entirely exclude human behavior from the field of science (2, 3).

A society cannot exist without some degree of commitment to a value system. A society cannot progress without some objective verification of its beliefs. The problems of reconciling commitments with investigations, faith with reason, is one that can never be finally solved. It is like the problem of airplane manufacturing in war. Commitment to a design is necessary for mass production. But such commitment if too rigorous will prevent the incorporation of improvements which may be decisive in winning the war. Compromise between maximizing the rate of production and keeping design up to date is necessary. So a society must continually compromise between maintaining the belief of its members in its values and maintaining a quality in its values capable of intelligent belief.

An illustration may also be drawn from a barn raising. The effort to raise the heavy framework will fail and may end in disaster unless *all* the participants believe in advance of actual experience that it can be done and bend their efforts to the task, but it will also fail if that conviction is not soundly based and the framework is actually too heavy for the group to raise.

The dilemma may be further illustrated by Stephen Decatur's famous toast. He answered in favor of loyalty to "my country, right or wrong." But he recognized the duty of citizenship to investigate and criticize so that the hope "may she always be right" would be realized. A society must continually justify its actions by its values, but it must also continually verify its values by its science.

In considering international relations as a discipline, this ambiguity in the conception of truth is important to have in mind. All the varieties of truth are involved in the study of international relations. At a later stage of this book international relations will be considered as history, as science, as philosophy, and as art. As history and as science the discipline of international relations seeks to organize propositions which are objectively verifiable by evidence or observation, or by logical inference from such propositions. In these approaches, the discipline should consist of truth in the sense that its propositions are convincing and correct.

As philosophy and as art, on the other hand, the discipline of international relations seeks to organize propositions which will maintain belief in the *best* values of civilization and will instruct in the conduct of affairs to forward those values. The success of these approaches is to be found in the results. The proof of the values of a free democratic society lies in its capacity to survive while serving its members. The proof of a good general is in winning wars with minimum cost and of a good diplomat in maintaining the peace without sacrificing national interests. In these approaches, the discipline of international relations should consist of truth in the sense that the propositions are persuasive and effective.

A discipline that seeks to give due weight to these divergent types of truth encounters difficulty in retaining the unity and coherence normally associated with the term *discipline*. In the next chapter we will consider whether international relations is a discipline and if so, in what sense.

REFERENCES

1. BUTTERFIELD, H., *The Origins of Modern Science, 1300-1800* (London, Bell, 1949).
2. CAMPBELL, Norman, *What Is Science?* (New York, Dover Publications, 1952).
2a. CASSIRER, Ernst, *An Essay on Man* (New York, Doubleday, 1953).
3. CONANT, James B., *Science and Common Sense* (New Haven, Yale University Press, 1951).
4. DESCARTES, René, *Discourse on Method* (1636), Parts 3, 4.
5. HAYAKAWA, S. I., "Semantics," *ETC*, Vol. 9 (Summer, 1952), pp. 243 ff.; also "Semantics," *Encyclopædia Britannica*.
6. HOLMES, Oliver Wendell, Jr., "Dissenting Opinion in Abrams v. United States," 250 U.S. Reports 616, 1919.
7. LANGER, Suzanne K., *An Introduction to Symbolic Logic*, 2nd ed. (New York, Dover, 1953).
8. ——, *Philosophy in a New Key*, 2nd ed. (Cambridge, Harvard University Press, 1951).
9. MORRIS, Charles, *Signs, Language and Behavior* (New York, Prentice-Hall, 1946).
10. MYRDAL, Gunnar, *An American Dilemma* (New York, Harper, 1944).
11. RAPAPORT, Anatole, *Operational Philosophy* (New York, Harper, 1953).
12. VAIHINGER, Hans, *The Philosophy of "As If,"* trans. by C. K. Ogden, 2nd ed. (London, Kegan, Paul, 1935).
13. WRIGHT, Quincy, *A Study of War* (Chicago, University of Chicago Press, 1942), Ch. 30.
14. ——, *Problems of Stability and Progress in International Relations* (Berkeley, University of California Press, 1954), Ch. 14.

Development of International Relations as a Discipline

INTERNATIONAL RELATIONS has only begun to emerge as a recognized discipline treated comprehensively and systematically in textbooks and academic curricula. There has, however, been a great deal of writing about international relations since man began to write in the fourth millennium B.C. (28, 35) and if one can judge from contemporary preliterate people, men had ideas about international relations long before that (27, 55).

Man is a social animal. Language and writing are products of society. It is therefore natural that the earliest writing should be about the society in which man found himself. But the recognition of his own society implied recognition of other societies with which his society was in relations of peace or war. No society has ever been so isolated from its neighbors that it was unaware of them. In fact the *out-group* was an important element in making its members aware of their own *in-group*. Recognition of the group and recognition of intergroup relations developed together and such recognitions were an immediate stimulus for discussion, analysis, and formulation of the phenomena recognized.

A discipline, however, implies more than sporadic writing about a subject which later historians may bring together and analyze. Some say a discipline exists only in so far as a body of data has been systematized by a distinctive analytical method. This definition would deny the title to most academic *disciplines,* but at the least a discipline implies consciousness by writers that there is a subject with some sort of unity; a concept of the scope of the subject and of the boundaries which separate it from other subjects; a certain consensus on its subdivisions, its organization, and its methods; and some recognition of the persons who are expert on the subject and of the criteria for establishing such expertness (2, 25, 56).

The degree in which any of the recognized disciplines—physics, zoology, economics, law, medicine, linguistics, mathematics—actually conforms to all these criteria can easily be exaggerated. The closer one examines any one of them the more he becomes aware of the vagueness of its boundaries, the uncertainty of its scope, the disagreements about its organization and methods, and the doubt as to the personnel who profess it and as to their qualifications. The ways in which the possible subjects of thought and study can be divided into disciplines are legion.

Geniuses have imagined hypotheses or conceptual systems, have organized materials for their verification or utilization, and have developed their implications, as did Euclid, Newton, Einstein, Ricardo, Mendel, and Freud. Others were inspired to labor in the same vineyards, until the disciplines of geometry, physics, economics, genetics, and psychoanalysis emerged. Such systematic unity bringing a large body of observations and ideas into a logical system with a minimum of assumptions is the ideal of all disciplines but the achievement of only a few.

Practical difficulties obstructing a developing activity have sometimes led to the initiation or development of a discipline. The need for a correct calendar to carry on agricultural activities had much to do with the early development of astronomy. The demands of war compelled the development of military science. Problems of trade and currency pressed for a discipline of political economy in the period of mercantilism. The increasing utilization of aviation necessitated the rapid development of the discipline of meteorology. Most disciplines probably owe something to the pressure of social needs, although in the pure sciences curiosity and the feeling for order may be a more immediate factor.

The discovery of a technique permitting the investigation of a new type of phenomena or of a method applicable to the analysis of a wide variety of phenomena may also initiate disciplines. Invention of the microscope led to such disciplines as histology and bacteriology, and development of statistical methods made possible the disciplines of demography, econometrics, and mathematical genetics.

Convenience in dividing labor and the classificatory impulse may create disciplines. Philosophers have attempted to subdivide all knowledge into disciplines, thus facilitating specialization in and more rapid development of each. Such attempts were made by Aristotle in antiquity, Thomas Aquinas in the thirteenth century, Francis Bacon in the seventeenth century, and Auguste Comte and Herbert Spencer in the nineteenth century. Teaching practice has resulted in classifications of knowledge. Thus medieval universities recognized the trivium (grammar, rhetoric,

and dialectic) derived from Roman educational practice, and the quad-
rivium distinguishing the modes of mathematical thought developed in
practice (geometry, arithmetic, music, and astronomy). Both were distinct from what were then considered the highest ranges of thought
(theology and philosophy). Modern universities usually recognize the
physical sciences, the biological sciences, the social sciences, and the
humanities, as well as the professions and the arts. Such subdivisions may
group easily distinguishable objects of thought and observation such as
man and nature (32). In the former, strivings for the good, the true, and
the beautiful, may be distinguished, and in the latter, animals, vegetables,
and minerals. Aristotle in this way distinguished ethics, politics, and
economics; metaphysics and logic; esthetics, rhetoric, and poetics; psychology, biology, and physics. Evolutionary conceptions provided Spencer
the distinctions between the inorganic (physics and chemistry), the
organic (biology), and the superorganic (psychology and sociology).
Specialized human activities provided the distinctions between law,
medicine, theology, education, engineering, business, agriculture, strategy,
and diplomacy. The basic means of human intercourse—speaking, writing,
and reasoning—and their respective standards of excellence provided the
basis for the ancient and medieval trivium—grammar, rhetoric, and
dialectic—and for the fundamentals of modern elementary education—
reading, writing, and arithmetic.

History has been no less important than logic, necessity, feasibility,
and convenience in initiating and maintaining disciplines. Once textbooks
have appeared or academic chairs have been established under a given
name; once curricula have been offered, degrees given, and learned journals initiated in a given field; once libraries have been organized according
to a given scheme, a discipline has achieved a solidity and position which
it is difficult to change however illogical or inconvenient that particular
subdivision may in time prove to be. Professional associations have been
factors in establishing disciplines, through presenting prerequisites to
entry into the profession, as in the cases of medicine, law, and theology.
Such professional requirements become organized in schools and departments of universities, and stabilized through the legislation of governments.

The proliferation of disciplines during the last two centuries of modern
history is made evident by comparing the universal scope of the French
Academy, the British Royal Society, and the American Philosophical
Society of the seventeenth and eighteenth centuries with the specialized
interest of contemporary learned societies each with its officers, journal,
and annual meetings. Their name is legion: physics, biology, bio-chemistry,
geology, genetics, ecology, bio-physics, geography, psychology, psy-
chometry, economics, political science, statistics, education, mathematics,
philosophy, ethics, modern languages, classics, archaeology, history, and

many others. They are grouped in the United States, with some overlapping, into the National Research Council, the Social Science Research Council, and the American Council of Learned Societies, dealing respectively with the natural sciences, the social sciences, and the humanities.

International relations is today an emerging discipline manifesting little unity from the point of view of method, logic, and convenience but much from that of necessity and history. It is most developed in the United States although there are chairs of international relations in Great Britain, Switzerland, Germany, France, and elsewhere. The discipline as a whole cannot be traced much back of World War I when the effort to organize the world through the League of Nations occasioned a more systematic examination of the contributory disciplines such as international law, international politics, international economics. The textbooks by Paul Reinsch on world politics in 1900 (34) and international unions in 1911 (33) and the publications of the Carnegie Endowment for International Peace of New York and of the World Peace Foundation of Boston perhaps went further in surveying the field than any other publications before World War I.

Since World War I numerous textbooks have attempted to integrate the subject under such titles as International Politics (7, 24, 26, 37, 39), International Relations (5, 6, 12, 13, 19, 21, 23, 29, 35, 44, 50), World Politics (3, 4, 11, 15, 18, 22, 34, 40, 42), Power Politics (38, 53), International Organization (31), International Government (8), and International Psychology (30, 45). It cannot be said, however, that any have succeeded in integrating all the points of view or all the contributory disciplines into a systematic treatment. During this period several societies for studying international relations as a whole were initiated. These included the Royal Institute of International Affairs in London; The Council on Foreign Relations in New York; The Foreign Policy Association in New York; The Graduate Institute of International Studies in Geneva; and the International Studies Conference under the Institute of Intellectual Cooperation in Paris. The Conference of Teachers of International Law, initiated before the war by the Carnegie Endowment for International Peace, extended its interest to "related subjects." These associations generally published journals, yearbooks, and monographs covering the whole field of international relations. They also organized conferences sometimes of international character bringing together professional and academic persons interested in the development of the discipline. Older societies in the social sciences such as the American Political Science Association, the American Economic Association, the American Society of International Law, the American Academy of Social and Political Sciences, and the Academy of Political Science gave increasing attention to international relations as a whole. Specialized institutes such as the

Norman Wait Harris Memorial Foundation at the University of Chicago; the Conference on Science, Philosophy, and Religion; the Institute of International Studies at Yale; and the Committee on International and Regional Studies at Harvard devoted much attention to international relations as a discipline (36, 51).

During the interwar period colleges and universities began to increase their offerings in the field. Previous to World War I courses in the field had generally been confined to diplomatic history, international law and international economics. After the war, courses in international relations and international organization became popular (47). In the 1930's international politics, political geography and public opinion were especially emphasized (16, 51). The difference perhaps reflects some decline in the optimism with which professors viewed the world order. Many universities began to organize curricula sometimes leading to advanced degrees in the field of international relations. These were sometimes under the supervision of an interdepartmental committee as at Chicago, Harvard, and Columbia; sometimes under an institute as at Yale and Geneva; sometimes under special professorships as at Oxford, London, and the University of Wales; sometimes, in a professional school as at Fletcher, American University, and Georgetown; sometimes in an undergraduate school as at Princeton; and sometimes under a department of International Relations (1, 2, 20, 48a, 51).

The advent of World War II and the creation of the United Nations and the Specialized Agencies gave a new impetus to the subject and led to popular demands for "world government" especially in the United States (14, 46). Because of the increased attention given to public relations activities by national governments and international organizations, the psychology and sociology of international relations, international education, and international communications have gained increasing attention. International associations in each of the social sciences were organized under the leadership of UNESCO. At the same time, the wide impact of World War II, the development of the atomic bomb and other exceptionally destructive methods of war, and the continuance of "cold war" between the Western and Soviet worlds, resulted in greater attention to the art of war (9, 42), to power politics (24, 38, 41, 53), and to political geography (52). The problem of balancing consideration of the needs of national security and of international co-operation, of war and peace, in a discipline of international relations became exceptionally difficult. Yet the demand for trained personnel in the field steadily increased as international contacts became more complicated and international organizations proliferated. This demand, together with an increasing number of research fellowships in the field, of government supported international student exchanges, and of government educational grants to ex-soldiers with a natural interest in international affairs has produced a larger number of students in the field, both graduate and undergraduate, than ever before.

The progress in integrating the subject academically and professionally has been accompanied by a great increase in the literature of all aspects of the field, in the number of learned journals devoted to it, and in the analysis of the progress of international relations as a discipline. Studies have been made by Symons (47), Ware (51), Zimmern (56, 57), Bailey (1, 2), Kirk (16), and Manning (20) on the progress of the discipline, and by Russell (35) on the history of the discipline. The Carnegie Endowment for International Peace, the Social Science Research Council, the International Studies Conference, the Royal Institute, the Council on Foreign Relations, and the Brookings Institution have all supported studies of the development of work in the field since World War I. These studies indicate that the undergraduate instruction in the field varies greatly from institution to institution. There is also great variation in the place which the discipline occupies in the general curriculum and the amount of attention given to it. There is similar variation among graduate and professional schools.

International relations has not yet achieved a definite form in either curricula, textbooks, or treatises. Sometimes the subject is integrated to conform to professional interests of the particular student. Sometimes it is organized around a particular functional approach such as international politics, international law, or international organization. Sometimes it is organized by grouping regional approaches such as the Far East, the Middle East, or Latin America. The subject as an academic discipline, when not supervised by a special committee, institute, or department of international relations, has been most frequently offered by political science departments and, as a consequence, international politics, international organization, and international law have tended to be emphasized. Economics departments have always given some attention to international trade and commercial policies. Political geography has been emphasized in certain institutions. Only recently have psychology and sociology departments given much attention to the field.

The quantity of work in international relations, both academic and in adult education, has greatly increased both in the United States and elsewhere. Improvement in the quality of the work has been parallel but less rapid. The intellectual integration of the discipline has progressed through discussions in meetings of educators, administrators, and the scholarly world on particular international problems requiring use of all of the relevant disciplines. The status of the subject as a discipline is indicated by the appearance of textbooks, histories, and bibliographies (17, 54) intended to cover the entire field. International relations is, in short, an emerging discipline, but its nature and character cannot be understood without considering the disciplines which have contributed to its creation, the subdivisions into which it is organized, and the objectives which it seeks.

REFERENCES

1. BAILEY, S. H., *International Studies in Great Britain* (London, Royal Institute of International Affairs, 1933).
2. ———, *International Studies in Modern Education* (London, Royal Institute of International Affairs, 1938).
3. BARNES, Harry Elmer, *World Politics in Modern Civilization* (New York, Knopf, 1930).
4. BROWN, Francis J., HODGES, Charles and ROUCEK, Joseph H., eds., *Contemporary World Politics* (New York, Wiley, 1940).
5. BRYCE, James, *International Relations* (New York, Macmillan, 1922).
6. BUELL, Raymond L., *International Relations* (New York, Holt, 1925).
7. BURNS, C. Delisle, *International Politics* (London, Methuen, 1920).
8. EAGLETON, Clyde, *International Government* (New York, Ronald Press, 1932; rev. ed., 1948).
9. EARLE, Edward M., ed., *Makers of Modern Strategy* (Princeton, Princeton University Press, 1944).
10. ———, "Impact of Scientific Discovery on International Relations," *Conference of Teachers of International Law and Related Subjects (C.T.I.L.)*, Vol. 8 (Washington, Carnegie Endowment, 1946), pp. 39 ff.
11. GIBBONS, Herbert A., *Introduction to World Politics* (New York, Century, 1922).
12. HILL, Norman, *International Relations, Documents and Readings* (New York, Oxford University Press, 1950).
13. HODGES, Charles, *The Background of International Relations* (New York, Wiley, 1931).
14. HUTCHINS, R. M., and BORGESE, G. A., *Committee to Frame a World Constitution, Common Cause* (Chicago, University of Chicago Press, 1947-1952).
15. KALIJARVI, Thorsten J., and associates, *Modern World Politics* (New York, Crowell, 1942; 3rd ed., 1953).
16. KIRK, Grayson, *The Study of International Relations* (New York, Council on Foreign Relations, 1947).
17. LANGER, William L., and ARMSTRONG, Hamilton Fish, *Foreign Affairs Bibliography, 1919-1932* (New York, Council on Foreign Relations, 1933).
18. LASSWELL, Harold D., *World Politics and Personal Insecurity* (New York, McGraw-Hill, 1935).
19. MAXWELL, Bertram W., *International Relations* (New York, Crowell, 1939).
20. MANNING, C. A. W., *The University Teaching of Social Sciences: International Relations* (Paris, UNESCO, 1954).
21. MIDDLEBUSH, Frederick G., and HILL, Chesney, *Elements of International Relations* (New York, McGraw-Hill, 1940).
22. MOON, Parker T., *Imperialism and World Politics* (New York, Macmillan, 1926).
23. ———, *Syllabus on International Relations*, Institute of International Education (New York, Macmillan, 1925).

24. MORGENTHAU, Hans J., *Politics Among Nations* (New York, Knopf, 1948; 2nd ed., 1954).

25. ———, "Area Studies and the Study of International Relations," *International Social Science Bulletin,* UNESCO, Vol. 4 (Autumn, 1952), pp. 647 ff.

26. ———, and THOMPSON, Kenneth W., *Principles and Problems of International Politics, Selected Readings* (New York, Knopf, 1950).

27. NUMELIN, Ragnar, *The Beginnings of Diplomacy* (New York, Philosophical Library, 1950).

28. NUSSBAUM, Arthur A., *Concise History of the Law of Nations* (New York, Macmillan, 1947).

29. PALMER, Norman D., and PERKINS, Howard C., *International Relations* (Boston, Houghton Mifflin, 1953).

30. PILLSBURY, W. B., *The Psychology of Nationalism and Internationalism* (New York, Appleton, 1922).

31. POTTER, Pitman B., *An Introduction to the Study of International Organization* (New York, Appleton, 1922; 5th ed., Appleton-Century-Crofts, 1948).

32. REDFIELD, Robert, "The Primitive World View," *Proceedings,* American Philosophical Society, Vol. 96 (February, 1952), pp. 30 ff.

33. REINSCH, Paul, *Public International Unions* (Boston, World Peace Foundation, 1911).

34. ———, *World Politics* (New York, Macmillan, 1900).

35. RUSSELL, Frank W., *Theories of International Relations* (New York, Appleton-Century-Crofts, 1936).

36. SAVORD, Ruth, *American Agencies Interested in International Affairs* (New York, Council on Foreign Relations, 1931, 1942).

37. SCHUMAN, Frederick L., *International Politics* (New York, McGraw-Hill, 1933; 5th ed., 1953).

38. SCHWARTZENBERGER, Georg, *Power Politics* (London, Cape, 1941).

39. SHARP, Walter R., and KIRK, Grayson, *Contemporary International Politics* (New York, Farrar and Rinehart, 1940).

40. SIMONDS, Frank and EMENY, Brooks, *The Great Powers and World Politics* (New York, American Book, 1935).

41. SPROUT, Harold and Margaret, *Foundations of National Power* (Princeton, Princeton University Press, 1945).

42. SPYKMAN, Nicholas, *American Strategy and World Politics* (New York, Harcourt, 1942).

43. ———, "Methods of Approach to the Study of International Relations," *C.T.I.L.,* Vol. 5 (Washington, 1933), pp. 58 ff.

44. STEINER, H. Arthur, *Principles and Problems of International Relations* (New York, Harper, 1940).

45. STRATTON, George M., *Social Psychology and International Conduct* (New York, Appleton, 1940).

46. STREIT, Clarence, *Union Now* (New York, Harper, 1938).

47. SYMONS, Farrell, *Courses in International Affairs in American Colleges, 1930-1931* (Boston, World Peace Foundation, 1931).

48. THOMPSON, Kenneth, "The Study of International Politics," *Review of Politics,* Vol. 14 (October, 1952), pp. 433 ff.

48a. UNESCO, *The Teaching of the Social Sciences in the United Kingdom* (Paris, UNESCO, 1953).

49. VINACKE, Harold M., "The Teaching of International Relations in the Post War World," *C.T.I.L.,* Vol. 5 (Washington, 1946), p. 105.

50. WALSH, Edward A., *The History and Nature of International Relations* (New York, Macmillan, 1922).

51. WARE, Edith E., *The Study of International Relations in the United States, Survey for 1937* (New York, Columbia University Press, 1938).

52. WEIGERT, Hans W., and STEFANSSON, Vilhjalmur, *Compass of the World* (New York, Macmillan, 1944).

53. WIGHT, Martin, *Power Politics* (London, Royal Institute of International Affairs, 1946).

54. WOOLBERT, Robert Gale, *Foreign Affairs Bibliography, 1932-1942* (New York, Council on Foreign Relations, 1946).

55. WRIGHT, Quincy, *A Study of War* (Chicago, University of Chicago Press, 1942), Chs. 4, 6, 7.

56. ZIMMERN, Alfred, *University Teaching of International Relations* (Paris, International Institute of Intellectual Co-operation, 1939).

57. ———, *The Development of the International Mind, Problems of Peace*, Geneva Institute of International Studies (London, Oxford University Press, 1925), Lecture 1.

CHAPTER
5

The Root Disciplines of International Relations

THE DISCIPLINE of international relations has developed synthetically and this has militated against its unity. Other disciplines have developed through analysis and subdivision of older disciplines, as did genetics from biology and classical economics from moral philosophy. These disciplines began with a theory and developed from an initial unity. In international relations, on the other hand, an effort is being made to synthesize numerous older disciplines, each with a specialized point of view into a unity. The contrast may be observed by comparing the disciplines of economics and political science. The first grew from the analysis by Adam Smith of the significance of trade and the division of labor in increasing wealth and from the application of the Benthamite theory of human motives to economic activities by Ricardo and the Mills. While many aspects of economic policy, business practice, and institutional development became incorporated in the discipline of economics, the initial theory has served as a unifying system of analysis. This system, it must be admitted, has proved progressively less satisfactory as free markets have become impaired through the rise of monopolies and the increasing intervention of government in economic life for military, political, social, and ideological purposes.

Political science, on the other hand, arose because people interested in political theory, political history, or comparative government; in constitutional, administrative or international law; or in the practical problems of public administration, party politics, military affairs or diplomacy came to realize that they had a common interest in the state and government. These various groups had no common theory of human nature or of social processes. Political science was, therefore, less integrated at its start than was economics, although the fact that it developed bibliographies, textbooks, academic departments, professional journals, and professional associations has given it a certain unity arising from the common background and understanding of its professors. Efforts have been made to unify the subject by defining the term *politics*. No definition has, however, commanded general consent. Politics is usually conceded to be an art, but is it the art of operating the *state*, the *government*, or the *party*; of organizing group *power*, group *will*, or group *unity*; of achieving group ends against the *opposition* of other groups; or simply of making group *decisions?* The multiplicity of definitions has hampered integration of the discipline.

International relations in this respect resembles political science rather than economics. At least eight disciplines (international law, diplomatic history, military science, international politics, international organization, international trade, colonial government, and the conduct of foreign relations) have contributed to its development (24). Each of these disciplines has long had recognized sources, methods, and professors; a considerable literature; and a respectable history. Other disciplines, because of their world point of view, have also contributed to the development of international relations less directly. These will be considered in the next chapter.

Of the root disciplines contributing to international relations, the best integrated is perhaps *international law*. While figuring in the practical relations of ancient Greek cities, in the legal thought of ancient Rome, in the speculations of medieval philosophy and theology on just war, and in the commentaries of the glossators and post-glossators of thirteenth and fourteenth century Italy (19), international law began as a discipline with the work of Francis of Victoria in the sixteenth century. His interest in the subject developed when, as a professor at the University of Salamanca, he became aware of the problems consequent upon the contact of Spain with the civilization of Mexico after the conquest by Cortez. He applied medieval speculations concerning just war and the contacts of peoples of different civilizations in a realistic spirit. The theory of natural law, originating in Greek philosophy and developed by Roman jurisprudence and medieval thought, provided a theoretical basis for his work. Francisco Suarez, also a Spaniard familiar with medieval thought, followed his lead. The unifying theory of natural law, however, soon came into competition with ideas derived from observation of international behavior by soldiers and diplomats like Balthasar Ayala and Albericus Gentili. In the early seventeenth century Hugo Grotius systematically developed the subject on the basis of both ethical theory and interstate practice—both the *jus naturale* and the *jus gentium*—somewhat modifying the scope of these words as used by Roman jurists (11).

Classical writings on international law of the *naturalist, positivist,* and *Grotian* or synthetic schools continued through the seventeenth and eighteenth centuries. The French Revolution and the Industrial Revolution completed the process which had been underway for three centuries of undermining belief in *natural law,* but a relatively stable balance of power developed in Europe in the nineteenth century, and international law became firmly established on the basis of treaties, diplomatic practice, and judicial decisions. Its principles, sources, and sanctions were clarified during this comparatively tranquil century by the practice of national and international tribunals, of foreign offices, and of international conferences; by the teaching of numerous courses in colleges, universities, and law schools; and by the writings of numerous commentators in all languages (1). The extensive collections of documents, treaties, and cases compiled by individuals, governments, and international institutions has provided in the twentieth century ample materials for detailed studies on a positivistic basis. The leading American text by Charles Cheney Hyde and the leading British text by Lassa Oppenheim are positivistic in tendency, although Lauterpacht, the editor of the recent editions of Oppenheim, and Jessup, who was Hyde's colleague at Columbia University, have in their writings recognized the need for drawing upon general principles of law to adapt international law to rapidly changing conditions. The establishment of international law as a *discipline* is indicated by the production of several histories of this discipline (1, 11, 16, 19). Numerous treatises and many college and university courses expound the subject. Several national and international societies and numerous journals are devoted to its development. Official international agencies exist to apply and develop it, such as the International Court of Justice and the International Law Commission of the United Nations.

Diplomatic history figured in the work of the ancient historians such as Thucydides and Polybius. Machiavelli and other practical diplomats of the Renaissance also wrote on the subject. As a discipline, however, the subject emerged with the systematic publication of collections of treaties and diplomatic correspondence beginning with Leibnitz's *Codex Juris Gentium Diplomaticus* in the late seventeenth century. Rymer, Dumont, Garden, and Martens followed in the eighteenth century. In the nineteenth century all governments began to publish diplomatic correspondence and treaties with more or less completeness. Records of important international conferences became available and memoirs of officials and diplomats multiplied. Source materials were therefore increasingly available and diplomatic historians made full use of the opportunity presented. Diplomatic history tended to emphasize the formalities, strategies, and tactics of statesmen and diplomats. It, however, provided the basis for topical treatises on diplomatic practice drawing also from the literature of international law and of the conduct of foreign policy, and from knowledge of human nature derived from personal experience. The well-known treatises by Wicquefort, Callières, Foster, and Satow (16) are of this type. The literature of the art of diplomacy like that of the art of war has always combined history and analysis with practical advice.

American diplomatic history has become a regular academic subject with such well-known texts as those by Carl Russell Fish, Samuel F. Bemis, and Thomas A. Bailey. European diplomatic history has been dealt with since the mid-eighteenth century by men like Koch, Gentz, Dupuis, Donnadieu, and Ferrero. Extensive diplomatic histories have been written by David Jayne Hill, Sir Charles Petrie (12), and Vladimir Potiemkin. The post-Napoleonic period has been made the subject of intensive study by Sir Charles K. Webster, H. W. Temperley, and Alison Phillips. Among other writers in the field mention may be made of W. L. Langer, E. L. Woodworth, and Harold Nicholson. During the interwar period the governments of Germany, Austria, Russia, Great Britain, France, and other of the early participants in World War I published extensive collections of prewar documents inspiring historians like Bernadotte Schmitt, Sidney Fay, and Pierre Renouvin to narrate the diplomatic origins of that war in detail.

The League of Nations and the United Nations have published their records in full and the publication of documents by national governments and of memoirs by statesmen and diplomats have become so voluminous in the period of World War II that diplomatic historians are presented an embarrassing wealth of material, although increasing international rivalries have continued to cast a veil of secrecy over much of the most important material. Furthermore, the relations of foreign offices to other departments of government and the involvement of diplomacy in economic, social, and propaganda problems has made it more difficult to treat diplomatic history as a subject capable of being written from the traditional materials alone.

Older than the disciplines of either international law or of diplomatic history is the discipline of *military science* or the art of war. Military history, strategical and tactical advice, military organization, military technology, and problems of discipline and morale have been combined to constitute this discipline. The commentaries of Caesar, Frontinus, and Vegitius in classical antiquity, of Sun-Wu in Confucian China, and of Kautilya in ancient India, contributed to the subject (9, 20). As a modern discipline, however, the subject was revitalized by the use of firearms. Machiavelli wrote on the art of war in the sixteenth century, Turenne and Vauban in the seventeenth century, and Marshal Saxe in the eighteenth century. After the Napoleonic period Jomini and Clausewitz systematized the subject which has subsequently been developed by soldiers like Von Der Goltz, Bernhardi, Foch, Maurice, and Fuller; sailors like Mahan and Fiske; and historians like Delbrück, Oman, and Winston Churchill (4). More recently, with the development of economic and psychological weapons and with problems of mass organization and total war involving the use of aircraft, radar, and atomic bombs, the subject has expanded and has been contributed to by physicists, psychologists, sociologists, economists, and administrators, as well as by strategists and historians. Studies by Vannevar Bush, Bernard Brodie and Samuel Stouffer are typical of this trend.

International politics has figured in the three disciplines already referred to. The classical international lawyers contrasted the precepts of justice with those of political expediency, especially in the initiation of war. The diplomatic historians often inserted generalizations about sound political practice in their narratives, frequently giving prominence to the principles of the balance of power. The writers on the art of war recognized in varying degree that war was politics carried on by other methods. Lord Shang and Kautilya attempted more or less systematic treatises on international politics in ancient China and India, and Aristotle's *Politics* extended briefly into the problems of war and peace.

As a distinct discipline in the modern world, however, international politics hardly antedates the Renaissance and can, in fact, be conveniently dated from Machiavelli's treatise on *The Prince* in 1511. Sir Francis Bacon, Lisola, and Sir William Temple in the seventeenth century; Bolingbroke, David Hume, and Alexander Hamilton in the eighteenth century; Montague Bernard and Treitschke in the nineteenth century; and numerous recent writers have continued Machiavelli's tradition of placing the analysis of political power and the conditions of its equilibrium at the center of the study. Political scientists in the tradition of Aristotle were usually more interested in domestic than in international affairs, but such writers as Hobbes, Locke, Montesquieu, Rousseau, de Tocqueville, and Bryce, touched on international politics as one aspect of their subject (6). Since World War II the subject has come to figure at the center of curricula on international relations in the United States, utilizing textbooks such as those by Frederick Schuman (18), William T. R. Fox (5), and Hans Morgenthau (10).

International politics has been regarded as a branch of political science, itself a synthetic discipline which emerged as an academic subject in the late nineteenth century. Political science, which deals with all aspects of the state and government, is usually subdivided functionally into political theory, politics and public opinion, public administration, and public law, and geographically into local government, national government, and international relations, the latter including international law, international politics, international organization, and international administration. Diplomatic practice, the conduct of foreign relations, colonial government, and military science are also sometimes included. There are historic, geographic, economic, psychological, sociological and humanistic approaches to international relations but the subject as a whole has usually been treated as an aspect of political science in American universities.

International organization did not become a recognized discipline nor was the name used until after World War I (14). Since then it has become the subject of numerous textbooks and numerous college courses. The stimulus for this development has, of course, been the creation first of the League of Nations and then of the United Nations, concrete manifestations of general international organization capable of analysis and evaluation.

Much earlier, however, the subject had been considered by practical reformers and statesmen interested in stability or peace. Consideration of the inconsistencies between international law and international politics during the post-Renaissance period could hardly fail to induce speculation about the possibility of reconciliation through political organization above or among states. The basis for such speculation was provided by the illustration of such superorganizations in the Holy Roman Empire and the Catholic Church. There were also historic memories of the ancient Roman Empire and practical experience with political alliances and with confederations like that of the Swiss.

The signs that medieval Christendom was disintegrating in the struggle of Emperor and Pope and the failure of the Crusades early in the fourteenth century stimulated Pope Boniface VIII's Bull *Unum sanctum,* Dante's *De Monarchia,* and Pierre Dubois' *Recuperatione Terra Sancta.* These discussions hoped to secure unity respectively through dominance of the Pope, the Emperor, or a federation of the princes. The collapse of Christian unity and the development of claims of sovereignty by the princes in the sixteenth century induced actual efforts at international federation by Henry VIII of England and Henry IV of France. A definite literature on the subject began in the seventeenth century inspired by the so-called Grand Design of Henry IV. This was set forth long after Henry's death in the memoirs of his minister Sully who may have utilized a tract by Emeric Crucé. The latter, published in 1623, was called *Le Nouveau Cynee* after a character in Plutarch and developed a plan of international organization in considerable detail. During the next two centuries eminent writers such as William Penn, Abbé St. Pierre, Jean Jacques Rousseau, Jeremy Bentham, and Immanuel Kant added to the literature of the subject, but it continued speculative and utopian rather than analytic until the effort of Czar Alexander I to realize the "Grand Design" during the Napoleonic Period (17).

The actual functioning of the Great Powers as a quasi-government of Europe during the post-Napoleonic Period, the multiplication of international conferences during the nineteenth century, the frequent use of arbitration and conciliation to settle controversies between nations, the establishment of several public international unions in the latter half of the nineteenth century, and the successful functioning of several federations of previously sovereign states provided a wealth of material for students of international organization to work on and the discipline became more tangible, analytical, and practical.

The Hague Conferences of 1899 and 1907 called by Czar Nicholas II stimulated new interest in the subject. Reinsch's study of Public International Unions in 1911 is probably the first effort to analyze the historic materials on international organization, although the compilation by Darby in 1904 pointed the way.

After World War I international organization became an established academic discipline utilizing textbooks by Potter, Rappard, Eagleton, Mander, and others. Tendencies may be observed on the one hand to relate institutions of international organization to international politics and international law, and on the other to relate them by analogy to national governments and federations. The latter tendency increased after World War II and was especially remarkable among the numerous writers and organizations who advocated a world government more intensive than the United Nations (17). As a reaction, empirical methods, measuring opinion, communication and other sociological indices in selected historic situations, have been applied by Deutsch, Pool, Klingberg, Snyder, Van Wagenen, Levi and others to formulate the conditions and estimate the prospects of effective organization integrating groups of states.

The subject is still greatly affected by political propagandas, but since World War I it has acquired the status of a discipline. Textbooks cover the whole subject, special treatises deal with particular aspects such as international adjudication, international legislation and international administration, and detailed studies and articles deal with the League of Nations, the United Nations, and the Specialized Agencies. Histories of the discipline have appeared by Lange, Termeulen, Hemleben, Marriott, Schuman, and others (17).

International trade has developed as a discipline parallel to that of international politics. During the seventeenth and eighteenth centuries peace and plenty were the stated objectives of governments, sometimes parallel, sometimes complementary, and sometimes conflicting. As peace was thought to require a favorable balance of power so plenty was thought to require a favorable balance of trade. The national accumulation of gold and silver, which resulted from the excess of exports over imports, was thought to assure prosperity and also national power, because such available wealth could purchase soldiers, military equipment, and allies. Mercantilist writers explained the technique of international trade and the means of regulating it for the national advantage. Emeric Crucé, who initiated the systematic study of international organization, was among the first to look upon trade not as an instrument of national policy, but as an end in itself, the development of which would unite the nations and assure their co-operation. Adam Smith tended to this point of view, and from his analysis of the economic gains to all from division of labor and trade developed classical economic theory carried on by Ricardo, the Mills, Bastiat, and others (21). The analysis of international trade was a major interest among most of these writers. They pointed to the general economic gain, through each nation specializing in the production in which it had a relative advantage and the tendency of trade to establish hostages in favor of peace.

The classical theory of international trade was contested by Marxists, protectionists, and autarchists who advocated the use of tariffs, exchange controls, quotas, government monopolies, and other methods for diverting trade to favor national power, to frustrate political enemies, to support particular economic groups, or otherwise to make trade an instrument of policy. More recently the influence of the network of commercial treaties, of the numerous international economic organizations, and of new means of transport and communication have become aspects of the broader discipline of international economics (2, 3). Not only are there textbooks, monographs, compilations, bibliographies, and numerous college courses on the subject, but there are many histories, both of international commerce and of the literature about it. The subject, although one aspect of the discipline of economics—parallel to economic theory, industrial relations and labor, taxation and finance, and economic history and institutions—is sufficiently specialized and integrated to constitute a discipline in itself.

Colonial government was dealt with by writers of ancient Greece and Rome whose theories differed radically. The Greeks assumed that a colony would naturally become independent when established, and the Romans that it would naturally remain as an enlargement of the Empire. There was little colonial enterprise in the Middle Ages, but with the explorations and discoveries of the fifteenth century and the establishment of relations between European nations and peoples of very different culture, attention was again paid to the subject. The early international lawyers touched on it. Rivalries for colonies played an important part in diplomatic history. The significance of colonies for national power and for national prosperity was also recognized. As strategic outposts, as sources of raw material, as markets for manufactured goods, and as outlets for population, colonies played an important role in the economics and policies of the colonial powers. Theories as to the value and destinies of colonies were developed by writers in the fields both of politics and of economics (8).

The interest of the natives of the colonies had from the first aroused some interest among writers of the metropole, and in the nineteenth century, the constitutional relation of the colony to the metropole, its status with respect to other countries, and the protection which should be afforded its inhabitants by international law and international organization became subjects of discussion, especially after certain colonies had by arms or agreement achieved an independent status under international law. The principal colonial powers developed distinctive practices on these subjects. National historians and analysts explained and evaluated their policies. In the latter nineteenth century comparative studies of colonial policy were made. Paul Reinsch, who contributed to the discipline of international politics and international organization, contributed also to the discipline now under discussion by writing textbooks on Colonial Policy and Colonial Administration. The embarkation of the United States upon overseas colonialism by acquiring the Philippines stimulated his work and also several histories of colonial activities.

The establishment of the Mandate System (23) under the League of Nations and later the Trusteeship System under the United Nations further developed the literature on the subject, establishing it as a discipline with textbooks, monographs, histories, bibliographies, and some college courses. Most writers agree that the colonial status is transitional, but opinions still differ, as they did among the ancients, as to whether the tendency is toward independence or toward absorption in the metropole. Fundamentally, the problem concerns the relationship between peoples of vastly different economic, military, technological, and educational advancement, and will continue as a subject of study so long as such differences exist in the world. The most recent literature of the subject is concerned with technical aid to underdeveloped areas (7).

The *conduct of foreign relations* is an emerging discipline which has to do with the constitutional structure and administrative methods of states in conducting foreign relations. With the development of the diplomatic and consular systems in the seventeenth and eighteenth centuries, writers on diplomatic practice such as Wicquefort and Callières began to deal with the perquisites of these officials in international law as well as with their relation to their own governments. As constitutional checks began to penetrate into the conduct of foreign affairs, especially with the establishment of the United States constitution, the problem of maintaining unity in international dealings with a proper respect for these constitutional inhibitions attracted attention. Hamilton, Madison, and Jay dealt with the subject in *The Federalist* and later writings. American history provided an abundance of material on the subject, and with the rise of democracy in the nineteenth century, legislative and federal qualifications of executive power in the making of treaties and of war, developed in other countries.

While books on international law and diplomatic history, as well as books on the constitutional law of particular countries, dealt with the problem briefly, interest in the subject was greatly increased when the problem thrust itself on the world scene through failure of the United States to ratify the treaty of Versailles and the League of Nations Covenant. Several treatises on the subject appeared as an aspect of American constitutional law (22). Similar studies were made of the constitutional practices and theories of other countries (6). In 1924 Dewitt C. Poole produced a comparative study of the conduct of foreign relations under democratic conditions (13). Subsequent studies have dealt with the matter not only as the problem of reconciling constitutional power with international responsibility, but also as the problem of reconciling the unity of national administration with the work of international administration, as the problem of reconciling the demands of the national public opinion with the demands of a developing world public opinion, and, in general, as the problem of gearing national governments, claiming sovereignty, into the developing international government and society. Carl Friedrich's book on *Foreign Policy in the Making* published in 1938 and Richard C. Snyder's on *Decision-Making as an Approach to the Study of International Politics* published in 1954 give some indication of the scope of this emerging discipline (5a, 19a). The increasing complexity of international organization with the establishment of the United Nations and its many specialized agencies has had an important impact on the organization and administration of all aspects of the member governments.

It will be observed that the eight disciplines discussed in this chapter emerged for the most part independently at different times and places in response to the professional interests of particular groups whose activities necessarily extended beyond the national domain. Lawyers, diplomats, soldiers, merchants, colonial administrators, foreign office officials, and officials of international organizations could not avoid international contacts and in some cases their entire activity consisted in dealing with such contacts. These groups differed, however, in objectives and methods, and the disciplines which guided them, and perhaps progressively improved their practices, were not closely related to one another. Military science, it is true, paid attention to the international law of war; international politics drew its material from diplomatic history; international organization rested upon international law; and international trade could not ignore international politics, but the aims of the soldier, diplomat, administrator and merchant were different and the disciplines which each understood often failed to reconcile these differences. The problem of a new discipline of international relations is to achieve such a reconciliation. The conditions of a shrinking world accentuate the effects of disharmonies in the action of different private and public organs within the nation, of the governments of different nations, and of different international organizations public and private. Pressure for a discipline which may produce more harmony in thought and as a result more harmony in practice therefore increases.

These disciplines have all in some degree assumed the sovereignty of the state. It may be that the shrinking world has required a modification of this concept and that disciplines based, not on *international relations*, but on a *world society* are required (17). There are such disciplines and they will be considered in the next chapter.

REFERENCES

More extensive references on the disciplines mentioned in this chapter are appended to the chapters dealing with each discipline. Useful summaries with bibliographies can be found in the *Encyclopædia of the Social Sciences* under the topics: International Law, Diplomacy, Militarism, War, International Relations, Political Science, International Organization, International Trade, Economics, Colonial Administration, Treaties. The following histories or treatises on these disciplines usually include extensive bibliographies.

1. Butler, Geoffrey, and Maccoby, S., *The Development of International Law* (London, Longmans, 1928).
2. Condliffe, John, *The Commerce of Nations* (New York, Norton, 1950).
3. Day, Clive, *A History of Commerce* (London, Longmans, 1907; 4th ed., 1938).
4. Earle, Edward M., *Makers of Modern Strategy* (Princeton, Princeton University Press, 1944).
5. Fox, William T. R., *The Super-Powers* (New York, Harcourt, 1944).
5a. Friedrich, Carl J., *Foreign Policy in the Making* (New York, Norton, 1938).
6. Heatley, D. P., *Diplomacy and the Study of International Relations* (Oxford, Clarendon Press, 1919).
7. Hoselitz, Bert, ed., *The Progress of Underdeveloped Areas* (Chicago, University of Chicago Press, 1952).
8. Knorr, Klaus E., *British Colonial Theories, 1570-1850* (Toronto, University of Toronto Press, 1944).
9. Montross, Lynn, *War Through the Ages* (New York, Harper, 1944).
10. Morgenthau, Hans J., *Politics Among Nations* (New York, Knopf, 1946).
11. Nussbaum, Arthur, *A Concise History of the Law of Nations* (New York, Macmillan, 1947).
12. Petrie, Sir Charles, *Earlier Diplomatic History, 1492-1713; Diplomatic History, 1713-1933* (New York, Macmillan, 1949).
13. Poole, Dewitt C., *The Conduct of Foreign Relations Under Modern Democratic Conditions* (New Haven, Yale University Press, 1924).
14. Potter, Pitman B., *An Introduction to the Study of International Organization* (New York, Appleton, 1922; 5th ed., Appleton-Century-Crofts, 1948).
15. Russell, Frank M., *Theories of International Relations* (New York, Appleton-Century-Crofts, 1936).
16. Satow, Sir Ernest, *Diplomatic Practice* (London, Longmans, 1917).

17. SCHUMAN, Frederick, *The Commonwealth of Man* (New York, Knopf, 1952).

18. ———, *International Politics*, 5th ed. (New York, McGraw-Hill, 1953).

19. SERENI, Angelo P., *The Italian Conception of International Law* (New York, Columbia University Press, 1943).

19a. SNYDER, Richard C., BRUCK, H. W., and SAPIN, Burton, *Decision-Making as an Approach to the Study of International Politics* (Organizational Behavior Section, Princeton University, June, 1954).

20. SPAULDING, O. L., NICKERSON, H., and WRIGHT, J. W., *Warfare* (London, Harff, 1924).

21. VINER, Jacob, *Studies in the Theory of International Trade* (New York, Harper, 1937).

22. WRIGHT, Q., *Control of American Foreign Relations* (New York, Macmillan, 1922).

23. ———, *Mandates Under the League of Nations* (Chicago, University of Chicago Press, 1930).

24. ———, *A Study of War* (Chicago, University of Chicago Press, 1942), Ch. 18, pp. 701 ff.; Appds. 26, 27, pp. 1365 ff.

CHAPTER
6

Disciplines with a
World Point of View

THE DISTINCTION between an international and a cosmopolitan or world point of view is not easy to define precisely (40, 43). The internationalist assumes the existence and importance of the nations though he may recognize that in their own interests they must co-operate with one another and accept responsibilities toward the world order. As the internationalist urges further responsibilities, more extensive co-operation, and a reduction of international oppositions, he approaches the cosmopolitan. On the other hand, a cosmopolitan who says like Socrates "the world is my country" may recognize that in fact there is a nation to which he owes allegiance and that the autonomy of the nation ought to be preserved insofar as it does not impair the "higher" loyalty to the world. He may even regard the cultural variety and cultural competition consequent upon the existence of relatively independent nations as a necessary condition for a progressive and interesting world. He thus approaches the internationalist.

But instead of approaching each other, the internationalist and the cosmopolitan may diverge. The former may so stress national sovereignty as to reduce international law, international organization, and international trade to a minimum, thus exaggerating the oppositional relations of nations and approaching the opinion of the extreme nationalist who brooks no limitations on the sovereignty of his nation and accepts a condition of *bellum omnium contra omnes* as normal in international affairs. The cosmopolitan, on the other hand, may stress world citizenship and freedom of transnational communication and movement to the extent of demanding a unified world government, eliminating the nations, reducing them to administrative subdivisions by agreement, or subjecting all to one in a universal empire. The cosmopolitanism of Dante, Charles V, Louis XIV, Napoleon, Stalin, and some recent advocates of world government looked in that direction (1, 38, 41). Such cosmopolitanism merges into the most extreme nationalism leading toward the dominance of the one successful nation in the world.

The disciplines to be discussed in this chapter, therefore, while attempting to view the world as a whole, take cognizance in varying degrees of the actual existence of nations. Consideration will be given to world history; world geography; pacifism; the psychology and sociology of international relations; humanistic, social, and biological disciplines; and to the recent development of regional studies, operational research, and group dynamics.

The first of these disciplines to be considered is *world history*. The idea is to be found in the historical books of the Old Testament which, like the historical literature of most religions, interpreted a mixture of myth and fact in accordance with a philosophical theory of origins. The idea of world history is also to be found in Herodotus who chronicled a similar mixture, but without a theory and with continued warnings that some of the reports he narrated might not be true.

In Western civilization, medieval histories assumed the potential universality of Christendom and warped the facts to fit that assumption. Bossuet's history written in the late seventeenth century was of this type. The theories of Hegelian dialectics, of Darwinian evolution, of constitutional federalism, and of technological and scientific progress which developed in the nineteenth century provided new bases for assuming an inevitable trend toward world unity and resulted in such universal histories as those of Hegel, Marx, and H. G. Wells.

Other historians have attempted to view the world as it is with its oppositions and co-operations, its disintegrations and integrations, without any theory of inevitable trend. The theory that history moves in cycles or fluctuations, of progress toward unification followed by retrogression and break-up, was envisaged by philosophers of ancient India and classical Greece. Among universal historians, Guizot, Freeman, Spengler, and Toynbee illustrate this tendency. They break history up into certain "civilizations" each of which includes many nations or lesser groups. Both nations and civilizations have life spans and consequently world history goes through fluctuations, although a tendency toward integration through technological or scientific advance is not excluded (31).

Other world histories, following the tradition of Herodotus, have sought to avoid any general theory either of persistent direction or sporadic oscillation, and to relate particular changes to particular circumstances, meteorological, technological, or ideological; social, economic, or political. Such writers, however, usually find it necessary to break history into minute parts, in each of which, as Ranke said, detailed research may make it possible to discover exactly what happened. But the process is so time-consuming that no one man can cover world history from the sources, and if secondary sources are relied upon or collaboration is attempted, the work becomes merely a reference work and the idea of world history is lost. As a history broadens in time and space, its exposition increasingly implies a theory, philosophical or scientific, as a criterion for selecting from the innumerable facts. World histories, therefore, tend to be philosophies or sciences of history rather than history itself (38).

World history, which seeks to recreate the development of the world as a whole in all its aspects, is to be distinguished from specialized histories on a universal scale. The latter may emphasize the unity of man as is usually true of histories of science, technology, art, and literature. They may also emphasize the diversity of man as is usually true of diplomatic and military histories. Historians of political and economic man are concerned with both the co-operative and oppositional activities of human groups and may, therefore, maintain a balance between these two tendencies.

The literature of world history is voluminous and has had its own historians, although the types of world history are so various that its study can hardly be called a discipline. The writing of world history has, however, had implications for international relations both as explanation and as builder of effective opinion. The awareness by mankind as a whole of the relations in time and space of the groups into which his species has been divided tends to develop an idea of unity, whether these relations are reported as predominantly co-operative or predominantly oppositional; whether change is found to have a direction toward cultural uniformity, material unification, spiritual union, or political unity; whether history is believed to move in greater or lesser oscillations of integration and disintegration; or whether historic changes are considered entirely sporadic and contingent (38, 41). The most recent and comprehensive effort to produce a world history is that undertaken by UNESCO in 1950 (32).

World geography, like world history, tends to encourage a universal point of view. The world may be looked upon as the environment of a particular nation, culture, or religion as it was by medieval cosmology, exemplified in Dante's *Divine Comedy* with Christendom at the center, not only of the world, but of the universe. Progressive understanding of the actual character of the world and its detailed mapping, description of the various peoples and nations, and explanation of their distribution in terms of the physical and economic characteristics of their habitats, and modes of utilizing their resources tends to give them all a certain equality in importance as denisons of the earth, and to create a realization of the world as a whole composed of many peoples related in space and time (9).

Ancient geography based on actual exploration, modified by ideas of necessary perfection and symmetry, facilitated this point of view and contributed to such objective histories as that of Herodotus. Classic geographic thought appears to have been initiated by Thales, Pythagoras, and Hecataeus in the sixth century B.C. It was continued by Aristotle and Eratosthenes and finally formulated by Strabo and Ptolemy in the first and second centuries A.D. Medieval geography, with its flat maps of the world usually with Jerusalem at the center and surrounded by the indefinite *ocean*, facilitated self-centered histories and philosophies and provided an obstacle to exploration and discovery. Modern geography utilizing the classical knowledge transmitted and added to by the Arabs, developed in the age of discovery, rediscovered the spherical character of the globe, and facilitated an objective view of its resources, peoples, and nations. Illusions continued because of the methods of projection of the spherical globe on flat surfaces. Divisions into Eastern and Western Hemisphere tended to perpetuate the idea of a radical distinction between the old and the new world. Mercator projections exaggerated the temperate zones at the expense of the tropics and obscured relations between the continents across the poles. New modes of projection, introduced since man learned to fly, and more extensive familiarity with globes have reduced these illusions. Insistence upon correct visual presentations has been at the center of modern political geography as illustrated in the work of Spykman (27).

Geographers, like historians, have tended to divide into the objective school which seeks, by reducing the field of a particular study, to discover and describe with increasing accuracy everything within it, and the subjective school that seeks a theory by which the field may be expanded indefinitely and the whole realized by the human mind. Writers of the first school tend to describe more and more about less and less until they describe everything about nothing of importance, as do some doctoral dissertations, while writers of the subjective school tend to describe less and less about more and more until they say nothing about everything as do mythologies about the origin and early development of the world and man (38).

The literature of geography consists of maps and descriptions of methods of mapping and projection; of detailed descriptions of areas, their physical, economic, and social characteristics, and the change of these characteristics in time; the establishment and exposition of relations capable of generalization between the geographical, including the geological, meteorological, and biological characteristics of an area and its human and social characteristics; and the exposition of geographical features in an area of the world significant for human action. The story of discovery and exploration also constitutes a dramatic feature of geographic literature which should not be omitted. The literature relating man to his environment and describing the utilizable resources and features of particular areas are obviously of most significance for international relations (9).

Writers like Friedrich Ratzel, Ellsworth Huntington, and Griffith Taylor following in the footsteps of Vico, Montesquieu, Kant, Humboldt, and Ritter have attempted to demonstrate broad relations between position, topography, resources and climatic fluctuations, and types of culture and civilization of mankind, the divisions into nations, and the movements of migration and conquest. Such generalizations, like those of world history, frequently extend beyond the data, although sometimes, as in the work of Ritter, the mass of detail obscures the whole. Writers like Mackinder, Kjellen, and Haushofer have attempted to assemble geographical data for practical purposes of foreign policy, thus following the tradition of military geographers and meteorologists who have always understood the relations of position, terrain, and weather to military operations; of economic geographers who have always understood the relations of the location of soils, minerals, skills, and other resources, and of markets, cities, and land and maritime highways to the planning and conduct of agriculture, industry, and trade; and of political geographers who have always understood the relation of the geographic, demographic, economic, cultural, and political character of the state's domain to policies for promoting its unity, security, and prosperity. The relation of boundary features to defense, offense, smuggling, irredentism, and local political attitudes has been of particular interest to political geographers.

Geography became during the nineteenth century a definite discipline with academic departments and textbooks. Histories have been written of both geographical discovery and geographical writing. Political geography, which organizes those aspects of geography especially pertinent to international relations, has been emerging as a more specialized discipline. Textbooks have been produced by Bowman, Colby, Jones, Whittlesey, Weigert, and others (9, 36).

Pacifism or peace education includes the effort to demonstrate the value of peace, to encourage its pursuit, and to instruct in the method of maintaining it. It has often been closely related to religious activity. As an international movement, pacifism resembles proselytism or missionary activity in that it seeks to exert influence by persuasion, but differs as does international organization, from colonial government in not assuming the inequality of cultures and value systems. Pacifism like proselytism is less a discipline than a propaganda, but it has an extended literature and has been the objective of numerous associations with activities which range from popular propaganda to learned research and publication. Histories of both the literature and the practices of peace have been written (3).

The influence of the peace movement on international relations has been important. Peace movements have usually tended toward a cosmopolitan view of the world, have often been inspired by the religious idea of human brotherhood, and have frequently looked to moral regeneration as the path toward realization. Peace, however, has also been asserted as the goal of international law, of international organization, of world government, and even of policies of nationality, empire, and balance of power (3, 38).

Peace and harmony have figured as ideals in most religions. Ancient Greek philosophy tended to view war as natural, though the dramatists produced pacifist literature and the Stoics were cosmopolitan pacifists. Hinduism and Buddhism were pacifistic in tendency. Confucianism has had both pacifistic and militaristic interpretations. Judaism balanced between peace and war, the Old Testament recommending both that swords be beaten into plowshares and the reverse. In Islam the doctrine of the Jihad asserted perpetual war with the infidel and peace only when the world was converted. Early Christian writers inspired by the Sermon on the Mount were pacifistic. They urged nonresistance and would not admit the propriety or necessity of war in any circumstances. When, however, the sheltering Roman Empire, of which Christianity had become the official religion, was threatened with invasion by the barbarians in the third century, St. Augustine developed the distinction between just and unjust war, placing war to defend the empire in the first of these categories. Catholic Christianity has continued to support this theory. While it accepts peace as the ideal, it recognizes that in an imperfect world, war to promote justice, considered an essential element of peace, may be necessary (8).

The Renaissance and the Reformation renewed interest in the texts of the Bible and primitive Christianity and led dissenting sects such as the Mennonites and the Quakers to deny the Catholic distinction and to insist upon nonresistant pacifism. Erasmus, writing at about the same time as Machiavelli, may be considered the originator of modern pacifism in contrast to Machiavelli's militarism. The writings of Erasmus influenced the international politics, international law and international organization of his time, and also peace movements both religious and secular. Such movements tended to flourish after unusually devastating wars and developed, particularly in England and the United States, after the Napoleonic Wars. These movements have continued and have inspired significant financial foundations such as the Carnegie Endowment for International Peace and the Nobel Peace Prize. The maintenance of international peace was the leading objective of the Hague Peace Conferences, the League of Nations, and the United Nations. The Charter of the latter organization states as its first object "to save succeeding generations from the scourge of war," and one of its Specialized Agencies, UNESCO, declares in its Preamble: "since wars begin in the minds of men, it is in the minds of men that the defenses of peace must be constructed," and peace must be founded "upon the intellectual and moral solidarity of mankind."

The literature of the peace movement has been voluminous, but it has often been inspired by emotional hatred of war rather than by intellectual analysis of the nature of peace, of the obstacles to achieving it, and of practical means to that end. Peace education has emphasized the costs of war in terms of economic loss and human suffering and the inconsistency of war with other national and international objectives and policies, and has proposed moral and political reforms sometimes of a rather sweeping character. Different schools of thought have varied greatly in the steps advocated. These schools may be roughly classified as the nonresisters and the world organizers. The first advocate individual nonsupport of violence in varying degrees from absolute nonparticipation in all war and physical coercion to nonparticipation only in the most military aspects of war, tolerating support of domestic police, international police, and civilian work contributing to victory in national war. The world organizational school often criticizes individual pacifism on the ground that so long as it is not universally accepted its effect is to make the peaceful vulnerable to attack by the unregenerate. The world organizers fear that a world mostly sheep will encourage attack by the wolves that remain, and therefore advocate organization of the sheep so that they can resist effectively. Following Pascal's suggestion that force without justice is tyranny and justice without force is anarchy, they seek to organize force behind international or world law deemed to embody justice. The nonresistant pacifists, therefore, tend to universal anarchy and the world organizers to universal government.

Moderates of the two schools approach one another and often come together on concrete proposals such as improvements in early education to prevent the development of aggressive sentiments, methods for influencing adult opinion generally, and development of substitute targets for aggressive dispositions. International agreements have been urged and made, for outlawing war, for disarmament, and for establishing procedures of pacific settlement. Education, propaganda, diplomatic agreements, and world institutions have been suggested to develop a world society within which peace could be maintained.

Pacifism is hardly capable of becoming an academic discipline itself, but it has increasingly felt the need of an adequate psychology and sociology of international relations to provide it with intelligible foundations. Perhaps its most important function has been its contribution to the building of these disciplines. It has also contributed to the developing disciplines of international education and international communications, both stimulated by the activities of UNESCO, though they have roots in a more distant past.

Theories of the *psychology of international relations* have been assumed by most political philosophers. Aristotle considered man a social animal, but wars between societies seemed to him *natural*. He considered war a sociological rather than a psychological phenomenon. A similar view underlay the medieval theory, that man, born in sin, with warlike tendencies, could be converted to Christianity and to peace. But even Christians came to recognize that war was a frequent consequence of grave social injustices and until such injustices were eliminated, war was justifiable in certain circumstances (8).

The Renaissance philosophers, however, interpreted the state of nature, which in the Middle Ages meant the state of man unconverted to the faith, in a psychological sense, as the nature of man apart from society. They, therefore, discussed whether this original nature of man was peaceful or warlike. Thomas Hobbes took the second view. Holding that man by nature was inspired by fear and greed, he defined the state of nature as one of war, by each against all, from which man could only rescue himself by the social contract establishing society and government to enforce law for the preservation of peace. War was, therefore, a psychological phenomenon; peace a sociological phenomenon. Rousseau, on the other hand, thought natural man was peaceful. The corruptions of society had made man warlike. In his *Social Contract*, however, Rousseau urged the need of government, no less comprehensive, but more democratic, than that urged by Hobbes. Locke's views were more moderate. Human nature, he thought, had its good and evil side. A man, however, could not be trusted to do justice in his own case, so government was necessary to maintain justice and peace. If, however, it exceeded the powers which it derived from the consent of the governed, revolution was justified. Other theories of human nature inspired Adam Smith, Jeremy Bentham, Immanuel Kant, and G. W. F. Hegel (35, 39).

It was not until the mid-nineteenth century, when psychology began to develop as a discipline based on observation more than on introspection, that the complexity of human nature could be understood. The dynamic psychology of Freud, the behaviorism of Watson, the conditioned reflexes of Pavlov, the social interactionism of Durkheim, Simmel, Dewey, and Thomas, the statistical measurements of Thorndike and Thurstone, and the *gestalt* approach of Koehler, Koffka, and Lewin, as well as the practical experience of educators, propagandists, and advertisers, showed that the manifestations of human drives are malleable, that *human nature* springs as much from early social conditioning as from original *instincts,* and that the manipulation of attitudes and opinions to accomplish specific objectives is an art requiring concrete knowledge of those to be manipulated as well as of the symbols and media to be used (19, 30). Psychology is, therefore, difficult to distinguish from sociology. In fact *social psychology* has developed as a discipline with roots in both and with several schools and methods of interpretation.

Specific application of this new psychological knowledge to the fields of politics and international relations began to be made shortly before World War I by Graham Wallas, Walter Lippmann, and A. Lawrence Lowell, utilizing to some extent the insights of Walter Bagehot. Such efforts received an impetus from the extensive use of propaganda in World War I and through the efforts of Harold Lasswell and others, the psychology of international relations has approached the status of a discipline with extensive bibliographies, monographs, journals, and practical activities guided by its assumptions (18). These activities extend into the guidance of international informational, educational, and propaganda activities, and into the analyses of propagandas to aid national and international policy.

Sociology and social anthropology deal with human groups, but since the period of the great evolutionary systematizers, Comte, Spencer, Ward, Morgan, Sumner, and Gumplowitz, these disciplines have been most interested in compact and integrated groups such as the family; the local community; the gang; the crowd; the primitive clan, village, or tribe; the political party; the cultural or professional association; or the business concern. These groups provide easier material to study in detail than the large and relatively amorphous groups such as nations, states, international organizations, and mankind as a whole. It is only recently that sociologists have again devoted attention to such groups and have applied to them concepts developed by more concrete studies, such as community, society, culture, institution, contact, co-operation, standardization, integration, conflict, opposition, competition, differentiation, diffusion, accommodation, assimilation, organization, social entity, social process, social force, social relation, *gemeinschaft, gesellschaft,* in-group, and out-group. Such concepts, while imperfectly stabilized in meaning, provide the bases for sociological theory (4, 5, 41).

The sociologists, though concentrating attention upon the group, have not been able to ignore the fact that the group is composed of individuals whose attitudes and opinions make it cohere, and that changes in these attitudes and opinions modify the group's policies and character, or cause it to disappear altogether. The sociologist, therefore, tends to become a psychologist, while the psychologist, who, though concentrating on the individual as a biological and psychic entity, cannot ignore the major contribution to his psychic character made by the group in which he was born and lives, tends to become a sociologist. Sociology and psychology tend, therefore, to be different approaches to a psychological sociology, or a social psychology which assume close relationship between group and individual, culture and personality, community and communicant, society and socius, organization and participant.

The sociology and the psychology of international relations approach one another but they differ in origin and emphasis. Sociology originated in history rather than philosophy, in observation rather than introspection. The earlier sociologists of international relations were philosophical historians and geographers, like Herodotus in antiquity, and Montaigne in the Renaissance, who compared the manners and customs of diverse societies; like Aristotle and Lucretius in antiquity, Vico and Montesquieu in the eighteenth century who sought to relate social laws to differences in environment, race, or tradition; or like Quesnet, Malthus, Hegel, and Marx in the eighteenth and nineteenth centuries who sought to explain history in terms of agriculture, population, ideas, and technology. It was not until the mid-nineteenth century that sociology began to emerge as a discipline, partly through the detailed study of primitive peoples by men like Morgan, Tyler, Wundt, and Sumner; partly through the philosophical generalizing of history by men like Comte and Buckle; partly through the application of concepts drawn from organic evolution by men like Spencer, Ratzel, and Gumplowitz; and partly through the sharpening of concepts by men like Emile Durkheim, Lester Ward, Georg Simmel, Max Weber, and Karl Mannheim.

Sociology is still an imperfectly integrated discipline, and the sociology of international relations remains even less integrated. There has, however, been much writing in the field particularly since World War I. The sociology of war and conflict was dealt with by Gumplowitz, Novicov, Havelock Ellis, LeTourneau, Steinmetz, Simmel, Bloch, and others. This literature greatly increased during the interwar period and since World War II studies in the field have been officially sponsored, particularly by UNESCO which has organized collaborative studies on International Tensions.

Other aspects of international relations dealt with by the sociologists include the sociology of intercultural relations and of intercultural communities; the social consequences of inventions such as the radio, the airplane, and atomic energy on world affairs (24), and the sociology of opinion, law, and value systems. The analysis and measurement of attitudes and opinions has been considered in the field of psychology rather than of sociology, but the explanation of opinions, beliefs, and evaluations, in particular social circumstances has been undertaken by sociologists. In this connection the contributions by anthropologists like R. R. Marrett, Carr-Saunders, Radcliffe-Brown, Bronislaw Malinowski, Ralph Linton, Ruth Benedict, and Margaret Mead, many of them drawn into practical applications of their knowledge of primitive peoples during World War II, is especially notable (4, 5, 41). The objective work of W. F. Ogburn, Talcott Parsons, Robert Angell, Robert MacIver, and Gunnar

Myrdal has been significant, and the more generalizing efforts of Ellsworth Huntington, Vilfreda Pareto, Gaetano Mosca, and Pitirim Sorokin have provided hypotheses stimulating to investigation (16).

The sociology of international relations is in need of a bibliography and of comprehensive analysis. There seems to have been no comprehensive textbook devoted to the subject. The sociology and the psychology of international relations have not been clearly differentiated from each other or from world history, political geography, and international politics.

The list of disciplines contributing to international relations could be indefinitely extended. *Philosophy, ethics, theology,* and the *humanistic studies* have had points of view on the subject. In these disciplines can be found the beginnings of psychology, the social sciences, international law, and world history. Among the social sciences, in addition to political science, economics, sociology, anthropology, social psychology, education and communications which have been mentioned, population, statistics, technology, and linguistics have shown tendencies to emerge as specialized disciplines, although all may be included in either sociology or economics. The significance of biology for social science has also attracted attention. The emerging disciplines of regional study, operational research, and group dynamics were emphasized by official action during World War II, and may prove of great significance for the study of international relations.

Studies of *population* development in relation to the food supply, to military potential, and to the differences in the relative power of nations, classes, and groups are of major importance in explaining international politics and international economics (14).

Statistics figure in studies of population, international trade, and finance. The statistics of military activity, of armaments, and of opinion have also been assembled and analyzed to verify mathematical theories of international politics, international tensions, and oscillations of war and peace. The concepts of distances between groups and of tensions within groups may also lend themselves to mathematical treatment and to statistical verification (38).

Technological change has figured in the theories of history and social change, and the influence on international affairs of particular inventions such as gunpowder, the printing press, the steam engine, electrical communication, the airplane, and the atomic bomb have been studied in detail (24).

Language is one of the most significant human techniques and students of linguistics and semantics find in it objective evidence of changes of knowledge, values, methods, and sentiments within groups and of differences in these respects between groups (7, 23). Opinions, policies, laws, values, and philosophies rest in some degree on linguistic habits. Nations and international relations can be studied as phenomena springing from linguistic symbols and their communication, and if studied from other points of view, such as those of economics, political science, and sociology, the distorting influence of the symbols of communication must be taken into account. Anthropology has recognized the language of primitive people as no less important in understanding them and their relations, than their physical and racial characteristics and their patterns of behavior, culture, and value.

Biologists have developed an interest in international relations. The study of social insects suggests interesting analogies to human societies and the study of animal behavior patterns throws light on human drives, unconditioned by language and culture. The problem of organization in general is dealt with by students of morphology and of animal aggregations, communities, and societies (2, 13). Plant and animal ecology is concerned with problems similar to human ecology and human geography (11). The balance of power resembles the balance of nature in many respects. Organic evolution provided the starting point for theories of social evolution, and the analysis of factors, such as mutation, geographic barriers, random variation, hybridization, and the relative size of groups and subgroups, which influence the stability and change of organic species, has proved suggestive for the internationalist viewing mankind as an organic species (42).

Intelligence agencies and occupying forces necessarily function in particular *regions*. Knowledge of the distinctive geography, language, history, civilization, economic institutions, religions, and attitudes of each region is of obvious utility to the participants in such activities. Studies grouping material from many disciplines about a particular region have, therefore, been developed for practical purposes of hot or cold war (6, 28, 33). Regions have been administratively and politically organized into states, federations, alliances, international organizations, and regional arrangements within the United Nations. The Economic and Social Council of the United Nations has set up commissions for Asia and the Far East, for Europe, and for Latin America. The Caribbean and South Pacific Commissions have been set up to study colonial problems of these regions. The social and political arts almost necessarily tend to be practiced regionally. The appropriate allocation of functions to local, provincial, national, regional, and world organs is the center of these arts (10, 39).

Certain disciplines such as history, geography, humanistic studies, and anthropology have always tended to concentrate studies upon particular regions. For these disciplines a world point of view involves a philosophical sophistication. The *natural* point of departure is local. The significance of recent regional studies lies in the regional integration of these disciplines with other disciplines which like psychology, sociology, economics, and politics have tended to generalize (12).

Regional studies lead to consideration of the *natural* regions of the world, of the criteria for determining them, and of the political, economic, social, and cultural consequences of increasing contact between diverse regional complexes (25). Scholarly institutes have developed, specializing in some one of the great regions of the world such as Latin America, the Slavic countries, the Middle East, the Far East, South Asia, and Western Europe and Africa. Careful consideration of such divisions, however, makes it clear that neither these nor any other regional scheme of the world is absolute. Regions within, between, and around such great continental divisions can be usefully studied for particular purposes as, for example, the North Atlantic, the Caribbean, the British Commonwealth, Central Europe, Central Asia, Southeast Asia, the Arab countries, the South Pacific, North Africa, South Africa, Central Africa, the Arctic. The regional point of view facilitates certain kinds of specialization and certain kinds of integration, but it also tends to certain types of distortion through exaggerating the significance of a particular region or a particular mode of dividing the globe (6, 22).

If regional studies properly emphasize the relativity of all time and space circumscriptions and dispel the illusion that any historic, political, legal, economic, cultural, social, or other region is absolute or inevitable, particularly with the modern means of communication, they may facilitate the world point of view. The whole will be seen through study of its parts.

Operational research occurs in a broad sense whenever practical operations are consciously used to increase theoretical knowledge, and the knowledge so acquired is then used reciprocally to increase the efficiency of the operation. The term has been used especially when quantitative methods are applied, only possible when the terms employed are *operationally* defined. Operational research is therefore related to practical action and to operational philosophy (26). Operational research has developed in the international field in recent years because it was found useful in military and political operations using modern technology to concentrate knowledge from many disciplines upon a particular operative problem.

During World War II problems were set by the military and political high command such as: How can the submarine menace to shipping be best met? How can a maximum tonnage be delivered to China from India? How can propaganda be best used to undermine the morale of the Japanese people? What will be the probable casualties in launching an amphibious attack upon Japan? What targets in Germany would maximize military results with minimum expenditures? What is the most efficient method for producing fissionable materials for the manufacture of atomic bombs? What will be the probable curve of change in relative airplane availability of the Allies and Germany on the Western front with maximum feasible production effort by the United States and Great Britain?

Efforts were made to define such problems precisely and in terms which could be dealt with by comparisons of probabilities and other quantities. Experts in various disciplines collected data as quantitative and objective as possible, and experts in mathematics devised methods of analysis, often using elaborate calculating machines. Such problems often involved physical, psychological, and cultural assumptions. From operational research have developed the science of Cybernetics (37), having to do with calculations involving many variables, some of them with "feed-back" effect; operational philosophy seeking to unite logical positivism, semantics, and pragmatism into a theory of science (23, 26); and applied anthropology adapting to the study of modern nations methods used in the study of primitive peoples (4, 21). Effective research has in the past been in large measure an individual activity, but operational research has lent itself to new forms of co-operative and directed research. The close co-operation between research and operations and the continual testing of the results of research in operations, gives its peculiar characteristics to this discipline (29).

It has been the tradition of modern science that major discoveries have been made when considerations of practical utility and subordination of the scientist to administrative direction have been minimized. The scientist, it is said, must be free to follow his curiosity, his hunch, or his insight without thought of practical results, of meeting a time schedule, or of pleasing a superior. Regional research and operational research which seek to co-ordinate many workers and many disciplines about a defined region or a defined problem run against this tradition. They are applied sciences, probably better adapted to forwarding the arts of strategy and statecraft than to advancing the fundamental disciplines of international relations. As will be seen, however, in the next section of this book, international relations like all the social sciences is as much a history, an art, and a philosophy as a science. It is synthetic rather than analytic. Its problem is to bring together knowledge and techniques in order to solve problems whether of national tactics, strategy, or policies; of international conciliation, adjustment, or organization; of world stability, justice, or progress.

Recent experience has shown that the traditions of law, diplomacy, and war which have guided international statesmen in the past are not adequate, and that the resources of all the disciplines and all the experts must be mobilized (16). There was a hint of this in descriptions of the studies necessary for diplomats in the sixteenth and seventeenth centuries (15, 20), but today the knowledge required is far beyond the competence of any one man. Methods for the integration of the skills of many experts in many methods is necessary. National foreign offices are seeking to meet the need by establishing closer relations with all other departments of government and with national scientific and educational institutions. Similarly, the United Nations, with its dozens of Specialized Agencies, its many committees, its trained experts in the Secretariat, and its innumerable contacts with private organizations, national and international, seeks to mobilize all the world's resources of knowledge and skill to accomplish particular tasks. The facilities available for practicing the art of adapting means to ends are perhaps superior to those available for developing a philosophy of international relations and for achieving agreement on what, at a given moment, the end should be.

The discipline of *group dynamics* has developed from social psychology under the inspiration of Kurt Lewin's interpretation of the *gestalt* theory (19). It distinguishes the individual's *life space* or subjective picture of the situation from the external *hull* or the objective reality of the situation. All individual and social behavior is determined directly by the configuration of the *life space*. The *hull* exerts influence only indirectly as it effects this configuration through the individual's experience, which, however, is always selective and distorted by sensory inadequacies, perceptual expectations, habitual conceptions, symbolic meanings, cultural assumptions, and individual and group prejudices. It is, however, the *life space* in a given situation as a whole that determines behavior not any particular aspect of it. Behavior is determined by the *gestalt*, not by a particular sensory, perceptual, or conceptual experience.

Groups function through achievement of sufficient concordance of the *life spaces* of the members so that in a given situation the members will act co-operatively with common understanding and common goals. The representation of *life spaces*, the analysis of the behavior to be expected within a given *life space*, the determination of the way in which the *life space* is influenced by experience, and the art of co-ordinating the *life spaces* of the members of a group constitute the discipline of group dynamics (30).

In its application to international relations, group dynamics seeks to analyze the conditions making for agreement or disagreement among the members of international groups such as diplomatic conversations or conferences; international secretariats or organizations; private international conversations, transactions or associations; and the international public as a whole in such activities as interpreting official or unofficial communications of international importance. Certain studies initiated by UNESCO have had this orientation, especially those concerning the technique of international conferences and the functioning of international secretariats (34).

Consideration of philosophy and world history, of politics and administration, of economics and technology, of sociology and biology may evolve a theory of the relation of values and techniques, of subjective and objective truth, of potential and actual reality, of the universal and the special which will keep ends and means, thought and action, the whole and the part, general and expert opinions in proper relation to one another. Such a theory might avoid the assumption, sometimes made by applied science that because means are effective the end which they tend toward must be good, or the assumption sometimes made by practical philosophy that because the end is good, the means necessary or convenient to achieve it must be good. While the latter exaggeration tended to dominate thought in the Middle Ages, the former has perhaps dominated thought in the modern world. Scientists have tended to consider the advancement of human knowledge good irrespective of its social consequences. When they had created the atomic bomb, however, some of them paused to consider whether they might not have erred in giving a dangerous weapon to an immature world. Theologians, political philosophers, and statesmen have tended to develop philosophies, religions, or political opinions into dogmas and to assert that any methods effective for the advancement of the favored doctrine is justifiable. Modern totalitarian rulers, whose dogmas were widely questioned and whose methods were intolerable, impressed the world with the error of such thinking, even more than had the excesses of the Inquisition in the late Middle Ages. Liberals insisted that the justice of social action was to be judged no less by the procedures employed than by the ends achieved.

A synthetic discipline appears to be needed which may moderate the zeal of the scientist and technician so that he will consider the social consequences of his formulas and inventions, and which may also moderate the zeal of the theologian and politician so that he will consider the social consequences of employing dubious methods which may appear immediately effective in spreading and realizing values deemed important. Such a discipline may also moderate the zeal of the reformer so that he will consider the special and vested interests which his reform will discommode, and may also moderate the zeal of the lobbyist or individualist so that he will give consideration to the general good, likely to be impaired by realization of his particular interests. The advocates, respectively of world government and of national sovereignty, the socialists and the individualists, the idealists for whom the possibilities of the future are real and the realists for whom only the past and the present exist—all of these might, through such a discipline, perceive the relativity of their positions and find grounds for compromise. The relativism, pragmatism, adaptability, and moderation observable in the healthy organism, in the well-adjusted personality, and in the stable culture, is needed in the world community. These qualities apparently flow from complex and continually changing equilibria. It should be the function of a discipline of international relations to analyze the entities, processes, forces, and relations in the international field, and to seek means for so regulating and balancing them that the opportunity for individuals and groups to achieve their values may be maximized.

REFERENCES

Further references may be found on most of the disciplines mentioned in this chapter at the end of subsequent chapters dealing with each discipline. The *Encyclopædia of the Social Sciences* contains valuable articles on History, Geography, Education, Pacifism, Internationalism, Psychology, Social Psychology, Sociology, Statistics, Technology, Language, Pan-Movements, Regionalism Group, Society.

1. ADLER, Mortimer J., *How to Think About War and Peace* (New York, Simon and Schuster, 1944).
2. ALLEE, W. C., *The Social Life of Animals* (New York, Norton, 1938).
3. BEALES, A. C. F., *The History of Peace* (New York, Dial Press, 1931).
4. BENEDICT, Ruth, *The Chrysanthemum and the Sword* (Boston, Houghton Mifflin, 1946).
5. ———, *Patterns of Culture* (Boston, Houghton Mifflin, 1934).
6. BENNETT, Wendell C., *Area Studies in American Universities* (New York, Social Science Research Council, 1951).
7. BLOOMFIELD, Leonard, "Linguistic Aspects of Science," *International Encyclopedia of Unified Science* (Chicago, University of Chicago Press, 1939).
8. CADOUX, C. J., *The Early Christian Attitude Toward War* (London, Oxford University Press, 1919).
9. COLBY, Charles C., ed., *Geographic Aspects of International Relations* (Chicago, University of Chicago Press, 1938).
10. Commission to Study the Organization of Peace, *Regional Arrangements for Security and the United Nations,* 8th Report (New York, 1953).
11. EMERSON, Alfred E., "The Biological Basis of Social Co-operation," *Illinois Academy of Science, Transactions,* Vol. 39 (1946), pp. 9 ff.
12. FRIEDRICH, Carl J., "The Problem of Communication Between Cultures Seen as Integrated Wholes," in *Approaches to National Unity,* Fifth Symposium on Science, Philosophy and Religion (New York, Harper, 1945), pp. 10 ff.
13. GERARD, Ralph W., "A Biological Basis for Ethics," *Philosophy of Science,* Vol. 9 (January, 1942), pp. 92 ff.
14. GINI, Corrado, and others, *Population* (Chicago, University of Chicago Press, 1930).
15. HEATLEY, D. P., *Diplomacy and the Study of International Relations* (Oxford, Clarendon Press, 1919).
16. HUSZAR, George B. de, ed., *New Perspectives on Peace* (Chicago, University of Chicago Press, 1944).
17. ———, "Regional Approach to the Study of the Contemporary World," in *Approaches to World Unity,* Fifth Symposium on Science, Philosophy and Religion (New York, Harper, 1945), pp. 691 ff.
18. LASSWELL, Harold D., *World Politics and Personal Insecurity* (New York, McGraw-Hill, 1935).
19. LEWIN, Kurt, *A Dynamic Theory of Personality* (New York, McGraw-Hill, 1935).
20. MAGGI, Ottaviano, *De Legato* (1566).

21. MEAD, Margaret, *And Keep Your Powder Dry, An Anthropologist Looks at America* (New York, Morrow, 1942).

22. MORGENTHAU, Hans J., "Area Studies and the Study of International Relations," *International Social Science Bulletin*, Vol. 4 (Autumn, 1952), pp. 647 ff.

23. MORRIS, Charles, *Signs, Language and Behavior* (New York, Prentice-Hall, 1946).

24. OGBURN, W. F., ed., *Technology and International Relations* (Chicago, University of Chicago Press, 1949).

25. PARMELEE, Maurice, *Geo-Economic Regionalism and World Federation* (New York, Exposition Press, 1949).

26. RAPAPORT, Anatol, *Operational Philosophy, Integrating Knowledge and Action* (New York, Harper, 1953).

27. SPYKMAN, Nicholas, *The Geography of the Peace* (New York, Harcourt, 1944).

28. STEWART, John H., "Area Research: Theory and Practice," *Social Science Research Council Bulletin*, No. 63 (New York, 1950).

29. STONE, Marshall, "Science and Statecraft," *Science*, Vol. 105 (May 16, 1947), pp. 507 ff.

30. THELEN, Herbert A., *Human Dynamics Laboratory* (Chicago, University of Chicago Press, 1950).

31. TOYNBEE, Arnold J., *A Study of History* (London, Oxford University Press, 1934, 1939, 1954), 10 vols.

32. UNESCO, "Project for a Scientific and Cultural History of Mankind" (C 4.123), *Records of the General Conference, Fifth Session* (Florence, 1950), p. 42; see also *Journal of World History* (1954).

33. ———, "Area Studies, Symposium with Bibliography," *International Social Science Bulletin*, Vol. 4 (Autumn, 1952), pp. 633 ff.

34. ———, *The Technique of International Conferences, A Progress Report* (1951).

35. WALLAS, Graham, *The Great Society* (New York, Macmillan, 1914).

36. WEIGERT, Hans W., and STEFANSSON, Vilhjalmur, *Compass of the World* (New York, Macmillan, 1944).

37. WIENER, Norbert, *Cybernetics* (New York, Wiley, 1948).

38. WRIGHT, Quincy, *A Study of War* (Chicago, University of Chicago Press, 1942), pp. 158 ff, 423 ff, 438 ff, 701 ff, 885 ff, 1079 ff, 1365 ff.

39. ———, "Fundamental Problems of International Organization," *International Conciliation*, No. 369 (April, 1941), pp. 468 ff.

40. ———, "Specialization and Universal Values in General International Organization," *Approaches to Group Understanding*, Sixth Conference on Science, Philosophy and Religion (New York, Harper, 1947), pp. 207 ff.

41. ———, ed., *The World Community* (Chicago, University of Chicago Press, 1948).

42. WRIGHT, Sewall, "Population Structure in Evolution," *American Philosophical Society, Proceedings*, Vol. 93 (December, 1949), pp. 471 ff.

43. ZIMMERN, Alfred, "Education for World Citizenship," *Problems of Peace*, Fifth Series, Geneva Institute of International Relations (London, Oxford University Press, 1931), pp. 304 ff.

PART
II

Objectives in the Study of
International Relations

CHAPTER
7

Educational and Research Objectives

TEACHING, RESEARCH, and writing in the field of international relations have at least four objectives—improvement of citizenship, improvement of leadership, development of professional competence, and increase of human knowledge. It is assumed that good citizens, able leaders, skilled experts, and increasing knowledge are good for the individual, the nation, and the world, and that education and research in international relations can contribute to these ends. The meaning of these assumptions is not entirely clear and some possible meanings may be questioned.

EDUCATION FOR CITIZENSHIP

What is a good citizen? Is he a good follower or a good critic? Perhaps reliable followers are more to be expected from the ignorant than from the intelligent. Erasmus commented *dulce bellum inexpertis* suggesting a critical attitude toward war and participation in it, in contrast to the well known statement by Horace, *dulce et decorum est pro patria moris.* The latter statement is often quoted as the appropriate attitude for good citizens. But if Erasmus is right, knowledge about war may not promote good citizenship as Horace interpreted it. It is by no means certain that Erasmus' aphorism is convincing under modern conditions. Some investigations suggest that familiarity with military discipline and war develops "war mindedness" (47).

Whatever may be the validity of these quotations, they suggest that there has been doubt as to the attitude which good citizens should have

65

toward war and also as to the effect of knowledge about war upon attitudes toward war (17, 31).

Stephen Decatur's famous toast has been alluded to at an earlier point in this book: "Our country! In her intercourse with foreign nations may she always be in the right; but our country, right or wrong." Socrates, although he drank the hemlock in obedience to the laws of Athens, said on a different occasion, "When you are asked your country, never reply 'I am an Athenian' or 'I am a Corinthian'—but 'I am a citizen of the world.'" Under modern conditions, is a good citizen a citizen of a city, a citizen of a nation, or a citizen of the world? What symbol of supreme allegiance does understanding of international relations tend to develop (17, 53)?

Reflection on these statements and upon others whose wide appeal is attested by their frequent repetition in "familiar quotations" suggests that the characteristics of a good citizen and the kind of education which will develop those characteristics are not free from controversy.

Earnest advocates of a considerable injection of international relations into the college curriculum in America believe that objective knowledge and comprehensive understanding of the field will provide a sound combination of patriotism and criticism in the rising generation. By objective knowledge they imply information about the entities, processes, forces, and relations of the past and present and about those which competent scholars think are likely to be relevant in the future. By comprehensive understanding they imply comprehension of the points of view, motives, values, and purposes which account for the attitudes, opinions, policies, and actions of leaders and peoples, and appreciation of the human quality of these states of mind. Understanding implies that criticism of the states of mind of others is accompanied and toned down by realization that all human behavior, however censurable, has roots in a common human nature and can attract some sympathy from a critic who is able to understand his fellows through understanding himself. It was implied by the Christian doctrine of charity and was given classic expression in Lincoln's Second Inaugural.

Such education in international relations is widely believed to be good for citizenship, but it is well to have in mind that the leaders of education in totalitarian states appear to believe that the combination of loyalty and criticism appropriate to the citizen requires that his knowledge be confined to those facts of the contemporary and past world which have been sifted through a comprehensive censorship, that interpretative ideas be confined to those that are believed by the government to conform to the accepted ideology, and that attitudes, policies and actions which result from different information or different interpretative ideas are not only wrong, but wicked and subversive. In lesser degree this opinion is entertained by many nontotalitarian governments. Surveying the various civilizations of the world, education for citizenship has generally in theory and practice consisted in disciplining the immature mind to attitudes of unreflective and uncritical loyalty to symbols, rituals, ideas, and theories deemed by tradition, law, and prevailing opinion to be true, and to absolute condemnation of those deemed untrue. It is only rarely that societies have taken the risk of permitting the individual to observe and read freely, to think as personal reflection and experience suggest, and to embrace whatever ideas and theories carry conviction after this process. The assumption of such a risk involves more faith in human nature than has been found in the leadership of many societies. Among the religions including Christianity, there has been great variation in the degree of that faith. Among states variations have been even more pronounced.

The assumption that objective knowledge of international relations by the undergraduate will make for good citizenship is, in fact, an application of the theory of democracy and human rights expounded by philosophers and statesmen in the tradition of liberalism. This tradition includes such names as John Milton, John Locke, Thomas Jefferson, Abraham Lincoln, Oliver Wendell Holmes, Jr., Woodrow Wilson, and Franklin D. Roosevelt, to mention those probably most familiar to Americans. This tradition accepts the equality of man, not in ability or intelligence or power, but in possession of a common human nature which makes understanding of differences possible, and in the right to common human opportunity without which society cannot rest upon general consent (20, 36, 37, 50, 53).

The idea that maximum objective knowledge and maximum freedom of opinion make for good citizenship has been incorporated in the bills of rights of many national constitutions and in the Universal Declaration of Human Rights approved by the General Assembly of the United Nations in 1948. It has been supported pragmatically by the historic fact that under this theory the British Commonwealth and the United States have grown in power and influence and have obtained formal commitment to the theory by most other states. This theory is, however, still competing with the opposing doctrine of dogmatic truth maintained by indoctrination and censorship under which states and churches have also thrived and have also acquired imitators (20, 23, 24).

If one accepts the liberal view that freedom of opinion promotes knowledge of the truth and that knowledge of the truth promotes moral and civic virtue, there is certainly a case for giving more emphasis to international affairs in education today than there was in periods when men's lives were less affected by happenings in distant parts of the world. If the good citizen should contribute by his opinion to adapting his local community, his nation, his world, to its environment, he must know something of that environment, and the relations of nations has become a major element in that environment. These relations increase in importance with the shrinking of the world and the acceleration of history consequent upon the rapid communication of information and ideas, propaganda, and military threats throughout the world (51, 55).

A number of writers, assuming in the liberal tradition that objective knowledge contributes to good citizenship and that in the modern world knowledge about international relations is relevant to the citizen's functions, have asked the more modest questions: What curriculum, what stage in education, what methods of instruction, will give the greatest amount of objective knowledge about international relations with the least encroachment on other items of the curriculum (3, 5, 15, 16, 17, 18, 26, 28, 42, 48, 54)? To answer such questions one must ask what is the citizen's function in respect to international relations? He has little opportunity to initiate policy, but he can vote in the United States for candidates for the Presidency or Congress who usually stand for certain international policies, and he can, through conversation, participation in organizations, or writing to political leaders, contribute his opinion for or against national or United Nations policies which have been initiated by governments or leaders of opinion (1). In deciding whether he prefers the views on international affairs of candidate X or Y; whether he is for or against this appropriation, that treaty, or the other policy; whether he thinks the recommendations of the Security Council, the General Assembly, or some other international organ should be supported and how vigorously, the citizen contributes to the formation of "public opinion." For this purpose he does not need expert knowledge, but a capacity to weigh many factors, to judge the probable consequences of the alternatives presented, to communicate his opinions effectively, and to maintain such confidence in his community as the circumstances permit with neither cynicism nor superenthusiasm.

The citizen's capacity to make these judgments may be assisted by the broadened experience resulting from the reading of history and the habits of reflection resulting from the study of philosophy, more than by detailed knowledge of how international relations are conducted or what results are to be expected from practical maneuvers or operations. Most of the disciplines which figure in the undergraduate curriculum on international relations—international politics, international organization, international law, and international economics—can be taught as history, as philosophy, as art, or as science. It seems probable that to educate for citizenship, emphasis should be placed upon the history and philosophy of the subject, rather than upon its techniques and methods. Without some attention to the latter, however, the subject may seem theoretical and remote from practical reality.

Apart from the emphasis on method, is there a choice among the disciplines for the undergraduate course (18)? Before World War I the courses in the international field open to undergraduates at American colleges were usually confined to international law and diplomatic history, especially American diplomatic history. The former tended to present a world point of view, and the latter a national point of view, but both probably tended to support isolationist policies. International law emphasized sovereign rights rather than world responsibilities and gave much attention to neutral rights and obligations with the implication that neutrality, with its repudiation of responsibility for world order, was a natural and even moral policy. Courses in American diplomatic history emphasized Washington's Farewell Address, the Monroe Doctrine, freedom of the seas, nonintervention, *de facto* recognition, hemispheric solidarity, and other policies tending toward irresponsibility of the United States for the world community. Such courses also usually created an aura of American moral superiority on the assumption that the United States favored disarmament, arbitration, and peace, while the European countries were generally engaged in armament races, power politics, and war. Higher education in international relations in the United States before World War I, therefore, did little to moderate a self-centered public opinion ready to repudiate Wilson's call for a policy founded upon a sense of international responsibility. While policy had actually begun to develop in that direction, at least since the Spanish-American War, opinion, as frequently happens, especially in the international field, lagged behind practice during the first decade of the twentieth century, and the effort to justify the repudiation of the League of Nations in 1920 kept it behind for two decades more.

College education in international relations, however, tended to follow the Wilsonian leadership after World War I. While international law and American diplomacy stayed in the curriculum, the content of those courses tended to change. International law began to emphasize duties as well as rights and suggested, as had Theodore Roosevelt and later Woodrow Wilson, that neutrality in a war involving principles is immoral. Courses in American diplomacy began to emphasize new interpretations of the Farewell Address and the Monroe Doctrine as the United States moved into the position of a great power, and were more cautious in suggesting any superior morality and peacefulness of American policy in the past, noting the backward role the United States had come to play in the development of international arbitration because of Senate obstruction, the refusal of the United States to arbitrate cases which involved political considerations like that of the *Maine* disaster in 1898, the exceptionally rapid growth of American territorial domain and military power, and the exceptional bloodiness of American history in the century between Waterloo and the Marne during which the American Civil War alone cost as many lives as all European wars combined.

Furthermore, during the interwar period, courses on international organization assumed a prominent role in most undergraduate curricula in the field. These courses usually assumed that effective international organization was the appropriate way to reduce war and to increase justice and respect for law in the relations of states, usually criticized the American policy of repudiating the League, and often doubted whether that institution could succeed in its political work so long as a great power, such as the United States, remained aloof. It is often said that the emphasis in courses on international organization during this period tended to create attitudes of utopian optimism in the League of Nations, oblivious to the war-engendering forces of power politics, and that attitudes of cynicism resulted when those forces and the failure of the League to control them became obvious in the middle 1930's (18). My own experience in teaching courses in international organization in that period, in discussing courses given by others, and in reading the textbooks most used does not confirm this theory. Courses in international organization during this period consisted in the main of historical analyses of the practice and ideas of international organization in modern history, of objective analyses of the League's activities with due emphasis upon its political difficulties, and of critical comment on the capacity of the League to meet the situation, especially if the United States refused to undertake more active responsibilities (3, 44).

Whatever may have been the influence of higher education on opinion, it is the fact that in the late 1920's, after the generation of college students exposed to the postwar courses became old enough to gain positions of political influence, opinion about the League of Nations and policies in respect to it began to take a more favorable turn, but not quite sufficient to put the United States into the League or even into the World Court. The depression of the early 1930's, the failure of the League in Manchuria, and the rise of dictatorships undoubtedly caused a reaction toward isolationism manifested in the Nye Committee report on the Arms Trade and the isolationist neutrality legislation of 1935. The outbreak of war four years later convinced almost all Americans that the assumptions concerning the causes of war on which that legislation was based were erroneous and that isolationist policies were both unwise and impossible, with the consequence of a general acceptance of international responsibility and international organization as the proper bases of policy. Public opinion suddenly seemed to believe what courses in international organization had been teaching for two decades. It appeared to consider that the United States had made a mistake in repudiating the League in 1920 and to support American entry into an even stronger United Nations.

Opinion appeared, for the moment, to be ahead of the government. Both Franklin D. Roosevelt and Cordell Hull, who had throughout their political lives been advocates of American entry into international organization, seemed unable to appreciate how rapidly public opinion had progressed to their point of view, and hesitated in order to avoid Woodrow Wilson's mistake of committing himself in advance of public opinion. It seems quite possible that the public would have accepted more important qualifications of sovereignty than were to be found in the San Francisco Charter. The difference in the Senate vote in 1945 compared with that of 1920 may be accounted for by the difference in the political methods of Wilson and Roosevelt, but the generation of courses in international organization may also have played a part.

In the late 1930's there was another shift in the emphasis in undergraduate courses in international relations (34). Courses in international politics began to take a predominant position. They emphasized the importance of national security and the struggle for power in the foreign policy of the major states. They analyzed the components of national power and the methods of "power politics." They gave historical illustrations of practices of imperialism and of the operation of the power equilibrium with some attention to military strategy, and maintained a certain skepticism as to the possibility of a law-governed world, of extensive international co-operation, or of effective international organization. Such courses have held the front rank for a decade in undergraduate instruction, and discussions among teachers of international relations in the 1940's suggested a prevailing opinion that they should occupy that position (18).

If public opinion follows, after a lag of two decades, what college courses emphasize in the field, one may well ask with concern what will public opinion be demanding in the late 1950's? By 1949 American opinion had fallen away from the determination to make the United Nations work manifested in 1946, had accepted a bipolar world of power politics, and seemed ready to support any policy designed to give the United States and its allies a military edge over the Soviet Union and its satellites. Some elements of public opinion, also disillusioned about the United Nations, demanded more intensive world government, and some joined the two points of view by demanding federation, not for the world, but for the democracies, a policy which might strengthen the North Atlantic Alliance against the Soviet Union. In the early 1950's minor elements of opinion manifested a return to isolationism. Some sought amendments to the Constitution which would impair the capacity of the government to promote United Nations objectives by restricting the treaty-making power. Some extremists even urged withdrawal from the United Nations (35, 40, 55).

The Department of State, while still formally supporting the United Nations as a means toward an eventual world order of justice and peace, tended, under the joint pressure of public opinion and Soviet obduracy, to build military power, regional alliances, and diplomatic understandings against the Soviets, and as *cold war* intensified to utilize the United

Nations as an instrument of American national policy rather than as an organization of the entire world to develop peace with justice (21, 55).

This review suggests that there has been a degree of indoctrination in American undergraduate education in international relations hardly compatible with the theory of what education should be in a liberal democracy (24). During a half century college education has successively and in a measure, successfully guided opinion in the United States toward isolationism, toward international organization, and toward power politics as the central theme of American foreign policy. It may be suggested that if education had actually gone to the roots of the subject, perhaps in the realm of social psychology, such rapid shifts would not have occurred. Students need to understand the circumstances and conditions which account for the shifts in public opinion and policy, and to have criteria for appraising the consequences if policy is based on one or the other opinion under varying circumstances and conditions. They need to see the world steadily and as a whole in all its complexity of changing technology and population; of changing opinion and policy; of changing power position of states, regions, alliances, and parties; of changing procedures of war, diplomacy, conciliation, adjudication, and sanctions. With such a view they may be able to judge of policies, not because of their association with a cliché or a symbol, but because they can see how it is likely to work in the short and in the long run with reference to fundamental values.

To present so vast a subject in the limited space possible in the undergraduate curriculum is a matter of great difficulty. In many institutions no more than one course is possible. In such a course efforts should be made to present the basic assumptions underlying international politics, international organization, international law, and international economics, and their influence on opinion and policy; to explain the divergencies of these assumptions in terms of more fundamental concepts of psychology, sociology, and ethics; and to suggest the conditions under which these or other assumptions are likely to dominate international relations in practice. Such a course would, however, be in danger, of becoming excessively abstract and intangible unless the student had already had courses presenting a wealth of factual material. A course in diplomatic history emphasizing the national point of view, and a course in political geography emphasizing the world point of view might serve this purpose (5, 18, 23, 54).

EDUCATION FOR LEADERSHIP

The world is no less in need of leaders to propose than of citizens to judge of their proposals. Is understanding of international relations essential for those who would be leaders in the world, and if so, what kind of education in the subject would be most helpful for them? We assume that we are discussing the subject in the orbit of liberal democracy and, therefore, exclude the kind of personalities and opinions which might be suitable for the leaders of an absolutistic government.

The leader in a democracy needs to know how the citizens he is to lead think on public issues. His leadership consists in crystallizing the public opinion of the group he leads and in modifying it so far as its demands are inadequate to the situation. It is no less important that he listen and respond sympathetically to the vague demands of opinion, than that he formulate issues for the public to judge, formulations which may include hitherto unthought-of alternatives. Autocratic leadership decides what policy shall be and then creates opinion to support it through monopolistic control of the instruments of communication. Democratic leadership understands what the fundamental demands of opinion are and for-mulates, for acceptance or rejection, policies which will progress toward their achievement under existing conditions. The democratic leader, therefore, should be as well educated in the history and philosophy of international relations as the citizen. He should, however, in addition be sufficiently sophisticated in the art and science of the subject to ap-praise the opinions of experts. The aspirant for political position should, therefore, in addition to the general undergraduate course in international relations, have had courses more or less specialized in international law, international politics, international organization and international eco-nomics informing him of the techniques and analyses used in these sub-jects sufficiently to enable him to distinguish policies from panaceas. He need not, in fact should not, be a professional himself, but he should be able to choose among the experts. Too much expertness in any one technique may be a handicap for a leader because it may blind him, through professional distortion, to the value of expert advice from those sophisticated in different techniques.

If the citizen needs to view the world steadily and as a whole, this is all the more true of the leader. He must particularly beware of the institutional delusion. If specialists tend to exalt their specialty as a cure for all evils, so the leader tends to regard the institution which he leads as the final cause of all effort. The churchman so regards his church, the businessman his corporation, the educator his university, and the states-man his state, and indeed the executive of an international organization, his international organization. It is the assumption of democracy that institutions are for men, not men for institutions. The democratic leader should always be prepared to judge the value of his church, his business, his university, his state, or his international organization, even its title to continue its existence, by its contribution to the people subject to it and to humanity in general (47).

National statesmen find this standard of judgment particularly difficult to apply because their continuance in office and capacity to serve depends, and in the theory of democracy should depend, upon support of the national public. The national public, however, is by definition committed to the proposition that the power position and glory of the nation is an end in itself. It is rare that statesmen like Lincoln can see, even in times of great emergency, that the nation deserves to exist only if it continues as a government of, by, and for the people, or, like Wilson, can see that the nation that fails to contribute to the advancement of mankind has lost its title to respect.

It is, therefore, particularly important that the education of leaders should be based as broadly as possible in time and space. In the modern age the world as a whole, persisting through the pulsations and fluctuations of its peoples and institutions from millennium to millennium, may provide a perspective in which existing institutions can be seen in proper proportion, and policies, immediately demanded by the requirements of the moment or the decade, can be shaped with a view to human justice, welfare, and progress through the centuries. It, therefore, seems important that education for statesmanship should include a course in world history.

EDUCATION FOR PROFESSIONAL SERVICE IN INTERNATIONAL RELATIONS

Experts in the field of international relations are in increasing demand. Most students of the subject in graduate and professional schools expect to make a living out of it. The number who do so is increasing by leaps and bounds. What are the professional opportunities? There were some 200 recipients of graduate degrees in international relations or in one of the social sciences with primary emphasis upon international relations at the University of Chicago in the quarter-century from 1923 to 1948. About 50 per cent of these were at the latter date teaching international relations at a college or university or in a few cases in a high school. Most of them were doing research with teaching and a few were engaged in research alone at academic or research institutions. About half of the remainder were in the public service. The Department of State Home Service, the Foreign Service of the United States, some other governmental agency of the United States, foreign governments, international organizations were, in that order, the beneficiaries of their services. Over half of those teaching in 1948 had had government service, mostly during World War II, other than the military service. Of the remaining 25 per cent, the majority were in public relations work dealing with international affairs, in private organizations, in journalism, in radio, or in free lance writing. Among these students the professional practice of international law and activity in the international aspects of business, both often thought of as professional opportunities in the field, played a relatively small role. Only a few had gone into politics. Teaching, government service, and public relations activities seemed to be the major professional opportunities.

Obviously the kind of graduate or professional education needed depends on the kind of position aimed at. Until rather recently courses on international relations were normally taught in the departments of political science, economics, history, or geography. Degrees were normally taken in one of these departments and therefore implied that the candidate was equipped in all, not merely the international, aspects of the field. At present many universities give advanced work in international relations to meet the demand for specialists in that field. General fields, such as international law, international organization, international politics, and international economics, are usually combined in the curriculum with regional fields such as the Far East, the Near East, the Slavic countries and Latin America. Capacity to teach courses in at least one regional field, as well as several general fields, is professionally desirable for the prospective teacher of the subject and is also advantageous for other professional service in international relations. General principles if applied in one region which has been studied intensively become concrete and tangible.

There is an increasing tendency for graduate schools to organize the teaching of international relations under an interdepartmental committee or even in a department devoted to the subject. It is probable that this tendency will continue and will make a well-rounded course in international relations a requirement for college or university teaching in the field. This academic integration of the various disciplines of international relations is a significant development in the contemporary world, and is important, not only for the education of specialists, but also for providing texts and supervision for undergraduate education of citizens and leaders.

Entry examinations into government service in the United States have tended to emphasize general culture and ability rather than specific professional equipment. This is notably true in the Foreign Service. Not until the period of World War I, was this service emancipated from the spoils system (25). Examinations which at first required knowledge of the specialized disciplines of international relations, have since World War II, emphasized general history, economics, and social science (39). Successful candidates obtain knowledge of professional subjects in the Foreign Service Institute within the Department of State before entering upon active duty. This tendency to give specialized training within the Service rather than before entering it has long been the practice in the British Civil Service (56) and is a manifestation of the changing character of technical and professional knowledge. Change takes place so rapidly that academic training may become obsolete if taken long in advance of actual service.

In spite of this situation, persons who have a broad academic background in international relations advance more rapidly in the Foreign Service and such a background, as well as specialization in some general field or region, is necessary for admittance to professional positions in the Home Service of the Department of State. Specialists with expert knowledge of international law, or international economics, and particularly those with detailed knowledge of a region, including its languages, are in demand.

In-service training, increasingly relied on to maintain professional competence in the services concerned with international relations, has often fallen short of adequacy, as it has in the Foreign Service Institute of the Department of State, because of inadequate support. A continuous professional training for career officers, such as the Army, Navy, and Air Force provide for officers in their War Colleges, is desirable. A limited number of Department of State officers participate in the National War College in Washington and a few are occasionally delegated to do advanced work in universities. There is, however, much room for improvement.

Of particular importance is the expert at the policy-making level or directly advising the policy-maker. Persons who have achieved distinction as economists, lawyers, administrators, public relations experts or regional specialists usually serve in such positions, often as political appointees. Their role merges with that of the statesman and they usually discover that the combination of specialist and policy-maker presents problems of exceptional difficulty (4, 43).

Agencies of the government other than the Department of State give extensive attention to international affairs. This is particularly true of the Department of Defense, the Department of Commerce, and the Treasury, but Labor, Agriculture, and Justice all have many contacts with international organizations and international relations. The professional personnel of international organizations has also been increasing rapidly. Before World War I there were only a few hundred employees of such organizations. After World War I the number arose to several thousand and today the United Nations, the Specialized Agencies, and other international organizations employ over 10,000 persons. Many of these employees are, of course, custodial or clerical rather than professional, but new types of professional service both at home and in the field are coming into demand. In international organization, it is, of course, necessary to distribute positions among the member states, and, in general, some supplementary languages as well as professional knowledge is necessary.

For public relations activities in international affairs a well-rounded background in the central disciplines of international relations is desirable, although the actual work may prove to be mainly organizational and literary. A capacity to meet people and to write is essential in most positions involving public relations. The specific professions of journalism, law, and business are entered through the normal channels, and it is usually only after entry that a student who has specialized in international relations can move into branches of the profession with an international content.

The turning out of well-qualified professionals is an important task of education in international relations, but less important than the development of citizens and leaders with a broad grasp of the subject. It will always be true that those engaged in professional activities in the field are less numerous and less influential than those who contribute to public opinion and public policy through leadership or participation as citizens. While the latter can profit by listening to the advice of experts, and require experts to carry out their decisions, they cannot entrust decision on basic objectives to experts. International affairs is fundamentally a political not a technical operation (27, 30, 56).

Political leaders, however, must exercise restraint. The consequences can be disastrous if they fail to recognize that in international affairs detailed decision-making depends on expert knowledge and current "intelligence" about foreign governments which the public cannot have. Public opinion and politics can deal only with general goals, leaving to the responsible official, guided by experts, details of implementation (5, 9).

RESEARCH IN INTERNATIONAL RELATIONS

As a discipline the prime object of international releations is to advance human knowledge in the field. In the education of citizens, leaders, and experts, the discipline of international relations co-operates with other disciplines. Its unique task is to advance knowledge in the field by aiding research. Research in international relations seeks to assemble and verify pertinent facts and relationships, to classify them in ways which will suggest fruitful generalizations, and particularly, because it is a synthetic discipline, to maintain contact with numerous other disciplines whose observations and generalizations it can utilize.

Research goes on in universities, institutes, governments, and international organizations. Governments and international organizations have primarily practical aims and while they have access to many pertinent facts not otherwise available and their publications are indispensable for all other researchers, they cannot be expected often to develop fundamental generalizations or insights (11, 38, 45). Those who control the budgets of public organizations tend to demand immediate practical results. Furthermore, public opinion is likely to oppose research which might lead to results casting doubt upon institutions, policies, and prejudices which are widely accepted. In international organizations there is a peculiar delicacy in research which might arouse national susceptibilities in any of the numerous members of these organizations. There is undoubtedly an increase of the relative proportion of research done by public institutions, both national and international, but because of these hampering conditions it is undesirable that publicly supported research should monopolize the field.

Academic research goes on in the preparation of graduate theses and in the individual work of most academic men (8). This has been the major source of research in the field of international relations and the product, appearing in learned journals and in numerous published and unpublished monographs, is usually the work of individual investigators. The quality of such work is, of course, dependent upon the quality of the men who enter the academic profession. The attractiveness of the profession to able men and the unbiased quality of research has depended to no small extent upon the tradition of academic freedom and academic tenure. Continuance of the present trends toward a qualification of academic freedom through investigations of scientists, scholars and institutions by government agencies motivated by "security" or "patriotic" reasons, toward the financing of academic research by public funds and toward political and military influence in planning projects, would undoubtedly deteriorate the quality of such research and hamper the growth of knowledge in the field of international relations (20, 50, 53).

Universities and certain institutes and organizations in the field have encouraged collective research (6, 7, 8, 12, 17, 32, 33, 41). This can vary all the way from group consultation to aid an individual researcher to group responsibility for the ultimate conclusions arrived at. New insight and new generalization is more to be expected from the former than from the latter. The protracted thought, which perceives new relations and suggests fruitful generalizations for verification, is the work of an individual mind. Discussion may be suggestive of new ideas and consultation in results may prevent mistakes, but for fundamental research the individual must be primarily responsible (47).

Group research, however, makes possible the assembling of more material than would be possible for one person, and gives an authority to conclusions because they embody a collective judgment which can be relied upon not to depart radically from the prevailing opinion of the time. Group research also permits experts in different disciplines to contribute their special knowledge, although unless such varied information is synthesized, the result may be little more than a symposium. Group research both in conclusions and presentation tends to be pedestrian and uninspired, but safe. Individual research can reach novel conclusions and can be persuasively presented, but it may be erratic. The individual researcher is a pioneer. The group research is a body of immigrants who occupy the territory.

Research may be carried on in the history, the art, the philosophy, and the science of international relations. If it combines all these methods about a topic of outstanding interest such as war, power politics, pacific settlement, nationalism, underdeveloped areas, or trade, ideas resulting from each point of view may contribute to the others.

The particular disciplines of international relations such as international law, international politics, international organization, and international economics, can, and usually do, provide certain assumptions for a particular research. Most doctoral dissertations attempt to verify hypotheses in one of these fields accepting the assumptions characteristic of the field. The more pioneering researchers, however, tend to combine several of these disciplines or to develop an area outside any of them. Such investigations question existing assumptions and may advance science to new points.

Vilfredo Pareto, following Machiavelli, distinguished the *lions* who apply *aggregates* or combinations of ideas which have been accepted at face value, from the *foxes* who break up such *aggregates* into their elements and make new combinations. Researchers, especially in international relations, are *foxes*. They analyze and criticize popular formulations and synthesize the elemental phenomena into new formulations. They have no respect for the established modes of thought and articles of faith, but seek for new and better ones. They are not likely to be welcome in the public service and they may even be suspect in teaching undergraduates. They may not always make good citizens or good leaders. They initiate ideas which influence the future for better or for worse. The world of tomorrow depends on their ability and judgment, their combination of analytic competence with a sense of human responsibility.

An understanding of the difference between the historical, practical, philosophical, and scientific approach to international relations may throw light upon their methods. Such an understanding may also suggest the types of instruction useful for researchers in the field. Education for research, however, is not easy to formalize. Basic research, like the creative arts, is the product of the experiences of a peculiarly sensitive mind. The essence of research is the perception of hitherto unobserved likenesses and differences; classes and entities; sequences, processes, associations, and relationships; causes and consequences; means and ends. Education can train in the use of techniques of observation and experiment for verifying hypotheses and in the use of systems of logical and mathematical inference for developing consequences to be verified. It can also stock the mind with information and ideas which may prove useful in formulating hypotheses. The sensitivity of mind indispensable to original research, is, however, as likely to be blunted as to be sharpened by education. When new ways of looking at things is of the essence, familiarity with the traditional modes of thought may do more harm than good. Familiarity with the personality, incentives, and methods of those who have in the past made significant contributions to the history, the art, the science, and the philosophy of international relations, may be useful, and the remaining chapters of this part will be devoted to a consideration of those four approaches to the subject.

REFERENCES

1. ALMOND, Gabriel, *The American People and Foreign Policy* (New York, Harcourt, 1950).
2. BAILEY, S. H., *International Studies in Great Britain* (London, Oxford University Press, 1933).
3. ——, *International Studies in Modern Education* (London, Oxford University Press, 1938).
4. BLOUGH, Roy, "The Role of the Economist in Federal Policy Making," *University of Illinois Bulletin,* Vol. 5 (November, 1953), No. 28.
5. Brookings Institution, The International Studies Group, *Report on a Conference on the Teaching of International Relations, Charlottesville, Virginia, January, 1950* (Washington, 1950).
6. Commission to Study the Organization of Peace, *A Ten Year Record, 1930-1949* (New York, 1949).
7. Council on Foreign Relations, *A Record of Twenty-Five Years, 1921-1946* (New York, 1947).
8. DEAN, Dorothy-Arden, ed., *Current Research in International Affairs* (New York, Carnegie Endowment for International Peace, 1952).
9. DUNN, Frederick S., "The Scope of International Relations," *World Politics,* Vol. 1 (October, 1948), pp. 142 ff.
10. ——, "The Present Course of International Relations Research," *World Politics,* Vol. 2 (October, 1949), p. 80.
11. FEIS, Herbert, Research Activities of the League of Nations, A Report to the Committee on International Relations of the Social Science Research Council, June, 1929 (Old Lyme, Conn., 1929).
12. Ford Foundation, *Report of the Study for the Ford Foundation Policy and Program* (Detroit, 1949).
13. FOX, William T. R., "Interwar International Relations Research: The American Experience," *World Politics,* Vol. 2 (October, 1949), pp. 67 ff.
14. GOODWIN, Geoffrey L., ed., *The University Teaching of International Relations,* International Studies Conference at Windsor, March, 1950 (Oxford, Blackwell, 1951).
15. HUDSON, Manley O., "The Teaching of International Law in America," *Conference of Teachers of International Law, Proceedings (C.T.I.L.),* Vol. 3 (Washington, Carnegie Endowment, 1928), pp. 68 ff., 178 ff.
16. ——, HULL, W. I., POTTER, P. B., and FITE, Emerson, "Teaching of International Relations," *C.T.I.L.,* Vol. 4 (Washington, 1929), pp. 137 ff.
17. International Studies Conference, *see* 14, 22, 38, 57.
18. KIRK, Grayson, *The Study of International Relations in American Colleges and Universities* (New York, Council on Foreign Relations, 1947).

19. KIRK, Grayson, "Materials for the Study of International Relations," *World Politics,* Vol. 1 (April, 1949), p. 426.

20. KIRKLAND, Edward C., "Do Anti-subversive Efforts Threaten Academic Freedom?" *American Academy of Political and Social Science* (May, 1951), pp. 132 ff.

21. McKEEVER, Porter, "Charges U.S. Weakens U.N.," *New York Times,* June 12, 1952, p. 1; June 14, 1952, p. 7.

22. MANNING, C. A. W., *The University Teaching of Social Sciences: International Relations* (Paris, UNESCO, 1954).

23. MERRIAM, Charles E., "The Making of Citizens, Chicago, 1931," *Civic Education in the United States,* American Historical Society, Report of the Commission on the Social Studies, Part VI (New York, Scribners, 1934).

24. MOORE, Willis, "Indoctrination in Education," *Bulletin,* American Association of University Professors, Vol. 38 (Summer, 1952), pp. 220 ff.

25. National Civil Service Reform League, *Report on the Foreign Service* (New York, 1919).

26. OGDEN, Montell E., "Purpose and Method of Teaching International Law in the Smaller College," *C.T.I.L.,* Vol. 6 (Washington, 1938), p. 84.

27. PASVOLSKY, Leo, "The Brookings Institution Program of International Studies," *World Politics,* Vol. 1 (January, 1940), p. 243.

28. QUIGLEY, Harold S., "Scope, Organization and Aims of Courses in International Relations," *C.T.I.L.,* Vol. 2 (Washington, 1925), p. 71.

29. RIESMAN, David, *The Lonely Crowd, A Study of the Changing American Character* (New Haven, Yale University Press, 1950).

30. ROOT, Elihu, "The Need of Popular Understanding of International Law," *C.T.I.L.,* Vol. 1 (Washington, 1916), p. 1.

31. ROSENHAUPT, Hans W., *How to Wage Peace* (New York, John Day, 1949).

32. Royal Institute of International Affairs, *Annual Report of the Council, 1951-1952* (London, 1952).

33. SAVORD, Ruth, ed., *American Agencies Interested in International Affairs* (New York, Council on Foreign Relations, 1940).

34. THOMPSON, Kenneth, "The Study of International Politics, A Study of Trends and Developments," *The Review of Politics,* Vol. 14 (October, 1952), pp. 433 ff.

35. UHL, Alexander, *The Assault on the UN* (Washington, Public Affairs Institute, 1953).

36. UNESCO, *A Handbook for the Improvement of Textbooks and Teaching Material as Aid to International Understanding* (Paris, 1949).

37. ———, *Some Suggestions on Teaching About the United Nations and Its Specialized Agencies.*

38. ———, *International Social Science Bulletin,* quarterly. Includes notes on research by Organizations of the Social Sciences, the United Nations, and the Specialized Agencies. See especially meeting on the "University Teaching of International Relations," Vol. 2 (Summer, 1950), p. 235 and "Education for the World Community," Vol. 4 (Spring, 1952), p. 147.

39. U. S. Department of State, *Preparing for a Career in the Foreign Service of the United States* (Washington, 1950).

40. U. S. Senate, Committee Hearings, *Revision of the United Nations Charter,* February, 1950; *Treaties and Executive Agreements,* February-April, 1953.

41. Van Wagenen, Richard W., *Research in the International Organization Field* (Princeton, Center for Research on World Political Institutions, 1952).

42. Vinacke, Harold M., "Teaching of International Relations," *C.T.I.L.*, Vol. 8 (Washington, 1946), p. 50.

43. Viner, Jacob, "The Short View and the Long in Economic Policy," *American Economic Review*, Vol. 30 (March, 1940).

44. Ware, Edith, *The Study of International Relations in the United States, Survey for 1937* (New York, Columbia University Press, 1938).

45. Wright, Quincy, *Research on International Law Since the War* (Washington, Carnegie Endowment for International Peace, 1930).

46. ——, Dickinson, E. D., and Hull, W. I., "Instruction in International Relations," *C.T.I.L.*, Vol. 5 (Washington, 1933), pp. 105 ff.

47. ——, *A Study of War* (Chicago, University of Chicago Press, 1942), pp. 409 ff, pp. 1203 ff, pp. 1347 ff.

48. ——, "Teaching of International Law in the Post War World," *C.T.I.L.*, Vol. 8 (Washington, 1946), pp. 22 ff.

49. ——, "Barriers to World Peace and Steps in Removing Them," *The School Review*, Vol. 54 (December, 1946), pp. 576 ff.

50. ——, "The University and the World Order," *Bulletin*, American Association of University Professors, Vol. 33 (Spring, 1947), pp. 43 ff.

51. ——, ed., *The World Community* (Chicago, University of Chicago Press, 1948).

52. ——, "Method in the Study of War," *World Politics*, Vol. 1 (January, 1949), p. 243.

53. ——, "The Citizens' Stake in Academic Freedom," *Journal of Higher Education*, Vol. 20 (October, 1949), pp. 339 ff.

54. ——, "Comments," in *Goals of American Education*, Ninth Symposium on Science, Philosophy and Religion (New York, Harper, 1950), pp. 501 ff.

55. ——, *Problems of Stability and Progress in International Relations* (Berkeley, University of California Press, 1954).

56. Young, George, *Diplomacy Old and New* (London, Swarthmore Press, 1921).

57. Zimmern, Alfred, ed., "University Teaching of International Relations," *Proceedings 11th International Studies Conference*, International Institute of Intellectual Understanding (Paris, 1938).

CHAPTER
8

The History of
International Relations

HISTORY IS DEFINED as the systematic record of past events, especially those in which man has taken part. The word is also used to refer to the events themselves, including the acts, writings, and speeches that cause or influence them. In this chapter we are concerned with the history of international relations in the first sense. History as a form of writing which presents international relations as a narrative is distinguished from the practical or professional literature of the subject (the arts of international relations), from evaluative and qualitative analyses (the philosophy of international relations), and from predictive and quantitative analyses (the science of international relations). These four kinds of writing expound respectively the four types of reality referred to in the second chapter—the actual, the possible, the desirable, and the probable—and should illustrate respectively the four kinds of truth referred to in the third chapter—the convincing, the persuasive, the effective and the correct.

In this sense history consists on the one hand of the process of determining exactly what happened and exactly when and where it happened, and on the other hand of evaluating and organizing the verified facts in a narrative. The first is facilitated by the historical sciences which instruct on the finding or interpretation of evidences of the past—paleography which deals with ancient writing; diplomatics which deals with official documents; epigraphy which deals with inscriptions; archeology which deals with pottery, buildings, and other nonliterary remains; numismatics which deals with coins; sphragiatics which deals with seals.

The writing of history or historiography usually follows a chronological form, but the selection of events to be presented, their evaluation and organization, depends upon some theory of the nature of history.

Historiography is sometimes called an art because the historian frequently seeks to interest the reader by arousing his emotions, to instruct the reader in appropriate methods of social action, to persuade the reader to accept certain attitudes or opinions, or to incite the reader to action by stimulating certain sentiments or loyalties. On the other hand, it is also said that history written to be edifying or inciting is propaganda and not history.

History is also sometimes called a science because the historian seeks to verify every fact by objective evidence and, as Ranke said, to state things as they actually happened. It is, however, impossible to include everything that happened and the narrative would be unreadable if all facts which are included were given equal weight as in a chronology. Consequently the historian must continually exercise judgment in selection and arrangement of his material.

Sometimes history is called a philosophy on the supposition that its proper presentation discloses a moral or causal order in human events. History was said by Lord Acton to be philosophy speaking by example and by Hegel to be the realization of an idea. On the other hand it is said that such an assumption, which tailors history to theory, results not in history but in philosophy.

History has relations to art, science, and philosophy, but it differs from all. Its object is to aid the reader in realizing a social entity of the past. History, in the proper sense, does not try to assist or induce action in the future; to formulate generalizations of predictive or control utility; or to demonstrate values, principles, or trends, although any of these objectives may be incidentally served by history. Rather history tries to identify social entities or *wholes* that have existed and can be differentiated from their surroundings, to describe the relation of the parts of such entities to one another and to the whole, to trace their changes in time, and to inform the reader of their character and life in such a way that he can sense and know objectively, and can feel and wish subjectively, as the people who lived in the time and place knew and felt. That is what is meant by historical *realization*—to recover today the total mental and emotional outlook characteristic of a society which is gone. The builder *realizes* the architect's plan by constructing the building in brick and mortar so that any observer can see it, but the historian *realizes* a past century when he presents it so that it lives again in the mind of the reader. Historians often tend to emphasize the aspects of the past which are important to the present because they disclose the origins of present problems, or because they are similar to present problems, or because they suggest how present problems can best be dealt with or how they are likely to turn out. History may thus contribute to the art, philosophy, or science of politics or social affairs, but, it is submitted, that insofar as it aims at these objectives it departs from its proper role. History should emphasize not what is important to us, but what was important to the people that the history is about, not how we would explain, relate, and evaluate events, but how people at the time actually explained, related, and evaluated them.

This ideal of history is seldom realized. Historians of each generation tend to create bygone ages in their own image, so history tends to change as historians change. Such extraction from the past of ideas or generalizations, useful or inspiring or informative for the present, is not to be criticized, but it is fundamentally an adjunct of philosophy, art, or science, and not history.

Carl Sandburg (14) points out that the theories of history have been numerous. He quotes Woodrow Wilson's comment that:

If it were possible to tell all, it would take as long to write history as to enact it, and we should have to postpone the reading of it to the leisure of the next world. A few facts must be selected for the narrative, the great majority left unnoted. But the selection—for what purpose is it to be made? For the purpose of conveying *an impression* of the truth. Where shall you find a more radical process of judgment? The "essential" facts taken, the "unessential" left out! Why, you may make the picture what you will, and in any case it must be the express image of the historian's fundamental judgments (21).

He also quotes Paul Angle. "It is hard to know what actually happened. If we do know what actually happened it is harder yet to know why it happened. And if by any chance we do know what happened and why, nobody gives a damn." He refers to Henry Ford's assertion that "history is bunk" as voicing Voltaire's slant that "History is a series of fables agreed upon." Sandburg's own view is that "The writer of history colors his work with his own personality." Sandburg's *Lincoln,* however, approaches my idea of history. By selection and presentation of events which actually happened in sufficient abundance, he makes the reader realize Lincoln as he was and the United States as it was at the time.

Historians have to decide what entity they wish to write about and they usually choose an individual, a nation, or a civilization, entities which have both subjective and objective aspects, and which appear to have some autonomy of choice. Arnold J. Toynbee (19) prefers a *civilization* as the unit of history because it makes a nearer approach to self-containment than lesser entities. A man or a nation cannot be explained fully without an understanding of the civilization in which he or it lived. A civilization, however, though influenced by other civilizations, changes in time and space primarily through the activity of internal groups and persons. It is, therefore, a more perfect subject for a history, especially if it is dead. A living civilization can be a subject of history only in respect to that part which is past, but, because the historian as such cannot yet judge the importance of the events even of that part in terms of their consequences for the civilization as a whole, much of which is still in the future, he cannot write the history of any part of a still living civilization adequately.

The self-sufficiency of all entities is however relative, and consequently individuals, associations, periods, cities, and nations can be selected as entities about which a reasonably adequate history can be written. Entities should, however, be selected that can be defined by concrete boundaries of time and space or are unified by concrete organization. A history of physics, a history of philosophy, or a history of international relations implies an abstract definition separating the subject of the history from its surroundings. Such abstract definitions can never establish such tangible and objective boundaries as can for instance such concrete definitions as England in the seventeenth century, classical civilization, the Papacy, or Napoleon. If the subject of a history is defined by an abstract concept, many circumstances which may actually influence the events embraced by the concept are ruled out of consideration. The distinctiveness of history lies in its comprehensiveness in appraising all the factors influencing the events narrated, and this distinctiveness is lost if some of those factors are eliminated by definition.

The study of history is said to have several peculiar advantages. In the first place it gives a sense of the continuity of human affairs, particularly if limited periods are studied intensively. "We cannot," said Lincoln, "escape history." What statesmen do today affects the world of tomorrow and what they did yesterday clings like mud to the shoes of their successors, limiting the possibility of action. *Natura non fecit saltum.* The more history is studied, the more the rhetoric of great changes, such as "the fall of the Roman Empire," "the Renaissance," or "the French Revolution," is found to divert attention from much that went on as before. *Plus le change, plus la même chose.*

On the other hand, the study of history gives a sense of change, sometimes more and sometimes less rapid, particularly if long periods are studied or if somewhat separated periods are compared. Those living at the death of Romulus Augustus in 476 A.D. were probably not aware of a sudden change. Yet Rome fell and Western Europe of the Venerable Bede was radically different from that of Claudius. So also the Europe of Francis Bacon was radically different from that of Roger Bacon, and the Europe of Louis Philippe from that of Louis the Sixteenth.

The study of history also gives a sense of the uniqueness of every nation, every period, and every individual, particularly if the study is intensive. Historians insist that history does not repeat itself, an insistence which may tend to make itself true because, following their doctrine, historians tend to emphasize the unique character of the entities with which they deal and to ignore the features those entities have in common. This characteristic of history often makes it disappointing to the social scientist searching for common features as a basis for generalization and prediction.

On the other hand, history studied over long periods often discloses apparent repetitions. Civilizations, like nations, rise and fall as noted by Guizot (8), Spengler (16), and Toynbee (19). Groups, like individuals, seem to have a life span. There seem to be similarities in the conditions of their progress and decay and in their characteristics at comparable stages of life (22).

The study of history also throws light upon the causation of human action. Historians recognize that men do not act in a vacuum and they try to explain the circumstances, conditions, motives, and intentions behind their acts. But historians, insofar as they stick to their trade, are careful to confine the generalizations they make to the historical period with which they deal. They are aware that there are unstated factors in every historic period which influence the operation of human fears and ambitions, of group policies and demands, and of the interpretation of events in ways which might differ greatly from their operation in other times and places.

Along with its emphasis upon causes of action and underlying conditions, history emphasizes the role of contingency. The unexpected is to be expected. Historians are, perhaps, less likely to be determinists than are scientists or philosophers. In their emphasis upon contingency they provide a healthy antidote to the overenthusiastic social scientist (4).

The study of history tends to give a sense of the influence of choice and of values in human affairs. Historians are seldom materialists, as may be philosophers of history like Marx or Buckle. They cannot ignore the influence of personality, of leadership, and of human choice.

Finally, the study of history can provide standards of evaluation. Historical entities can be realized as units in which each part is related to the others and to the whole. Each whole can be appraised as better or worse than others and the elements of character and action which compose it can be appraised in relation to this judgment of the whole. Historians, like other men, differ in their preferences. One historian may like the Greece of Pericles; another the Rome of Augustus; another the France of Aquinas. But at least the reasons for appraising any element of the admired period can be made explicit in terms of its contribution to the particular civilization as a whole.

While the statesman or citizen should look to social science rather than to history for reliable rules or precedents to guide his expectations, his policy, or his action, he can acquire from extended historical reading a balanced sense of continuity and change in human affairs; of the peculiarities and similarities of historic periods; of the role of causation and contingency in historic change; and of the possibilities of choice and evaluation in the making of history. Against this background we may ask, what is the meaning of the history of international relations and what is its value.

If my analysis is correct, the subject of a history should be a concrete *whole* bounded by time and space or unified by concrete organization. *International relations* does not in itself constitute such a *whole* and is not, therefore, a suitable subject for a history. If by international relations we mean the discipline or literature of the subject, to write its history, it would be necessary to abstract certain writings from others and to define the contributory disciplines and the writings to be included in each. Such a *history* would differ from a philosophy or a science of international relations mainly in employing a chronological rather than a topical outline, and even then the writer would probably find it necessary to break the chronology into long periods each of which would be dealt with topically.

If by international relations we mean the conduct of international affairs, we refer to an abstraction from the total life of the world—to the official and unofficial relations of states. This involves a definition of *relations* and *states*, and does not constitute a concrete entity which exists in a defined time and place or has a concrete organization, and which, therefore, has a *history*.

Diplomatic history is undoubtedly a discipline, but it is as much an analysis as a history and gains its unity through utilization of a concrete body of material—diplomatic archives and treaties. A comprehensive history of diplomacy should consider not only this material but also all evidence bearing on international and trans-national relations, on the domestic policy of each of the nations, and on the progress of business, education, art, literature, science, and philosophy throughout the world insofar as these activities influenced diplomatic decisions. The history of international relations, therefore, turns out to be the history of the world.

In earlier times a *civilization* such as that of classical antiquity or of ancient China could be dealt with as a unit with a beginning, an end, and a geographical span. Its heroic age of conflicting ideas and adventure, its time of trouble with states in power-political relations fighting increasingly bitter wars, its universal state emerging from conquest, and its decline often under the dominance of a universal church looking forward to a new heroic age and a new civilization could be delineated, as has been done by Toynbee, with suggested ideas as to the present state and probable future of our civilization (19).

Since the age of discoveries, however, no less an entity than the world can be taken as the basis for a history of international relations and such a history would have to include the histories of the earlier civilizations which provided its roots and of the nations and international organizations which are its present fruits. But as the emerging world civilization is still in its early stages, history can do little to define its character or prognosticate its future. Until world history has run its course and the last man searches among its records, the history of international relations in which we now exist, even of its earlier stages, cannot be adequately written.

International relations is not, therefore, in itself a suitable subject for a history, but history is unquestionably an important subject of international relations. The student of international relations can gain from the study of history and particularly world history a balanced sense of continuity and change, of uniqueness and repetition, of causation and contingency, and of choice and standards. He can better realize the complexity and uncertainty of human affairs, the many factors to be considered in making judgments, the dangers of abstraction, of dogmatism, of prediction, of action, and of inaction. He can better understand the abundance and variability of human values and the opportunities as well as the insecurities in any situation. Above all he can acquire a conception of the world as a whole, in which numerous distinctive civilizations and nations have become progressively more closely interrelated.

Unfortunately, historians have often been unaware of, or have concealed their major premises and have written history, not to create a realization of the entity they are writing about, but to promote a cause or to point a moral. Such history may fail in the virtues either of history, or of philosophy, art, or science. It may breed dogmatism and feed violent revolution militating against the tolerance and wisdom which should be the fruit of history. History has been no less productive of the enthusiasms which breed war and revolution than of the wisdom which breeds peace, stability, and steady progress.

REFERENCES

1. ACTON, Lord, *A Lecture on the Study of History* (London, Macmillan, 1896).
2. ADAMS, Brooks, *The Law of Civilization and Decay* (New York, Macmillan, 1896).
3. ADAMS, Henry, "A Letter to History Teachers" in *The Degradation of Democratic Dogma* (New York, Macmillan, 1919).
4. BERR, Henri, and FEBVRE, Lucien, "History," *Encyclopædia of the Social Sciences*.
5. BOLINGBROKE, Lord, *Letters on History* (1735).
6. FREEMAN, Edward A., *Historical Essays*, 1st Series (London, Macmillan, 1871).
7. GEORGE, H. B., *Historical Evidence* (London, Oxford University Press, 1909).
8. GUIZOT, F. P. G., *The History of Civilization in Europe* (1828); rev. ed. (New York, A. L. Burt, 1899).

9. HALDANE, Richard Burdon, Viscount, "The Meaning of Truth in History" (London, 1914), in *The Conduct of Life and Other Addresses* (New York, Dutton, 1915).

10. HARRISON, Frederic, *The Meaning of History* (London, Macmillan, 1894).

11. LECKY, W. C. H., *Historical and Political Essays* (New York, Longmans, 1908).

12. RICE, Stuart A., ed., *Methods in Social Science* (Chicago, University of Chicago Press, 1931), chapters by Ferdinand Scheville and Henri Pirenne.

13. ROBINSON, James Harvey, *The New History* (New York, Macmillan, 1912).

14. SANDBURG, Carl, "How Should History Be Written," Notebook, *Chicago Daily News* (August 16, 1930).

15. SEELEY, J. R., *Introduction to Political Science* (London, Macmillan, 1896).

16. SPENGLER, Oswald, *The Decline of the West* (New York, Knopf, 1932).

17. STUBBS, William, *Seventeen Lectures on the Study of Medieval and Modern History* (Oxford, Clarendon Press, 1886).

18. TEGGERT, F. J., *Theory of History* (New Haven, Yale University Press, 1925).

19. TOYNBEE, Arnold J., *A Study of History* (London, Oxford University Press, 1935), Vol. 1, Introduction.

20. TREVELYAN, George M., "History and Literature," *History* (n.s.), Vol. IX (1924), pp. 91 ff.

21. WILSON, Woodrow, *Mere Literature and Other Essays* (Boston, Houghton Mifflin, 1896), p. 170.

22. WRIGHT, Quincy, *A Study of War* (Chicago, University of Chicago Press, 1942), pp. 25 ff., 103 ff., 438 ff.

CHAPTER
9

The Arts of
International Relations

ART IMPLIES the skillful and systematic adaptation of means for the attainment of some end. Writing about an art consists of instruction in, or exposition of, techniques or practices for accomplishing ends. Writing is itself an art which may be employed with more or less skill to achieve the ends of the writer.

In the fine arts the end is the creation in the mind of the observer of a state of mind deemed valuable by the artist, such as realization of the possibilities of human life and behavior, or appreciation of complex combinations of sensation, feeling, symmetry, and form. In the practical arts, which include invention, engineering, negotiation, administration, war, medicine, and education, the end is any activity, object, or condition deemed valuable such as flying, communicating at a distance, a skyscraper, a treaty of peace, victory in a war or a law suit, restoration of the health of a patient, or the development of a person's capacities.

Art is like history in that it deals with the concrete rather than the abstract, but it deals with concrete objects or states of mind which are in process of creation while history deals with concrete events, acts, things, or passions which have been. Art is also like history in assuming a dualism of subject and object. Both distinguish man from the world, the moral from the material, the possible from the actual. Both are more interested in the subjective than in the objective. According to Lord Balfour:

What has, in the main, caused history to be written, and when written to be eagerly read, is neither its scientific value nor its practical utility, but its

91

aesthetic interest. Men love to contemplate the performance of their fellows, and whatever enables them to do so, whether we belittle it as gossip or exalt it as history, will find admirers in abundance. . . . Directly it appears (however) that the governing preoccupation of an historian is to be picturesque, his narrative becomes intolerable. This is because the interest—I mean the aesthetic interest—of history largely depends upon its accuracy, or (more strictly) upon its supposed accuracy. . . . Fact has an interest, because it is fact; because it actually happened. . . . On this interest the charm of history eventually depends (1).

Art differs from history in being manipulative and forward-looking, while history is contemplative and backward-looking. Art manipulates the actual of the present to realize the desires of the future, while history contemplates the actual of the past to realize the ideals of the past.

The novel is the form of art that most resembles history and the two are sometimes combined in the historical novel. It is, indeed, sometimes said that a novel may be more real than history. This is because the novelist, unhampered by the necessity of documenting his statements and free to draw from his entire experience of human behavior, can provide more details about his characters than is possible for the historian. The novelist may be more convincing to his readers than is the historian, but he can only convince them that what he writes might exist or could have existed, while the historian may convince them that what he writes actually did exist. The historian, therefore, is on the safe side of the possible. "Truth," said George Trevelyan, "is the criteria of historical study, but its impelling motive is poetic. The poetry consists in its being true. There we find the synthesis of the scientific and literary views of history" (22).

Instruction in an art gives the learner manipulative skill, whether the art is that of shoeing horses, designing buildings, painting pictures, operating businesses, arguing law cases, breeding cattle, constructing bridges, administering government, negotiating treaties, or winning wars. Such instruction involves indoctrination in the objectives of the art; information about its tools, its vocabulary, and its methods; and acquisition of skills in their use through training and discipline. Such instruction involves practice in doing, rather than reading about. Its value is primarily for those who are going to practice the art, trade, or profession, although knowledge of the objects and techniques of the arts can aid in understanding society and human nature. Furthermore, the welfare of society depends in considerable measure upon the skill of professionals and the objectives they pursue. Public opinion cannot contribute to appraising performance, maintaining standards, and reforming abuses unless it is somewhat aware of the modus operandi of the experts.

Any art has a tendency to become secret and exclusive in order to protect its practitioners from competition and to prevent misinterpretation or premature application by the public; to become rigid in methods and objectives because persons indoctrinated in the objects and trained in its skills find it difficult to modify skills and practices; and to attach exaggerated importance to itself and its objectives in society. These professional distortions render the arts and professions inadequate critics and reformers of themselves. Consequently public opinion and leadership must continually scrutinize the arts and professions, and reform them when they have become unadaptable to changing society. For this reason it is important that citizens and leaders as well as the experts themselves be informed about the arts. But this knowledge need not be skill in doing, but knowledge about (27).

This is particularly true of the arts relevant to international relations. These include, besides the master art of international politics (3, 9, 11, 16) the more technical arts of diplomacy and war, public administration and the conduct of foreign affairs, investigation, public relations, education, economic management, and the practice of international law. The opportunities in these arts and professions have been considered earlier (Chapter 7) and their relations to the various disciplines in the field will be discussed later (Chapter 31). Here some attention will be given to the arts themselves.

Most of them are practiced by persons in the employment of national governments. But to increasing extent, international organizations employ experts in the same arts. Some of these arts—public relations, education, economic management, and international law—may be practiced by independent professionals or by employees of private organizations.

It is to be observed that all of these arts can be utilized in either the oppositional or the co-operative relations of nations, and they may be utilized in both at the same time. The art of international politics, in fact, instructs statesmen in how and when to shift allies and opponents in order to promote policies, whether of stability or expansion, as changing circumstances suggest.

Diplomacy is the most characteristic of these arts with a history as ancient as that of human relations. In the modern period when permanent diplomatic missions began to be sent, it developed a tradition of aristocracy, ostentation, secretiveness, and prevarication. "An ambassador," said Sir Henry Wotton in the sixteenth century, "is an honest man sent to lie abroad for the good of his country" (25). Claims of privilege to assure prestige and protect from local pressures led to abuses. Diplomats quarrelled about precedence in audiences, processions, and international conferences, engaged in espionage and sabotage, and gave asylum in diplomatic premises to refugees from the local police. International law has ironed out many of these problems by establishing rules of precedence based on the alphabet, on titles mutually agreed upon, or on the length of residence at a court, and rules limiting immunities to those essential for performing diplomatic functions. The members of diplomatic services are now selected and trained to perform functions which extend into economic and political observation as well as representation and negotiation, with little regard for aristocratic background (11, 20, 30).

The diplomat aims to maintain the prestige, position, and policies of his state and, when relations are bad, these functions may involve operations of "cold war" or, reversing Clausewitz's statement, war by other methods, but it is more common to think of diplomacy as an agency of co-operation, as continuous effort to achieve agreement and settle controversies. The arts of accurate statement, argument from principles of law or morals, compromise, conciliation, persuasion, and bargaining are more important than espionage, bribery, double dealing, and veiled threats. The function of diplomacy in keeping the peace was recognized even in the sixteenth century when writers sometimes referred to diplomats as agents of the community of nations as well as of their own states. When the undeveloped state of communications made it inevitable that instructions should be general and frequently outdated by the march of events, this function, as well as that of forwarding particular policies of the nation, was necessarily kept in mind by diplomats (3).

The art of diplomacy has developed an even more co-operative tendency with the growth of international organizations. Periodic conferences, such as the meetings of the Security Council and the General Assembly of the United Nations, bring diplomats together who are in principle committed to maintain the purposes and principles of the Charter as well as the policies of their states. The United Nations Secretariat itself has found it necessary to maintain a core of conciliators and mediators to assist the Security Council and the General Assembly in dealing with cases such as those of Palestine, Indonesia, and Kashmir (6). With the development of the United Nations this use of professional diplomats skilled in persuasion, conciliation, and compromise, responsible to the United Nations alone, will doubtless increase. Collective diplomacy, however, has not eliminated oppositional relations and has in fact provided public forums for their expression.

The art of war, including grand strategy, strategy, logistics, and tactics, is second only to diplomacy in the practice of international relations. Like diplomacy, it has been regulated by rules of international law. Their tendency during the seventeenth century was to protect officers, their prerogatives and honor; during the eighteenth, to protect private property and neutrals; and during the nineteenth century to protect civilians and to limit the inhumanities of war so far as military necessity permitted. The totalitarian wars of the twentieth century have enlarged the sphere of military necessity and indicated the relativity of both states of war and rules of war to military inventions (4, 8, 24, 28).

War has been used characteristically in the oppositional relations of states but in case of insurrection or rebellion the same art has been used as an auxiliary to civil police in maintaining domestic order. In international relations, collective military operations to suppress violations of the law of nations have, in principle, the character of international police. The theory of the vast operations undertaken by the United Nations against Germany, Japan, and their satellites from 1941 to 1945 was that of international police, not of war, as was evident in the practices of non-neutrality, unconditional surrender, and prosecution of war criminals, as well as in the Declaration of the Atlantic Charter, the Declaration of the United Nations, and the declarations of the Casablanca, Cairo, Teheran, Yalta, and Potsdam Conferences (28, 29).

The United Nations Charter contemplates utilization of the art of war as international police through the co-operation of national forces to maintain international peace and security. The procedure was employed to suppress aggression in Korea from 1950 to 1953. The United Nations Secretariat initiated a Police Force of quasi-military character wearing its own uniform to guard its mission in Palestine in 1948, and has urged a permanent force of this character (6). Like diplomacy, war is moving from an instrument of states in oppositional relations to an instrument of the world community to maintain peace.

Public administration has become a recognized profession in municipal and national governments. In dealing with foreign affairs, with colonial affairs, and with international organizations, national governments are confronted by problems different from those faced in domestic administration. Responsibilities flowing from international commitments must of necessity be reconciled with constitutional requirements of legislative participation. International conventions and agencies often impose qualifications upon the administration of dependent territories. International conventions regulate the whole field of international administration and co-operation. These complexities of public administration concerned with foreign and colonial affairs and with international organization has given it a special professional character (21).

The problems of reconciling executive and legislative agencies in the conduct of foreign policy; of gearing functional with regional experts in foreign offices; of gearing experts in other departments of the government with responsible foreign office experts; of gearing national experts with experts in international organizations; of recruiting, training, organizing, and maintaining the independence of international civil services; and of gearing the various divisions of the United Nations with the Specialized Agencies are problems of recent decades and have only begun to be solved. Issues of language, of differing national traditions, of national susceptibilities, and of standardizing tests of competence are only a few of the difficulties involved (9, 11, 15, 18).

Investigation is used to cover all means for acquiring information or *intelligence*. It is an art that has been utilized by both diplomacy and war. International law has regulated it by seeking to exclude espionage from diplomacy and subjecting it to grave penalties in war. Investigation, however, goes beyond the obtaining of secret information in oppositional relations of states, although that aspect may be expected to continue so long as such relations exist.

Both embassy attachés and consuls are engaged in observing and reporting on political, military, legal, economic, cultural, and other activities going on in the state or district in which they function. Often special agents are sent out by departments of government other than the foreign office to investigate or report on conditions abroad. Investigation relevant to international relations extends into observation and interviewing in the field, into library research, and into content analysis of newspapers, broadcasts, and other media of foreign propaganda and information. It even extends into science and technology (2).

During World War II the United States organized the Office of Strategic Services to co-ordinate information for the conduct of the war, an activity which contributed to the discipline of *operational research*. It also organized the Office of Research and Development to co-ordinate information about inventions for military purposes (2). After the war the Office of Research and Development was established in the Department of Defense, and the Central Intelligence Agency was established under the National Security Council. The latter employs professional investigators, both secret and public, both in the field and at home, to co-ordinate information from all sources and to provide relevant information to all departments of government, particularly to the State Department and the Department of Defense. The problem of gearing expert advice and intelligence into the decision-making process is one of unusual difficulty in the international field (5).

Information obtained by national governments is often made available to international organizations and thus serves co-operative as well as oppositional relations. International organizations, themselves, however, devote major attention to the assembling of relevant information but never of a secret character. Investigatory commissions are often sent to troubled areas, and member governments are requested to provide information on such matters as trade, population, labor conditions, cultural activities, and even armaments and troop movements.

Besides governments, private organizations with public service objectives such as the New York Council on Foreign Relations and the Royal Institute of International Affairs, organizations with objectives of commercial profit such as the *Encyclopedia Britannica*, the *Statesmen's Yearbook,* and the *Annual Register,* and numerous journals—daily, weekly, and monthly—broadcasting companies, and news commentators engage in gathering and giving publicity to information. The professions of investigation and reporting have a major task in international relations (5).

Public relations and propaganda activities have, like investigation, been adjuncts of the professions of diplomacy and war since these professions existed. Governments have always realized that the manipulation and communication of symbols is cheaper than the destruction of enemy armies or the occupation or blockade of enemy territory, and can sometimes be even more effective in achieving desired results.

It is only since World War I, however, that public relations activities both domestic and foreign have become part of the regular activity of foreign offices, embassies, and departments of defense (14). With this development, international law has taken cognizance of these activities and has attempted to adapt to modern conditions older rules designed to protect the state and its ruler from libel and from subversive, revolutionary, and warmongering propaganda. The effort to distinguish between propaganda by governments and by private agencies and between improper utterances and proper exercises of the freedom of the press has given rise to no little controversy in which liberal and totalitarian countries generally differ.

In the United States the Office of War Information, which conducted both domestic and foreign public relations activities during World War II, was transferred to the Department of State and has engaged in extensive activities abroad including radio broadcasts (The Voice of America), distribution of periodicals, maintenance of libraries, and association with international organizations with the object of circulating correct information about the United States and its policies. The distribution of information to prevent error is not easy to distinguish from propaganda to influence attitudes, opinions, and actions (14).

Private agencies for investigating and reporting also engage in publishing information and influencing opinion. The professions of investigation and of public relations are as closely related to each other as are the eyes and the ears to the voice and the pen. It is to be anticipated that as development of knowledge of the psychology and sociology of international relations proceeds, these professions will acquire increasing importance, particularly for international organizations now hampered by the disposition of national governments to monopolize or control instruments of information and propaganda. The United Nations and its affiliated organizations, particularly UNESCO, have sought to enter this field.

Education as a profession relevant to international relations is closely related to investigation and public relations. Systems of education have been used both to inform and to indoctrinate. The weight given to each varies greatly according as the government is democratic or authoritarian. Properly speaking, information is to inform, propaganda to influence opinion, and education to impart knowledge, to train in skills, to maintain culture, and to form the attitudes and character of the young.

Attention has already been called to the growth of the disciplines of international relations in higher education in the United States and other countries. Doubtless many of the attitudes most relevant to national and world opinion on international issues are formed in preschool and elementary education. This phase of education is perhaps deserving of more attention than education in the disciplines of international relations at a higher level. Aggressive attitudes and habits of projecting them on a scapegoat or displacing them on an external enemy may emerge from the system of family discipline. Attitudes toward the state and other nations may be fixed by symbolisms and readings in elementary school experience. These attitudes and predispositions are no less important in the development of public opinion than are the information and ideas in the field acquired as an adult. For this reason the profession of education in international relations should be considered to include not only college teachers of the subject but all teachers and even parents. Some professional knowledge in this field is a requirement of good citizenship.

In modern times, education has been treated as a function either of local communities or of national governments, although other institutions of society such as the church, business corporations, private schools, and families have in varying degrees provided education. All institutions of importance comprehend, as pointed out by Plato, that their existence depends in no small degree on early inculcation of their purposes and principles in the minds of the young. It is therefore not surprising that international organizations have taken an interest in education and have sought to moderate attitudes of excessive national loyalty which tend to produce oppositional relations between states and to emphasize attitudes of international co-operation and awareness of the world community. As yet the educational experience of most people is but little affected by these efforts.

Economic management has been an adjunct of diplomacy and war and has served equally to draw nations together and to keep them apart. Loans to friends rather than to potential enemies, discriminatory trade regulations, and manipulation of government monopolies for navigation and trade have always been instruments of diplomatic pressure and coercion. In time of war, blockade, contraband seizures, and confiscation of enemy property at sea have been utilized by all belligerents and have been major instruments of sea power. International law has been concerned with freedom of the seas and with property rights at sea of both belligerents and neutrals since the maritime codes of the middle ages. Many bilateral treaties have dealt with these topics (7, 10, 12, 13, 28).

The classical economists regarded international trade as a major source of national wealth and during the nineteenth century influenced governments to emphasize the regulation or freeing of trade and the facilitation of production and international loans for co-operative purposes of mutual benefit. This trend has been recognized in the many general international conventions and organizations for facilitating communication, transportation, and trade during the late nineteenth and twentieth centuries (21).

The industrialization of war, however, has increased the use of economic regulation as an instrument of war and diplomacy during the period since World War I. The mercantilist practices of the seventeenth and eighteenth centuries have again come into vogue augmented by the development of socialistic theories urging a governmentalization of national economies, by the rise of totalitarian states able to control the national economy, and by the rise of pressure groups in democratic states demanding government intervention in economic life to protect industry, agriculture, labor, and other special interests. All foreign offices have economic divisions which gather economic information, analyze it, and advise on economic policies.

These activities gear into those of international economic and financial organizations which seek to free or to regulate the movements of goods and capital for purposes of general welfare. The intricacies of the relations of law, policy, trade, finance, and management require a special competence both in economic theory and in factual knowledge, and practical skill in judging the consequences of changing conditions and of government action. Experts in this profession are needed by foreign offices and by international institutions (7, 21, 23).

The practice of *international law* has developed as a profession in connection with diplomacy, war, and public relations. The immunities of diplomats, the procedures of negotiation, and the form, interpretation, and validity of treaties came to be regulated by general rules of customary law. Limitations upon the conduct of hostilities, the rights of prisoners of war, of civilians, and of private property, and the procedures of reprisal and military justice came to be recognized by generals and admirals and to be formulated in both customary and conventional law (26).

In the seventeenth and eighteenth centuries, civil and admiralty courts began to listen to pleas based on international law, especially in cases involving diplomats, neutral property, and aliens. Military tribunals have referred to international law in dealing with war criminals, spies, and requisitions.

As the practice of international arbitration developed in the nineteenth century after the revival of this institution in the Jay Treaty of 1794, and as international jurisdiction developed in the Hague Court of International Arbitration of 1899, the Permanent Court of International Justice of 1920, and the International Court of Justice of 1945, the opportunities for the professional practice of international law increased (19). The profession of international law is not large, but throughout the world many international lawyers are needed as advisers to foreign offices, military establishments, and international organizations, and as judges, and advocates in both national and international tribunals. They also have a role in advocacy and enlightenment in the form of public opinion (12, 13).

Like all disciplines, international relations acquires tangibility and reality through its utilization in the practical arts and professions. Familiarity with these arts gives the citizen or leader a sense of practicability, warning him against theoretical solutions, and an appreciation both of the possibility and the difficulty of changing situations through human action. The political leader with some understanding of several of the arts may be able to avoid the professional distortion which often affects the master of only one. Knowledge of the arts tends toward a salutary relativism in appraising values which may, however, degenerate into the cynicism said often to characterize diplomats. Familiarity with all points of view may lead to their equal evaluation and to willingness to put skills at the service of the highest bidder. To avoid such degeneration is the task of the philosophy of international relations.

REFERENCES

1. BALFOUR, A. J., *Theism and Humanism* (New York, Hodder and Stoughton, 1915), pp. 91-92.
2. BAXTER, James Phinney, *Scientists Against Time* (Boston, Little, Brown, 1946).
3. BERNARD, Montague, *Four Lectures on Subjects Connected with Diplomacy* (London, Macmillan, 1868).
4. BRODIE, Bernard, *A Guide to Naval Strategy* (Princeton, Princeton University Press, 1944).
5. BRYSON, Lyman, "Notes on a Theory of Advice," in *Freedom and Authority in Our Time,* Twelfth Symposium on Science, Philosophy and Religion (New York, Harper, 1953), pp. 27 ff.
6. Commission to Study the Organization of Peace, United Nations Guards and Technical Field Services (New York, September, 1949).
7. FISK, George M., *International Commercial Policies* (New York, Macmillan, 1915).
8. FISKE, Rear Admiral Bradley A., *The Art of Fighting* (New York, Century, 1920).
9. FRIEDRICH, Carl J., *Foreign Policy in the Making* (New York, Norton, 1938).
10. GORDON, David L., and DANGERFIELD, Royden, *The Hidden Weapon, The Story of Economic Warfare* (New York, Harper, 1947).
11. HEATLEY, D. P., *Diplomacy and the Study of International Relations* (Oxford, Clarendon Press, 1919).
12. HISTORICUS, *Letters on Some Questions of International Law* (London, Macmillan, 1863).
13. HOLLAND, T. E., *Letters on War and Neutrality* (London, Longmans, 1914).
14. LASSWELL, Harold D., *Propaganda Technique in the World War* (New York, Knopf, 1927).

15. McCamy, James L., *The Administration of American Foreign Affairs* (New York, Knopf, 1950).

16. Machiavelli, Niccolò, *The Prince* (1513).

17. Maurice, Major General Sir Frederick, *Principles of Strategy* (New York, R. R. Smith, 1930).

18. Poole, Dewitt C., *The Conduct of International Relations Under Modern Democratic Conditions* (New Haven, Yale University Press, 1924).

19. Ralston, Jackson H., *The Law and Procedure of International Tribunals* (Stanford, Stanford University Press, 1926).

20. Satow, Sir Ernest, *Guide to Diplomatic Practice* (London, Longmans, 1917).

21. Sharp, Walter R., *Co-ordination of Economic and Social Activities*, United Nations Studies, No. 2 (Washington, Carnegie Endowment for International Peace, 1948).

22. Trevelyan, George M., "History and Literature," *History* (N.S.), ix (1924), p. 91.

23. Viner, Jacob, "The Short View and the Long View in Economic Policy," *American Economic Review*, Vol. XXX (March, 1940), pp. 1 ff.

24. Von der Goltz, Lieutenant General Colmar Freiherr, *The Conduct of War* (London, Kegan, Paul, 1908).

25. Walton, Izaak, "Life of Sir Henry Wotton," in *Reliquiae Wottonianae*, 4th ed. (London, 1685).

26. Wilson, George Grafton, *Handbook of International Law*, 3rd ed. (St. Paul, West, 1939).

27. Wright, Quincy, "Specialization and Universal Values in General International Organization," in *Approaches to Group Understanding*, Sixth Symposium on Science, Philosophy and Religion (New York, Harper, 1946), pp. 206 ff.

28. ———, *A Study of War* (Chicago, University of Chicago Press, 1942), pp. 1299 ff.

29. ———, *The World at the Cross Roads* (Chicago, World Citizens Association, 1946).

30. Young, George, *Diplomacy, Old and New* (New York, Harcourt, 1921).

The Philosophy of
International Relations

PHILOSOPHY MEANS the love of wisdom. It refers not only to wise formulations but also to the process of obtaining them and the state of mind of the possessor. The word would generally be recognized to differ from history and art in that it deals with the abstract rather than the concrete, and to differ from science in that it emphasizes *wisdom* which pays attention to subjective qualities, values, and aspirations as distinct from *knowledge* which emphasizes the objective and disinterested character of its evidence (13). Caution is necessary because philosophy is applied to systems of generalizations like those of Aristotle (1) and Spencer (16), based on observation rather than introspection. Judging, however, from the majority of writings in the two fields, philosophy seems to apply logic to introspections while science applies it to observations, with the consequence that philosophy is concerned more with values, purposes, and ends while science is concerned with relations, behaviors, and origins. Philosophy tends to be qualitative and rational; science quantitative and mathematical. Utilizing the distinction familiar to psychoanalysis, philosophy develops the *wish principle* of men and of societies, seeking to perceive the universe so that it conforms to the natural configurations of the human mind or to particular traditions, while science develops the *reality principle* so that the human mind may adjust itself to the universe as it *really is*. In this sense philosophy is a sophistication of religion which often conceives the tribe, the world, or the universe as a child perceives the family in early experience with a protective father and a loving mother. Philosophy moderates the wishful faith coming from these early and half-forgotten memories by reason resting on experience, but seldom entirely abandons those memories as does science.

The philosopher does not make God or the universe in his own image, but in interpreting the world he never quite forgets his own image or the image of the value system implicit in the culture and tradition in which he was brought up. The idols of the tribe, the market place, the theater, and the cave usually, as Francis Bacon recognized, have influenced the philosophies more than they have the sciences (2). Philosophy is particularly likely to be influenced by the language in which it is written. What can be said grammatically is likely to be considered real, at least in the sense of possible, and what cannot be said easily is likely to be considered impossible. Every language has within it values, distinctions, and classifications which arise from the customs, beliefs, and convictions of those who have used it and which do not exist for people who use a different language. The philosopher conversant with many languages has, therefore, a broader base for judging values and classifications. He can detect those which have at least the objectivity which flows from their recognition by all mankind. He may not eliminate the idols of the tribe, but may get rid of the idols of the market place, the theater, and the cave.

This is not to disparage philosophy. In the experience of the average man the *wish* principle is undoubtedly more important than is the *reality* principle. He knows what he wants better than he knows what can be obtained. His life consists in ordering wants and seeking to realize them. The man who has lost all interest in, or sense of, values has lost interest in life and may commit suicide.

Philosophy is related to history because the historian cannot neglect the philosophy of the people about whom he writes, but if history seeks to propagandize for a particular philosophy, as did the histories of Hegel, Marx, and Acton, it ceases to be history and becomes philosophy (18). Perhaps it should be noted that Acton, seeking to reconcile a clear conception of objective history with his religious convictions of what history ought to teach, found it extremely difficult to write at all.

Philosophy is also related to art because every art has ends which it seeks to realize, and philosophy may assure the artist that his ends are sufficiently valuable to justify this effort. In fact the artist usually assumes the value of his ends from tradition, faith, or intuition and leaves it to the philosopher of aesthetics, ethics, economics, or politics to make what justifications he can.

Sophistication in philosophy creates familiarity with abstractions, with the processes of logical inference, with value systems, and with the general characteristics of systems of thought. It is necessary to assume something in any process of reasoning. Consequently something must be accepted from faith, from experience, from introspection, from observation, or from some source other than reason itself. The philosopher will, therefore, be alert to the assumptions, axioms, postulates, beliefs, or opinions which consciously or unconsciously constitute the major premise of any argument, ideology, value system, or philosophy which may be presented to him.

Philosophy differs from science in the nature of its assumptions. The major assumption of science is the reliability of the senses, particularly the sense of sight extended by the microscope, the telescope, and various instruments of measurement. The major premise of most philosophies, on the other hand, is the reliability of introspection. *My* basic categories of thought, *my* feelings and desires, *my* intuitions of right and wrong must be susceptible of comprehension by everyone else and must be reliable, if I define them clearly, because all men are alike in their *innate ideas* (4). Sometimes philosophers place main reliance upon opinions which have been widely believed. The utterances of the founder of Christianity, of Buddhism, of Islam, must be susceptible of comprehension by everyone else and must be reliable, if clearly defined, because they have been so widely believed. In the western tradition, the first has been called *natural law*, the second *revelation*. These introspections and revelations are usually believed to have the peculiarity that if their logical inferences were acted upon by everyone, a more perfect state of society would result. Thus philosophy tends to deal with the type of proposition which becomes true by being widely believed in a society. In this it is distinguished from science which tends to deal with propositions the truth of which is independent of human belief. Science finds its special field in the behavior of nonhuman entities and philosophy in the behavior of man (17).

The study of philosophy is often supposed to develop attitudes of calmness, deliberation, toleration, and reasonableness. To view a problem *philosophically* is to view it without excitement, without pressure of time, and without prejudice or bias, and with appreciation of the merits of all points of view. This may be true, but on the other hand, persons may become wedded to a particular philosophy, ideology, or religion which enjoins its devotees to achieve their ideals as soon as possible. Such absolutistic beliefs can be dangerous to the world. Unless a philosopher has acquired a moderate skepticism in regard to every particular system of beliefs, including the one he favors, he may, through overanxiety to convert the world to his belief, engender great enmities and encourage methods of extraordinary barbarism and an attitude opposed to the discussion of major premises. This is obvious from the extraordinary barbarities in the Crusades and inquisitions and wars of religion committed in the name of Christianity in spite of the peacefulness and toleration attributed to its founder. This suggests that any philosophy believed dogmatically can promote very unphilosophical attitudes (7).

Sophistication in a particular philosophical system develops standards of evaluation and judgment in the various contingencies of life. Without some philosophy the only guide is the feeling of the moment, which the slightest experience shows is often an unsafe guide in a complicated society. Life consists in the gradual accommodation of biological urges and wishes to the conditions, inherent in society and nature, which obstruct their realization. Every society and culture involves some value system to assist in this accommodation. Philosophy, in the general sense, contributes to the understanding of this value system, and in a complex society, to an understanding of the competing value systems of church, state, business, and education, which may co-exist in the same community and may require adjustment to one another. Philosophy can therefore be of great practical use in ordering the competing preferences and value systems from which no one can escape.

Sophistication in a particular philosophy can also provide a point of view for ordering ideas. Justice Holmes said he viewed all ideas and experience through the keyhole of the law. Doctors, educators, engineers, teachers, and artisans, all acquire more or less familiarity with the philosophy underlying their art or profession. Without some system of thought with which to relate them, new ideas cannot be retained or their meanings analyzed. The philosophy inherent in any art or profession is by nature one-sided and in itself tends to cultivate professional distortions through excluding from consideration in any problem the ideas which, though relevant, do not fit easily into that philosophy. The study of philosophy should, but sometimes does not, provide an antidote to this professional distortion by disclosing the limitations of these practical and professional philosophies and providing a broader frame of reference and a more elaborate system for dealing with ideas (10).

The object of a particular philosophy may be individual serenity and adjustment, it may be social cohesion and progress, or it may be knowledge and understanding. A philosophy may be presented as a value in itself on the supposition that it presents objective truth which is the basis of knowledge and understanding good for both men and society. In view, however, of the multitude of competing philosophies, this form of presentation invites controversy and tends to a dogmatism by each which can be dangerous to both men and society. Premature consumption of the apple of wisdom may promote discord. Pearls should not be spread before swine. A little learning is a dangerous thing.

Since it confines itself to objective truth, science is less dangerous than philosophy, although it has dangers of its own. The devotees of science can consistently say that its propositions remain true whether anybody believes them or not and thus avoid the urge for propaganda. The devotees of philosophy, on the other hand, assume that the truth of any particular philosophy depends upon its wide acceptance, and consequently have no defenses against the urge for missionary activity to justify the faith. This is observable not only in the missionary religions and utopias which can be considered activist philosophies, but also, in a more subtle way, in the legal systems and conservative ideologies which can be considered quietist philosophies (11, 12).

A philosophy intended to promote individual serenity and adjustment, can assume the variability of man and can, therefore, recommend itself only to particular human types, acknowledging that others may need a different philosophy. It thus presents itself, not as absolute, eternal, and universal truth, but only as truth relative to a particular personality or a particular type of personality. Charles Morris has presented valuable data suggesting that the religions should be thus interpreted (9). Some people are naturally Moslems, others naturally Buddhists, other naturally Christians. If this relativistic interpretation of religions were generally accepted, religion might contribute more to the peace and order of the world than it has in the past. In view of the relative distinctiveness, if not uniqueness, of every personality and the probability that ultimate values constitute the summation of the individual's personality and experience, this line of thought suggests that there should be as many religions as there are people in the world. Everyone should make his own.

Philosophy and religion, however, serve not only an individual, but also a social, purpose. They bind the members of a society together by common values which provide a basis for social relationships and for co-operation under changing conditions. Men cannot act unitedly and spontaneously to meet emergencies or to adapt institutions and practices to changing circumstances unless they share some values and purposes. This line of thought suggests that in a shrinking world, where all peoples are in contact with one another, there should be only one religion or philosophy. While acknowledging their indispensable social function, one must point to the danger of religions and philosophies professing to be absolute, universal and eternal (11, 12).

A value system tends to be hierarchically organized with supreme values for the realization of which other values serve as means (13). Thus they tend to support the opinion that the end justifies the means. Since no society entirely realizes the highest values of its philosophy, it can easily be argued that all means are justifiable that will hasten their realization, in other words, that the present, which will surely suffer by the application of some of these means, must be sacrificed to the future. Consequently the world is afflicted by Hitler's Gestapo, by Stalin's G.P.U., by Torquemada's Inquisition, by Salem witch hunts, and by "Un-American" investigations.

The alternative type of value system is competitive, assuming that the best values will triumph in a free market of opinion (6, 8). Such a system, however, if it is to exist in an orderly society must recognize limitations upon the procedures which the adherents of any opinion may utilize in order to persuade others to their view. Procedures of discussion, propaganda, legislation, and adjudication, with proscription of fraud and violence, therefore, tend to become the essence of the system. They are the suitable means for permitting the better opinions, the better values, the better ends to emerge. The means, therefore, justify the ends. Ends achieved through the utilization of these means tend to be considered good.

Such a philosophy clearly has some resemblance to science whose test of truth is the adequacy of the methods of observation, measurement, analysis, and verification which have been used (3). The physicist assumes that if he follows the techniques of his profession, the facts will be found and the conclusions will be sound. The lawyer assumes that if the judge and jury function, observing the established procedures, the facts will be found and the verdict will be just. Both scientific method and legal procedure will establish *law*, the one in the jural sense, the other in the scientific.

A society operating on the basis of a competitive philosophy tends to establish its basic procedures by constitutional prescriptions which cannot themselves be easily changed. Since these procedures usually make it easier for opinions which rest on the traditions of constitutionalism to triumph, than others, they tend to exaggerate the values of law, tradition, and the prevailing ideology and so to sacrifice the present and the future to the past.

Hierarchically organized value systems tend to subordinate established institutions to ideology and to be absolute, rational, and active. Competitively organized value systems, on the other hand, tend to subordinate ideology to established institutions and to be relative, traditional, and quietist. The first tend to revolution; the second to stagnation. If society is to be both progressive and stable, reason must continually be balanced by tradition, Rousseau by Burke.

This discussion may suggest that life is greater than logic, that any philosophical system if it is to serve a society must be taken with many grains of salt. Pushed to its logical conclusion, any philosophy will straitjacket or strangle any society. Every philosophy should teach that all philosophies, including itself, are only relatively true. Each applies to some persons, some situations, some societies better than to others, and each maximizes its values, if it confines itself to the sphere of its greatest efficiency, tolerantly acknowledging the value of other philosophies in their proper spheres (5, 7). This need not, however, preclude the continual effort of philosophy to broaden its syntheses by refining its analyses. Even though acknowledging the present *truth* of pluralism it is the nature of philosophy, as of reason itself, to strive for the more comprehensive *truth* of a still unattainable monism.

It is clear that philosophy has much to contribute to all the disciplines of international relations (14, 15). It justifies and reconciles the arts by comparing their ends. It extracts values from history by comparing the consequences of different philosophies in different circumstances. It shows the limitations of science by pointing out that the policies which science endorses and the probabilities which science foresees have no meaning for mankind unless they contribute to ends or tend toward results which man can evaluate. To evaluate is the function of philosophy.

It is clear, however, that in the field of international relations, more than in other fields, a profound sense of the relativity of all philosophies is necessary for peace. The world is composed of many states, many religions, many legal systems, many languages, many cultures. The claim of one to be absolute has been a major cause of wars and disorders. Most wars are fundamentally ideological wars, wars to make *my* vision of the perfect world prevail. There are many visions of the perfect world and they cannot all prevail in one world (18).

The task of the philosophy of international relations is therefore one of synthesis and accommodation. What do the many ideologies have in common that can become a world philosophy or a world culture sufficiently to reconcile the great variety of value systems? What procedures can be devised which will permit those aspects in which cultures and philosophies differ to co-exist in peace?

It has been the effort of UNESCO, of the Human Rights Commission, of the Specialized Agencies, and of the Economic and Social Council of the United Nations to forward this synthetic task by co-operative methods. It has been the effort of the United Nations and the International Court of Justice to forward the task of accommodation by solving conflicts as they arise. Philosophical insight may contribute to this task (9, 11). It cannot be accomplished, however, unless the probable results of alternative formulations and alternative courses of action can be predicted within reasonable margins of error. This is the task of science.

REFERENCES

1. ARISTOTLE, *Metaphysics; Politics.*
2. BACON, Francis, *Novum Organum, or True Suggestions for the Interpretation of Nature* (1620).
3. COHEN, Morris, *Studies in Philosophy and Science* (New York, Holt, 1949).
4. DESCARTES, René, *Discourse on Method* (1636).
5. DEWEY, John, "Philosophy," *Encyclopædia of the Social Sciences.*
6. ———, *Reconstruction in Philosophy* (New York, Holt, 1920).

7. FRANK, Philipp, "Relativity, Truth and Values," in *Perspectives on a Troubled Decade,* Tenth Symposium on Science, Philosophy and Religion (New York, Harper, 1950), pp. 203 ff.
8. JAMES, William, *A Pluralistic Universe* (London, Longmans, 1912).
9. MORRIS, Charles, *Paths of Life, Preface to a World Religion* (New York, Harper, 1947).
10. ———, "Philosophy as Symbolic Synthesis of Belief," in *Approaches to Group Understanding,* Sixth Symposium on Science, Philosophy and Religion (New York, Harper, 1947), pp. 626 ff.
11. NORTHROP, F. S. C., *The Meeting of East and West, an Inquiry Concerning World Understanding* (New York, Macmillan, 1946).
12. ———, "Philosophy and World Peace," in *Approaches to World Peace,* Fourth Symposium on Science, Philosophy and Religion (New York, Harper, 1944), pp. 642 ff.
13. PLATO, *Gorgias; Meno; Protagoras; Republic.*
14. RUSSELL, Frank M., *Theories of International Relations* (New York, Appleton-Century-Crofts, 1936).
15. SABINE, G. H., *A History of Political Theory* (New York, Holt, 1937).
16. SPENCER, Herbert, *First Principles of a New System of Philosophy* (New York, Appleton, 1879).
17. STRAUSS, Leo, *Natural Right and History* (Chicago, University of Chicago Press, 1953).
18. WRIGHT, Quincy, *A Study of War* (Chicago, University of Chicago Press, 1942), pp. 446 ff., 705 ff.

CHAPTER
11

The Science of
International Relations

SCIENCE IS popularly defined as knowledge gained and verified by exact observation and correct thinking, but among scientists it is more often conceived as the process of acquiring such knowledge. This process involves observing, classifying, measuring, and experimenting with concrete data; formulating relations among quantitative variables, parameters, and constants which seem consistent with these data; devising new observations, classifications, measurements, and experiments to verify the formulations; and as new data and ideas are obtained, revising and verifying formulations *ad infinitum*. James B. Conant (5) has described science as the process of developing conceptual systems on the basis of observation and experiment with the object of stimulating new observation and experiment. He says its peculiarity lies in the organization of close, continuing, and reciprocal relations between speculative reflection, logic, and mathematics on the one hand and observation, experiment, practice, and technology on the other. Its validity depends upon the free intercourse and mutual criticism of a body of qualified persons devoted to its progress. To science there is no absolute truth and no final goal. Science is a process which, as it goes along, yields relative truths of more or less value for theoretical insight or practical action. Its test is in the capacity of its formulations actually to predict or to control.

Modern science has roots in the post-Renaissance rationalism which, skeptical of revelation, sought to demonstrate all truth by the application of reason, but its more important roots are to be found in the habits of accurate observation and generalization from them by men like Archimedes among the ancients and Roger Bacon in the middle ages, and in the traditions of mathematical reasoning initiated by the Pythagoreans in antiquity and emphasized by the Arabs in the middle ages (3, 6, 22). Twentieth-century science has grown from all these roots and its relation to rationalism is one rather of opposition than of acceptance. It recognizes the dependence of its conclusions upon the logically unprovable assumptions of common sense, that nature is continuous, and that observations are an index of reality (18). A relation which, after isolation, description, and measurement, is found to be invariable in every time and space in which it has been observed is believed by science to constitute a reliable rule or law likely to recur in every time and space even of the future. As the result of the experiments of Boyle and others in the eighteenth century, it has been concluded that the density of a gas has a definite relation to conditions of temperature and pressure in London, Chicago, Rome, or Peiping; at sea level, on the top of Mount Everest, or on Mars; in pre-Cambrian, Jurassic, modern, and future times. The scientist need not attribute such generality to all the relatively invariable relations which he discovers. He may limit some of his generalizations to particular times and places. For instance he may recognize that their applicability is limited to dimensions normal to human observation, excluding the sub-atomic and the super-galactic. He may even believe that the invariability of some frequently observed relations cannot be relied upon in other times and places. He may recognize that conditions not considered in his formula are likely to intervene. He may recognize that his generalizations rest basically on the statistical stability of large numbers or the organizational stability of complex equilibria and therefore are only relatively true even within the stated field of applicability (23). Science is founded on a belief in relativism and a profound skepticism of all absolute truths. The scientist anticipates that his most cherished formulae will be outmoded, but he considers that today they constitute better truths than any others. His formulations are comparative, not superlative; hypothetical, not absolute; probable, not certain (8, 17, 18, 19, 20). "The laws of science are not immutable," writes Thurstone. "They are only human efforts toward parsimony in the comprehension of nature" (24).

The scientist is therefore skeptical of qualitative distinctions or of the assumption that the number of alternatives in a practical situation is limited. He attempts to reduce all differences to quantitative variables. His careful observations suggest that within the dimensions which normally concern human activity there are few sharp lines or sudden jumps. Consequently, solutions of complex problems can often be found which differ from any of the limited number of alternatives which first spring to mind (1, 21).

In this, science differs from law, morals, religion, and aesthetics, which usually assume sharp lines of distinction. The judge has to decide that the defendant is innocent or guilty. The moralist has to decide that this action is right or wrong, the priest that this doctrine is true or false, the critic that this work of art is significant or trivial. For practical purposes of human behavior, such qualitative decisions are adapted to most cultures and perhaps to the configuration of the human nervous system and the character of language. They are, therefore, useful in human affairs, but the scientist does not find them in nature. The boundaries of objects and events shade off gradually if examined minutely. Most differences are differences of degree and can be represented by positions on a curve better than by discrete symbols. Consequently the reduction of qualitative to quantitative differences is a scientific desideratum. To the scientist the defendant is less liable or more liable than the plaintiff. This behavior is in the circumstances better or worse than that. This doctrine is more persuasive or less persuasive than that. This picture is more or less valuable than that.

The primary test of science is its capacity to predict and control. A formula is not a scientific formula unless it works in practice, no matter how correct the reasoning or effective the presentation or persuasive the conclusion. If competent experimenters or observers cannot get the expected results in practice, the formula must be rejected or revised. Its postulates may be inadequate or some essential variables may have been neglected. Science is, therefore, pragmatic. Pure science seeks formulae which will relate causes and effects with such a high degree of probability and such a slight margin of error that its predictions are reliable. Applied science seeks to translate these predictive formulae into control formulae stating the means which will produce desired ends (4, 5).

Science assumes that observation is the most reliable guide to reality. It utilizes rational inference and introspective suggestion but insists that the conclusions be stated in terms of predictions which can be verified by observation or experiment. This assumption may be justified by the repeated observation that men are more alike in reports of the senses, particularly in the sense of sight, than in any other kind of experience. Reports which depend on introspection or feeling cannot be verified by others. The intuitions of one man differ from those of another, but a reading on a dial or a description of a microscopic or telescopic photograph by one can be verified by anyone else who is properly trained (4).

Assuming the continuity of nature, science expects a universal consistency in its results, and therefore the second test of a formulation is its consistency with other well-verified formulae. Internal consistency, implying a minimizing of assumptions and of independent variables and a continuous simplification and unification of science as a whole, is a desideratum because it adds to the predictive scope of science (9, 15). But it is secondary to the verifiability of any formula from objective data. Two inconsistent formulae, each of which is reliable within its field, are preferable to one formula with a high margin of error. The resolution of inconsistencies and simplification of the complex gives opportunity for scientific ingenuity in deriving new hypotheses and for inventive ingenuity in devising new tests and experiments.

The desiderata of science, therefore, include accuracy in observation and description; operational clarity in definition and terminology; measurability through reduction of qualitative to quantitative differences; correctness of reasoning within the symbol system employed; objectivity in elimination of personal and cultural biases from observation, reporting, and reasoning; economy in the making of assumptions and the positing of variables; concern for the consistency, unity, and simplicity of science as a whole; and creative imagination in devising hypotheses and methods of verification (19, 27).

Scientists differ in the priority they give to study of the concrete and the abstract. Observers and inductivists, like Bacon, Boyle, Darwin, Mendel, and Michelson, begin with the observation of concrete facts under the conviction that only after much precise description and careful induction can hypotheses be formulated in such operational and quantitative terms as to be susceptible of verification. On the other hand, thinkers and deductivists like Descartes, Newton, Laplace, Poincaré, and Einstein begin with reflection on, and deduction from, an abstract conceptual system with the conviction that only on the basis of clear conceptions can relevant observations and experiments be devised. Both types have contributed to science. Both recognize that the essence of science is the organic union of the concrete and the abstract, whichever may have been contemplated first. Probably if the workings of the scientific mind could be probed, it would be found that the observers usually had a vague theory in mind from the beginning but feared they would bias their observations if they formulated it until examination of the facts had given it considerable substance and probability. It might also be found that the thinkers usually had past observations or experiments in mind which they believed gave support to the concepts and conceptual systems which were the prime objects of their attention but thought it useless to look further until a clarification of concepts had suggested what to look for. Some historians of science emphasize the dominant role of conceptual systems in the actual development of the pure sciences, especially the physical sciences. They find that the imaginative proposal of a broad conceptual scheme in terms of operational definitions has been the major stimulus to scientific deduction, observation, and experiment, either to verify or to refute it. Pure scientists, the historians insist, have been interested in conceptual schemes and not in practical utilities. However, nonutilitarian motivation does not necessarily mean prime interest in theory. Important scientific contributions have undoubtedly been made because of the curiosity of men to see how concrete things behave or what can be learned from the application of a new technique of observation or experiment (3, 5, 19).

Science is related to philosophy because it makes use of the logical systems which philosophy provides, and because it criticizes the assumptions in all philosophical systems. It differs from philosophy in emphasizing objectivity rather than evaluation, nature rather than man, probability rather than desirability, verifiability rather than consistency. Philosophy may speculate to elucidate the possible and to persuade opinion, but science must ceaselessly check its generalizations by observation and practice. It cannot roam far from its data.

Science is related to art because it criticizes the methods of any art in respect to their efficiency in achieving the desired results and because it utilizes the techniques of the arts in its process of verification. It differs from art in being contemplative rather than manipulative, in being guided by curiosity rather than utility or value, in concerning itself with probabilities rather than possibilities and desirabilities, and in being interested in abstract rather than concrete problems.

Science is related to history because it provides methods for discovering and weighing historical evidence and because it utilizes some of the facts and relations which history discovers in verifying its generalizations. It differs from history in its concern for the repetitive rather than the unique, the common rather than the interesting, the probable rather than the certain, the universal rather than the particular.

Science is distinguished from philosophy, art, and history by its nonhumanistic orientation. To science, man is a part of nature. The special position assigned to him in the dualism which pervades history, art, and philosophy has no place in science. To science the subjective and objective are simply two ways of looking at the same thing. Its effort is to present explanations which are objectively verifiable with the hope that such explanations may be possible in all fields. Consequently in the opinion of the natural scientists, to introduce the subjective is to duplicate in the fields where objective explanations are available or to abandon science in the fields where such explanations have not yet been discovered. The natural scientist as a man may doubt whether his method can serve in all fields of human interest and may welcome the work of philosophers in such fields. But as a natural scientist he must quiet his doubts and labor in the faith that science may be expanded into fields, which, from his point of view, are still in the unknown (29).

The social scientist may proceed from the same theory, but often he believes that human motivations and behavior with which he deals can hardly be studied successfully without utilizing reports of subjective experience. Such evidence, he believes, provides more adequate data in his field than could be obtained from observing such objective facts as individual or group behavior or neural structure and functioning. Man and society may be explainable in terms of behavioral effects and neural causes, but they are easier to explain in terms of words and symbols expressive of purposes, attitudes, policies, decisions, and other subjective conditions or events. It is not impossible that these evidences of the subjective world can acquire considerable objectivity through such refinements of methods for describing, analyzing, measuring, and interpreting them as have been proposed by the disciplines of semantics, group dynamics, communications, and attitude measurement (2, 12, 13, 14, 20). Some social scientists believe that sensory experience, which purports to connect the objective and the subjective worlds, is of such a selective nature as to preclude the application of the methods of natural science in the social sciences, and to necessitate the assumption of philosophical dualism and the analysis of the mind (7, 10, 11).

International relations is a field extraordinarily difficult for science to enter. If sovereign states are considered the units of study, it deals with the relations of a small number of large entities, each of which seems to be independent and *unique*. Neither the statistical stability of large numbers nor the organizational stability of complex equilibria are therefore to be expected. If the world as a whole is taken as the unit, there is no other world with which it can be easily compared.

Predictability is a consequence either of the random action of innumerable similar entities or of the regulated action of complementary entities in such equilibrium that the behavior of the whole can be controlled from a single point and by a single purpose. Determinism, permitting completely reliable predictions, therefore is possible only in situations controlled by an infinite number of atoms or by one supreme power. The number of statesmen controlling the behavior of states has always been small and in the modern world has tended to become smaller with the result of diminishing the reliability of predictions based on a statistical analysis of their behavior. But on the other hand, the instability of the equilibrium, considering the high degree of freedom of states from external conditions and the imperfect organization of governments to manipulate such equilibria as exist, is not sufficient to permit reliable predictions based on knowledge of the policies of governments. In fact, the internal stability of most states and their external independence has been diminished by the shrinking of the world with the consequence that predictions based on political knowledge have become progressively less reliable (27, 28).

Nevertheless, science has often been able to solve such difficulties by making observations at a wholly different level of magnitude. There may be a statistical regularity in the behavior of electrons and protons even when the molecules into which they are organized become, as in the case of many organic molecules, so large and complex that the behavior of the molecules themselves is statistically unreliable. There may be an organizational reliability in our galaxy even though we discover that our solar system is so dependent on other heavenly bodies as to be organizationally unreliable. By further analyzing the parts, or further expanding the concept of the whole, prediction and control, even at the intermediate levels of magnitude, may be facilitated. The internationalist may therefore develop a measure of statistical reliability by lowering his gaze to the multitude of men and attitudes in the world, or by raising his gaze to the single relatively independent and potentially stable and controllable world community. The behavior of states, nations, and governments may prove amenable to scientific treatment when they are conceived as compositions of men or attitudes, or as parts of a world order.

International relations shares with all the social sciences other difficulties in the application of the scientific method. The persons and organizations with which the social sciences deal may be influenced by the scientific generalizations themselves, and thus once such a generalization has been formulated and has become known to the persons whose behavior it attempts to predict, they may react in ways different from their past behavior, the observation of which justified the generalization. The generalizations about the movement of planets or molecules may influence the behavior of men, but not that of the planets or molecules. But generalizations about the behavior of men as investors, as patriots, or as soldiers, may influence not only the men who manage—the investment bankers, the governors, the generals—but also the investors, the patriots, or the soldiers themselves. They may be induced to persist in their behavior even after they have become conscious of its consequences or they may behave differently. Such generalizations, therefore, cannot have the scientific character that their truth is independent of human beliefs (27, 28).

This "feed-back" effect operates in other fields where contingencies of varying probability continually affect the process, and it is not entirely unamenable to mathematical treatment as illustrated in Cybernetics (26) and the theory of games (25), but its operation is so much the essence of social behavior, in which anticipated consequences are major causes of action, that scientific analysis is peculiarly difficult (20). Science normally considers that time is one directional, that causes precede effects in time. In human behavior, however, time may be reversed in contemplation by means and end analyses. The end to be achieved in a distant future may be a major cause of a series of steps from that point in time to the present. The last step in this mental analysis of ends and means is the first step in realization but subsequent steps do not follow automatically. The continual interaction of mental analysis in which time moves from future to present and practical action in which it moves from present to future creates a self-correcting process not easily susceptible of prediction on the scientific assumption that relations repeatedly observed in the past will recur in the future under the same observable conditions. Purposes may change rapidly and neither the purposes nor the causes of their change are easy to observe. Among movements or behavior normally attributed by the physical sciences to relations, forces, or conditions external to the moving object, *activity* or internally determined behavior may be distinguished as the main concern of biology. Among such activities *purposive* or goal-directed activity may be distinguished as the main concern of psychologists and within that class *self-correcting* purposive activity may be identified as the main concern of social science. The study of such activity requires methods of observation and analysis radically different from those of the physical sciences and even from those of biology and psychology (20).

The influence of purpose and self-correction is only one aspect of the sensitivity of the human mind to influence by a multitude of occurrences widely separated in time and space. Because of this sensitivity, the number of variables in a formula involving human behavior is inevitably very great, and the orbit of events which must be considered in formulating those variables becomes incredibly large as human communication, history, and science expands. Behavior within a primitive tribe is influenced by a limited history incorporated in tribal traditions and by events in a limited geographic space. But behavior in a civilized state is influenced by millennia of history, by news from all over the world, and by a mass of scientific and popular knowledge, and of religious and cultural traditions which can be grouped under the general head of opinion. As a result, most variables have to be treated as if they were constants. Propositions in social science therefore usually include, more often implicitly than explicitly, the dubious qualification *other things being equal.* This means that the generalization is applicable only where the general conditions of culture, society, and opinion are identical with those which prevailed when the observations were made upon which the generalization was founded. Because, in fact, culture, society, and opinion are always changing, and therefore generalizations are never identical in different parts of the world or different historic periods, this means that many social-scientific generalizations are limited in application to the time and space in which made, that is, they are in reality historic rather than scientific generalizations. Their applicability is at best limited to the society which provided the observations and to a short period in its future during which it is fair to assume that the general conditions of that society will not change (1, 27).

Because of these circumstances, social-science generalizations share the characteristic of many philosophic generalizations, that their truth depends in a measure upon their persuasiveness. The validity of most social-scientific *laws* depends on the continuance of the beliefs and opinions which were assumed when the *law* was formulated. But the *law*, by disclosing the consequences of these beliefs and opinions, may influence people either to continue or to abandon them. If the desirability of these consequences is presented persuasively, men will continue their beliefs and opinions, and behavior will meet the expectations of the *law*. This indicates that social science and social propaganda are not wholly unrelated (28).

Social science, however, differs from philosophy in that its generalizations are based on observation of the past rather than ideals of the present. Its truth, therefore, is supported, not only by its persuasiveness, but also by human inertia. Insofar as men act by habit and custom, the continuity of nature applies to human as well as to nonhuman affairs, and social-science generalizations have a scientific rather than a philosophic character. Clearly these conditions apply more completely to primitive than to civilized peoples.

The influence of science on human affairs is, therefore, somewhat paradoxical. Natural science, assuming the continuity of nature, expands man's control over his natural environment and tends to create inventions and new conditions to which ancient faiths, customs, and opinions are ill adapted. Natural science, therefore, often lends support to reformers who wish to change social ideas and institutions in order to adjust society to present and future conditions, and to utilize the opportunities which scientific advance has made available.

Social science, on the other hand, assuming the continuity of most human and social relations, makes generalizations which will be valid in the future only so far as fundamental customs and traditions continue. Social scientists, therefore, are likely to have a conservative influence on society because their professional distortion makes them propagandists for the assumptions on which the validity of their work depends. Their expectation that trends in the past will continue in the future and that relations observed to be invariable in the past will be invariable in the future color their wishes and they become skeptical of novel ideals and aspirations (1, 9, 14).

There are, however, very few social scientists in the world. The majority of so-called social scientists are in fact social philosophers who interpret the past not by careful observations, but by discreet selection to justify ideals or aspirations acquired from introspection, early education, or cultural tradition. Their generalizations are ruled by the Baconian idols, not by scientific ideas, and may be either radical or conservative according to the character of the particular idols.

We may therefore conclude that the social sciences have peculiar difficulties because of human purpose which makes anticipations of the future a factor in the present, and because of the contingency of its generalizations upon conditions composed of so many variables that they are unsusceptible of complete analysis. Consequently, there is in social affairs a universality of change and lack of reliable constants, presenting difficulties to measurement. There is also a universality of relations among all the entities in the entire human community presenting difficulties to division of the disciplines and specialization of effort, either functionally or regionally. The variations of no social relation can be measured in isolation from a vast uncontrolled and unanalyzed environment. All human experience—past, present, and future—should enter into every equation about human behavior. In greater degree than in any other phase of nature the whole controls all its parts in the human community. This control is of such degree that explanation of the behavior of sub-wholes in terms of their parts or of parts in terms of sub-wholes is subject to an exceptional margin of error.

The social sciences are, therefore, as near to philosophy as they are to natural science. While observing the past and formulating expectations of the future, the social scientist cannot ignore the desires men have for the future nor the necessary relation between expectations and desires. Men cannot labor effectively for ends which are deemed impossible, and it is difficult for men to maintain expectations which conflict with what they ardently desire. The social scientist can, therefore, as a man hardly avoid being a philosopher, and as a citizen he cannot feel irresponsible concerning the effect of his generalizations upon the future of humanity and of the society of which he is a member.

In spite of these difficulties, it would be premature to limit the scope of social science or to assert arbitrarily that utilization of different scales of observation, application of mathematical methods which give consideration to the feed-back of purpose and self-correction on action, and utilization of machines capable of solving equations of many variables may not continually diminish the margin of error in formulations and thus expand their capacity to influence and in some aspects to predict and control human affairs.

Furthermore, many of the criteria of science—objectivity, accuracy, quantification, logic—may be useful in influencing the point of view of the citizen, the leader, and the professional on international relations. In a field so largely made up of conflicting emotions and symbols, appreciation of the scientific virtues can prevent hasty opinions, ill-considered decisions, and the application of methods unlikely to achieve the ends desired.

All disciplines have tended in the modern period to become sciences, however resistant their material may be to such treatment. They usually begin as arts or histories, then become generalized into philosophies, and then struggle to become sciences. This may be because man, in addition to being a social and rational animal, is a tool-using animal. He has used tools to control his environment, and to control himself. In the modern period, perhaps because of the opportunities presented by the discovery of a new world in the Americas and because of innumerable technical inventions, he has preferred the former. In other ages and civilizations men have been more devoted to self-discipline than to the disciplining of nature and society. They have found religion and philosophy useful for that purpose. In the modern age, however, they have looked out on the world rather than in on themselves. History and philosophy may contribute to self-orientation and personal adjustment. But they help little, except as they are hand-maids of science, in man's effort to predict the future and to control his environment. Art is under the same limitation unless it rests upon applied science. In the modern world, therefore, disciplines have been considered tools for man's use in achieving his ends. Science is therefore preferred for the same reason that a farmer prefers a plow that will plow to one that will not, or an orator prefers a phrase that will move his audience to one that will not. In the next part of this volume attention will be devoted to the progress which the various disciplines have made toward becoming sciences.

REFERENCES

1. BARNARD, Chester I., "On Planning for World Government," with appendix by Lawrence J. Henderson on the "Defectiveness of Chains of Deductive Reasoning," in *Approaches to World Peace*, Fourth Symposium on Science, Philosophy and Religion (New York, Harper, 1944), pp. 825 ff.

2. BLOOMFIELD, Leonard, "Linguistic Aspects of Science," *International Encyclopedia of Unified Science*, Vol. 1, No. 2 (Chicago, University of Chicago Press, 1938).

3. BUTTERFIELD, H., *The Origins of Modern Science, 1300-1800* (London, Bell, 1950).

4. CAMPBELL, Norman, *What Is Science?* (New York, Dover, 1952).

5. CONANT, James Bryant, *Science and Common Sense* (New Haven, Yale University Press, 1951).

6. DAMPIER, Sir W. C., *History of Science*, 3rd ed. (New York, Macmillan, 1942).

7. EASTON, David, *The Political System* (New York, Knopf, 1953).

8. EINSTEIN, Albert, *The World as I See It* (New York, Covici-Friede, 1934).

9. FRANK, Philipp, "The Logical and Sociological Aspects of Science," in *Contributions to the Analysis and Synthesis of Knowledge*, Proceedings American Academy of Arts and Sciences, Vol. 80 (July, 1951), pp. 16 ff.

10. HAYEK, F. A., *The Counter-Revolution of Science* (Glencoe, Ill., Freepress, 1952).

11. ———, *The Sensory Order* (Chicago, University of Chicago Press, 1952).

12. KNIGHT, Frank, "Social Science," *Ethics*, Vol. 51 (January, 1941), pp. 136 ff.

13. KORZYBSKI, Alfred, *Science and Sanity*, 2nd ed. (Lancaster, Pa., Science Press, 1941).

14. LERNER, Daniel, and LASSWELL, Harold D., eds., *The Policy Sciences* (Stanford, Stanford University Press, 1951).

15. NEURATH, Otto, BOHR, Niels, DEWEY, John, RUSSELL, Bertrand, CARNAP, Rudolf, and MORRIS, Charles, *Encyclopedia of Unified Science*, Vol. 1, No. 1 (Chicago, University of Chicago Press, 1938).

16. PARSONS, Talcott, and SHILS, Edward, *Toward a General Theory of Action*, 2nd ed. (Cambridge, Harvard University Press, 1949).

17. PEARSON, Karl, *Grammar of Science*, 2nd ed. (London, 1899).

18. PLANCK, Max, *Scientific Autobiography and Other Papers* (New York, Philosophical Library, 1949).

19. POINCARÉ, Henri, *Science and Method* (London, Thomas Nelson, n.d.).

20. RAPAPORT, Anatol, *Operational Philosophy, Integrating Knowledge and Activity* (New York, Harper, 1953).

21. RICE, Stuart A., *Quantitative Methods in Politics* (New York, Knopf, 1928).

22. SARTON, George, *Introduction to the History of Science* (Washington, Carnegie Institution, 1927, 1931).

23. SCHROEDINGER, Erwin, *What Is Life?* (New York, Macmillan, 1946).

24. THURSTONE, L. L., *The Vectors of Mind* (Chicago, University of Chicago Press, 1935).

25. VON NEUMAN, John, and MORGENSTERN, Oscar, *Theory of Games and Economic Behavior* (Princeton, Princeton University Press, 1947).

26. WIENER, Norbert, *Cybernetics* (New York, Wiley, 1948).

27. WRIGHT, Quincy, *A Study of War* (Chicago, University of Chicago Press, 1942), pp. 681 ff., 1355 ff.

28. ———, "The Social Sciences and Policy Formation," in *Approaches to World Peace*, Fourth Symposium on Science, Philosophy and Religion (New York, Harper, 1944), pp. 83 ff.

29. WRIGHT, Sewall, "Gene and Organisms," *American Naturalist*, Vol. 87 (January, 1953), pp. 5 ff.

PART
III

Practical Analyses of
International Relations

Modes of Analyzing
International Relations

THERE ARE MANY ways in which international relations might be analyzed. In Part I of this volume the study of international relations was analyzed historically by indicating some twenty disciplines which have actually emerged dealing with the subject directly or indirectly. Each of these disciplines makes certain assumptions, serves certain purposes, and pursues certain methods, and therefore each constitutes an analysis of international relations from a point of view which historically has been sufficiently important to engage the efforts of writers and practitioners. Many of these disciplines, however, are imperfectly conscious of their assumptions, purposes, and methods and, therefore, lack integration and logical coherence. What unity they have is a consequence of an historical process, not of an abstract analysis.

In Part II the study of international relations was analyzed under the fundamental categories of history, art, philosophy, and science. Each of these categories implies a particular conception of the nature of truth, of its relation to reality, and of its value to man and society. The character of a particular discipline can be understood by the weight which has been given in its literature to one or the other of these categories.

It would also be possible to analyze the study of international relations according to the methods employed (3). Thus the *historical-descriptive* method used especially, but not exclusively, in the writing of history has figured in the study of diplomatic history, international politics, and political geography, demography, and technology. This method starts with the observation and description of concrete phenomena and proceeds to their classification in obvious categories of spatial or temporal proximity, or of similarity or difference in structure or function. Temporal variations in concepts derived from these classifications may be described and related to one another or to specified conditions. More abstract concepts based upon motive and intention, cause and effect, means and ends, may eventually be developed and related to one another.

general → specific The historical-descriptive method may be distinguished from the *analytic-rational* method frequently employed in philosophy and characteristic of the study of international law and international ethics. This method begins with rational inference from abstract assumptions usually about human nature, human motives, and human values, and continues with the objective elucidation of these inferences by concrete instances selected from history. As the historical method moves by induction from the concrete to the abstract, so this method moves by deduction from the abstract to the concrete. The difference, however, resides actually in the relative weight given to inference and instance. All thought must pay some attention to both.

Each of these methods can be distinguished from the *synthetic-practical* method employed in the arts and figuring especially in the study of international organization, colonial government, international education, and international communications. This method starts with the imaginative construction of subjective ends and proceeds to the practical means requisite for their realization.

Finally, some use has been made in the field of international relations of the *statistical-mathematical* method characteristic of science, especially in the study of international economics, and the psychology and sociology of international relations. This method may begin with the objective classification of data chosen with special reference to its susceptibility to quantitative treatment and measurement. It then employs mathematical methods to assess the probability that observed relationships will be sufficiently persistent to permit within reasonable margins of error predictions or controls of importance to mankind. This method may also begin with the mathematical analysis of hypothetical relations among defined variables and constants and proceed with observations or experiments for the purpose of verifying the results obtained. As the synthetic-practical method proceeds from subjective ends to objective means, so the mathematical-statistical method proceeds from objective classes and relations to subjective values.

No one method, however, characterizes any of these disciplines. All of them utilize the historical-descriptive method and all are to some extent both analytic and synthetic, both inductive and deductive, both logical and mathematical.

The analysis of international relations may be applied not to the study of the subject, but to the subject matter of the study. From this point of view attention may be focussed on the *entities* related, on the *processes* of change, on the *forces* at work, or on the *relations* of the variables involved (5).

The *entities* of importance to international relations may be studied, their characteristics and policies distinguished, and the outcome of future situations inferred through the application to the data of any of the methods described. Among the entities involved, the state, the government, the nation, and the people may usefully be distinguished according as the groups of dominant importance in the world are considered as territorial and legal, as administrative and political, as psychological and sociological, or as racial and cultural entities.

Processes such as diplomacy, war, arbitration, trade, administrative management, may be taken as the center of study. The methods and the consequences of the application of each may be examined, and conclusions may be drawn as to their relative utility in different circumstances. These processes may be usefully classified as juridical, administrative, political, and psychological according as they seek to settle controversies by the application of generally accepted procedures and principles; by the utilization of effective means to accomplish accepted ends; by the manipulation of power and influence to preserve and advance the interests of a group against the opposition of other groups; and by the manipulation of symbols to create, maintain, and develop groups and to promote policies.

Forces can be studied, in some cases measured, and their consequences under various conditions appraised. Among *forces* usually considered important in international relations are nationalism, imperialism, pacifism, militarism, and other group opinions; sentiments, beliefs, religions, and other individual attitudes; technical, administrative, legal, and other innovations; and charismatic personalities, plans, ideologies, propagandas, and other sources of political initiative. These forces may be classified as movements, drives, inventions, and ideas according as they embody an emotional opinion or *ism*, stimulating group demands; individual dispositions, derived from heredity or experience, to act in a definite way when faced by the appropriate stimulus; a mechanical or social technique making new services or controls available; or a dynamic theory of society, program of action, or passion for leadership.

Finally, the *relations* of groups to one another may be defined and the consequences of these relations appraised. The relation of one group to another may be usefully conceived as the "distance" which separates them (5). And these *distances* may be analyzed into technological, strategic, psychological, political, legal, ideological, sociological, anxiety, and other aspects. If many groups are concerned, their relationships may be conceived as constituting a super group or system, and the relations of anxiety, organization and power in the whole may be conceived by analogy to the relations of tension, resistance, and energy in an electrical or mechanical system (6). Such relations may be expressed as quantitative variables susceptible of mathematical treatment and sometimes yielding results useful for prediction and control. Social relations significant in the international field may be conveniently classified by the words community, organization, society, and culture according as they manifest more or less communication within or among groups; more or less centralization of authority; more or less co-operation; more or less standardization of values and behavior patterns (4, 7). It will be observed that an emphasis upon society, organization, culture, and community, respectively characterize the state, the government, the nation, and the people.

In this and the following part of this volume, sixteen disciplines will be considered in accord with these different forms of analysis. They have been grouped into two classes. Those with an objective primarily *practical* are dealt with in this part, and those with an objective in considerable measure *theoretical* are dealt with in the next part. These two classes are not concerned with the method of study employed in the discipline, with the subject matter with which it deals, or with its value or effectiveness (1), but with the general orientation of the discipline. The practical disciplines are designed to contribute to an art, practice, or profession, or to solve a problem, while the theoretical disciplines are intended to contribute to the general advance of human knowledge and understanding (2).

The practical disciplines include international politics and the subsidiary arts of war, diplomacy, and the conduct of foreign relations; colonial government and international organization; international law; international economics; international education; and international communications. The theoretical disciplines include political geography, political demography, technology, the sociology of international relations, the psychology of international relations, and international ethics. Some of these disciplines view the world as essentially divided into sovereign states while others view human and group behavior mainly from a world point of view. The practical disciplines have to do with social structures and policies, and may be included among the *policy sciences* (3). The theoretical disciplines fall into three classes respectively emphasizing conditions (geography, demography, technology), behavior (sociology, psychology), and institutions (ethics), and respectively included among the *ecological, behavioral,* and *social* sciences. Such practical disciplines as political science, economics, law, education, and communications are, however, often included in the latter class and they have developed theoretical aspects though their orientation is primarily practical.

The history of the development of these and other disciplines has been considered in Chapters 5, 6, and 9. In the following chapters an attempt will be made to define each of them; to state its underlying assumptions and the conditions under which these assumptions are applicable; to analyze its principles and methods; and to criticize it with reference to the entities, processes, forces, and relations significant in contemporary world affairs.

An effort will also be made to indicate the extent to which each discipline has evolved from a history, an art, or a philosophy into a science; the extent to which it has utilized, not only the historic-descriptive, the analytic-rational, and the synthetic-practical methods, but also the statistical-mathematical method; and the extent to which its interest has shifted from the study of entities, processes, and forces to that of relationships.

REFERENCES

1. HERZ, John H., *Political Realism and Political Idealism* (Chicago, University of Chicago Press, 1951), and review by Quincy Wright, *World Politics*, Vol. 5 (October, 1952), pp. 116-128.
2. HUSZAR, George B. de, ed., *New Perspectives on Peace* (Chicago, University of Chicago Press, 1944).
3. LERNER, Daniel, and LASSWELL, Harold D., eds., *The Policy Sciences, Recent Developments in Scope and Method* (Stanford, Stanford University Press, 1951), and review by Quincy Wright, *American Political Science Review*, Vol. 46 (March, 1952), pp. 234-238.
4. OGBURN, William F., ed., *Technology and International Relations* (Chicago, University of Chicago Press, 1949).
5. WRIGHT, Quincy, *A Study of War* (Chicago, University of Chicago Press, 1942), pp. 423-451, 701-739, 1227-1250, 1432-1444, 1456-1471.
6. ———, "Measurement of Variations in International Tensions" in *Learning and World Peace*, Eighth Symposium on Science, Philosophy and Religion (New York, Harper, 1948), pp. 54-62.
7. ———, ed., *The World Community* (Chicago, University of Chicago Press, 1948).

CHAPTER
13

International Politics

DEFINITION

INTERNATIONAL POLITICS is the art of influencing, manipulating, or controlling major groups in the world so as to advance the purposes of some against the opposition of others. As a discipline, it includes expositions instructing in the practice of this art, predicting the consequences of its application, evaluating it, and narrating its history (9, 10, 28).

Politics is ordinarily used to describe an art rather than a history, philosophy, or science, that is, to designate a procedure or a series of acts adapting means to ends. As a discipline it refers to concrete instruction on how to perform such acts efficiently and effectively. There may be a pure science of politics demonstrating generalizations, rules, or principles useful for predicting the course of politics in a given area or under given conditions. There may also be an applied science of politics interpreting these generalizations in categories of means and ends in order to promote understanding of the art. There can also obviously be histories of politics narrating the actions, reactions, and intentions of the participants, and their consequences in time sequence for a specified area, and there can be philosophies of politics appraising the ends pursued and the means employed in accordance with qualitative resemblances and differences. These studies, however, are auxiliary or consequential. The essence of politics is doing, not contemplating or comprehending. Political writing is not usually intended to contribute to the discipline of politics, or political science, but to influence opinion or action in the interest of political ends.

Politics has to do with groups. An individual may seek to advance his

130

own power or position, but he is not engaged in politics unless he does so by influencing, manipulating, or controlling groups, his own or others. He may put himself at the center of a clique, faction, party, nationality, government, state, church, or international organization, enabling him to influence or control its action. To this end he may employ threats, bribes, or rhetoric, and he may lead the group to institute propaganda, economic, administrative, or military action to influence or compel desired behavior by other groups, parallel, subordinate, or superordinate.

Politics, therefore, always involves oppositional relations of groups. The groups may be relatively independent and unrelated to one another by social or political ties as is usually the case in international politics. They may be groups opposing one another within a social or political organization, as parties within a state, factions within a party, departments within a government, or states within a federation. They may be lesser political groups opposing the inclusive political group of which they are parts, as in insurrections or rebellions, or in political controversy between a local or provincial government and the central government or between nations and the United Nations.

A group may find achievement of its ends opposed not by another group, but by natural conditions. Thus a group may struggle to improve its material conditions against the niggardliness of nature, to maintain profits in a competitive market, to recover from a natural disaster of flood or drought, to defend itself against disease, or to protect its food supply against insect pests. Such activities, however, are not politics but economics or agriculture or medicine or engineering. Politics may enter into such activities because frequently different groups will oppose one another as to the best means to conduct such operations. But such activities are primarily technical, not political. Economics, particularly, tends to become politics under competitive conditions when the number of firms have become small and each business tends to identify its difficulties with one or more particular competing firms. As government intervention or management becomes important, the government seeks to subordinate business to its own ends, usually in opposition to the ends of the business concern or department, and consequently economic activities become political. Totalitarianism implies an extreme degree of functional and geographic centralization of decision-making within a group. It seeks to eliminate politics from economics by reducing production, distribution, and opinion to problems of technology and administrative management. In fact it has the opposite effect. It makes all economic, technological, and even educational, religious, and scientific activity political by attempting to settle the major problems in all these fields by decisions or plans of broad and enduring effect, certain to arouse controversy among major interests. These interests become identified as cliques, factions, or parties according to the institutional forms by which plans, policies, and decisions are made. The controversies among these groups can only be solved by political methods such as elections, parliamentary votes, negotiations, pressures, threats, bribes, demotions, or assassinations. The more centralized and totalitarian is the regime, the more the latter methods tend to supersede the former. Politics is driven underground and functions within agencies and by methods not open to the general public view.

Groups may differ in opinions, beliefs, ideas, standards, objectives, methods, or other characteristics, and these differences may involve inconsistencies, logical, or practical, but they do not constitute oppositions which may lead to political controversy, conflict, tension, or hostility unless a procedure is initiated to solve the difference. Groups may peacefully coexist for a long time so unaware or tolerant of their differences that there is no opposition and no political problem. Politics does not arise until the focussing of attention upon differences between groups leads to efforts to solve them (30).

A group may express its ends or its opinions in abstract terms, based on asserted major premises, and debate with other groups which accept the same major premises, thus proceeding by pure logic. This method is most frequently employed in theological, philosophical, scientific, and legal controversy. Such oppositions between advocates of differing interpretations or conclusions within an accepted universe of discourse are usually differentiated from politics. The opposition is said to be between ideas, interpretations, or inferences, not between groups. In proportion as the advocate identifies the opposing formulations with the groups that sustain them, the activity becomes political. Thus politics is frequently near at hand even in the most abstract arguments. Rhetoric and other means of persuasion, or perhaps even methods of compulsion, as the treatment of heretics by the inquisition and deviationists by the communists, are added to logic, and truth is established by inducing or compelling belief and agreement rather than by inference from premises or observation of phenomena.

Man is a political animal and tends to organize his friends in a group in order to frustrate the group identified as his enemy, whatever ends or means or opinions may be involved.

The ends of politics may be anything. The preservation of the existence of a group, the forwarding of the interests of its members, and the expansion of its opinions or values to others are characteristic political ends, but political activity tends to wane as the attainability of ends is believed to be remote in time. Politics is sometimes defined as the art of the possible contrasted with utopianism, the art of the impossible, and religion, the art of the ultimate. There may be vigorous groups striving politically to attain ends generally thought to be impossible, as, for example, to prove that the earth is flat or that the sun moves around it, or to be highly improbable in any near future as that all men shall observe the Golden

Rule or that all men shall submit to centralized world government. If there are such groups, and if they arouse the opposition of other groups, the activity is political. Ordinarily, however, the impossibility or improbability of such ends come to be seen by many of the advocating group whose energy in their behalf flags. These characteristics of the ends sought are usually observed even sooner by nonbelievers who then consider political activity to oppose them as a waste of energy. Religions or utopias or ideologies whose advocates believe that the millennium is around the corner tend to be highly political and the supporting groups tend to be militant in their activities and often compel their opponents to similar energy in self-defense. But once the advent of the millennium is postponed for several centuries or several millennia, the groups which believe in it, and the end itself cease to be political.

Furthermore, once an end is achieved, as in the passage of legislation, or once an opinion comes to be accepted by practically everyone, as is true of much of science, oppositions may die out and the end will cease to be political.

Thus objectives or opinions tend to be nonpolitical when they are accepted as attainable goals or valid rules or standards by no one or by everyone. In proportion as the entire public which discusses an objective or method or opinion is equally divided as to its desirability or validity, the subject is political.

The methods of politics are infinite. The words *influence, manipulation,* and *control* have been used. Influence may proceed by logic, rhetoric, propaganda, dissemination of information, or education. Manipulation may proceed by bribery, blackmail, threats, negotiation of compromises or bargains, and giving or withholding economic advantages, honors, or positions of power. It may include prevarication, perfidy, patronage, and electioneering. Control may proceed by invocation of the civil law, by criminal prosecution, assassination, intervention, insurrection, rebellion, reprisals, and war. The methods available differ in different situations.

International politics differs from other kinds of politics in its means, in its ends, and in the groups that participate in it. It has been distinguished from national politics by the fact that fewer methods are barred by law. Within most states direct violence, fraud, and corruption are in theory, and in some degree in practice, prohibited by law. Among sovereign states, until recently, war was permissible and few methods of war were forbidden if they promised to contribute to victory. Such was the principle of *military necessity* as understood in the law of war. In its control of the methods of politics available to groups within it, national law has as a rule been both more comprehensive and better enforced than has international law in controlling the political methods available to the states and other major groups which together compose the world community.

International politics has also differed from national politics in that its characteristic end has been the continued existence of the groups that participate in it. Because of the relative freedom of these groups to use all available means to forward political ends, the existence of each group is more threatened by others than is usual in domestic political situations. Consequently, other ends of these groups, such as the development of group prosperity and the maintenance and propagation of group values, have tended to be subordinated to the major end—the continuance of the existence of the group.

The fact that international politics has been distinguished from other politics by the savagery of the means commonly used and the absoluteness of the ends commonly pursued is due to the peculiar institutional structure of international politics in many periods of history. During the past few centuries the groups mainly concerned in the system have been sovereign territorial states. Such a system has occurred at other times in history, and is generally known as a *state system* or as a system of international politics in the narrow sense. If, however, international politics is viewed broadly, it may be applied in circumstances in which sovereign states, with their characteristic ends and means, do not exist. International politics can then be distinguished only by the fact that the groups involved are those of major importance in the *world* as viewed at the time, a *world* which might be confined to a region, continent, or *civilization,* less than the world in a literal sense. Politics among such groups, whether territorial, ideological, economic, cultural, or other, might be better designated as *world politics,* and politics among lesser groups within them as *domestic politics.* In medieval Europe, world politics from the European point of view concerned the opposition of the Pope and Emperor, each claiming universal authority, and in the crusading period it concerned Christendom and Islam. In the later Roman Empire, it concerned the opposition of the Eastern and Western Empires. In the sixteenth and seventeenth centuries, it concerned the opposition among the five or six *great powers* of Europe, especially the Hapsburg and Bourbon monarchs claiming to rule by divine right. Smaller states, feudal principalities, and free cities played a lesser role. In the eighteenth and nineteenth centuries the *powers* tended to become corporate and constitutional, public opinion tended to become a limitation upon governments and non-European powers entered the system. In the twentieth century, world politics has mainly concerned the opposition of great powers—European, American, and Asiatic—tending to diminish in numbers as a result of world wars. Some seventy smaller states in all continents, certain nonterritorial entities such as the United Nations, the Roman Catholic Church, the Communist International, and World Zionism, and certain regional arrangements such as the North Atlantic community, the Soviet bloc, the British Commonwealth, the Arab League, the organization of American states, and various organizations of Western European states, have played a lesser role (4).

Groups rise and fall in power and importance. The groups which at any moment have such power and exert it so persistently and effectively that they can be considered *major* groups can be discovered only by historical examination. In this field, legal position, traditional position, and forms of language often exert a distorting influence. The Holy Roman Empire was considered important in world politics centuries after it was a hollow shell. The Ottoman Empire, the Hapsburg Empire, the Chinese Empire continued to enjoy prestige after their power was greatly reduced. Yet legal and traditional position and prestige are elements in actual power. Consequently it would be as erroneous, in estimating the major groups at any moment, to consider military power alone as it would be to exaggerate former military power which continued in language and prestige. All the elements which contribute to political power including morale, reputation, capacity to make allies and friends, as well as arms, resources, and geographic position, must be considered and weighed in deciding what are the major groups in the world at any moment (29).

ASSUMPTIONS

The only assumptions that need to be made in the discipline of world politics are (*a*) that there is a *world*, whose peoples are in contact with one another, (*b*) that the people of that world are divided into major groups whose objectives or interests are to some extent inconsistent with one another, and (*c*) that each group when opposed by other groups in pursuit of an interest uses in order to overcome that opposition whatever means it considers most effective and least inconsistent with its other interests. With these assumptions, it would be possible to discuss the politics in any kind of world—a system of sovereign states, a world confederation or federation, a universal empire, or a universal church. It is difficult to discover historically, or to imagine, a world in which these assumptions would not be applicable. As pointed out, in most historic periods large sections of the world's population were so separated from one another that their contacts were unimportant, consequently the *world* in past systems of world politics has usually consisted only of a particular *civilization* such as that of the Mediterranean, the Far East, and India in ancient times, or of Europe, the Far East, Mexico, and Peru during the period before Columbus.

It is perhaps possible to conceive of the world's population becoming so unified through general acceptance of a single value system or religion that there would be no major political groups at all, or if there were, their differences would concern only logical inferences from the universal doctrine and would not engender political opposition. Persons conversant with the influence of different geographical environments and different traditions upon opinion, of the ease of concealing vast areas of disagreement under a common phraseology, and of the history of all efforts to unify whole civilizations by a common doctrine are not likely to consider such a possibility seriously. Biologists have observed the tendency of all animal forms separated by natural barriers or subjected to different conditions to diverge through processes of mutation, random variation, hybridization, and selection. It is difficult to believe that in any measurable time man will so control his environment and so communicate with his neighbors that groups manifesting social differences and working for conflicting ends will be eliminated from the human race.

It is also conceivable that man might become so rational that inconsistent ends would be resolved by logical argument proceeding from a common philosophy, or that the world would become so organized that men would be compelled by effective government to utilize only such means to settle their differences. No national state has actually achieved either of these conditions. Political activity, including parliamentary debate, electioneering, and party organization, go on in the best regulated democracies, and less respectable methods such as distribution of patronage, undisclosed expenditure of campaign funds, intimidation of voters, stuffing of ballot boxes, coercion or liquidation of minorities, and control of the media of opinion formation have been used in states both of the past and the present, both democratic and autocratic. The idea of eliminating all political methods is as utopian as is the idea of eliminating all political groups, although both ideas seem to have captured the imagination of both secular and religious leaders from time to time. Such leaders have not succeeded in eliminating politics but in degenerating its methods. Their efforts have driven dissent underground to emerge sporadically as sedition, sabotage, or heresy, and to induce official persecution, genocide, concentration camps, and massacres in vain efforts to extinguish it.

World politics cannot be improved by attempting to eliminate it altogether, but by altering the groups engaged in it, by altering the methods available to them, and, as a consequence, by altering the ends for which they struggle. It would seem that political ends are more likely to be modified by altering political conditions than by moralizing. Since the effectiveness of the latter depends upon the acceptance by those addressed of certain ultimate social values, it is unconvincing to those who do not accept those values. If, however, conditions render certain methods unavailable and thus make the achievement of certain ends impossible or improbable in any but the most distant future, such ends are likely to fade in political importance. Groups always have several ends, and their relative importance will be modified as changing conditions make some more easy and some more difficult to attain.

The actual discipline of international politics has usually made much narrower assumptions than those just stated, thus permitting a richer body of conclusions but at the expense of rendering the discipline applicable to a narrower range of historical circumstances. Modern political science has centered around study of the sovereign territorial state and consequently has assumed the continued existence of such states.

International politics as a branch of political science has therefore assumed: (a) sovereign, territorial states with conflicting policies exist in contact with one another, (b) the major value of each is its own continuous, independent, existence, (c) the only reliable means available to maintain this value is self-help supported by military power and alliances.

In the history of the past four or five centuries there is much to justify these assumptions. After the Peace of Westphalia, international law, supported by such world public opinion as there was, recognized sovereign territorial states as superior to other groupings, particularly religious groups. The Erastian doctrine that the king could choose the religion for his people was accepted in those treaties by peoples who had suffered from over a century of religious war culminating in the "Thirty Years War." The long period of religious wars, first between Christians and Moslems and then between Catholics and Protestants, was succeeded by a period of political wars between territorial states. Territorial states have differed greatly in power but there has been no period since Westphalia when any other grouping—church, ideological party, international organization, or business firm—could have effectively competed in power with the greatest states. The great powers have not always been the same. Great Britain and France have persistently occupied that position. Turkey, Poland, Spain, the Netherlands, Sweden, and the Habsburg Empire, once great powers, have departed from that position. Germany, Italy, and Japan rose to that position, but do not occupy it today. Russia and the United States, nonexistent or unimportant at the time of Westphalia, are now the greatest of powers. China, once great but distant, became weak and long occupied a position of nominal greatness. Its potential greatness, inherent in its population and resources, may be in process of realization under the communist regime. India, long divided or controlled externally, shows signs of developing a great power position. There have been many fluctuations in the possession of political power, but during the modern period, territorial states claiming legal sovereignty have been the major groups in the world.

At the time of Westphalia, the system was confined to the states of Europe which had a superiority over the rest of the world in military technique because of their development of gunpowder and economic technology, and which also had close contacts with one another. The development of the communication and transport inventions during the past century, facilitated in the nineteenth century by the practical application of science, has increased contacts of all powers throughout the world. Consequently, today substantially all of the land territory of the globe is under the legal sovereignty of some state which enters into the system of international politics.

States have many values. *Peace and plenty* was a characteristic phrase for the objectives of policy in the eighteenth century. *Security and prosperity*, with little difference in meaning, is more commonly used today. Power and resources is another way of contrasting political and economic objectives. Maintenance of the traditional way of life and of civilization are also sometimes described as major values of national policy. The welfare of its citizens and of humanity is a generalized phraseology with similar meaning. There can be no doubt of the complexity of the goals which guide the policies of states and of the variation in priorities among different states and, under different conditions, in the same state. Democracies tend to give greater weight to domestic economic needs than do autocracies. When peace seems in prospect for a long future, both government and public opinion in any state are likely to pay more attention to prosperity, welfare, and culture, less to security and power.

There are, however, few illustrations of voluntary abandonment of independent existence by a state which has enjoyed that status, and none of such voluntary abandonment by a great power. Great powers have always fought when they deemed it necessary to defend their independence. Any temporary failure to emphasize self-preservation as a major goal of national policy has been due to the fact that independence seemed not at the moment to be threatened. While it is conceivable that prosperity or culture or welfare might flourish by union of several states, and while small states have sometimes united or voluntarily accepted the protection of, or annexed themselves to, a great power with such ends in view, states in general have considered their continued independence a necessary condition of assuring the prosperity, the culture, and the welfare of their people. The possible qualifications to this assumption, even in modern times, must be noted, but among the great powers there is certainly much to justify the assumption that continuous independent existence is the major value of the sovereign state.

The third assumption is more questionable. Grotius took the view that general respect for international law was the only secure bulwark of state security. Statesmen, however, have considered international law, lacking a world organization with capacity to enforce it, a slender reed, and have looked primarily to their power position assuring their own capacity to defend themselves against any probable attack. Power position is composed of many elements—*armaments in being* including land, sea, and air forces, stores of arms, fortifications, bases, strategic plans, and military preparedness generally; *military potential* including geographic position, population, food supply, natural resources, industrial plant, economic and financial system, level of education, and human skills in leadership, strategy, science, and technology; *national morale* including patriotic spirit, national character, level of prosperity, health of population, and suitable institutions; and *international reputation* manifested by allies, actual and potential, favorable treaty commitments and success in negotiation and international organization (24). States differ greatly in the degree in which they possess these varied elements of power and security. International politics requires continuous evaluation of those both of the state itself and of its probable enemies, and development of those in which the particular state is best endowed. A small state has to rely on geographic position and on reputation and diplomacy, gaining allies, while a great state can rely on its armaments in being and capacity to make more. Such evaluations have frequently been inaccurate. Statistics of past wars suggest that even among great states a favorable world opinion, and the capacity to gain allies which goes with it, have been more important in winning wars than superior military preparedness when the war began. The political activity of foreign offices seems to have been more important than the military preparedness of defense departments both in assuring security and in winning wars, although the latter cannot be overlooked.

When *self-help* depends on alliances more than on military forces, and when it takes the form of *collective self-defense* rather than individual self-defense, the meaning of this assumption and the conclusions to be drawn from it take a radically different form.

Writers on international politics have, however, usually given a primary weight to military force and military potential as the most reliable means of self-preservation and have analyzed the requirements of international politics in accord with the characteristics of the system of international relations created by this assumption (7, 13, 24, 31). They seek to justify this position by pointing out that, since a state's independence is of primary interest only to itself, it can rely only on its own efforts to secure that independence. The disciplines of international law and international organization, and the analysis of international politics itself, indicate, however, that this interest may be translated into terms of wider appeal.

ANALYSIS

The discipline of international politics consists of the detailed analysis of assumptions, such as those which have just been stated, to assist in estimating the expectations inherent in changing circumstances and conditions, and in deciding upon policy and action most suitable for maintaining the state's existence in both the short and the long run. Such an analysis, whether in the form of a logically organized system or of a commentary on a period of history, may be of practical value to statesmen and diplomats under the conditions which have existed during the past few centuries and this has been their primary utility (1, 13, 15). No such analysis can be attempted here.

To the scientifically or philosophically minded certain general conclusions flowing from these assumptions may be of interest and they may even be of value to statesmen who take a long run view of their policies. Among these conclusions are the following: (*a*) international politics tends to assume the form known as *power politics;* (*b*) whatever stability the system has results from a *balance of power;* and (*c*) the stability of such an equilibrium tends to deteriorate through internal forces within the system itself.

[margin note: contrast elsewhere]

In a certain sense, all politics is power politics. In the broadest sense power is the capacity to accomplish ends and politics is the art of adapting means to accomplish group ends against the opposition of other groups. Thus politics consists in developing group power. That power ranges, however, from capacity to influence to capacity to compel and may be manifested in various ways adapted to various circumstances. Rational argument; education and information; emotional propaganda; appeals to tradition, custom, law, and ideals; criminal and civil action; economic inducements ranging from bribery to co-operation for the general welfare; withholding of expected benefits; threats of violence, subversive activity, infiltration, espionage, sabotage, and assassination; display of superior armed force; maritime seizures, blockade, invasion, and war are all forms in which power may be exerted. It is difficult to find any common measure by which one of these forms for exerting political and social power can be equated with others as is true of the physical concept of power measured in horsepower or watts (11, 19).

Particularly difficult is it to equate persuasive forms of power which operate on the mind, such as promises of rewards or punishments, or invocation of habits or ideals, with coercive forms which act on the body such as imprisonment or execution of individuals, bombing of armies and cities, blockades and starvation of peoples, and occupations of territory. The distinction between the two is also difficult to formulate precisely. When does a threat of destruction or a withholding of means of subsistence become so imminent as to pass from the realm of persuasion to that of coercion? It may, in fact, be said that all social and political power is only persuasive. The so-called coercive forms have the object of persuading either the person against which they are immediately directed or others. Criminals are executed to persuade others to abstain from crime. Armies are destroyed to persuade governments to surrender. Political leaders are assassinated to persuade their successors to follow a different policy. Territory is occupied to persuade the population to observe the occupant's decrees. All political power can with this line of thought be subsumed under the category persuasion, the so-called coercive forms coming under the head *propaganda of the act*. Occupation of territory followed by total destruction of the population may be *pure* coercion, but even here the ruthlessness is often designed to persuade others not to attempt seizure of the territory.

On the other hand, all political power can be subsumed under the head coercion on the assumption that arguments, threats, and promises that fail will be followed by compulsions affecting the bodies of those of recalcitrant mind. If the arguments of the grand inquisitor fail to move the heretic, the heretic will be burned. If negotiation fails, war will follow.

Difficult as it is to make the distinction between persuasion and coercion the concept of *power politics* rests on this distinction. In a well-ordered state, politics is limited to methods of persuasion. The state alone coerces, and it coerces, not to achieve political ends, but to maintain the law. Where there is no well-ordered state above the groups engaged in politics, those groups can be expected to use coercive measures, and politics among them becomes *power politics*. Under such conditions a group has nothing but itself to rely on for security. If persuasion of its opponents to compromise and of its allies to come to its assistance fails, it may cease to exist unless it can defend itself by its own resources from invasion, occupation, and extinction. Under those conditions, greatest weight will be given to those elements of power high in the coercive scale. Armaments in being will outweigh potentialities, technical skills, morale, and reputation. Little states that cannot compete in armaments will have to make the best they can of the other forms of power, but their independence will be qualified unless the balance of power among the great prevents aggression by any of the latter. Among the great powers themselves, armament rivalry will be the central theme, and politics will consist largely of each government calculating: What other is its probable and most dangerous opponent? What is its relative military power in general and *vis à vis* that potential enemy in particular? What is the relative impact of its own and its probable opponents power in particular places? What is the effect which general changes in population, invention, and industrialization is having in time upon the general and local relativities of power? Realizing the possibilities of conflict, each power must prepare to withstand attack from whatever quarter it may be launched as the price of its continued existence. Power politics, therefore, is not a game which statesmen can play or not at discretion. It is a necessary condition of the assumptions stated—that is that states exist with conflicting policies, that each gives first value to its continued independent existence, and that each can ultimately rely on no form of power other than its capacity to defend itself by arms (14, 15).

Under these conditions it is obviously wise for each state to take measures in time to prevent any other from getting so powerful that it can conquer a neighbor. If state *A* conquers its neighbor *B*, its power will be so augmented that it can more easily absorb C and D, and then E and F. State Z cannot fail to observe the process and will therefore seek to persuade its probable predecessors in the process to act with it in order to curb state A before even its first conquest is complete. Such behavior to maintain the balance of power does not need to posit any altruism or particular disposition of states to help one another for reasons of law or morality, but only a moderate foresight by each state in defending its own existence. The balance of power, therefore, means the condition in which any state attempting aggression will find itself faced by such a coalition that it cannot succeed (6, 16, 27, 29). A balance of power policy means that each state, in addition to preparing directly for its own defense, will indirectly act for its own defense by joining with other states in preventing any state from getting so powerful that it can conquer any state. It adds to the concept of *individual self-defense* that of *collective self-defense* referred to in Article 51 of the United Nations Charter.

Clearly adhesion to a balance of power policy always leaves much room for differences of opinion. Is A or B the more dangerous state? If A, should not C or D join with it equally dividing B rather than in protecting B from A? Should not Z remain neutral and conserve its defensive strength while A temporarily weakens itself in conquest of B? Because of such uncertainties in the action which a balance of power policy requires and the frequent errors of states in calculating the probabilities, there has never been a condition in which every state was certain of insuperable obstacles to its success in conquest. The opportunities for greatly improving his power position looked favorable to Louis XIV, to Napoleon, and to Hitler. But all eventually failed. The balance of power functioned, but its functioning did not carry conviction in advance.

It is to be observed that the following of balance of power policies by states does not require the assumption that a certain state or states is by nature imperialistic or expansive. The assumptions of power politics imply that every state will continue to seek to improve its relative power position as a measure of defense and, therefore, that each will increase its power when the opportunity presents itself. The only deterrent is the improbability of success. There is, therefore, from the point of view of international politics no essential distinction between aggressive and defensive policies. Power politics implies that all states will be aggressive when they can and defensive when they must.

This is an oversimplification. In fact, particular leaders or states through a combination of circumstances may embark upon policies which justify alarm among their neighbors, and therefore become the objects of general defensive preparation and coalitions. These developments, however, are adventitious and not necessary developments of the assumptions underlying the discipline of international politics. Aggression can be used as a term of law to refer to illegal resorts to force and as a term of sociology to refer to characteristics in the social and political composition of a state inclining it to attack its neighbors for purposes of aggrandizement rather than defense. These concepts are of importance in international politics, but *power politics* might continue even if there were no legal aggression and no aggressive state so long as states lack confidence in the effectiveness of law and each strives to improve its power position for defense (29).

The stability of the equilibrium in a system of power politics within a developing civilization tends to deteriorate because the number of states in the system tends to decrease, war tends to increase in destructiveness, natural defenses tend to diminish in effectiveness, and the states tend to increase in economic and cultural interdependence (29).

The first of these tendencies may be observed in the reduction in the number of states in the modern system from thousands in the sixteenth century to a few score in the twentieth. Similar reduction was recorded in the ancient Chinese system of states from the Confucian period to the period of warring states terminated by the establishment of the Ts'in Dynasty, and also in the Mediterranean system from the age of Pericles to that of Augustus.

In operating the balance of power, small states tend to federate or to seek protection. Great states will frequently find it possible in spite of the balance of power to annex a small neighbor and will sometimes compensate one another by dividing, rather than defending, the small. Furthermore, the conditions of developing military technology tend to increase the relative disparity of the great and the little. This process of eliminating the lesser, then the middle sized, and finally some of the great states, tends toward a bipolar world—Athens vs. Sparta, Rome vs. Carthage, Bourbon vs. Habsburg, France vs. Britain, Triple Alliance vs. Triple Entente, Soviet Union vs. United States.

The greater the number of states and the more nearly equal their power, the more stable is the equilibrium. In a system composed of a large number of equal states, no one can defy all successfully. Consequently, if all are ready to curb aggression, no aggression can be successful. As the number of states diminishes, the relative power of each against the whole becomes greater and the hope of successful aggression by the more powerful increases. When bipolarity is reached each of the centers of power fears attack by the other. No allies are possible because all are now associated with one or the other center of power and consequently the center of power against which time appears to be running is likely to start a war. Eventual war is likely to be considered inevitable and consequently, even though the chances of success are not good, it would be better to run the risk now than later. Such conditions have in the past often led to a termination of a system of power politics by the establishment of a universal state through conquest.

Power politics breeds inventiveness in military technology. Such inventions may increase the relative power of the offensive, in which case the state with priority in an invention is likely to start aggression in order to cash in on its advantage before the other acquires the invention as it almost inevitably will in time. Such a development increases general anxiety and decreases stability. Invention, may on the other hand, increase the power of the defensive, in which case war if it comes tends to be a war of attrition remarkably destructive of life and property. The prospects of such a war may augment anxiety, accelerate armament races, and produce eventually the war which all hoped to avoid.

If wars are relatively innocuous, as they are likely to be when the military technology of all states is only slightly developed, they are likely to be frequent but their effect is to restore rather than destroy the basic stability of the system. If, on the other hand, wars are very serious, they are likely to be less frequent but more destructive to basic stability when they occur. It has been the historic experience that in power political systems, wars have become progressively more destructive but they have occurred, eventually destroying the system. Whether extreme destructiveness of weapons, as in the jet planes and H-bombs of the 1950's "enabling everyone to kill everybody else" will result in a stable situation in which "nobody will want to kill anyone at all" is not certain, although Winston Churchill considered it the major hope of peace in 1953. Others had made the point earlier (2, 30).

Military technology continually seeks to bridge natural obstacles of river, mountain, desert, and sea. Inventions consequently tend to increase the vulnerability of all states. Those which formerly were sheltered by natural defenses and could act as balancers, throwing their weight always against the dangerous aggressor as did Great Britain from the time of Elizabeth to that of Churchill, become themselves so liable to attack that they must pay more attention to their immediate danger, less to maintaining general equilibrium.

The shrinking of the world and the progress of communication and trade which results from the military contact and the borrowings among states, from their rivalries and their co-operation in power politics, tend toward economic and cultural interdependence, constitutionalism, democracy, and attention to the arts of civilization rather than of war. The result is that many states become less self-sufficient, less centralized, and less able to shift alliances, to threaten war and to engage in the maneuvers necessary for maintenance of a stable equilibrium. Democratic and constitutional statesmen cannot easily follow Machiavelli's advice to pay first attention to the arts of war. Their constituencies demand more attention to the arts of peace. In such a situation, opportunities are presented to the autocratic states that remain. The development of civilized characteristics by most of the states provides an opportunity to the barbarians, who have acquired the arts of war developed by the civilization, but not the antipathy to war which is likely to be an ultimate fruit of civilization. As a consequence, the system of power politics becomes less stable.

The effect of these tendencies has been to deteriorate the stability of balance of power systems. There are fewer states, all are more worried, all are more vulnerable, and many are thinking of security in terms of a universal law or a universal culture. The consequence has usually been a universal conquest, after efforts to establish an effective regime of law by general consent have failed.

CRITICISM

It is clear from this analysis that useful as is the discipline of international politics, based on the narrower assumptions stated, for applying the arts of statesmanship during periods when these assumptions are relatively valid, it is of little value for long-range prediction or control. These assumptions while applicable during certain historical periods have been by no means applicable in all such periods. A science of international relations based exclusively on these assumptions cannot predict the development of conditions which will make these assumptions no longer applicable. A discipline of international politics may, however, have within itself criteria of self-correction permitting prediction, if not control, of the process of deterioration which tends to undermine the validity of these assumptions. For this, the discipline must be based on the broader assumptions stated earlier in this chapter which posit only the existence of a world, of major groups within it, and of political action by each of these groups to achieve its ends. These broader assumptions do not preclude consideration of the changes of the major groups from sovereign territorial states to members of universal federation, to world political parties, or to something else as the world shrinks, and of the changes in political methods to be expected as military technology changes. Such considerations can be facilitated by the disciplines of international organization, international law, international economics, and the psychology and sociology of international relations.

The sovereign territorial state is ephemeral. As it emerges into new forms, new processes, new forces, and new relations develop, and with their development the rate of change in the entities about which world politics revolves accelerates. The states of today are radically different from those in the time of Machiavelli, of Charles V, of Louis XIV, of William III, of the two Pitts, of Napoleon, of Bismarck, and of the other artists of power politics in modern history. The terms and the techniques they employed are still used, but perhaps a better understanding of the nature of modern states, of the processes of change in them and in the system in which they participate, of the forces welling up in the opinion of their peoples, and of the relations significant and measurable in the present world will disclose the degree of the obsolescence of the assumptions underlying much writing on current international politics.

REFERENCES

1. BOLINGBROKE, Henry St. John, *Idea of a Patriot King* (1738).
2. BRODIE, Bernard, ed., *The Absolute Weapon; Atomic Power and World Order* (New York, Harcourt, 1946).
3. BURNS, C. Delisle, *International Politics* (London, Methuen, 1920).
4. Commission to Study the Organization of Peace, Eighth Report, *Regional Arrangements for Security and the United Nations* (New York, June, 1953).
5. FOX, William T. R., *The Super-Powers* (New York, Harcourt, 1944).
6. HUME, David, "Of the Balance of Power," *Philosophical Works* (Boston, Little, Brown, 1854), Vol. 3, pp. 364 ff.
7. KAUTILYA, *Arthasastra,* trans. by R. Shamasastry (Mysore, Wesleyan Mission Press, 1929).
8. KENNAN, George, *American Diplomacy, 1900-1950* (Chicago, University of Chicago Press, 1951).
9. LANGER, William L., *The Diplomacy of Imperialism, 1890-1902* (New York, Knopf, 1935).
10. LIPPMANN, Walter, *The Cold War* (New York, Harper, 1947).
11. MERRIAM, Charles E., *Political Power, Its Composition and Incidence* (New York, McGraw-Hill, 1934).
12. ———, *Prologue to Politics* (Chicago, University of Chicago Press, 1939).
13. MACHIAVELLI, Niccolo, *The Prince* (1513).
14. MORGENTHAU, Hans J., *Scientific Man Versus Power Politics* (Chicago, University of Chicago Press, 1946).
15. ———, *Politics Among Nations, The Struggle for Power and Peace* (New York, Knopf, 1948).
16. ———, and THOMPSON, Kenneth, *Principles and Problems of International Politics, Selected Readings* (New York, Knopf, 1950).
17. POLYBIUS, *Histories,* E. S. Shuckburgh, ed. (London, Macmillan, 1889).
18. REINSCH, Paul S., *World Politics at the End of the Nineteenth Century Influenced by the Oriental Situation* (New York, Macmillan, 1900).
19. RUSSELL, Bertrand, *Power* (New York, Norton, 1938).
20. RUSSELL, Frank M., *Theories of International Relations* (New York, Appleton-Century-Crofts, 1936).
21. SCHUMAN, Frederick L., *International Politics* (New York, McGraw-Hill, 1933; 4th ed., 1948).
22. SCHWARZENBERGER, Georg, *Power Politics* (London, Jonathan Cape, 1941).
23. SHARP, Walter R., and KIRK, Grayson, *Contemporary International Politics* (New York, Farrar and Rinehart, 1940).
24. SPROUT, Harold and Margaret, *Foundations of National Power* (Princeton, Princeton University Press, 1945).
25. SPYKMAN, Nicholas, *American Strategy and World Politics, The United States and the Balance of Power* (New York, Harcourt, 1942).
26. THUCYDIDES, *History of the Peloponnesian War.*

27. WEIGERT, Hans W., and STEFANSSON, Vilhjalmur, *Compass of the World*, a Symposium on Political Geography (New York, Macmillan, 1944).

28. WIGHT, Martin, *Power Politics* (London, Royal Institute of International Affairs, 1946).

29. WRIGHT, Quincy, *A Study of War* (Chicago, University of Chicago Press, 1942), pp. 372-405, 743-860, 955-986, 1389-1391, 1472-1492.

30. ———, *Problems of Stability and Progress in International Relations* (Berkeley, University of California Press, 1954).

31. YANG, Kung-sun, *The Book of Lord Shang*, trans. by J. J. L. Duyvendak (London, Probsthain, 1928).

152

The Art of War

DEFINITION

WAR IS THE art of organizing and employing armed force to accomplish the purposes of a group. As a discipline it includes the practical, historic, philosophic, and scientific studies contributing to this art.

Though usually defined as an art, and therefore consisting of a co-ordinated group of voluntary acts, war has also been defined objectively as a contention by force or as a social situation characterized by conflict, tension, and large-scale violence in the relation of groups. In the legal sense, this conception has been narrowed to include only situations which *equally permit* the participating groups to contend by armed force. Armed contentions arising from the effort to suppress insurrections and aggressions in which the participants are not accorded equal status are not, therefore, "war in the legal sense," but if of considerable magnitude, they are referred to as "war in the material sense." Studies of the sociology, psychology, and law of war usually accept an objective conception of war, but practical studies of military science and of the art and history of war usually treat war subjectively, as a method for achieving a group's will, and it is in that sense that studies of war constitute a distinct discipline (41).

While war has usually been employed by states as a method of international politics, it has also been employed by insurgents and rebels to gain independence, by national governments to suppress domestic and colonial revolts, and by international organizations to suppress aggression. The objectives of war have been territorial, economic, and cultural expansion; national independence, security, and solidarity; and interna-

148

tional stability, law, and peace. War is, therefore, related to the subject matter of all of the disciplines of international relations. The study of each of these disciplines can throw light on the causes of war, and the art of war may be useful to the practitioners of any aspect of international relations (41).

War, like politics, is a matter of fact or of action rather than of theory or words. It has, however, been the subject of a vast literature which extends into the realms of political science, economics, history, international law, psychology, sociology, philosophy, and belles lettres. In most of this literature war figures only incidentally, but in the body of writing known as military science or military history, the theory of war, or the art of war, war occupies the center of the scene. These four terms suggest that the discipline dealing primarily with war extends into science, history, and philosophy as well as practice. But the central idea of this literature has been practical advice on how to win wars, and consequently the term *art of war* used by Machiavelli (23) and Jomini (18) seems most appropriate. Military history, like diplomatic history, is less historical than technical in purpose, and is usually designed primarily to assist the practitioners of the art. The science and theory of war, while they may seek explanations in sociology, psychology, or geography, or justifications in law, ethics, or philosophy, are concerned primarily with the building of systems of thought which will guide the soldier, general, statesman, or citizen to appreciate the situation and to act so that victory may be won.

Armed force carries the idea of disciplined or purposefully controlled violence, whether the instruments are fists, stones, clubs, spears, arrows, guns, or air-borne atomic bombs, and whether the group employing this method consists of half a dozen or ten million persons (13).

Like politics, war implies group action in opposition to other groups. Duels or prize fights are not war unless the individuals involved act as champions of opposing groups.

While modern war is waged on the diplomatic (19), economic (17), and propaganda (20) fronts, as well as on the military front, and while in the broadest sense, the art of war co-ordinates all these elements to the purpose of victory, yet in the narrower sense used in the discipline, the art is confined to the military aspect. This embraces the organization, discipline, and maintenance of the morale of the armed forces on land, sea, and air; the invention, development, and procurement of weapons; the provision of transport and the movement of forces; the conversion of policies into military objectives, such as enemy territory to be occupied, enemy forces or resources to be destroyed, and civilian or neutral interests or morale to be attacked; and the strategy of campaigns and tactics of battles, sieges, blockades, or air raids to achieve these objectives. The larger problems of military policy, such as determination of the national policy it is to serve; the preparation of national opinion, economy, and institutions for war; the co-ordination of military preparation and action with diplomacy, policy, and government; the co-ordination of national military action with that of allies; the determination of specific war aims and peace terms; and the conduct of diplomacy, propaganda, and economic relations with enemy, neutral, and allied countries lie in the realm of international politics and diplomacy. Yet the conduct of war is so closely related to these activities that the art of war cannot entirely ignore them. It is in fact subordinate to the art of politics.

ASSUMPTIONS

The discipline concerned with the art of war rests on the same assumptions as the discipline of international politics: (*a*) that there are groups in contact with one another, (*b*) that their purposes and policies sometimes conflict, (*c*) that each uses the means most effective and least objectionable to achieve its ends—with the addition (*d*) that the use of armed force to destroy the opposition is an available and permissible means, and (*e*) that such use may, in certain circumstances, achieve the desired end, usually defined by the short, but frequently ambiguous, word *victory*.

War might become obsolete because either or both of these last two assumptions failed to be realized. Well-ordered states forbid the use of armed force in domestic politics by law which may be so effective that this method is not considered available by political parties or other groups however bitter their contentions may become. Furthermore, in such states, the will to maintain law is so general that its maintenance is possible by police action against the individual, and war by the state against organized internal groups resisting by arms is not necessary. International organization seeks to produce similar conditions in the community of nations. There are, however, few states in which circumstances may not arise when groups will contemplate the possibility of insurrection or rebellion, and a war to suppress such movements becomes necessary. The problem of organizing the world with its varied cultures and powerful national sentiments so that states will not regard armed force as an available means is still more difficult to solve.

Even if the combined influence of law, ethics, international organization and other social sanctions fails to make war unavailable, the development of international politics and military technology may make its use obviously suicidal or ineffective to accomplish its ends. This would be the situation in an equilibrium of power so perfect that any potential belligerent would be confronted by an insuperably powerful combination. A state of military technology which gives an advantage to the defense above the offense contributes to such an equilibrium. War may also become useless if its technology becomes excessively destructive, whether because of the probability of stalemate and mutual attrition or because of the probability of mutual air raids laying waste cities. Even under such conditions, which tend to make *victory* a meaningless term, wars may occur from accident, intense emotion, or blind loyalty to an ideology, but they can hardly occur from rational design because the initiators' chance of gain greater than loss or even of survival is reduced to a minimum. Men do not fight duels if one has only his hands and the other a sword, nor do they fight if both have machine guns at close range. War, like the duel, implies that each side thinks it has some chance both of victory and of survival (5, 16, 41, 42).

Exception may be made in case a group is dominated by an ideology realizable in a supernatural or a subnatural world. Some religious devotees may willingly face total annihilation on the supposition that death for the cause will translate them to heaven and hasten the coming of the kingdom of God. Some utopian devotees may willingly face defeat and almost total annihilation of the group if, in the process, they can so devastate their enemies as to create a favorable environment for the acceptance of their revolutionary ideology by the few survivors.

The discipline of war cannot be defined by the assumptions underlying the narrower conception of international politics. Even though a system of world politics developed in which there were no sovereign territorial states, each struggling to maintain its existence through self-help and *ad hoc* alliances, still war might exist whether between functional groups or between the organized world and seditious groups within it. War cannot be defined by the difference between international and national politics, that is, by the absence or presence of effective government, because wars have frequently occurred within a state and international systems have got along without war over considerable periods. During the century between Waterloo and the Marne, the American Civil War cost as many lives as all the international wars in Europe put together (42).

So long as there are groups of any kind whatever in contact with one another, so long as their purposes and policies may conflict, and so long as armed force may be both an available and a useful means for forwarding those purposes and policies, war may be resorted to and knowledge of the art of war will remain useful (15).

ANALYSIS

The analysis of war has ordinarily taken the form either of critical history (24, 26, 28, 29, 30, 33, 36) or of systematic exposition (2, 4, 7, 14, 18, 23, 25). Its object has usually been to assist generals and statesmen in practicing the art, that is, in utilizing war most effectively as an instrument of policy, whether that policy is defense or expansion, maintenance or change of law. This object of the art of war is to be distinguished from the narrow usage of the term *instrument of national policy* in treaties such as the Kellogg-Briand Pact. That term includes only policies in pursuit of national interest in violation of law. In this legal sense, war as an instrument of national policy does not include war as an instrument of national defense, of international sanction, or of international policy (41).

Treatises on the art of war analyse the principles of military organization, strategy, tactics, and logistics. They also consider the application of those principles in the varied contingencies of relative resources, positions, and forces; of technology, geography, and climate; and of policy, information, and morale. The description of the way problems have been solved by great generals and admirals of the past figure largely in these treatises whether their organization is systematic or historic (9). Recently the extensive industrialization of war and the significance of new inventions and technologies has raised the question whether there are principles of strategy which are applicable under all conditions of technology. In any case the utilization of advancing technology and invention has become a major aspect of the art of war (6). So also military law (11, 31, 37), military medicine (34), military economics (17, 40), and military psychology (20) are aspects of the art of war of increasing importance.

It is not the purpose of this chapter to develop an analysis of the subject, but rather to state certain broad deductions concerning the tendency of war in the life of a civilization and the probable future of the art of war. Four propositions may be hazarded. War tends (*a*) to become absolute, (*b*) to become obsolete, and, as a result of these conflicting tendencies, (*c*) to become less frequent and more destructive, and (*d*) eventually to eliminate the civilization in which it develops.

Under the social conditions which usually characterize the early stages of a civilization, war tends to be a controllable instrument of policy, thus distinguishing it from war among primitive peoples which tends to be ritualistic rather than instrumental. Fighting groups are relatively small, socially integrated, and without much capital accumulation. They are also numerous, independent, and of relatively equal power. Weapons are not very destructive. The initiative, the accumulation of supplies, and the superior generalship which usually belongs to the offensive tends to give it an advantage over the defensive. Furthermore, the armed forces tend to be controlled by leaders free to act in accord with considerations of rational policy. Under such conditions, the leader is in a position to balance costs against gains and to order his forces to fight, retreat, or surrender according as that calculation suggests, without great risk of losing his position.

The progress of civilization, however, tends to make the fighting groups larger, less socially integrated, and richer. Their unity depends less on culture and more on policy, and they are more capable of sustaining the costs of war, consequently, once war is embarked upon, it is both more necessary to continue to victory if political solidarity is to be preserved, and more possible to attempt to do so for a long time.

The progress of civilization also tends to the invention of superior means of mobility, communication, and destruction. Larger forces can be mobilized and concentrated and greater losses of personnel and property can be visited upon the enemy. Heavy losses develop a spirit of hate and a demand for vengeance which makes it difficult to stop hostilities so long as equal losses are being imposed upon the enemy. War aims shift from the original policy for which arms were taken up to compensation for the losses suffered. Instead of war being an instrument of policy, all policy becomes subordinated to military victory (41).

The progress of civilization also tends to a greater knowledge of the art of war, to a wider distribution of military inventions, to more effective intelligence services, and, thus, to a continuous reduction of the advantage of the offensive. Within a developed civilization the victim is usually somewhat prepared, is not easily surprised, and understands the proper defense to every maneuver of the enemy. Generalship has become less a function of gifted personalities than of adequate staff work which can be provided in any highly civilized nation. Thus the power of the defense tends to increase and the probability of early and inexpensive victory to diminish. This is especially true because the balance of power principle tends to bring allies to the victim rather than to the aggressor. It is true that weapons of great mobility, protection, and striking power, such as the air-borne atomic bomb, may create tremendous capacity for destruction for which there is no direct defense. In this sense the progress of military technology increases the power of the offensive. But if knowledge of such inventions is distributed, all participants in war are equally vulnerable because it is not possible for the aggressor to destroy the defender's capacity to retaliate. The offensive, therefore, has no continuing advantage. War tends to become a process of attrition, as it always is when the defense has an advantage, although with such weapons making effective retaliation the only defense, the mutual attrition proceeds very rapidly (5, 42).

The progress of civilization furthermore tends to increase the economic and political consciousness of the people, converting the group from a personal autocracy to a corporate democracy in which the leaders are controlled by public opinion and constitutional law. The public, once induced to embark upon war by government propaganda or external attack, convinced that their cause is just, and suffering from earlier losses for which vengeance is demanded, cannot be easily stopped in their warlike activity. The leaders must continue to promise victory or lose their positions.

The progress of civilization finally tends, as noted in the discussion of international politics, to develop greater inequalities of power; to eliminate, subject, or neutralize small states; to reduce the number of great states; and to develop coalitions and alliances among them producing eventually a bipolar world. Wars, therefore, tend to spread and to have large and relatively equal forces on each side, capable of prolonged resistance and great powers of mutual destruction. Victory cannot be achieved by sudden surprise, mass attacks, or skillful manoeuvres, but only by enduring attrition longer than the enemy.

These factors mean that war ceases to have the character of a sword which the ruler can use so long as he is winning, but can abandon and parley, or flee, when defeat seems certain. It rather has the character of a heavily loaded truck without brakes going downhill at an accelerating rate, with the leader sitting at the wheel incapable of stopping it and urged by the passengers to keep on the road whatever disasters may be ahead (41).

All of the factors mentioned, when summed up, mean that with the progress of civilization, war tends to create two hostile poles, each with an implacable will to victory, about which all the energies of the civilization gathers and which engage in mutual destruction, until, after both have suffered serious attrition, one succumbs.

Some or all of these conditions may develop at any stage of a civilization. War always tends to become absolute as Clausewitz (7) noted, but the tendency is augmented with the development of civilization.

The factors which tend to make war absolute, also tend to make it obsolete, if one assumes that civilization has the effect of making men more rational in adapting means to ends. Absolute war is not a useful instrument of policy to either party. Consequently, in proportion as statesmen are rational, they will not resort to war. The essence of civilization is to turn human interests to general welfare, broader cooperation, and individual freedom; to more far-sighted adaptation of means to ends; and to rational modes of settling controversies by negotiation, arbitration, or law.

No civilization, however, has experienced the complete obsolescence of war. This is due to a number of factors. The development of civilized appreciation of the uselessness of war proceeds unevenly. Some groups exist which are unaware of the risks of war, or value power in itself to such an extent that they will assume the risk, or are composed of persons so politically unconscious or uninformed as to be the willing followers of a leadership with strong nerves and weak intelligence.

It only takes one to start a war. Consequently as long as one group of considerable power exists arming for war, others must arm in defense in case the general political situation makes each group dependent for survival on self-help.

The contingencies of war and the possibilities of new inventions are such, furthermore, that the obsolescence of war as a useful instrument of policy cannot be entirely certain. There is always the possibility that skillful leadership can use war effectively.

Furthermore, the more war becomes absolute, and the more civilized states seek to avoid it, the more vulnerable they become to threats of war. Thus as war itself becomes obsolete as a useful instrument, threats of war become a useful instrument of diplomacy in the hands of reckless leaders, and threats may lead to war.

Effective international organization to assure the nipping of incipient aggression in the bud and to enforce general armament reduction is difficult to achieve for reasons which will be discussed in the chapter on international organization. As a consequence the danger of war has never been entirely eliminated in any civilization. The tendencies of civilization have, consequently, been to make war less frequent, but more absolute when it comes. War has therefore occurred in the life of a civilization, in oscillations of increasing length and increasing amplitude. The total costs of war to a civilization have tended to increase as the civilization has developed (41).

The end of such a development is war of such absolute character that the civilization either collapses because of excessive destruction of life, property, social solidarity, and morale, or becomes excessively integrated, because all groups are subordinated to a single survivor which establishes a *universal state* incapable of adaptation to changes in its material or moral environment. The tendency of international war is therefore similar to that of international politics. Both tend to destroy the system they originally built, to become obsolete as means to the ends desired, and to develop potentialities of absolute destruction or of absolute power. Under such conditions, the freedom, competition, flexibility, and adaptability necessary for the development of a civilization come to an end. The absolute universal state, if established, collapses from internal disruption and with it the civilization that it was designed to protect passes into history.

CRITICISM

So long as war is a possibility the discipline concerning its use is indispensable to sovereign groups that are to survive. Furthermore, the discipline, in throwing light on the character and tendencies of war, illuminates the future course of world politics in which war plays so important a role.

If, however, war is studied merely as a means to political ends, the antinomy between its absoluteness and its obsolescence presents an impasse. The study of war must be broadened to include its sociological and psychological roots if the disposition of groups to be guided by reason and to eschew absolute war is to be reconciled with the tendency of groups to seek to enforce their wills until they are ruined by such war.

The discipline of war as usually presented gives a distorted view of the nature of man and society. It underestimates the possibilities of adjustment by diplomacy and law, and also the risks of resort to war. Those absorbed in the study of military organization, strategy, and tactics tend to overlook the excessive costs and uncertain consequences of war, and the danger of excessive military preparation to freedom and democracy, and even to effective war itself. Excessive military preparation results in the stockpiling of weapons which soon become obsolete, in the freezing of military plans, and in an arms race which bankrupts budgets, stimulates aggressive tendencies at home, and convinces both potential allies and potential enemies that aggressive intentions exist. Professionals in the art of war, intent on immediate requirements, are doubtful guides to foreign policy. Democracies have wisely adopted the principle that the military should always be subordinate to the civil authorities in making political decisions (19, 22, 32). That is another way of saying that the art of war should be subordinate to the art of international politics.

REFERENCES

1. ASTON, Major General Sir George, ed., *The Study of War for Statesmen and Citizens* (London, Longmans, 1927).
2. BERNHARDI, Friedrich von, *On War of Today* (London, Hugh Rees, 1912).
3. BRODIE, Bernard, *Sea Power in the Machine Age* (Princeton, Princeton University Press, 1941).
4. ———, *Guide to Naval Strategy* (Princeton, Princeton University Press, 1944).
5. ———, ed., *The Absolute Weapon* (New York, Harcourt, 1946).
6. BUSH, Vannevar, *Modern Arms and Free Men* (New York, Simon and Schuster, 1949).
7. CLAUSEWITZ, Carl von, *On War* (London, Kegan Paul, 1911), 3 vols.
8. DUPUY, R. E., and ELIOT, G. F., *If War Comes* (New York, Macmillan, 1937).
9. EARL, Edward Mead, CRAIG, G. A., and GILBERT, Felix, *Makers of Modern Strategy* (Princeton, Princeton University Press, 1943).
10. EISENHOWER, Dwight D., *Crusade in Europe* (New York, Doubleday, 1948).
11. FEILCHENFELD, Ernst H., *The International Economic Law of Belligerent Occupation* (Washington, Carnegie Endowment for International Peace, 1942).
12. FISKE, Rear Admiral Bradley A., *The Navy as a Fighting Machine* (New York, Scribners, 1917).
13. ———, *The Art of Fighting, Its Evolution and Progress with Illustrations from Campaigns of Great Commanders* (New York, Century, 1920).

14. FOCH, Marshal Ferdinand, *The Principles of War* (London, Chapman and Hall, 1914).
15. FULLER, Major General J. F. C., *The Reformation of War* (New York, Dutton, 1923).
16. ———, *Armament and History* (New York, 1946).
17. GORDON, David L., and DANGERFIELD, Royden, *The Hidden Weapon, The Story of Economic Warfare* (New York, Harper, 1947).
18. JOMINI, Baron Antoine Henri, *The Art of War* (1838).
19. KERWIN, Jerome G., ed., *Civil-Military Relationships in American Life* (Chicago, University of Chicago Press, 1948).
20. LASSWELL, Harold D., *Propaganda Technique in the World War* (New York, Knopf, 1927).
21. LIDDELL-HART, B. H., *Remaking of Modern Armies* (London, Murray, 1927).
22. MCKINLEY, Silas Bent, *Democracy and Military Power* (New York, Vanguard, 1941).
23. MACHIAVELLI, Niccolo, *The Art of War* (1520).
24. MAHAN, Admiral A. T., *The Influence of Sea Power on History, 1660-1783* (Boston, Little, Brown, 1890; 16th ed., 1902).
25. MAURICE, Major General Sir Frederick, *Principles of Strategy* (New York, R. R. Smith, 1930).
26. MONTROSS, Lynn, *War Through the Ages* (New York, Harper, 1944).
27. NICKERSON, Hoffman, *Can We Limit War?* (London, 1932).
28. OMAN, Charles, *History of the Art of War in the Middle Ages* (London, Methuen, 1924), 2 vols.
29. ———, *History of the Art of War in the Sixteenth Century* (New York, Dutton, 1937).
30. POLYBIUS, *Histories*, E. S. Shuckburg, ed. (London, Macmillan, 1899).
31. PUTTKAMMER, Ernst W., *War and the Law* (Chicago, University of Chicago Press, 1944).
32. SMITH, Louis, *American Democracy and Military Power* (Chicago, University of Chicago Press, 1951).
33. SPAULDING, Oliver L. Jr., NICKERSON, Hoffman, and WRIGHT, John W., *Warfare, A Study of Military Methods from Earliest Times* (New York, Harcourt, 1925).
34. TALIAFERRO, William H., *Medicine and the War* (Chicago, University of Chicago Press, 1944).
35. TAYLOR, F. L., *The Art of War in Italy, 1494-1529* (Cambridge, Cambridge University Press, 1921).
36. THUCYDIDES, *History of the Peloponnesian War*.
37. U. S. War Department, *Basic Field Manual, Rules of Land Warfare* (Washington, 1940).
38. UPTON, Major General Emory, *The Military Policy of the United States* (Washington, Government Printing Office, 1912).
39. VON DER GOLTZ, Lieutenant-General Colmar Freiherr, *The Conduct of War* (London, Kegan, Paul, 1908).
40. WRIGHT, Chester W., ed., *Economic Problems of War and Its Aftermath* (Chicago, University of Chicago Press, 1942).
41. WRIGHT, Quincy, *A Study of War* (Chicago, University of Chicago Press, 1942), pp. 8, 291 ff., 423 ff., 575 ff., 698, 707, 792 ff., 1228, 1236.
42. ———, *Problems of Stability and Progress in International Relations* (Berkeley, University of California Press, 1954).

CHAPTER
15

The Art of Diplomacy

DEFINITION

DIPLOMACY in the popular sense means the employment of tact, shrewdness, and skill in any negotiation or transaction. In the more special sense used in international relations it is the art of negotiation, in order to achieve the maximum of group objectives with a minimum of costs, within a system of politics in which war is a possibility. As a discipline it includes practical, historic, philosophic, and scientific studies contributing to this art.

Diplomacy, like war, is most commonly employed as a method of international politics, but like war, the term cannot be confined to relations between sovereign states. While negotiations figure in all human transactions, the peculiarity of diplomacy lies in its relation to war. Negotiation with war as a possible alternative constitutes diplomacy. Where the possibility of war does not exist, as is usually the case in negotiations between business men, between party leaders, or between states in a federation, the term *diplomacy* is hardly applicable.

Diplomacy, however, is not attached to a particular institution such as a system of permanent missions with legally regulated ranks and procedures. *Ad hoc* representatives of groups which enjoy, *de facto* or *de jure,* a sovereign capacity to make war, are, when carrying on negotiations, engaged in diplomacy.

Diplomacy differs from war in that it uses words rather than material weapons. Display of force and threat of war are among the instruments of diplomacy, but if war itself begins diplomacy is usually interrupted between the belligerents.

Diplomacy always balances advantages against costs in a way which war, once it is embarked upon, cannot do. Consequently, diplomacy appears to be a method of international politics in contrast to that of war. It has sometimes been thought of as negotiation to achieve the maximum of group objectives without war. In this sense the outbreak of war marks the failure of diplomacy. Since, however, diplomacy may function to create favorable conditions for war, to assist in winning war, to extract the maximum advantage from winning war, or to reduce the disadvantages from losing war, this conception is imperfect. Diplomacy is a supplement to, as well as, on occasion, a substitute for, war. Diplomacy is, however, a narrower term than politics. Politics has sometimes been defined as the art of forwarding group purposes against the opposition of other groups *without war*, but the more common usage, especially in the field of international politics, recognizes war as a possible method of politics. Politics, therefore, includes all methods available in any situation of opposition between groups, while diplomacy is concerned only with the agents, procedures, purposes, and methods of negotiation and only with situations where war is a possibility.

Diplomacy proceeds by compromise, conceding as little as possible to the opponent; by bargaining, giving in one area in order to receive in another; by rewards, paying for benefits received; by preparation or display of force, often accompanied by honeyed words—the mailed fist in the velvet glove; by threats of war, economic embargo, trade discriminations, refusal of loans or other hostile measures; by gaining the support or assuring the neutrality of third parties; by bribes to key personalities; and by propaganda or promises to divide the opposing group and to gain the support of public opinion. These methods are especially applicable when the parties are comparatively equal and are opposed in most matters, and when the negotiation is bilateral.

Diplomacy also proceeds by emphasizing the need of a common front against a dangerous third party; by appealing to principles of law, morality, humanity, and civilization; and by emphasizing the common advantages to be gained by co-operating for common ends. These methods become increasingly applicable as the relation of the parties becomes in lesser degree oppositional and in greater degree co-operative, and in proportion as the number of parties involved in the negotiation becomes greater.

When the parties in a bilateral negotiation are of unequal power, the weaker is certain to be aware of the threat implied by this fact, especially if the more powerful succeeds in isolating him from possible friends, though the more powerful may be especially careful to keep discussion on a high plane of principle. Appeals to principles, public opinion, and international law are likely to be the actually effective bases of negotiation in proportion as the participants are numerous, the most interested are relatively equal in power, and many are relatively disinterested. Such appeals are more useful in the United Nations General Assembly than in bilateral negotiations, although even in the latter they are frequently utilized to create an atmosphere of public opinion among third states, or in the world generally, favorable to the proposals set forth and unfavorable to those of the opponent (33).

As diplomacy becomes institutionalized, it may make use of good offices and mediation; of commissions of inquiry and conciliation, and of arbitration and judicial settlement thus approaching the methods of adjudication familiar within the state. It may also make use of consultation, conference, or periodic meetings of councils and assemblies as in the League of Nations and the United Nations, thus augmenting the role of common opinion and of disinterested parties and approaching the legislative procedures familiar within the state. It may also make use of permanent alliances, guarantees, obligations of mutual assistance, and international procedures to determine and stop aggression as in the United Nations Charter, thus approaching the executive function familiar within the state. Finally, it may establish consultative and administrative agencies for performing common functions as in the international unions and the specialized agencies of the United Nations, thus approaching the administrative activity familiar within the state.

With these institutional developments, diplomacy tends to become merged in international organization, but so long as the relations of the participants are more oppositional than they are co-operative and, as a consequence, war is a possibility in fact whatever it may be in law, the structure depends primarily upon negotiation among the major members, and the system is fundamentally diplomatic and military. There is a certain logical progression, exemplified in the history of the Swiss, American, and German federations, from a system of international politics resting upon the procedures of war and diplomacy to a federation resting upon central powers of execution, adjudication, legislation, and administration (35). International organization can be considered a transitional stage in this progress. Each of these systems, however, rests upon somewhat different sociological and psychological assumptions. The progression, therefore, historically depends upon the development in fact of the social and psychological conditions which realize the assumptions of one or the other system. It should be added, however, that the institutionalization of one or the other system tends to perpetuate the conditions of its viability. Efforts, even though slightly premature, to establish a system inappropriate to existing conditions may contribute to creating more favorable conditions, but if too premature the effect may be the opposite. The examination of the relation between such differing political systems as diplomacy, international organization, and world government, and of the social and psychological conditions of their functioning, belong to the realm of the sociology and the psychology of international relations and will not be further pursued here.

The literature of diplomacy, like that of war, has been both historical and systematic. The existence of historical source materials in the abundant publication of treaties and diplomatic correspondence, especially in the nineteenth century, and in the considerable opening of national archives for research, coupled with the appreciation that the art of diplomacy consists less in the understanding of principles than in their application to particular circumstances, has tended to emphasize the historical form (2, 4, 10, 15, 16, 18, 21, 24, 25, 29, 30). Diplomatic history is a well-recognized discipline, but it merges into the history of international politics. Treatises have also been written systematically bringing together information on the agents and procedures of diplomacy (19, 27, 34), on the principles and wisdom developed in diplomatic practice (1, 7, 11, 14, 22, 37), on the formalities of international and national law applicable to the subject (12, 20, 23), and on the policies pursued by diplomats in general (6), by particular diplomats (5, 13, 26, 28, 31, 32), or by particular countries (3, 8, 9, 17, 29, 36). The latter treatment of diplomacy differs from topical expositions of national foreign policy and international policy only in emphasizing methods rather than ends, but the two are usually treated together.

ASSUMPTIONS

The assumptions underlying the discipline of diplomacy are no different from those underlying the discipline of the art of war. Both assume groups with inconsistent ends in contact with one another, among whom the use of armed force as an instrument of policy is possible. If world politics should become so organized that war was eliminated, diplomacy, in the sense here used, would not exist, although negotiation would continue, as it does within and among organs of a constitutional state and among private individuals and groups within such a state.

While war and diplomacy exist under the same conditions, and one can hardly exist without the other, yet the relative roles of the two may vary. If contacts among groups are few and inconsistencies of policy and culture are consequently great, war assumes the dominant role. Thus the normal relation when contacts are first established among groups which have hitherto developed wholly independently is war, as exhibited, for example, in the first contacts of European nations with those of America and Asia in the fifteenth and sixteenth centuries. If contacts increase, common values, cultural understandings, and co-operation toward common ends are also likely to increase and diplomacy will assume a more important role. The development of relations of the Western powers with China illustrates this change. As commerce, missionary, and educational contact increased, common understandings of international law and diplomatic institutions developed and, in the latter part of the nineteenth century, relations became less warlike and more diplomatic. Diplomacy of the quarter-deck merged into diplomacy of the court. A reverse trend can be observed in the relations between the democratic and communist worlds since World War II. As the Iron Curtain became more impervious, trade and communications were reduced and the relations became less diplomatic and more those of cold war.

These observations suggest that for the art of diplomacy to be applicable, it is necessary to assume that the groups involved have some principles, standards, rules, and objectives in common. The art of war, on the other hand, is applicable even though the groups involved have nothing in common, although, as war has actually developed among civilized nations, belligerents acknowledge a law of war and expect to make peace after hostilities; consequently the art of war has assumed that the groups involved have much in common.

ANALYSIS

Diplomacy assumes more of co-operation than does war. There may, as already noticed, be some co-operation even in war, for example in the treatment of prisoners, observance of military conventions, and expectations of eventual peace. But as war becomes absolute, all co-operation in the present or hope of co-operation in the future fades away. Relations become exclusively oppositional. Each desires only the total destruction of the other. Diplomacy, on the other hand, seeks to widen areas of agreement and co-operation, and cannot function unless there are some such areas to begin with. The tendency of diplomacy is, therefore, toward international organization and world government. The phrase *absolute diplomacy* has been coined apparently as a synonym for cold war. The entire nation devotes itself to victory in *cold war,* as the nation in arms devotes itself to military victory in *absolute war.* In this sense absolute diplomacy may be a precursor of absolute war, although it may, if successful, avoid war altogether. The tendency of diplomacy, however, is away from such absolutism. Diplomacy tends both to broaden the area and to increase the objectives of co-operation among the participating groups. For this, several reasons may be adduced.

The position of third states is likely to be important. State *A,* if it is to succeed in a negotiation with state *B,* may find it convenient to strengthen its friendship with states *C, D,* and *E,* and state *B* similarly seeks allies. While such efforts may tend toward creating a bipolarity of opposition, so long as the system remains flexible and the expectations of success in negotiation are great, *A* and *B* are both likely to feel that in the future each will need the friendship of the other in negotiations with *C* or *D.*

Consequently, the area of agreement expands. Oppositions do not become hardened so long as the future relations of friendship or opposition are uncertain. This uncertainty of the future, which is destroyed with the establishment of bipolarity and the possibility of calculating which side time favors, is a condition under which peace and diplomacy thrive in a system of international politics.

In diplomacy advantages and costs are calculated and weighed against one another with the result that political problems of security are likely to be linked with economic problems of trade. Diplomacy, though it may use trade embargoes as an instrument of pressure, tends to use trade advantages as an instrument of bargain or reward. Diplomacy, therefore, tends to develop trade and peaceful co-operation which, once developed, serve as hostages against war. War, on the other hand, destroys trade and its preparation tends toward policies of self-sufficiency and autarchy.

Diplomacy recognizes the principle of equilibrium as a basis of stability and security in a power political system. But a policy of balance of power implies that each state looks upon the stability of the whole system as the essence of its own security. The beginning is, therefore, made for subordinating the sovereignty of the state to the stability of the world community. Policies of balance of power naturally lead to policies of collective security which become institutionalized through common organs, procedures, and rules of law to assure that aggression will be always confronted by insuperable force. International organization to promote collective security is, therefore, only a planned development of the natural tendency of balance of power policies. It is the natural tendency of states, when faced by an emergency, to gang up against the aggressor who, if successful against his first victim, will eventually turn on the others. Collective security seeks to supplement this natural tendency by positive obligations and convenient agencies and procedures to enlist common action. Whether the gain in certainty compensates for the loss in flexibility depends upon the presence or absence of general conditions favorable to co-operation among states (14, 35).

A system of diplomacy tends to create bonds of personal friendship among the diplomats and this in turn develops feelings of mutual responsibility. With institutionalized and permanent missions a sense of solidarity in the *corps diplomatique* in each capital is likely to develop because of common interest in preserving diplomatic prerogatives. The privileges and immunities of the diplomats, without which they can hardly perform their functions, themselves depend on formalities of international law and procedure, sanctioned by mutual interest, reciprocity, and custom. Reliance upon law to serve their own interests tends toward a similar reliance to secure the interests of the states they represent. Thus diplomacy contributes to developing the system of international law supported by custom, good faith, reciprocity, and common interest, but once developed, law itself tends to develop systems of arbitration, adjudication, and enforcement which imply international organization.

These tendencies inherent in diplomacy itself are augmented by the natural tendencies of a civilization to develop closer contacts among its members with the progress of trade, travel, and migration; to accelerate invention in the fields of transport and communication facilitating such contacts; and as a consequence to increase mutual understandings of the different cultures and to establish certain common standards of human rights and international law. These developments also tend to give greater weight to the human values contingent upon peaceful co-operation and less to the heroic values contingent upon struggle. The natural tendencies of a developing civilization are therefore to augment the role of diplomacy and to diminish that of war.

The consequences of these conditions, which tend to make war obsolete for rational man, as it becomes absolute, tend to make diplomacy obsolete because it becomes merged in international organization with the object of preventing war and promoting international co-operation.

War and diplomacy are both characteristics of a system of international politics and the disciplines instructing in each will be useful only so long as such a system exists, yet the tendencies of the two are opposite. War, seeking to project the will of the part upon the whole, tends to chaos or world empire, while diplomacy, intelligently merging the interests of the part with the stability of the whole, tends to international co-operation and world federation.

CRITICISM

The discipline of diplomacy is insusceptible of formulation in a rigid system. Its essence is flexibility and adaptation to continually changing conditions. It escapes the rigidities of military tactics on the one hand and of the application of law on the other. Although in both law and war, as in all the practical arts, the circumstances alter the means or even the ends of action and the applicability of generally accepted principles and rules, yet this is true in diplomacy to an exceptional degree (31, 32, 33). The art of war proceeds by deciding upon objectives and then seeking to achieve them even at great sacrifice. The will to achieve the objective is the essence of war. The art of law proceeds by establishing rules and principles to which behavior must conform and tends toward a system of *positive law* in which the opportunities of interpretation are reduced and rigidity increases. Negotiation, however, cannot be successful if it assumes the logical form either of a plan to be realized, of a principle to be applied, or of a rule to be observed. It must rather assume the logical form of a dialectic or conversation in which each event is in a degree creative of the next. Diplomacy, more than either war or law, proceeds by a process of action and reaction. Initial plans, general principles, and customary rules are adapted and modified until at the end those relied upon by both of the participants may have been radically altered. History is, therefore, the natural form for expounding the art of diplomacy. Its essence is in the process by which a result, unplanned, unforeseen, and undetermined at the beginning, emerges at the end. The possibility of such a result depends upon a certain vagueness and flexibility of expression, upon attitudes of opportunism and expediency, and particularly upon a refusal to close doors. Ultimata mark the end of negotiation. It has been observed that a lady says "no" when she means "perhaps," and "perhaps" when she means "yes." If she says "yes," she is no lady. A diplomat, on the other hand, says "yes" when he means "perhaps," and "perhaps" when he means "no," but if he says "no," he is no diplomat. Diplomacy always leaves every possible solution open. It closes only those which are impossible.

It has been noted that the methods of diplomacy are highly varied, ranging all the way from the quasi-parliamentary methods of winning votes in the General Assembly of the United Nations to the grim but silent calculations of military potentials in cold war negotiations. As its methods are varied, so its values are relative. Peace and plenty, security and prosperity are set against one another. Gains and losses, though on incommensurate subjects, must be weighed and balanced. The diplomat tends to view the world as a moving equilibrium of relative values and forces, not as a hierarchy of values and forces each pyramiding up to an absolute. This again indicates why the art of diplomacy is better learned from historical example than from precept or rule. The exceptions to any principle of diplomacy will be more numerous than the applications and no plan can be realized in its entirety. The historical episode illustrates the application of a principle without the implication that there is a general rule. It also illustrates the process by which plans are compromised and modified with the development of understanding by each of the total situation as perceived by the other.

The discipline of diplomacy, however, though broad in its methods and relativistic in its philosophy, breeds a certain narrowness of outlook. With its merits of relativity, flexibility, and balance, it tends to overemphasize the role of individuals in shaping the destiny of groups. The state under an absolute ruler able to maneuver freely tends to become the .ideal of the diplomat and the diplomatic historian (21). The forces of public opinion, of law, of cultural ideas, and of social ideals tend to be minimized or viewed with a certain cynicism. The diplomat no less than the soldier and lawyer is subject to professional distortions and his art should be kept to its role of instrument rather than maker of policy.

REFERENCES

The list includes a sampling of general treatises on diplomatic agents, their rights, methods, standards, and objectives, and of general diplomatic histories of the United States and Europe. The literature of diplomacy also includes the voluminous source materials of official archives, published and unpublished; numerous biographies, autobiographies, and memoirs of diplomats and foreign ministers; and many analyses of the foreign policy and diplomacy of particular states or diplomats at particular times or on particular matters. The present list includes only a few such detailed treatments of diplomacy in action (5, 13, 24, 26, 28, 29, 31, 32), although they are among the most valuable materials for understanding the art of diplomacy.

1. ANDERSON, Frank Maloy, and HERSHEY, Amos S., *Handbook for the Diplomatic History of Europe, Asia and Africa, 1870-1914* (Washington, Government Printing Office, 1918).
2. BAILEY, Thomas A., *A Diplomatic History of the American People*, 5th ed. (New York, Appleton-Century-Crofts, 1955).
3. BARBER, Hollis W., *Foreign Policies of the United States* (New York, Dryden Press, 1953).
4. BEMIS, Samuel Flagg, *The Diplomatic History of the United States* (New York, Holt, 1936).
5. BENEDETTI, Count, *Studies in Diplomacy* (London, Heineman, 1896).
6. BERNARD, Montague, *Four Lectures on Subjects Connected with Diplomacy* (London, Macmillan, 1868).
7. CALLIÈRES, Francois de, *On the Manner of Negotiating with Princes* (1716), trans. by A. F. Whyte (Boston, Houghton, Mifflin, 1919).
8. CHAMBERLAIN, Lawrence H., and SNYDER, Richard C., *American Foreign Policy* (New York, Rinehart, 1948).
9. DULLES, John Foster, *War or Peace* (New York, Macmillan, 1950).
10. FISH, Carl Russell, *American Diplomacy*, 4th ed. (New York, Holt, 1923).
11. FOSTER, John W., *The Practice of Diplomacy* (Boston, Houghton Mifflin, 1906).
12. GENTILI, Alberico, *De Legationibus*, trans. by Gordon J. Laing (New York, Oxford University Press, 1924).
13. GREW, Joseph C., *Turbulent Era, A Diplomatic Record of Forty Years, 1904-1945*, Walter Johnson, ed. (Boston, Houghton, Mifflin, 1952).
14. HEATLEY, D. P., *Diplomacy and the Study of International Relations* (Oxford, Clarendon Press, 1919).
15. HILL, David J., *A History of Diplomacy in the International Development of Europe* (New York, Longmans, 1905-1914), 3 vols.
16. KENNAN, George F., *American Diplomacy, 1900-1950* (Chicago, University of Chicago Press, 1951).
17. LIPPMANN, Walter, *United States Foreign Policy, Shield of the Republic* (Boston, Little, Brown, 1943).
18. MACHIAVELLI, Niccolo, *Florentine History* (1527), trans. by W. K. Marriott (Everyman's Library).
19. MAGGI, Ottaviano, *De Legato* (1566).
20. MARTENS, Charles de, *Le Guide Diplomatique* (Paris, 1832).
21. PETRIE, Sir Charles, *Earlier Diplomatic History, 1492-1713; Diplomatic History, 1713-1933* (New York, Macmillan, 1939).
22. REINSCH, Paul S., *Secret Diplomacy* (New York, Harcourt, 1922).

23. SATOW, Sir Ernest, *A Guide to Diplomatic Practice* (London, Longmans, 1917).

24. SCHMITT, Bernadotte E., *The Coming of the War, 1914* (New York, Scribners, 1930).

25. SEELEY, Sir John R., *The Growth of British Policy* (Cambridge, Cambridge University Press, 1895).

26. STETTINIUS, E. R., Jr., *Roosevelt and the Russians, The Yalta Conference,* Walter Johnson, ed. (New York, Doubleday, 1949).

27. STUART, Graham H., *American Diplomatic and Consular Practice* (New York, Appleton-Century-Crofts, 1936; 2nd ed., 1952).

28. TEMPERLEY, H. W. V., *The Foreign Policy of Canning* (London, Bell, 1925).

29. VAN ALSTYNE, Richard W., *American Diplomacy in Action* (Stanford, Stanford University Press, 1947).

30. WALSH, Edward A., ed., *The History and Nature of International Relations* (New York, Macmillan, 1922).

31. WEBSTER, Sir Charles, *The Foreign Policy of Castlereagh, 1815-1822* (London, British Book Centre, 1925), 2 vols.

32. ————, *The Foreign Policy of Palmerston, 1830-1841* (London, British Book Centre, 1951), 2 vols.

33. ————, *The Art and Practice of Diplomacy* (London, School of Economics and Political Science, 1952).

34. WICQUEFORT, *The Ambassador and His Functions,* trans. by John Digby (London, 1681).

35. WRIGHT, Quincy, *A Study of War* (Chicago, University of Chicago Press, 1942), pp. 249 ff., 708, 743 ff., 767 ff., 1255 ff.

36. ————, ed., *A Foreign Policy for the United States* (Chicago, University of Chicago Press, 1947).

37. YOUNG, Sir George, *Diplomacy, Old and New* (New York, Harcourt, 1921).

CHAPTER
16

The Conduct of
Foreign Relations

DEFINITION

THE CONDUCT of foreign relations is the art by which a government ascertains the state's rights, obligations, interests, and responsibilities in international relations, and makes decisions in order to protect those rights, observe those obligations, promote those interests, and discharge those responsibilities. As a discipline it differs from diplomacy in that it rests less upon an understanding of human nature and more upon an understanding of particular institutions; it differs from international politics in that it rests less upon an understanding of the international system and more upon an understanding of the constitutional system of the particular state; it differs from international law in that it must balance national interests against international obligations; and it differs from international organization in that it must balance the policies and procedures of the national order against those of the international order. It is, therefore, even less adapted to treatment as a science or philosophy than any of these disciplines and lends itself to historical or practical treatment. Flexibility, adaptability, and sensitivity to many continually changing factors is the essence of this art.

A government's conduct of foreign relations differs from its conduct of domestic affairs in that policies and decisions must be weighed, not only in relation to national law and opinion, but also in relation to international law and the probable reactions of foreign governments (44). With the shrinking of the world manifested by the more abundant penetration of the trade, peoples, communications, and anxieties of each nation into the domain of others, and the consequent increase in the impact of any action by any government upon the interests of others, it has become increasingly difficult to differentiate foreign from domestic affairs and to formulate foreign policies.

International controversies and negotiations today continually deal with postal, radio, rail, maritime, and aviation regulation; with labor, educational, and scientific standards; and with individual rights, judicial procedures, agricultural production, financial policy, public health control, armament manufacture, and many other matters formerly considered *domestic* in character. Articles 1 and 55 of the United Nations Charter indicate the broad scope of matters which states have agreed are of international concern. The international character of a policy or decision arises from the legal fact that the state is bound by international obligations limiting its competence or its right to deal with the matter at discretion, from the political fact that the interests of other states may induce them to oppose the action proposed, or from the administrative fact that the co-operation of other states may be useful or necessary to achieve the national objective. If any one of these legal, political, or administrative facts is involved in a situation, its solution cannot in practice be treated entirely within the domestic sphere of the state most interested. Article 2, Paragraph 7 of the Charter requires, it is true, that the organs of the United Nations regard a matter as "essentially" within a state's "domestic jurisdiction" unless that state's international obligations are involved or "the maintenance of international peace and security" requires the United Nations to apply "enforcement measures," yet political considerations of less gravity or administrative considerations may in fact require that the matter be dealt with by international consultation or agreement.

The soldier and diplomat usually have, in any situation, a clear conception of the policy of the group they represent, whether victory in war or achievement of the maximum of specified national objectives possible by negotiations. But the person who conducts foreign relations, at least in a constitutional and democratic state, has no such clear conception of his objectives. He is faced on the one hand by national laws of more or less explicitness and by national opinions and traditions of more or less coherence, and on the other hand, by foreign threats and demands variously supported by force, international law, and world public opinion. These pressures often make it necessary that he modify what he would consider in the national interest or that he do something when he would consider it in the national interest to do nothing. He is also faced by changing circumstances and conditions of economy, power, diplomacy, and opinion in the world which continually influence conceptions about the national interest and the national power position. Out of this confusion of pressures, domestic and foreign, he must make decisions applicable to each issue but without ignoring the requirements of the total situation and of the long run. Foreign policy in a complex and changing world must be flexible and adaptive.

As the complications of the national constitution increase with the multiplication of official agencies, parties and pressure groups interested in a given problem, and as the complications of the international situation increase with the proliferation of international organizations, self-determining nations, regional blocs, and transnational opinion groups, the problem becomes more and more difficult. A Louis XIV who *was* the state did not face the same problem. The arts of war and diplomacy, tinctured by respect for international law, could be his guides to achieve the policy which he had formulated in his own mind or in consultation with a small number of trusted advisors. This is in less degree true of modern dictators, but even a Hitler or a Stalin is faced by a conscious, although controllable, public opinion and by organizations of both party and government, including especially the Army and secret police, which must be persuaded.

The discipline described in this chapter has developed with the evolution of constitutional and democratic controls of the foreign relations of the state. It has come to be a discipline of major importance for democratic states measuring the applicability, in given circumstances, of the disciplines of war and diplomacy, and even those of international politics, international law, and international organization.

ASSUMPTIONS

The assumptions underlying this discipline are:

1. Only the *state* has international relations, but it cannot act except through organs of government acting within the scope of their constitutional powers.

2. All organs of government should, in a democracy, exercise these powers under guidance of national law and opinion.

3. The Constitution must, however, authorize a definite organ to represent the state in relations with other states, to communicate officially with them in the name of the state, and to discharge the state's international responsibilities. This organ is usually the chief of state advised by the foreign office.

4. This representative authority must, in order to meet these responsibilities, have power to perform national obligations, and wide initiative and discretion to determine national interests, and to formulate and execute national policies (44).

These assumptions are, in a measure, inconsistent. The requirement that the chief executive in conducting foreign relations respect constitutional limitations and observe national law and opinion may in certain constitutions largely deprive him of the capacity to meet international responsibilities and to protect national interests. Secretary of State Hull pointed out that during the first six years of the Franklin Roosevelt administration, both he and the president realized that a more active policy in thwarting potential aggression was in the national interest, but the state of national legislation, the attitudes of congress, and the prevailing public opinion compelled them to pursue a policy of neutrality and isolation (24, 42). Such a situation is not exceptional. It frequently presents a moral dilemma to the officials conducting foreign relations in a constitutional state, although it is exaggerated in the United States because of the constitutional system of checks and balances (6, 15, 44).

The representative authority of the modern state has a dual inheritance of power and responsibility. In respect to power he is an organ of democratic constitutionalism and can act only as authorized by the constitution and within the limitations of law, but in respect to international responsibility, he is the heir of the absolute monarchs among whom international law and diplomacy originated in the modern state system of the sixteenth and seventeenth centuries. The president of the United States is responsible, as was Louis XIV, in international politics for pursuing policies which will assure the security, prosperity, power, and prestige of the state, and in international law for observing and enforcing the obligations of the state. If these responsibilities are not discharged, the state may find itself involved in serious international difficulties. If a neglect of diplomatic precautions or of international obligations results in the United States becoming the victim of diplomatic defeat, reprisals, or war, the president is responsible even though the neglect was due to an adverse public opinion or election, to the failure of congress to approve appropriations or to legislate as required by treaty, to the insistence by Congress or the states on enacting legislation conflicting with international obligations, or to the refusal of the courts to be guided by international standards.

In the conduct of negotiations, the essence of which is compromise and concession on both sides, this inadequacy of power to meet responsibility creates exceptional difficulties, especially if the negotiation involves political compromises, matters traditionally regarded as domestic, or multilateral agreement or organization. If the president refuses to disclose his policy during a political negotiation, he will be accused of secrecy and of sacrificing national interests under foreign pressure. If he does disclose his policy, public opinion is not likely to accept any recession and negotiation may become impossible. In any case, his policy cannot be published at home without its being published abroad. Such publicity will weaken the nation's bargaining power by disclosing its hand to the opposition (4).

If he declines to negotiate on such matters as human rights or labor

standards he will be accused of negligence in failing to advance democratic and humane objectives, but if he does sign treaties on such matters
he will be accused of encroaching on "domestic jurisdiction," on "states
rights," or on "congressional prerogatives" and may encounter serious
opposition in implementation (50).

In activities in organs of the United Nations where many states are
involved, the dilemma between formulation of policy at the national and
at the international level becomes exceptionally difficult. If the president
seeks to formulate a national policy only after consulting all interested
agencies of the executive, the Congress, and the leaders of the opposition
party, with due appreciation of prevailing public opinion as manifested
by the press, the polling agencies, and the numerous private organizations, a policy will emerge which is so rigid and so incumbered by inhibitions that instructions based upon it will leave the American representative in the United Nations little opportunity for concession, and stalemate
may result (23). Insofar as constitutional provisions limit the treaty-
making power, the situation becomes even more serious because new
instructions cannot remedy it (50). American opinion has deplored the
rigidity of instructions characteristic of Soviet representatives in the
United Nations. This rigidity results from the excessively centralized
character of the Soviet regime, but rigidity resulting from constitutional
limitations upon the central authority are no less frustrating to negotiation.

If, on the other hand, the president follows the policy of building the
authority and prestige of the United Nations and leaves the American
representatives wide opportunity to be influenced by debate and wide
discretion to accept resolutions or agreements that command general
consent in the United Nations, the resulting resolution is likely to be
attacked by the opposition party, by Congress, and by various executive
agencies who feel that they should have had an influence in making
policy. Such opposition may impair the possibility of giving practical
effect in the United States to the resolutions of the United Nations, and
it may engender movements for constitutional amendment designed to
prevent treaty-making on matters deemed to be domestic in character
but which nevertheless are of vital international importance (49).

While illustrations have been drawn from the situation of the United
States, the problem exists in greater or less degree in all modern states,
even in the modern autocracies and dictatorships (4, 20, 22, 25, 37, 41).

ANALYSIS

A detailed examination of the course of legal interpretation and of national and international understanding which have developed to meet these problems cannot be attempted. A few observations may, however, be made on the approach to the problem.

The problem can perhaps best be approached by considering the practical influences and legal limitations which the representative authority of the state is obliged or expected to consider in conducting foreign relations. The conduct of foreign relations includes the instruction of negotiators and the conclusion of treaties (10, 12, 30, 43, 47); the utilization of armed forces and resort to war (2, 19, 31, 32, 36, 38, 48); the recognition of states and governments; the making of representations, protests, demands, and declarations of national policy; the participation in international institutions and submission of controversies to pacific settlement; and the fulfillment of international obligations and making of reparation for failure to do so (44). In some of these acts, the executive may be obliged to obtain the concurrence of one or both houses of the legislature. Others he may have power to perform independently. Even in the latter case, he may be expected to respect numerous technical, legal, and moral considerations, and he necessarily needs detailed information. Consequently he requires advice from agencies that are qualified by both factual and legal capacity to give it. In the modern state the executive is, therefore, a large and complex organization of civil and military servants divided into departments of which the foreign office is only one and subdivided into innumerable offices, divisions, bureaus, and services.

The foreign office is usually a complex of geographic and functional divisions, many of which must be consulted before action can be taken on any matter of foreign affairs (3, 29, 39). Furthermore, most international problems usually involve military, legal, financial, commercial, labor, agricultural, or other problems, the principal experts in which are outside of the foreign office. Consequently, the opinion of the other departments of the government usually must also be co-ordinated, requiring an elaborate system of interdepartmental committees and commissions, of cabinet meetings, and of special consultations.

Related to the organizational problem of discovering among the thousands of government agencies the relevant repositories of information on any question, is the personnel problem—the problem of recruiting, training, encouraging, and if necessary dismissing officials at home and in the field. The problems of public administration are of particular importance and difficulty because of the high qualifications necessary in the personnel, the need of maintaining an *esprit de corps*, especially in the foreign service, and the necessity that the personnel retain the political confidence of the administration in power. Investigatory activities of congressional committees may complicate this problem as well as the problems of policy (11, 29).

Once the administrative system is organized to assure a rapid coordination of advice from all interested agencies of government and to assure the approval of all private or public agencies of political importance whose co-operation is constitutionally, legally, or factually required, the problem arises of the considerations which should enter into policymaking and the weight to be given to each of them. No foreign office in a democracy can give single-minded attention to practice of the art of international politics under guidance of the intelligence reports which come in by daily cable from the foreign service (1). Public opinion, the position of political parties, and the demands of major pressure groups must be discovered and considered and perhaps influenced by astute fireside chats or personal conferences by the chief executive. National traditions, which constitute a crystalization of public opinion, must be studied and interpreted so as to avoid any apparent departure, even though conditions have greatly changed since the tradition was formulated. Rules of international law, treaties, and relevant national legislation must similarly be studied and interpreted so as to avoid violation. The equilibrium of power, the situation of trade and finance, the intentions of other states, particularly the great powers, and other conditions in the outside world which seem of primary relevance in determining policy must be considered, but the conclusions they suggest must usually be modified in the light of the other factors. The foreign-policy-maker in a modern state is always torn between the policies which seem best adapted to serve national interests in the light of world conditions as disclosed by the cables and by expert knowledge of international politics, international law, and international economics, and the policies which will best serve the national interests as interpreted by national laws, traditions, and opinions. The latter may be conflicting, may have developed under other conditions, or may be based on views distorted by misinformation, prejudice, or propaganda.

Such a system involves compromise and adjustment, and precludes a logically defined end or persistent adherence to policies once formed, a condition which de Tocqueville considered the greatest weakness of democracies (13).

What long-run tendencies can be expected when foreign relations are conducted under the complex conditions of constitutional democracy? It appears that (a) a tendency toward dictatorial executive control is opposed by (b) a tendency toward popular democratic control, and that (c) a tendency toward organized international control is opposed by (d) a tendency toward autonomous national control.

a. In times of stress, complexities tend to be ignored and foreign relations tend to be conducted dictatorially. The foreign relations of a state cannot be conducted effectively in a world of power politics unless power and responsibility are combined in the hands of an authority able to make rapid decisions in the light of the international situation, unhampered by domestic opinion. The arts both of war and diplomacy require centralization of national authority even though the former tends in the long run to destroy, and the latter to develop, international authority. As a result, autocracies have an advantage in international politics over democracies. All states, therefore, tend to become autocratic in this field as a necessary measure of security in proportion as the international situation is unstable and the existence of the state is threatened. Since international politics tends toward an unstable bipolar world, the special art of conducting democratic foreign relations tends to become inapplicable and the discipline concerned with that art tends to become obsolete (26).

  b. Under conditions of stability and technological progress, legislative bodies and public opinion increasingly demand influence on, or even control of, foreign relations. As the world shrinks the conduct of foreign relations becomes increasingly important for national welfare, and all aspects of domestic government and administration become increasingly affected by it. As a result legislatures utilize appropriation, legislative, and investigatory powers to control diplomatic action. Parliaments raise issues of confidence on matters of foreign policy. Opposition parties insist on a voice in the making of policy. Judicially enforcable constitutional restrictions on treaty-making or other action in the foreign field may even be invoked. In short, in proportion as threats to security are not immediate, all states tend to abandon the tradition handed down from the age of absolute monarchy that the conduct of foreign relations is largely executive and to apply democratic and constitutional principles in this field (4, 11, 34, 50). The sudden development of widespread war or conditions of general international insecurity is, therefore, likely to find many states unprepared to conduct foreign policy effectively in the new situation. Constitutional limitations may be widely abandoned in respect to foreign affairs and in some instances in respect to domestic affairs. Dictatorships may be established and they may become permanent (27, 46). Such was the situation in which the Roman Empire succeeded the Republic, in which militant feudal monarchies developed after Charlemagne, in which divine right monarchies arose in the fifteenth century, and in which modern dictatorships have arisen in the twentieth century in Europe and Asia. Avoidance of such revolutionary changes and continued maintenance of democratic and constitutional principles is one object of the discipline under consideration. The reconciliation of democratic and constitutional controls with the exigencies of international politics through better constitutional understandings, and a more skillful civil service, a more educated public, and more tolerant and informed parties and pressure groups becomes a major problem of international relations (15, 44, 45).

c. A solution of these opposed tendencies in the conduct of foreign relations with the advance of civilization, on the one hand toward militant autocracy and on the other toward constitutional democracy, on the one hand toward elimination of a special discipline concerning the conduct of foreign relations and on the other towards its exaggeration, is not likely to be found except through the continued maintenance of more stable international conditions. Such was the conclusion of Elihu Root in commenting on De Tocqueville's statement that democracies could not successfully conduct foreign affairs (13, 35, 49). If wars recur with increasing frequency and destructiveness, democracy can be expected to disappear in the conduct, not only of international, but also of domestic affairs. All states will become autocratically governed, *garrison states,* until perhaps one has conquered all the rest (26). But even then, the overcentralization, characteristic of empires composed of peoples of very diverse culture, will be unlikely to leave much opportunity for constitutional democracy. More effective international organization, reducing the danger of war and increasing the role of international law, of world public opinion, and of conference, debate, and negotiation may increase stability and contribute to the vitality of democracy. The survival of democracy may therefore depend upon progress in the disciplines of international organization and international law, as well as upon the discipline here under consideration (46, 49).

d. Even if stable conditions were established under the United Nations or other international organization, the discipline here under consideration would continue to be important. The problem of adjusting procedures of democratic decision-making at the international level with those at the national level is, as already noted, inherently difficult though it does not differ in kind from that faced by confederations and federations, or, in fact, by all states that recognize the value of local self-government. The solution of the problem tends to develop confederations into federations, that is, to develop a functional division between the powers of the constituent units and those of the union. Thoroughgoing democratic control by each state of its delegation in an international assembly is incompatible with the possession by these delegations of sufficient discretion to make the international assembly capable of action. International bodies therefore find that they cannot function effectively in a shrinking world unless they have legislative powers resting, not on national public opinions, but on a world public opinion. In striving for efficiency, before a powerful world opinion exists, the autonomy of national democracies may be unduly restricted, the system may become overcentralized, and countermovements emphasizing *domestic jurisdiction* and *national sovereignty,* or even rejecting international organization altogether may arise. Excessive *internationalism* is likely to induce movements of excessive *nationalism*.

Effective international organization may be the alternative to increasing instability in a world of sovereign, autocratically organized states in perpetual cold or hot war with one another, but a world of varied cultures, economies, and polities is likely to remain decentralized and to function by co-ordinating national policies rather than by organizing a system of world legislation, administration, adjudication, and enforcement. The discipline here under consideration will continue necessary to co-ordinate the national institutions and policies of each state with international institutions and policies and to maintain a balance between nationalism and internationalism.

CRITICISM

It has been pointed out that officials responsible for conducting foreign relations face four types of criticism under conditions of constitutionalism and democracy: (*a*) that they deceive the public and pursue unpopular foreign policies, (*b*) that they neglect national interests in order to win popular favor and elections, (*c*) that they use international institutions only to forward national policies, thus weakening the international institutions, and (*d*) that they neglect national policy under the influence of international law and organization (4).

These criticisms illustrate the internal contradictions in the discipline here considered under world conditons of power politics. It is not possible to win a war with an army whose strategy and tactics are controlled by the votes of the soldiers, nor is it possible to succeed in a negotiation conducted by diplomats whose instructions are made public and unchangeable by parliamentary vote. War and diplomacy, the instruments of foreign policy in a power political world, are inherently autocratic institutions. The authority that conducts foreign policy must be able to control these instruments in action with wide discretion in the light of changing conditions or they cannot function effectively (1, 2, 20, 28, 29, 32, 40, 50).

When the representative authority of a state is constitutionally responsible to domestic public opinion and legislative enactment, it cannot formulate policies and commit the nation to them on its own initiative. Constitutionalism implies that government should not decide until the public has been convinced. The representative authority, however, will court disaster, if it follows the opinion of legislative bodies and popular leaders. They are usually uninformed on foreign affairs and more interested in domestic matters. Decisions which ignore the actual situation of the world cannot be wise. The representative authority can, therefore, only succeed under democratic conditions if the public is educated, tolerant, and appreciative of the inevitable dilemma in the situation, and is able to delay decisions until the public and the necessary constitutional agencies have been persuaded. If emergencies arise frequently, so exigent that this is not possible, democratic constitutionalism will be abandoned or the state will suffer disaster (11, 12).

The maintenance of stable international relations is therefore vital for democracy, and the issue concerning the relation between national policy and international organization is fundamental to this end. Under present conditions care in steering between the Scylla of rigid national policies and the Charybdis of unacceptable international policies is the essence of a satisfactory solution. Instruction to national representatives should include the essential but only the essential limitations which national opinion requires, and this implies enough prior consultation to maintain bipartisanship and congressional support, but no more. Resolutions passed by international organizations in accord with their constitutional procedures should be respected. National organs should weigh possible injury which might result to national interests from implementing such resolutions, against the certain injury to national interest in the weakening of international organization if such resolutions are ignored.

REFERENCES

The books listed at the end of Chapters 13, 14, and 15 usually touch on the control of foreign relations. Those listed here give especial attention to the subject.

1. ALSOP, Joseph, and KINTNER, Robert, *American White Paper, The Story of American Diplomacy and the Second World War* (New York, Simon and Schuster, 1940).
2. BERDAHL, Clarence A., *War Powers of the Executive in the United States,* University of Illinois Studies in the Social Sciences, No. IX (1920).
3. Brookings Institution, *Governmental Mechanism for the Conduct of United States Foreign Relations* (Washington, 1949).
4. BRYCE, James, *Modern Democracies* (New York, Macmillan, 1921), Vol. 2, pp. 367 ff.
5. CHAMBERLAIN, Lawrence H., and SNYDER, Richard C., eds., *American Foreign Policy* (New York, Rinehart, 1948).
6. CHEEVER, Daniel S., and HAVILAND, H. Field, *American Foreign Policy and the Separation of Powers* (Cambridge, Harvard University Press, 1952).
7. COLEGROVE, Kenneth, *The American Senate and World Peace* (New York, Vanguard, 1944).
8. CORWIN, Edward S., *The President's Control of Foreign Relations* (Princeton, Princeton University Press, 1917).
9. ———, *The Constitution and World Organization* (Princeton, Princeton University Press, 1944).
10. CRANDALL, Samuel B., *Treaties, Their Making and Enforcement* (Washington, Byrne, 1916).

11. DAHL, Robert A., *Congress and Foreign Policy* (New York, Harcourt, 1950).
12. DANGERFIELD, Royden, *In Defense of the Senate* (Norman, University of Oklahoma Press, 1933).
13. DE TOCQUEVILLE, Alexis, *Democracy in America*, Vol. 1 (New York, 1862), pp. 254 ff.
14. DENNISON, Eleanor, *The Senate Foreign Relations Committee* (Stanford, Stanford University Press, 1942).
15. ELLIOTT, William Yandell, and others, *United States Foreign Policy, Its Organization and Control* (New York, Columbia University Press, 1952).
16. FLEMMING, Denna F., *The Treaty Veto of the American Senate* (New York, Putnam, 1930).
17. ———, *The United States and the League of Nations, 1918-1920* (New York, Putnam, 1932).
18. ———, *The United States and World Organization, 1920-1933* (New York, Columbia University Press, 1932).
19. FLOURNOY, Francis R., *Parliament and War* (London, King, 1927).
20. FRIEDRICH, Carl J., *Foreign Policy in the Making* (New York, Norton, 1938).
21. HAMILTON, Alexander, MADISON, James, and JAY, John, *The Federalist*, Nos. 3, 4, 5, 24, 25, 42, 64, 74, 75.
22. HEATLEY, D. P., *Diplomacy and the Study of International Relations* (Oxford, Clarendon Press, 1919).
23. HISS, Donald, *United States Participation in the United Nations* (New York, Commission to Study the Organization of Peace, 1947).
24. HULL, Cordell, *Memoirs*, 2 vols. (New York, Macmillan, 1948), Vol. 1, pp. 176 ff., 211 ff.
25. HURST, Sir Cecil J. B., and others, *Great Britain and the Dominions* (Chicago, University of Chicago Press, 1928).
26. LASSWELL, Harold D., *National Security and Individual Freedom* (New York, McGraw-Hill, 1950).
27. ———, *The World Revolution of Our Time, A Framework for Basic Policy Research* (Stanford, Stanford University Press, 1951).
28. LIPPMANN, Walter, *United States Foreign Policy, Shield of the Republic* (Boston, Little, Brown, 1943).
29. McCAMY, James, *The Administration of American Foreign Policy* (New York, Knopf, 1950).
30. McCLURE, Wallace, *International Executive Agreements* (New York, Columbia University Press, 1941).
31. MAURICE, Major General Sir Frederick, *Governments and War* (London, Heinemann, 1926).
32. OMOND, Lieutenant Colonial J. S., *Parliament and the Army, 1642-1904* (Cambridge, Cambridge University Press, 1933).
33. PLISCHKE, Elmer, *Conduct of American Diplomacy* (New York, Van Nostrand, 1950).
34. POOLE, Dewitt C., *The Conduct of Foreign Relations Under Modern Democratic Conditions* (New Haven, Yale University Press, 1924).
35. ROOT, Elihu, "The Effect of Democracy on International Law," *Proceedings, American Society of International Law* (1917); p. 7 ff.
36. ———, *Military and Colonial Policy of the United States* (Cambridge, Harvard University Press, 1916).

37. SCHUMAN, Frederick L., *War and Diplomacy in the French Republic* (New York, McGraw-Hill, 1931).

38. SMITH, Louis, *American Democracy and Military Power* (Chicago, University of Chicago Press, 1951).

39. STUART, Graham H., *The Department of State* (New York, Macmillan, 1949).

40. SUTHERLAND, George, *Constitutional Power and World Affairs* (New York, Columbia University Press, 1919).

41. TAKEUCHI, Tatsuji, *War and Diplomacy in the Japanese Empire* (Garden City, Doubleday, Doran, 1935).

42. U. S. Department of State, *Peace and War, United States Foreign Policy, 1931-1941* (Washington, Government Printing Office, 1943), p. 3.

43. WILCOX, Francis O., *The Ratification of International Conventions* (London, Allen and Unwin, 1935).

44. WRIGHT, Quincy, *Control of American Foreign Relations* (New York, Macmillan, 1922).

45. ———, "Domestic Control of Foreign Relations," in *Survey of American Foreign Relations* (New York, Council on Foreign Relations, 1928), pp. 83 ff.

46. ———, *A Study of War* (Chicago, University of Chicago Press, 1942), pp. 262 ff., 819 ff.

47. ———, "The United States and International Agreements," *American Journal of International Law,* Vol. 38 (1944), pp. 341 ff.

48. ———, "Constitutional Procedures in the United States for Carrying Out Obligations for Military Sanctions," *American Journal of International Law,* Vol. 38 (1944), pp. 678 ff.

49. ———, "Constitutionalism and World Politics," *University of Illinois Bulletin,* Vol. 49 (1951), No. 32 reprinted in *Problems of Stability and Progress in International Organization* (Berkeley, University of California Press, 1954).

50. ———, "Congress and the Treaty Making Power," *Proceedings, American Society of International Law* (1952), pp. 43 ff.

Colonial Government

DEFINITION

COLONIAL government is the art of organizing, administering, and developing *backward* peoples and areas, geographically separated from the governing state. As a discipline, it includes the practical, historic, philosophic, and scientific studies contributing to this art.

The art is a progressive one. It is assumed that backward peoples like adolescent individuals will eventually graduate from that condition into full maturity (12). Consequently, the art of dealing with them involves not only control or guidance, in a broad sense, government, but also development of the area and people so that they will cease to be in the unequal situation of backwardness (50).

The art of colonial government involves action with respect both to the people and the area. The people must be organized, controlled, guided, educated, and advanced to bring them to a condition of responsibility and, as was said in the League of Nations Covenant, "capacity to stand by themselves under the strenuous conditions of the modern world" (Art. 22), and in the United Nations Charter capacity for "self determination" (Art. 55), for "self government" (Arts. 73, 76), or for "independence" (Art. 76). The area must be developed economically and its resources converted to use. The weight to be given to these two aspects of the art has been highly controversial. If attention is directed exclusively to the welfare and development of the people, the area may long lie fallow, but if attention is devoted exclusively to the area, the people are likely to be exploited, subjected to forced labor if not slavery, or even exterminated, to make way for immigrants or contract labor.

The problem is somewhat arbitrarily limited by inclusion in the definition only of areas geographically separated from the governing state.
The art of dealing with indigenous peoples and distinctive national
minorities in the homeland, like the Indians in the United States, the
numerous tribes in Siberia, and the Slavic nationalities in the Hapsburg
Empire is, in many respects, similar. But where the political destiny of
the area is linked by geographical conditions with that of the governing
state, the international interest in the economic and military development
of the area, in its trade and strategic relations, and in the welfare and
political development of its people has usually been less, and there has
been a greater disposition to recognize the problem as one of domestic
government (25, 47).

The theory of territorial sovereignty under international law has, it is
true, been applied to geographically separated colonies, and in principle,
their government is also within the domestic jurisdiction of the governing
state, yet in practice, many geographically separated, non-self-governing
areas actually have a distinct international status such as protectorate,
vassal, mandate, or trusteeship, or the governing state has accepted specific treaty obligations in respect to them (22, 23). Under the Berlin Act
of 1885, for example, the parties accepted certain principles in respect to
their colonies in the conventional basin of the Congo and under Article 23
of the League of Nations Covenant, the members of the League accepted certain vague limitations upon their action in the interest of the
welfare of the native inhabitants of their colonies. Under Chapter XI of
the United Nations Charter all members accept extensive obligations,
including the obligation to report annually to the United Nations, in
respect to all their territories "whose peoples have not yet attained a full
measure of self-government." While this does not explicitly confine the
obligation to geographically separated territories, in practice it has been
so interpreted.

The treatment of aliens; of backward peoples; of racial, religious, and
linguistic minorities; and of other categories of peoples liable to discriminatory treatment or persecution in the home territory of a state has also
been a subject of international interest. The diplomatic protection of nationals abroad and humanitarian intervention under customary international law (40), the protection of minorities on the basis of treaties supervised by the League of Nations (25), and the promotion of respect for
human rights of all persons, as required by provisions of the United
Nations Charter (21), have given some effect to that interest. These activities, however, belong to the disciplines of international organization
and international law rather than to that of colonial government. They
are not guided by the assumptions of geographical separation, temporary
backwardness, and inferiority of status which are the essence of the discipline of colonial government.

The discipline of colonial government might, it is true, be treated as one aspect of a discipline of imperial government, which may be defined as the art by which a politically organized people subjects and governs other peoples whom it considers politically inferior because of geographical, cultural, ideological, economic, military, or other difference. The art of empire in this sense would be concerned with the acquisition and government, not only of colonies, but also of unincorporated territories, protectorates, trusteeships, satellites, spheres of influence and interest, national minorities, aboriginal tribes, and ideological dissidents (6, 15, 26, 27), whether originating in migration from the metropole as the British colonies in America, Australia, and New Zealand; in conquest by the metropole as the Spanish colonies in Mexico and Peru and the British Empire in India; in political absorption by the metropole as in the Hapsburg empire and the Soviet satellites (19); in peripheral growth combining all as in the ancient Roman expansion in the Mediterranean basin (3, 38), the English expansion over the British Isles, the Russian expansion in Asia (45), and the American expansion in the west (48); or in the acquisition of predominant influence by economic, legal, and political means as by the powers in their spheres in China during the nineteenth century (51). Such a discipline of imperial government would include the disciplines of national government, of colonial government, of international organization, of international law, and of international politics so interpreted as to serve the cause of imperial expansion and rule. The concepts that minorities, colonies, and protectorates are permanently inferior, that international law and international organization recognize the inferiority of some peoples (8, 23), and that international politics and geography can serve programs of imperial expansion (13, 14, 41, 42) have been assumed by certain writers. The modern trend in these disciplines, however, has been to accept the theses of equality and democracy which have been increasingly approved in modern civilization.

ASSUMPTIONS

The assumptions underlying the discipline of colonial government are: (1) there are backward peoples at present incapable of self-government or of developing the areas they inhabit, (2) this is a temporary condition and in course of time all *backward* peoples will achieve full status either of independence or of full incorporation in the metropole and will enjoy the normal degree of self-government, (3) in the interval, these peoples must be governed and developed by an outside authority which, for this purpose, has an acknowledged position of superiority, and (4) the governing authority should give primary consideration to the social, economic, and political interests of the inhabitants of the area and to the interest of the world community in international peace and prosperity, and only secondary consideration to its own interests (50).

1. Colonial government rests upon the assumption of the inequality of human groups. In this it resembles empire and aristocracy rather than international organization and democracy. This assumption is not merely the recognition of cultural and institutional differences inherent in the division of the world into nations and states, but recognition of differences which make some groups at the moment generally inferior to others. The criteria for measuring this inferiority are not, however, clearly established.

Legal inferiority is one aspect. It is clear that there are degrees of legal sovereignty and subordination. Some geographically distinct groups do not enjoy full sovereignty under international law but have the inferior status of a colony, unincorporated territory, protectorate, vassal, mandate, or trusteeship (22, 50). It is assumed, however, that this legal inferiority exists because of other conditions that require it. The inferior legal status is a consequence, not a cause of *inferiority*. The criteria of inferiority must, therefore, be sought elsewhere.

Economic backwardness is also of importance. Some areas are undoubtedly exploited for economic purposes much more efficiently than others, but the difference in legal status does not depend entirely on these differences. Jamaica, a colony, is probably more efficiently developed than the independent state of Haiti. While non-self-governing areas may in general lag behind independent states in economic development, this is by no means universally true. The concept of *underdeveloped areas* is not identical with that of *non-self-governing territories* (16).

Political backwardness is of major importance in determining inferior legal status, but is not a criterion of easy or precise application (32). Although doubtless, in principle, capacity to maintain self-government should be the criterion to distinguish independence from subordination, such capacity is difficult to determine and is not, in fact, always considered. It is probable that certain Caribbean Republics have no more capacity to maintain justice and stability internally and independence externally than do such protectorates as Tunisia and Morocco. Many independent states lack an habitual respect for human rights and institutions of self-government, notably those in the Soviet orbit.

The race and culture of the inhabitants of an area, although often deemed to indicate inferiority requiring colonial government, fail to provide clear criteria. The black, red, yellow, and white races each dominate in some independent states, and anthropologists have not been able to detect a general inferiority or superiority of any race. Some cultures are less competent in the technological control of nature than others. All have made claims of moral superiority and have accused others of moral inferiority. The cultural differences among independent states are very great. Doubtless the modern colonial period began with the assumption by Europeans of a general racial superiority of the white man, and a general cultural and technological superiority of European nations. Peoples were rated as *backward* in proportion as they differed in race, culture, and technology from the conquering nations of Europe. These assumptions find little support among modern anthropologists. In a practical sense, however, a culture that is so technologically backward that it cannot exploit its territory or maintain its people in the modern world of production, trade, and war will doubtless have difficulty in achieving and maintaining independent legal status (26, 50). Furthermore, a culture that hampers realization of certain of the psychic and social needs of all human beings will have difficulty in surviving when faced by the competition of cultures better adapted to human nature.

Power, in all its aspects—technological, psychological, political, and economic—has been an important criterion of backwardness. Groups that had power to gain independence ceased being *backward*. Those that lacked that power continued as colonies or protectorates, though even in this respect there have been many exceptions. Such colonies and protectorates as Algeria, Morocco, and Tunis are probably more powerful than such independent states as Liberia and Costa Rica. Geographic position and habitual political relations moderate the influence of other aspects of power.

The policy of states in recognizing new states and emancipating dependencies, and the policy of international organizations in admitting states to membership and in emancipating mandates and trusteeship territories disclose some criteria for independence. These criteria vary considerably, but in general include (*a*) clearly established boundaries and reasonable prospect of maintaining them, (*b*) an administration with *de facto* capacity to govern the area, (*c*) laws and institutions capable of giving reasonable protection to aliens and minorities, and of maintaining reasonable standards of justice among all inhabitants, and (*d*) a public opinion, and institutions for manifesting it, which give reasonable indication of a desire for independence and reasonable assurance of the permanence of the two preceding conditions (32, 44).

These criteria for independence ignore racial, cultural, and economic factors, and are primarily concerned with political power, domestic law, public opinion, and administrative capacity. These criteria are all relative and depend in part on the external surroundings and the world situation. A group may have capacity to maintain frontiers and govern internally if the surrounding area is tranquil, or if world conditions favor stability and collective security, whereas a similar group in a disturbed area or under general conditions of international instability and unmitigated power politics would not have that capacity. Relative and vague as these criteria are, we may assume that the clear absence of any one marks the group as *backward* in the sense that its independence should not yet be recognized.

It can therefore be said that a country is *backward* and requires some form of tutelage or colonial government when available evidence indicates that under the existing conditions of its domestic order, of its neighborhood, and of the world, its people either lack the desire for independence or are incapable of maintaining law, order, and justice within the boundaries they claim. While application of these criteria would probably elevate the legal status of some groups which are not now self-governing, they might reduce the status of some states now recognized as independent (9).

2. While colonial government rests on the assumption of inequality, in modern times, this assumption has been qualified by the further assumption that this inequality is temporary.

Artistotle assumed that some men are born to be slaves and others free. Modern thought repudiates this theory and accepts the legal equality of man as an assumption of domestic government. While men vary in capacity, all resent inferiority of status and all, except the immature, the insane, and the criminal, are moderately able to discharge the responsibilities of freedom. Consequently the assumption of legal equality has been found to be more likely to produce a stable society than any system of inequality, whether based on physical or mental capacities; on hereditary position, wealth, occupation; or on race, religion, sex, or other condition. This pragmatic argument for equality has often been buttressed by religious or philosophical theories of the dignity of man and the ends of society, which assert that human personality is a value in itself and should be treated as an end and not as a means, and that the state is for man and not man for the state. Whatever the theory, most of the states of the world have formally accepted the principle of equality in ratifying the United Nations Charter (21).

Similar arguments have been applied to human groups. Empires have rested on the theory that some races, cultures, or areas are designed by nature to be dependent upon a superior, or governing group whether that group is defined as a race, a culture, a nation, or a state. This theory expressed in modern times by Hitler (14) is not new. Rome acted on this assumption and did not make equal treaties with the peoples it conquered, but at first accorded them a position in the empire inferior to that of the Roman citizen. Eventually, however, Rome abandoned this theory and Roman citizenship was extended to all (3, 38). The Greek city-states formed colonies by migration rather than by conquest and acted on the different theory that colonies were potentially equal to the mother country and when firmly established would naturally become independent (28).

Modern states, since the period of discoveries in the fifteenth and sixteenth centuries, have acquired dependencies by both conquest and colonization. They originally accorded inferior status to both types of dependency but the trend has been either to grant independence or to accord equal status within the state. The British, after loss of the American colonies by war, and after the Durham Report on the Canadian insurrection of 1838, adopted the theory of self-government, later called *dominion status* for dependencies formed by colonization from Europe. After World War I the dominions were recognized as having all the attributes of independent statehood although they continued members of the British Commonwealth of Nations (17). After World War II, dominion status was extended to dependencies formed by conquest in Asia and Africa and the adjective *British* was eliminated from the *Commonwealth of Nations.* The French adhered to the different policy of anticipating eventual assimilation of all colonies in metropolitan France, a result in a measure achieved in regard to the *old colonies* formed by migration, in the West Indies, Reunion, and Algeria. But more recently, self-determination has been contemplated for the African and Asiatic colonies and protectorates (33). Most modern colonial countries have followed the policy of independence in regard to some dependencies and assimilation in regard to others (35). Whichever course is followed, however, the colonial status is regarded as temporary. Dependencies are treated as wards or children that will eventually achieve equal status, not as imbeciles, slaves, or criminals that will permanently be subjected to special controls and indignities. Colonial government has, therefore, been compared to the treatment of adolescents or to the tutelage of infants (12), the latter term, used in the mandates article in the League of Nations Covenant, was applied, especially by French writers, in the interpretation of the status of mandated peoples (50).

The disintegration of colonial empires has proceeded at accelerating pace. The United States won independence in the late eighteenth century, the Latin American colonies of Spain and Portugal became independent in the early nineteenth century, the movement of British colonies toward dominion status and independence began in the mid-nineteenth century, and the United States withdrew from Cuba and promised independence to the Philippines in the early twentieth century. The two world wars resulted in mandate or trusteeship status looking toward independence for Turkish, German, and Italian dependencies. Denmark recognized the independence of Iceland, the United States that of the Philippines, and the British, Dutch, French, and Japanese that of their major dependencies in Asia. Without considering the recent extension of the Soviet dominance in satellite states, it can be said that in 1950 less than 10 per cent of the world's population remained in a condition of dependency, while in the mid-nineteenth century half of the world's population were in that condition and in the mid-eighteenth century two-thirds.

3. The assumption of superiority of the administering authority during

the period of colonial government is no less fundamental to the discipline under consideration than is the assumption that the period of tutelage is limited. Consequently, the qualifications of the administering authority are important. The mandates articles of the League Covenant required that the mandatory be competent by reason of its experience or its geographical position. Perhaps these two bases of qualification are not equally relevant, and it cannot be said that in practice any qualifications have been important in determining what states shall administer dependencies even mandates and trusteeships, except the power to acquire and hold them and the interest in, and capacity for, overseas exploration, colonization, and conquest.

States have in fact become colonial powers by the accidents of discovery, colonization, and war (26, 28). Spain and Portugal initiated the modern movement followed by England, France, and the Netherlands, which poached on the preserves of their predecessors. Denmark, Norway, and Sweden acquired small colonial claims which have been subsequently abandoned with the exception of Denmark's possession of Greenland and Norway's of Spitzbergen. Belgium, Germany, Italy, the United States, and Japan acquired important dependencies in the late nineteenth and early twentieth centuries. One common characteristic of these countries is their easy access to the sea, their extensive maritime activities, and their sea power during the period of colonial acquisition. Land-bound powers like the Hapsburg, Ottoman, Manchu, and Romanoff empires expanded from their land frontiers. They were not colonial powers in the sense here used, but the formation and later disintegration of their empires followed a similar course. The Soviet Union has sought to re-establish and even to expand the Romanoff empire in a new form.

The colonial powers have also had proficiency in science and technology, thus enjoying advantages over the colonial peoples whom they have governed, in war, transportation, and communication, and in the agricultural and industrial utilization of resources. The tendency of the dependent peoples to acquire these proficiencies as well as the ideas of nationality and independence, through contact with, and education by, the colonial power has been an important factor in the break up of empires.

The modern colonial powers were, in the main, Christian. Missionary activity was often closely related to colonial activity, and the colonial powers characteristically credited themselves with superior moral capacity as a justification for their colonial activity. This claim was usually not accepted by the colonial peoples as illustrated by the Rivera frescoes in the Cortez palace at Quernavaca, Mexico. It exhibits at one end the auto de fe's of the Spanish inquisition and at the other the Aztec sacrifices of living victims, suggesting that there was little to choose in the morals of conquerors and conquered at the time of Cortez. However, the western concepts of individuality and nationality brought by missionaries tended to develop resistance to imperial domination among colonial peoples.

The qualifications requisite for assuming the responsibilities of colonial government, like the qualifications requisite for emancipation from dependency, were hardly discussed objectively, until the advent of the mandates system. Historically both rested on the power, in the one case, to hold colonies, and, in the other, to gain independence.

4. Colonial governments have always assumed that in addition to securing their own commercial, strategic, and other interests they should give consideration to the welfare and development of the inhabitants of the area; and to the interests of third states and of the world community in equality of missionary and commercial opportunity, in utilization of the resources of the area, in international peace and security, and in the eventual equal participation of the colonial people in international relations. The degree of weight to be attached to those considerations has, however, varied greatly both in theory and practice (35, 50). In the early history of colonial practice during the modern period, the metropole governed almost entirely in its own interest, exploiting the natives and excluding the citizens of other states. The occasional recognition of *the white man's burden* to assume humanitarian and international responsibilities in his colonial activity was considered hypocritical by both colonial peoples and nations without colonies. In the nineteenth century, these responsibilities were given greater effect as manifested by such international agreements as the Berlin Act of 1885, and the recognition of dominion self-government in British imperial conferences. The United Nations Charter, going beyond the League of Nations Covenant, states that "the interests of the inhabitants" of all non-self-governing territories "are paramount," and requires consideration for their culture, their economic and social advancement, and their political aspirations including self-government. Due attention must also be given to the general interests of the world community in international peace and security, in the productiveness of the colonies and in information about them. While the Open Door to trade and equality in the treatment of aliens is not required by the Charter for all non-self-governing territories, these principles are to be applied in the trusteeship territories, as they were in most of the mandated territories during the period of the League of Nations.

If the limitations stated in the Charter were given full effect, little special advantage would remain for the governing state. In respect to trusteeship territories, as was true of mandated territories, the principle was accepted that the administering state should gain no material advantage, whether in finance, trade, or strategy, from its administration. An exception is made in the Charter in respect to "strategic area" trusteeships, provided for in Article 82, and in practice the governing state can doubtless gain advantages through its capacity to appoint its nationals to administrative posts, to place contracts for public works with national firms, and to gain commercial, strategic, and other advantages through superior information and administrative control. In principle, however, the government of colonies has approached the condition of the Roman Law Mandate or the Common Law Trusteeship, that is, an uncompensated activity for the benefit of someone else. The interests of the people in the area and of the world community are to be given primary consideration (50).

ANALYSIS

The analysis of colonial government as an art based on the assumptions stated in the preceding section was hardly attempted prior to the twentieth century. Earlier writings on the subject had usually been of an historical character, relating the colonial experience of particular colonial powers or the general changes in colonial objectives and methods as history proceeded. The subject was sometimes treated as the historical movement by which Western Europe as a whole had imposed itself on the outer world, including not only the establishment and exploitation of actual colonies or dependencies, but also the activities of European traders, missioners, travelers, soldiers, and diplomats in distributing European ideas and techniques and in creating for themselves special advantages even in formally independent countries like China and Japan. This was accomplished through the conclusion of one-sided treaties giving the European states extraterritorial jurisdiction; commercial privileges; naval and commercial bases; missionary, consular, and diplomatic establishments; and spheres of interest, and through the practice of diplomatic protection of nationals and of intervention with military force for protective or intimidating purposes. In this process of the expansion of Europe, the rivalries among the European powers themselves, so fruitful of wars in the seventeenth and eighteenth centuries, played an important part. Each was stimulated to establish its sovereignty or influence in an area of strategic or economic importance before a rival did so. The spirit of private enrichment, of adventure, and of zeal for the expansion of Christianity, European civilization, or national empire also played parts in the drama, enlivened by the exploits of such picturesque personalities as Cortez, Raleigh, Gordon, and Cecil Rhodes.

Philosophies of colonialism comparing the theories of different colonial powers were also written (18). The British tendency to favor indirect government and the development of indigenous institutions and customs so far as compatible with commercial development has been contrasted with the French tendency to emphasize their *mission civilatrice*, to educate the colonial elite, and through them, in time, the whole colonial population with the view of eventual assimilation of the colony in France (33).

When the United States acquired overseas possessions as a result of the Spanish-American War, interest was aroused in the experience of older colonial powers, and Paul Reinsch produced volumes on colonial government (30) and colonial administration (31). He tried to survey past practices systematically with a view to assisting American administrators in the Philippines and Puerto Rico.

The work of the Permanent Mandates Commission gave an impulse to similar studies in many countries. The Commission needed objective standards going beyond those stated in the texts of Article 22 and of the mandates to guide them in criticizing the activity of the British, French, Belgian, Japanese, and Dominion mandatories, influenced by a variety of colonial traditions (50). The studies of colonial problems by the International Labor Organization and by such unofficial agencies as the Royal Institute of International Affairs and the Institute of Pacific Relations also stimulated the development of a systematic and practical discipline (35, 51).

The status in international law of different dependent areas has also been analyzed under the stimulus of the new term *mandate*. Such terms as *dependency* and *colony* tended to give way to such terms as *protectorate* and *vassal state*, which in turn had in some cases been superseded by such terms as *dominion, unincorporated territory, mandated territory, trusteeship territory*. These terms, whose precise analysis cannot be undertaken here, gave increasing indication of the theoretically temporary character of the *colonial* relationship, of the increasing weight to be accorded the interests of the inhabitants of the area, and of the increasing responsibility of the governing authority to the world community. The terms *tutelage, trust,* and *mandate,* which appear in the League Covenant, respectively emphasize these three aspects of modern colonial government.

The analysis of the discipline of colonial government utilizes historical materials and compares reports of colonial powers. It also uses anthropological data about the governed people, the principles of public administration, of economic geography, political economy, and of world politics. It has emphasized the importance of close study of each particular region, its ethnography, demography, geography, resources, economy, strategic position, and political history, and the danger of adhering to any principles without adapting them to the special conditions of the region (10, 16, 24, 35).

In such analyses, one source of inequality may be emphasized above another by particular specialists. Thus, the anthropologist and ethnologist tends to emphasize the differences between the culture and values of the backward people and the governors, the aspects in which the former can or cannot be adapted to *civilization,* and the methods by which adaptation or supersession can be accomplished with a minimum of disturbance or violence. Anthropologists, however, in making such suggestions, tend to characterize cultures as different but not as superior or inferior. Missionaries and educators may share the interests of anthropologists in culture and values, but are likely unconsciously to accept the superiority of their own and to be uninformed concerning native values. They, therefore, seek to inculcate novel ideas by education and evangelism, often resulting in strange ambivalences, repressions, and periodic outbursts, especially in the second generation, more aware than their parents had been of the conflict between the traditional and the imported beliefs and values.

The economists and economic geographers tend to emphasize the inferiority in the technologies and in the efficiencies of land and resource utilization by the natives. In recommending improvements in transportation, agriculture, and mining, and in initiating trade, wage labor, new systems of land tenure and taxes, they may ride roughshod over indigenous cultures, give the natives revolutionary ideas of economic progress, and introduce forced labor, contract labor, and epidemic diseases. Violence, suppression, and depopulation may result. In colonial areas of relatively advanced agriculture and dense population, economic development is likely to introduce trade and a money economy superseding subsistence farming by cash crop agriculture; to introduce sanitary and health measures, decreasing the death rate; to disseminate ideas of nationalism and acquisitiveness; and to develop a vague comprehension by the natives of the greater freedom and wealth of the governors. A population rising more rapidly than the food supply, and the supersession of communal and customary values by European political and economic values often creates problems without any easy means of solution (16).

The political and military administrators in colonial areas tend to emphasize the strategic importance of the area and its relation to the condition of international politics. The development of naval bases and airports, the exploitation of strategic materials, and the training of natives for military purposes may augment the unrest consequent upon the activities of traders, missionaries, and technicians, and may eventually create among the natives the motives and the means for successful revolt. The involvement of the colony in international war may result in a change of hands or in extermination of the native population.

The public administrators and the lawyers may ignore native practices and superimpose a foreign system of administration and law which the natives do not understand, or they may interpret native customs and institutions in terms of legal and administrative relations familiar to themselves. Ideas of status, tenure, family, property, contract, and government may be applied which distort the natives' customs and institutions and lead to conflict. The influence of anthropological studies upon colonial law has, however, tended to develop among lawyers and administrators a more realistic comprehension of native customs and values, to encourage them to conform their own preconceptions of administration and judicial action to the native institutions, and to utilize in greater degree the existing system of authority and law and the native personnel to administer it (7, 35, 46).

Accepting the theory that colonial dependency is a temporary situation, the modern colonial or *technical aid* administrator, sophisticated in anthropology, administration, and technology, tends to supersede the naive traders, missionaries, educators, soldiers, and lawyers in influence, and his art tends to make itself obsolete by its very success. By advising administrators how most rapidly to educate the colonial peoples, to develop the area economically, and to advance the society to a condition ripe for emancipation from its dependent status the discipline of colonial government hastens the situation when there will be no *backward* areas and hence no need for a discipline about them. The situation differs from that of the education of adolescent individuals because there will always be a new crop of children when one has reached maturity. Similarly, past civilizations which were less than universal could expect always to have barbarians on the periphery, and consequently might expect the process of colonial government to go on indefinitely. Since the modern age of discoveries, however, the world has tended to develop a single civilization by contact and mutual accommodation of the civilizations which existed in Europe, the Middle East, China, India, and America, and to diffuse this developing world civilization among less developed peoples through the process of colonial government, trusteeship, and technical aid. Since the world is now all known, this process is affecting all its parts, and colonial government will, in time, come to an end unless, indeed, a new civilization arises by which the older civilization is regarded as barbarian and in need of colonial government. This doubtless is the theory of communism which regards itself as a superior civilization destined to subject the capitalist world to colonial and satellite government as a preparation for communism. The West may similarly regard the communist areas and may tend to treat them as inferior and in need of re-education. Thus the rise of communism may modify the prospects for a termination of the art of colonial government envisaged in the pronouncements of colonial powers in the early twentieth century, and in the relevant provisions of the League of Nations Covenant and the United Nations Charter.

Attention cannot be given here to the art of communist infiltration, revolution, education, and control beyond noting that it is analogous to the art of colonial government, looked at from the communist point of view (19). From the Western point of view which accepts self-government, human rights, economic development, and establishment of an equal position for all peoples in the community of nations, the problem of a body of colonial administrators properly educated and increasingly recruited from the governed population itself has been a matter of major importance. By stressing knowledge of the area governed above knowledge of the imperial power, by establishing schools for administrators in the area, and by employing in both civil and military administration adequately educated persons of the locality, the colonial government hastens conditions for self-determination and the end of its own functioning. The process can be observed in the British administration of India, the American administration of the Philippines, and the Dutch administration of Indonesia in the generation before the emancipation of these areas.

Even if a colonial government does not consciously adopt these policies, its activities will inevitably educate the natives in its superior techniques of arms, agriculture, transportation, and industry. Its development of the area will contribute to the natives' wealth and to their need to employ these techniques, and its theories will indoctrinate them with nationalism and the desire for independence. Consequently, apart from the assumptions of the discipline, colonial activity tends to create conditions favorable to self-determination in a colony. Certain factors, however, tend to slow down this process. Among them are pressures of home interests with trade or investments in the area, of colonial officials and candidates for such jobs, of enterprisors and adventurers who look to colonies for opportunities, and of the rivalry of other states against whom colonial bases or raw materials may be strategically useful or who may threaten to pick up the colony if it is prematurely emancipated. Adjustment of these tendencies on the one hand toward emancipation and on the other toward exploitation is one important aspect of the modern art of colonial government.

One important aspect of the art is the appraisal of the interests of the inhabitants of the colonial area, of the world community, and of the administering authority in order to develop policies which will ignore none of these interests and will keep them in proper balance. Should the interests of the inhabitants be approached socially or individually? A social approach suggests that these interests be appraised by standards of the area rather than of the governing authority. The cultural and social institutions indigenous to the area may be regarded as of value even though they differ greatly from those of the governing authority. They will usually be so regarded by the peoples of the area themselves, yet a policy based on their appraisal may tend to perpetuate a society incapable of developing the area or of accommodating itself to world civilization.

On the other hand, the individual may be regarded as a prime value, and efforts may be made to educate him so he can develop the area economically and participate in institutions preparing the area for self-government and accommodation in the world community. Application of such a standard tends to play havoc with pre-existing customs and value systems of the area.

Compromises between these standards of appraisal are doubtless necessary. The world will not tolerate the preservation of incompetent indigenous cultures as museum pieces even though anthropologists would like to study them, nor will it tolerate the oppressive measures often necessary if individuals are too rapidly torn from their ancient customs and values (16, 24).

The interest of the world community in developing the area economically and in opening its opportunities to trade, undoubtedly militate against respect for the native culture. Transnational communication and trade, and missionary activity tend rapidly to destroy many cultures. Consequently, some restraint upon such communication is doubtless required, but conditions should be developed in which the native community can prepare itself for more contact with the world, a contact which it can, in the long run, hardly avoid.

As early colonial administrators considered too exclusively the interests of the governing power, recent principles of mandate and trusteeship administration may minimize that interest over much. Colonial development is an expensive business and states will not engage in it for nothing. Yet the vast majority of states that have no colonies and view the possession of colonies by a few as an accident of history will not tolerate complete exclusion from the advantages to be gained from the colonial areas. The Open Door, not only for trade but for concessions and even for colonial jobs, and military neutralization of the area, was urged, especially in the mandate system and the Washington treaties of 1922. A careful discrimination between legitimate advantages of the administering state and just demands of other states has occupied much attention in the Permanent Mandates Commission and in the Trusteeship Council.

An important change in regard to the military status of the areas was accepted in the United Nations Charter. The mandated territories were to be neutralized while the trusteeship territories are required to provide facilities for collective action against aggression. Furthermore, the transfer of the major control of these areas from the League Council dominated by the great powers who were mostly mandatories to the General Assembly of the United Nations dominated by noncolonial powers increases the influence of the latter. The proposals made in the General Assembly to fly the United Nations flag along with that of the administering power in the trusteeship territories emphasized this position, as did the effort to increase United Nations control of non-self-governing territories, which are not trusteeships, by broad interpretations of the terms of Chapter XI of the Charter.

CRITICISM

This review indicates that colonial government is not likely to become a rigorous discipline. Its assumptions indicate its pragmatic character designed for a transitional period. Its principles must be flexible and adaptable to highly varied conditions. Its practice is less the application of principles than continual compromise among conflicting pressures and competing values.

Nevertheless, the continual study of colonial problems by relatively impartial international bodies under the League and the United Nations has developed a more systematic comprehension of the nature of the problem, has assisted in easing the transition from dependency to independent statehood of many millions of peoples, and has assisted empires in unburdening themselves of the profit and loss of colonial rule without war or serious loss of prestige.

REFERENCES

1. BOWMAN, Isaiah, *The Pioneer Fringe* (New York, American Geographic Society, 1931).
2. BRYCE, Lord, *The Relations of the Advanced and the Backward Races of Mankind* (Oxford, Clarendon Press, 1902).
3. ———, *The Holy Roman Empire*, 4th ed. (London, Macmillan, 1873).
4. BUELL, Raymond L., *The Native Problem in Africa* (New York, Macmillan, 1928), 2 vols.
5. CLARK, Grover, *A Place in the Sun* (New York, Macmillan, 1936).
6. CROMER, Lord, *Ancient and Modern Imperialism* (London, Murray, 1910).
7. DEKAT ANGELINO, A. D. A., *Colonial Policy* (Chicago, University of Chicago Press, 1931), 2 vols.
8. DICKINSON, Edwin D., *The Equality of States in International Law* (Cambridge, Harvard University Press, 1920).
9. HAAS, Ernst B., "The Reconciliation of Conflicting Colonial Policy Aims; The Attempts to Terminate Colonialism," *International Organization*, Vol. 6 (1952), pp. 521 ff.; Vol. 7 (1953), pp. 1 ff.
10. HAILEY, Lord, *An African Survey* (New York, Royal Institute of International Affairs, 1939).
11. HALL, H. Duncan, *Mandates, Dependencies and Trusteeships* (Washington, Carnegie Endowment for International Peace, 1948).
12. HALL, G. Stanley, *Adolescence* (New York, Appleton, 1904), 2 vols., Ch. 18, "Adolescent Races."
13. HAUSHOFER, Karl, *Wehrgeopolitik* (Berlin, Junker und Dünnhaupt, 1941).
14. HITLER, Adolf, *Mein Kampf* (New York, Reynal and Hitchcock, 1939).
15. HOBSON, J. A., *Imperialism* (London, Constable, 1905).
16. HOSELITZ, Bert F., ed., *The Progress of Underdeveloped Areas* (Chicago, University of Chicago Press, 1952).
17. HURST, Sir Cecil J. B., and others, *Great Britain and the Dominions* (Chicago, University of Chicago Press, 1928).
18. KNORR, Klaus, *British Colonial Theories, 1570-1850* (Toronto, University of Toronto Press, 1949).
19. KOLARZ, Walter, *Russia and Her Colonies* (New York, Praeger, 1953).

20. LANGER, William L., *The Diplomacy of Imperialism, 1890-1902* (New York, Knopf, 1935).

21. LAUTERPACHT, H., *International Law and Human Rights* (London, Stevens, 1950).

22. LINDLEY, M. F., *Acquisition and Government of Backward Territory in International Law* (London, Longmans, 1925).

23. LORIMER, Sir James, *The Institutes of the Law of Nations* (Edinburgh, Blackwood, 1883), 2 vols.

24. MACK, Robert T., *Raising the World Standard of Living, The Conduct and Effectiveness of Point Four,* United Nations Technical Assistance and Related Programs (New York, Citadel Press, 1953).

25. MAIR, L. P., *The Protection of Minorities* (London, Christopher, 1928).

26. MOON, Parker T., *Imperialism and World Politics* (New York, Macmillan, 1926).

27. MORGENTHAU, Hans, *Politics Among Nations,* 2nd ed. (New York, Knopf, 1954).

28. MORRIS, Henry C., *The History of Colonization* (New York, Macmillan, 1908), 2 vols.

29. OLIVIER, Lord, *White Capital and Coloured Labour,* 3rd ed. (London, Woolf, 1929).

30. REINSCH, Paul S., *Colonial Government* (New York, Macmillan, 1902).

31. ———, *Colonial Administration* (New York, Macmillan, 1906).

32. RITSHER, W. H., *Criteria of Capacity for Independence* (Jerusalem, Syrian Orphanage Press, 1934).

33. ROBERTS, S. H., *History of French Colonial Policy, 1870-1925* (London, King, 1929), 2 vols.

34. ROBINSON, H., *The Development of the British Empire* (Boston, Houghton Mifflin, 1922).

35. Royal Institute of International Affairs, *The Colonial Problem* (London, Oxford University Press, 1937).

36. SALTER, Sir Arthur, *Peace and the Colonial Problem* (London, National Peace Council Conference, 1935).

37. SEELEY, J. R., *The Expansion of England* (London, Macmillan, 1883).

38. ———, *Roman Imperialism* (Boston, Roberts, 1871).

39. South African Institute of International Affairs, *Africa South of the Sahara, an Assessment of Human and Material Resources* (London, Oxford University Press, 1951).

40. STOWELL, Ellery C., *Intervention in International Law* (Washington, Byrnes, 1921).

41. TRIEPEL, Heinrich, *Die Hegemonie, ein Buch von führenden Staaten* (Stuttgart, Kohlhammer, 1938).

42. TREITSCHKE, Heinrich von, *Politics* (New York, Macmillan, 1916), 2 vols.

43. UNESCO, *The Race Concept, Results of an Inquiry* (Paris, 1952).

44. United Nations, General Assembly, Ad Hoc Committee on Factors (Non-self-governing Territories), *Reports* (1952-1953).

45. VLADIMIR, *Russia on the Pacific and the Siberian Railway* (London, Sampson Low, 1899).

46. VANDENBOSCH, Amry, *The Dutch East Indies* (Grand Rapids, Eerdmans, 1933).

47. VAN LANGENHOVE, F., *The Sacred Mission of Civilization, To Which Peoples Should the Benefits Be Extended* (New York, Belgian Government Information Center, 1953).

48. WILLOUGHBY, W. F., *Territories and Dependencies of the United States* (New York, Century, 1905).

49. WOOLF, Leonard S., *Empire and Commerce in Africa* (New York, Macmillan, 1920).

50. WRIGHT, Quincy, *Mandates Under the League of Nations* (Chicago, University of Chicago Press, 1930).

51. ——, *Legal Problems in the Far Eastern Conflict* (New York, Institute of Pacific Relations, 1941).

52. ——, *A Study of War* (Chicago, University of Chicago Press, 1942), pp. 278 ff., 313, 965 ff., 1134 ff., 1177 ff., 1189 ff.

CHAPTER
18

International Organization

DEFINITION

INTERNATIONAL ORGANIZATION is the art of creating and administering general and regional societies composed of independent states to facilitate co-operation in realizing common purposes and objectives. As a discipline it includes the philosophy guiding that art and appraising its methods, and the science predicting the results to be expected from the application of the art in given circumstances. It also includes practical and historic studies contributing to this art, philosophy, and science.

The term *organization* suggests either a condition involving a hierarchy of authority and procedures of action, or a process by which authority develops and acts to realize group objectives. The difference resembles that between potential (latent) and effective (kinetic) energy. The first is a condition in which energy may be released and utilized and the latter a process in which energy actually flows and does useful work. The difference also resembles that between the intellect and the will. The former is the mind conceived as a system of files, classifications, indices, and documents which make it easy to obtain and to relate items of information when needed, while the latter is the mind conceived as an active process using such a system to realize plans and purposes. The word *law* is also used in both of these senses, but perhaps the potential and intellectual sense is more characteristic of law, while the effective and volitional sense is more characteristic of organization. If law is referred to in the effective sense, the terms *law in action* or *the legal process* are frequently used. If organization is referred to in the potential sense, the term *an organization* or *a constitution* may be used, though

199

sometimes the term *organization* is used in the potential sense in distinction from *administration* or *organization in action*. As an art, organization is used in the effective sense. The term *international administration* has been used (32), but while it emphasizes the dynamic character of the art, it also suggests the narrower meaning of administration excluding legislation, adjudication, and execution which are included, along with administration, in the term organization.

As in the cases of international politics and international law the adjective *international* is used in preference to the adjective *world*. The latter would have the advantage that it would make it clear that the discipline includes examination of the possibility of *world federation* or other form of *world government* more centralized than *international organization*, but since these differences are ones of degree rather than of kind, and no one contemplates a total elimination of nations in a universal society, the term *international* seems appropriate. Furthermore, use of the adjective *world* would exclude from the discipline, as the adjective *international* does not, independent organizations of large regions of the world. The inter-American organization of states is an *international organization* but not a *world organization*. Neither term is entirely satisfactory, but *international* seems preferable in deference to practice and in recognition of the probability that both regional and universal organizations will remain predominantly *international* in character. Sovereign nations are the major groups with which the art has been concerned, and its method has been more to influence and co-ordinate national policies than to initiate and execute supranational policies, though the latter method has never been wholly lacking.

The discipline of international organization has usually described existing institutions, legal relations, and procedures, and analyzed the consequences to be expected from their operation; presented the history of their changes; and dealt critically with the objectives and purposes they avow and with their effectiveness in achieving these avowed objectives or purposes.

Such scientific, historic, or philosophic treatments are useful to the art, but studies more closely related to the detailed operation of international organizations are more useful. Such studies relate the details of policy formation, administration, and adjudication with the conditions of opinion on the one hand and with procedures of efficient accomplishment on the other. The practice of international organization is both guided by, and exerts influence upon, public opinion. It also adapts itself to and realizes objectives. Organization is the nexus between group opinion and group accomplishment, between external conditions and internal adaptations. It involves on the one hand the interpretation and formulation of opinions into concrete plans and programs, and the realization of these plans and programs through legislative, adjudicative, executive, and administrative activities including in the latter supervision, investigation, regulation, and management. It involves on the other hand the discovery and analysis of conditions affecting group purposes, the invention of suitable adjustments to them, the formulation of procedures and plans for making such adjustments, and the influencing of opinion, by dissemination of information, by education, and by propaganda, to accept such plans and procedures. A successful organization applies opinion to improve conditions if it can, and it influences opinion to adapt to conditions if it must. It regards neither group opinion nor external conditions as implacable, nor does it regard either as entirely malleable, but it regards each as more or less resistant and as more or less susceptible to change. The art of organization consists in judging the relatively implacable and the relatively malleable aspects of each situation. If opinion is rigorously insistent upon policies which conditions make impossible of achievement, organization is frustrated and collapse may occur, but skill in the art of organization may persuade even an implacable opinion to postpone accomplishment of its aims until more propitious circumstances develop and may devise means for somewhat modifying even the most implacable conditions. Timing is, therefore, the essence of successful organization and administration. Like war and diplomacy, the art of organization always appreciates the historical context of events. As accomplishments now possible were once impossible, so the future may hide as yet undisclosed possibilities of accomplishment.

International organization may be universal, regional, or bilateral, but the shrinking of the world through invention has tended to create a universal system of interdependence which tends to subordinate regional and bilateral organizations to universal organizations. The United Nations contemplates, more than did the League of Nations, such a subordination. The inter-American system, the Brussels Pact, the North Atlantic Pact, and the Arab League are in principle part of the United Nations covered by Articles 51 and 52 of the Charter. This principle of subordination may not, however, be observed in all instances in practice. The important regional organization of the Soviet Union and its satellites constituted by a network of bilateral treaties and Soviet administrative and military controls has little relationship except of opposition to the United Nations. Regional organizations unintegrated with the universal organization are still possible (12). Furthermore, neither the United Nations nor any of its Specialized Agencies are literally universal. Some states voluntarily abstain from or have been refused membership in each of these organizations. Thus every international organization formally extends only to a part of the world community, although, in accord with Paragraph 2, Article 6 of the Charter, the United Nations asserts authority to maintain certain principles for the entire community of nations.

The principal members of international organizations are sovereign states, but in some cases dependencies and other nonsovereign entities have been admitted, and influence may be exerted by international ideological groups such as the Catholic church, the Zionist organization, and the Cominform; by regional and functional international organizations both official and unofficial; and by national foundations and associations interested in international affairs. The United Nations and many of its Specialized Agencies permit representatives of other international organizations to participate in some meetings and have given a certain consultative status to numerous nongovernmental organizations interested in their objectives. In a world of power politics, however, influence is closely related to power, and consequently, the opinion and objectives of the great powers have been of major influence in shaping the purposes of international organizations. But because of the equality of all members in the General Assembly and in the Conferences of the Specialized Agencies, the lesser states exert considerable influence which can be conclusive if they unite. The opinions, objectives, and interests of territorial states as such have been of predominant importance in determining the objectives of international organizations although the possibility that international blocs, regions, associations, or parties may increase in influence should not be discounted (74).

The interests of states fall into two classes, usually designated political and nonpolitical. The first includes the interest of each state in self-preservation, independence, and increase in its own power, an interest which tends to put it into opposition to other states, because power is relative and the gains of one tend to be the losses of others. Nonpolitical interests concern such matters as international trade, international communication, world health, international finance, the development of a world public opinion and other objectives which necessarily require, or may be facilitated by, co-operation across national boundaries. In these matters the gain of one tends to be the gain of others.

This distinction is not, however, absolute. Political interests can be forwarded by co-operation. Alliances, regional arrangements, or general organizations for collective security and pacific settlement are designed to facilitate concerted action to suppress aggression, and consultation, conciliation, or adjudication to prevent it. Nonpolitical interests on the other hand, can seldom be forwarded without some political controversy. All states, for example, want to engage in some international trade, and each tends to develop a commercial policy. That policy, however, is designed not only to facilitate international trade, but also to obtain revenue, to protect local industries, to create conditions of trade favorable to itself, or to increase its power. It maintains these policies by tariffs and other commercial regulations which often conflict with the interests of other states and lead to political controversy. Even the common interest of states in world health may encounter political difficulties such as, for example, the unwillingness of certain states to permit the export to potential enemies of medical supplies or facilities for their manufacture, which might also be of military value.

Whether the interest is predominantly political or predominantly non-political, international organization, differing in this respect from international politics, is concerned with the common interest of states. It is concerned primarily with the co-operative aspects of international relations while international politics is concerned primarily with the oppositional aspects.

International politics tends to develop balance of power policies by which each state appreciates that it has an interest in combining with others against any one that is becoming dangerously powerful. This implies that each state is aware of a common interest in the stability of the whole system of states. Such awareness tends to develop international organization for facilitating the co-ordination of balance of power policies or for organizing collective security, but the discipline of international politics assumes that the interest of each state in its independence, and its consequent political opposition to others, will frustrate the effectiveness of such organization; that the balance of power will be maintained by armament policies, limited alliances, *ad hoc* collaboration, and occasional wars; and that, therefore, a balance of power system is to be distinguished from international organization (18, 86, 87).

International organization differs from colonial government and empire in that it tends to assume the equality of states (68). The United Nations Charter is said to be based on the principal of "the sovereign equality of states" (Art. 2, par. 1). Discriminations are assumed to be odious. An inferior and a superior do not often have a common interest in perpetuating that relationship. States, even though regarded by others as *backward,* cannot be expected to relish membership in an organization the purpose of which is to perpetuate their inferior status. The United Nations Charter explicitly states that the trusteeship system shall not apply to members (Art. 78), and it also recognizes the principle of *self-determination* promising eventual equality of status to groups which are not yet self-governing (Art. 1, par. 2; Arts. 55; 73; 76). International organizations may admit nongovernmental, regional, or specialized organizations with a status different from that of sovereign states for certain purposes, but sovereign states are the principal members. UNESCO has been careful to avoid formulating a philosophy which might accord with the ideologies of some states and not with those of others, and the United Nations has been careful to avoid services or observances at headquarters which might seem to favor any one religion.

International organization, therefore, differs from a balance of power system and from an empire, though each of the latter are possible world structures, actually realized in large areas for long periods of history.

International organization is more centralized that a balance of power system and less centralized than an empire. It differs from a balance of power system as art differs from nature, and from an empire as democracy differs from aristocracy. It assumes the rationality and foresight of states while a balance of power system assumes their bondage to custom and tradition. It maintains the equality and freedom of states while an empire maintains their inequality and the subjection of some to others. International organization seeks to minimize, though it may not be able wholly to eliminate, discriminations, coercions, threats, and hostilities. It seeks to act through consultation, negotiation, and conciliation to gain consent to settlements of international problems or to procedures for settling them, and to act through co-operation, adjudication, administration and, if necessary, international sanctions for implementing such agreements.

Does international organization also differ from world federation? This distinction has been insisted upon by advocates of the latter (64, 71). They assume that international organization implies that states alone govern individuals and that central organs deal only with the governments of states. World federation, on the other hand, implies a division of governmental functions between the states and the federation, each exercising within the scope of its functions all the powers of government over individuals. This distinction between *leagues, confederations,* or *staatenbunden* on the one hand, and *unions, federations,* or *bundestaaten* on the other is, however, relative, as observed by Freeman who, in his history of *federal government,* applied that term to both of these types (24). Federations have varied greatly in the scope of federal powers, in the extent to which the states have controlled the effective exercise of these powers even by such means as nullification or secession, and in the extent to which the federation, as in the case of the Soviet Union, has been able to disregard legal limitations by the use of extra-constitutional agencies of party, propaganda, and police.

The functions of international organizations have often extended into domains of individual interest such as human rights, social security, standards of living, health, education, and culture. In proportion as such functions are effectively implemented, the organization becomes a *federation.* The United Nations Charter is ambiguous on this point. On the one hand it requires the United Nations to promote such ends and pledges the members to act and to co-operate with it for their achievement (Arts. 55, 56), but on the other hand it forbids the United Nations to *intervene* in matters essentially within the domestic jurisdiction of any state (Art. 2, par. 7). Since a matter concerning which a state has assumed an international obligation has ceased to be within its domestic jurisdiction, this does not preclude United Nations *intervention* to enforce obligations which states have undertaken by the Charter or other treaties, and such obligations may include acceptance of United Nations procedures dealing directly with individuals. The United Nations has the potentiality, therefore, within the Charter, of becoming a *federation* through practice and supplementary conventions. Efforts to prevent such a trend have been manifested in proposals, especially in the United States, to limit the national treaty-making power. Such efforts, however, in seeking to thwart any qualification of national sovereignty through a developing *federalism* in international organizations would actually impair the sovereign capacity of the state to make treaties. Future possible qualifications of sovereignty would be prevented by a present major qualification of sovereignty.

Whether in principle a considerable capacity for direct action on individuals, especially in the fields of law enforcement, taxation, and opinion control is essential for effective international organization is controversial, the differences of opinion being reflected in the ambiguities of the Charter. Historians have reported that confederations have been weak and transitional forms of organization (24), and sociologists have asserted that *secondary societies,* that is, societies whose members are societies and not individuals, are inherently unreliable and unstable (38, 59, 89). Governments tend to act in accord with the present will of the society they govern at the expense of obligations which it may have undertaken in the past to a super-society. Consequently a society is only strong if it lives, not only in formal obligations and central organs, but also in the minds and hearts of the people who ultimately compose it.

For this reason the discipline of international organization has concerned itself with a wide range of political forms between loose systems of power equilibria on the one hand and centralized empires on the other, including leagues, confederations, federations, and unions. The issue of the degree of intervention of the central organs in the structure and functioning of the parts is a major practical problem with which such organizations must deal, and it is likely that they will deal with them most effectively if they act in the exigencies of circumstances, in accord with changing conditions of technology and opinion, avoiding commitment to abstract definitions or irrevocable principles (12, 18, 90).

Federations, confederations, and regional and general international organizations have been created by agreement of sovereign states and have functioned for long periods of history. Some have eventually disintegrated. Some have become centralized states. None has wholly avoided internal war. The opinion has been expressed, with the support of social psychology, that the most successful have resulted from the decentralization of empire rather than from the voluntary union of states (1). There has been sufficient of both coercion and consent in the formation and history of most such organizations to make such an interpretation possible, but not to make it conclusive.

ASSUMPTIONS

In the widest sense the discipline of international organization needs to make only three assumptions: (*a*) that there is a world or super-group whose peoples are in contact with one another, (*b*) that the people of the world are divided into major groups which have some opinions and objectives in common, and (*c*) that these groups co-operate to forward their common opinions and objectives. These assumptions, it will be recalled, resemble the broader assumptions of the discipline of international politics with the difference, however, that common rather than inconsistent objectives, and co-operation rather than opposition, are emphasized. International politics merges into international organization as the objectives of states become identical and as co-operation supersedes strife as the means for obtaining the objectives of all.

In all historical civilizations these assumptions have been to some extent realized, as have also those of international politics. A civilization implies a world among whose parts some communication and contact exists. It also implies some common interests as well as some inconsistent interest of the parts, and some co-operation as well as some opposition among them. Sociologists, in fact, insist that the very conception of organization implies both co-operation and opposition because it implies both a whole and parts. The co-existence of a whole and its parts implies that the parts are not wholly identified with or absorbed in each other or in the whole. Thus they have some independence and consequently some inconsistency of purposes. While the assumptions which make international organization possible have been to some extent realized in all civilizations, the development of international organization has actually varied greatly in different civilizations. The art of international organization has been more developed and more effective in some civilizations than in others.

Within these broad assumptions, organization could take many forms. The *empire* in a measure realized by Rome in ancient times, the *universal ideology* in a measure realized by the Catholic church in the Middle Ages, the *balance of power* in a measure realized under British leadership in the nineteenth century, the *confederation* or *international organization* in the narrow sense, which the League of Nations and the United Nations have attempted to realize in the twentieth century, and the *universal federation* urged by many world government groups are all a possibility, though with varying degrees of probability in any immediate future (86, 89).

In a narrower sense, international organization may be contrasted with empire, ideology, balance of power, and even federation. In this sense it assumes (*a*) that sovereign territorial states exist in contact with one another, (*b*) that they have common interests in preserving their sovereign equality and in gaining the advantages of co-operation in many fields, and (c) that they are disposed to co-operate to achieve their common interests, and to organize in order to facilitate that co-operation.

These assumptions are related. The definition of sovereignty inevitably changes as contact, common interest, and co-operation increases. The scope of common interest, in contrast to inconsistent interests, tends to increase with contact, with actual co-operation, and with reduction of the absoluteness of the concepts of sovereignty and equality. Increased contact, consequent upon an improving technology of communication and trade; increased perception of the advantages of intercourse and co-operation through experience; and increased willingness to reinterpret such values as independence and sovereignty permit efficient co-operation and promote international organization. All of the terms employed in the assumptions are interrelated and flexible, as are the assumptions of democracy. Government of the people, by the people, and for the people can assume many forms. Similarly, organization of sovereign states, by sovereign states, and for sovereign states can assume many forms. But as the ideas of liberty, equality, and fraternity of some kind are inherent in any form of democracy, so the ideas of sovereignty, equality, and co-operation are inherent in international organization in the narrow sense.

International organization is a democratic organization of sovereign states, but it is to be observed that such an organization tends to make the state rather than man the objective of its activity, and, therefore, to conflict with domestic democracy. International organization may perpetuate autocratic governments which claim to represent their states and to suppress democratic movements in the interest of international stability. Such was the effect of the organization of Europe in the age of Metternich. International organization could promote co-operative efforts toward democracy, self-determination of nations, and respect for human rights and human welfare, and these objectives are stated in the United Nations Charter. National governments, however, decide the policies of international organizations and they are likely to be primarily interested in their own positions and in preserving the situation in which they have risen to power, and to diverge in their views of desirable change. International organizations are, therefore, likely to put stability and collective security ahead of reform and peaceful change. They tend to be conservative.

If, however, the ultimate purpose of democracy is man, and the state is merely an instrument for promoting his welfare, international organization, if it is to serve democracy, should look back of the government to the people, should insist on respect for human rights and group self-determination and, therefore, should seek to establish direct relations between the world and the individual. Democratic opinion, and the international assemblies, in so far as they reflect it, therefore tend to see the states, not as sovereign entities which are a value in themselves, but merely as instruments of human justice and welfare. Such a tendency emphasizing the equality of man militates against an absolute interpretation of the equality of states. The latter differ greatly in population and power, in the democracy of their institution, and in their capacity to forward human welfare. Thus democratic opinion and the effort to achieve reforms formally accepted, tends to move international organization in the direction of federation.

The tendency of civilization to increase international contacts, to diffuse cultures, and to augment co-operativeness, buttresses this tendency of international organization. International organization in the restricted sense, like international politics and colonial government, tends to make itself obsolete and to become universal federation. The opposite tendencies of international politics and war and of national governments and loyalties hamper the speed and may frustrate the realization of this tendency. It is not inevitable that international organization should develop into universal federation any more than it is inevitable that international politics should develop into a universal empire by conquest. The two tendencies moderate each other and international organization and international politics may both continue to exist in the world for a long time.

ANALYSIS

The analysis of international organization may proceed, among others, from the legal, the administrative, the political, and the sociological points of view.

The legal point of view concentrates on legal texts and their interpretation through the investigation, on the one hand, of *travaux preparatoire*, practice, and other evidence of the intention of the parties under the assumption that a state does not willingly restrict its sovereignty, and, on the other hand, of ideas of legal coherence, workability, and effectiveness in achieving expressed purposes. The practical jurist seeks to reconcile inconsistencies, to apply analogies, to minimize unworkable procedures, and to emphasize precedents illustrating procedures found to be effective. The theoretical jurist, on the other hand, may attach exaggerated importance to the literal meaning of texts or the opinions expressed during the course of negotiating the legal instrument. Most jurists in dealing with the Charter and other international constitutional documents recognize the validity of Chief Justice Marshall's method of interpreting the Constitution of the United States, favoring a liberal interpretation, which permitted adjustment of the Constitution to new conditions, which profited by experience in its working, and which accepted new methods for better realizing its purposes. Practical jurists also usually discriminate between political and legal provisions recognizing that political organs are better adapted to interpreting the former and courts the latter. This appreciation doubtless accounts for the hesitancy of the organs of the United Nations in the early years to ask the International Court of Justice for advisory opinions on the provisions concerning the scope of *domestic jurisdiction* and the meaning of *sovereign equality*. Premature definitions of such terms might hamper healthy development of the organization (26, 40, 41, 87).

The administrative point of view differs from the legal in giving greater weight to effectiveness in achieving ends and less to the texts. The officials of the Secretariat and the members of commissions assume that the purposes stated in the Charter or in resolutions of the principal organs of the United Nations are to be realized, and that hampering procedures or apparent restrictions in the texts are to be interpreted, evaded, or even ignored when they get in the way. The steady pressure of wise and inventive administrative action may modify meanings, establish precedents, and make the institution live and grow. It is especially in the field of administration that the art of international organization can be usefully applied (23, 67).

The political point of view recognizes the importance of national policies flowing from national public opinions, and appreciates the importance of timing in the making of decisions. This point of view is characteristic of the national representatives in the principal organs of the United Nations and is guided by the arts of international politics and diplomacy. It is not unaware of the potential influence of world public opinion and the possibility of mobilizing it in the atmosphere of the General Assembly, but it also appreciates the danger that national opinion may, in the different atmospheres of the national capitals, compel governments to neglect to implement what the delegates have accepted. The balancing of world and national opinion, the calculation of the power behind each, and the proper timing of initiatives constitutes the art of international organization from the political point of view. Historians have emphasized the significance of political parties cutting across state boundaries in the stabilizing of confederations and federations (74). Such parties, by opposing different views of national interest, have reduced the influence of the oppositions between different states and regions and have augmented loyalties to the whole at the expense of loyalties to the parts. National parties are, however, only one of the political devices by which related groups, whether clans, tribes, city states, or national states have been organized into larger wholes throughout human history (7, 9, 22).

The sociological point of view devotes attention to long-run trends, to the influence of charismatic personalities and of technological, ideological, and demographic changes on public opinion, to the tendency of national public opinion to develop by reaction to progress in the development of world opinion, and so to appraise in a larger span of time the relative importance of the factors emphasized by the politicians, the lawyers and the administrators of international organizations. The sociologists recognize that organizations cannot exist without communication among the members; that abundant communication tends to build common opinions, values, and standards; that from these common interests and goals develop; and that it is soon seen that co-operation to achieve such goals will be facilitated by central organization for gearing means to ends. These processes of communication, standardization, co-operation, and organization, though tending, each to develop from the other in this order, are interdependent (59, 89). Relatively isolated groups may become organized from conquest or other fortuitous circumstance of international politics, but once a central organization is established it may increase communication and encourage the general acceptance of common laws and policies, thus creating the conditions for its own survival after the circumstances which initiated it have ended. So also unorganized education and propaganda may bring about a genuine commitment by people to goals and standards which have been formally accepted by their governments and thus make possible organizations for realizing such goals and standards in practice. The American Declaration of Independence, by asserting in 1776 that all men are created equal may have contributed to the Emancipation Proclamation, followed by the thirteenth, fourteenth, and fifteenth amendments to the Constitution, four score and seven years later. Thus the processes of legal interpretation and international administration, respectively related to the standardization of values and the organization of authority, may progress even before political action has developed a will to co-operate or social and technical developments have assured an abundance of transnational communication. Students of international organization have differed on the issue of whether the establishment of formal international organizations should await the development of the common moral and cultural standards, necessary for their effective functioning, or should, if circumstances have thrust such organizations into premature existence, create those conditions by education and propaganda (87, 89).

CRITICISM

The art of international organization in which international lawyers, international administrators, international statesmen, and scientific internationalists seek to strengthen the common interests and the co-operation of states is, in a measure, opposed by the art of international politics by which national lawyers, administrators, statesmen, and patriots seek to strengthen the power of their states and, therefore, to augment oppositions and conflict within the international community. The two often merge, however, because national and international statesmanship may meet in the same person. International politics, tends with the advance of the civilization, toward world conquest or world chaos. The art of international organization may avoid either, by evolving a world confederation which compromises between national and world sovereignty, but history shows that the task is not easy to accomplish. As has been previously suggested, international organization and international politics may long co-exist. While they do, the art of conducting foreign relations so as to gear national policies into the policies of international organizations is the key discipline.

The essence of international organization is the equality of states and the world point of view. It therefore resembles international law, but is more flexible, less bound to the past, more rapidly responsive to opinion, and more capable of influencing opinion. The establishment of the United Nations and the Specialized Agencies with thousands of employees devoting themselves to this art and educating the national statesmen, who represent their states in Council and Assembly meetings, in the elements of the art, may provide a leadership for public opinion which will in time develop a sufficient sentiment of internationalism to accommodate the need for world unity with the need for national individuality. Against this possibility, the tendency of international politics to bipolarize the world, offers serious obstacles. No science, either of international politics or of international organization, permits a reliable prediction of the future. Only a broader science of international relations, resting upon psychological and sociological foundations, could approach that task.

REFERENCES

This list includes a small selection of the publications on international organization. None of the documentary sources are included. The official documents of the League of Nations have been catalogued by Hans Aufricht (*Guide to League of Nations Publications*, Columbia University Press, 1951). A selection of the documents of the San Francisco Conference of 1945 was published by the United States State Department (*The United Nations Conference on International Organization*, Washington, 1946). The activities of the United Nations and the Specialized Agencies can be followed in the biweekly, *United Nations Bulletin*, and the *United Nations Year Book* published by the United Nations, and in the quarterly, *International Organization*, published by the World Peace Foundation of Boston. This contains significant articles on International Organization, as do the *American Journal of International Law*, published quarterly, the *International Social Science Bulletin*, published quarterly by UNESCO, and the *Annual Symposia* published by the Conference on Science, Philosophy and Religion of New York.

This list includes a selection of general treatises on international organization, descriptive analyses of the League of Nations and the United Nations, histories of plans of international organization, and a few classical and more recent analyses of the problem, especially those stimulated by the two world wars of the twentieth century leading to the League of Nations and the United Nations.

None of the numerous studies on regional organizations, policies of particular states in the League of Nations and the United Nations, and the work of international organizations in special fields have been included.

1. ALEXANDER, Franz, *Our Age of Unreason,* rev. ed. (New York, Lippincott, 1951).
2. ARECHAGA, Eduardo Jiminez, *Voting and the Handling of Disputes in the Security Council* (New York, Carnegie Endowment, 1950).
3. BARR, Stringfellow, *Citizens of the World* (New York, Doubleday, 1953).
4. BARTLETT, Ruhl J., *The League to Enforce Peace* (Chapel Hill, University of North Carolina Press, 1944).
5. BENES, Eduard, and others, *International Security* (Chicago, University of Chicago Press, 1939).
6. BEVERIDGE, Sir William, *The Price of Peace* (London, Pilot Press, 1945).
7. BONNET, Henri, *The United Nations, What They Are and What They May Become?; The United Nations on the Way; Outlines of the Future* (Chicago, World Citizens Association, 1942, 1943).
8. BORGESE, G. A., ed., *Common Cause,* monthly, University of Chicago Press, 1947-1951.
9. BRINTON, Crane, *From Many One* (Cambridge, Harvard University Press, 1948).
10. BURTON, Margaret E., *The Assembly of the League of Nations* (Chicago, University of Chicago Press, 1941).
11. CHASE, Eugene P., *The United Nations in Action* (New York, McGraw-Hill, 1950).
11a. CHEEVER, Daniel S., and HAVILAND, H. Field, *Organizing for Peace* (Boston, Houghton Mifflin, 1954).
12. Commission to Study the Organization of Peace, *Reports,* Nos. 1-9 (New York, 1941-1954).
13. CONWELL-EVANS, T. P., *The League Council in Action* (London, Oxford University Press, 1929).
14. CORBETT, Percy, *Post War Worlds* (New York, Institute of Pacific Relations, 1942).
15. DARBY, W. Evans, *International Tribunals,* 4th ed. (London, Dent, 1904).
16. DAVIES, Lord, *The Problem of the Twentieth Century,* 3rd ed. (London, Benn, 1938).
17. DERUSSET, Alan, *Strengthening the Framework of Peace* (London, Royal Institute of International Affairs, 1950).
18. DOUGLAS, William O., and others, "Syposium on World Organization," *Yale Law Journal,* Vol. 45 (August, 1946), pp. 865 ff.
19. DULLES, John Foster, *War, Peace and Change* (New York, Harpers, 1939).
20. ———, *War or Peace* (New York, Macmillan, 1950).
21. EAGLETON, Clyde, *International Government,* rev. ed. (New York, Ronald, 1948).
22. *Federalist, The,* by Alexander Hamilton, James Madison and John Jay (1789).
23. FELLER, A. H., *The United Nations and the World Community* (Boston, Little, Brown, 1952).
24. FREEMAN, Edward A., *History of Federal Government,* 2nd ed. (London, Macmillan, 1893).
25. Geneva Institute of International Relations, *Problems of Peace,* Five Series (London, Oxford University Press, 1926-1931).

26. GOODRICH, Leland, and HAMBRO, Edvard, *Charter of the United Nations, Commentary and Documents*, rev. ed. (Boston, World Peace Foundation, 1949).

27. GREAVES, H. R. G., *The League Committees and World Order* (London, Oxford University Press, 1931).

28. HAMBRO, Carl J., *How to Win the Peace* (New York, Lippincott, 1942).

29. HAVILAND, H. Field, *The Political Role of the General Assembly* (New York, Carnegie Endowment, 1951).

30. HEMLEBEN, Sylvester J., *Plans for World Peace Through Six Centuries* (Chicago, University of Chicago Press, 1943).

31. HILL, Martin, *Immunities and Privileges of International Officials, The Experience of the League of Nations* (Washington, Carnegie Endowment, 1947).

32. HILL, Norman, *International Administration* (New York, McGraw-Hill, 1931).

33. HOBSON, J. A., *Toward International Government* (New York, Macmillan, 1915).

34. HOOVER, Herbert, and GIBSON, Hugh, *The Problem of Lasting Peace* (New York, Doubleday, 1942).

35. HUDSON, Manley O., *By Pacific Means* (New Haven, Yale University Press, 1936).

36. ———, *International Tribunals* (Washington, Carnegie Endowment, 1944).

37. ———, *The Permanent Court of International Justice, 1920-1942* (New York, Macmillan, 1943).

38. HUSZAR, George B. de, ed., *New Perspectives on Peace* (Chicago, University of Chicago Press, 1944).

39. KANT, Immanuel, *Eternal Peace* (Boston, World Peace Foundation, 1914).

40. KELSEN, Hans, *The Law of the United Nations* (London, Stevens, 1950).

41. ———, *Recent Trends in the Law of the United Nations* (London, Stevens, 1951).

42. KOHN, Hans, *World Order in Historical Perspective* (Cambridge, Harvard University Press, 1942).

43. LAVES, Walter H. C., ed., *The Foundations of a More Stable World Order* (Chicago, University of Chicago Press, 1941).

44. League of Nations Secretariat, *The Aims, Methods and Activities of the League of Nations* (Geneva, 1935).

45. LEVI, Werner, *Fundamentals of World Organization* (Minneapolis, University of Minnesota Press, 1950).

46. LIPPMANN, Walter, *U.S. War Aims* (Boston, Little, Brown, 1944).

47. LISSITZYN, Oliver, *The International Court of Justice* (New York, Carnegie Endowment, 1951).

48. LOEWENSTEIN, Karl, *Political Reconstruction* (New York, Macmillan, 1946).

49. MacIVER, Robert M., *Toward an Abiding Peace* (New York, Macmillan, 1943).

50. MADARIAGA, Salvador, *The World's Design* (London, Allen and Unwin, 1938).

51. MANDER, Linden A., *Foundations of Modern World Society*, rev. ed. (Stanford, Stanford University Press, 1947).

52. MARRIOTT, Sir John, *Commonwealth or Anarchy* (New York, Columbia University Press, 1939).

53. MAZUNDAR, Haridas T., *The United Nations of the World* (New York, Universal Publishing Co., 1942).

54. MERRIAM, Charles E., *On the Agenda of Democracy* (Cambridge, Harvard University Press, 1941).

55. MILLER, David Hunter, *The Drafting of the Covenant* (New York, Putnam, 1928).

56. MORGENTHAU, Hans J., ed., *Peace, Security and the United Nations* (Chicago, University of Chicago Press, 1946).

57. MORLEY, Felix, *The Society of Nations, Its Origin and Constitutional Development* (Washington, Brookings Institution, 1932).

58. MYERS, Denys P., *Handbook of the League of Nations* (Boston World Peace Foundation, 1935).

59. OGBURN, William F., *Technology and International Relations* (Chicago, University of Chicago Press, 1949).

60. PASTUHOV, Vladimir, D., *A Guide to the Practice of International Conferences*, 5th ed. (Washington, Carnegie Endowment, 1945).

61. POTTER, P. B., *An Introduction to the Study of International Organization*, 5th ed. (New York, Appleton-Century-Crofts, 1948).

62. RAPPARD, W. E., *The Quest for Peace* (Cambridge, Harvard University Press, 1940).

63. REINSCH, Paul S., *Public International Unions*, 2nd ed. (Boston, World Peace Foundation, 1916).

64. REVES, Emery, *The Anatomy of Peace* (New York, Harpers, 1945).

65. SALTER, Sir Arthur, *Security, Can We Retrieve It?* (New York, Reynal and Hitchcock, 1939).

66. SCHUMAN, Frederick L., *The Commonwealth of Man* (New York, Knopf, 1952).

67. SCHWEBEL, Stephen M., *The Secretary General of the United Nations* (Cambridge, Harvard University Press, 1952).

68. SCHWARZENBERGER, Georg, *The League of Nations and World Order* (London, Constable, 1936).

69. SHOTWELL, James T., *On the Rim of the Abyss* (New York, Macmillan, 1936).

70. SOHN, Louis, *Cases and Materials on World Law* (Brooklyn, Foundation Press, 1950).

71. STREIT, Clarence, *Union Now* (New York, Harper, 1939).

72. SULLY, Duc de, *The Great Design of Henry IV*, Introduction by E. D. Mead (Boston, Ginn, 1909).

73. TINGSTEN, Herbert, and others, *Peace and Security After the Second World War*, A Swedish Contribution to the Subject (Uppsala, Swedish Institute of International Affairs, 1945).

74. TURNER, Frederick Jackson, "American Sectionalism and World Organization," *American Historical Review*, Vol. 48 (April, 1942), pp. 545 ff.

75. United Nations, *Everyman's United Nations* (New York, Funk and Wagnalls, 1953).

76. U. S. Senate, *Revision of the United Nations Charter*, 81st Cong., 2nd Sess., Report No. 2501 (September 1, 1950), and Hearings, Subcommittee of Committee on Foreign Relations (February, 1950).

77. Universities Committee on Post War International Problems, Ralph Barton Perry and Arthur O. Lovejoy, eds., *Reports* (Boston, 1942-1945). See **also**, *International Conciliation* (1944-1945), Nos. 401, 405, 410, 414.

78. VANDENBOSCH, Amry, and HOGAN, Willard N., *The United Nations, Background, Organization, Functions, Activities* (New York, McGraw-Hill, 1952).

79. VAN WEGENEN, Richard, *Research in the International Organization Field* (Princeton, Center for Research on World Political Institutions, 1952).

80. WALTERS, F. P. A., *History of the League of Nations* (London, Oxford University Press, 1952), 2 vols.

81. WELLES, Sumner, *Seven Decisions that Shaped History* (New York, Harper, 1951).

82. WERTHEIMER, Egon F. Ranshofen, *The International Secretariat* (Washington, Carnegie Endowment, 1945).

83. WHITTON, John B., ed., *The Second Chance, America and the Peace* (Princeton, Princeton University Press, 1944).

84. WILLIAMS, Sir John Fischer, *Some Aspects of the Covenant of the League of Nations* (London, Oxford University Press, 1934).

85. WOODWARD, Ernest L., and others, *Foundations for World Order* (Denver, University of Denver Press, 1949).

86. WRIGHT, Quincy, *A Study of War* (Chicago, University of Chicago Press, 1942), pp. 776 ff., 817, 917 ff., 934 ff., 955 ff., 1012 ff., 1043 ff., 1332 ff.

87. ———, *Problems of Stability and Progress in International Relations* (Berkeley, University of California Press, 1954).

88. ———, ed., *Neutrality and Collective Security* (Chicago, University of Chicago Press, 1936).

89. ———, ed., *The World Community* (Chicago, University of Chicago Press, 1948).

90. ———, and others, *The World at the Cross Roads* (Chicago, World Citizens Association, 1946).

91. YOUNG, Sir George, *Federalism and Freedom* (London, Oxford University Press, 1941).

92. ZIMMERN, Sir Alfred, *The League of Nations and the Rule of Law, 1918-1935* (London, Macmillan, 1936).

93. ———, *The American Road to World Peace* (New York, Dutton, 1953).

International Law

DEFINITION

INTERNATIONAL LAW has been variously defined as the body of rules, principles, and standards (a) to which independent states are bound by common consent (14, 30, 47), (b) for violation of which such states habitually and reciprocally consider one another liable (17, 21, 52), (c) which are most suitable for maintaining order and justice within the world community (26, 48), and (d) which are actually invoked because deemed most useful for dealing effectively with international controversies (1, 13, 37). These four somewhat inconsistent concepts emphasize respectively the historical, scientific, philosophical, and practical approaches to international law. The discipline of international law gives some weight to all of them.

The first two conceptions have been designated *positivistic* in that they assume that law proceeds from the will of sovereign states, manifested either by their prior consent or their subsequent protests. The historical school recognizes that jural law cannot be deduced from mere behavior of the subjects of law, as could sociological law, but it considers custom— that is, practice with a sense of obligation—evidence of tacit consent. Treaties provide evidence of express consent and are therefore a source of positive law so long as they are observed. The historical school insists that consent and practice must combine to make positive law. The scientific school takes the same point of view but emphasizes the *sanction*, manifested by the practice of states in making protests followed, if they are not heeded, by reprisals, when a rule is violated, as the prime evidence of the jural character of a rule (21). They assume that in protesting against the violation of a rule by another a state manifests its own obligation to observe the rule (17).

Adherents of the third concept have been designated *naturalists* in that they assume a *natural law* existing apart from the will of states but derived by reason from *self-evident principles*. They put reason ahead of will as a source of law. The fourth conception permits utilization of the sources of law characteristic of both *positivism* and *naturalism*, and its adherents have been called *eclectics*, or Grotians after the seventeenth-century jurist who accepted this point of view in his book which established modern international law on a firm foundation (13). Advocates, judges, and diplomats tend to be eclectics weighing various sources of law with an eye to their relative persuasiveness in the particular situation.

In proportion as the world community becomes organized with central agencies of effective law-making and enforcement, these four schools tend to unite and international law tends to become positive law expressive of the will of the world community as manifested through the processes of these agencies and presumably tending to conform to universal reason (20).

A law in the most general sense is a realized generalization. A scientific law is realized in the order of nature. Insofar as observation and experiment have verified logical deductions from a generalization, the generalization is promoted from the status of hypothesis to that of law. Jural law is realized in the order of a society. Insofar as the system of sanctions maintained by a society induces the members of the society to observe deductions from a generalization, the generalization is promoted from the status of an ethical or practical norm to law.

The norm (rule, principle, or standard of jural law) is usually stated as an end and the sanction (penalty or remedy) as a means to maintain it. "You shall not kill with malice, but if you do you will be executed." Certain jural positivists, however, prefer a form of statement more analogous to scientific law, though it relates cause and effect by "shall" rather than "is." Nonobservance of the norm (delict) is stated as a condition or cause, and the sanction as a consequence or effect in the legal rule. "Whoever kills with malice shall be executed." This form tends to divorce jural law from ethics, to reduce the discretion and the influence of the biases of magistrates, to separate the functions of adjudication and legislation, to prevent adaptation of treatment to the delinquent, and to maintain the ideal of government by law rather than by men. Advanced systems of law are torn between these desiderata and ideas of individual justice, scientific penology, and social expediency which conceive sanctions as means of enforcement adaptable to the particular circumstances (22).

The concept of law implies some generalization. One does not describe a single observation that a stone fell to the earth as a scientific law nor does one describe a single instance in which a judge condemned an individual to pay a fine as a jural law. The observation that all stones fall to the earth might be described as an empirical law and the observation that persons who drive over fifty miles an hour on a given highway are usually fined ten dollars might be described as a legal regulation. The term *law*, however, seems more appropriately applied to comprehensive generalizations such as Newton's law of gravitation, the rule that violators of traffic regulations shall be fined, or the even more general rule that drivers who do not exercise reasonable caution shall be penalized.

There is, however, an inverse relation between the degree of generalization and the degree of realization. It is much easier to prove that this stone fell to the ground than that all stones fall to the ground, and it is more easy to prove the latter than that the motion of all bodies conforms to Newton's law of gravitation or to Einstein's even more general law of relativity. It is more certain that the decree of a judge in a particular case will be maintained than that a general legislative rule or general principle of justice will be observed in all instances. It is the effort both of scientific and jural law to formulate conceptual systems which have at the same time the utmost generality and the utmost reliability. But for practical purposes less general rules which are of more certain reliability may be more useful. The technical arts, like engineering, transportation, agriculture, and medicine, and the social arts like administration, commerce, communication, and education, utilize mainly a less general type of rule. Jural law consists in the reciprocal processes of individual and official decisions concretizing general principles of justice for practical purposes and of juristic writing and judicial opinion generalizing concrete decisions for theoretical purposes. Through this reciprocal process a society develops a system of law which is at the same time rationally integrated by broad principles and concepts, and effectively applied by concrete rules and decisions (36, 41).

The broad principles and concepts which integrate a system of jural law gain their authority from their conformity to the values which are inherent in the culture, and which are supported by the public opinion of the society. Consequently from this point of view jural law may be regarded as both a crystallization and a maintenance of public opinion. Public opinion accepts certain principles of justice; these are concretized in specific rules of law and the latter are enforced by decisions of official agencies. This process is illustrated in the development of American law after the Declaration of Independence, itself distilled from a public opinion originally manifested in the revolutionary Committees of Correspondence. This opinion was formulated in broad principles of justice in the Articles of Confederation presently superseded by the Constitution and the Bill of Rights. This basic law was subsequently concretized through action of the legislative, judicial, and executive authorities established by these instruments. In democratic theory law springs from the people.

From the autocratic point of view, officials who have the power to govern make decisions to carry out their will, but administrative convenience, or even necessity in a complex society, urges that these decisions be generalized by orders, decrees, or rules of law assuring that subordinate officials shall carry out the will of the ruler. The desire to make enforcement of such rules easier urges that they be rationalized in terms of principles of justice comprehensible to, and acceptable by, the people who are to be ruled. To achieve this, opinion must be consulted and representative institutions to express it may be established. This process is illustrated in the development of the English Common Law from the Norman Conquest, through the establishment of the King's Courts and finally the development of Parliament in the thirteenth century. But still, in the theory of the British Constitution, law is an expression of the King's will.

There obviously may be degrees of realization as well as of generalization. A scientific hypothesis or conceptual system may be supported by experiments or observations to verify many deductions made from it but some deductions may still resist such verification. The stage at which the degree of realization justifies calling the generalization a *law* may be controversial. So, also, an ethical norm or principle of justice may have been enforced within a society in many instances but some acts of members of the society, which appear to be contrary to logical deductions from the norm, may have been tolerated or ignored. The stage at which the degree of realization of such a norm justifies calling it law may be controversial. The issue has been extensively debated in connection with the Nuremberg judgment finding certain individuals guilty of the crime of aggressive war. Opinions have differed as to whether the initiation of aggressive war was a crime under international law when the defendants committed the acts for which they were indicted. The tribunal held that it was, that the rule relied upon by the prosecution was not *ex post facto*, and that it had not become obsolete through nonobservance (3, 21, 55).

Jural law differs from scientific law in that it is assumed that it can be violated. Scientific law in principle cannot be violated. An apparent nonconformity of an observation with a rule, which has been generally verified by past observations and experiments and by logical inference from a broader conceptual system generally accepted, may be tolerated for some time but this is possible only on the assumption that there have been errors in observation, reporting, measurement, or deduction, or that relevant factors have been neglected. If in spite of the correction of these errors the observations continue to defy the generalization, the latter must be reformulated to take cognizance of the new observation if it is to continue as *law*. Jural law, however, concerns the behavior of persons and official agencies assumed to have *free will*. Thus it is to be expected that occasionally individuals bound by the law will violate it and that official agencies because of negligence or malfeasance will fail to remedy such violations. A considerable failure of realization is, therefore, to be expected of any rule of jural law. Its status as law depends not only on objective observation that persons and official agencies within the society generally conform to the rules but also on subjective assumption of a duty to conform by such persons and agencies. If that assumption is generally made in the society, the rule may be valid law even though its imperfect observance and enforcement makes it ineffective. The American prohibition amendment, for example, was considered law until its repeal by the twenty-first amendment, although the frequency of its violation was notorious. Excessive and protracted violations may, however, render a jural law obsolete and no longer law. The moment at which this stage has been reached may be controversial. A British court applied the law which permitted a person to exonerate himself from certain charges by "wager of battle" as late as 1829, although the procedure of battle had not been invoked for centuries and was widely considered to be obsolete.

In determining the legal character of an ethical norm, therefore, it is necessary to examine its *sources* no less than its *sanctions*. The former refer to the evidence that a given ethical norm is considered obligatory within the society while the latter refers to the evidence that such a norm is enforced within the society. Some writers distinguish evidence of the origin of a rule (historical source) from evidence of its obligatory character (jural source), and some distinguish the consequence of violation (jural sanction) from factors assuring observance (effectiveness). These distinctions indicate that *jural sources* are closely related to *jural sanctions,* but for present purposes the broad distinction between source and sanction seems sufficient (21).

The sources of jural law have usually been classified as agreement, custom, reason, and authority. It is generally assumed that a sense of obligation can be inferred from express consent to a rule, from long continued observance of a rule manifesting that consent, from logical consistency of a rule with generally accepted principles of justice, and from explicit enactment or declaration of a rule by authority of the society. Each particular system of law defines precisely the circumstances under which agreement, custom, and general principle are to be treated as sources of law and the competence of its official agencies to make and declare law.

The sources of international law available to the International Court of Justice are defined in Article 38 of the statute as follows:

The court, whose function is to decide in accordance with international law such disputes as are submitted to it, shall apply:

a. International conventions, whether general or particular, establishing rules expressly recognized by the contesting states;

b. International custom, as evidence of a general practice accepted as law;

c. The general principles of law recognized by civilized nations (23);

d. Subject to the provisions of Article 59, judicial decisions and the teachings of the most highly qualified publicists of the various nations, as subsidiary means for the determination of rules of law.

Article 59 declares that "the decision of the court has no binding force except between the parties and in respect of that particular case."

It will be observed that the final category indicates very imperfect authority in the society of nations to make law by explicit enactment. To determine law within modern states, the order of importance of these sources would normally be reversed. Enactment by legislative or executive authority would come first, followed by maxims or principles of justice often explicitly stated in constitution or code but sometimes found only in judicial or juristic literature. Customs established by local, commercial, or professional practice of long duration, and agreement established by contract or consent would come last, and would be valid only in so far as permitted by legislation or by accepted general principles of the law.

This difference in emphasis upon the sources available distinguishes international law from systems of municipal law. In the former the prime evidence of legal obligation is assumed to be agreement by the states bound, and in the latter enactment by legislative authority established by the state. The difference in respect to sanctions are no less important. The sanctions, in the broad sense of factors contributing to the observance of jural law include such psychic factors as conscience, habit, interest, and fear. It is generally assumed that a rule will be observed if it is prescribed by the culture or religion of the society, if it conforms to the habits of the peoples bound by it, if observance will serve the self-interest of most of these people on most occasions, and if violation is almost certain to be followed by unpleasant consequences. All social institutions— the schools, churches, and associations as well as government—contribute to putting ethical values, social customs, public opinion and judicial agencies behind the law. Few such institutions function throughout the society of nations but public opinion, diplomatic inertia, and national self-interest, as well as fear of reprisals, often contributes to the observance of international law.

In the narrow sense, the term *sanction* is limited to *jural sanctions,* that is, the consequences which the law attaches to violation of a norm or the punitive or remedial procedures which it authorizes. Fear is, therefore, relied upon, but so far as it recognizes agreement, custom, and general principles of justice as sources, the law by implication acknowledges the importance of interest, habit, and conscience as sanctions. Legislative enactments not conforming to these sources, and consequently not able to rely on these sanctions, are in special need of coercive or *jural* sanctions if they are to be maintained. Frequently, if the social sanctions do not function, the resources of a society will prove unable to enforce a formally enacted law, as illustrated again in the case of the American prohibition amendment. International law and municipal law are alike in depending ultimately on social sanctions for effectiveness, but international law with feeble jural sanctions is mainly dependent on them, and they are less effective in the society of nations than they are in most nation states.

In spite of its weaknesses international law does spring from recognized sources and is supported by recognized sanctions. Its rules, principles, and standards are established by a subjective sense of legal obligation and an objective probability of observance by governments. International law may, therefore, properly be called *law* but the vagueness of its sources, the inadequacy of its sanctions, and the uncertainty of its content, reflecting the changing and disordered state of the world society which it purports to regulate, makes it impossible for states to rely upon it for securing all their rights and interests. The world is still far from being law-governed.

ASSUMPTIONS

International law assumes (*a*) that there is a world society whose peoples are in contact with one another, (*b*) that the people of this society are divided into major groups whose interests are sometimes consistent and sometimes inconsistent, (*c*) that each group guided by reason perceives that its interests will be best served if all observe rules of law formulating their common interests and regulating their conflicts, and (*d*) that the world society through its own organs, or the organs of the groups acting in individual or collective self-interest, will generally prevent flagrant violations of the law from succeeding.

These assumptions it will be observed differ from those of the discipline of international politics in emphasizing that the major groups in the world have some interests in common as well as some in conflict, and that they are sufficiently guided by reason to formulate these interests as law. These assumptions differ from those of international organization in emphasizing that the major groups have some interests in conflict as well as some in common, and that they are guided by rational principles regulating both their common and conflicting interests rather than by a will to co-operate for the common good.

International law may, therefore, be said to occupy an intermediate position between international politics and international organization. It gives greater weight than does international politics, but less than does international organization, to the disposition of statesmen to subordinate the necessities and interests of their groups to the interests of the world as a whole.

While these general assumptions underlie all schools of international law, narrower assumptions are made by each of the schools of international law mentioned at the beginning of this chapter. The historical school, which defines international law as the body of rules, principles, and standards to which independent states are bound by common consent, assumes that the major groups in the world are independent states and that the major interest of each state is the preservation of its independence. The object of international law is, therefore, to maximize national independence or to assure the utmost sovereignty to each state comparable with equal sovereignty to others. This school of thought, however, keeping close to practice does not hesitate to recognize that neutralized states, protectorates, vassal states, members of confederations and unions, mandated and trusteeship territories, and other dependent states with some international status exist, and that consequently the society of states includes some members with less than equal sovereignty (3). This school of thought recognizes custom, and treaties, observance of which is prescribed by custom, as the main sources of international law, and it recognizes habit and inertia, as the main sanction for particular rules of international law. Self-interest, however, often manifested by the disposition of states to form alliances in order to prevent aggressions by any state so serious as to disturb the balance of power, is recognized as the fundamental sanction of the system as a whole. This school following closely the *realism* of international politics sees the equilibrium of power as the only basis of stability in a system of independent states, and consequently assumes that resort to hostilities to preserve that equilibrium, even though not justified by any wrong done by the overpowerful state, is politically justifiable (30). The dilemma arising from this distinction between the legal justifiability of war to prevent or punish violations of law and the political justifiability of war to protect the state's basic interest in its existence, independence, and power position is solved by recognizing the initiation of war for *reason of state* as a prerogative of sovereignty. This view, treating war as an exercise of sovereign power rather than as an act of legal sanction or defense, followed the observed practices and attitudes of post-Renaissance statesmen and ignored the Medieval distinction between just and unjust war. This paved the way for impartial neutrality by third states. War therefore came to be defined as a legal relation of states equally entitling them to pursue their policies and to settle their differences by armed force (43, 54).

With these assumptions international law did not attempt to prevent war, and since war might result in the elimination of states it could not protect the basic security of states. The function of international law was therefore to regulate a limited range of peaceful relations (diplomatic privileges and immunities, treaty validity and interpretation, boundaries, citizens abroad, rights at sea), to regulate the conduct of war (prisoners, private property, occupation, armistices, forbidden methods), and to define the status of neutrals in order to prevent war from spreading (neutral rights at sea and neutral duties of abstention, prevention, acquiescence, vindication, and reparation).

Once war was admitted as a lawful process for acquiring new rights, the status of "international law" as law became doubtful (21) and the art of power politics tended to become the only guide to state behavior. Imperial-minded statesmen and realistic jurists in such circumstances sought to rationalize this art in terms of an *international law* that had abandoned the basic concepts of state independence and equality, and consisted only of procedures rationalizing imperial expansion. This was true of the *auspices* of the Roman *jus feciale* (32), the *Jihad* of Moslem law (22a), the unequal treaties of modern imperial and hegemonic law (26, 46), the Nazi *Ausserstaatsrecht,* and the Soviet law of the *transitional period* destined to terminate in a universal communist society (10).

If a system of law follows practice too closely it becomes history or science and ceases to be normative. The essence of jural law is that it seeks to maintain standards which may be, and sometimes are, violated. It seeks to realize in a society values superior to actual practice. While the historical school of international law does recognize the legal value of state independence, of international negotiations, of freedom of the seas, of the regulation and localization of war, and of the stability of the state system as a whole, it gives international law a position subordinate to that of international politics. It does not view international law as a constructive force that can maintain basic justice among states, rather it conceives it as a law of *co-ordination* dependent upon maintenance of the balance of power by political methods (30). The *society* or *family* of nations is treated by this school as a convenience of jural reasoning, not as a jural society that makes and enforces law to which states are subordinate, and it may be considered less than universal (4, 6, 10, 22a, 29).

The *scientific* school of international law which defines international law as the body of rules, principles, and standards for the violation of which independent states habitually and reciprocally consider one another liable, shifts emphasis from the general behavior of states to their behavior in the one field of diplomatic or legal protest (52). The law is determined not by what states do but by what they object to. An Irish member of the House of Commons, on being asked how one determined what the rules of the House were, said "by violating them." So, according to this school, states discover what international law is by violating it. International law might be defined as the rules indicating the reactions to be expected from other states by the acts of a state or its agents.

The legal advisors of foreign offices tend to take this point of view. On examining a proposed decision or policy of their government, they attempt to advise on the probability that it will be acquiesced in, that it will stimulate mild or vigorous representations, or that it will cause reactions of more or less vigorous protest which if ignored may lead to reprisals or other measures of forcible self-help. It is assumed that states will hesitate to make formal protests against acts by others except on the basis of a rule which they acknowledge as applicable to themselves in similar circumstances. Consequently, on the assumption that states reciprocally acknowledge one another's equality under law, the practice of states in protesting the action of others provides evidence that the rule, violation of which is protested, is one of law (17, 22, 26).

This point of view while recognizing states as the only subjects of international law in the sense that they alone are responsible under it, tends toward a development of procedures for better maintaining this responsibility. The primitive procedure of diplomatic representation and protest may be improved by the utilization of investigating commissions, arbitral tribunals, international courts, and international political agencies like the General Assembly and the Security Council of the United Nations (42). The definition of international law accepted by this school assumes that the society of nations should develop procedures able to determine impartially the liabilities asserted and to provide remedies.

This school of international law may be regarded as *scientific* because it infers the content of international law from objective evidence of the rules which states believe should be sanctioned and because it thereby provides a clear criterion for distinguishing international law from international practice on the one hand and from international ethics on the other (22).

The scientific and historical schools may be regarded as *positivist* in holding that international law flows from state sovereignty whether manifested by the observance of rules and principles in actual conduct or by the demand that rules and principles be observed by others. In this they are to be contrasted with the third school which defines international law as the body of rules, principles, and standards which are most suitable for maintaining order and justice within the world community. The *Naturalist* or philosophical school which accepts this conception of international law assumes that the nature of man and society requires that certain principles be observed. International law is necessarily universal.

This is not the place to examine the history of natural law as it developed in Greek philosophy, in Roman juristic thinking, and in Patristic and Medieval speculation (41). Its basis was introspection and the ethical system inherent in Classical-Christian civilization. The influence of the theory of natural law upon the classical formulation of international law in the sixteenth and seventeenth centuries was very great (4,

8, 29). The concepts of a state of nature and of a natural law which applied among men apart from the institutions of positive law was transferred to international relations on the assumption that sovereign monarchs were, in relation to one another, in a *state of nature* governed only by natural law. When states began to be considered as corporate entities, rather than as sovereign monarchs, the analogy of the state to man in a state of nature, though far from perfect, continued to be applied (8).

The concept of natural law may be given a more scientific connotation, as indeed it had in the writings of Aristotle, by considering that the *natural law* governing human relations is not unlike that governing the relations of nonhuman entities. It is concerned with the actual more than the ethical. Social psychology and sociology may be able to develop valid generalizations relating social norms, institutions, and practices to conditions of communication, population, technology, and culture. Such *natural laws* of society might provide the basis for predicting the effective international law in a given state of world civilization. While the *naturalist* approach has usually been *philosophical,* drawing deductions from such metaphysical assumptions as the equality of states, with this interpretation, *naturalism* might be eligible, even more than the second school discussed, to the designation scientific. Writers with this point of view have denied the equality of states, and have assumed, as did Hobbes, that states have a *natural right* to do what is expedient to increase their freedom and power (26), consequently for them international law differs from international politics only in assuming that states interpret this expediency rationally.

A natural law of the world society need not, however, assume that the sovereignty, or even the existence, of territorial states is inevitable. It should doubtless assume that major groups differing from one another will always exist in the world, but it should not exclude the possibility that individuals, regional groups, and universal functional organizations may be subjects of universal law. Such a natural law would be valid whether the universal society is anarchic, international, federal, or cosmopolitan and might therefore be described as *world law.*

This term has in fact been utilized to describe the law of the United Nations including the relations and procedures of its organs, and the relations of states to individuals and to the specialized agencies in distinction from international law utilized to describe the relations between independent states (40). This school of thought draws its assumptions from the developing science of international relations, particularly as manifested in the disciplines of geography, demography, technology, psychology, sociology and ethics (55).

The practical school of international law, which defines that subject as the body of rules, principles, and standards which are actually invoked because deemed most useful for dealing effectively with international controversies, is eclectic and flexible. It assumes that international law is a practical instrument for dealing with practical problems (24). Diplomats and arbitrators in arguing cases have not hesitated to utilize broad principles of justice and expediency as well as precise rules of custom and treaty (23). The sources of international law available to the International Court of Justice are sufficiently broad to permit the lawyers before the court to find materials to support almost any cause, and the court, as its opinions and dissenting opinions indicate, is able to embrace a wide range of ideas from positivism to naturalism, from *restrictiveness,* interpreting international instruments on the assumption of state sovereignty, to *effectiveness,* interpreting such instruments on the assumption that purposes formally accepted by the parties are to be achieved (25). It is clear in the practice of the International Court and in the writing of contemporary jurists that international law is not today bound by assumptions which prevent it from developing as the needs of a changing world require. There is nothing in the nature of international law to prevent individuals, international organizations, and nonstate associations from being or becoming its subjects, to prevent the community of nations from developing effective organization, or to prevent international law from becoming a *world law* developed and maintained by that organization. While these developments may not be prevented by the nature of international law they may be seriously hampered by the present condition of international politics and international organization (37, 40).

It appears that while all schools of international law assume the existence of both a universal society and subordinate groups, the historical and scientific schools tend to attribute juridical reality only to states from whose will they derive international law, thus reducing the universal society to a mere name. The naturalist and eclectic schools, on the other hand, tend to attribute juridical reality to the universal society and to the sources and sanctions of international law which it has established and from which the jural position of states is derived.

These two points of view if pushed to their logical conclusions lead respectively to national monism and international monism (22, 28). The first asserts that in final analysis the national or *municipal* law of a state must prevail over international law while the second asserts that international law must eventually prevail. Both monistic schools assume that law must constitute a logically consistent system, and are therefore to be contrasted with the *dualistic* or more properly *pluralistic* school which recognizes the distinctiveness of the sources and sanctions of international law and of the municipal law of each state, and the possibility or even probability of inconsistency among them (45). Pluralists point out that in practice national courts apply rules of national law unequivocally expressed by their constitutional authorities even though they may pay respect to the rules of international law as evidence of the probable intention of those authorities (28, 52). International courts, on the other hand, have repeatedly made it clear that within the scope of their jurisdiction they apply international law, anything in the national law of the parties to the contrary notwithstanding. They, however, recognize that national legislation and practice may in some circumstances be a source of international law (37).

The flexibility of legal pluralism, leaving important areas for political adjustment between competing or conflicting national and international legal systems, seems to accord with the facts of contemporary international practice. That practice, guided by moderate interpretations of the scientific and eclectic schools, refuses to accept the logical consequences of monism, either national or international, thus recognizing that law is not a philosophy but a process. Its "life," as Justice Holmes remarked, "has not been logic: it has been experience" (16).

ANALYSIS

As a body of rules and principles applied by diplomats, statesmen, and officials of international organizations, international law is today in a state of flux. The traditional international law, developed in the practice, judicial precedents, and juristic writings of the eighteenth and nineteenth centuries and based on assumptions of historical and jural positivism, is in many respects inconsistent with the new international law, developed in generally ratified conventions of the twentieth century combining Medieval and Renaissance conceptions of natural law with new conceptions of international organization. This change began with recognition of the general interest of all states in preventing war in the Hague Convention for the Pacific Settlement of International Disputes of 1899 and was widely accepted in the League of Nations Covenant and the Kellogg-Briand pact. The change was formally achieved in the Nuremberg Charter, the United Nations Charter, and the interpretations given them in the War Crimes trials and the Universal Declaration of Human Rights (19, 55).

The old international law assumed that states are the only subjects of international law, that they enjoy sovereignty and independence except in so far as modified by explicit rules of customary or conventional international law, that they are free to initiate war for *reason of state,* and that nonparticipating states are obliged to observe impartial neutrality. While approving procedures of international fact-finding conciliation and arbitration to deal with disputes, of international conference to codify international law, and of administrative union to facilitate co-operation in nonpolitical matters, the old international law regarded bilateral diplomacy as the major procedure for the maintenance of international law, and forcible self-help as its major sanction. Controversies and hostilities were regarded as matters of primary concern only to the litigating states.

The new international law assumes that individuals and international organizations, as well as states, are subjects of international law; that the sovereignty and independence of states is limited by rules of international law and procedure intended to realize the purposes and maintain the principles of the United Nations Charter; that the initiation of aggressive war is an unlawful act and does not protect the responsible individuals from criminal prosecution even if committed in the name of a state, and that nonparticipating states must not help the aggressor and must assist the United Nations in maintaining and restoring international peace and security (19, 33, 55). It therefore assumes the indivisibility of war and the indivisibility of peace. Hostilities anywhere and controversies which may lead to hostilities are of interest to all states and to the community of nations as a whole. War in the sense of a situation which equally entitles the participants to contend by arms, as in a duel, is outlawed. If hostilities occur, the aggressor and the defender must be differentiated. International relations are, therefore, in considerable measure, multilateral and the society of nations as a whole should consider and deal with serious controversies and situations, should act to maintain international peace and security, and should facilitate co-operation among nations to develop conditions favorable to a just and stable world.

Juristic opinion is divided as between advocates of the old and the new international law. It is urged on the one hand that the political and social conditions of the world will not in any foreseeable future permit realization of the new international law; that assertion of a law incapable of realization, produces disillusionment, contempt for law, and retrogression to chaos; that the new international law implies a centralization of world authority favorable to administrative tyranny and dangerous to human liberty; and that, in any case, such centralization presupposes a uniformity of world civilization which would eliminate the competition of value systems essential for human progress. It is, therefore, alleged that the realization of the new international law is both improbable and undesirable, and that attention should be turned to the traditional rules of international law, developing them in accord with the basic principles of territorial sovereignty and creating conditions favorable to their observance such as a more stable equilibrium of power, a broader spirit of international co-operation, and more effective agencies of pacific settlement (20).

The advocates of the new international law, on the other hand, urge that the old international law developed in the seventeenth, eighteenth, and nineteenth centuries is not adapted to the shrinking world in which all peoples are vulnerable to military, economic, and propaganda attacks from distant quarters and that civilization or even the human race itself will be destroyed unless the world organizes effectively to maintain the principles of the new international law. The obsolescence of the old international law is said to be demonstrated not only by the consequences of recent wars but by the practical action of governments and peoples in demanding effective measures to outlaw war and protect human rights and in ratifying general conventions to realize these demands. The new international law, it is insisted, need not involve a degree of legal or political centralization or cultural uniformity incompatible with human progress, in fact the social and cultural differences among nations and regions are so embedded in geographic, climatic, economic, and historic conditions that fear of too much uniformity in the world is fantastic. Concerted effort on the political, economic, educational, and cultural fronts can, it is said, create conditions under which the new international law can be realized. It is, therefore, asserted that the old international law has become obsolete and undesirable beyond hope of revival, and that the peoples and governments must strive to realize the new international law to which they have committed themselves (7, 9, 19, 26, 33, 54, 55).

The new international law in principle changes the world society from a system of sovereign states to a world union in which the United Nations protects human rights, punishes international crimes, and enforces its law against both states and individuals. In principle there is, therefore, a functional division of governmental authority between the United Nations and the nations similar to the division of powers between the United States and states of the union. This functional division is, however, imperfect in law because the United Nations does not include all states and the powers of its central organs are mainly of persuasive rather than coercive character. Legislative power is vested only in the Security Council and only in respect to the restoration and maintenance of international peace and security. Executive power outside of the Secretariat is also vested only in the Security Council and only in respect to forces provided by states in agreement with it. Judicial power is vested in the International Court of Justice but extends only to cases between states submitted by specific or general agreement of the parties. Furthermore, the exercise of the limited legislative and executive powers of the Security Council is seriously hampered by the voting procedure requiring unanimity of the great powers. The United Nations has not been able to recruit military forces, collect taxes, or influence world opinion so as to develop a power comparable in fact to that of the major nations. These nations have not to date been willing to limit their own armaments or to contribute armed forces to the United Nations. Their financial contributions have averaged less than one part in a thousand of their national budgets and they have carefully controlled United Nations information in their mass media and educational systems. They have not rallied to the United Nations but have tended to cluster around two poles of power, making the world's political equilibrium very unstable (37, 55).

From the factual point of view, the problem of realizing the new international law lies in the realm of international politics, international organization, international economics, international education, and international communications. Can political conciliation, organizational activity, trade, propaganda, and education develop a more stable and united world in which the United Nations can so develop its power in relation to that of the nations that it can perform the functions attributed to it by the charter? These problems are considered in other chapters of this book.

From the legal point of view, the problem of realizing the new international law concerns in the long run the continuous process of legal practice and interpretation, but in the short run it concerns the amendment, interpretation, implementation, and supplementation of the United Nations Charter.

Formal amendment of the charter requires unanimity of the great powers. That procedure is likely to block important amendments unless there is a change in the attitude of the Soviet Union which has insisted upon full retention of its sovereignty as defined by traditional international law even at the expense of frustrating realization of the purposes stated in the charter. Because of its minority position in the world and the radical difference between the communist type of world order which it desires and the democratic type of world order desired by the Western powers, such a change in attitude in respect to amending the charter implies a radical change of outlook by the Soviet leaders.

A general conference for reviewing the charter may however be summoned by vote of the Assembly and Security Council without great power veto, and the summoning of such a conference will be considered automatically in 1955. Such a conference can propose amendments which, however, become valid only if approved by two-thirds of the members of the United Nations including the principal powers. Such proposals might develop sufficient world opinion to induce the Soviet government to modify its position at least in minor matters.

Without formal amendment the charter might be made much more effective if suitable standards of interpretation were adopted. Certain members of the United Nations, particularly the Soviet Union, have on occasions insisted on the principle of *restrictive* interpretation which operates on the presumption that the members preserve their sovereignty except insofar as explicitly renounced by the charter or other treaty. In general, however, the organs of the United Nations have followed the principles of *effective* interpretation which operate on the presumption that the members intended to realize the purposes and principles stated in the charter and therefore intended to contribute power to the organs of the United Nations and to qualify the sovereignty of states to the extent necessary to that end. Application of this standard of interpretation has made it possible for the organs of the United Nations to make recommendations on matters within the scope of the charter even though the member affected has considered it essentially within its *domestic jurisdiction* (Art. 2, par. 7) and has made it possible for courts to protect human rights within the territory of members on the ground that the latter pledged themselves by the charter (Art. 56) to respect those rights. The principle of effective interpretation has also made it possible for the General Assembly to recommend action by the members concerning the maintenance of international peace and security, whenever the Security Council, because of the veto or other reasons, has been unable to function, and has made it possible for members to organize under Article 51 in *collective self-defense* against aggression when the United Nations as such proves unable to act. It is clear that this principle of interpretation opens up a wide opportunity to develop new procedures within the charter when the procedures specified prove unworkable. The organs of the United Nations, including the International Court of Justice, have increasingly adopted the effective standard of interpretation of the charter as did the Supreme Court of the United States in interpreting the Constitution under the leadership of John Marshall.

The problem of implementation involves effective administration by the Secretariats of the United Nations and its Specialized Agencies; efficient procedures in the conduct of business by the political organs; adequate gearing of the governments of the members into the activity of international organizations; effective co-ordination of the activities of the United Nations and its Specialized Agencies; continuous informational and educational activity to develop a world public opinion behind the United Nations and the Specialized Agencies; and political ingenuity in making decisions and recommendations by these agencies, in inducing members to conform to them, and in devising new procedures when those that have been used prove unworkable (40).

Much can be accomplished by the day to day activity of able and devoted civil servants in the Secretariats and of representatives of governments in the political organs of the United Nations and the Specialized Agencies. The process is slow, but custom and interest may in time conspire to develop a machinery of international organization and an opinion giving it vigor, particularly if the principle of effective interpretation is utilized. In this way hampering restrictions may be avoided and progress may be possible without breach of legal continuity and without sudden or radical innovations which might induce revolt.

Supplementation refers to action by the members in committing themselves to obligations within the general purposes of the United Nations but beyond the specific commitments of the charter. The creation of the Specialized Agencies was of this character. So also was the establishment of regional arrangements among American, Soviet, Western European, North Atlantic, Arab, and Pacific states. The effect upon the charter of such arrangements requires careful scrutiny. They are contemplated by that instrument, but if they become too powerful, they may contribute to a weakening of United Nations control, to a bipolarization of the world, and to a decrease of international stability. The charter assumes that authority in the use of force to "maintain and restore international peace and security" should be centralized and consequently that defensive action by states or groups of states should be controlled by the central authority of United Nations (Arts. 51-54). Frequent failure of the Security Council to function because of the veto has made such regional and collective self-defense arrangements seem necessary. The supervision of these arrangements by the General Assembly, contemplated under the Uniting for Peace resolution of 1950, may moderate their inherent danger. However, the problem of adjusting world and regional defense arrangements so as to maximize stability is far from being solved. There can be no doubt but that an uncontrolled development of regional security arrangements would frustrate achievement of the basic purposes of the charter (6).

CRITICISM

The discipline of international law is in a state of crisis. As understood by traditionalists it appears to be obsolete, and as understood by modernists it appears to be premature. A system of law must look to the past and the values of continuity, predictability, and stability, but it must also look to the future and the values of justice, progress, and peace demanded by the public opinion of the community. A valid legal discipline must reconcile vested interests with public policies and in a progressive society, whose visions of the future and interpretations of the past are continually changing, it must include means of continuous self-correction. In times of exceptionally rapid change the gap between custom and aspiration may become too wide to bridge.

Systems of municipal law faced by rapid social change have often been altered by revolution. The change in the condition of the world community during the first half of the twentieth century has been of revolutionary proportions. The invention of the airplane, the radio, and the atomic bomb; the spread of ideologies of democracy, of communism, of human rights and of human welfare; the self-determination of hitherto dependent peoples; the shifts in the location and relative magnitude of centers of political and military power; and the organization of world authority to eliminate war, to secure national and individual rights, and to promote human welfare have produced a wide gap between the nineteenth and the twentieth centuries (55). The nations have formally accepted revolutionary changes in international law to accommodate their rights and obligations to these momentous changes in the conditions of the world. The obstacles which the condition of world politics and national opinions, and the traditions of diplomacy, war, and international law itself, offer to the utilization of the new international law are tremendous. Little help in surmounting these obstacles can be expected from the traditional arts of international relations which assume conditions that are vanishing. A science of international relations based on more fundamental assumptions of geography, technology, culture, and human nature might prove helpful.

REFERENCES

This selection from the voluminous literature of international law includes a few of the histories and *"classics,"* a few of the general treatises on jurisprudence and international law, and some of the studies on recent tendencies of international law. Reference may here be made to the collections of source materials (treaties, diplomatic correspondence, documents of international organizations, and cases). These include the *Digests of International Law* edited by John Bassett Moore (Washington, Government Printing Office, 1906) and Green Hackworth (Washington, Government Printing Office, 1940); the collections of *International Legislation* (Washington, Carnegie Endowment, 1932-1948) and *World Court Reports* edited by Manley O. Hudson, (Washington, Carnegie Endowment, 1934-1943); and the *Annual Digest of Public International Law Cases,* edited by Hersh Lauterpacht (London, Longmans and Butterworth, 1932 on). Numerous studies on special topics have appeared as monographs or in journal articles, of which the Draft Conventions of the Harvard Research on International Law (Supplements, *American Journal of International Law,* 1929-1939) deserve special mention. Such materials constitute the principal working library of the practicing international lawyer.

1. BRIERLY, Sir James L., *The Law of Nations,* 4th ed. (New York, Oxford University Press, 1949).
2. ———, *The Outlook for International Law* (New York, Oxford University Press, 1944).
3. BRIGGS, Herbert W., *The Law of Nations: Cases, Documents and Notes,* 2nd ed. (New York, Appleton-Century-Crofts, 1952).
4. BUTLER, Sir Geoffrey, and MACCOBY, Simon, *The Development of International Law* (New York, Longmans, 1928).
5. BYNKERSHOEK, Cornelius van, *Questionum Juris Publici,* Libro Uno, English trans. by Frank (Oxford, Carnegie Endowment for International Peace, 1930).
6. Commission to Study the Organization of Peace, *Regional Arrangements for Security and the United Nations,* Eighth Report, New York, 1953.
7. CORBETT, Percy, *Law and Society in the Relations of States* (New York, Harcourt, 1951).
8. DICKINSON, Edwin D., *The Equality of States in International Law* (Cambridge, Harvard University Press, 1920).
9. FENWICK, Charles G., *International Law,* 3rd ed. (New York, Appleton-Century-Crofts, 1948).
10. FLECHTHEIM, Ossip K., and HERZ, John H., "Bolshevist and National Socialist Doctrines of International Law," *Social Research* (February, 1940).
11. GENTILI, Alberico, *De Jure Belli,* Libri Tres, English trans. by Rolfe (Washington, Carnegie Endowment for International Peace, 1933).

12. GOEBEL, Julius, *The Equality of States, A Study in the History of Law* (New York, Columbia University Press, 1923).

13. GROTIUS, Hugo, *De Jure Belli ac Pacis,* English trans. by Kelsey (Oxford, Carnegie Endowment for International Peace, 1925).

14. HALL, William E., *A Treatise on International Law,* 8th ed. (A. P. Higgins, Oxford University Press, 1924).

15. HOLLAND, T. E., *Studies on International Law* (New York, Oxford University Press, 1898).

16. HOLMES, Oliver Wendell, Jr., *The Common Law* (Boston, 1881; rev. ed., Little, Brown, 1923).

17. HURST, Sir Cecil J. B., *International Law, Collected Papers* (London, Stevens, 1950).

18. HYDE, Charles Cheney, *International Law, Chiefly as Interpreted and Applied by the United States* (Boston, Little, Brown, 1945), 3 vols.

19. JESSUP, Philip C., *A Modern Law of Nations* (New York, Macmillan, 1948).

20. KEETON, George W. and SCHWARZENBERGER, Georg, *Making International Law Work* (London, New Commonwealth Institute, 1939).

21. KELSEN, Hans, *Law and Peace in International Relations* (Cambridge, Harvard University Press, 1942).

22. ——, *Principles of International Law* (New York, Rinehart, 1952).

22a. KHADDURI, Majid, *The Law of War and Peace in Islam* (London, Luzar, 1940).

23. LAUTERPACHT, Hersh, *Private Law Sources and Analogies of International Law* (London, Longmans, 1927).

24. ——, *The Function of Law in the International Community* (New York, Oxford University Press, 1933).

25. ——, *International Law and Human Rights* (London, Stevens, 1950).

26. LORIMER, Sir James, *Institutes of the Law of Nations* (Edinburgh, Blackwood, 1883), 2 vols.

27. MAINE, Sir Henry Sumner, *International Law,* 2nd ed. (New York, 1894).

28. MASTERS, Ruth D., *International Law in National Courts* (New York, Columbia University Press, 1932).

29. NUSSBAUM, Arthur, *A Concise History of the Law of Nations* (New York, Macmillan, 1947).

30. OPPENHEIM, L., *International Law,* 1905, 7th ed. rev. by H. Lauterpacht (London, Longmans, 1948, 1952), 2 vols.

31. ——, *The Future of International Law* (New York, Oxford University Press, 1921).

32. PHILLIPSON, Coleman, *The International Law and Custom of Ancient Greece and Rome* (London, Macmillan, 1911), 2 vols.

33. POLITIS, N., *New Aspects of International Law* (Washington, Carnegie Endowment for International Peace, 1928).

34. PUFENDORF, S., *De Jure Naturae et Gentium,* Libri Octo, English trans. by Oldfather (Oxford, Carnegie Endowment for International Peace, 1934).

35. ROOT, Elihu, *Addresses on International Subjects* (Cambridge, Harvard University Press, 1916).

36. SALMOND, Sir John, *Jurisprudence or the Theory of Law* (London, Stevens, 1902).

37. SCHWARZENBERGER, Georg, *International Law as Applied by International Courts and Tribunals* (London, Stevens, 1945).

38. SCOTT, James Brown, *The Catholic Conception of International Law* (Washington, Georgetown University Press, 1934).

39. SERENI, Angelo P., *The Italian Conception of International Law* (New York, Columbia University Press, 1943).

40. SOHN, Louis, *Cases and Other Materials on World Law* (Brooklyn, Foundation Press, 1950).

41. STONE, Julius, *The Province and Function of Law, Law as Logic, Justice, and Social Control* (Cambridge, Harvard University Press, 1950).

41a. ———, *Legal Controls of International Conflict* (New York, Rinehart, 1954).

42. STOWELL, Ellery C., *International Law* (New York, Holt, 1931).

43. STURZO, Luigi, *The International Community and the Right of War*, English trans. by B. B. Carter (New York, R. R. Smith, 1930).

44. SUAREZ, Francisco, *De Legibus ac Deo Legislatore* (1612), English trans., by Williams (Oxford, Carnegie Endowment for International Peace, 1944).

45. TRIEPEL, Heinrich, *Völkerrecht und Landesrecht* (Leipzig, 1899).

46. ———, *Die Hegemonie, ein Buch von führenden Staaten* (Stuttgart, 1938).

47. VATTEL, Emerich, *Le Droit des Gens*, English trans. by Fenwick (Washington, Carnegie Endowment for International Peace, 1916).

48. VICTORIA, Francis de, *De Indis et de Jure Beli Relectiones*, English trans. by Bate (Washington, Carnegie Endowment for International Peace, 1917).

49. WESTLAKE, John, *International Law*, 2nd ed. (Cambridge, Cambridge University Press, 1910, 1913), 2 vols.

50. WILSON, George Grafton, *International Law*, 3rd ed. (St. Paul, West, 1939).

51. WOLFF, C. von, *Jus Gentium Methodo Scientifica Petractatum*, English trans. by Drake (Oxford, Carnegie Endowment for International Peace, 1934).

52. WRIGHT, Quincy, *The Enforcement of International Law Through Municipal Law in the United States* (Urbana, University of Illinois, 1916).

53. ———, *Research in International Law Since the War* (Washington, Carnegie Endowment for International Peace, 1930).

54. ———, *A Study of War* (Chicago, University of Chicago Press, 1942), pp. 152 ff., 329 ff., 694 ff., 707, 863 ff., 895 ff., 923 ff., 1229 ff., 1294 ff., 1332 ff., 1392 ff., 1416 ff., 1425 ff.

55. ———, *Problems of Stability and Progress in International Relations* (Berkeley, University of California Press, 1954).

CHAPTER
20

International Economics

DEFINITION

INTERNATIONAL ECONOMICS is the art of managing the world economy and the foreign aspects of national economies. As a discipline it is the philosophy guiding this art and appraising its methods; the science relating national economies to one another and relating economic activity to world politics; and the history both of international economic activities and of theories about them.

Economic activity includes all activity rationally designed to achieve human objectives when faced by the niggardliness of nature, that is, by the scarcity of material or human resources (55, 74, 95). It is therefore contrasted with political activity which includes all activity designed to achieve group objectives when faced by the opposition of other groups. Scarcity is the essence of economics as opposition is of politics. In economics the problem is to overcome obstructions to achievement arising from physical nature, in politics to overcome obstructions arising from human nature. Technology, geography, and demography are basic to economics, as psychology, sociology, and ethics are basic to politics.

Both international politics and international economics assume that the world is divided into sovereign states, each with distinct policies and economies. Economics, however, assumes that men are rational, at least in some of their activities; that in making choices, they will calculate the probable results and the relation of means to ends; and that such choices will, therefore, tend to employ limited resources to maximize the satisfaction of these ends. Politics, on the other hand, recognizes that men frequently act on the basis of irrational emotional drives and erroneous

237

beliefs; consequently political scientists study attitudes and opinions as they are and the choices which they suggest. They often find that political behavior can best be explained by psychological analyses of masses and of individual leaders, and that insight may be obtained from infantile and neurotic behavior. They study biological and cultural drives and practices of ambivalence, repression, scapegoating, displacement, projection, and inertia. Only in special circumstances do they anticipate rational adaptation of clearly defined means to clearly defined ends. Economists, on the other hand, attempt to predict opinions from a fundamental human desire to satisfy long-run wants and a fundamental human rationality in adapting means to ends. Economists, however, recognize that much of human behavior, particularly that involved in the occurrence and continuance of wars and the rivalries for power cannot be explained on that basis and so tend to confine their study to the limited fields in which human action is in considerable measure rational, especially agricultural, industrial, business, and financial activity. They thus tend to relegate the causation of war and of international relations to the realms of politics, sociology, and psychology (72).

Economists have seldom accepted the idea, popularized by Marxism and supported by some historians, that the major causes of war are economic. They usually agree that "the passions that lead to war do not arise from hunger, privation and fatigue," but from "wounded self-respect, helpless hatred and thwarted affection" (9). "Hunger, privation and fatigue" are easier to define than are "wounded self-respect, helpless hatred and thwarted affection," and the means for dealing with them are less controversial. If *rationality* consists in a clear definition of ends and the application of effective means to realize them, politics is less likely to be *rational* than economics because its ends are so vague and its means are so controversial. Economics, however, is by no means free of these difficulties (89, 95).

While the various schools of economic thought have been together in associating economic activity with scarcity of resources, conscious wants, and deliberate choices based upon calculation of causes and consequences, they have differed in the definition of economic values. Some have distinguished economic values from other values by their objective necessity for maintaining life or the standard of living [classical (55, 64, 74) and ethical schools (83)], and others by their measurability, actual or potential [mathematical school (11, 59, 90)]. Still others hold that all subjective values do [marginal utility school (2, 37, 54)] or ought [neoclassical school (41, 51)] to enter into the economic calculus. Most economic schools have been interested in the factors determining market values, measured by prices, but some have attached greater importance in this determination to producers' costs [classical school], dependent on the "state of the arts" [Marxists], and others to consumers demands [marginal utility school], dependent on the prevailing value system [neo-classical school], and institutional arrangements [historical school (47, 75)], including government policy [Keynsians (24, 40)].

In spite of their differences the fields of economics and politics overlap. A shortage of resources leads to competition between different persons or groups to obtain them and this may lead to rivalry, conflict, and political activity by each to overcome the obstruction offered by others to attaining its objectives. Conversely, a group may persuade an opposing group to yield to its demands by offering economic rewards or withholding economic advantages. Politics may therefore be an instrument of economics and economics may be an instrument of politics.

Foreign policies of states were often said, during the seventeenth and eighteenth centuries, to seek *peace and plenty* and much the same idea has been expressed in the nineteenth and twentieth centuries by the phrase *security and prosperity* (28, 84). Peace or security has been said to be the objective of *political* policy, and plenty or prosperity of *economic* policy. Sometimes security has been sought in order to secure conditions in which the people might prosper; sometimes prosperity has been sought in order to develop national wealth with which to build armaments to increase the state's power position and better to assure its security. Within the United Nations these two objectives are pursued together—the "maintenance of international peace and security" by the Security Council and the "promotion of the economic and social advancement of all peoples" by the Economic and Social Council.

On the other hand, economic and political activities may conflict with one another. Prosperity may be sacrificed for power, but on other occasions power may be sacrificed for prosperity. The exclusive pursuit of economic policy by a state may result in neglect of military preparation, in expansion of international trade rendering the state vulnerable to blockade, and in a decline in the military spirit, all tending to impair the state's political power. Reciprocally, exclusive pursuit of political policy may result in excessive taxes and excessive barriers to international trade, reducing the prosperity of all, and in a regimentation and militarization of the people, hampering technological development, economic enterprise, and the commercial spirit. Governments, therefore, continually find it necessary to balance economic against political policies, attempting to achieve as much national security as is possible without undue impoverishment of the people, and as much prosperity as is possible without undue impairment of national defense (34). Such moderate policies, maintaining a balance between domestic pressures and foreign necessities, between economic policy and political policy, guiding the first by the effort to maintain a balance of trade and the latter by an effort to maintain a balance of power, have been characteristic of most states during the modern period. But there have been exceptions in practice and efforts have been made to justify them in theory.

Both nationalists and internationalists have sought to reconcile politics and economics. The extreme internationalists have tended to become cosmopolitans and to assert that general pursuit of economic policy will result in free trade, economic interdependence, and a world community devoted to human prosperity, welfare, and economic progress in which war will be so obviously unnecessary and irrational that it will not occur. Sound economic policy, they therefore contend, is the means for peace and security as well as for plenty and prosperity for all. This position was maintained by the Manchester School of Cobden and Bright in the mid-nineteenth century and by such "liberals" as Cordell Hull and Norman Angell in the twentieth century. It undoubtedly influenced British free trade policy in the Victorian period and, in lesser degree, the American Reciprocal Trade policy of the "New Deal" (9, 17, 86, 92). In neither instance, however, was political policy wholly neglected. Britain maintained a dominant navy during its free trade era and the United States developed its military and naval power during the New Deal period. The economic policies advocated by the League of Nations and the United Nations have been in considerable measure based on this theory, but again these economic policies have been associated with political policies of collective security to maintain peace and prevent war (9, 34, 92, 96).

On the other hand, the extreme nationalists have tended to become imperialists and to assert that general pursuit of political policy will result in such augmentation of national power that effective opposition can be eliminated. A universal empire can then be established in which peace and security for all can be assured and economic life can prosper in a universal market as it did in the Pax Romana of the Antonine Caesars, the India of Asoka, and the China of the Mings (26, 38, 61). However, efforts in this direction of the Hapsburgs, the Bourbons, the Bonapartes, the Hohenzollerns, and the Nazis at successive periods of modern history have produced neither security nor prosperity but universal war and economic deterioration.

The British during the nineteenth century, by balancing a national and imperial political policy with an international and cosmopolitan economic policy, achieved the *Pax Britannica* in which peace and prosperity advanced more, at least in Europe, than at any period since the age of the Antonines (12, 95). The League of Nations and the United Nations have both sought to achieve a similar balance of international political policy and international economic policy, but faced by the new imperialism, first of the Nazis and then of the Soviets, results have to date been disappointing. The experience, however, suggests that the maintenance of balance among economic and political ends is better adapted to modern conditions than efforts to reconcile these ends through either a universal economy or a universal state.

Economic policies have tended toward pacifism and cosmopolitanism and political policies have tended toward militarism and imperialism. Neither has been successful, if pursued exclusively, in achieving its aim. Only through balance have people been able to enjoy either moderate security or moderate prosperity.

Theory has reached the same conclusion. Economics, centering attention on the problem of man against physical nature and assuming human rationality, concludes that men will in the long run co-operate with, rather than fight, one another whether this co-operation takes the form of fair competition or organized planning. War is generally uneconomic; peace is generally economic. This conclusion of economic thinking is sometimes obscured by the laymen's identification of competition with conflict. While both are species of opposition, the two are sharply distinguished by most economists and sociologists (56, 95). Competition refers to opposition among social entities independently striving for something of which the supply is inadequate to satisfy all, while conflict refers to oppositions among social entities directed against one another. Competitors need not be aware of one another's existence while entities in conflict always are. Competition may, it is true, result in conflict, as it does when political methods are used by a government to achieve economic ends or when a business concern resorts to direct methods to eliminate a particular competitor. Competition may also result in elimination of the unsuccessful without such awareness. Such competition, called by Darwin the struggle for existence and survival of the fittest, has been a more important factor in organic evolution than conflict. The results of competition need not, however, be so drastic. In human affairs, the unsuccessful competitor may move to greener pastures; both competitors may improve their techniques or discover new resources or new markets; or they may combine to share resources, techniques, and markets. The normal effect of competition is, therefore, to promote division of labor, trade, technological advance, and co-operation, increasing production and lowering prices. Competition can, and usually does, improve the economic position not only of competing producers but also of the consumers who obtain economic goods more cheaply (3, 27, 29, 55, 64, 65, 73, 74).

Conflict on the other hand in the short run injures both parties to the conflict and may do so in the long run. Furthermore, the struggle for power in preparation for the conflict is very likely to reduce the prosperity of all participants. That struggle may be spoken of as a competition for power. But such political competition differs radically from economic competition for a living. Political power is necessarily relative—one man's superiority in power is another man's inferiority. Economic gain, however, may be mutual—one man's prosperity may increase that of others. Both participants in a trade or bargain may profit (74). Political competition, therefore, tends toward conflict while economic competition tends toward co-operation. Economics can therefore be considered the science of human co-operation to conquer nature, while politics can be considered the science of group co-operation to conquer other groups. The phrase *beat 'em or join 'em* may apply to either economic or political competition, but in the first the natural trend is toward a joining of all humanity to fight nature, while in politics the natural trend is toward the joining of half of humanity to fight the other half in a universal and mutually suicidal war.

The art of diplomacy may, it is true, long maintain an unstable equilibrium by continually uniting the weaker and isolating the over-powerful, but the trend of politics among sovereigns is toward conflict and war. This trend may only be reversed through recognition by each that its security depends on the stability of the whole (i.e., that its sovereignty is in part qualified). In so far as the opposition between parallel groups, inherent in politics, is moderated by opposition between a superior and an inferior group—between the United Nations and each nation, between a federation and each member state, between the state and each citizen—politics may become an instrument of peace. Wise diplomats, in pursuing international politics, conceive the equilibrium of the system of states as a whole as in opposition to the policy of whatever state at the moment threatens to disturb the peace.

Maintenance of balance between the political end of power and the economic end of prosperity must be distinguished from the maintenance of balance between military preparedness and sound economy, both treated as instruments of power, and also from the maintenance of balance between government intervention in business and free enterprise, both treated as instruments of prosperity. Most politicians today recognize that a prosperous civilian economy is an element of state power, no less essential than armaments in being. So, also, most economists, repudiating extremes of both socialism and *laissez faire,* recognize the need of some government intervention in economic life to sustain the conditions of free markets, to prevent monopoly and exploitation, to moderate economic fluctuations, and to assure continuous economic expansion (6, 7, 24, 40, 41, 45, 46, 65, 68, 69, 73, 77).

While international economics and international politics are both primarily arts, the former has made greater strides toward becoming a science.

Modern economics has behind it practice as old as human existence (12, 31). It also has behind it empirical generalizations and philosophical speculations extending into antiquity (23, 30). It began to become a discipline during the mercantilist period of early modern history (28).

However, the discipline became established only after Adam Smith and the classical economists had asserted certain general hypotheses and these had been integrated into a conceptual system resting on the assumptions of Benthamite hedonism and utilitarianism. Among these hypotheses were the following: that production will be maximized by the utmost division of labor (occupational or geographic) and the utmost freedom of trade among all producers and consumers; that such trade will benefit both buyer and seller if each is guided by rational self-interest, the buyer seeking the cheapest and the seller the dearest market; that free markets equating prices of commodities, wages of labor, interest on capital, and profits of management will distribute the product according to the contribution of each to the productive process; that automatic adjustments to changes in population, technology, and values will, with only temporary lapses, maintain employment, demand, and production, permitting the free market to expand indefinitely (25); and that individual and national wealth, and individual and social justice will be promoted by such maximization of production, such equitableness of distribution, and such expansion of the market. The classical economists sought in the approved scientific method to verify deductions from these hypotheses by observation and statistics (51, 55, 64, 74, 78).

Political science, on the other hand, while it has an equally long history of practice and an even longer history of empirical generalization and philosophical speculation behind it, became a discipline even more recently than economics and not because of any general hypotheses, but because of practical interests. Constitutional and international lawyers, political philosophers, public administrators, political historians, politicians, and diplomats found that they had a common interest in recording, systematizing, and increasing their knowledge about the state which had come to be the focus of politics and the center of interest to all of them. While both the economists and the political scientists have been divided into a number of schools, the schools of economics have arisen through divergent criticisms of the classical hypotheses, while schools of political science have been distinguished by different definitions of their subject arising from the different aspects of the state—philosophical, practical, juristic, psychological, or institutional—which have attracted the attention of each.

Furthermore, economic phenomena—production, demand, and trade—lend themselves to precise definition, to quantification, and to objective verification better than do political phenomena—organizations, policies, and procedures.

While the conceptual system of the classical economists has not withstood unscathed the criticism and testing to which it has been subjected, and the arguments for the rival conceptual systems which have combatted it, discussion has on the whole proceeded by the scientific processes of precise formulation, concrete observation, and logical deduction and induction under the assumption that the test of the truth of a proposition is its capacity to predict or control. In political science, on the other hand, as in jural law, generalization has consisted of expositions of ideals, goals or principles to be achieved, of practical measures for achieving them, and of the systematic relationships of such measures. The goals or principles are usually drawn from subjective aspiration or public opinion and the methods from law, precedent, or history. Political science has only begun, through the rise of psychological and sociological concepts and of statistical methods, to formulate, in the manner of science, precise relationships between causes and effects, between ends and means, between the abstract and concrete, and between generalizations and facts, and to verify such formulations by logic or objective observation convincing to all who understand the symbols and techniques.

Political generalizations, like jural laws, have usually claimed to be true only in the sense that human groups, the members of which generally believe in them, may be able to make them true by appropriate organization and action. Economic generalizations, on the other hand, have claimed to be true whenever or wherever the conditions postulated exist. The two styles of generalization may, it is true, differ more in form than in substance. Goals and conditions approach each other in the social sciences. Political science may describe its ideals and the state of opinion and organization which can and will achieve them in the form of conditions implicit in its generalization, while economics may be obliged to acknowledge that its generalizations are true only under conditions of human opinion and organization sustaining its implicit values and goals (27). The "conditions" of most "truths" in the social sciences include states of human opinion and belief as well as of natural resources and environment. Subjective values are no less important than material conditions.

ASSUMPTIONS

Several assumptions, not always consistent with one another, have been made by the various schools of economics. As noted, modern economics began with a logical theory elaborated by the classical school upon certain assumptions concerning (a) economic resources, (b) human welfare, (c) the political division of the world, and (d) the rationality of man. Each of these assumptions may be examined.

Resources. The classical economists assumed that the supply of economic goods and services was inadequate to serve human needs and that consequently production should be maximized. They were faced by the facts of human necessities for food, clothing and housing, and the scarcity of resources and skills to provide them in sufficient abundance. Consequently the outstanding problem was that of more efficient production.

Efficiency implied more goods for less work, thus a distinction was assumed between work or labor which was burdensome and leisure or play which was pleasurable. Production, generally involving burdensome labor, was assumed to constitute *economic* activity while consumption was pleasant and constituted *noneconomic* activity. Economic value was, therefore, measured by the cost of production or the amount of labor required to produce the commodity in question (55, 74).

Presently it was observed that economic value as measured by price was not actually determined by cost of production but fluctuated widely according to consumers' demand. Also, luxury goods and services had economic value and were exchanged in the market for necessities of life. As a result the marginal utility school developed (2, 37, 54). This school explained economic values by comparison within the mind of each consumer of the relative subjective value of the alternative purchases which his means would permit and comparison among consumers of the subjective value or utility each attributed to a given commodity. The economic demand resulting from these comparisons induced exchanges, the *marginal* utility, or least utility satisfied in the market, determining the price. The mathematical school combined the classical and marginal utility schools by ascribing the economic process to the changing relation of supply and demand in the market. It explained market value by simultaneous equations involving many variables such as production costs, output, effective demand, and subjective values (13, 44, 59, 90). The historical, institutional, and ethical schools underlined the dependence of these complicated relations upon the opinion, culture, institutions, policies, and progress of the society as a whole (47, 75, 83). This *macroeconomic* approach was accepted by the *neo-classicists* although they did not entirely abandon the *microeconomic* approach of the earlier schools (25, 41). The structure and changes of the whole society seemed to them more significant for either prediction or control than the motives and activities of the individual *economic man*. Both the mathematical and the institutional points of view tended to eliminate the classical distinction between economic activity (labor and production) and noneconomic activity (leisure and consumption), and to shift the problem of economics from that of production to meet human necessities to that of accounting for economic values and realizing them.

Welfare. The classical economists had assumed that human welfare would be served by equitable distribution of the goods and services produced, but they were inclined to interpret equity as the natural result of exchange in free markets. They argued that such exchange would assure to every element in the production process—land, capital, labor, and management—a return proportionate to its contribution to that process. If production were maximized—and they thought it would be maximized by freeing enterprise from government regulation—distribution would take care of itself in free markets. The desirability of separating economic activity from political activity became, therefore, a conclusion of the classical school from their analysis of the processes of production and distribution. The superiority in both production and distribution of the *invisible hand* of competition and exchange over the *visible hand* of government was, they thought, demonstrated (74).

To others, however, the problem of distribution was the major economic problem. Observing the exploitation of the weak by the strong, the vast differences of income, and particularly the low income of labor which seemed directly to put most into the production process, the socialists insisted that the important problem was not the quantity of production, measured by the abstract symbols of money value in a market, but the kind of things produced and their distribution. The needs of the poor and underprivileged must be satisfied before the desires of the rich and powerful, said the Marxists, and to do this a society, controlled by the masses, must intervene to control the processes both of production and distribution. It could not do this effectively, they concluded, unless it exercised exclusive control over production goods—land and capital— and planned production and distribution so as to maximize social welfare (52, 53).

This assumption of the socialists, however, involved further assumptions as to the ethical principle of distribution and the authority to enforce it. Society as a whole was sufficiently organized to perform these tasks only through the state. Consequently the socialist school of economics reached the conclusion, opposite to that of the classical school, that economics and politics must be united in the totalitarian state.

The Marxists, it is true, were originally cosmopolitans and anti-nationalists. They assumed that as equitable production and distribution developed, antagonistic classes would disappear, the coercive state would *wither away*, and national differences would become unimportant. The temporary *dictatorship of the proletariat*, necessary to destroy the other classes, when its task had been accomplished, would also disappear in a universal voluntary cosmopolitan society.

Classical critics anticipated the opposite results. They pointed out that an entire economy could be planned and operated only by a powerful state, and that as the state assumed economic functions it would become more arbitrary, coercive and military, and that differentials in wealth power and privilege both among classes and among states would increase (63, 70). Experience with socialist and communist economic practice has in some measure supported these conclusions. As application of Marxist economies have progressed in the application of ethical theories of distribution from *collectivism* (everyone gives according to his desire and receives according to his contribution) through *socialism* (everyone gives according to his capacity and receives according to his contribution) to *communism* (everyone gives according to his capacity and receives according to his needs), the results anticipated by the critics have been observed with increasing completeness. Communist states have been marked by extraordinary centralization of government, suppression of individual freedom, inequality of privilege, and international tension (46, 48).

Territorial states. The classical economists assumed that political authority in the world would remain divided territorially among sovereign states and that the activity of these states would greatly influence economic processes. Among such activities they recognized the special economic significance of those concerning the monetary and taxation system, the law regulating property and contract, the police system defining and punishing crime and preventing disorder, and the legislation regulating foreign trade and exchange. While the classical school believed that reduction to a minimum of state interference in the economic sphere would contribute to individual, national, and human welfare, they recognized that there was a legitimate and inevitable sphere of political action to maintain order, to protect civil rights, and to provide revenue, and that this would necessarily exert influence on economic life. They hoped, however, for a maximum freedom of trade, both within and between states, thus permitting the development of a universal economic society whose members would be influenced only by the profit motive in applying resources to production. If action in the economic field were guided by consideration of the supply of, and the demand for, commodities, capital, labor, and management, they thought production would be maximized, distribution would be equitable, peace would be established, individual liberty would increase, and government regulation and taxation would diminish. They, however, recognized that in the field of politics conflicts would arise preventing a perfect operation of the competitive economic system and that, in any case, differences in legal, monetary, taxation, and police systems would present some barriers to the free movement of workers, commodities, capital, management, and information across national frontiers. Consequently the theory of international economics would necessarily differ from that of national economics (15, 55, 60, 84).

The communists, pending the *withering away of the state*, assumed state control of production, trade, and distribution, and thus identified economy with public policy. For them national economy was the domestic policy of the state and international economy was its foreign policy. In a power political world the former tended toward autarchy and the latter toward the use of the economy as a weapon of power politics. The subordination of economics to politics, characteristic of all states in time of war (19), thus became a characteristic of the communist state at all times. Consequently the Marxist hope that socialist economics would eliminate politics has in practice, and indeed in the theory of its critics if not of its advocates, been reversed. Communist politics has eliminated economics. The communist state tends to abandon welfare for power. The balance in policy between peace and plenty of the mercantilist state and that between security and prosperity of the liberal state has tended to be eliminated in the communist state in which economic activity becomes an instrument to maintain the power and policy of the government internally and externally (48).

The extent to which this is a necessary consequence of socialist economics applied by sovereign territorial states is controversial. Socialist Britain under the Labor Government with a liberal and welfare tradition sought to organize a socialist economy for welfare rather than power, but it is recognized, even in Britain, that socialism reverses the tendency of liberal economics toward a cosmopolitan economic community. It tends toward autarchy within the nation or within the sterling bloc (1, 27, 65, 66).

Rationality. The classical economists assumed that men are reasonable at least in handling their economic affairs. Producers would, they thought, if free and particularly if spurred by competition, seek to utilize the limited resources available to them to maximize income and minimize labor. They would, therefore, utilize the most advanced technology; locate industry where material, labor, and markets can be combined most effectively; organize industry efficiently; and buy in the cheapest and sell in the dearest markets. Specialization, invention, division of labor, and trade would progressively lower prices, benefit consumers, distribute income equitably, and promote individual wealth, national prosperity, and international peace. By the application of individual reason to individual interest, society would prosper, as Mandeville pointed out in his "Fable of the Bees or Private Vices, Public Benefits" (49), which influenced Adam Smith to discover the divine harmony in *laissez faire* economy (74).

The subsequent classicists have been less certain of this divine harmony but have assumed that human reason through democratic legislation providing social security for underprivileged and nonproductive classes, managing the financial system to smooth out economic fluctuations, planning government works to maintain full employment, and enforcing regulations to prevent monopoly and unfair competitive methods would maintain conditions for the functioning of a free economy in the social interest (6, 7, 14, 22, 24, 25, 33, 41, 43, 45). They assumed that the Benthamite formula of "the greatest good for the greatest number" would assure legislation of this type if all interests were represented in making it. "The agenda of liberalism" (46) and "planning for *laissez faire"* (73) are modern formulae for legislation which will protect social interest without hampering the functioning of a free and competitive economic system.

The communists have also relied on human reason to plan for a vast economy maximizing production and equalizing distribution of the product, but their critics point out that in eliminating the stabilizing influence of large numbers they have widened the gap between individual and social interest. Each of numerous producers will under the spur of competition apply reason to increase the efficiency of his own concern, thus maximizing the influence of economic reason in the economy as a whole to the benefit of the consumers. A small board, on the other hand, in planning and administering the economy as a whole is not spurred by competition in the direction of efficiency, but is likely to be influenced by the human urge to hold and augment its own power. Reason may function, but a reason which serves the interest of the planner and not that of the people. *Society* becomes distinct from the *people* who are compelled to submit to its will (43, 46, 70). The communists, however, hope that the *dictatorship of the proletariat* will rise above the corrupting influence of power and will formulate plans with the sole object of achieving the theoretical aims of maximum production and equitable distribution. They thus exhibit greater confidence in reason guided by principle than do the liberals. Their optimism has hardly been confirmed by experience, but they believe that eventually education in *social consciousness* and the elimination of *capitalist encirclement* will produce the human types and the political conditions suitable for universal communism (44).

ANALYSIS

International economics has developed from the assumptions of general economics that scarcity of resources requires continuous devotion of human energy to production; that the great differentials of wealth and poverty urge more equitable distribution of this product; that the territorial division of the world into sovereign states differentiates international from national economic activity; and that men are generally reasonable and can be relied upon to adjust their opinions concerning the suitability of means to achieve economic ends. The last of these assumptions is probably less applicable to international than to national economic activity. The theory of international economics is more complicated and difficult to understand than that of national economics. Furthermore, the practice of international economics is more directly affected, even in liberal states, by political decisions and conditions influenced by irrational and unpredictable mass opinions. Nevertheless, the idea of maximizing the material welfare of mankind is easy to grasp and a rational discipline of international economics might well have as its ultimate object to formulate the conditions for realizing this idea in the existing state of the arts. The discipline as it exists will be criticized from this point of view in the final section of this chapter.

The first assumption concerning the scarcity of resources is the essence of economics, and becomes increasingly applicable to international relations as industrialization and population growth augment the economic interdependence of nations. While colonies of migrants are, in their early life, more dependent on the mother country for imports than they are at later stages, on the whole, general technological and economic progress increases the interdependence of all peoples. If every state were completely self-sufficient there would be no international economics. But today most states would be unable to sustain their populations without the importation of foodstuffs, raw materials, or manufactured products, and even states with great areas and resources, such as the United States and the Soviet Union, able to maintain a balance in agriculture, mining, and industry, need to import some indispensable industrial or fertilizing minerals and require many other imports to sustain their standards of living (10, 15, 29, 33, 68, 69, 87, 92).

The second assumption which concerns the urge for equitable distribution is also less applicable to international economics. Social sympathy extends more to fellow citizens than to foreigners. To many Americans the idea of a bottle of milk a day to every Hottentot seems absurd while the idea of a bottle of milk a day to every American school child seems reasonable. Congress has appropriated for economic aid to underdeveloped countries (33) as well as for school lunches. In both cases sympathy for the underprivileged may have played a part as also the political expediency in the one case of getting votes from the poor citizens and in the other of preventing the penetration of Soviet influence in underdeveloped areas. The proportion of sympathetic to political consideration was, however, probably greater in the votes for school lunches. In each case there may also have been an economic motive of widening the domestic and international market for American industry and agriculture, but this motive was probably slight, particularly in the case of school lunches.

The existence of international economics as a special discipline has depended upon the third of these assumptions—that concerning geographical boundaries of economic, as well as of legal and political, significance. If states were absorbed in a world empire or federation there would be a world economy indistingiushable in principle from a national economy. As a special discipline international economics has dealt with the general effects on the world's economy of types of (a) frontier regulation, (b) domestic economy and (c) foreign policy orientation, and with (d) the art of controlling economic activity as an instrument of national and international policy.

Frontier regulations. The political division of the world tends to hamper the natural division of labor and the course of trade which would otherwise be influenced only by physical geography and demography. Political boundaries are obstacles to movements of *population, commodities, capital, management,* and *information,* not only because of legal regulations, but also because the familiarity of producers and consumers with national law, administration, language, and culture and their identification with national symbols and territory favor the home market. Domestic trade bulks larger than international trade in all countries, but international movements do take place in spite of these obstacles, and in spite of added obstacles imposed by the national peculiarities of monetary, taxation, and banking systems, and by restrictions, regulations, and formalities of more or less significance concerning all movements across political frontiers. Economic movement has been likened to a river which will eventually rise above any dam, however high, and it has also been likened to the movement of the bloodstream in the body, stoppage of which will kill the limb or perhaps the entire body (80). Trade is difficult to kill and its killing may be disastrous.

Human migration has occurred on a large scale motivated often by religious and political considerations but tending to be influenced by the push of overpopulation and lack of opportunity in the land of emigration and even more by the pull of economic opportunity, and especially the reports of such opportunity by friends and relatives, in the land of immigration. Because of the cultural and social inhibition upon migration, motives have to be strong to bring it about, and because of the social and political implications of large scale population movements, legislation usually regulates it. New countries, while first welcoming immigration, tend in time to restrict it on grounds of health, subversive ideas, cultural difficulty of assimilation, or protection of domestic labor. Old countries may restrict emigration in order to maintain a domestic monopoly of industrial information and skill and to retain military man power. Emigration restrictions are, however, usually less significant than immigration restrictions. Migration has increasingly been regulated by international agreement especially to deal with minority and refugee problems and to facilitate seasonal migration of agricultural workers. The long-run influence of migration on economies is very great, but the short-run effect is economically less significant than that of other economic movements across frontiers (18, 81).

Commodity trade tends to move in channels of comparative advantage —that is, each country tends to concentrate its production on commodities in which, because of its resources, technology, and skill, it has greatest comparative advantage. Country A may be inferior to country B in the production of all commodities of commerce, yet mutually advantageous trade will occur if country A produces and exports that commodity in which its comparative inferiority is least, assuming that its population is relatively immobile. If that immobility did not exist the entire population of country A might migrate to richer pastures.

Restrictions on exports are often imposed for purposes of revenue, re-source conservation, military preparation, or political pressure upon a rival, but restrictions on imports are more common. They are imposed to raise revenue; to protect domestic industry, especially infant industries; to facilitate diversification of economic opportunity; to bring political pressure upon another government; to establish economic autarchy or national self-sufficiency; to facilitate economic planning; and to eliminate vulnerability to foreign blockade or embargo. Such restrictions may be enforced by tariffs, quotas, exchange controls, health regulations, embargos, or customs formalities.

All trade restrictions are in general uneconomic as they prevent efficient geographical division of labor and promote less efficient utilization of resources. But they persist because of their political and social utility or even necessity. Revenue, defense and diplomatic requirements, vested interests and policies of social welfare, and economic planning often make them appear immediate expedients, even desirable permanent policies (10, 60, 82, 85).

Capital movements across frontiers were seldom restricted during the nineteenth century when the gold standard, managed in large measure from London, facilitated such movements, contributing to the development of underdeveloped territories, the maintenance of a multilateral trade equilibrium, and the promotion of more efficient division of labor. The pressure of exporters to prevent the export of capital when it would build up a commercial rival has been increasingly important. The direction of capital movements has been used as a method of political pressure and persuasion by both capital importing and capital exporting countries. The economic dislocation consequent upon war and the widespread repudiation of debts and confiscation of foreign property have increased the natural tendency of capital to stay at home. At the same time exchange controls and managed currencies to promote national financial and currency stability, and regulations of capital importing countries motivated by fears of imperialism or of diplomatic interventions to protect foreign investments, have greatly hampered capital movements. Intergovernmental loans, the establishment of branch firms, or direct investment in foreign concerns have become more important than private portfolio investments in foreign securities. Regulative and developmental services formerly performed by movements of private capital have therefore been in a large measure transferred to national and international agencies such as the U. S. Reconstruction Finance Corporation, the U. S. Export and Import Bank, the U. S. Mutual Assistance Administration, the Point IV Program, UNRRA, the technical assistance program of the

United Nations, and the operations of the International Bank and the International Fund (1, 5, 16, 33, 36, 67, 87, 96).

Movements of management and skill across frontiers have been hampered by the imperialistic fears and nationalistic sentiments of underdeveloped countries. Such countries have increasingly insisted that the managers of important industries, and even of educational and religious activities, shall be nationals. Experts and technologists may be utilized, but those provided by international organizations are preferred over those sent by national governments or corporations. The influence of economic management from the technologically more developed countries upon both the economic development and the political orientation of underdeveloped areas was of great importance in the nineteenth century. By its success in supporting the western ideologies of political nationalism and economic progress, it created counter movements based upon these ideologies but hostile to the leadership of western business or political management characterized as *imperialism*. The propaganda of communism, also adopting the western slogans of political nationalism and economic progress, has contributed to the identification of western *imperialism* with opposition to these movements, especially in Asia, but increasingly in Africa (33, 61).

The movement of information across frontiers has often been hampered in connection with restrictions upon the other types of economic movement discussed. Migrants, commodities, and managers carry information with them. Even movements of pure capital have sometimes been restricted with the thought that it would draw experts and managers with information calculated to develop a commercial or military rival. Countries wishing to monopolize techniques, especially techniques of war manufacture, have imposed heavy penalties upon the transmission of technical information abroad and have prevented the migration of laborers, experts and managers with this knowledge. They have also prevented export of commodities incorporating new inventions (9).

While economic considerations have been of some importance in restraining movements of information, they have been less important than political and social considerations. Governments have sought to prevent the importation of information or ideas, propagandas or missionary activities which might undermine the established culture, religion, society or polity. They have also tried to prevent the export of information which might induce diplomatic protest, disturb diplomatic relations, or disclose to the foreign eye conditions of shocking inhumanity or domestic unrest. Barriers of this kind, perhaps even more than barriers of more strictly economic character, can contribute to sustaining group solidarity and unity especially if the latter is founded upon ideas which are generally rejected by the outside world and which are especially vulnerable to objective information and rational thought. For this reason primitive cultures have great difficulty in surviving the impact of civilized ideas (31) and doubtless the effort of the Soviet rulers to make the Iron Curtain impervious is influenced by the same conditions (48, 95).

International law has in the past recognized the competence of sovereign states to impose whatever barriers they see fit to the export or import of information and ideas, thus recognizing and protecting the distinctiveness of national cultures, ideologies, and institutions, and conceding the vulnerability of all to such influences from the outside. The modern movement for international recognition and protection of human rights, including freedom of information, is founded upon the democratic concept of a freely formed public opinion and the objectivity of scientific truth tending toward a world community of mankind. Which of these positions is preferable? That is the primary question to be answered in dealing with the problem of political barriers between nations, but the answer can be found in the fields of law, communication, and education rather than in that of economics.

Like war, economic restriction at the frontier manifests the identity and unity of the state and prevents its absorption into the universal community. The function, which among primitive people was performed by natural barriers of mountains, deserts, oceans, and distances, is performed among people with advanced technology by artificial barriers. Political barriers of opinion, tension, conflict, and war, and economic barriers restricting movements of people, trade, capital, management, and information across frontiers are of major importance for this purpose. The continuous economic pressure of industry seeking opportunities to exploit new resources and technologies and to trade is balanced by the political pressure of groups to manifest their existence, to demand the exclusive loyalty of their members, and to act as units against affronts to the national pride. Under conditions of political tension and war economic barriers increase, while in times of peace and mutual confidence they diminish (95).

The relationship between barriers and peace is reciprocal. Economic barriers increase political tension, and political tension increases economic barriers. Thus once a process of building tension is started, it tends to increase cumulatively ending in war. If the opposite process of diminishing political tensions and diminishing economic barriers is started, it also may develop, cumulatively ending in federation or union. Usually, however, the progress of such a movement arouses a counter movement of national loyalty and states rights, initiating a reverse trend toward barriers, tensions, and hostilities. The result of these tendencies is an oscillation of rising and falling tensions in international relations, like that observed among primitive people in which periods of feuding and hostility between neighboring tribes may oscillate with periods of intertribal ceremony and friendship (91).

Domestic economies. Agrarian, feudal, socialistic, and capitalistic states naturally pursue different foreign economic policies (95).

Agrarian states tend to be decentralized and static. The political activities of the government tend to be dissociated from the routine economic life of the peasant population. The tendency of agrarian populations to increase may urge government policies of territorial expansion but the usual political unconsciousness of agrarian populations permits governments a wide freedom in transferring territories with their inhabitants. An illiterate peasantry often lacking in national sentiment may be equally available as a source of taxation and recruitment to any government which controls it.

With rising political and economic consciousness and transition from subsistence to cash crop farming, agrarian populations may make demands for government action to provide irrigation systems; river, canal, and railroad transportation for crops; credit for agricultural improvement; and insurance or storage granaries against crop failure and famine. Such demands, which are more likely to occur when agrarian economies are in contact with industrial and capitalistic economies, may develop a system of state socialism and perhaps, a spirit of active nationalism or even imperialism.

The older agrarian economies more frequently developed into feudalism through the concentration of land holding, the weaker seeking the protection of the stronger in times of domestic disorder or foreign invasion.

Feudal states tend to be decentralized, each feudal domain being almost a state by itself. They also tend to be militaristic and aggressive, partly because of the urge of the ruler to unite dissident feudal lords in a common cause. Feudal society develops a mass of economic restrictions to protect powerful interests, but as those interests become co-ordinated in a national state, these regulations tend to be modified to promote the political interests of the state in accord with the system of ideas known as *mercantilism* (28). Policies to assure domestic military industries, to provide the government ready funds to pay soldiers, to withhold economic advantages from political rivals, to exploit colonies for the benefit of domestic interests, and to monopolize profitable trade routes and trades are applied with the asserted purpose of promoting peace and plenty. Such policies both stimulate war and serve as instruments of war, especially by naval powers which rely for victory upon the economic strangulation of their enemies by blockade, seizure of enemy property at sea, and prevention of neutral navigation and trade of advantage to the enemy.

Mercantilism with its loosening of domestic economic regulations and its conception of broader national interests tends to develop industrialization and capitalism, especially after the development of technologies facilitating division of labor, mass production, and overseas trade.

Capitalistic states tend toward a policy of economic *laissez faire,* the removal of economic regulations, and the general policy of economic liberalism. The separation of economic from political activity, inherent in this policy and the development of international trade, tend to increase general prosperity, to equalize economic conditions among nations, and to oppose military adventure, thus promoting peaceful international relations and the development of a universal economic community—a situation characteristic of the Victorian period (75).

However, as agrarianism tends with population growth to develop into feudalism, so capitalism tends to the concentration of economic power in huge corporations, to monopolies restricting competition, to economic fluctuations of increasing amplitude, and to increasing government intervention for protection of vested interests, for protection of exploited classes, for military preparation (increasingly important as war becomes industrialized), and for hampering the economic and military development of political rivals. This new protectionism resembles the old mercantilism. Remedy for the inequity inherent in this situation has sometimes been sought in a return to liberal capitalism and sometimes in state socialism under which weaker elements submit to the state in exchange for protection as in disintegrating agrarian societies they submitted to feudal lords.

State socialism has sometimes developed in agrarian or feudal states from the need of military defense; of recovery from war, famine, or other disaster; of nationally planned land and water control systems; or of rapid industrialization to remedy technological backwardness. In most capitalistic states the natural tendency to substitute the monopoly of the state for the monopoly of corporations and cartels has developed aspects of state socialism. Nationally planned economies have tended to promote autarchy and international friction, both economic and political, consequently statesmen, aware of the economic interdependence of all sections of the world developed during the period of capitalist economics and of the economic advantage to all of freer international trade, have urged freer international economic policies (72). This situation, together with the inherent difficulties of large-scale economic planning, have tended in the past to confine socialistic systems to periods of crisis. Recent combinations of dynamic ideology and administrative efficiency have extended the scope of such systems.

In the twentieth century totalitarian states have pursued policies of autarchy and subordination of economic to political goals while the liberal states have urged policies in the economic agencies of the League of Nations and the United Nations to expand international trade and to reduce economic barriers in the interest of prosperity, though they have not always observed these policies in practice. Countries have tended to vary in their acceptance of state socialism or of liberal capitalism according to their general level of prosperity. Poorer countries of Eastern Europe and Asia have tended to accept fascism or communism. Richer countries, especially the Americas and the British Dominions, have tended to maintain free economies. The intermediate countries of Western Europe have tended to compromise with liberal socialism or mixed economies. In no country is any system applied unequivocally. Even the Soviet economy permits some private property and includes elements of *socialistic competition.* Communist Yugoslavia and China appear to have gone further in this direction. The United States has under its Reciprocal Trade Agreement Policy initiated in 1934 theoretically adhered to a free and nondiscriminatory international economic policy, but many practices initiated by the "New Deal" and sustained by subsequent administrations have had a socialistic character. Other countries have been equally ambivalent. Great Britain has moved from theoretical free trade to a considerable measure of state socialism with extensive restrictions on trade and capital movements. Keynesian economics, insisting on the necessity of extensive government intervention to maintain free economy under changing conditions of population and technology, has been widely accepted (17, 24, 40, 77).

The economic foreign policy of a state is undoubtedly influenced by factors other than the form of its domestic economy, but it seems probable that the considerable trend away from capitalism and toward socialism has influenced the deterioration both of international trade and of international political stability in the twentieth century.

Foreign policy orientation. Long-run objectives of foreign policy influence national economic policies and world economy. Among such general foreign policy orientations attention will be given to nationalism, imperialism, cosmopolitanism, and internationalism (95).

A *nationalistic economy* places the political unity of the nation first. It utilizes economic regulation to develop a degree of economic self-sufficiency and diversity of economic opportunity, to induce leading elements of society to support the government, to increase general prosperity, and to develop national political and military power. By placing the horizon of economic consideration at the national frontiers, regulation tends to be protectionist or socialistic and hampering to international trade. A relatively small number of nations are however geographically, morally, technologically, or historically suitable for a national economy that is in any large degree self-sufficient. No state in the modern world can be wholly self-sufficient.

An *imperial economy* is an enlarged national economy. States that have colonies tend to identify the empire with the nation for economic purposes and to create a self-sufficient unity of this larger block. In the same spirit regional economic policies tend to group neighboring states into customs unions or economic blocks (85). Such policies, seeking to give economic unity to areas of great cultural and economic diversity, usually find it necessary to decentralize government and to recognize considerable local autonomy. This militates against economic unity. Imperial and regional economies, therefore, tend to break up unless they become military empires or federations utilizing a high degree of central coercion.

A *cosmopolitan economy* can only develop on the basis of *laissez faire* unless the world becomes organized under a central government. The variety of cultures and economies in the world militates against such a government. Consequently, cosmopolitan economy implies separation of politics and economics, leaving the latter to develop on a world scale without the hampering influence of government. This was the tendency of liberal economy in the latter part of the nineteenth century. Some central planning was, however, essential to that economy. Management was necessary to maintain the stability of the gold standard, to regulate credit, to collect debts, and to protect property. These functions were performed in the nineteenth century by the Bank of England, the British capital market, and the British foreign office and navy. Their performance was facilitated by the general acceptance of certain rules of monetary regulation in accord with the gold standard and certain standards of international law concerning the honoring of obligations and the respecting of private property. These conditions have been greatly changed, and the rise of the new nationalism and of new concepts of social justice makes restoration of such a cosmopolitan economy unlikely (5, 24, 94).

An *international economy* implies that national economic policies are made and maintained with consideration for standards and objectives accepted by agreement of states. Such agreements are facilitated by international organization. The specialized agencies and commissions of the United Nations dealing with instruments of communication and transport, with international trade and finance, with the social and economic interests of agriculture, labor, underdeveloped areas, and people generally seek to formulate such standards and objectives. Some of these organizations particularly the International Bank and the International Fund have considerable operating power to maintain exchange stability and to provide credit for long term investment (96).

The complexity of these organizations conforms to the complexity of the situation but their effectiveness is dependent upon the capacity of the United Nations to reduce international tensions and to maintain moderate political stability. While a cosmopolitan society of traders and bankers is not likely to develop, an international economic society may develop within which the national governments could form their policies and agree upon certain universal standards, and upon international institutions to perform stabilizing functions similar to those performed by British agencies in the nineteenth century. This result, however, is not likely to be achieved unless the United Nations becomes able to exert a pacifying influence comparable to that exerted by the British Foreign Office and Navy during the nineteenth century.

Economic control as an instrument of policy. The applied science and art of international economics concerns the imposition of particular economic restrictions, usually for political purposes. While such restrictions are often supported by economic arguments, and in some cases, the arguments have had economic merit, in general progress toward the economic goals of maximum utilization of resources for production and equitable distribution of the product is hampered by restrictions upon international economic movement. Such regulation, therefore, must usually be justified by arguments outside the realm of economics. Foreign *economic* policy is usually not an end in itself, but an instrument of foreign *political* policy. That policy may be to defend the state as a whole against invasion, threats, pressures, or infiltrations from other states, real or imagined, or to defend the government against domestic pressure groups, special interests, or ideological phantasies which may unseat it at the next election or raise banners of sedition and disunity. The influence in economic policy making of *public interest* and of *private interests* is often difficult to distinguish. *Rationalizations* are usually in terms of the former, but *reasons* may often spring from the latter.

Since the aims of state policy differ greatly, among different states, at different periods in the life of a state, among different parties in a state, and even among different agencies in the same government, few generalizations useful for practicing the art of international economics can be offered, but analysis of the methods and spirit of policy-making and of economic research is instructive.

Methods of policy-making. The actual character of national economic regulation is influenced in no small degree by the methods and agencies of economic policy-making. In the nineteenth century period of free economy, government regulations were usually made by the legislature or by international agreement and enforced by the courts. Trade restrictions took the form of a general tariff, usually free of political discrimination and relatively permanent. It might be reduced by conventions usually generalized by most-favored-nation clauses. The objective of such tariffs was primarily revenue, but even if protective, trade could adjust to them. Capital movements were in the nineteenth century largely controlled by central banks and particularly by the Bank of England which maintained the gold standard and regulated credits by the application of well-understood rules and statistically determined signals to maintain stability.

As economic policy has become an instrument of national policy, administrative and military regulations have become more important. Legalistic controls have been superseded by bureaucratic controls. The general staff and the bureaucracy make regulations on the basis of vague legislative directives and general policies, opening the way for favoritism, compromise, sudden change and unconsidered decisions. Such forms of regulation are far more inimical to international economic movements than are legislative and conventional tariffs (9).

Planned economies under such military and bureaucratic controls reach a high point in the utilization of economic regulation for political purposes. The government may use the economy primarily as an agency for keeping itself in power. It may also use it to aid friends and weaken enemies. The usefulness of such a system in playing the game of power politics cannot be doubted, and as the world shrinks and the exigencies of power politics increase all states find themselves under pressure to adopt such methods of economic control, however hostile the methods may be to peace, democracy, human freedom, economic prosperity, and social progress (66).

Spirit of policy-making. The general characteristics of the national economy and the organization of its controls influence the spirit of economic policy-making in the state, though that spirit reciprocally influences the organization and characteristics of the economy.

This spirit may be, and usually is, highly *opportunistic*. The pressure of domestic interests and of foreign exigencies often require rapid decisions, the consequences of which are not and cannot be foreseen. Long run policy becomes simply the unforeseen consequence of many and apparently necessary decisions. Though made with little consideration for long run policy or effects and perhaps with insufficient understanding of the consequences of taking the path of least resistance, decisions must be justified by arguments appealing to public understanding and sentiment. Later, after they have led to other decisions in the same direction they may be rationalized as a step in a general policy which was not in fact thought of at the time the first step was taken. The reasons, the justifications, and the subsequent rationalizations should be distinguished (9).

Policy may be largely *routine*, as it was in the administration of tariffs and the maintenance of the gold standard in the late nineteenth century. Administrators whether of government or of banks make routine decisions when the need arises to maintain stability and enforce the law. Economic science may contribute to this kind of regulation by devising both the rules and the statistical indices guiding their application. It is hoped that this kind of regulation may be exercised internationally by the Fund under the United Nations to maintain that stability in exchanges formerly provided by the gold standard.

Policy may be *rational*, adapting means to long-run objectives. The difficulty with planning a whole economy in this spirit lies in the virtual impossibility of formulating clear objectives for a large and varied society which would be widely acceptable for any length of time. There is a high probability, therefore, that the objectives which are formulated can be carried out only with much regimentation and coercion of the popula- tions. The unpredictability of the economic consequences of the plan under changing conditions and the lack of means for maintaining initia- tive and devotion to the public interest among the planners present further problems. In proportion as the scope of the plan is broad, its duration long, the population to which it is to apply varied, and the conditions of economic life dynamic, planning is likely to prove another word for tyranny, generating rigidity, unrest, internal tensions, and ex- ternal hostility (63, 65, 95). Planning, in the sense of adapting means to clearly defined ends, is, of course, another word for reason, said to be the characteristic distinguishing man from the animals, but the effort to apply it too broadly ignores the inevitable divergence of opinions characteristic of human beings and seeks to evade the political problem of continually reconciling divergent ends and controversial means.

Democratic governments, therefore, prefer the spirit of *balance* which moderates the spirit of opportunism by recognizing that several long range policies must be kept in mind; moderates the spirit of routine by appreciating that, in a dynamic society, stability must not be static and regulatory rules and indices must be continually adjusted to changing conditions; and moderates the spirit of planning by subjecting all plans to political debate and reconsideration by bodies representative of the major elements of public opinion, and by subjecting the administration to continuous public scrutiny of its activities and to responsibility to political authorities. Such balance requires consideration of domestic prosperity versus international security, of government enterprises in the general interest versus private freedom to compete, of long-range objectives versus short-range necessities, and of social justice in distribution versus economic efficiency in production.

Operational research. A policy of balance requires the continual serv- ices of economists in appraising the practical effect of economic regula- tion under the extremely complicated conditions of the modern world. Much of the science of international economics consists in analysis coupled with observation and the preparation of statistical indices to accomplish this task. In this work theory and practice must be closely related. Use may be made of *operational research* in which the decision- making agencies of government or of international organizations con- tribute data and policy objectives to the economist and permit him to check the results of operations. The art of applied economics and the science of pure economics thus come into continuous and intimate contact.

CRITICISM

Considered in its broadest context, the task of international economics is to define the conditions under which production will be maximized and equitable distribution assured for the world. It is clear from the preceding analysis that the simple formulae neither of nineteenth-century free trade nor of twentieth century social planning will suffice in the complicated, dynamic, interdependent but nationalistic world of the twentieth century. Mixed economies, balancing government planning, regulation, and operation with private initiative, enterprise, and competition have tended to prevail, and they have tended to be guided by national, regional, and universal considerations and to operate through a variety of agencies at all levels.

Adjustment, compromise, insight, and flexibility rather than rigid formulae seem to be required. It would appear, however, that a moderate independence of economic from political activity is desirable. Economic policies solely the handmaid of international political maneuvering tend to domestic tyranny and international war, while foreign policies solely the handmaid of economic interests tend to an impersonal system of cosmopolitan trading oppressive to underprivileged peoples and classes and vulnerable to movements of militant nationalism and imperialism. The peculiar conditions of the nineteenth century by which such a system was for a time maintained through the powerful but liberal British Empire is not likely to recur.

The science of international economics can perhaps best serve by guiding the international and national agencies into moderate and balanced policies, aiming at human prosperity but aware of the limitations imposed by international politics (3, 6, 9, 24, 34, 77, 87).

Ultimately, the problem of human prosperity is the problem of relating the world's population to the earth's resources. It at once becomes evident, however, that estimate of the needs of a population involves demographic, cultural, social, and political considerations outside of the realm of economics, and that estimate of the earth's resources involve geographic, technological, transportation, and social problems on the periphery of economics. These peripheral factors prevent the isolation of economics as a pure science. International economics is today controlled by international politics. Demands of people springing from their cultures, institutions, traditions, and power positions tend to divert production and distribution to purposes remote from human welfare and even from group prosperity. Men will usually sacrifice butter for guns under emergency conditions and today bipolar power politics tends to make emergency permanent.

The great human problems underlying economic problems are the waste and inequitable distribution of resources, the growth of population, the corruption of power, and the shrinking of the world.

The mining of minerals, the cutting of the forest cover, the exhaustion and wash-out of soils, the wastage of human resources by disease and undernourishment, the monopolizing of scarce resources for political purposes and the destruction of both human and material resources in war threaten to decrease production perhaps more rapidly than technology, preventive medicine, specialization, trade, and international organization can overcome (58, 68, 88).

The potentialities of population growth in underdeveloped areas where the average expectation of life is less than thirty, by improvements in preventive medicine and increases in available food, threatens to outstrip any possible economic surplus and to lower the standard of living. The Malthusian problem has not been solved. While better health and longer life may increase productivity more than they increase consumption in some circumstances, they do not do so in all circumstances. There is usually a long lag between reduction of a high death rate in a high birth rate population and establishment of a higher standard of living, which may eventually reduce the birth rate. The immediate effect of technological improvement of underdeveloped areas may therefore be more overpopulation, more unrest, and more disposition to accept a revolutionary ideology (4).

"Power corrupts, and absolute power corrupts absolutely," according to Lord Acton. An economic plan must be administered and the administrators, if they combine political with economic power, tend to become tyrants. Centralized economic power can be more dangerous than centralized political power because efficient economic management, like military management, requires technical skill, rapid decision, and concentration of power. Civil government can be divided among the legislative, executive, administrative, and judicial authorities, each checking excesses of the others. Functions of public order, defense, justice, and regulation can be performed on the basis of general laws equally applicable to all. But an administration that plans and operates an entire economy in a large area must be centralized, must rapidly make decisions which will affect different groups differently, and must, therefore, control people as well as economic processes. Economic regulation differentiates and classifies people by function and controls their day-to-day activity. Such widespread discriminatory interferences with freedom are certain to be resented and are impossible to maintain without coercion. The good society seeks to balance government, economy, religion, and education against one another in order to prevent each from becoming overpowerful. With the same objective, it seeks to maintain checks and balances in government, competition in economy, freedom in religion, and many independent educational institutions. The *easy* solution seeking to rectify economic ills by comprehensive government planning has been better for propaganda than for human welfare. Economy should balance political power rather than fortify it, if human freedom is to continue (26, 95).

The world is shrinking under the influence of new inventions in the fields of communication, transportation, and war (71, 95). This provides both the opportunity and the incentive for more effective organization for peace and more efficient utilization of the world's resources, but at the same time it increases national anxiety, stimulates defensive policies, and extends international tension. Underdeveloped peoples become aware of their inferior economic position and demand improvement. All people become aware of their vulnerability to attack by economic regulation, by psychological propaganda, or by military aggression. Thus opinions favorable to world unity and world economy are faced by policies of nationalism, and self-sufficiency, dividing peoples by artificial geographical lines, while social ideologies divide them by artificial party lines and political systems divide them by artificial concentrations of power. These policies, ideologies, and systems create group opinions more powerful than economic interests and hamper the utilization of world resources for the satisfaction of individual wants of all groups and classes. Under these conditions the assumptions of international economics and the analyses which may develop from them are not in themselves adequate to solve the major problems of the world. The social and psychic conditions under which these assumptions are valid must be studied.

REFERENCES

This list includes a few classical treatises of each of the leading schools of economic thought, some histories of economics and economic thought, several recent treatises on international economics, and a few detailed studies of contemporary problems in the field. Many articles in the *Encyclopædia of the Social Sciences* deal with the subject, of which those by Francis Eulenberg on "International Trade," by Eli Heckscher on "Mercantilism," by Frank H. Knight on "Value and Price," by Werner Sombart on "Capitalism," and by Jacob Viner on "International Trade, Theory," may be mentioned.

1. ASHWORTH, William, *A Short History of the International Economy, 1850-1950* (London, Longmans, 1952).
2. BÖHM-BAWERK, Eugen von, *Capital and Interest*, trans. by Smart (London, Macmillan, 1890).
3. BOULDING, Kenneth E., *Economic Analysis*, rev. ed. (New York, Harper, 1952).
4. CARR-SAUNDERS, A. M., *World Population* (New York, Oxford University Press, 1936).
5. CASSEL, Gustav, and others, *Foreign Investments* (Chicago, University of Chicago Press, 1928).
6. CLARK, Colin, *The Conditions of Economic Progress*, 2nd ed. (London, St. Martins, 1951).

7. CLARK, John Maurice, *Social Control of Business*, 2nd ed. (New York, McGraw-Hill, 1939).
8. CLOUGH, S. B., and COLE, C. W., *Economic History of Europe*, rev. ed. (Boston, Heath, 1946).
9. CONDLIFFE, John B., *The Reconstruction of World Trade*, Report of International Studies Conference, Bergen, 1939 (New York, Norton, 1940).
10. ———, *The Commerce of Nations* (New York, Norton, 1950).
11. Cowles Commission for Research in Economics, *Economic Theory and Measurement,* A Twenty Year Research Report, 1932-1952 (Chicago, University of Chicago, 1952).
12. DAY, Clive, *A History of Commerce* (London, Longmans, 1907; 4th ed., 1938).
13. EDGEWORTH, F. X., *Papers Relating to Political Economy* (London, Macmillan, 1925).
14. EGLE, Walter P., *Economic Stabilization* (Princeton, Princeton University Press, 1952).
15. ELLSWORTH, P. T., *The International Economy* (New York, Macmillan, 1950).
16. FEIS, Herbert, *Europe, The World's Banker, 1871-1914* (New Haven, Yale University Press, 1930).
17. ———, *Seen from E. A., Three International Episodes* (New York, Knopf, 1947).
18. FERENCZI, I., and WILLCOX, W. F., eds., *International Migrations* (New York, National Bureau of Economic Research, 1929-1931), 2 vols.
19. GORDON, David L., and DANGERFIELD, Royden, *The Hidden Weapon* (New York, Harper, 1947).
20. GRAHAM, Frank D., *The Theory of International Values* (Princeton, Princeton University Press, 1953).
21. GRAS, N. S. B., *An Introduction to Economic History* (New York, Harper, 1922).
22. HABERLER, Gottfried, *Prosperity and Depression: A Theoretical Analysis of Cyclical Movements* (Geneva, League of Nations, 1937).
23. HANEY, Lewis H., *History of Economic Thought*, 4th ed. (New York, Macmillan, 1949).
24. HANSEN, Alvin H., *Economic Stabilization in an Unbalanced World* (New York, Harcourt, 1932).
25. ———, *A Guide to Keynes* (New York, McGraw-Hill, 1953).
26. HAWTREY, R. G., *Economic Aspects of Sovereignty* (London, Longmans, 1930).
27. HAYEK, F. A., *The Road to Serfdom* (Chicago, University of Chicago Press, 1944).
28. HECKSCHER, Eli F., *Mercantilism* (London, Macmillan, 1935), 2 vols.
29. HEILPERIN, Michael G., *The Trade of Nations* (New York, Knopf, 1947).
30. HEIMAN, Eduard, *History of Economic Doctrine* (New York, Oxford University Press, 1945).
31. HERSKOVITS, Melville J., *Economic Anthropology* (New York, Knopf, 1952).
32. HOOVER, Glenn E., ed., *Twentieth Century Economic Thought* (New York, Philosophical Library, 1950).
33. HOSELITZ, Bert F., ed., *The Progress of Underdeveloped Areas* (Chicago, University of Chicago Press, 1952).
34. HUTCHINS, Robert M., and others, *International Economic Relations* (Minneapolis, University of Minnesota Press, 1934).

35. INGRAM, John K., *A History of Political Economy* (New York, Macmillan, 1893).

36. International Studies Conference, *The State of Economic Life* (Paris, International Institute of Intellectual Co-operation, 1934); see also Condliffe.

37. JEVONS, William Stanley, *The Theory of Political Economy* (London, 1871; 4th ed., 1911).

38. JONES, John Harry, *The Economics of War and Conquest* (London, King, 1915).

39. KEYNES, J. M., *The Economic Consequences of the Peace* (New York, Harcourt, 1919).

40. ———, and others, *Unemployment as a World Problem* (Chicago, University of Chicago Press, 1931).

41. ———, *The General Theory of Employment, Interest and Money* (New York, Harcourt, 1936).

42. KLEIN, Lawrence R., *A Text Book of Econometrics* (Evanston, Row, Peterson, 1953).

43. KNIGHT, Frank H., *Freedom and Reform, Essays in Economic and Social Philosophy* (New York, Harper, 1952).

44. LANGE, Oskar, *On the Economic Theory of Socialism* (Minneapolis, University of Minnesota Press, 1938).

45. LERNER, Abba P., *The Economics of Control* (New York, Macmillan, 1944).

46. LIPPMANN, Walter, *The Good Society* (1937); rev. ed. (Boston, Little, Brown, 1943).

47. LIST, Friedrich, *The National System of Political Economy* (1841), trans. by Lloyd (London, Longmans, 1904).

48. LOUCKS, William N. and HOOT, J. Weldon, *Comparative Economic Systems: Capitalism, Socialism, Communism, Fascism, Co-operation*, 4th ed. (New York, Harper, 1952).

49. MANDEVILLE, Bernard de, *The Fable of the Bees, or Private Vices, Public Benefits* (1714); 4th ed. (London, 1925).

50. MANTOUX, Etienne, *The Carthaginian Peace, or the Economic Consequences of Mr. Keynes* (London, Oxford University Press, 1944).

51. MARSHALL, Alfred, *Principles of Economics* (1891); 8th ed. (London, Macmillan, 1948).

52. MARX, Karl, *Capital, A Critical Analysis of Capitalist Production* (1886) (London, Swan-Sonnenschein, 1902).

53. ———, *A Contribution to the Critique of Political Economy*, 2nd ed. (London, 1904).

54. MENGER, Karl, *Principles of Economics* (1871); trans. by Dingwell and Hoselitz (Glencoe, Ill., Free Press, 1950).

55. MILL, John Stuart, *Principles of Political Economy* (1848); Ashley, ed. (London, Longmans, 1909).

56. OGBURN, W. F., and NIMKOFF, M. F., *Sociology* (Boston, Houghton Mifflin, 1940).

57. OHLIN, Bertil, *Interregional and International Trade* (Cambridge, Harvard University Press, 1933).

58. OSBORN, Fairfield, *The Limits of the Earth* (Boston, Little, Brown, 1953).

59. PARETO, Vilfredo, *Cours d'Economie Politique* (Lausanne, 1896-1897), 2 vols.

60. Patterson, Ernest M., *An Introduction to World Economics* (New York, Macmillan, 1947).

61. Pavlovitch, M., *The Foundations of Imperialist Policy* (London, Labour Publishing Co., 1922).

62. Pigou, A. C., *The Political Economy of War* (New York, Macmillan, 1921).

63. ———, *Socialism vs. Capitalism* (New York, Macmillan, 1937).

64. Ricardo, David, *The Principles of Political Economy and Taxation* (1817); (Everyman's Library, New York, Dutton, 1926).

65. Robbins, Lionel, *Economic Planning and International Order* (London, Macmillan, 1937).

66. ———, *The Economic Causes of War* (London, Cape, 1939).

67. Royal Institute of International Affairs, *The Problem of International Investment* (London, 1937).

68. Schultz, Theodore W., ed., *Food for the World* (Chicago, University of Chicago Press, 1945).

69. ———, *Production and Welfare in Agriculture* (New York, Macmillan, 1953).

70. Schumpeter, Joseph A., *Capitalism, Socialism and Democracy*, 3rd ed. (New York, Harper, 1950).

71. Schurr, Sam H., and Marschak, Jacob, *Economic Aspects of Atomic Power* (Princeton, Princeton University Press, 1950).

72. Silberner, Edmund, *The Problem of War in Nineteenth Century Thought* (Princeton, Princeton University Press, 1946).

73. Simons, Henry, *A Positive Program for Laissez Faire* (Chicago, University of Chicago Press, 1934).

74. Smith, Adam, *An Inquiry into the Nature and Causes of the Wealth of Nations* (1776); Cannon, ed. (London, Methuen, 1904).

75. Sombart, Werner, *The Quintessence of Capitalism* (1913); trans. by Epstein (London, Unwin, 1915).

76. Staley, Eugene, *War and the Private Investor* (New York, Doubleday, 1935).

77. ———, *World Economy in Transition* (New York, Council on Foreign Relations, 1939).

78. Taussig, F. W., *Principles of Economics* (1911); 4th ed. (New York, Macmillan, 1939), 2 vols.

79. ———, *Notes and Essays Contributed in Honor of, Explanation in Economics* (New York, McGraw-Hill, 1936).

80. Teggart, F. J., *Rome and China* (Berkeley, University of California Press, 1939).

81. Thomas, Brinley, *Migration and Economic Growth, A Study of Great Britain and the Atlantic Economy* (Cambridge, Cambridge University Press, 1953).

82. Towle, Lawrence W., *International Trade and Commercial Policy* (New York, Harper, 1947).

83. Veblen, Thorstein, *The Theory of the Leisure Class* (1899); (New York, Macmillan, 1908).

84. Viner, Jacob, *Studies in the Theory of International Trade* (New York, Harper, 1937).

85. ———, *The Customs Union Issue* (New York, Carnegie Endowment for International Peace, 1950).

86. ———, *International Economics* (Glencoe, Ill., Free Press, 1951).

87. VINER, Jacob, *International Trade and Economic Development* (Glencoe, Ill., Free Press, 1952).

88. VOGT, William, *Road to Survival* (New York, Sloane Associates, 1948).

89. WALLAS, Graham, *Our Social Heritage* (London, 1921).

90. WALRAS, Leon, *Elements of Pure Economics*, 1874, trans. (London, Allen and Unwin, 1954).

91. WARNER, Lloyd, "Murngin Warfare," *Oceania*, Vol. I (January, 1931), pp. 417 ff.

92. WILCOX, Claire, *A Charter for World Trade* (New York, Macmillan, 1949).

93. WRIGHT, Chester W., *Economic History of the United States*, 2nd ed. (New York, McGraw-Hill, 1949).

94. WRIGHT, Quincy, ed., *Gold and Monetary Stabilization* (Chicago, University of Chicago Press, 1932).

95. ———, *A Study of War* (Chicago, University of Chicago Press, 1942), pp. 75, 133-35, 200, 281-85, 367, 380-82, 708-10, 1146-97, 1365-75, 1439.

96. ———, ed., *The World Community* (Chicago, University of Chicago Press, 1948).

287 (text
291 (class

International Communication

DEFINITION

INTERNATIONAL COMMUNICATION is the art of using symbols to express, to inform, to formulate, or to influence the opinion and policy of groups on matters of importance for international relations. In a narrower sense it is the art of using symbols expressive of one nation to influence another. As a discipline it is the philosophy guiding that art and the science analyzing international communications, determining their purposes, and measuring their effects. The discipline also includes historical studies bearing upon the art, philosophy, and science.

The form and structure of language has been studied wherever writing exists. Rhetoric has been an art and a discipline since ancient times, as has literary criticism (5). The medieval trivium—grammar, rhetoric, and dialectic—dealt with the correctness, effectiveness, and logic of communication. Communication as a whole, however, hardly began to become a discipline in the west until after the invention of printing in the fifteenth century. This greatly increased the radius and speed of diffusion of information, ideas, and opinions, and permitted a periodical press to arise. As a result, democratic institutions could expand to much wider areas and public opinion could directly influence public policy (96). Attention to the subject further increased in the nineteenth century after postal and telecommunication had augmented the abundance and speed of directed communications, and in the twentieth century, after the radio, cinema, and television had permitted mass communication at a distance and had made it immediately available to the relatively illiterate (93, 97, 106). Recently, the development of social psychology, sociology, and anthropology has disclosed the major significance of communication to individual and group behavior and to institutions (48, 70, 78). According to the social psychologist Charles H. Cooley: "The more closely we consider this mechanism (of communication) the more intimate will appear its relation to the inner life of mankind. Without communication, the mind does not develop a true human nature but remains in the abnormal and nondescript state; neither human nor properly brutal " (26).

In no field of social activity have the changes in communication been more important than in that of international relations. With these changes diplomats have been able to keep in immediate contact with their governments (103) and transnational communication among peoples has been added to diplomatic correspondence between governments (104). International relations have been transformed in character. The influence of diplomacy has declined and the influence of world opinion and international organization has increased (21, 39, 45, 90, 111).

Communication has been regarded as the unifying principle in biology, psychology, and sociology. An organism can be considered a system for communicating nervous impulses to control the functioning of muscular, digestive, circulatory, and sexual systems so that the organism can survive and multiply. Biologists have discussed the different patterns of communication—radial, bisymmetrical, linear, and so forth—and their relative efficiency (24, 61). A personality can be considered a system for the communication of internal drives and impulses on the one hand, and on the other, of external experiences immediately sensed and perceived or stored in memories and conceptions, into such close relations as to permit choice, action, achievement, orientation to changing situations, and survival (50, 61, 70).

Societies exist by virtue of communications. Here the term is used in a narrower sense of transmissions of meanings from one person to another permitting them to interact. From such interactions develop communities, societies, institutions, social movements, cultures, and civilizations (24, 26, 56, 61, 78).

The developing disciplines of mathematical biophysics (82, 84, 85, 94), cybernetics (105), and operational philosophy (83) may in time develop formulae and techniques useful in all aspects of communication. To these disciplines, the essence of communication, differentiating it from a mechanism, is its capacity to produce effects grossly disproportionate to the physical energy of the immediate cause. The impact of symbols, transmission of which involves only minute quantities of physical energy, may revolutionize the behavior of complex psychic and social equilibria. A single communication may exhibit a magnified "trigger effect," initiating a chain of events of tremendous importance. The movement of a billiard ball is proportionate to the energy expended by the player, but the movement of "Operation Overlord" on the Normandy beach was disproportionate to the energy expended by General Eisenhower and his staff in ordering the operation to begin on June 6, 1944 (15, 25, 35, 95).

Anthropologists recognize the pervasive importance of communications in their field. "Every culture pattern and every single act of social behavior," writes Sapir, "involves communication in either an explicit or implicit sense" (91). Among primitive people, several modes of communication have been distinguished. *Formal language* which exists among all people, perhaps marking the primary distinction of man from other animals (13, 17, 107, 110), is of first importance and is always adapted to and adequate for the transmission of the culture from generation to generation and of its maintenance in action. *Gesture* is less social and more individual than language and may even contradict it. Voluntary or involuntary gestures may verify or contradict the meaning of a verbal communication (91), thus manifesting the difference between opinion—what is said—and attitude—what is thought (110). Communication also takes place through the process of *imitation*. Example may be more effective than precept in transmitting culture. *Artistic representation* and *departures from customary observances* are other means of social suggestion (91). In 1917, the Russian soldiers manifested their attitude toward the war, not by voice or gesture, but by departing from the front for their homes. They talked with their legs.

Communication becomes easier in proportion as the persons involved have similar experiences and predispositions. Within a group with a wealth of common professional experience, or educated in a culture or ideology establishing many common predispositions, precise and complete meanings as well as vague connotations may be conveyed by a minimum of word or gesture (91). The conversation of lawyers and the command system of an army illustrate this. International communication, on the other hand, implies a minimum of shared culture or ideology. Consequently communication becomes difficult unless indeed the participants are talking shop about professional or other activities in which they have much experience in common (83). In diplomatic correspondence misunderstanding is likely, even if efforts are made to compose notes with great precision, explicitness, and completeness (103).

Primitive peoples are usually distinguished from civilized peoples by their lack of written language (37). Writing permits a great extension of communication in time and space. Communications can be stored in manuscripts for centuries and dispatched by courier for long distances without any deterioration in accuracy. Writing, which permits the inscription of treaties and the regular transmission of dispatches and instructions, greatly extends the range of international relations.

The invention of the printing press and the newspaper followed by other means of mass communication (radio, cinema, and television) has greatly developed the power of propaganda both within groups and between groups. These inventions initiated the era of universal mass communication and changed human affairs as radically as did the invention of writing (9, 45, 89, 90).

The development of these new means of communication has, however, accentuated the distinction between opinion and attitude, manifested among primitive peoples by the difference in meaning, sometimes carried by simultaneous word and gesture. Diplomatic historians seek to compare the official correspondence of a statesman with the same statesman's private letters and diaries (1). Content analysts seek to differentiate the motives and intentions of the propagandist, which may be inferred from his communications in a given situation, from the meaning which he expected the audience to receive from them (9, 55, 61, 99).

Communication is always an organization of symbols, about something, from someone, to someone. A communication can, therefore, be studied in itself analyzing its symbols relating them to one another and to the whole in order to extract all of its possible meanings. These possible meanings can be related to the objective world to which they refer in order to derive objective information of descriptive, predictive, or control value. A communication can also be studied in relation to the author or communicator to gain possible insight into his motives, attitudes, intentions, and personality. Finally a communication may be related to the person or audience to which it is directed, in order to ascertain its influence, tranquilizing or inciting, upon attitude, opinion, policy or action, and to relate this reaction to the particular predispositions or characteristics of that person or audience. Discrimination of these syntactic, semantic, expressive, and pragmatic types of analysis indicate the scope and meaning of the discipline of communications as a science (41, 48, 50, 71, 72, 75, 83, 88). To practice the art of communication, the communicator requires precise knowledge of his purpose, his medium, and his audience. From this, he can formulate precisely his message and form of presentation.

His purpose may be to express himself, to interest, to entertain, to inspire, to inform, to instruct, to direct, or to incite others. The fine arts (87), religion, philosophy, science (14), history, administration (68, 98), and politics (55) all depend on communication. Their media include music, painting, literature, conversation, rumor (2), and "mass communication." The intended audience may be no one, anyone, or everyone. It may be a particular individual, group, elite, party, or nation; everyone now living; or all posterity. Communication with any of these purposes, media, or addressees may influence international relations. It has been widely assumed that political purposes, mass communications, and national audiences are of particular importance in contemporary international relations, and the term *propaganda* is especially applicable to communications based on these assumptions (46, 51, 99).

In propaganda each of the media which may be employed—press, radio, cinema, television, rumor, infiltration—implies a different limitation upon the presentation. Unless the culture of the audience to be addressed, including existing attitudes and opinions, present potentialities of action, and nuances of language are thoroughly understood, mass communication will probably fail to be established or will lead to unexpected reactions. The message to be transmitted, must be considered in relation to the purpose of the communicator and also in relation to the feasibility of the desired action by the group addressed at the time of presentation (61, 99). The actual presentation, if it is to achieve the desired reactions, must give due consideration to all of these aspects. Its effectiveness can sometimes be determined in advance by pre-testing or by follow up studies after initial presentation (55).

The art of transnational communication is one of extreme difficulty whether between governments or between peoples. The latter is still in its infancy. Doubtless, a large proportion of transnational informational and propaganda programs are either so uninteresting or so unadapted to the audience that they have no effect or an opposite effect from that intended (99, 103, 104).

ASSUMPTIONS

The discipline of communications rests upon assumptions derived from the findings of sociology and psychology. They include the following:

1. Communities, cultures, societies, and institutions *exist* because of interaction among persons, only possible if communication permits a sharing of information, ideas, feelings, and values among members of the group (78).

2. Persons and societies control their impulses and *act*, in accord with standards of selection and of evaluation implicit in the attitudes, opinions, cultures, and ideologies established within them through communication (48, 91).

3. The *solidarity* and integration of a community increases as the key symbols used in communication become *internalized* or *sentimentalized* by the members; thus developing common interests, attitudes, and values, and establishing procedures and institutions for maintaining law and realizing social goals (53, 55, 61).

4. The individual's education and experience condition his inherited drives, internalize the values of his culture in his personality, and establish his roles and skills, but only if information on conditions and situations is currently and accurately communicated to the relevant persons can the action of individuals or societies be *adaptive* (41, 50, 70).

It is, therefore, assumed that communication is essential for the existence of societies, and for their action, and that the character of communications influences the solidarity of societies and the adaptiveness of their action.

International communication takes place among, or concerning the relations of, societies, each of which exhibits far more solidarity and far greater capacity for unified action, than does the super-society of which they are members. International relations, therefore, differs from relations within nations because the body of predispositions or internalized values and beliefs common to the world's population is small as compared with that common to the population of any nation, and because the flow of communications between nations is smaller than that within each nation (106, 110). Transnational communication, whether between governments or peoples, is, therefore, likely to be misunderstood. Conditions and situations are likely to be differently interpreted by the people of different nations, and the development of a universal culture is retarded by the more rapid integration of national cultures and by their differentiation from one another. The special assumptions of the discipline of international communications may therefore be stated as follows:

1. A world community, a universal culture, a world society, and world institutions have been developing since the fifteenth century because of the extension of the radius and rapidity of communication by inventions in ocean, land, and air transport and in the press, postal service, and telecommunication. This development will tend to continue if the abundance and ease of world communication systems increase relative to that of national communication systems (112). It has been suggested that animals are guided mainly by instinct; primitive man by custom; civilized man by conscience; and modern man, in the age of abundant communications, by public opinion (89). States may recapitulate this development. When contacts are slight, they are guided only by the instinct of self-preservation and power augmentation. This tends to be moderated, as diplomatic contacts develop, by customary international law. In time, developing by analogy to national systems of law, international custom becomes modified by concepts of international justice and international ethics. With more abundant international communications, not only between governments but also between peoples, a world public opinion tends to develop and to influence government actions, especially when that opinion is organized in international institutions (34, 90, 110).

2. The United Nations and other international institutions are systems of action, capable of making decisions in accord with standards of selection and evaluation. The effectiveness of these decisions will increase in proportion as the development of international communications increases the solidarity and integration of the world community (91, 110).

3. The world community today lacks solidarity or integration because its key value symbols are not in any large degree internalized in the per-

sonalities of the world's population. It is only an *international* community whose value symbols, though formally accepted by governments, are not sentimentally accepted by the peoples who eventually control the governments. It rests therefore on government opinion, not on personal attitudes. Transnational communications are therefore interpreted by the peoples in the light of their national cultures, national opinions, and national beliefs, and tend to increase misunderstanding and conflict rather than to further understanding and co-operation (111).

4. Because of the great diversity in the cultures and conditions of the peoples of different nations, a world culture will probably always be relatively loose and ambiguous, the world society will always be relatively lacking in solidarity and integration, and world institutions will always be relatively weak, but the difference is one of degree. More adequate communication can develop a world society within which world institutions can be more effective than they are today in maintaining international peace and security and promoting international co-operation (112, 113).

The first two of these assumptions—there is a world community and it is organized for action—rest upon the historical facts of geographical discovery, technological invention, and international organization, which have been increasing the radius and rapidity of transmission and the abundance, pervasiveness, and accuracy of communications throughout the world, thus facilitating the acceptance of universal standards and goals of action by the world community as a whole. Exclusive attention to these historical facts, discloses a picture of steady progress from the slow and infrequent sailboats, horseback riders, and locally circulating pamphlets and papers; through the more rapid and abundant steamboats and railroad trains carrying the "penny post" and world newspapers; to the greatly accelerated speed and frequency of air-borne persons, mails, and newspapers between all parts of the world and the instantaneous communication directed to particular destinations by telegraph, cable, and radio, and for mass consumption by radio and television. A similar picture of steady progress is also disclosed from the system of *ad hoc* diplomatic missions; through the net work of permanent missions and consulates and occasional international conferences for developing international law; through the establishment of international administrative unions to facilitate postal and telegraph communication, sea and land transportation, exchange of information by governments and humanitarian and commercial co-operation; to the organization of universal institutions to assure peace, security, pacific settlement, and the achievement of common economic, social, humanitarian, scientific, educational, and cultural goals. In the last fifty years such universal institutions have progressed from the Hague System, through the League of Nations, to the United Nations. Scrutiny of these developments can easily create the conviction of an emerging "one world."

The last two assumptions—the relative weakness of the world community and its continuing weakness compared with states—qualify this impression by noting the actual superficiality of the effect of world communications compared to that of national communications upon culture and personality, and the divergent conditions of the different parts of the world that account for, and are likely to continue to maintain, great diversities of culture and value systems. The sentiment of nationalism has developed more rapidly than the sentiment of cosmopolitanism. National communications systems have developed more effectively than the world communication system. Artificial barriers have been added to the influence of national languages, national postal and telegraph rates, national education, and national institutions in dividing the world into many national communication systems rather than uniting it in a single world system (3, 4, 10, 23, 31, 34, 56, 64, 66, 80, 109, 110).

Opposing tendencies continue side by side. On the one hand, material and technological tendencies make for world unity, and on the other, moral and sentimental tendencies make for national societies. The actual condition which a discipline of international communications must assume is a world community continually balancing these opposing tendencies. Material progress favoring cosmopolitanism develops world communication, world culture, world co-operation, and world institutions; but these tendencies stimulate reactions toward traditional beliefs and loyalties, and national barriers, national differentiations, and national conflicts for a time augment sentiments of national self-determination and sovereignty. Eventually, the destructiveness of war, and the general cultural and economic deterioration consequent upon it, initiates a reaction toward a period of cosmopolitanism and world unity. The amplitude of these oscillations may be unnecessarily great and unnecessarily disturbing to civilization. The art of international communications might have as its object reduction of this amplitude so that the diminution of communication distances between nations, inevitable with the progress of science and technology, might be accompanied by parallel diminution in the cultural distances, thus maintaining the world community in a dynamic equilibrium and avoiding violent oscillations of nationalism and cosmopolitanism.

ANALYSIS

The analysis of international communications has proceeded on the basis of the assumptions stated and has dealt with (a) the content of communications, (b) the process of communication, (c) the effectiveness of communications, and (d) the relations established by communications. In other words, communication has been treated as an entity, as a process, as a force, and as a field of relations. These respectively emphasize the form and content of the communication itself, the characteristics and reactions of the audience, the intentions and purposes of the author, and the objective meaning of the communication. They are respectively related to the syntactic, the pragmatic, the expressive, and the semantic analysis of a particular communication (71, 72).

Content analysis. A particular symbol, communication, document, or flow of communications may be analyzed as a value in itself, or as evidence concerning the addressee, the author, or the subject discussed. The literary critic usually has the first of these points of view; the historian, the second; the philosopher, theologian, or psychiatrist, the third; and the scientist, the fourth. Subsequent sections of this chapter on the process of communication, the effectiveness of communication, and the relations established by communication can deal more adequately with the last three of these aspects of communication. *Content analysis* has acquired a specialized meaning referring to the quantitative analysis, not only of single documents, but of a flow of documents (9, 55), and can throw light on all four aspects of communication.

Literary criticism, following the *Poetics* of Aristotle, has usually sought to explain and to evaluate the aesthetic effect of a literary document in its own terms—the relation of parts to whole, the harmony of imagery, meaning, allusion, rhythm, and sound; the appropriateness of form to content; and in general, the total effect of the document upon the sophisticated reader (6, 12, 28, 42, 92). Some schools of criticism have adopted less comprehensive criteria and have appraised a literary document according to its affective impact upon the average reader, thus leaving judgment to individual taste, or according to its meaning and value in the experience of the author or the history of the period. Others have criticized such a document from the point of view of its significance in the history of ideas or of literary forms. Literary critics, statisticians, and mathematicians have on occasion sought to explain the effect of a literary masterpiece by the frequency of typical terms or classes of terms (114); by the economy, redundancy, and arrangement of terms (37); or by the precision, ambiguity, or connotative plurality (portmanteau character) of terms (75, 87), with the hope of making criticism objective.

From the point of view of international relations, literary criticism is undoubtedly important. Works of art are a common heritage of mankind, and the international communication and criticism of works of literary art, as well as of the other fine arts, can contribute much to understanding among the elite of all nations (73). Appreciation of the interplay of precision and ambiguity, of denotation and connotation, of part and whole, of objective and subjective meanings, which give value to works of literature and art may contribute to evaluation of societies, particularly of the society of nations. Its contradictions, so baffling and disturbing to many, may disclose valuable unity in diversity to the aesthetic critic. To these ends, aesthetic criticism may have more to contribute than have emotional, scholarly, or philosophical criticism. The latter, however, may respectively disclose common elements of spontaneous human nature, common strivings of men and of civilizations toward expression of their aspirations, and common sharing by all of philosophical ideas and forms of expression, awareness of which may contribute to the solidarity of the world community.

The importance, from the point of view of world citizenship, of international contacts among leaders in the fine arts, of transnational communication of works of art and literature, and of more widespread appreciation of aesthetic values has been recognized by UNESCO and by numerous unofficial organizations in the field. Critical analysis of literary and artistic works is a necessary element in such transnational communication. People with varied cultural traditions need more than mere translations to appreciate the works of literature produced by one another.

Similar to literary criticism is the evaluation of documents with reference to their probable propaganda, educational, or informational influence. Will people read or listen? If they do, how will their attitudes, opinions, and ideas be affected? These subjects will be considered in dealing with the effectiveness of communication.

Historical criticism. Content analysis of documents produced within a nation during a period of time can provide information about the people who prepared them or the audience for whom they were prepared and who presumably read them. Historians rely mainly upon qualitative analysis of such documents known as *source materials* in order to construct narratives which enable their readers to realize past civilizations. Lawyers and judges utilize such documents, as well as oral testimony, as *evidence* to settle controversies about past events. Modern content analyzers have subjected diplomatic, parliamentary, and other official documents, and the press, radio, film, television, and other materials of mass communication to *quantitative analysis* in order to discover the interests and opinions of contemporary governments, elites, and peoples, and the changes of those interests and opinions through time. Attention surveys have been based on counts of the relative frequency of the appearance of key symbols in the press of different countries at the same time, and of the same country at different times. Assuming that the press both influences and reflects the interests and opinions of the readers, such surveys may indicate the extent to which a given public at a given time is dominated by sentiments of nationalism or internationalism, of imperialism or cosmopolitanism, of militarism or pacifism, of constitutionalism or revolutionism, of optimism or pessimism, or by combinations of these and other sentiments. Such surveys may also indicate the rate at which movement is taking place from the domination of one of these sentiments to domination by another. The *public* of importance in a particular area, whether a small elite or a general voting population, can be identified by study of the particular social and political structure and culture of the area. Movements of its attention and interest constitute the very heart of international relations and their precise measurement may provide statesmen, national and international, with important guidance for regulatory action (61, 90, 113).

More precise surveys have been made to determine the direction, intensity, homogeneity, and continuity of opinions concerning given symbols, interests or policies in a given public. Questionnaires and polls, responded to by a carefully selected sample of the population, and counts of *opinion statements* and *themes* in the press and other media of mass communications have been analyzed for this purpose (80, 110).

Comparatively little has been done in relating such opinion studies to studies of the attitudes of samples of population, although methods have been devised for the measurement of *attitudes* as distinct from *opinions* (101). Precise determination of attitudes doubtless requires a prolonged individual examination as in the psychoanalytic interview, but questionnaires have been devised which may indicate the extent to which symbols have been *internalized* or *sentimentalized* and may permit rough measurement of several *dimensions* (direction, intensity, continuity, and integration) of the attitudes they represent (54, 110).

Continuing studies of this kind, disclosing both the opinions of the public and the attitudes of persons with reference to the major symbols of international politics, might have a profound effect upon the conduct of foreign policies and of international organizations for peace and security. The technique for making such surveys is, however, only on the threshold of development, and in any case the conditions in a world divided by iron curtains are not propitious for surveying the world public as a whole.

Philosophic criticism. Content analysis of communications may indicate not only the interests, opinions, and attitudes of the audiences but also the purposes, intentions, and policies of the authors. Literary critics and psychoanalysts have interpreted the personality of authors by analyzing their works (88) and historians have interpreted the intentions of political leaders from their letters and papers (1). Content analyzers have successfully interpreted the policies of governments by inference from the themes and the audience of government propagandists. Thus some of Hitler's military moves were predicted from the analysis of the propaganda issued by Goebbels. Such analysis, of course, requires knowledge of much besides documents. Does the success of political and military measures depend on a suitable state of opinion at home and abroad (55, 61, 99)? What does the government studied think about this dependence?

Diplomatic correspondence and speeches of public men have long been scrutinized to determine the policies they manifest or conceal, and the power with which such policies are likely to be supported. For this purpose, analysis of the content of such documents is supplemented by knowledge of the personalities of the authors, of the history and policy of the state they represent, and of the conditions of public opinion and military preparation. Such documents often indicate radical inconsistencies among opinions, attitudes, policies, and capabilities in a given situation. The public expression in a document may vary greatly from the private attitude of the statesman in whose name it is issued, and also from the policy which the government has decided to follow and from its capacity to implement that policy in the situation. Important as is the content of diplomatic communications, analysts recognize that they must be interpreted and supplemented by much extraneous material. Interpretation is difficult, but in the practical conduct of international relations, whether by national governments or by international agencies, the analysis of communications to discover currently the policy and power of the main actors, is of the greatest importance (61, 99, 113).

Scientific criticism. Finally a communication may be analyzed from the point of view of the information it purports to convey. Scientific treatises are usually read from this point of view. They provide little information about the author or the audience, and while they may be criticized with reference to elegance and clarity of presentation, this literary point of view is usually subordinated to the utility of the document for conveying information about the facts and relations which it discusses. Precise operational definitions and correct logical inferences are essential for this purpose (14, 82).

Learned writings, diplomatic communications, and even the press must be resorted to for information relative to international relations. That subject, however, is far from being a scientific discipline. Its terminology lacks clarity and its expounders lack objectivity. Consequently information can be obtained only if the documents are subjected to scientific criticism. The bias, policy, or propagandistic intention of the author, or of the government or society which has permitted publication, must be considered. Social as well as official censorships are here involved (21, 47).

It must also be recognized that ambiguity may be the essence of political symbols and communications. It may be the means by which diverse persons and organizations can be brought together for political action. Ambiguity concerning ultimate values and goals may be the price of international co-operation on immediate objectives in proportion as national cultures are diverse (55). The operational definition, comprehensive analysis, and precise inference expected in science is not to be found in the vocabulary, propositions, and expositions in the documents which constitute the only source of information on international relations.

Communications provide the bases for knowing, understanding, evaluating, and acting in the international field. They are, however, likely to mislead rather than to guide the scholar unless read carefully. The art of criticizing communications is therefore of prime importance in developing the discipline of international relations, whether from the point of view of aesthetic appreciation, of audience reaction, of author's intention, or of factual information on the subjects discussed.

The process of communication. As a process, communication is concerned with the interaction of persons, with the transmission and interpretation of signs and symbols, with the activation of personalities and organizations, and with the development of cultures and ideologies. These psychic, technical, social, and cultural processes proceed together, and they are in high degree interdependent.

Interaction is a complicated process in which a speaker apprehends the expectation of the listener in respect to the speaker's role and intentions, and the listener apprehends the expectation of the speaker in respect to the listener's reaction. If the conventions of language and other symbols are sufficiently understood by both speaker and listener and if they are appropriately interpreted in the given situation—only possible if there is some sharing of a common experience and a common culture—neither of these expectations will be disappointed and interaction will take place. The meaning of the speaker will enter into the personality of the listener and he will react in the manner expected by the speaker, in response to which the latter will react in the manner expected by the listener. Interaction develops through conversation progressively integrating the participants into a society (26, 78, 82).

Obviously a great deal of communication does not produce interaction in this sense. The audience does not listen or does not understand or misunderstands. This may result from its ignorance either of the language or of the subject matter (83). The sentence, "I saw a giraffe," means nothing to an African ignorant of English or to an Englishman ignorant of giraffes. Failure of interaction is especially likely in international and transnational communication. Because of the usual differences of language and of cultural background of the speaker and audience, diplomatic conversations do not usually proceed as smoothly as conversation between old members of a social club. Such conversations may be assisted through occasionally surrounding them with the convivial atmosphere of a club, but only if the participants and personalities involved have much experience and culture in common and have considerable freedom in the application of their instructions. Interaction between diplomats divided by the iron curtain has been exceptionally difficult to achieve. As already noticed, where cultural backgrounds are diverse, some ambiguity, permitting diverse interpretations, may be a condition for the efficacy of political communications. Exaggerated efforts at precision in the communication of doctrine or policy, even among people of common culture, has led to heresy, sectarianism, or partisanship rather than to unity (55, 112, 113).

Transmission. Communication is the art of using signs and symbols to influence others. Clearly unless signs and symbols are transmitted through time and space so as to affect the eye or ear of the person to be influenced, unless conventional meaning is attached to the signs and symbols, and unless the users have some experience with what is meant, there can be no communication. Modern invention has greatly increased the possibility of disseminating combinations of signs and symbols accurately, rapidly, and widely, and of preserving them for long periods of time. The sensory impact and conventional definition of a sign or symbol is, however, a small part of its meaning in communications. According to logical positivists and pragmatists a term conveys information only if operationally defined and the amount of information conveyed varies with the user's familiarity with the operation (83). Furthermore, the interpretation of a term depends not only upon its denotation but also upon its connotation, which, as the semanticists have pointed out, may be more significant in expressing or rousing emotion, than in giving information (75). Some semanticists have classified terms in accord with their predominantly, informative, appraising, inciting, or formulating meaning (72). Communications can be misunderstood if a fighting word is given a literal meaning or if a merely descriptive word is translated into another language which gives it affective qualities. Communication will fail if a word intended to describe is accepted as an insult or if a word intended to evaluate is accepted as a statement of fact (41, 50). The character of a communication as a whole can usually be classified as exposition, as evaluation, as propaganda, or as formulation, and its classification may indicate the interpretation to be given particular terms. Conversely the character of the terms predominantly used may indicate the character of the communication as a whole. The whole and the parts react upon one another. Often, however, the characteristics of a communication is ambiguous. Propaganda may be concealed in apparent exposition as often happens in the news columns of the daily press, or evaluations may be embodied in apparently unbiased formulations. Such ambiguity is a common method of exerting influence upon the unwary reader and also a frequent source of misunderstanding and suspicion (46, 60).

For this reason, if official international relations are to be peaceful, diplomatic communications should be unusually explicit, and translations into another language should be scrutinized with great care. In international conferences, preliminary preparations and discussions should establish a basis of common purposes and values, and a common understanding of the agenda if the negotiation is to succeed. If these precautions are neglected, the conference is likely to achieve no results or formulæ will be announced which manifest merely formal agreement on a document but no interaction among delegates or agreement in substance. But as noticed, some ambiguity, implying margins of disagreement irrelevant for the immediate purpose, may be a necessary means of political integration (112, 113).

It has been hoped that continuous contact of the delegates of different nations in international organizations would create a common spirit and understanding, converting them from *delegates* to *representatives* and facilitating interaction. This result has been hampered, however, by the practice of explicit instruction, leaving delegates little freedom, or by reserving the right of ratification. The latter practice has sometimes rendered genuine agreements among representatives of many nations, achieved in the "Spirit of Geneva" or the "Spirit of the United Nations," impotent because unratified and unacceptable to the "Spirit of Paris," the "Spirit of London," the "Spirit of Washington," or the "Spirit of Moscow." The technique of diplomatic conference to achieve both genuine agreement among representatives and approval of governments is, therefore, of great importance in the practical conduct of international communications and international relations. The problem, which has for centuries faced resident diplomats in establishing social relations with local officials and other diplomats at the same capital without losing understanding of their own government, is faced at a different level in the establishment of social relations and understanding among representatives in international organizations. The agency co-ordinating communication at the point where nationalism and internationalism come to grips is, as pointed out in Chapter 16, at the heart of the art of conducting international relations. The controversial character of this agency was well illustrated in the Senatorial hearings in 1953 on proposals to amend the United States Constitution with the object of transferring control over international agreements from the executive in direct touch with foreign and world opinion, to Congress in direct touch with only national opinion, or to the states in direct touch with only local opinion (113).

The growth of mass communication and its extension to transnational communication has increased both the range and the difficulty of communication. The communicator frequently fails to understand the influence of the varied cultural backgrounds of his audience and the varied connotation of symbols among them. Transnational communication between peoples is therefore an art of peculiar difficulty. Unless conducted with great skill, it may augment conflict, even when the intention is to produce understanding (61, 99, 104).

Activation. International communication usually has for its object the influencing of the action of persons and institutions or the changing of attitudes, beliefs, and opinions. A *system of action*, whether a person or an organization, is a highly sensitive organization of drives, dispositions, and evaluative standards capable of making choices when presented with a stimulating situation. Communication may provide the stimulus by presenting a situation, but the reaction will be that desired by the communicator only if that presentation is accepted by the audience, if appropriate drives or dispositions are activated, and if evaluative standards leading to the desired choice are suggested. These conditions are not likely to be met unless the communicator is well aware of the nature of the personality or organization he is trying to influence and with the evaluative standards embodied in the culture or ideology which the recipient has *internalized*.

Diplomatic proposals or transnational communications often fail to produce desired results, or even produce opposite results, because of the imperfect knowledge of the system of action dealt with. A threat may bring submissions but is more likely to bring a counterthreat. A conciliatory gesture may assist negotiation but it may encourage further aggression by creating an impression of weakness. Seldom are diplomats certain which results to expect, and if they think they are certain, they are likely to be mistaken (55, 62, 103).

Acculturation. Communication, if abundant and productive of interaction, leads to the spread of ideologies and the growth of a common culture among those in communication with one another. Within that common culture, further interaction, can take place more easily and the culture can develop in depth and comprehensiveness. This process, however, of cultural diffusion, ideological circulation, and the formation of super-cultures, is likely to be a slow one with many set backs. Transnational communication, which does not produce interaction, does not tend toward a universal culture, but rather to the augmentation of national differences (29, 64, 91, 110).

Culture depends upon the internalization or sentimentalization of meanings. Persons must understand, accept, and incorporate in their personalities the meaning of the communication if the process is to take place. The process could be expressed as a movement from symbols to opinions, from opinions to attitudes, and from attitudes to values. A mere transmission of symbols means very little. If they are understood, common opinions may develop permitting common action at a superficial political level, in a state, alliance, party, or pressure group. If these opinions become sentimentalized as attitudes, a common society is in the process of developing. If finally, these attitudes become basic values of the personality, and if institutions develop to realize them, a common culture is established, and common action at the social level becomes possible. International relations, in the present historical period, have seldom passed beyond the stage of common opinions. They have functioned only at the political level. Such movements as those which propose to develop the North Atlantic Treaty Organization into a federation or the United Nations into a World Government can only be realized if the common opinions established by these treaties, become internalized as attitudes which predominate among the peoples to be united (82, 84, 90, 110).

The effectiveness of communications. Those who employ communications as a force to realize their purposes are concerned with the organization of agencies of initiation, co-ordination, and control; the theme or message to be communicated; the medium to be employed; and the predispositions and general characteristics of the audience to be influenced. From all these considerations, the detailed content of the communication can be composed and the time and circumstances of its publication determined. There is a very large literature on all of these aspects of communication. Doubtless if all education, parliamentary debate, electioneering, preaching, journalism, advertising, public relations activity, lecturing, propagandizing, social conversation, and literary production is included, this activity absorbs more money and energy than any other human activity except, perhaps, military preparation and economic production. Even in these fields, communication in the form of reports, instructions, and orders plays a major role.

The problem of the communicator is to maximize the efficiency of his communication. The section on "relations established by communications" deals with the general effect on society and international relations of changes in the degree of regional or functional centralization of communication control, and with the influence of new inventions, facilitating mass and directed communication at a distance. The present section seeks to suggest some of the problems of those who initiate and control international communications.

Communicators must of course be aware of the different forms of communication and their relevance to different situations. A distinction is usually made between information, education, propaganda, and instruction, but no sharp line can be drawn between them. In a general way, these terms conform to the semantic distinctions already referred to between informing, appraising, inciting, and formulating statements. After considering these forms of communication, attention will be given to the significance of the agency, theme, medium, and audience in making communications effective.

Information in a broad sense refers to the operationally defined content of any message or communication (31) but in a narrow sense it means a communication of *facts* about conditions, persons, sentiments, ideologies, institutions, laws, positions, or demands without efforts to evaluate, to persuade, or to incite to action. Information is a preferred term for government agencies engaged in communication because it is assumed that an *information agency* will not arouse the anxiety among others which a *propaganda agency* might. Nevertheless, information programs are selective. The materials are chosen because they are thought to be useful for preparing the ground for education, propaganda, or negotiation, or for initiating currents of thought in the addressees, leading them to desired opinions or attitudes. So far as information programs are what the name implies, they are in less need of adaptation to peculiarities of the audience than are other types of communication. Bona fide information programs, however, present certain problems. Because of the general suspicion of audiences in respect to transnational communication, care has to be taken to avoid information which might seem highly improbable to the audience. Accurate information on the distribution of automobiles in the American laboring population is said to have seemed so improbable to Russian audiences as to convince them that the "Voice of America" was not to be believed. The reputation for truthfulness is the essence of an information program and such a reputation cannot be maintained unless the information is always, not only objectively true, but also geared to the audience's conception of probabilities (61, 99).

Education adds to information, standards of appraisal and evaluation to guide action. The subject will be dealt with further in the next chapter but a brief comment is in point here. Education usually seeks to transmit a culture or system of values and thus assumes that the audience to be educated is actually or potentially a participant in the culture which the communicator is interested in transmitting. Transnational education should, therefore, assume that some cultural values are universal or at least apply to all the nations involved and should confine itself to education in these supranatural standards. Insofar as this assumption is not justified, educational programs in the field of international relations tend to become transnational propaganda of particular national cultures. To avoid such propaganda, transnational education sometimes confines itself to giving objective information about the values and beliefs of different societies. But if education is to be differentiated from both information and propaganda, it must seek to *internalize* values and standards so that the learner will have the attitudes, predispositions, and patterns of action necessary for his successful functioning in society. The term is, therefore, used especially in reference to the young who do not yet have such attitudes. Transnational educational programs encounter the difficulty, not only that the audience is suspicious of such programs, but also that its members are mature and have attitudes which will often be in conflict with those which the program seeks to establish. Few values, even though formally accepted by most governments in diplomatic instruments, escape frequent conflict with the parochial values actually accepted by many peoples (20, 104).

Propaganda differs from education in that its aim is to influence opinion and incite action. The propagandist is not interested in developing the

personality of the members of his audience and inducing in them attitudes and modes of thought conforming to the culture he professes, but
only in developing an opinion which, however verbal and ephemeral,
may be sufficient at the critical moment to support the action desired. He
operates in a much more superficial level of the mind than does the
educator. He may appeal to drives of sex, security, dominance, and greed,
but these are not very far below the surface in most personalities. He
may also appeal to generalities such as peace, justice, progress, and welfare of such character that their specific application is undetermined. He
utilizes the device of associating his proposal with attitudes or values
already existing in the audience, such as patriotism, loyalty, and sympathy. Special devices of *name calling, glittering generality, prestige,
plain folks, card stacking,* and the *band wagon* have been described and
have proved effective because they may conceal from the audience the
aspect of his personality which is being stimulated and through which he
is being unwittingly led to adopt an opinion, the purport of which he
does not clearly apprehend. A certain ambiguity is therefore usually
to be found in political propaganda and is a condition of its effectiveness
in proportion as the audience is heterogeneous (40, 46, 60, 67).

Propaganda is not equivalent to untruthfulness or unfair argument or
unworthy appeal. It is not immoral but amoral. The issues of factual
truth, fairness, and sound values are irrelevant to the propagandist, except
insofar as neglect of them may, in the long run, prevent the effectiveness
of the propaganda. The aim of the propagandist is to get results and he
judges the validity of his methods by this standard. Transnational propaganda, which implies a suspicious audience because of the general expectation of conflict in contemporary international relations, is a delicate
business. It will almost certainly misfire or backfire unless the propagandist has accurate information about his audience and wins their
confidence before he attempts to influence their opinions. The Jesuits who
went to China in the seventeenth century adopted Chinese costume,
learned the Chinese language, practiced much of Chinese culture, and
utilized their knowledge of astronomy and other arts and disciplines
useful to the Chinese to acquire prestige. For ten years they integrated
themselves into Chinese civilization before they began their religious
propaganda, and, as a result, the latter was remarkably effective, but only
so far as they were able to avoid direct conflict with the basic values of
Chinese culture. Eventually, the *rites question,* involving the compatibil-
ity of Chinese ancestor worship and Catholic Christianity, presented an
obstacle, frustrating the success of their movement. This case admirably
illustrates the methods necessary for the success, and at the same time,
the limits, of transnational propaganda.

Since the object of propaganda is to induce action, the symbols employed may be closely related to action. Threats and offers of reward may

be employed, and, to make them convincing, acts may be committed because of their propaganda significance. Military and economic operations in war may, for example, be regarded as a form of *propaganda of the act* designed to change the opinion of the enemy population and government, substituting the will to surrender for the will to resist. More commonly, *war propaganda* or *psychological warfare* is regarded as merely an auxiliary to military or economic action, but, unless total annihilation of the enemy is contemplated, the former point of view, is more suitable. War is an operation on the mind of the enemy as a whole through attacking the bodies of a few (51).

Instruction (sometimes used as equivalent to education) is used here to refer to communication to an audience from which obedience can be expected. Foreign offices instruct their diplomatic agents, executives instruct their administrative inferiors, and party chiefs instruct the rank and file of the party. While information can be given to any audience, education to an audience with some cultural characteristics in common, and propaganda to an audience whose characteristics are well known to the propagandist, instruction can only be given to an audience in a subordinate position. Its significance in international relations arises from the development of fifth columnist and subversive movements in one country subject to instruction by agencies in another. Instructions interpret, formulate, and apply to concrete circumstances the attitudes, opinions, or policies to which the audience is already committed. To be effective the terms of instructions must be operationally defined.

Negotiation and war have been the most characteristic types of action in international relations and both of them depend upon instructions although they employ all types of communication. Negotiation involves informational dispatches from the negotiator in the field to his own foreign office; instructions from the foreign office to the negotiator in the field; and notes from one government to another or verbal communications between the negotiators. The latter may include information, education, and propaganda. Their object is to persuade, but appeals to law or ethical principles and to mutual interests may be supplemented by suggestions of threat or reward. General propaganda, creating a suitable atmosphere of opinion or bringing pressures upon the negotiator from segments of his national public, may also be used (103).

War also involves all types of communication—instructions and orders by superior to subordinate officers; education and indoctrination of the armed forces; information from scouts, spies, and staff officers to the command; and propaganda designed to sustain national morale and unity, to win the good will of neutrals or to convert them to allies, and to discourage and disunite the enemy (15, 51). Negotiations involving all forms of communication take place between allies, and even between enemies for armistice or surrender.

This survey suggests that if transnational communication is to be effective, the communicator must be aware of the conditions which favor or hamper the successful use of such communication for informing, for educating, for propagandizing, or for instructing a given public, as well as the results to be expected from each of these activities under favorable conditions. More concretely the communicator must pay attention to the organization of his operation, to the theme and form of his message, to the media to be utilized, and particularly to the predispositions of the audience to be influenced.

Communication agencies. Should the national or international agency directing transnational communications be independent or should it be linked with the policy-making organ? If independent of government, a national agency may be relatively free from the inhibitions flowing from the national legislature and public opinion, and from the limitations which international law and comity imposes upon official agencies. An independent agency may, therefore, be in a better position than a government agency to win the confidence of the audience, usually suspicious of the propaganda of foreign governments, and to shape its message to the predispositions of that audience in a way which national opinion, judging from its own predispositions, might deem subversive. On the other hand, propaganda is closely related to action. Unless presented and timed in close relation to policy and action, propaganda may create false expectations, induce premature moves, and defeat itself. An audience cannot be asked to engage in revolutionary or insurrectionary movements unless they can expect military and diplomatic support. Propaganda urging revolt will not assist a policy which is, at the moment, aimed at conciliation. For this reason, there has been an increasing tendency for governments to organize transnational communications in close contact with foreign offices. This has been a response to increasing nationalism and increasing international tension. Expedient as this policy may be from the point of view of the national policy of the sending state, provided the communication agency can escape hampering restrictions of its own legislature, it is likely to be interpreted by the government of the receiving audience as an effort to influence the people over the head of their own government, to subvert their national loyalty, and to win in psychological warfare. It therefore tends to solidify national states, to rigidify national policies, to differentiate between the nation's friends and enemies, to increase international tensions, and thus both to raise obstacles to its own success and to hamper the development of an international society (61, 99).

International organizations probably gain from the activities of independent transnational communication agencies, especially if many such agencies compete with one another, if they are free from national political censorships, and if they operate under professional standards designed to prevent deception and incitement to violence. The United Nations has sought to maintain these conditions by including freedom of transnational communication in its Universal Declaration of Human Rights and by seeking to gain official acceptance of covenants and conventions on the subject. International Organizations have also maintained official communication agencies of their own with the object of informing the people of member states of the activities of the organization and of educating them to accept the standards and objectives established by their charters. The member governments, even though formally committed to these standards and objectives, have often been reluctant to permit such communications to their people. The progress of integration of national policies and international responsibilities of states can be measured by the freedom of official international agencies to communicate directly to the national publics.

Theme and form of message. The themes of transnational communication particularly of propaganda, must, it is said, be simple, consistent, and related to all other aspects of policy. All communications must support the central theme unless a total change is intended, as, for example, when a government is about to change its diplomatic alignments. It is said that while the United States is engaged in cold war with the Soviet Union, patriotic American communication agencies should pursue single mindedly either the theme of encouraging revolt by the satellites and the oppressed nationalities, or the theme of trade, friendship, and co-operation between the American and Soviet peoples, but not both. One can not, at the same time, it is said, encourage hostility to, and create conditions for conciliation with, the Kremlin. This argument assumes the necessity of policies either of hostility or of friendship with a given state in a given situation. However, it may be that inconsistencies in propaganda, keeping several avenues open for development as the occasions arise, may sometimes have advantages. Relations are in most instances not black or white, but some shade of gray. They may even be multidimensional, exhibiting aspects outside of any linear continuum (31).

Independent communication agencies can be expected to present a variety of themes, thus encouraging individual thought, choice, and responsibility by the members of the public, a condition usually considered necessary for democracy.

Official communication agencies of international organizations usually limit their themes in accord with the standards and purposes expressed in their charters. The inconsistent interpretations of these standards and purposes often given by different member governments will of course be reflected in informational reports about the activities of the organization. If such agencies seek to propagandize interpretations or policies which remain highly controversial among the member governments, their activity is likely to prove disruptive and self-defeating.

No less important than the theme is the form in which it is presented. In communication with a sophisticated audience, standards of criticism and analysis of the kind discussed in the section of this chapter on "content analysis" will have to be studied. In mass communication, problems of language, terminology, logic, and style are important. The message will not be understood if the grammatical construction is complex, if terms are abstract and remote from the individual's immediate experience, if the reasoning appears to be confused and difficult to follow, and if the style fails to produce a receptive atmosphere.

Communication media. The medium chose for the transnational communication of a message influences the size of the audience reached, the accuracy and impact of the message upon the members of that audience, and the possibility of confining the message to a selected audience. A larger proportion of some publics can be reached by radio, of others by the press, and of others by rumor. The wealth, literacy, and customs of the audience are all important in determining the medium which will achieve the widest coverage. Diplomatic correspondence and press reports can convey messages more accurately than radio or rumor. Where ambiguity is desired the latter method may be preferable. Television and cinema probably have the greatest impact upon the individual of all mass communication media, and radio probably has more impact than the press. Individualized communication by conversation, group discussion, and lecture may, however, have greater impact than any means of mass communication. The grapevine of rumor or the instruction of subversive agents can be selective and can therefore distribute inconsistent messages in different places and to different classes of people without immediate detection as would be true of inconsistent press or radio communications. Diplomatic correspondence can make inconsistent suggestions to different countries so long as secrecy can be preserved, but in the modern era of rapid publication of such correspondence, there is considerable risk in such methods. A reputation for sincerity and consistency is an asset which no government or communication agency can afford lightly to part with (16, 20, 79).

Audience response. In all transnational communication, as has been repeatedly emphasized, the characteristics of the audience is the vital consideration. What are its predispositions? its capabilities? its tendencies? Measurements of attitude and opinion in all their dimensions, pretesting, and checking are indispensable, if transnational communication is to succeed (61). Especial attention may be paid to the predisposition of the audience with respect to the importance of the subject discussed, to the probability of the *facts* asserted, to the reliability of the sources cited, and to the desirability of the conclusions pointed to in a message. Does the message have such relevance to the current values, interests, and anxieties of the audience that it will attract and hold their attention? Are the facts presented of a character which the audience, guided by its culture, knowledge, and experience, will consider highly improbable or even impossible? Is the concrete evidence presented or the person presenting it convincing to persons with the experience, habits, and beliefs of this audience? Is the evidence sufficient to convince them of *facts* which they are predisposed to consider improbable? Do the conclusions which the message suggests tend to support the values, wishes, and interests of the audience and thus to enlist their *will to believe?* All of these questions are involved in determining the credibility of a communication to a given audience.

Transnational and international communication, whether informational or educational, propagandistic or instructional, is certain to meet resistances in some quarters and may increase conflict rather than co-operation even if it proceeds from an international agency. In the long run, such communication, utilizing all of the devices of modern technology probably tends to move the world from a predominant loyalty to national symbols to a predominant loyalty to international symbols, but in the short run, much opposition to this tendency can be expected. The very success of internationalist propaganda and education may be expected to stimulate the vigor of nationalist movements. The increasing nationalization of the United States in the first half of the nineteenth century promoted by congressional oratory, presidential action, national political parties, and supreme court interpretations of the constitution, as well as by the rapid increase in communication among the people of all sections of the country, stimulated a countermovement of states' rights in one section of the country leading to civil war (29). In the same way the internationalizing influence of the League of Nations in the 1920's may have contributed to the nationalistic excesses of Fascism, Nazism, and Nipponism in the 1930's.

The long-run tendency of universal and abundant communication toward developing a world society may be postponed or even frustrated by short-run movements toward more intensive nationalism and regionalism (106). For this reason the conduct of transnational communication, especially by international agencies, is of major importance. The skill and wisdom of that conduct may decide whether the world society will move continuously toward stability and solidarity at a rate no more rapid than the various peoples can generally absorb, or whether countermovements, opposing the tide, will increase divisions, precipitate hostilities, and perhaps frustrate the general tendency, ushering in a prolonged period of political instability, social disintegration, and cultural degeneration (110, 113). The impact of a communication upon the existing values of the audience is no less important than its credibility to that audience in determining its effectiveness.

Relations established by communications. The system of international communication can be thought of as establishing a field of social relations in the world community which gives objective meaning to all communications. That field determines the centers of power and, in a measure, their relative power; the distances between these centers; the atmosphere of opinion and of tension which conditions their action; and the values, goals, and policies which guide their decisions.

Man has been called a social animal, and that means a communicating animal. He has been called a tool-using animal, and his major tool is language. He has been called a power-seeking animal, and communication is a major element of power (31).

Economic activity involves not only production and transportation, but also trade, markets, and finance of which communication is the instrument. Communication is also indispensable for production and transportation when they become more complicated than the single artisan who designs, fabricates, carries, and disposes of his product.

Domestic political activity involves not only the employment of policing forces and public administrators, and the conduct of major public utilities, but also the making, applying, and administering of laws and the leading of opinion, entirely matters of communication. Even police activity, public administration, and utility management require the communication of instructions and orders, increasingly as the scale of government increases, regionally and functionally.

Wars are waged not only on the military front and the economic front, but also on the propaganda and diplomatic fronts where communication is the instrument employed. Even on the military front, the maintenance of morale and the realization of strategic plans and tactical movements depends upon skill in communication (49). The fighting unit, whether conceived as an army, a state, a nation, or a people, is a unit only because of communication among its members.

The importance, the complexity, and the inefficiency of communication increases in all human activity as the scale of operations increases. All societies rest upon interaction and communication, but in small primitive tribes and in rural households the individual engages in much solitary activity, and communication is limited to voice, gesture, and models for imitation. As division of labor, interdependence, separation of co-operating workers by time and space increases, communication becomes more indispensable for operations, more elaborate in form and content, and more likely to fail in its objectives.

International relations is the activity in which this expansion of the significance of communication has reached its maximum. Communication has tended to be the essence of all international activities. War and diplomacy, international organization and administration, international journalism and propaganda, and international education and law are, in the main, forms of communication. In all, efforts are made to influence the mind and behavior of people, usually at a distance and usually by symbols, though propaganda of the act may sometimes be important. International relations, therefore, more than other of the social arts depends on communication to influence opinions, attitudes, values, and policies. The world can be thought of as a field, a network of communications, the character of which determines the character of international relations. As compared with lesser fields of communication—the family, the local community, or the nation—the world field is characterized by considerable, though diminishing, distances between centers of communication; by extensive discontinuities in the flow of communication, especially at national frontiers; and by frequent discrepancies between the attitude of the communicator and the opinion he expresses, and between his intention in that expression and the audiences interpretation of it (31).

The centers of power in the world are the agencies which initiate, co-ordinate, and control communication. At different historic periods, these agencies have varied in degree of centralization, both functional and geographic.

A high degree of centralization concentrating power at a single point is called absolutism. A low degree of centralization distributing power at many points may be called democracy. Many different combinations are, however, possible. If there were one central agency in the world which initiated and controlled all communications, whether political, economic, religious, educational, or artistic and which instructed all local authorities, heads of families, teachers, preachers, administrators, business organizers, military officers, and workers in order to implement the values it accepted, absolutism would be maximized. If, on the other hand, there were complete independence from external interference in communication control in the principal geographical divisions of the world; if there were also very great independence of initiative in different functional institutions within each area such as the state, the church, the universities, the schools, the business corporations and the families; and if within both geographical and functional groups, local and lesser authorities had wide areas of free initiative and all individuals enjoyed a wide freedom to initiate ideas and to communicate them through the spoken word and easily accessible facilities of press, radio, and television, there would be a maximum of democracy, a condition which would approximate anarchy. It is of course recognized that the terms *absolutism* and *democracy* are here used in a particular sense. Perhaps the terms *authority* and *freedom* would be more suitable, although all such terms are extremely ambiguous.

The problem of organizing agencies of communication so as to maximize stability and progress, involves a balance, avoiding either of these extremes. In spite of the lack of instruments of mass communication at a distance, medieval Europe had a high degree of unity because of the capacity of the Pope to communicate to his agents, the bishops and priests, throughout Europe without interference by secular authority, and because of the capacity of these agents to communicate freely with the people whose attitudes were formed by a culture which attributed major authority to ecclesiastical communications even when those communications called for economic boycotts such as excommunication and interdict or for wars such as the crusades. However, the decentralized communication initiatives of barons and of merchant guilds, and the relative inefficiencies of ecclesiastical censorships and controls prevented the system from becoming extremely autocratic. The Soviet system is similar within its area. It is, however, equipped with instruments of mass communication and of directed communication at a distance, and it operates far more efficient methods of censorship and punishment to prevent deviant or defiant communications. Therefore, it is a more autocratic system than was that of the church in medieval Europe.

The modern state system as it arose in the fifteenth century sought to transfer initiative in communications from the ecclesiastical authorities to the secular monarchies. Luther emphasized this change in urging obedience to secular authorities. The doctrines of sovereignty and the legitimacy of power proclaimed by Machiavelli and Bodin systematized the new order of communications. International law recognized the unlimited authority of the state to control all incoming and outgoing communications. In practice, however, such censorships and controls could not be enforced efficiently by the autocratic governments, and liberal governments incorporated in their constitutions guarantees of freedom of opinion, speech, and press for both transnational and national communications (47, 96). Even the Soviet Union, with modern devices of censorship and of radio interference, has not been able to exercise with complete efficiency the power of controlling all incoming and outgoing communications. The modern state system differs from the medieval system in that in principle, the control of communications, while theoretically absolute in each sovereign state, is divided among many sovereign states, each controlling a limited territory, and is exercised with moderation by most states.

The advance of liberalism and democracy has initiated a change in international law, recognized in principal by the United Nations Charter and the Universal Declaration of Human Rights. These instruments seek to establish individual freedom of communications, both national and transnational; to eliminate national censorships; and to permit communications from international organizations to the peoples of all nations. These principles of a new international law have not yet been established in practice. Their realization would tend to a major modification of state sovereignty because the freedom of individuals and of international organizations to communicate would tend toward a development of a universal culture and universal values, increasing the power of universal institutions committed to these values and diminishing the power of national institutions committed to local values. It is, therefore, not surprising that the movement for freedom of communications has been subjected to serious attacks, not only by the Soviet states, but in some degree, by most other states. It is also not surprising that serious attacks upon this movement have occurred in the United States itself, whose government was the initiator and major supporter of this change in international law (10, 113).

It must be realized that, while rules of international law qualifying the nation-states' control of communications have been proposed in the name of freedom, the enforcement of such rules, if pushed too far, might result in even more effective control by universal institutions, thus establishing a more comprehensive absolutism and a more serious threat to freedom. Some diversity of national cultures is valuable and this implies some national control of communications. In the present period a wider distribution of communication control would probably make for a better balance between stability and progress. This implies reduction of national controls, increase of the initiative and authority of the United Nations and its agencies, maintenance of the independent initiative of churches, universities, the press, business concerns and other major institutions, and protection of a high degree of individual freedom of communication (112, 113).

The geographical centers of communication control are continually changing, but certain centers may persist for a long time, as they have in Rome, Paris, and London. While military forces including personnel, materiel, and military potential—population, geographical position, economic resources, and industrial plant—are important aspects of power, their organization and utilization depend upon a center of communications able to organize a society, to maintain its solidarity and morale, and to establish a reputation and conduct a diplomacy, winning allies and sustaining a favorable atmosphere of world opinion. Such a center can draw to itself the material resources and build the material forces necessary for political power (31). The location of centers of power is, of course, greatly influenced by the location of natural resources and populations capable of being organized, but these resources will remain fallow unless a center of communications organizes them. The determination of the location of these centers of power and the measurement of their relative power in all aspects is of major importance for the guidance of international relations, whether for a national or an international purpose. Research might well be devoted to the problem of describing precisely the location and changes, and measuring precisely the relative power of the major centers of communication in the world. As a result of such research, methods might be established for making periodic surveys of the field of world communications indicating the location of centers, the relative power of each, and the rapidity of change in relative power of, and distances between, centers. Such a survey, like a world weather map, might provide useful data for predicting gathering storms and perhaps even for their control (113).

The distances of these centers of communication and power from one another can be measured in terms of miles, but this is of small significance. It is more important to measure the technical and strategic distances between them in terms of ease of trade and communication and of vulnerability to military, economic, and propaganda attack. The course of invention has obviously decreased these distances but, in terms of existing facilities, very unequally among different parts of the world.

No less important is the measurement of legal and ideological distances between these centers in terms of degrees of inequality in legal recognition and in the understanding of science and logic. Such inequalities tend to diminish with abundance of communication. While they exist they indicate areas of superiority and subordination.

The states of friendship or hostility and of anxiety or confidence between pairs of such centers can be conceived respectively as psychic and expectancy distances. Though rapidly fluctuating, these also can roughly be measured and indicate the immediate dangers threatening world stability.

Finally, political and social relations measured in terms of the degree, respectively, of sharing common political institutions, and of similarity of culture, values, and social institutions, can be conceived as distances, political and social.

All of these distances are related to the field of world communication, and upon their variations and relations to one another depends, in a measure, the probability of war or peace between any two centers of power. Indications of these various aspects of distance might be represented on a world map of the centers of power, adding to its value (110, 113).

Atmosphere of opinion. Apart from influencing the centers of power and the distances between them, the field of communications influences the general atmosphere of opinion and the general state of tension, energy, and resistance in the world. In principle, changes in the symbols of attention and interest of the various parts of the world's population, and changes in opinions about these symbols, measured in respect to direction, intensity, homogeneity, and continuity can be determined and roughly measured. A plotting of the variations and changes of world opinion, indicating points of tension, will illuminate the significance of the separate centers of communication, initiative and control in the world. The magnitude of such tensions can perhaps be regarded as a function of the energy and power of these centers and of the resistances of each to change in its symbol structure as in electrical systems, tension may vary as the product of energy and resistance (90, 110, 113).

Decision-making. Finally, communication influences the persistence of the culture of an area, defining the values and goals of its people, and the policies of their governments or centers of communication and power. From these may be deduced the decisions and actions of governments to be expected in given circumstances. These circumstances have reference to the capability of governments determined by power, distances, and the atmosphere of opinion.

The order of thought set forth in this section suggests that a total plotting of the field of communications in the world at a given moment, and of the tendency of that field to change might provide a basis for the prediction and control of international relations. The concept implies that the total status of the communication field at a moment influences the movement of the parts, but that the field itself is continually being modified by independent changes of the parts. Research might indicate whether the elaboration of a model embodying these characteristics of the field of world communications lies within the possibilities of mathematical or other precise method of exposition (31, 61, 82, 84, 105). The subject is further considered in Chapter 32.

CRITICISM

The system of communication is of key importance to international relations. The great turning points in civilization were marked by changes in the communication system—the use of symbolic language separated man from animals, the use of written language separated primitive from civilized man, the invention of printing followed by telecommunication separated local civilizations from the world civilization which has been emerging since the fifteenth century (110).

In a narrower sense, types of societies and of social standards are determined by the forms of communication. Among animals without symbolic communication, culture and tradition are impossible, information is available only for restricted times and spaces, and action must be based on *instinct* developed by organic evolution and conditioned by the limited experience of each animal. Among preliterate peoples using symbolic language, culture and tradition can be accumulated and can be transmitted from generation to generation, but precise knowledge drawn from a large area is not possible, nor can there be a steady influx of new values and ideas. Consequently, action is largely based on *custom* developing slowly with tribal experience and integrated in a stable culture which relates values, goals, techniques, and action by language. Among people who write, accurate information and generalizations can be preserved and accumulated, ideas can circulate over wide areas, societies can be progressive in the sense of continually adjusting values, goals, and techniques to changing conditions in a more perfect adaptation. Values can be institutionalized in systems of justice, religion, art, government, and technology, and individuals can guide their conduct by a *conscience*, manifesting these institutionalized values. With more widespread systems of communication, subjecting every group to ideas from both historic and contemporary peoples living under very diverse conditions, invention of new techniques and new values can continue at an accelerating pace; institutionalized value systems can become more flexible; guidance by conscience established in earlier education and maintained by rigid institutions can give way to guidance by developing science and changing *opinion* (89). Under these conditions society may become so amorphous as to disintegrate. On the other hand, communication may expand so unevenly and discontinuously as to provide the natural conditions out of which political leaders can develop larger and more powerful nation-states in rivalry with one another (31). A technology permitting universal communication also has the possibility of continuous adaptation of humanity to changing conditions, thus moderating the great fluctuations, the declines and falls of civilizations, which in the past have marked the cumulative maladaptation of values to conditions (110).

Considering all its aspects, communication can be studied as central in all the social sciences. It unites the biological and psychic aspects of man, conditioning the *id* by the *superego* and creating the *ego* as a system of action. It unites the psychic and social aspects of man, permitting interaction among men by creating expectations, roles, and understandings, and permitting societies to exist as systems of action. It unites the social and intergroup aspects of human experience by developing the technology of communication at a distance, which permits primary groups to unite into secondary and tertiary groups, and permits communities, cultures, societies, and institutions to expand so as to include the entire human race. The art of communication is involved in all of man's enterprises—practical and theoretical, political and economic, artistic and utilitarian, social and technical. Particularly important is the influence of communication upon the forms and processes of international relations. Without communication at a distance, international relations can only concern limited relations of neighboring tribes or states. With present techniques international relations concerns all groups in the world. Communication has increased the vulnerability and interdependence of all peoples and at the same time has created opportunities for international co-operation for human benefit and the possibility of a universal culture and a world organization capable of maintaining peace and order and assuring justice and progress for all mankind.

The study of communication is more fundamental than the study of power or of trade because it is the condition for both. It is more fundamental than the study of organization and of law because both are developments of the system of communications. It is more fundamental than the study of geography and demography because the human significance of both depends on the state of the arts of which the technology of communication is primary. It provides a nexus for the integration of psychology, sociology, and ethics.

In spite of this broadly integrative power of the discipline of communications it must always be recognized that communication takes place between persons and groups, and that it is about things, including persons and groups, as well as ideas and values. Communication is the web that connects them, but for prediction and control it is necessary to know something concrete about the conditions of the objective world which includes *organisms* and persons capable of social reaction; *organizations,* groups, and societies also capable of social reaction; *mechanical systems* and material objects, both natural and artificial; and *ideologies,* composed of words and other symbols, with a meaning derived from the culture. Description of the field of communication can be useful only to one who knows something concrete about the persons figuring in the situation as systems of action, as bundles of conditioned impulses, and as organizations of social roles and cultural traits; and something about the concrete groups figuring in the situation as systems of action and organizations of purposes and procedures. It is necessary also to know something concrete about the material things in the environment—the conditions and trends of population; the conditions of climate, terrain, and resources; and the state of the arts and technologies. Finally, it is necessary to know something concrete about the culture, the specific beliefs, ideologies, and values which compose it and by which expectations and wants of persons and groups are guided. It is true, much of this can be learned from the content of communications but much cannot. Acquaintance with the facts must be added to the knowledge which any or all of the disciplines can give about them.

REFERENCES

All printed and written materials illustrate the subject of communication, and all books on social science analyze the subject, explicitly or implicitly. History is rooted in the *historical sciences* elucidating and criticizing *historical sources* which include all communications of the period written about, and its fruit is a narrative indicating the effects of communication on human attitudes, opinions, and actions in the particular time and place. Treatises on politics, diplomacy, war, law, administration, economics, and education discuss and appraise the forms of communication used in the practice of these arts. Treatises on rhetoric, literary criticism, linguistics, logic, and ethics treat the subject philosophically, while treatises on social psychology, sociology, and technology deal with it scientifically. Books in all these fields could find a place in a comprehensive bibliography of the subject.

The discipline of communications began in antiquity as an aid to the arts of oratory, argument, composition, and poetry, but with the invention of means of mass communication the modern discipline has been concerned particularly with the arts of political propaganda, *public relations,* journalism, and advertising. It has sought to define and measure *public opinion,* to analyze and even quantify the *meaning* of symbols and documents (semantics and *content analysis*), to describe the forms and measure the properties of communication systems (cybernetics and mathematical biology), and to ascertain the social consequences of the introduction of new instruments of communication (technology and *mass media*).

Some of this literature has been classified in two bibliographic volumes sponsored by the United States Social Science Research Council (*Propaganda and Promotional Activities,* H. D. Lasswell, Ralph D. Casey, and Bruce Lannes Smith, eds., University of Minnesota Press, 1935; *Propaganda, Communications and Public Opinion,* Smith, Lasswell and Casey, eds., Princeton University Press, 1946) and in the selected bibliographies attached to the contributions in the symposia on *Public Opinion and Communications* edited by Bernard Berelson and Morris Janowitz in 1950 (Glencoe, Free Press) and in *The Policy Sciences* edited by Daniel Lerner and H. D. Lasswell in 1951 (Stanford University Press). The scope of the subject is further indicated by numerous articles in the *Encyclopædia of the Social Sciences* each with a bibliography. Of these the following are particularly significant: "Communication," "Language," and "Symbolism" by Edward Sapir; "Censorship" and "Propaganda" by H. D. Lasswell; "Public Opinion" by Wilhelm Bauer; "Advertising" by Leverett Lyon; "Journalism" by Allen Nevins; "Publicity" by Ernest Gruening; "Government Reporting" by Wylie Kilpatrick; "Government Publication" by Henry Furst; "Fictions" by Morris R. Cohen; "Writing" by Bernhard Stern; "Printing and Publication" by R. L. Duffus; "Public Libraries" by Pierce Butler, Richard H. Hart, and Douglas Waples; "Press" by Dexter M. Keezer; "Postal Service" by J. C. Hemmeon; "Telephone and Telegraph" by J. Warren Stehman; "Radio" by H. T. Lewis, W. A. Orchard, and Harry Shulman; "Transportation" by Kurt Widenfeld; "Literacy and Illiteracy" by Helen Sullivan; "Literature" by Max Lerner and Edwin Mimm, Jr., "Theatre" by Julius Bab; "Motion Picture" by H. T. Lewis and W. A. Orton; "Freedom of Speech and Press" by J. M. Landis; "Debate, Parliamentary" by Lindsay Rogers; and "Criticism, Social" by R. M. Lovett. The Symposia of the Conferences on Science, Philosophy and Religion, edited by Lyman Bryson, Louis Finkelstein, and R. M. MacIver (New York, Harper, 1942-1954), especially the 13th and 14th Symposia on *Symbols,* and the Monographs of the *International Encyclopedia of Unified Science* (University of Chicago Press, 1938-1954) further illustrate the scope of the subject.

The following list includes a few books of selections illustrating different forms of communication and a few "classics" of the subject, but consists mainly of recent studies dealing with the techniques, controls, analysis and criticism of communications, and with the forms, policies, and social importance of communication systems, with special reference to international communications.

1. ADAMS, Charles Francis, *Memoirs of Mrs. Adams in Familiar Letters of John Adams and his Wife Abigail Adams During the Revolution* (New York, Hurd and Houghton, 1876).
2. ALLPORT, Gordon W., and POSTMAN, Leo, *Psychology of Rumor* (New York, Holt, 1947).
3. ALMOND, Gabriel, *The American People and Foreign Policy* (New York, Harcourt, 1950).
4. ANGELL, Norman, *The Public Mind* (London, Douglas, 1926).
5. ARISTOTLE, *Rhetoric, Poetics, Politics.*

6. AUERBACH, Erich, *Mimesis*, trans. from German by Willard R. Trask (Princeton, Princeton University Press, 1953).
7. BALLARD, G. A., *America and the Atlantic* (New York, Dutton, 1923).
8. BENTHAM, Jeremy, *Handbook of Political Fallacies*, rev. ed. (Baltimore, Johns Hopkins University Press, 1952).
9. BERELSON, Bernard, *Content Analysis in Communication Research* (Glencoe, Ill., Free Press, 1952).
10. ———, and JANOWITZ, Morris, *Reader in Public Opinion and Communication* (Glencoe, Ill., Free Press, 1950).
11. BERGSON, Henri, *Creative Evolution* (New York, Holt, 1911).
12. BLACKMUIR, R. P., CROCE, Benedetti, and others, *Lectures on Criticism* (New York, Pantheon, 1949).
13. BLOOMFIELD, Leonard, *Language, 1914* (New York, Holt, 1933).
14. ———, "Linguistic Aspects of Science," *International Encyclopedia of Unified Science*, Vol. 1, No. 4 (University of Chicago Press, 1939).
15. BRADLEY, Omar N., *A Soldier's Story* (New York, Holt, 1951).
16. BRIGANCE, William Norwood, *Speech, Its Techniques and Disciplines in a Free Society* (New York, Appleton-Century-Crofts, 1952).
17. BRIGGS, Harold E., ed., *Language, Man, Society: Readings in Communication* (New York, Rinehart, 1949).
18. BRITTON, Karl, *Communication, A Philosophical Study of Language* (London, Kegan Paul, 1939).
19. BRUNER, Jerome S., *Mandate from the People* (New York, Duell, Sloan, 1944).
20. BRYSON, Lyman, ed., *The Communication of Ideas* (New York, Harper, 1948).
21. BURCKHARDT, Jacob, *Force and Freedom, Reflections on History* (New York, Pantheon, 1943).
22. CANTRIL, Hadley, *Gauging Public Opinion* (Princeton, Princeton University Press, 1944).
23. ———, *Public Opinion, 1935-1946* (Princeton, Princeton University Press, 1951).
24. CHILDS, Charles Manning, *Physiological Foundations of Behavior* (New York, Holt, 1924).
25. CHURCHILL, Winston S., *The Second World War* (New York, Houghton Mifflin, 1948-1953), 6 vols.
26. COOLEY, Charles Horton, *Social Organization, A Study of the Larger Mind* (New York, Scribner, 1929).
27. COPELAND, D. B., ed., *Liberty and Learning* (Christchurch, N.Z., 1950).
28. CRANE, Ronald S., and others, *Critics and Criticism, Ancient and Modern* (Chicago, University of Chicago Press, 1952).
29. CURTI, Merle, *The Roots of American Loyalty* (New York, Columbia University Press, 1940).
30. DAVIDSON, Philip, *Propaganda in the American Revolution* (Chapel Hill, University of North Carolina Press, 1941).
31. DEUTSCH, Karl W., *Nationalism and Social Communication* (New York, Wiley, 1953).
32. DEWEY, John, *The Public and Its Problems* (New York, Holt, 1927).
33. DICEY, A. V., *Lectures on the Relations Between Law and Public Opinion in England* (London, Macmillan, 1914).
34. DUNN, Frederick S., *War and the Minds of Men* (New York, Council on Foreign Relations, 1951).

35. EISENHOWER, Dwight D., *Crusade in Europe* (New York, Doubleday, 1948).
36. GARDINER, Alan H., *The Theory of Speech and Language* (Oxford, Oxford University Press, 1932).
37. GELB, Ignace, J., *A Study of Writing* (Chicago, University of Chicago Press, 1952).
38. GILBY, Thomas, *Between Community and Society* (New York, Longmans, 1953).
39. GRANDIN, Thomas, "The Political Use of the Radio," *Geneva Studies*, Vol. 10, No. 3 (August, 1939).
40. HARTER, D. Lincoln, and SULLIVAN, John, *Mass Persuasion* (Philadelphia, Twentieth Century Publishing Co., 1953).
41. HAYAKAWA, S. I., *Language in Action* (New York, Harcourt, 1941).
42. HUGHES, Ernest R., *The Art of Letters, Lu Chi's "Wu Fu," 302 A.D., A Translation and Comparative Study* (New York, Pantheon, 1951).
43. HUTH, Arno, "Mass Communication in Underdeveloped Areas," *International Conciliation*, No. 477 (New York, Carnegie Endowment for International Peace, January, 1952).
44. HUXLEY, Julian, ed., *Freedom and Culture* (London, Wingate, for UNESCO, 1951).
45. INNIS, Harold, *Changing Concepts of Time* (Toronto, University of Toronto Press, 1952).
46. IRION, Frederick C., *Public Opinion and Propaganda* (New York, Crowell, 1950).
47. JORDAN, Wilbur K., *The Development of Religious Toleration in England* (Cambridge, Harvard University Press, 1932-1940), 4 vols.
48. KECSKEMETI, Paul, *Meaning, Communication and Value* (Chicago, University of Chicago Press, 1952).
49. KENT, Sherman, *Strategic Intelligence for American World Policy* (Princeton, Princeton University Press, 1949).
50. KORZYBSKI, Alfred, *Science and Sanity* (1933); 3rd ed. (Lakeville, Conn., Institute of General Semantics, 1948).
51. LASSWELL, Harold D., *Propaganda Technique in the World War* (New York, Knopf, 1927).
52. ———, and BLUMENSTOCK, Dorothy, *World Revolutionary Propaganda* (New York, Knopf, 1939).
53. ———, *Democracy Through Public Opinion* (Menasha, Wis., Banta, 1941).
54. ———, *Public Opinion in War and Peace* (Washington, National Economic Association, 1943).
55. ———, and others, *Language of Politics* (New York, Stewart, 1949).
56. ———, *The World Revolution of Our Time* (Stanford, Stanford University Press, 1951).
57. ———, LERNER, Daniel, POOL, Ithiel DeSola, and others, *The Comparative Study of Symbols* (Stanford, Stanford University Press, 1952).
58. LAZARSFELD, Paul F., and STANTON, Frank N., *Communication Research, 1948-1949* (New York, Harper, 1949).
59. ———, BERELSON, Bernard, and GANETT, Hazel, *The People's Choice, How the Voter Makes Up His Mind in a Presidential Campaign* (New York, Columbia University Press, 1944).
60. LEE, Alfred McClung, *How to Understand Propaganda* (New York, Rinehart, 1952).

61. LERNER, Daniel, and LASSWELL, H. D., eds., *The Policy Sciences* (Stanford, Stanford University Press, 1951).
62. LIPPMANN, Walter, *Public Opinion* (New York, Harcourt, 1922).
63. ———, *The Phantom Public* (New York, Harcourt, 1925).
64. LOEWENSTEIN, Karl, ed., "The Role of Ideologies in Political Change," *International Social Science Bulletin*, UNESCO, Vol. 5, No. 1 (Winter 1953). (Résumé of papers and discussions at 2nd Congress of International Political Science Association, The Hague, 1952).
65. LOWELL, A. Lawrence, *Public Opinion and Popular Government* (New York, Longmans, 1913).
66. ———, *Public Opinion in War and Peace* (Cambridge, Harvard University Press, 1922).
67. MACDOUGALL, Curtis D., *Understanding Public Opinion* (New York, Macmillan, 1952).
68. MCCAMY, James L., *Government Publications for the Citizen* (New York, Columbia University Press, 1949).
69. MANNHEIM, Karl, *Ideology and Utopia* (New York, Harcourt, 1936); 2nd ed., 1949.
70. MILLER, James G., ed., *Experiments in Social Process, A Symposium in Social Psychology* (New York, McGraw-Hill, 1950).
71. MORRIS, Charles, "Foundation of the Theory of Signs," *International Encyclopedia of Unified Science* (Chicago, University of Chicago Press, 1938).
72. ———, *Signs, Language and Behavior* (New York, Prentice-Hall, 1946).
73. MURRAY, Gilbert, "Work of the Committee on Intellectual Cooperation of the League of Nations," *Conference for the Establishment of the United Nations' Educational, Scientific and Cultural Organization* (UNESCO, 1945).
74. ODEGARD, Peter H., *The American Public Mind* (New York, Columbia University Press, 1930).
75. OGDEN, C. K., and RICHARDS, I. A., *The Meaning of Meaning* (New York, Harcourt, 1923).
76. ———, *Opposition* (London, Kegan Paul, 1932).
77. OGLE, Marbury B., Jr., *Public Opinion and Political Dynamics* (New York, Houghton Mifflin, 1950).
78. PARK, Robert E., and BURGESS, Ernest, *Introduction to the Study of Sociology* (Chicago, University of Chicago Press, 1924).
79. PIMLOTT, J. A. R., *Public Relations and American Democracy* (Princeton, Princeton University Press, 1951).
80. POOL, Ithiel DeSola, *Symbols of Internationalism* (Stanford, Stanford University Press, 1951).
81. POWELL, Norman J., *Anatomy of Public Opinion* (New York, Prentice-Hall, 1953).
82. RAPAPORT, Anatol, *Science and the Goals of Man, A Study of Semantic Orientation* (New York, Harper, 1950).
83. ———, *Operational Philosophy, Integrating Knowledge and Activity* (New York, Harper, 1953).
84. RASHEVSKY, Nicholas, *Mathematical Theory of Human Relations* (Bloomington, Ill., Principia Press, 1949).
85. ———, *Mathematical Biology of Social Behavior* (Chicago, University of Chicago Press, 1951).

86. REISS, Samuel, *The Rise of Words and Their Meaning* (New York, Philosophical Library, 1950).
87. RICHARDS, I. A., *Principles of Literary Criticism* (New York, Harcourt, 1925).
88. ———, *Practical Criticism, A Study of Literary Judgment* (London, Kegan Paul, 1939). See also Ogden and Richards.
89. RIESMAN, David, in collaboration with DENNEY, Reuel, and GLAZER, Nathan, *The Lonely Crowd, A Study of the Changing American Character* (New Haven, Yale University Press, 1950).
90. ROTHWELL, C. Easton, ed., *RADIR* (Revolution and the Development of International Relations) *Project* (Stanford, Hoover Library, Stanford University Press, 1950-   ). See Lasswell, Lerner, Pool.
91. SAPIR, Edward, *Language, An Introduction to the Study of Speech* (New York, Harcourt, 1921). See also "Communication," "Language," *Encyclopædia of the Social Sciences.*
92. SCHOENBERG, Arnold, *Style and Idea* (New York, Philosophical Library, 1950).
93. SEABURY, William M., *The Public and the Motion Picture Industry* (New York, Macmillan, 1926).
94. SHANNON, C. E., and WEAVER, W., *The Mathematical Theory of Communication* (Urbana, University of Illinois Press, 1949).
95. SHERWOOD, Robert, *Roosevelt and Hopkins*, rev. ed. (New York, Harper, 1950).
96. SIEBERT, Fred S., *Freedom of the Press in England, 1476-1776, the Rise and Decline of Government Controls* (Urbana, University of Illinois Press, 1952).
97. SIEPMANN, Charles, *Radio, Television and Society* (New York, Oxford University Press, 1950).
98. SIMON, Herbert A., SMITHBURG, D. W., and THOMPSON, V. A., *Public Administration* (New York, Knopf, 1950).
99. SPEIER, Hans, *Social Order and the Risks of War* (New York, Stewart, 1952).
100. STRAUSS, Leo, *Persecution and the Art of Writing* (Glencoe, Ill., Free Press, 1952).
101. THURSTONE, L. L., and CHAVE, E. J., *The Measurement of Attitude, A Psychophysical Method and Some Experiments with a Scale of Measuring Attitudes Toward the Church* (Chicago, University of Chicago Press, 1929).
102. WAPLES, Douglas, BERELSON, Bernard, and BRADSHAW, Franklyn R., *What Reading Does to People: A Summary of Evidence on the Social Effects of Reading and a Statement of Problems for Research* (Chicago, University of Chicago Press, 1940).
103. WEBSTER, Charles K., The *Art and Practice of Diplomacy* (London School of Economics and Political Science, 1952).
104. WHITE, L. W., and LEIGH, Robert D., *Peoples Speaking to Peoples* (Chicago, University of Chicago Press, 1946).
105. WIENER, Norbert, *Cybernetics, or Control and Communication in the Animal and Machine* (New York, Wiley, 1948).
106. WILLEY, Malcolm, and RICE, Stuart A., *Communication Agencies and Social Life* (New York, McGraw-Hill, 1933); Monograph accompanying Report of the President's Research Committee on Recent Social Trends in the United States, W. F. Ogburn, ed. (1933), 2 vols.

107. WILSON, Richard Albert, *The Miraculous Birth of Language* (New York, Philosophical Library, 1950), preface by George Bernard Shaw.
108. WOLFENSTEIN, Martha, and LEITES, Nathan, *Movies: A Psychological Study* (Glencoe, Ill., Free Press, 1952).
109. WRIGHT, Quincy, ed., *Public Opinion and World Politics* (Chicago, University of Chicago Press, 1933).
110. ———, *A Study of War* (Chicago, University of Chicago Press, 1942), pp. 29-41, 174-176, 317-319, 362-366, 402-405, 598-614, 958-964, 975-982, 1012-1042, 1049-1054, 1079-1117, 1231-1233, 1240-1260, 1276-1283, 1300-1304, 1442-1444, 1448-1453, 1466-1492.
111. ———, ed., *A Foreign Policy for the United States* (Chicago, University of Chicago Press, 1947).
112. ———, ed., *The World Community* (Chicago, University of Chicago Press, 1949).
113. ———, *Problems of Stability and Progress in International Relations* (Berkeley, University of California Press, 1954).
114. YULE, George U., *The Statistical Study of Literary Vocabulary* (Cambridge, Cambridge University Press, 1944).

International Education

DEFINITION

INTERNATIONAL EDUCATION is the art of developing the individual's attitudes, knowledge, understanding, and skills in order to adapt him to life in the contemporary world and to adapt the world community to civilized human life. As a discipline it is the philosophy guiding that art and the science seeking to predict the results of its application. It also includes historical studies contributing to this art, philosophy, and science (50, 78, 126).

International education has arisen from the movements of proselytism (72) and pacifism (11, 42), but in its modern form it is a branch of the general discipline of education. It merges into the discipline of international communications, and both have roots in the psychology, sociology, and ethics of international relations.

The term *international education* has several distinct connotations— education for internationalism, education in the discipline of international relations, education through international contacts, and education for international service. These four connotations respectively give propagandistic, informational, methodological, and practical emphasis to the term. All of these connotations are to be found in the general discipline of education (25, 35, 82).

The prime function of education, and its sole function among preliterate peoples, is to transmit the culture of the group to the rising generation and thereby to make it possible for the individual to live comfortably in the group, and for the group culture to survive. Among preliterate peoples, culture is static and unprogressive. However varied may have been methods of education utilized by such people, the results were always in a measure successful in achieving this limited objective. The rising generation learned the mores and folkways, lived in them, and passed them on with little change (71, 79). However, with the expansion of group contacts by trade or conquest to include different cultures, the problem of education became more complicated. The individual lived in a larger world in which customs and practices varied. The object of education therefore shifted from the group's culture to the individual's adjustment. Socrates, in seeking to found education on human truths independent of Athenian folkways, lost his life. Today, everyone lives in a world technologically united. Everyone is vulnerable to military, economic, and propaganda attacks from people with different values and customs. International educators, therefore, consider it necessary for everyone to be educated for life, not only in his particular nation, but in the varied and complex world from which he cannot escape. He must have not only a national mind, but an international mind (19, 124). His attitudes, values, beliefs, and knowledge must make him aware, tolerant, and even appreciative of the varied cultures and conditions of the peoples of the world. He must, it is said, be educated for internationalism (122).

In response to the increasing international contacts during the *Renaissance* and the *Enlightenment*, the literary genre of essays on manners of remote peoples such as those by Montaigne and Bacon, of satires describing imaginary peoples such as those by More and Swift, and of imaginary letters from the Orient such as those by Voltaire, Montesquieu, and Goldsmith sought to arouse Europeans to an awareness of the narrowness of their horizons (16, 49, 74). During the nineteenth and twentieth centuries such literature and also the publications of national and international organizations devoted to education in pacifism, cosmopolitanism, and internationalism became extraordinarily abundant (11, 43, 121). As a reaction, however, officially sponsored education in nationalism kept pace (64, 81, 87, 94, 128), with the result that the ideal of world citizenship is less popular in the west, and probably also in the east, than it was in the eighteenth century (88, 90).

Many enlightened educators and reformers, skeptical of the results of indoctrination, noting the failure of missionary religions to keep the peace among their converts who live under different conditions and with different historic antecedents, and the failure of pacifism and cosmopolitanism to stem the tide of rival and hostile nationalisms, have sought to avoid the implications of education for internationalism. They believe that knowledge makes virtue, and that objective education in the discipline of international relations will lead through the individual's own reflection to attitudes appropriate to life in the present day world. To them the problem is not that of developing and educating the rising generation in a value system adapted to the contemporary world, but of educating it on the facts of the world (9, 10, 68, 102, 115). Such a program, however, involves development of an objective discipline of international relations. Without such a discipline no selection can be made, among the innumerable facts concerning the world, of those which are important. Furthermore it is clear that no such discipline can escape the problem of values (8, 50, 126). No educational system has been able to evade the primary function of education—developing in the individual attitudes appropriate to the values of the society in which he is to live—and, in progressive societies, of adapting those values to changing conditions. A discipline of international relations can hardly be suitable for education unless it deals with values and their relationship to the changing conditions of the world (98, 114, 117, 118, 122, 125).

Can such values be gained through experience? In the Middle Ages the universities served as meeting places for youth from all sections of Europe. In modern times missionary activity has maintained direct contacts between peoples of diverse culture in all parts of the world. In the eighteenth century the *foreign tour* was part of the education of those that could afford it. Today student migrations, international houses, endowed scholarships and fellowships, and government-sponsored exchanges of persons serve a similar function (5, 63). It has been suggested that the problem of reconciling objectivity with the development of suitable attitudes in international education can only be solved by promoting actual contacts among people of different cultures. International education has, therefore, been used to refer to this method of education (46, 59).

To provide such contacts for all citizens is, however, impossible. International education has, therefore, often referred to the education of specialists in the field. Education among civilized peoples with differentiated institutions has always been closely related to preparation for practical service in the government, in the church, in the schools, in business concerns, in the professions and trades, or in other specialized activity. Formal education has in most civilizations been initiated through recognition of the need of special training for such services (35, 61, 95). Today service in foreign offices, in diplomatic, consular, and military careers, and in public international organizations has greatly increased in magnitude and influence. Closely related are careers in national and international civic organizations and in *public relations,* journalism, radio, television, adult education, and other activities intended to inform and lead public opinion on international issues. Education for such services has been called international education (15, 54, 123).

These four aspects of international education may be related to different classes of persons. All citizens, especially those who vote, need some education for internationalism. They need, in some sense, to feel themselves citizens of the world. The interested public, a more limited group, that seeks to understand international affairs and criticize policy, needs some education in the discipline of international relations. The still more limited group who lead opinion, initiate ideas, and propose issues need to add to such education, practical experience with different cultures, through international contact. Finally, the policy-makers and administrators need special education for international service (2).

The purpose of international education in the broad sense, including all four connotations, is to adapt the individual to life in the contemporary world, and to adapt the world community to civilized human life. The adult individual should be able to imagine, and to judge wisely among, alternative courses of policy and action for himself and for the various groups with which he is identified in the changing situation of the world. This implies that he have predispositions inducing both creative and adaptive reactions to information about the current world situation, and that current information be available to him which is accurate and complete in respect to events, attitudes, opinions, and values of importance. The provision of such information is the function of international communication discussed in the preceding chapter. The establishment of such predispositions is the function of international education. The individual is, however, a unit. He reacts to the total situation which includes family, occupation, local community, nation, region, and world. International education cannot, therefore, be sharply differentiated from all education. The term merely serves to emphasize the broader scope of education necessary for successful life in a world community which no one can escape (8, 56, 75, 100, 114, 122).

Parallel to the methodological, informational, propagandistic, and practical connotations of *international education,* the term *education* has been used in four senses: psychological, sociological, ideological, and professional (37, 38, 52).

In the psychological and methodological sense, education refers to the learning process. It is to be found in all human groups, and even among animals. Among men, it begins at birth and continues until death. Inherited drives begin to be conditioned by experience in the infant, and as life goes on they are reconditioned so as to prepare the organism for meeting the new types of situation to be expected. Among animals, such conditioning can only result from actual experience. Learning is by trial and error, assisted by imitation. But a man's experience can be vicarious, anticipatory, and teleological. The experience of others, living and dead, can be transmitted by communication, tradition, and history. Situations experienced by no one can in some measure be foreseen through the process of generalization and the development of scientific thought. Ends desired can, in some measure, influence the response to both actual and anticipated situations. Learning can proceed through the acquisition of attitudes, knowledge, skills, and understanding symbolically transmitted, although modern educators emphasize the importance of the roles of action and direct experience (13, 38, 47, 86, 107). Through this process, the disciplines of philosophy, science, art, and history have developed among the most advanced people as contributors to the educational process.

In the sociological and informational sense, education refers to the actual process by which the maturing individual is inducted into the life and culture of the group. It occurs within all human groups and continues through the life of the individual in progressive societies, but is applicable particularly to the young. Culture and tradition is impossible without education in this sense. At birth, individuals are equally adaptable to any language, culture, or society. The particular ones with which they are to live must be learned. If a particular culture is not transmitted to the rising generation, it will cease to exist. Education in this sense is, therefore, a necessary condition for the individual's life in his group, and for the continued existence of the group itself (12, 37, 52, 66, 67). Much of such education proceeds by children imitating elders and listening to their unplanned talk. Among primitive people, there is great variation in respect to the aspects of culture which are transmitted by these processes of unconscious education and those aspects which are consciously transmitted. Even among civilized people, much of education, as for example learning to walk and talk and to employ household facilities, is in large measure unplanned. While by such processes children can educate themselves, it may often be at considerable expense to the personality. The culture may be carried on, but many of its bearers who have learned it the hard way and at the wrong age may develop neurotic or warped personalities (79).

In the ideological and propagandistic sense, education refers to the conscious and purposeful control of learning by the more experienced members of society. In this sense, education occurs among all civilized people and in some degree among most preliterate peoples. Supervision of practice, admonition and example, initiation and ceremonies, variously administered by older children, by parent or relatives, or by older members of the group, and variously sanctioned by appeals to affection, fear, and shame are utilized by all groups, the method depending on the extent to which the group's culture or part of it is formulated in ideologies capable of precise expression (79). Among civilized peoples, education is designed not only to transmit, but also to improve the culture, in order that it may more completely realize values expressed in the doctrines of a religion or other ideology. Verbal exposition of such ideology and of the values it implies is necessary in such cases because it is assumed that practice falls short of these values. Consequently, imitation of adult practice and unconscious education, often adequate among the preliterate people whose culture, customs, and practices are closely parallel, cannot be sufficient among progressive peoples. In proportion, therefore, as societies are progressive, education involves a conscious and purposeful action of the older members of society who are aware of its values, both practiced and desired (14, 18, 29, 36, 37, 51, 85, 89, 112).

In the professional and practical sense, education refers to the work of certain specialized institutions, the schools and their personnel, the teachers. Such institutions do not exist among preliterate people. They were occasionally to be found among the ancient civilizations, in Egypt, Mesopotamia, India, and China. They were utilized more widely in the classic civilizations of Greece and Rome, in the Middle Ages, and in the Renaissance. In these instances, however, institutional education generally reached a very small proportion of the population, mainly those designed for special service in state or church. During periods when expansion of empire and continuous contact of different cultures introduced problems of adaptation of cultures to one another, and a need for adapting the rising generation to rapidly changing conditions not clearly defined by the traditional culture, education tended to expand ideologically, horizontally, and vertically. Schools sought to modify tradition and expression on the basis of a broader philosophy and science. They increased in number and admitted a larger proportion of the population. They developed from the centers of civilization into the provinces and colonies and into less developed areas. They included a larger range of age groups, moving down to the kindergarten and up to the university (35, 82, 95, 96).

In such circumstances, education tended to become more centered on the student and less centered on the culture. Knowledge and virtue came to be defined in terms more abstract than that found in the traditional culture, and conflicts developed between the liberals and radicals who wanted to inject values and ideas based on science and philosophy into education, and the conservatives and reactionaries who wished education to transmit the culture as it had been. Excessive influence of the former has disintegrated cultures and societies because it has exaggerated individualism and the pursuit of personal happiness without regard to social solidarity. Excessive influence of the traditionalists has been equally unfortunate. Culture has become rigid, institutions have become unadaptable to changing conditions, and civilizations have died in the pursuit of impossible loyalties (89). The usual failure of education, under conditions of rapid change, to preserve a proper balance between the requirements of continuity and change, have contributed to the wreckage of past civilizations (108, 121). The problem was not solved by the Platonic Academy, the Aristotelean Lyceum, the schools of Epicurus and Zeno, the Neo-Platonists or the ecclesiastical schools of classical antiquity, nor was it solved by the church schools and scholastic universities of the later Middle Ages, seeking to reconcile the faith of the Church with the reason of Aristotle. Napoleon said in 1805: "Of all political questions, that (of education) is perhaps the most important. There cannot be a firmly established political state unless there is a teaching body with definitely recognized principles" (35). What he said of the state could be said of civilizations, although it is clear that the definite recognition of principles must be balanced with the need of continuously adapting them to new conditions.

Formal education has expanded during the last century in all directions. In the United States, most children go through elementary school, over half go through high school, and a quarter get some college education (96). UNESCO is engaged in an effort to make fundamental education universal throughout the world (109). A science of education has developed, based on psychology and sociology, seeking to reconcile the needs of the individual and of society in a shrinking world, in which change becomes ever more rapid (14, 39, 67).

Controversy continues, however, between the claims of church and state to control education; between the demands for equal opportunity for all and superior opportunities for the more able; between the claims of tradition and of science in the curriculum of general education; and between the claims of general or liberal education and of professional and vocational training in the educational system as a whole. The rise to power of the nation state, the progress of democratic ideas, the requirements of industrial civilization, the use of education for revolutionary and reform purposes, and the advance of the science of education have all contributed to the development of these issues. Generally acceptable solutions have not been found (29). Whether solutions, in some measure adequate, will be found depends in no small measure upon advance of the special discipline of international education. Can that discipline develop a proper balance between education, on the one hand, to strengthen national cultures and national institutions and, on the other, to develop awareness of the diversity of cultures and the common interests of nations? Can it formulate standards and maintain institutions necessary to reconcile national diversity in world unity (84, 118, 122, 123, 125)?

ASSUMPTIONS

The modern discipline of international education has developed from the following assumptions:

1. International relations under present conditions concerns relations among sovereign states, and the existence, character, and policy of each state depends upon the state of mind of the individuals that compose it. Governments require the support of public opinion and the nature of that support is related to the individual's attitudes and predispositions.

2. Modern man lives in a world in which all states are vulnerable and interdependent; he cannot live satisfactorily in it without awareness of

its fundamental characteristics, history, and processes; and it will not develop satisfactorily unless opinion and leadership is based upon such awareness.

3. Some knowledge of the principal cultures, nationalities, and states of the world; some toleration for them; and some appreciation of the contributions each can make to the advance of civilization must be widespread among all peoples if diverse nations and cultures are to co-exist peacefully.

4. Mutual understanding, toleration, and appreciation among peoples of diverse cultures is not possible unless most men guide their behavior in some measure by attitudes, values and objectives common to all, that is, unless they combine some measure of world citizenship with national loyalties.

These assumptions rest upon the findings of political geography, economics, technology, and demography concerning the vulnerability and interdependence of all peoples and upon the findings of social psychology, sociology, and ethics concerning the relation of the individual and the group (122, 123).

Group behavior is a function of leadership and organization on the one hand, and, on the other, of culture and opinion. As fundamental education and democracy develop in a group, leadership and organization become more subject to public opinion within the group. A democratic government cannot pursue a foreign policy radically opposed by the opinion of the public on whose suffrage rests its power. Even autocratic governments must prepare public opinion to assure support for policies which may require the people to fight or to endure privations. Democratic governments which recognize freedom of the press, of discussion, and of opinion can only in limited degree create a favorable public opinion. While a government with monopolistic control of the system of communications can, in some measure, create a favorable public opinion, even its capacity is limited by resistances arising from the existing culture of the people. An established culture cannot suddenly be altered by propaganda using mass media or terror, although such methods may produce an apparent conformity of opinion. The culture of the group and the attitudes of the people are the product of education and can hardly be changed in less than a generation even by a government with full control of the educational, communication, and police systems. Culture controlled by education determines in large measure the attitudes and predispositions of people which, in turn, determine the interpretations they give to current information and propaganda and their obedience to leaders. Education, therefore, is fundamental in creating the conditions under which public opinion develops, leadership arises and persists, and policies are pursued (37, 100).

Insofar as education develops an autonomous, self-contained, narcissistic culture in each political group, as it tends to do within the primitive tribe and in lesser degree within the modern nation (71, 128), the individual is unprepared to adapt himself to the actual impact of foreign groups upon him and his group. Primitive peoples faced by the techniques and policies of *civilized* invaders find no guidance in their culture to adapt themselves to the situation. Their culture disintegrates and the people may die out from loss of values and incapacity to build a new society or to become assimilated in that of the conqueror (97). Cultures manifest traditional values and wishes and the techniques for realizing them under the conditions of the past. As human personality must adapt biological wishes to objective reality in order to attain sanity (70), so a group culture must adapt values to new conditions if it is to survive. Education must make the people of each culture and nation aware of the realities of vulnerability and interdependency in a shrinking world, and of the processes by which order is maintained and by which change takes place in the world as a whole. Unless men know the social and physical environment in which they live as it is and as it is becoming, adaptation is impossible. Faith in a culture which assumes an environment remote from actual conditions, leads to insanity, to suicide, or to social disintegration.

International education assumes the desirability of peace and order (41, 42, 65, 76, 103). There are, doubtless, nations so confident in the superiority of their culture and power that they regard the conquest and subordination of all others not only as necessary for their own defense, but also as desirable for the progress of civilization. Policies based on such confidence have more often led to ruin than to enduring achievement. History has, however, witnessed the repeated collapse of civilizations grown too soft to defend themselves against the attack of more warlike and more barbarous peoples. Since civilization implies a preference for peace and prosperity over war and poverty, progress in civilization has tended to be self-defeating. In time the superior techniques of war which a civilization invents become understood by the surrounding barbarians, but the will of the civilization to use these techniques for conquest or even for defense tends to suffer a steady attrition. Eventually the barbarians attack and destroy it. The progress of civilization has not, therefore, been continuous but oscillating (107, 108, 120, 121).

Today the reluctance of the more civilized peoples to fight or to prepare for war is maintained, not only by this natural tendency of civilization, but also by the conviction that with modern instruments of war civilization would be destroyed even if the more civilized nations were victorious. The price of civilization is no longer the capacity to win in war but the capacity to prevent war. Thus the object of policy must be peaceful coexistence of diverse nations, not merely national defense. Sufficient knowledge of the world environment by the public might be adequate for the latter, but for peaceful coexistence more is necessary—toleration and appreciation of other nations and comprehension of a world in which they can all live together (122).

Such mutual toleration and appreciation among people of different states, religions, ideologies, parties, and economic systems has in a measure been accomplished within some of the larger federations and empires. Unless a peaceful world among groups of even greater diversity is conceived, it cannot be achieved. But such a conception is not likely to be accepted by peoples of all cultures simultaneously. Barbarians intent on conquest can be expected to remain an aspect of the world, as criminals remain in even the best ordered national societies. Consequently, reality requires that international education, along with knowledge, toleration, and appreciation of the diverse cultures in the world, recognize the continued danger of aggression and prepare to deter or prevent it (68, 109, 117, 127).

Such deterrent or preventive action implies organization of the world as a whole to assure that aggression will always be confronted by insuperable power. Such organization, however, implies that most men (enough to create a predominant world opinion) have some attitudes, values, and objectives in common. They must prefer peace to war, civilization to barbarism, and collective security to individual defense. In short, there must be at least a rudimentary universal culture defining these terms. Peace must include policing action to deter or stop aggression. Civilization must be defined in terms of universal human rights and freedoms. Collective security must be defined in terms of specific procedures to determine aggression and of specific forces available for international policing. Until such a minimum of universal culture and world citizenship is established by international education, conditions will be lacking for effective international organization (50, 100, 118, 123).

ANALYSIS

If it is assumed that wise foreign policy and satisfactory individual adjustment requires that education be based on the realities of a shrinking and interdependent world; that civilization requires the peaceful coexistence of diverse nations; and that such coexistence implies attitudes of mutual understanding and toleration, general appreciation of the value of these diversities, and widespread acceptance of some universal values and goals, what should be the specific aims and methods of international education? The subject is a large one. Only a few positive suggestions can be made with some indication of the difficulties faced.

Values cannot be ignored. National systems of education have sought to create attitudes favorable to national values, and international education must seek to create attitudes favorable to the values necessary for a peaceful and progressive world (98, 100, 118). The problem of international ethics, raised by this statement, will be dealt with in a later chapter.

A discipline of international relations must be created. International education must inform on the reality of international relations, but what is that reality? Every nation sees international relations from its special point of view. How can the world as a whole be seen as it *really* is? A universal history, such as that proposed by UNESCO, seeks to present that reality genetically. The practice of universal organization, such as that exemplified by the United Nations, seeks to present that reality legally, politically, and administratively. Humanists, moralists, and logicians have sought to present the reality of the world as a philosophy of civilization. Social scientists have sought to present it as a science, organizing propositions about international relations into a self-correcting, logical system of predictive and control value. A discipline of international relations must integrate these various points of view concerning the world by a system of propositions, and a method of self-correction as conditions change and new insight is gained, if international education is to proceed from reality (68, 77, 78, 125).

International contacts must be increased. No description giving knowledge about the world can be a complete substitute for experience or knowledge of acquaintance. The elite of each nation who exert major influence on opinion and policy should have direct experience with cultures other than their own. Only thus can the abstractions of a discipline be interpreted with sufficient wisdom and flexibility to give guidance to action. Student exchanges, exchanges of leaders and specialists, international conferences of all kinds, and investigations by officials and commissions have been supported by governments, by the United Nations, and by private agencies such as the Institute of International Education (3, 63, 73, 109). Such efforts, together with improved facilities for private travel and preparatory education to make it effective, are contributions to this end.

Policy-makers must be properly educated. Examinations for foreign service have varied from professional subjects, such as diplomatic history and international law, to general subjects, such as literature, history, economics, and politics. In the United States the tendency has been toward the latter for admission to the foreign service with in-service training in more specialized matters after passage of the admittance examination. In the Home Service of the State Department more use has been made of persons with specialized education in particular regions of the world or in particular functional fields. In the United Nations the need for geographical distribution of the personnel has militated against adequate standards of educational preparation. The problem of suitable education for these services and for special international missions has been widely recognized and discussed in detail (92).

The education of the Civil Service, however, is less important than that of statesmen. The latter have not usually had anything resembling professional education in international relations. In the United States the first six presidents had extensive experience in international affairs through travel, diplomatic service, and special study. Subsequent presidents have often had experience in national politics, state government, or military leadership, but seldom in international relations, though this has been less true since 1900. Only if public opinion is aware of the importance of international relations will there be insistence that leaders be competent in the field. Education for international statesmanship requires a broad understanding of the world as a whole, a comprehension of its major peoples based upon extensive travel and acquaintance, and participatory experience with human nature in politics, rather than detailed acquaintance with the disciplines of international relations. A statesman should be a generalist rather than a specialist (123).

The demands made upon international education are easier to state than to achieve. What are some of the problems? Those arising from the capriciousness of the field, the biases of opinion, the requirements of cultures, and the conflict of long and short run goals deserve especial attention.

The capriciousness of international relations. The reality of international relations is capricious, fluid, intangible, and difficult to teach. The opinions of governments are the immediate source of policy and action in the international field. These opinions may change rapidly because they are based, not on permanent conditions or clear evidence, but upon interpretations of the opinion and policy of others often based on insufficient information, and upon fears, complacencies, and demands of the domestic public frequently influenced by erroneous information, propaganda, or domestic politics. Only as international education creates more enlightened and better informed publics can international relations become more predictable and can a reliable discipline be created in the field. So long as the reality is governed by erroneous information, irrational arguments, fickle opinions and capricious policies, prediction and control are necessarily difficult. It should not be said that they are entirely impossible. There may be a system even concerning action springing from error, unreason, and prejudice. It cannot, however, be denied that international relations is not a subject that lends itself to treatment as a reliable discipline. International education must, therefore, create the conditions for a discipline of international relations, but it has difficulty in functioning until that discipline is created.

National biases and international objectivity. The opinions which are real in the sense that they influence the conduct of international relations tend to be unreal in the sense that they are not founded on accurate knowledge of the situation with which they deal. Among factors contributing to this condition are the tendency of the public to accept over-simplifications, to confine attention to over-narrow-horizons, to insist on the inflexibility of national traditions, and to indulge in wishful thinking (17).

The world is complicated—sufficiently so if only the relatively stable facts of geography, technology, demography, culture, and institutions are considered, much more so if the unstable factors of opinion, policy, decision, and action are considered. A discipline of international relations, to be realistic, must be extremely complicated—too complicated for transmission by widespread education. Simplification is necessary and tends to take the form of simple models, such as the pioneer surrounded by friends and enemies, a competitive community of traders, the nations in a physical equilibrium of military power, or a world state governed by law. Such simplifications, one or other of which is usually assumed by each of the traditional disciplines of international relations, are often misleading (90).

National history, culture, and policy tend to be the focus of attention in each national system of education. Because the people identify themselves with the nation and know most about it, they find it difficult to view the world as a whole, especially when the world is so complicated and political opinion and law are so parochial. It is difficult and may even be dangerous for educators to attempt to broaden the horizons of understanding when national loyalties are believed to require self-sufficient attitudes within the nation, and when distrust of out-groups is deemed essential to preserve the solidarity of the in-group (21, 48, 89). The very sentimentalization of the national culture in the attitudes of the people makes the people resist a widening of their horizons to the world as a whole, even when objectively they realize that that world is important to them.

National traditions are often rigidified through the influence of institutions and loyalties and are thus difficult to modify even when unadapted to new conditions. Such traditions may include stereotypes of other nations which depart widely from reality but nevertheless influence attitudes, opinions, and policies, both of the people entertaining them and of the people misrepresented by them (69).

Francis Bacon noted that the idols of the den, the theatre, the forum, and the market place biased man's interpretation of reality. People see other nations and the world only through the distorting lenses of national culture, national stereotypes, national traditions, and national wishes of the moment. Wishful thinking is more difficult to moderate in public opinion than it is in individual observation. International education attempts to reduce these distortions, but to do so it must in a measure transcend the very culture in which it functions and which it would be sedition to repudiate.

International understanding and national solidarity. It cannot be denied that international education may, under certain circumstances, disintegrate a national culture. This tendency has often been evident when contact among different cultures has increased rapidly. Isolated primitive cultures are static, precise, and well-integrated but unadapted to radical changes in conditions (71). Civilized cultures tend to be dynamic, flexible and imperfectly integrated, but more adaptable to considerable change in conditions. Primitive cultures usually break down upon the introduction of new technologies or ideas consequent upon contact with more advanced peoples (53, 97). Some civilized cultures are more vulnerable to external influences than others. In proportion as they emphasize freedom of opinion and have within them groups of diverse character, they tend to be open and less vulnerable to new inventions and the introduction of new ideas, but at the same time less capable of coherent action (89). They tend to emphasize individual welfare and to reduce sentiments of group loyalty and solidarity, and thus their culture decays from within; their people become distintegrated as a whole and an easy prey to external invasion or internal revolt (29, 36).

International education, in emphasizing toleration, mutual appreciation, and universal standards may weaken allegiance to national cultures, and turn the world to individual self-seeking, with the result of a general disintegration of institutions and a decline of civilization. The task of international education in maintaining a proper balance between an unrealistic nationalism and a vague cosmopolitanism is not easy to achieve (123, 124).

Long run and short run. International education, though essential in the long run, may weaken the free world's capacity for defense, necessary in the short run, in a world of power politics. On the other hand, war, likely to be the fruit of short-run defense policies, may destroy the national cultures and set back the long-run goals of a free world, even if victory is won. Either war or conquest by barbarians would be disastrous for civilization. International education, teaching that in the long run civilization can be preserved only by preventing war through development of a universal society with appropriate institutions (65, 76), may, in the short run, sap the confidence of peoples in their capacity for national self-defense by convincing them of its hopelessness. International education faces the task of maintaining a balance between attitudes appropriate to the long run and those appropriate to the short run. Fear of aggressive war, justified by contemporary conditions, militates against long-run possibilities of a peaceful world because it augments rivalries, polarizes power and induces resort to preventive war, precipitating the very conditions feared. On the other hand, fear of war itself, justified by long-run considerations of the progress of science and the needs of a peaceful world, may be a cause of war in the short run because it discourages the peaceful in the possibilities of defense and encourages the warlike in the possibilities of aggression, thus weakening the equilibrium of power upon which present peace rests. International education has the difficult task of maintaining a balance between willingness to endure war if necessary and unwillingness to make war unless necessary, between defense and provocation, between conciliation and appeasement (121, 123).

CRITICISM

The problem of international education is no less formidable than its task is important. The importance of that task is being increasingly realized, not only by international organizations, but also by national governments, by national educational systems, and by universities.

The activities of UNESCO, geared to the long-run problem, seem unreal to peoples and governments faced by short-run dangers of war. Why, it is asked, worry about the international education of a generation which is likely to be blotted out by atomic war before it reaches a position of influence? This argument would be less convincing if the influence of UNESCO were universal. So long as important governments refuse to co-operate with UNESCO and seek to prevent it from influencing their people, the gap between long- and short-run requirements will continue. Nevertheless, civilization is a large stake and in the long run its salvation in a shrinking world requires a center for the investigation and dissemination of ideas, standards and values from the world point of view. If the United Nations and diplomacy can meet the short-run problems of balancing power and preventing war, an atmosphere of opinion more favorable to the functioning of UNESCO may spread throughout the world.

Foreign offices find difficulty in separating international education from national propaganda. They necessarily subordinate all effort to the policy of the moment. The "Voice of America," designed to spread valid information about the United States, is likely to be interpreted as propaganda of American superiority among less privileged peoples or as propaganda of sedition among peoples whose governments deprive minorities of human and national rights.

The possibility that international education may disintegrate the national culture and weaken the national morale is certain to be emphasized by politicians with the result that international education, and institutions like UNESCO committed to it, become targets of party politics. Campaigns are launched against teachers and textbooks with an international slant, and there is a reaction toward nationalism and isolationism. These difficulties can hardly be avoided until a discipline of international relations has achieved an objectivity and a balance of values both convincing and persuasive to the leaders and peoples of the important nations and cultures. In the meantime, courses in civics, history, geography, and literature may be made less biased. International criticism to this end may exert some influence in national education even at the lower levels.

It is in the colleges and universities that international education has its greatest opportunity. Future leaders may gain more objectivity, more suitable attitudes, and more understanding of the international process than they would otherwise have through college courses in the field. Marked progress has been made in the United States, both in the quality and quantity of such courses since World War I (68, 106, 115). The same is true in other countries (9, 10, 78). Such courses, and university research, may contribute to developing a discipline of international relations which can prove a key to more effective international education by all agencies—international, national, and private—as that discipline gains in objectivity and comprehensibility. For this very reason it is to be expected that universities and university teachers will become targets of attack by extreme nationalists, traditionalists, and ideologists as they have, particularly in Germany, Russia, and the United States, during the past generation. The preservation of academic freedom in universities is, therefore, an essential element in the progress of international education (21, 23, 48, 80).

REFERENCES

The bibliography of international education includes studies on educational methods and theories thus extending into the field of educational psychology. It also includes studies on the social functions and activities of educational institutions thus extending into the history and sociology of education. Only a few of the many books in these fields are included in this list. Some others are listed after the chapters on the psychology and the sociology of international relations. The *Cyclopaedia of Education,* Paul Monroe, ed. (New York, Macmillan, 1911-1913), 5 vols., and the *Encyclopaedia of Modern Education,* Harry N. Revlin, ed. (New York, Philosophical Library, 1950), deal with these subjects as do many articles in the *Encyclopaedia of the Social Sciences,* E. R. A. Seligman and Alvin Johnson, eds. (New York, Macmillan, 1930-1935), 15 vols., such as those on "Human Nature" by John Dewey; "Educational Psychology" by R. M. Ogden; "Education, Primitive" by Margaret Mead; "Education, History" by George S. Counts; "Education, Public" by I. L. Kandel; "Civic Education" by Carl Brinkman; "Civic Organizations" by W. B. Munro; "Universities and Colleges" by Stephen D'Irsay; "Teaching Profession" by Walter R. Sharp; and "Academic Freedom" by Arthur O. Lovejoy.

The bibliography of international education also includes studies of the picture of, and attitudes toward, the world which the art of international education has, or has attempted, to develop and the methods, formal and informal, utilized for developing such a picture and such attitudes. A few books on nationalism, internationalism, world citizenship, and pacifism are included in this list. Articles in the *Encyclopaedia of the Social Sciences* on "Internationalism" by H. N. Brailsford; "Pacifism" and "Peace Movements" by Norman Angell; "Cosmopolitanism" and "Nationalism, Theory" by Max H. Boehm; "Individualism" by A. D. Lindsay; "Humanism" by E. P. Cheyney and F. C. S. Schiller; "Humanitarianism" by Crane Brinton; "Pragmatism" by H. M. Kallen; "Nationalism, History" by Carleton J. H. Hayes; and "Patriotism" by Francis W. Coker illustrate this approach.

Finally such a bibliography should include publications by the numerous organizations engaged in international education. National governments, most of which, apart from educating the young, now engage in educating their adult citizens in international affairs and the United Nations with its predecessor the League of Nations and its Specialized Agencies particularly UNESCO (United Nations Educational, Scientific and Cultural Organization) are the most important public agencies in the field. But numerous private organizations, both national and international, also engage in international education, both scholarly and popular, both professional and general, some with a primary interest in education and others with a primary interest in international relations. Some like the Royal Institute in London; the Council on Foreign Relations, the Foreign Policy Association, and the Institute of Pacific Relations in New York; the Brookings Institution and the Middle East Institute in Washington; and the university institutes on international affairs at London, Geneva, Harvard, Yale, Princeton, Columbia, Chicago, and other universities have the object of extending knowledge; others like the many associations for the United Nations, for World Government, for Atlantic Union, for World Citizenship, for Peace have the object of influencing attitudes; others like the Institute of Education in London and the American Council on Education, the National Educational Association, and the American Association of University Professors in Washington have the object of improving the profession; while still others like the Ford, Carnegie, and Rockefeller foundations have all these objects. See Frederick S. Dunn, "Introduction," *Current Research in International Affairs* (New York, Carnegie Endowment for International Peace, 1952); Ruth Savord, *Directory of American Agencies Concerned with the Study of International Affairs* (New York, Council on Foreign Relations, 1931); Chester R. Read and Samuel Marble, *Guide to Public Affairs Agencies* (Washington, Public Affairs Press, 1946); National Educational Association, *Organizations Interested in International Relations* (Washington, 1939); George Galloway, *Postwar Planning in the United States* (New York, Twentieth Century Fund, 1942). A few of the hundreds of such organizations are here listed as authors of important publications.

1. ADAMS, John, *The Evolution of Educational Theory* (London, Macmillan, 1928).
2. ALMOND, Gabriel, *The American People and Foreign Policy* (New York, Harcourt, 1950).
3. American Association of University Professors, *Bulletin* (Washington), quarterly.
4. American Association for the United Nations, *Publications* (New York).
5. American Council on Education, R. B. Knapp, ed., *Studies on Orientation to America for Foreign Exchangees,* Conference (Washington, June, 1952), Report of Committees and Conferences, No. 54; H. L. Nostrand and F. J. Brown, eds., *The Roles of Colleges and Universities in International Understanding,* Conference (Estes Park, Colo., June, 1949), Report, No. 38. See also Kandel, I. L.
6. American Historical Association, Commission on the Social Studies, *Report,* Vol. 3 (New York, 1933); "Public Opinion and the Teaching of History in the United States," *Report* (New York, 1926).

7. American Society of International Law, *American Journal of International Law* (Washington, 1907–), quarterly.

8. ARNDT, Christian O., and EVERETT, Samuel, eds., *Education for a World Society*, 11th Year Book of the John Dewey Society (New York, Harper, 1951).

9. BAILEY, S. H., *International Studies in Great Britain* (London, Royal Institute of International Affairs, 1937).

10. ——, *International Studies in Modern Education* (London, Royal Institute of International Affairs, 1938).

11. BEALES, A. C. F., *The History of Peace* (New York, Dial Press, 1931).

12. BEAR, Robert M., *The Social Function of Education* (New York, Macmillan, 1937).

13. BODE, Boyd H., *How We Learn* (Boston, Heath, 1940).

14. ——, *Modern Educational Theories* (New York, Macmillan, 1927).

15. Brookings Institution, *Major Problems of United States Foreign Policy* (Washington, 1946–), annual.

16. BROWN, F. Andrew, "On Education: John Locke, Christian Wolfe and the Moral Weeklies, *University of California Publications in Modern Philology*, Vol. 36, No. 5 (1952).

17. BRYCE, James, *International Relations* (New York, Macmillan, 1922).

18. BRYSON, Lyman, FINKELSTEIN, Louis, and MacIVER, R. M., *Goals for American Education*, Ninth Symposium on Science, Philosophy and Religion (New York, Harper, 1950).

19. BUTLER, Nicholas Murray, *The International Mind* (New York, Scribner, 1913).

20. Carnegie Endowment for International Peace, *International Conciliation* (New York), quarterly. See also Conference of Teachers of International Law; Shaw, Roger; Ware, Edith; Wilson, Howard E.

21. CARR, Robert R., *The House Committee on Un-American Activities, 1945-1950*, Cornell Studies in Civil Liberty, R. E. Cushman, ed. (Ithaca, Cornell University Press, 1952).

22. Center of International Studies, Princeton University, *World Politics* (1948–), quarterly.

23. CHEYNEY, E. P., ed., "Freedom of Inquiry and Opinion," *Annals*, American Academy of Political and Social Science (Philadelphia, November, 1938).

24. COHEN, Bernard C., *World Affairs and the Education of Citizens* (Princeton, Princeton University Press, 1953).

25. COLE, Percival R., *A History of Educational Thought* (London, Oxford University Press, 1937).

26. COMENIUS, Johann Amos, *The Great Didactic, Setting forth the whole art of Teaching all things to all men* (1632), edited with Commentary by H. W. Keatinge (London, Black, 1921-1923), 2 vols.

27. Commission to Study the Organization of Peace, *Reports* (New York, 1940–).

28. Committee to Frame a World Constitution, *Common Cause*, G. A. Borgese, ed. (Chicago, University of Chicago Press, 1946-1951), monthly.

29. CONANT, James Bryant, *Education and Liberty: The Role of the Schools in a Modern Democracy* (Cambridge, Harvard University Press, 1953).

30. Conference of Teachers of International Law and Related Subjects, *Proceedings* (Washington, Carnegie Endowment, 1911–). See also Hudson, M. O.; Quigley, H. S.; Spykman, N.

31. Conference on Science, Philosophy and Religion, Annual Symposia (New York, Harper, 1942–). See also Bryson, Lyman; Strang, Ruth.
32. CORBETT, Percy E., *Post War Worlds* (New York, Institute of Pacific Relations, 1941).
33. Council for Education in World Citizenship, *Education and the United Nations* (Washington, Public Affairs Press, 1943).
34. Council on Foreign Relations, Richard P. Stebbins, ed., *The United States and World Affairs,* annual; *Foreign Affairs,* quarterly (New York, 1922–). See also Kirk, Grayson; Dunn, F. E.
35. COUNTS, George S., "Education, History," *Encyclopædia of the Social Sciences.*
36. DAY, Edmund E., *Education for Freedom and Responsibility; Selected Essays* (Ithaca, Cornell University Press, 1952).
37. DEWEY, John, *Democracy and Education: An Introduction to the Philosophy of Education,* 1916 (New York, Macmillan, 1938).
38. ———, *Experience and Education* (New York, Macmillan, 1938).
39. DUNN, Frederick S., *War and the Minds of Man* (New York, Council on Foreign Relations, 1950).
40. ———, Introduction to *Current Research in International Affairs* (New York, Carnegie Endowment, 1952).
41. EINSTEIN, Albert, and FREUD, Sigmund, "Why War?" in *Correspondence* (Paris, International Institute of Intellectual Co-operation, 1933).
42. ERASMUS, Disiderius, *Antipolemus, or the Plea of Reason, Religion and Humanity against War,* 1518 (London, 1794).
43. FARIES, J. C., *The Rise of Internationalism* (New York, Gray, 1915).
44. Ford Foundation, *Report of the Study for the Ford Foundation on Policy and Program* (Detroit, Mich., 1949).
45. Foreign Policy Association, *Bulletin* (New York), weekly.
46. Fox, Byron L., *International Cultural Relations* (Syracuse, Syracuse University Press, 1953).
47. Fox, Charles, *Educational Psychology, Its Problems and Methods* (New York, Harcourt, 1925).
48. GELLHORN, Walter, *The States and Subversion,* Cornell Studies in Civil Liberty, R. E. Cushman, ed. (Ithaca, Cornell University Press, 1952).
49. GOLDSMITH, Oliver, *The Citizen of the World, or Letters of a Chinese Philosopher residing in London to his friends in the East, 1762* (London, 1928), 2 vols.
50. GOODWIN, Geoffrey L., ed., "The University Teaching of International Relations," *Proceedings, International Studies Conference,* Windsor, 1950 (London, Blackwells, 1951).
51. GRACE, Alonzo C., and others, *Proceedings, International Conference on Comparative Education* (Chemissee, Germany, April, 1949).
52. HORNE, Herman H., *The Philosophy of Education,* rev. ed. (London, Macmillan, 1927).
53. HOSELITZ, Bert, ed., *The Progress of Underdeveloped Areas,* Harris Foundation Institute (Chicago, University of Chicago Press, 1952).
54. HUDSON, Manley O., *The Teaching of International Law in America,* Conference of Teachers of International Law, Vol. 3 (Washington, Carnegie Endowment, 1928), pp. 68 ff., 178 ff.
55. HUTCHINS, Robert M., *The University of Utopia* (Chicago, University of Chicago Press, 1953).
56. HUXLEY, Julian, *UNESCO: Its Purpose and Its Philosophy* (Washington, Public Affairs Press, 1948).

57. Institute of Education, University of London, *Year Book.* See also Kandel, I. L.

58. Institute of Pacific Relations, New York, *Far Eastern Survey,* fortnightly; *Pacific Affairs,* quarterly. See also Corbett, Percy.

59. Institute of International Education, *News Bulletin* (New York, 1925–), monthly.

60. International Institute of Intellectual Co-operation, *Publications* (Paris). See also Einstein, Albert; International Studies Conference.

61. International Studies Conference, Organized by International Institute of Intellectual Co-operation and UNESCO. See Goodwin, Geoffrey; Manning, C. A.; Zimmern, Alfred.

62. John Dewey Society, Year Books. See Arndt, C. O.

63. KANDEL, I. L., *United States Action in International Cultural Relations,* Report No. 23 (Washington, American Council on Education, 1945).

64. ———, "Nationalism and Education," *Year Book of Education 1949* (University of London, Institute of Education, 1949).

65. KANT, Immanuel, *Eternal Peace, 1795* (Boston, World Peace Foundation, 1914).

66. KILPATRICK, W. H., *Philosophy of Education* (New York, Macmillan, 1951).

67. ———, *Education for a Changing Civilization* (New York, Macmillan, 1927).

68. KIRK, Grayson, *The Study of International Relations in American Colleges* (New York, Council on Foreign Relations, 1947).

69. KLINEBERG, Otto, *Tensions in the Modern World,* UNESCO Studies in International Tensions (New York, Social Science Research Council, 1950).

70. KORZYBSKI, Alfred, *Science and Sanity* (New York, 1933); 3rd ed. (Lakeville, Conn., Institute of General Semantics, 1948).

71. KROEBER, A. L., ed., *Anthropology Today, An Encyclopaedic Inventory* (Chicago, University of Chicago Press, 1953). *An Appraisal of "Anthropology Today,"* Sol Tax, and others, eds. (Chicago, University of Chicago Press, 1953).

72. Laymans' Foreign Missions Inquiry, W. E. Hocking, Chairman, *Rethinking Missions* (New York, Harper, 1932).

73. League of Nations, International Committee of Intellectual Co-operation, Recommendation of Subcommittee of Experts, *How to Make the League of Nations Known and to Develop the Spirit of International Co-operation* (Geneva, 1927). See also International Institute of Intellectual Co-operation.

74. LOCKE, John, "Some Thoughts Concerning Education" (1693), *Works* (London, 1794), Vol. 8.

75. MACDONALD, John, *Mind, School and Civilization* (Chicago, University of Chicago Press, 1952).

76. MADARIAGA, Salvador de, *The World's Design* (London, Allen and Unwin, 1938).

77. MANNHEIM, Karl, *Ideology and Utopia: An Introduction to the Sociology of Knowledge* (New York, Harcourt, 1936).

78. MANNING, C. A. W., *The University Teaching of Social Sciences, International Relations* (Paris, UNESCO, 1954).

79. MEAD, Margaret, "Education, Primitive," *Encyclopædia of the Social Sciences.*

80. MEIKLEJOHN, Alexander, *Freedom and the College* (New York, Century, 1923).

81. MERRIAM, Charles E., *The Making of Citizens, A Comparative Study of Methods of Civic Training* (Chicago, University of Chicago Press, 1931), A Summary of Studies on Civic Education among the DucDucs and in the United States, France, Great Britain, Austria, Switzerland, Germany, Italy, and Russia.

82. MONROE, Paul, *A Textbook on the History of Education* (New York, Macmillan, 1905).

83. MYRDAL, Gunnar, "Psychological Impediments to Effective International Co-operation," Kurt Lewin Memorial Lecture, *Journal of Social Issues*, Supplement No. 6 (New York, 1933).

84. ———, *The Relation Between Social Theory and Social Policy*, Conference Address, British Sociological Association (March, 1953).

85. National Educational Association, Educational Policies Commission, *Education and the Peoples' Peace* (Washington, 1943); *The Education of Free Men in American Democracy* (Washington, 1941).

86. OGDEN, Robert Morris, *Psychology and Education*, new ed. (New York, Harcourt, 1932).

87. PIERCE, Bessie L., *Civic Attitudes in American School Text Books* (Chicago, University of Chicago Press, 1930).

88. PILLSBURY, W. B., *The Psychology of Nationality and Internationalism* (New York, Appleton, 1919).

89. POPPER, K. R., *The Open Society and Its Enemies*, 2nd ed. (London, Routledge and Kegan Paul, 1952), 2 vols.

90. POOL, Ithiel de Sola, *Symbols of Internationalism* (Stanford, Stanford University Press, 1951).

91. President's Commission on Higher Education, *Higher Education for American Democracy* (New York, Harper, 1948).

92. Public Administration Clearing House (Sayre, W. S. and Thurber, C. C., eds.) *Training for Specialized Mission Personnel* (Chicago, Public Administration Service, 1952).

93. QUIGLEY, Harold S., *Scope, Organization and Aim of Courses in International Relations*, Conference of Teachers of International Law, Vol. 2 (Washington, 1925), pp. 7 ff.

94. REISNER, Edward H., *Nationalism and Education since 1789, A Social and Political History of Modern Education* (New York, Macmillan, 1922).

95. ———, *Historical Foundations of Modern Education* (New York, Macmillan, 1927).

96. ———, *The Evolution of the Common School* (New York, Macmillan, 1930).

97. RIVERS, W. H. R., *Essays on the Depopulation of Melanesia* (Cambridge, Cambridge University Press, 1922).

98. ROSENHAUPT, Hans W., *How to Wage Peace? A Handbook for Action* (New York, John Day, 1949).

99. Royal Institute of International Affairs, *Survey of International Affairs*, A. J. Toynbee, and others, eds., annual; *International Affairs*, quarterly; *The World Today*, monthly; *Chronology of International Events*, bimonthly. See also Bailey, E. S.; Toynbee, A. J.

100. RUSSELL, Bertrand, *Education and the Modern World* (New York, Norton, 1932).

101. SHAW, Roger, *Policies and Programs of Institutes of World Affairs* (New York, Carnegie Endowment for International Peace, 1952).
102. SPYKMAN, Nicholas, *Method of Approach to Study of International Relations*, Conference of Teachers of International Law, Vol. 5 (Washington, 1933), p. 58.
103. SAWELL, Florence M., *The Growth of International Thought* (London, Butterworth, 1929).
104. STRANG, Ruth, *Education Against Aggression*, Seventh Symposium on Science, Philosophy and Religion (New York, Harper, 1948), pp. 205 ff.
105. STREIT, Clarence K., *Freedom and Union* (New York), monthly.
106. THOMPSON, Kenneth, "The Study of International Politics: A Survey of Trends and Developments," *Review of Politics*, Vol. 14 (October, 1952), pp. 433 ff.
107. THORNDIKE, E. L., *Educational Psychology* (New York, 1913-1914), Vol. 1, "The Original Nature of Man"; Vol. 2, "The Psychology of Learning"; Vol. 3, "Individual Differences and Their Causes."
108. TOYNBEE, Arnold J., *A Study of History*, Royal Institute of International Affairs (London, Oxford University Press, 1934, 1939, 1954), 10 vols. (Abridgements by D. C. Somervell and E. D. Myers.)
109. UNESCO, *A Handbook for the Improvement of Textbooks and Teaching Materials as Aids to International Understanding* (Paris, UNESCO, 1949); *Fundamental Education, Common Ground for all Peoples*, Report of Special Committee, Henry W. Holmes, ed. (New York, Macmillan, 1947); "The Enquiry into the Teaching of the Social Sciences," General Report of Conference, 1952, *International Social Science Bulletin*, Vol. 5 (Winter, 1953), pp. 151 ff. See also International Studies Conference; Huxley, Julian; Klineberg, Otto.
110. United Nations, *Bulletin*, weekly. See also UNESCO.
111. United World Federalists, Publications, New York.
112. VANDERBILT, Arthur T., and others, *Modern Education and Human Values* (Pittsburgh, University of Pittsburgh, 1952).
113. WATSON, Goodwn B., *Action for Unity* (New York, Harper, 1947).
114. WALLAS, Graham, *The Great Society* (New York, Macmillan, 1917).
115. WARE, Edith E., *The Study of International Relations in the United States* (New York, Carnegie Endowment, 1939).
116. WILDS, Elmer H., *The Foundations of Modern Education*, new ed. (New York, Rinehart, 1942).
117. WILSON, Howard E., *Universities and World Affairs* (New York, Carnegie Endowment, 1952).
118. World Citizens Association, Publications, Henri Bonnet, ed., 1942-1943; *A Platform of World Citizenship* (Chicago, World Citizens Association, 1942).
119. World Organization of the Teaching Profession, Proceedings of Fifth Delegates Assembly, Malta, 1951.
120. World Peace Foundation, *International Organization* (Boston, 1946–), quarterly.
121. WRIGHT, Quincy, *A Study of War* (Chicago, University of Chicago Press, 1942), pp. 166-217, 423-437, 970-982, 1012-1042, 1093, 1218-1224, 1334, 1347-1352, 1448-1455.
122. ――――, ed., *The World Community*, Harris Foundation Institute (Chicago, University of Chicago Press, 1949).

123. Wright, Quincy, *Problems of Stability and Progress in International Relations* (Berkeley, University of California Press, 1954).
124. Zimmern, Alfred, *The Development of the International Mind, Problems of Peace,* First Series (Geneva, Institute of International Relations, 1926).
125. ———, *Education for World Citizenship, Problems of Peace,* Fifth Series Geneva, Institute of International Relations, 1931).
126. ———, ed., *University Teaching of International Relations,* Proceedings International Studies Conference, Prague, 1938 (Paris, International Institute of Intellectual Co-operation, 1939).
127. ———, *The American Road to World Peace* (New York, Dutton, 1953).
128. Znaniecki, Florian, *Modern Nationalities: A Sociological Study* (Urbana, University of Illinois Press, 1952).

PART IV

Theoretical Analyses of International Relations

The Theoretical Social Disciplines

Disciplines seeking to analyze international relations theoretically cannot be sharply distinguished from those seeking to analyze it practically. The practical disciplines, discussed in the preceding part of this book, have in most cases attempted to develop a basic theory. Political science, economics, jurisprudence, communications, and education profess to be theoretical disciplines and as such to provide generalizations useful for the practical disciplines, but they have emerged mainly from the practical activities of statesmen, merchants, advocates, propagandists, and teachers. Their primary objective has been practice rather than understanding, manipulation rather than contemplation.

The disciplines to be considered in this part emerged from scholarly efforts to discover relatively permanent definitions, postulates, and principles, analysis of which would explain phenomena and their changes, and would thus promote understanding of man and his societies.

Geography, population, and technology, each refer to classes of phenomena which are readily susceptible to observation, description and, in some cases, measurement. The concepts of society, of personality, and of value, though less tangible, have been comprehended even by primitive peoples and have been distinguished in all systems of philosophy (1). It is not therefore surprising that each of these types of phenomena should have become the subject matter of a special discipline.

Each of these types of phenomena obviously differs from nation to nation and each apparently influences international relations. The six disciplines of political geography, political demography, the technology, sociology, and psychology of international relations, and international ethics have, therefore, emerged from the more general disciplines concerned with these six types of phenomena, as distinct efforts to establish theoretical foundations for the study of international relations. The first three have tended to remain disciplines of empirical character and the last has usually been treated as a philosophy, although efforts have been made to develop a science of international ethics. The sociology and psychology of international relations have, perhaps, been most successful in establishing theoretical bases for a science of international relations.

Universal history might have been discussed in this section. Its aim is to promote understanding of international and world relations through inducing realization of past conditions of the international community and the processes of change. Its objectives have usually been theoretical rather than practical but, as with all history, its method has been synthetic rather than analytic. The role of history in relation to science is to emphasize the uniqueness of historical situations, and thus to suggest limitations upon all disciplines which seek abstract analyses of human or group relations, and to criticize the results achieved by such disciplines through knowledge of the particular historical situations in which they are applied.

General philosophy might also have been considered in this section, but its scope is so broad that it can hardly be considered a discipline of international relations. As history criticizes the validity of the conclusions of these disciplines from the point of view of experience, so philosophy criticizes them from the point of view of logic. Universal history and general philosophy belong in a different category from the disciplines discussed in this part. They, in fact, constitute the sources from which these theoretical disciplines have emerged.

Historians have tended to become philosophers of history as they have moved from local and national to universal history and as such to abstract elements of explanatory value from the total stream of history. A particular philosopher of history has often given exaggerated emphasis to one such element as population change (Malthus); the material environment including climate (Buckle); inventions and technology, and the economic structures based upon them (Marx); the development of institutions (Maitland); the personality of leaders (Carlyle); or the striving to realize ideas (Hegel) or to meet challenges (Toynbee). Such abstractions, departing from the proper method of history, have contributed to the development of the analytic disciplines here discussed.

General philosophers have sometimes sought to give meanings more concrete than is possible by purely analytic activities to generalizations in the areas of experience which interest them particularly. Some of them have, therefore, specialized in a particular type of subject matter. As a result, philosophy came to be divided into "natural" and "moral" philosophy (Descartes, Leibnitz). The first of these, dealing with nonhuman nature, subsequently came to be divided into the many natural sciences and the latter, dealing with human nature, into the many social sciences, especially ethics (Kant), psychology (Hobbes), and sociology (Comte). There have, however, been philosophers who have emphasized the more material factors of environment, population, and technology (Vico, Montesquieu).

Thus the history of thought discloses a reciprocal influence of universal history and general philosophy in the emergence of the theoretical disciplines relevant to international relations, each striving to become a science.

REFERENCE

1. REDFIELD, Robert, "The Primitive World View," *Proceedings, American Philosophical Society*, Vol. 96 (February, 1952), pp. 30 ff.

Political Geography

DEFINITION

POLITICAL GEOGRAPHY is the science relating the physical environment to politics, and particularly to the state. As an aspect of international relations, it is the science relating the physical environment to world politics, and the art, sometimes called Geopolitik, of utilizing the physical environment in world politics. It may also refer to a philosophy which attributes determining, or at least major, influence upon culture, civilization, and policy to the physical environment or to particular aspects of that environment such as location, climate, terrain, and natural resources.

In common usage geography is a description of the earth's surface with special reference to those features of human or social importance. In this sense it is an aspect of history for the latter deals not only with the sequence of events in time, but with their location in space, and with their explanation not only by temporal antecedents but by spatial proximities. Apart from the techniques of mapping to manifest spatial relations, geography in this sense may be considered history which emphasizes the influence upon human behavior and institutions of the physical environment and spatial relations. Political geography from this point of view consists of the interpretation of political boundaries and of political history in terms of location, situation, and environment.

Since its development as an academic discipline, however, geography has come to refer to a science rather than an art, history, or philosophy, but a science of empirical character. Derwent Whittlesey in treating political geography gives "attention to the degree of correspondence between the pattern of states and the patterns of the natural environment, ranging from coincidence to complete discrepancy" (45).

ASSUMPTIONS

The discipline of political geography assumes (a) that the physical environment influences politics, and (b) that politics influences the human significance of the environment. As an aspect of international relations, the discipline usually assumes (c) that sovereign territorial states exist and that each seeks to maintain and improve its relative power position in order to assure its continued independence.

The physical environment clearly influences political facts such as the location, size, technology, culture, economy, and polity of states and other political groups; their foreign and domestic policies; the location and character of their boundaries; and the location of, and relation between, the major centers of political power in the world. To say that there is such an influence is not to say that that influence is determining or even of major significance in all cases.

It seems clear that the relationship between politics and geography is reciprocal. The establishment of a political group, the pursuit of a policy, the location of a boundary, and the location of major centers of power influence the physical environment or at least its significance to man directly or indirectly, consciously or unconsciously. Political groups utilize the physical environment to achieve their objectives—political, economic, social, and cultural—and this utilization influences the characteristics of the group. From the point of view of the science of geography, this reciprocal relationship is generally recognized. The environment demands adjustment of politics to its conditions whether from convenience or necessity. But politics reacts by encouraging utilization of the environment, by stimulating invention enlarging the possibility of such utilization, and by promoting the realization of those possibilities through the introduction of new technologies and new values. Social and economic changes especially in the realm of communication and transportation may revolutionize the human significance of the environment. This reciprocal relationship prevents easy expression of the relationship of geography and politics in terms of correlation, causation, or simultaneous equations. Geographers aware of this complexity often hesitate to commit themselves to generalizations and content themselves with chorography or detailed description of particular regions and of the empirical relations observed in such regions. Extended to the study of historical changes in regions, to the comparison of different regions, and to the classification of typical regions, this approach has been called *cultural geography* (32). *Human geographers* (3), on the other hand, have sought broad generalizations concerning the relation of man to his environment, either explaining history in the long run by geographical determinism (27, 28, 33), or seeking to guide practice by expounding the art of optimum land utilization or of adaptation of man to the environment for security and prosperity (29). Geography as an aspect of history has tended to emphasize the influence of the environment on man, while geography as an art has tended to emphasize the influence of man on his environment.

Political geographers interested in world politics have usually accepted the assumptions of international politics that sovereign territorial states exist as the principal political groups in the world, that the primary objective of each is preservation of its independence, and that to achieve this objective each seeks to maintain, or if possible, to improve, its relative power position. Political geographers have, therefore, sought to establish the best policy for each state in utilizing its position, territory, resources, boundaries, and other geographical features for purposes of power and prosperity. As a political geographer usually writes from the point of view of his own state, he often seeks to explain or criticize past policies and to advise on future policies of his state from an analysis of its geographical position, and to predict the probable policy of other states, particularly political rivals, from an analysis of their geographical positions. Such studies in the present age of world communication and transportation involve an analysis of the strategic relations of the entire world as determined under existing technological conditions by the location and relation of continents, oceans, islands, straits, deserts, resources, and political boundaries (20, 23, 34).

Political geographers in utilizing their knowledge to develop an applied science or art in the international field might accept the assumptions of international organization and international law, and from that universal point of view criticize past policies or advise on future policies of the United Nations in its effort to stabilize the equilibrium of power, to organize international co-operation, and to create conditions in which international peace and security may be maintained. There have been a few studies from this point of view, on such topics as the location of United Nations' bases, the character and location of United Nations' forces and contingents, the control of trusteeship and dependent territories to promote general security, the availability of strategic resources, and the control of sources of nuclear energy (6, 41, 43, 44).

Most political geographers have, however, adopted a national point of view, partly because as citizens they have put their own state's interests first, partly because as historians they are more familiar with national than with international policies, and partly because as scientists they have interpreted their function as prediction rather than control and have been obliged to accept the fact that the major concentrations of political power are today in the governments of nations and not in the organs of the United Nations.

Different schools of geography, though together in their basic assumptions, differ as to the interpretation of these assumptions. They differ, for example, as to (a) the importance of geographical factors relative to racial, cultural, social, and political factors in determining the character of states, their policies, the location of their boundaries, and the location of power centers in the world. They also differ as to (b) the relative importance of different geographical factors such as location, terrain, resources, climate, in influencing the policies, boundaries, and power of states. Furthermore they differ as to (c) the degree of persistence of the influence of geographic factors in time and (d) the degree of uniformity in the importance of geographical influences in all situations.

The determinists or environmentalists note the coercive influence of environment on the occupations and lives of primitive peoples. Dwellers in the forest, on the seashore, on the plains, in the Arctic, are obliged to adapt their economy to the conditions they face, and other aspects of culture are in considerable measure influenced by the economy. When, however, groups of men with established customs and values migrate to a new environment they seek to bend that environment to their traditional way of life and succeed in doing so in proportion as their technology is developed to utilize natural resources and to transport materials from a distance. Civilized man is not coerced by his environment but utilizes it to realize his values. Nevertheless there are limits to the process and, in particular, the location of a state determines in considerable measure the means of defense, whether land, naval, or air power, which can be successful (47).

The word *geography* covers a wide variety of environmental factors. Particular schools have emphasized particular aspects. The climatic school points to the influence of climate on human energy and on agricultural production. The peoples of the tropics and of the Arctic differ both from one another and from the peoples of the temperate zone who are more numerous and more powerful. Areas of optimum climatic energy have been mapped and correlated with the advancement of civilization (16). The resource school points to the location of soils, minerals, and other resources as of major significance. Only countries well supplied with coal and iron, with petroleum, and perhaps in the future, with uranium, it is said, can become great powers (5). The location school, especially important in world politics, emphasizes the influence of continental, insular, coastland, or other positions of the state's home territory on defense and, in the modern shrinking world, the significance of heartland, rimland, or insular location on the general pattern of world politics (21, 34, 36).

Some geographers have emphasized the persistence of geographic factors. The location of continents, islands, rivers, and harbors, and the soils, minerals, plants, and climate of a particular area change only in geological time. Through the centuries these factors are thought to exert a continuing influence on civilization and policy. Others, however, emphasize the varying importance of these factors on human life and their actual change through human action. Climates may fluctuate considerably in relatively short times, and man may modify its influence through artificial heating and refrigeration. Resources of mine and soil may be exhausted and hitherto unimportant resources may become of major importance through the progress of technology. Canals, railroads, steam navigation, and the airplane revolutionize conditions of transportation and change the importance of ports and bases for commercial or strategic purposes. The invention of the airplane has revolutionized strategy by greatly reducing the influence on logistics of barriers such as oceans, deserts, and the Arctic, and has induced many geographers to emphasize the mutability of the influence of the geographic environment upon men and society (29, 43, 44, 48).

Some geographers believe that environmental influences dominate society and policy at all times and places, while others believe that the importance of these influences are highly variable. They are determining in some situations such as the uninhabitability of the Arctic and Antarctic and the occupational patterns of primitive peoples, but are of relatively little influence in others such as the religious practices of city dwellers and the occupational choices of the middle class in modern states.

It seems clear that on each of these issues the eclectics have the better of the argument. Geographical influences are seldom or never entirely determining. No one geographical feature predominates generally over the others, none are entirely persistent in their influence, and the degree of geographical influence is highly variable. For these reasons the analysis of geographical influences on history, society, and policy, and of their optimum utilization in a given situation is extraordinarily complex and is contingent upon changing technological, cultural, economic, and political conditions. The result is that careful geographers hesitate to advance broad concepts and conceptual systems but recognize that their science is in high degree empirical. People may "think geographically," in the sense that they are always alert to environmental influences, but the importance and nature of these influences depends upon the total situation—geographic, cultural, social, and political in the area (45). If geography is a science, it is a science little removed from detailed description and the classification of historical precedents. The geographers who have ventured into universal propositions relating culture, institutions, policy, and strategy to particular climates, types of terrain, types of resources, types of locational relation, have been regarded as stimulating rather than as authoritative.

ANALYSIS

The lack of precision in the formulation of common assumptions, the divergence in interpretation of these assumptions by different schools of geography, and the consequently highly empirical character of political geography has resulted in a great variation in the analyses of the subject and the conclusions of different writers in the field. The topics usually discussed are (*a*) the relation of geography to political institutions, (*b*) to policies, (*c*) to boundaries, and (*d*) to centers of political power.

Political institutions. Most modern geographers recognize that earlier generalizations associating democratic and free institutions with mountainous and insular sites and associating authoritative and slave institutions with continental and plains sites are contingent upon the state of the arts and the tradition of the peoples. The institutions on the prairies of middle western America may be as free as those in mountainous Switzerland and much freer than those on the plains of Russia, although the latter are geographically similar. The Americans inherited free British institutions and faced the relatively weak American Indians, while the Russians faced the more powerful Mongols and had no experience with free institutions. These factors may have been more important than geography. It has frequently been pointed out that a state with natural defenses of mountain, sea, or desert finds it necessary to devote little of its social energy and resources to military discipline and preparations, and consequently is able to organize its economy for welfare and its polity for freedom. This generalization may have a measure of validity, though the autocratic regimes in Japan and China during their long period of isolation appear to be exceptions. The tendency of military technology to render previous geographic barriers to invasion abortive (as has the airplane for England and the United States) and the tendency for peoples sheltered by natural barriers from the need for external defense to divide and fight civil wars (as illustrated by periods in the history of England, Japan, the United States, and China) indicate that this generalization, if properly qualified, is one of sociology rather than of geography.

Climatic conditions undoubtedly impose limitations upon the advance of civilization and political power because of their influence upon human energy and upon agriculture. It is to be expected that great powers will develop only in the temperate zone and in view of the restricted temperate areas of the southern continents it is to be anticipated that such powers would have their centers in North America, Europe, and Asia. Nevertheless, improved technologies of air conditioning, refrigeration, and heating can do much to ameliorate the climatic difficulties of naturally inhospitable areas. Even Ellsworth Huntington, known as the expounder of climatic influences on civilization and power, recognizes that genetic selection and cultural traditions may exert an equal or in some cases, greater, influence (17).

A particular state of the arts may induce the flowering of one civilization in irrigable river valleys (Egypt, Mesopotamia, China, India), another in mountainous areas (Greece, Switzerland, Peru), another in plains areas of sufficient rainfall to produce staple crops (Northern Europe, United States, Russia, Argentina), another in areas of abundant coal and iron (Britain, Germany, United States), and still others in areas rich in petroleum, areas of great hydro-electric resources, areas rich in pitchblende, and perhaps in the future, areas suitable for tidal or solar engines. As in the case of climate, the identification of valuable natural resources and the extent and character of their influence is a function of technology and sociology as much as of geography.

Efforts have been made to rate the human potentialities of areas of the world by formulae giving consideration to many factors—climate; mineral, power, and agricultural resources; accessibility to the sea, to trade, and so forth (37, 38). Such formulae are stimulating to thought but the number of factors to be considered, the changes in their significance with invention, the influence of genetic, cultural, and nongeographic factors, the importance of the particular combination of factors, and the difficulty of properly weighing the relative importance of different factors, limits the practical utility of this method.

Other geographers have sought to develop geographic generalizations through the application of the biological conceptions of youth, adolescence, maturity, and age to the peoples inhabiting different regions of the earth. This conception has been applied to states (40), to nations, and to civilizations (39, 47). Youth is said to be a period of internal co-ordination, adolescence of external expansion, maturity of stability and defensive strength, old age of internal decay and invasion from abroad. It is recognized that societies in old age may have within them youthful movements usually seeking revolutionary change. No area can, therefore, ordinarily be classified as wholly old or wholly young. This concept, assuming an analogy between societies and organisms, suggests application of the Darwinian concept of struggle for existence and survival of the fittest to international politics. Successful war expanding the territory of the state is considered evidence of the fitness of a state, while stability or defeat is considered evidence of decay and unfitness. Whatever may be the value of these dubious analogies for limited purposes, their support lies in the realms of demography, sociology, social psychology, and world history rather than in that of geography.

Insofar as societies can be characterized as *old* or *young*, both types have existed at some time in most areas of the world, usually correlated with the degree of exhaustion of resources under a given technology. Rejuvenation may come through invention or trade, or through the discovery and utilization of new resources. Such a development may be the consequence of a revolutionary ideology or of foreign intervention. The old, soil-exhausted Italy of antiquity was rejuvenated by the energy of Christian faith in the Middle Ages and by the rivalry of territorial princes in developing handicrafts and trade in the Renaissance. Old Russia may have been rejuvenated through the industrialization and better exploitation of minerals and power resources by the Soviets. Old Arabia may be in process of rejuvenation through the exploitation of petroleum by American companies. While the aging and decline of states and civilizations may be attributed to changes in the environment through exhaustion of resources, revival is usually to be attributed to psychological, social, economic, technological, and political changes.

Policies. Governments develop domestic policies to preserve order, to administer justice, and to promote prosperity, and they develop foreign policies for defense against invasion, improvement of power position, maintenance of the balance of power, and increase of prosperity through international trade. Geographical influences can be traced in both foreign and domestic policies. Large states are usually composed of a number of distinctive geographical regions, the interests of which differ, requiring continuous compromise of domestic policies and militating against the pursuit of a foreign policy utilizing resources and geographical position to maximize the defense and prosperity of the state as a whole. Policies aimed at utilizing a state's resources with greatest efficiency, whether for domestic consumption or foreign trade, may be inconsistent with the policies best calculated to promote domestic tranquility and international security. Thus there may be conflicts, not only between domestic and foreign policies, but also between economic and political policies.

Solution of these problems involves knowledge of geographical facts, but the principles lie rather in the realms of politics and economics than of geography.

It is perhaps in the realm of global defense strategy that geography has been most emphasized. The Monroe Doctrine that dominated American policy during the nineteenth century was said to be founded upon the geographical fact of continental isolation. The British policy of maintaining a dominant navy and an equilibrium of power on the European continent was facilitated if not dictated by its insular position (23). The Prussian policy of military efficiency was influenced by its continental position and its lack of natural barriers to invasion from either east or west (36).

The sea power school of strategic thinking initiated by Admiral Mahan (23) held that a state with predominant sea power, including an adequate navy, a maritime-minded population developed by a large merchant marine, well-distributed bases, and control of narrow waterways could dominate world politics through use of this power to blockade and strangle its rivals.

More recently the land power school developed by MacKinder, Kjellen, and Haushofer has held that domination of the "heartland" (Eastern Germany, Russia, and Siberia) of the "world continent" (Eurasia) permits control of the "rim lands" (Western Europe, Middle East, India, and

China). Control of these permits control of the off-shore islands (Great Britain, Africa, Indonesia, and Japan and the transoceanic islands (the Americas and Australia (20, 36).

These theories are on the one hand an historic generalization of the position and policy of the British Empire during the seventeenth, eighteenth, and nineteenth centuries, and on the other, an hypothesis supporting efforts at world conquest by Germany or the Soviet Union. The latter theory could hardly command attention until the development of railroad networks and later the airplane had augmented the speed of land movement, made utilization of interior lines on a vast scale feasible, and made rim lands and off-shore islands more vulnerable to attack from the continent. Clearly the relative validity of these theories depends on the technology of war, of transportation, and of production. The steamship (more dependent on bases than was the sailing ship), the railroad, the airplane, and the high degree of autarchy maintainable by great powers through co-ordination of their resources have greatly reduced the influence of sea power.

Aware of these changes, even before the airplane had come into use, Sir Halford MacKinder, a Britisher, appreciated the extreme vulnerability of the British Empire if the "heartland" should come under the domination of a single power. He, therefore, reasserted the policy, always recognized by Britain, of preserving the continental balance of power and of maintaining alliances with "rim-lands" and island states (20). Nicholas Spykman from an American point of view has given a similar emphasis, pointing out the great disparity in power, both human and material, between the American and the Eurasian continents if the latter were united, the impossibility of continental defense of the Americas in the air and submarine age, and the strategic necessity that America ally itself with off-shore island and rim-land states of the Eurasian continent and that it maintain an equilibrium among the great powers of the heartland (34).

Significant as have been these generalizations in modern world politics, they are generalizations of the disciplines of international politics and the art of war rather than of geography.

Political boundaries present a point of view from which all of international relations may be examined. The problem of boundaries brings geography into close contact with international law, international economics, international organization, and international politics. This problem involves four processes which may be denominated demarcation, delimitation, territorial adjustment, and foreign policy (14).

Demarcation, a term differentiated from delimitation by Sir Henry McMahon in 1897 (1, 22), refers to the process of marking on the ground a boundary already delimited by agreement or by unilateral action. It involves surveying and setting monuments, but often there is a wide range for interpretation because agreements or other documents may have been made with imperfect geographical knowledge. International law may provide guides for demarcation if a boundary is delimited by such natural features as a river, a mountain range, a watershed, a bay, or a lake, and international organizations may provide procedures of arbitration, investigation, or conciliation to solve differences of interpretation.

Delimitation refers to the achievement of a documentary description of a boundary by agreement, legislation, decree, or award. Demarcation takes place on the ground while delimitation takes place on paper. In most periods of history boundaries have been zones of slight habitation, usually because of inhospitable geographic conditions, and precise delimitation by agreement has not been considered necessary. States have sometimes unilaterally both delimited and demarcated the limits of their territory by artificial structures such as the Great Wall of China or the Roman Walls in England, Syria, and elsewhere. As population grows in boundary zones between two states which recognize each other, precise delimitation by agreement becomes necessary. Treaties often terminating wars describe the boundary in more or less detail and with more or less precision sometimes following lines of military occupation (*uti possidetis*), and sometimes restoring prewar boundaries. This process, while indicated in the earliest known treaty, that between Lagash and Umma, states of Mesopotamia in the third millenium B.C. (25), has been characteristic of European states only since the sixteenth century and of Asian states only since the nineteenth century. Boundaries in the American and African continents often originated in decrees of imperial powers dividing their domains for administrative purposes or in treaties between European colonial powers, though subsequent treaties and arbitrations between independent states in these continents have more precisely delimited their boundaries. In the process of delimitation as of demarcation, international law and international organization may play an important part, as also may the processes of war and diplomacy (1).

Delimitation by treaty is not possible unless there has been a basic adjustment of territorial claims. Whenever a large area is in dispute, the problem of such adjustment arises. To effect it, different principles have been appealed to in different historical periods—hereditary title of princes; titles under documents supported by international law; the principles of nationality, of self-determination, and of plebiscite; diplomatic compromise on economic, strategic, political, and cultural interests; diplomatic bargaining and trading of areas in one part of the world for those in another or for considerations of different types; and superior power manifested by occupation and completed conquest of the area. Detailed geographic information concerning the disputed area may be of value for pacific settlement of such controversies. Most geographers, as well as diplomats and lawyers, recognize that there is no master principle for determining a perfect boundary or for settling boundary disputes. Natural barriers to sudden invasion such as seas, mountains, rivers, and deserts have often been accepted (15).

There have been differences of opinion as to whether states should be homogeneous in regard to geographic and cultural characteristics. Advocates of the principle of nationality like Mazzini have insisted upon the value of a considerable degree of homogeneity, and recent studies suggest that barriers to easy communication among groups militate against the success of a common government (9). In fact, however, states of large size have usually been in considerable measure heterogeneous in regard to geographic characteristics, culture, language, economic activities, and even law, though they have had to recognize increasing autonomy in differentiated areas as these areas developed in technology and knowledge. Some historians like Lord Acton have pointed out the advantage of the complementarity and toleration which may flow from such heterogeneity (50). It is clear that if heterogeneity is considered desirable, boundary claims cannot be settled by any political principle. War and conquest have often settled such controversies, but international law and international organization have increasingly discouraged this method (14, 18, 47, 49). International law can, it is true, in the present state of the world decide any boundary controversy by weighing claims of occupation, prescription, accretion, agreement, and documentary interpretation in accord with the support given them by the evidence and the sources. But such decisions will seldom settle a dispute, because usually at least one of the states bases its claim upon economic, political, cultural, or other considerations which it deems sufficiently important to justify ignoring the law. The problem of territorial adjustment is political rather than legal in character (14).

Back of territorial claims lies the general policy of a state, and back of that its culture, economy, and power. If statecraft is the art of maximizing the prosperity and security of the state, states might be expected to be as anxious to get rid of burdensome territory as to acquire desirable territory. A territory may be economically burdensome and strategically indefensible, its people may be politically dissident and socially unassimilable, yet states have seldom surrendered territory wholly voluntarily. The British recognition of the independence of the dominions, and acknowledgment of the dominion status of India, Pakistan, and Ceylon and of the independence of Burma, Egypt, and Iraq, and the American recognition of the independence of Cuba and the Philippines are in some measure instances to the contrary. The Dutch recognition of Indonesia and the French recognition of Syria, Lebanon, and the Indo-Chinese states were not entirely voluntary.

States have sometimes in fact abandoned useless territory as seems to have been true of the Falklands in the eighteenth century, but in such instances they have usually attempted to retain legal title resulting in subsequent controversy like that between Britain and Argentina in this instance.

More frequently states have sought to expand their territories, for such reasons as necessity for strategic defense, augmentation of great power position, increase in prestige, prevention of acquisition of the territory by a rival, certain access to economic resources or markets, more *lebensraum* for its population, union of people of the same nationality, or expansion of religion, ideology, or culture. Sometimes the development of backward people or of economic resources needed by the world's population have been given as reasons. The reasons given indicate the state of world politics, of strategy, of world economy, and of world opinion at the moment and also the particular philosophy dominating the policy of the state advancing the claim (14, 47).

In the modern state system territory has been regarded as an evidence of power and a universal value, much as money is a universal value in modern economics. This doubtless accounts for the reluctance of states to abandon territory and their general desire to acquire it whenever possible. It also gives support for, and is supported by, the evolutionary analogy, of dubious validity, which holds that a territorially expanding state is fit to survive and a territorially declining state is not. In fact, huge empires have not been more enduring than many small and compact states, and empires built rapidly such as those of Hitler, of Mussolini, and of Japan in the 1930's have often disintegrated with equal rapidity.

In modern times the concept of territorial sovereignty has manifested the universal value accorded to territory and has been manifested in the importance attached to the precise delimitation and demarcation of boundaries. The degree in which that concept dominates thinking is indicated by the actual functioning of boundaries. They may be characterized by barbed wire entanglements and fortifications; they may, on the other hand, be indicated by scarcely noticed markers in wheat fields, forests, deserts, or even in a city street traversed without obstruction. Where the latter condition prevails, tensions are slight and boundaries may become imaginary lines of little significance for travel, trade, and culture as are, with rare exception, boundaries between states of the United States. Where the former condition prevails, boundaries may be an iron curtain dividing populations in all aspects of life and manifesting extreme interpretations of sovereignty and extreme tension. These differences indicate that the significance of boundaries is a problem in the realm of politics, economics, or sociology rather than of geography.

Centers of power. World history has indicated a shifting of power in the western world from Egypt and Mesopotamia; to Greece and Rome; then to Spain, France, England and Germany; and finally to the United

States and Russia. There have also been shifts in the centers of power in South Asia and the Far East, in North Asia, in pre-Columbian Mexico, and in the power relations of Asiatic areas with the centers of Europe and America. Can geography provide evidence to predict these movements of the centers of power in the future?

As already noted, under a given state of the arts, one environment is more suitable for power development than is another. Furthermore, power may shift because of the exhaustion of resources or perhaps because of climatic changes. Major factors in these shifts, however, have been changes in the arts, in the economic and military value of resources, in the growth of population, and in skills in utilizing resources and in organizing political and military power. Geography can assist in interpreting the historical record, but the nongeographical factors are so important that it is unlikely that geography will ever be able to provide principles or evidence for predicting where the major centers of power will be in the future. Alexis de Tocqueville, in his famous prediction made in the 1830's that the United States and Russia would become the major power centers of the world, emphasized political institutions and capabilities as well as the geographic conditions of these two countries (8).

CRITICISM

It has been the hope of some geographers that because of the apparent permanence of geographic conditions, geography might become the master science of international relations. This hope seems vain. Geography is primarily a descriptive discipline. It provides evidence, as does history, for generalization by the disciplines of politics, economics, sociology, and psychology, and it may itself make a few empirical generalizations. Geography, however, does not determine international relations.

Furthermore, the apparent permanence of geographical conditions is illusory. The human significance of geography depends on the conditions of society, population, and technology. Civilized man uses his environment to serve ends which come from other sources. He must know the properties of his position, terrain, climate, and resources, as the chemist must know the properties of the elements. These properties can be put to many uses, can serve many ends, and can support many types of international relations. Geography cannot develop concepts and conceptual systems applicable beyond a limited time and area in which a given state of the arts, of population, and of society can be assumed. Political geography may be combined with demography and technology to develop a discipline concerning the material conditions of international relations, but to develop a general theory of international relations it must be combined with these and with social psychology, sociology and ethics.

REFERENCES

1. Boggs, W. Whittemore, *International Boundaries—A Study of Boundary Functions and Problems* (New York, Columbia University Press, 1940).
2. Bowman, Isaiah, *The New World, Problems of Political Geography* (New York, World Book Co., 1921; 4th ed., 1928).
3. ———, *The Pioneer Fringe* (New York, American Geographical Society, 1931).
4. Brunhes, Jean, *Human Geography*, trans. by T. C. LeCompte (Chicago, Rand McNally, 1920).
5. Colby, Charles C., ed., *Geographical Aspects of International Relations*, Harris Institute Lectures (Chicago, University of Chicago Press, 1938).
6. Commission to Study the Organization of Peace, *Security and World Organization*, 4th Report, International Conciliation, No. 396 (January, 1944); *Security Through the United Nations*, 5th Report, International Conciliation, No. 432 (June, 1947); *Regional Arrangements for Security and the United Nations*, 8th Report (June, 1953).
7. Davis, D. H., *The Earth and Man*, rev. ed. (New York, Macmillan, 1948).
8. De Tocqueville, Alexis, *Democracy in America*, 1832 (New York, Barnes, 1862).
9. Deutsch, Karl, *Nationalism and Social Communication* (New York, Wiley, 1953).
10. Febvre, L. P. V., *A Geographical Introduction to History*, trans. by E. G. Mountford and J. H. Paxton (London, Kegan Paul, 1925).
11. Fitzgibbon, Russell H., ed., *Global Politics* (Berkeley, University of California Press, 1944).
12. Gyorgy, Andrew, *Geopolitics: The New German Science* (Berkeley, University of California Press, 1944).
13. Hartshorne, Richard, "Recent Developments in Political Geography," *American Political Science Review*, Vol. 9 (October, December, 1935), pp. 785 ff., 943 ff.
14. Hill, Norman, *Title to Territory* (London, Oxford University Press, 1945).
15. Holdich, Thomas H., *Political Frontiers and Boundary Making* (London, Macmillan, 1916).
16. Huntington, Ellsworth, *Civilization and Climate* (New Haven, Yale University Press, 1915).
17. ———, *Mainsprings of Civilization* (New York, Wiley, 1945).
18. Langer, Robert, *Seizure of Territory* (Princeton, Princeton University Press, 1947).
19. Lebon, J. H. G., *Human Geography* (New York, Longmans, 1952).
20. MacKinder, Sir Halford J., *The Geographical Pivot of History* (Royal Geographical Society, London, 1904).
21. ———, *Democratic Ideals and Reality, A Study in the Politics of Reconstruction* (New York, Holt, 1919).
22. McMahon, Sir A. Henry, "International Boundaries," *Journal of Royal Society of Arts* (November, 1935), col. 84, pp. 2-16.
23. Mahan, Admiral Alfred T., *The Influence of Sea Power on History, 1660-1783* (1890); 16th ed. (Boston, Little, Brown, 1902).
24. Moodie, A. E., *Geography Behind Politics* (London, Hutchinson University Library, 1947).
25. Nussbaum, Arthur, *A Concise History of The Law of Nations* (New York, Macmillan, 1947).

26. PEARCY, G. Etzel, FIFIELD, Russell H., and others, *World Political Geography* (New York, Crowell, 1948).
27. PEATTIE, Roderick, *Geography in Human Destiny* (New York, G. W. Stewart, 1940).
28. RATZEL, Friedrich, *Anthropogeographie*, 2nd ed. (Stuttgart, 1899-1912), 2 vols.
29. RENNER, George T., *Human Geography in the Air Age* (New York, Macmillan, 1942).
30. ———, and others, *Global Geography* (New York, Crowell, 1944).
31. RUSSELL, Richard J., and KNIFFEN, Fred B., *Culture Worlds* (New York, Macmillan, 1950).
32. SAUER, Carl, "Geography, Cultural," *Encyclopædia of the Social Sciences*.
33. SEMPLE, Ellen C., *American History and Its Geographic Conditions*, rev. ed. (Boston, Houghton Mifflin, 1933).
34. SPYKMAN, Nicholas J., *American Strategy in World Politics, The United States and the Balance of Power* (New York, Harcourt, 1942).
35. ———, *The Geography of Peace*, ed. by Helen R. Nichol with introduction by Frederick S. Dunn (New York, Harcourt, 1944).
36. STRAUSZ-HUPÉ, Robert, *Geo-politics: The Struggle for Space and Power* (New York, Putnam, 1942).
37. TAYLOR, Griffith, *Environment and Race* (London, Oxford University Press, 1927).
38. ———, *Environment and Nations* (Chicago, University of Chicago Press, 1936).
39. TOYNBEE, Arnold J., *A Study of History* (London, Oxford University Press, 1934, 1939, 1954), 10 vols.
40. VALLAUX, Camille, "Geography, Human," *Encyclopædia of the Social Sciences*.
41. VAN VALKENBURG, Samuel, *Elements of Political Geography* (New York, Prentice Hall, 1940).
42. VON ENGELN, O. D., *Inheriting the Earth or the Geographical Factor in National Development* (New York, Macmillan, 1922).
43. WEIGERT, Hans W., and STEFANSSON, Vilhjalmur, eds., *Compass of the World* (New York, Macmillan, 1944).
44. ———, *New Compass of the World, A Symposium on Political Geography* (New York, Macmillan, 1949).
45. WHITTLESEY, Derwent, *The Earth and the State, A Study of Political Geography* (New York, Holt, 1939).
46. WOOLDRIDGE, S. W., and EAST, W. G., *The Spirit and Purpose of Geography* (New York, Longmans, 1950).
47. WRIGHT, Quincy, *A Study of War* (Chicago, University of Chicago Press, 1942), pp. 60-64, 109-110, 123-124, 137, 220-223, 278 ff., 450-470, 548-554, 702, 767 ff., 848 ff., 1151, 1240 ff.
48. ———, *Problems of Stability and Progress in International Relations* (Berkeley, University of California Press, 1954).
49. ———, *Legal Problems in the Far Eastern Conflict* (New York, Institute of Pacific Relations, 1941).
50. ZIMMERN, Sir Alfred, ed., *Modern Political Doctrines* (London, Oxford University Press, 1939).

Political Demography

DEFINITION

POLITICAL DEMOGRAPHY is the science relating population to politics and to the state. As a discipline of international relations it is the science relating the world's population to world politics, and the art of employing population and migration controls, and eugenics in world politics. It may also refer to a philosophy which attributes determining, or at least, major, influence upon culture, civilization, international relations, and foreign policies to the static and dynamic conditions of the world's population.

Demography in the general sense has been defined as "the science of population," as "vital statistics," and as "the mathematical knowledge of the general movements and the physical, social, intellectual and moral conditions of populations" (56). The world's population may be subdivided for statistical purposes by the areas of habitation (states, regions, continents, or other political or geographic divisions); by the age, sex, race, or other physical characteristics of its components; by the language, religion, nationality, ideology, or other cultural characteristics of its components; or by the technological skills, standards of living, urbanization, occupation, or other economic characteristics of its components. Correlations may be made between these various classes suggesting significant relationships. Basic information on these matters is provided periodically by censuses in many parts of the world, but in much of Asia, Africa, and South America this information is incomplete or entirely lacking (17, 20, 29).

More significant politically is information on the dynamics of population change, such as birth, death, marriage, fertility, fecundity, and migration rates, and rates of change in age and sex ratios and in standards of living, occupation, and cultural characteristics. Registrations of births, marriages, and deaths required by law in many countries add to the data of periodical censuses from which such rates of change may be derived (55). Such data on the dynamics of a population makes possible prediction of social, cultural, economic, and political changes, with, it is true, a considerable margin of error, due especially to the opportunity and the stimulus which such predictions give for governments, groups, and persons to control population movements (29, 30, 35).

Census taking was occasionally practiced by some states of antiquity, but the practice came to an end in the dark ages. Vital statistics began to be recorded in certain European countries in the sixteenth century. It was not, however, until the eighteenth century that modern states began to make periodical censuses and only in the nineteenth century was there sufficient data from censuses and registrations to permit the development of demography as a discipline (20, 30). The term was first employed by Achille Guillard in 1855 (21).

It cannot be said that a special discipline of *political demography* has emerged. The data for demographic study is, however, generally collected by national governments for political purposes, such as taxation, military recruitment, and economic and social planning. Consequently, it is nearly always classified primarily by states. Partly for this reason, demography as a discipline has always paid much attention to the influence of population movements on public policy, and especially on international relations. Demographers have recognized that the national differences in rates of change of certain population variables would influence the relative power position and standards of living of the nations, both matters of prime importance in the formulation of national foreign policies. Statesmen have recognized that the political significance of a territorial transfer was in considerable measure dependent upon the size and characteristics of the population inhabiting the area. Consequently, international political conferences have often had committees to provide such information in regard to controversial territories. This was true at Vienna in 1815 and at Paris in 1919. The conditions, therefore, seem to exist for recognizing political demography as a discipline distinct from economic and social demography, although the three are closely related.

ASSUMPTIONS

Political demography assumes (a) that the conditions and the changes of population influence national and international policies and institutions, (b) that national and international policies and institutions influence the conditions and changes of population, (c) that sovereign territorial states exist and that each seeks to regulate its population in order to improve its power position and the economic welfare of its people, and (d) that the rapid growth of the world's population, characteristic of the past few centuries, is likely to continue and to affect profoundly the general characteristics of international politics.

Some demographers have attributed a determining influence upon international politics to population changes, usually assuming that the population growth of a nation would inevitably produce pressures for expansion and war (4, 50). Many now recognize that these relations are far more complicated than this simple statement implies. A few assume that general increase in the world's population will produce pressure for more effective international co-operation (2, 6). Diverse as are opinions, no one questions that population change is an influence on world politics (59).

During much of history, people have looked upon the general situation and changes of population as part of the order of nature which, like climate and geographic conditions, could not be controlled, although in fact customs such as abortion and infanticide, war and migration, actually have maintained population stability among many peoples and have sometimes exerted a selective influence (9). It is now generally assumed by governments and international organizations that both the quantity and quality of population can be regulated by limitations or incentives to births (42, 45) and migrations (17), by development of medical and public health programs, and by technological changes improving agriculture, industry, and commerce (2, 6, 13, 15, 20, 26). Restrictive, expansive, and eugenic policies, both customary and legislative, are to be found in most states (49).

The vast differences in the rates of change of significant population variables among different countries indicate the effectiveness of policy and conditions in these fields. Thus birth rates vary from nearly 40 per 1000 in Bulgaria, Chile, Egypt, and India to less than half that number in Western Europe and the United States. Death rates vary from over 25 per 1000 in Chile, Egypt, India, and other countries to less than 10 per 1000 in Holland, New Zealand, and the white population of South Africa. Natural increases in population therefore vary from over 17 per 1000 in Bulgaria, Egypt, and South Africa to less than 2 per 1000 in France (30). Migration rates are even more variable. The United States has continually gained population from immigration, during some years in the early twentieth century as much as by natural increase, some 8 per 1000, while other countries have lost population by emigration (16, 17). Fertility rates, or the average number of children per woman of child-bearing age (15 to 49), have also varied greatly, the drop in all western countries since the mid-nineteenth century being of the order of 50 per cent (29). The effect of these quantitative changes and of the policies or conditions which produce them upon the quality of the population is highly controversial. Positive policies with eugenic intention have been more common in the field of migration regulations than of birth or death regulation (11, 12, 15, 28).

It is the assumption of international politics that states seek to improve their power position and the welfare of their people. Clearly population changes affect both of these policies though often in opposite senses, since rising population tends to increase the ease of recruiting soldiers but, according to the Malthusian theory (34), to diminish the standard of living. These tendencies are, however, influenced by developments in the field of technology and education. Thus the relations of population change to either security or welfare policies is not simple (2, 26, 59).

So also the precise effect on international politics of a rising world population is dependent on many factors. General changes in population have accompanied rises and falls of civilizations in the past. Population increased during the rise of classical civilization in the Mediterranean until the third century when a decline began which continued for several centuries. Europe's population in the seventh century was probably less than half of what it had been in the third century. With the development of medieval civilization in Europe there was another rise reaching a maximum in the early fourteenth century, perhaps equal to that of the classical period. A sharp decline began with the Black Death in the mid-fourteenth century continuing until a rise began a century later reaching unparalleled heights in the twentieth century, some nine times as great as the height of population in antiquity and the middle ages. The greatest gains were in the areas outside the ancient Roman Empire. Doubtless this parallelism in the rise and fall of civilization and of population is the consequence of complicated interactions. It can neither be said that rising civilization necessarily causes an increase in population, nor that an increasing population causes a development of civilization. The parallelism is to be noted, however, not only in Europe but also in other parts of the world (59).

It is to be expected that continued increase in the world's population, one aspect of the *shrinking world*, would in the future produce greater pressure on resources and closer contact of peoples, but the political and social consequences depend on numerous other factors, especially those in the realms of technology, social structure, and social policy. It is usually assumed that the world's population will continue to increase for a long time, consequently calculations have been made of the maximum population which the world's resources can support. These estimates have varied from twice to five times the present population (15, 20, 38, 59). In some areas, especially western Europe, population appears to have reached a condition of stagnation (29).

ANALYSIS

Assuming that population changes and public policies reciprocally influence one another, that national governments have basic objectives of security and prosperity, and that changes in the world's population exert an important influence on world politics, demographers have been concerned with (*a*) the rates and characteristics of changes in the population of the world and of the nations; and with the relation of these changes (*b*) to standards of living, and (*c*) social values; to the (*d*) power position, and (*e*) national policies of the various nations; and (*f*) to the system of world politics and international organization. Their prime interest has been in discovering the facts. Even the best censuses are insufficiently accurate and comprehensive to permit of some of the correlations which demographers would like to make. In vast areas of the world little but a bare enumeration is available and in some areas even this is uncertain. Estimates of the population of China, for example, vary from over 600 million to under 300 million (17, 30, 59). Demographers, though employing elaborate statistical methods to correlate diverse aspects of population change, appreciate that the data is sufficient to justify such refined methods only in a few countries and for short periods of time (20, 60). For most areas and for most of history the crude estimates of population change can be utilized, only as historians and geographers use them, to supplement other types of evidence concerning the causes of change (47, 49).

The future of population. In spite of the inadequacy of present data, demographers have sought to project the present population trends of the principal nations and of the world into the future. Some have attempted to develop a general logistic curve indicating the changes in time, not only of human population, but also of other organic populations, and to locate on such a curve the present position of each nation, thus permitting prediction of changes in growth rates and of the date at which each nation may reach a condition of stability. Such a curve can be fitted to the growth of an organism which can be regarded as a population of cells growing at a decreasing rate until a point of maximum size is reached after which there is little change during the life of the organism. Fruit flies in a bottle multiply up to a point of stability in accord with a similar curve (38, 47). Most demographers, however, believe that changes in technology, culture and social institutions, developments of international trade, exploitation of new resources, and other factors are so continuous in modern nations that a regular curve, dependent on the constancy of such factors, is not to be expected.

The method of projection favored by demographers depends on examination of fertility and fecundity rates and death rates at different ages, in different classes of the population. Such methods applied before World

War II suggested a maximum United States population of some 170 million by 1970, after which there would be relative stability (31, 35, 49). The census of 1950, however, tended to modify such predictions because of the unexpected increase during the preceding decade. There were predictions in 1953 that population would exceed 200 million in the 1970's, and would reach 375 million by 2050 (43).

Another method is to assume the unlimited capacity of man to invent technologies to exploit the earth's resources, and to estimate the quantity of the resource which sets the final limit to population expansion. The present tendency is to regard certain mineral fertilizers such as phosphates and sources of energy as the limiting factor in world population rather than the amount of arable land (43). On such bases demographers have estimated the maximum world population as from five to ten billion (15, 20). The development of energy from nuclear fission may modify these estimates.

Others have believed that rising standards of living and conventions of civilization lead to declining fecundity (capacity to bear children) or to declining fertility (actual bearing of children), and that, therefore, stability or even decline of the world's population will begin long before the maximum exploitation of resources has established a limit (20, 38, 59). While a decline in fecundity has not been established, it is clear that fertility has declined greatly in some states (29).

Finally, population projection has sometimes been based on the discrimination of fundamental population types such as (a) relatively stable populations with very high birth rates and very high death rates, (b) rapidly growing populations with high birth rates and low death rates, and (c) relatively stable populations with low birth rates and low death rates (10). Primitive peoples are to be found in all of these classes, as also are civilized peoples (9, 38). These types are not sharply distinguished, because both birth and death rates vary continuously between wide limits, but they provide bases for rational speculation upon probable population policies and trends.

The first type is represented by predominantly agricultural populations with no effective policies or techniques for dealing with either birth or death rates. Production determined by the area under cultivation and the customary agricultural techniques is stable. High birth rates soon push population to the point of subsistence and high death rates from famine and pestilence keep it there. China has apparently been in this situation.

The second type is marked by populations in the early stages of agricultural expansion or industrialization. The exploitation of new lands, or the activities of an efficient government, an enlightened rural aristocracy or an urban population managing industry and commerce have increased productiveness making possible population growth. Some progress in sanitation and medical practice has reduced the death rate, but the birth rate remains high because the higher standards developed for themselves by the aristocracy or the urban managers, have not penetrated to the masses of the agricultural and working population. Examples of this type were to be found in western Europe and the United States in the nineteenth century. India, Russia, and Latin America are in this class today.

The third type is marked by populations in the later stages of industrialization, when over half of the population is urbanized. Higher standards of living have influenced all classes of the population to limit family size, and technical devices to this end have become publicized and widely distributed. At the same time public health and medical practice have greatly prolonged the expectation of life diminishing the death rate especially infant mortality. The United States and most of western Europe are approaching this stage. Urbanized commercial populations even though based on servile classes have in past civilizations sometimes approximated this type for brief periods.

Clearly the criteria for predicting the future of these different types will be quite different. The first type may increase rapidly, moving into the second type through policies increasing production by industrialization and agricultural improvement, eliminating local famines by grain transport and storage, and eliminating epidemics by sanitary and medical measures. While the first type of population may suffer heavy temporary losses through war, famine, or disease, it will rapidly regain its normal size because of the high birth rate and the probability that the death rate will decline in the local areas where, after disaster, food will be more abundant. Public policy may bring about rapid increases in such a population but, apart from policy, relative stability can be anticipated. Prediction depends upon knowledge of, or influence upon, the policy of the government.

Changes in populations of the second type are difficult to predict. Continuance of the existing rate of increase depends upon continuance of a declining death rate, possible only if production keeps ahead of population growth, and continuance of a high birth rate, probable only if the average standard of living does not rise. Prediction of the growth of production involves consideration of the probabilities of invention or importation of new technologies, of capital growth, of international trade, of the health and economic efficiency of the population, in fact, of the whole economy. Is per capita income likely to increase or diminish with the existing rate of population growth? Prediction of the rapidity of the penetration of higher standards of living and population control methods among the masses depends upon estimate of the resistance which the social, cultural, and religious characteristics of the people offer to the acceptance of new values, and estimate of the disposition of the government and leaders of society to encourage such changes (2, 23, 39, 46, 57). While there was a tendency in the nineteenth century for populations of this kind to move into the third type because of improvements in both technology and living standards, the rate at which this occurred varied greatly.

The third type of population is perhaps less difficult to predict because its low birth rate is not likely to increase rapidly and sets a limit to the rapidity of population increase. Furthermore, the death rate is usually so low that it cannot be greatly reduced. Such populations may, however, decrease at an accelerating rate. The average age is much greater than in populations of the first and second type. A war or epidemic suddenly killing off many women of child-bearing age may be devastating. On the other hand certain improvements of economic conditions may result in some increase in the birth rate which, with the low normal death rate, will increase the population. It does not appear that such populations lack fecundity but rather that they limit fertility voluntarily (15, 18, 49).

Doubtless improved data, more refined classifications, and more elaborate statistical methods will increase the validity of population projections, but it seems likely that such projections will always be of slight validity for periods beyond a few decades into the future. It is certain that the influence of policies upon production and health, and the influence of education and communication upon technological advance and social standards, matters outside the study of population itself, will have to be considered if such projections are to be valid.

Standard of living. What is the effect of changes in population upon standards of living and levels of living? These terms, which refer respectively to the subjective and objective conditions of life, are closely related. Economic capacity to maintain a higher level of living is likely to develop the desire for a higher standard of living, and such a desire is likely to direct energy and effort in order that the actual level may reach the standard (31).

This was the problem considered by T. R. Malthus which initiated the modern discipline of demography (34, 56, 57). His conclusion was that population tended to increase more rapidly than the food supply. He suggested that the first grew by geometric progression, the second by arithmetic progression. Thus increases in production would permit more to live, increasing the population but not the level of living. He thought the positive checks on population—disease, famine, and war—would always be more important in keeping population down to the production capacity of the country than moral checks such as celibacy, delayed marriage, or sexual restraint.

The history of the nineteenth century in Europe seemed to refute Malthus' theory by exhibiting remarkable peacefulness, a rising average level of living, and in the latter part of the century a more equitable distribution of production together with an unparalleled increase in population. The Malthusianists, however, attributed this to the extraordinary increase in productiveness arising from inventions in the fields of production, transportation, and communication initiating the industrial revolution, coupled with the opportunity presented by the opening of overseas countries from which foodstuffs and raw materials could be imported cheaply. This condition, they thought, was not likely to recur (18).

However, production has continued to accelerate and in addition population has ceased to increase in western Europe. Thus Malthus' fatal proportion has seemed to many demographers far from inevitable. Production may, they think, continually keep ahead of population thus permitting a continuous rise in levels of living stabilized by the development of high standards of living in the culture and family limitation to realize them (2, 57).

Pessimists, however, point to the limitations of the earth's resources—top soils are being washed away, minerals are being mined and dissipated, and sources of power such as coal and petroleum, stored up through geological ages, are being burned up at an extraordinary rate. Furthermore, while in western Europe and North America population is relatively stable, it is still increasing rapidly in other parts of the world. Thus the human race as a whole is increasing while it dissipates irreplaceable resources. Eventually, it is insisted, there will be a day of reckoning and whatever technological advance may have been made it will be found that the raw materials of production will be insufficient to support the world's population (8, 37, 54).

Critics of this position do not deny the facts but point to the possibility of substituting new types of power (hydro-electric, tides, solar engines, nuclear fission or algae grown in trays for fuel), of revitalizing worn-out soils, of expanding agriculture by the suitable use of mineral fertilizers, and of utilizing minerals such as aluminum of which the supply is almost unlimited. By such technological developments they believe that the world's population can continue to grow for centuries with rising levels of living (2, 36, 43). The eugenicists believe the quality of the human race may be improved by sterilization of defectives and marital preference for the superior, thus increasing the rationality of human decisions and the average productiveness of populations (11, 15, 20, 27, 28). Others anticipate similar results from better dietetics, education, and public health (2, 6, 7, 13). While there is a limit to the world's population, it is believed that the development of higher standards of living and of intelligence generally will result in population limitations long before this limit is reached.

Certainly there is no simple relation between population and levels of living. With particular reference to political demography, there is no condition of population which creates a *necessity* for migration, conquest, or any other international policy of violent character as the only alternative to submitting to population decimations by famine or disease. Civilized man, different from his primitive ancestors, always has alternatives of policy to meet the basic problem of maintaining the national level of living or even of increasing it to meet higher standards, in the face of increasing population (59).

Social values. What is the influence of the population situation of a country upon its culture and values? It has been suggested that populations of the first type with a high birth rate and a high death rate tend to be guided by custom, those of the second type with a high birth rate and a declining death rate by conscience, and those of the third type with a low birth rate and a low death rate by opinion (44). In the first situation, life is hard. There is little leisure and little belief in the capacity of man to control the conditions of his life. Life becomes a routine governed by custom and tradition. Such people tend to be lethargic and not to disturb the peace of nations, however grievous may be their lot. Security and satisfaction is found not in material comforts but in family and local relationships. Through much of their history civilizations of the past have been of this type. Population has been stable and there has been a wide differential between the few governors and the impoverished masses.

Where population is increasing, actually or potentially, because man has begun to control his economy and his health, a larger leisure class develops given to thinking and planning, and the population more generally perceives the capacity of man to control the conditions of his life. Under such circumstances ideologies and religions develop designed in varying degrees to reconcile man to his conditions and to stimulate him to improve them. In the past, the religions and ideologies of the West have tended to the latter character while those of southern and eastern Asia have tended to the former. Through the influence of these ideologies and religions, man has become endowed with a conscience which has encouraged resignation or driven to activity, and society as a whole has acquired ideals of stability or of progress toward goals established by the ideology or religion. General conditions of living may not have improved because of the continued high birth rate but life has been guided more by conscious goals and less by customary routines. There appear to have been periods of rising population developing these conditions in ancient Egypt, Mesopotamia, Persia, India, and China and in the West during Roman expansion, the Crusades, and the last three centuries (40).

Under such conditions, the possibility of higher general standards of living may be perceived and movements to realize them may develop, perhaps leading to technological advances or expansion into new land, eventuating in higher levels of living and diminutions of the birth rate. When this happens, and population becomes stabilized with a low birth rate and a low death rate, higher standards of living may develop progressively; there will be more leisure, more education, more attention to eugenics and health, more belief in progress and in the efficacy of effort, more development of science and technology, and more active planning of human and social life by individual associations and governments. Under such circumstances, conditions change rapidly, there is less belief either in custom or in traditional ideologies and religions which originated under different conditions. People and societies tend to be directed by opinion. Public opinion tends to become the guide for law, morals, and practical action, superseding the idea of natural law derived from custom or of moral law derived from traditional ideologies. Such conditions may have existed in a measure in Periclean Greece, Virgilian Rome, and Renaissance Italy, but the structure rested on a servile class. Until the more general realization of these conditions in nineteenth century Europe and America, periods governed by opinion have been rare, unstable, and brief (59).

While the population situation doubtless has influence on these changes of value pattern, it is not the only factor. Conditions of communication are equally important. In fact, these three types of society may be related to the degree of use of language, of writing, and of mass communications. Only with the latter, can opinion, with its relative flexibility, become a major guide to individual and social conduct.

The techniques of production, the system of distribution, and the special characteristics of the cultural and ideological tradition are also influential. Some ideologies are more resistant to continuous change than are others.

Undoubtedly these three types of cultural characteristics tend to influence international relations. Under conditions of rapid change, *opinion directed* peoples may, if suitably educated, be more capable of international conciliation and adjustment than are *conscience directed* peoples, or *custom directed* peoples. The two latter tend to move with implacability in the direction demanded by ancient custom or by values treated as absolute. Only *opinion directed* people have the possibility of appreciating the relativity of values and of rapidly accommodating them to changing circumstances. As the world shrinks and history accelerates, flexibility in value patterns becomes more and more important if stability is to be preserved and devastating wars avoided. Historically the education of public opinion has never proved adequate to realize its possibilities and democracies have usually been short lived.

Power position. What is the effect of population change on the power position of the various nations? This question has often been faced by statesmen and they have usually assumed that population was a major element in power. They have, therefore, usually favored an increasing population assuring easier recruiting for the armed forces and, in some cases, they have supported ambitious policies in order to acquire new territories for settling the enlarged population. Population decline has usually been deplored as evidence of a diminishing position of the culture in competition with other cultures, a diminishing general economy and decreasing power (4, 51).

Before the rise of nationalism and the industrialization of war this argument had a degree of validity and today there undoubtedly is some relation between power and population. A state with very small population cannot be a *great power,* but a state with a very large population is not necessarily a *great power.* Today the morale and education of the people, the degree of industrialization of the country, the availability of resources, and the capacity to produce advanced weapons of war are as important in the calculation of power as is population. Furthermore moral reputation and the capacity to make allies is an element of increasing importance in the calculations of power politics. Modern war requires far more skill and specialized training of the individual participant, whether fighting at the front or handling transportation and manufacture in the rear, than has war of the past. Thus the average level of living is no less important than the total number of the population. Furthermore, the patriotism and loyalty of the citizen and the soldier is of increasing importance as the sacrifices called for by war increase. Members of the armed forces cannot be driven to fight by disciplinary methods of the officers in the same degree as was formerly possible. The highly trained air man or radio technician can only function if he does so voluntarily, and this implies a sense of participation in the national enterprise possible only with a relatively high level of living and education (59).

In spite of these factors, differential rates of population increase remain an important factor in rendering the balance of power unstable. In the latter half of the nineteenth century, France became increasingly alarmed at the superior rate of population increase in Germany. Later when Russia and France became allies, Germany became similarly alarmed at the high rate of Russian population increase. Today the greater rate of population increase in the Soviet group of states compared to the Atlantic group is a cause for alarm by the latter.

It has been suggested that under conditions of international rivalry a country falling behind in the population race perceives that time is against it and consequently initiates preventive war. Germany's aggressiveness in 1914 and 1939 has been attributed to the fact that it was faced by an increasing population disadvantage compared with eastern Europe. This factor, however, is only one in calculating the balance of power. Conditions of industry and alliance may be more important in estimating future power position (59).

It is to be noticed that this argument which attributes greater aggressiveness to states of less rapidly increasing population is the opposite of the economic argument which attributes greater aggressiveness to states of more rapidly increasing population seeking *lebensraum* for their surplus population. The latter argument may be strengthened by the suggestion that a young population, characteristic of a rapidly increasing population, is inclined to be more aggressive and expansive than an old population characteristic of a stable or declining population. In fact, because of the complexity of the situation, it is unsafe to draw conclusions in regard to policy from the population situation alone. All the other factors entering into the present and future power position must be considered (59).

National policy. While national policies are undoubtedly influenced by the population situation, that influence appears to be indeterminate. Overpopulation may lead to active policies of conquest, migration, industrialization, commercial expansion, or birth control, and it may also lead to passive policies of resignation, other worldliness, and social stratification. Similarly underpopulation may lead to active policies of alliance, rearmament, or preventive war to restore the balance of power, or to passive policies of abandoning great power position, disarmament and neutrality.

The phrases of political oratory asserting that expansive policies are *necessary* to acquire more *lebensraum* or a *place in the sun,* to convert a *have not* to a *have* position, to assure *self preservation* or to provide areas for migration, raw materials, or markets indicate at best the choice of one alternative rather than another to meet a problem, and, at worst, a rationalization of propaganda to conceal policies motivated by the ambitions of rulers or the special interests of certain groups. Reflection will usually indicate that there is no *necessity,* but a number of alternatives involving greater or lesser cost, greater or lesser risks, greater or lesser advantages (2, 6, 26, 45, 46, 52).

Policy emerges from the total situation involving many political, economic, social, and cultural factors other than population. The population situation is never historically the sole determinor of policy, nor can a policy, whether defined in terms of augmenting the state's power position, restoring the balance of power, improving the standard of living of the people, or promoting justice or progress, ever be implemented by consideration of the population situation alone, however completely and accurately that situation both now and in the foreseeable future may be defined. With the rise of democracy it is increasingly important that the complexity of the considerations, which must enter into choice of the alternatives of foreign policy, be widely understood (57, 59).

World politics. The influence of population development upon the characteristics of international relations in the world as a whole is equally indeterminate. While it is argued by Malthusianists that a continually increasing world population will eventually press upon the steadily depleting world resources, augmenting the struggle for existence of peoples and nations, it is also argued that increase in world population will augment communications, increase international and transnational contact, break down local values, and develop universal values in a universal society with universal organizations able to maintain peace and to exploit the world's resources to the maximum advantage of all without the wastes of war. The rapid increase of the world's population during the nineteenth and twentieth centuries has exhibited both of these tendencies. Both international rivalry and international co-operation have increased. There has been a development both of international tensions and of international procedures for dealing with them (2, 15, 59).

Historically, periods of relative peace, prosperity, and cultural progress, such as the Pax Romana of the Antonine Caesars, the Pax Ecclesiastica of the middle ages, and the Pax Britannica of the nineteenth century, have been periods of rapid population expansion, while periods of war, poverty, and cultural disintegration such as the dark ages from the third to the eighth centuries and the early renaissance from the fourteenth to the sixteenth centuries have been periods of population decline in Europe.

In an earlier work, the writer characterized the influence of population on contemporary world politics as follows:

(1) The rapid growth of world-population during the past century has augmented international communication, inter-penetrated cultures, increased international co-operation, and tended to bring the entire human race together into a single community. But it has also, in augmenting contacts between people of different cultural and political allegiance, increased opportunities for friction between nations, each of which often places retention of its cultural individuality, its political unity, and its relative power position above its economic prosperity. Thus while becoming more united, the world has become less stable, and tensions have increased. This situation gives the human race more capacity, if its various divisions can agree, to control its future through orderly processes. On the other hand, its eggs all being in one basket, if it cannot agree to exercise these now possible controls, its capacity to annihilate itself is also augmented.

(2) Policies of war and expansion have been less influenced by population changes than by the willingness of people to accept unsound economic theories on the subject. A more general knowledge of the economic value of the various alternatives for meeting particular population problems would under present conditions make for international peace and co-operation rather than for war, provided people really wished to make general welfare the object of policy.

(3) Differentials of population pressure in neighboring areas, if generally known to the inhabitants of the over-populated area and if maintained by artificial barriers to trade and migration, tend to international violence, provided the people of the over-populated area have energy and mobility, are accustomed to the use of violence as an instrument of policy, and are dominated, as people in the mass usually are, by political rather than by economic objectives.

(4) Population is one factor in military potential, and differential rates of population growth in neighboring states tend to disturb the balance of power if such neighbors are in positions of traditional rivalry and depend for their defense upon their own resources rather than upon the mutual jealousies of others. Such disturbances in the balance of power between the great powers have tended to the development of all states into a system of two rival alliances.

This is likely to lead to the conviction that war is inevitable and to general war initiated by the group against whose military potential time is running.

(5) The two preceding propositions suggest that imperial wars tend to be initiated by countries with the most rapidly rising populations, while balance of power wars tend to be initiated by the alliances with the less rapidly rising populations, provided other factors of the military potential are being equally affected by time.

(6) While population conditions in the broad sense are a major factor in international politics and establish limits to the possibilities of international relations during any historical epoch, the possible variations of policy within these limits steadily increase as civilization develops, and today such variations are very great. Consequently, today the character of the influence of a particular population change is so dependent on other factors that it is impossible to predict, from a study of population phenomena alone, what international policies or occurrences to expect (59).

CRITICISM

Demography is undoubtedly an important approach to the study of international relations. Human attitudes, opinions, institutions, and policies are influenced by the density and trends of population. But the density of population is a function, not only of the number of people but also of their resources and technology, and the significance of population trends is a function, not only of population projections but also of changes in culture, ideology, economy, and polity.

Studies relating aspects of population composition and development to international relations, and studies indicating the optimum size and composition of population under given conditions yield theoretical and practical insight into the problems of international relations. Such studies cannot, however, in themselves exhaust the subject. While wars are fought between populations, no statistical analysis of the populations can disclose all their causes. Changes in individual and group opinions; establishment of new national and international institutions; the evolution of treaties, legislation, and juristic analyses; technological discoveries and inventions, especially in the arts of war and economic production, all affect international relations rather directly. All these changes are affected by one another and also by population changes. The influence of the latter must be taken into account but in its proper relations and proportions. The temptation to state over-precisely and without adequate qualification, the international consequences of, or the remedies for, population conditions may thus be avoided. Alarming statements regarding the relation of population conditions to international affairs have often been made as propaganda for policies of value to the few rather than to the many; consequently, it is in the general interest that the indeterminateness of the actual relationship should be understood (59). "It is not in the circumstances of the external world but in the minds of men that the mainsprings of violent social conflict lie" (39).

REFERENCES

1. ALISON, Sir Archibald, *The Principles of Population and Their Connection with Human Happiness* (Edinburgh, Blackwood, 1840), 2 vols.

2. BARR, Stringfellow, *Citizens of the World* (New York, Doubleday, 1953); expansion of *Let's Join the Human Race* (Chicago, University of Chicago Press, 1950).

3. BARROWS, H. H., "Geography as Human Ecology," *Association of American Geographers, Annals,* Vol. 13 (1923), pp. 1 ff.

4. BERNHARDI, General Friedrich von, *Germany and the Next War* (London, Arnold, 1912).

5. BONAR, James, *Theories of Population from Raleigh to Arthur Young* (London, Allen and Unwin, 1931).

6. BOYD-ORR, Lord, *The White Man's Dilemma* (London, Allen and Unwin, 1953).

7. BRITTAIN, Robert, *Let There Be Bread* (New York, Simon and Schuster, 1952).

8. BROWN, Harrison, *The Challenge of Man's Future* (New York, Viking, 1954).

9. CARR-SAUNDERS, A. M., *The Population Problem, A Study of Human Evolution* (Oxford, Clarendon Press, 1922).

10. CHANDRASEKHAR, S., "Population Problems and International Tensions," *International Social Science Bulletin,* UNESCO, Vol. 1 (1949), pp. 54 ff.

11. DARWIN, Leonard, *What Is Eugenics?* 2nd ed. (London, Watts, 1929).

12. DAVIE, Maurice, *World Immigration* (New York, Macmillan, 1936).

13. DeCASTRO, Josue, *The Geography of Hunger* (Boston, Little, Brown, 1952).

14. DIXON, Roland B., "Migration, Primitive," *Encyclopædia of the Social Sciences.*

15. EAST, E. M., *Mankind at the Cross Roads* (New York, Scribner, 1923).

16. FERENCZI, Imre, "Migrations, Modern," *Encyclopædia of the Social Sciences.*

17. ———, and WILLCOX, W. F., *International Migration* (New York, Bureau of Economic Research, 1929), 2 vols.

18. FIELDS, James A., *Essays in Population* (Chicago, University of Chicago Press, 1931).

19. GALTON, Francis, *Hereditary Genius, An Inquiry into Its Laws and Consequences* (1869); (London, Macmillan, 1925).

20. GINI, Corrado, and others, *Population,* Harris Institute Lectures (Chicago, University of Chicago Press, 1930).

21. GUILLARD, Achille, *Éléments de statistique humaines ou démographie comparée* (Paris, Guillaumin, 1855).

22. HALPHEN, Louis, "Migrations, Ancient and Medieval," *Encyclopædia of the Social Sciences.*

23. HOSELITZ, Bert F., *The Progress of Underdeveloped Areas,* Harris Institute Lectures (Chicago, University of Chicago Press, 1952).

24. HUNTINGTON, Ellsworth, *The Human Habitat* (New York, Van Nostrand, 1927).

25. ———, *The Character of Races* (New York, Scribner, 1924).

26. International Studies Conference, *Peaceful Change,* 1937 Proceedings (International Institute of Intellectual Co-operation, Paris, 1939), 2 vols.

27. JENNINGS, H. S., *The Biological Basis of Human Nature* (New York, Norton, 1930).

28. ——, "Eugenics," *Encyclopædia of the Social Sciences.*

29. KUCZYNSKI, Robert R., *The Balance of Births and Deaths* (New York, Macmillan, 1928).

30. ——, "Population, History and Statistics," *Encyclopædia of the Social Sciences.*

31. LORIMER, Frank, "Population Factors Relating to the Organization of Peace," *International Conciliation,* No. 369 (April, 1941).

32. McKENZIE, R. D., "Ecology, Human," *Encyclopædia of the Social Sciences.*

33. MacLEAN, A. M., *Modern Immigration* (Philadelphia, Lippincott, 1925).

34. MALTHUS, Thomas R., *An Essay on the Principles of Population* (1798); 2nd ed. (1803); 6th ed. (London, Murray, 1826), 2 vols.

35. NOTESTEIN, Frank W., and others, *The Future Population of Europe and the Soviet Union, Population Projections, 1940-1970* (Geneva, League of Nations, 1944).

36. OGBURN, William F., ed., *Recent Social Trends in the United States,* Report of the President's Research Committee on Social Trends (New York, McGraw-Hill, 1933), 2 vols.

37. OSBORN, Fairfield, *The Limits of the Earth* (Boston, Little, Brown, 1953).

38. PEARL, Raymond, *The Biology of Population Growth* (New York, Knopf, 1925).

39. PENROSE, E. F., *Population Theories and Their Application* (Stanford, Stanford University Press, 1934).

40. PERRIS, G. H., *A Short History of War and Peace* (New York, Holt, 1911).

41. PETTY, Sir William, *An Essay Concerning the Multiplication of Mankind* (1682), summarized in *Economic Writings* (Cambridge, University Press, 1899), vol. 2, pp. 453-478.

42. PLACE, Francis, *Illustrations and Proofs of the Principle of Population* (London, Allen and Unwin, 1930).

43. PUTNAM, Palmer, *Energy in the Future* (New York, Van Nostrand, 1953).

44. RIESMAN, David, *The Lonely Crowd, A Study of the Changing American Character* (New Haven, Yale University Press, 1950).

45. SANGER, Margaret, ed., *Proceedings, World Population Conference* (Geneva, 1927); (London, 1927).

46. SCHULTZ, Theodore W., *Food for the World,* Harris Institute Lectures (Chicago, University of Chicago Press, 1945).

47. SWEENEY, J. S., *The Natural Increase of Mankind* (Baltimore, Williams and Wilkins, 1926).

48. THOMAS, Brinley, *Migration and Economic Growth, A Study of Great Britain and the Atlantic Economy* (Cambridge, Cambridge University Press, 1953).

49. THOMPSON, Warren S., *Population Problems* (New York, McGraw-Hill, 1930).

50. ——, *Danger Spots in World Population* (New York, Knopf, 1930).

51. TREITSCHKE, Heinrich, *Politics* (New York, Macmillan, 1916), 2 vols.

52. United Nations, Department of Social Affairs, *Preliminary Report on the World Social Situation* (New York, United Nations, 1952).

53. VIDAL DE LA BLACHE, P. M. J., *Principles of Human Geography,* 1922, trans. by M. T. Bingham (New York, Holt, 1926).

54. VOGT, William, *Road to Survival* (New York, Sloane, 1948).

55. WHIPPLE, G. C., *Vital Statistics*, 2nd ed. (New York, Wiley, 1923).
56. WOLFE, A. V., "Demography," *Encyclopædia of the Social Sciences*.
57. ——, "Population, Theory," *Encyclopædia of the Social Sciences*.
58. WRIGHT, Harold, *Population* (New York, Harcourt, Brace, 1923).
59. WRIGHT, Quincy, *A Study of War* (Chicago, University of Chicago Press, 1942), pp. 208-212, 466-467, 566-570, 599, 612, 714, 1118-1145.
60. YULE, G. U., "The Growth of Population and the Factors Which Control It," *Royal Statistical Society, Journal*, Vol. 88 (1925), pp. 1-58.

Technology and International Relations

DEFINITION

As A DISCIPLINE of international relations, technology is the science relating invention and the progress of material culture to world politics, and the art of developing mechanical devices for, and utilizing them in, war, diplomacy and international trade, travel, and communication. Governments have increasingly established commissions, institutes, or other agencies for promoting this art.

In a general sense, technology is the art of combining and utilizing materials, entities, forces, processes, and relations to serve human purposes, and the science seeking to predict and control the human and social consequences of the inventions and methods resulting from the practice of that art. It also includes historical studies of the making, development and use of inventions, and philosophical studies appraising the importance of technology for the development of cultures, nations, and civilizations.

The term *technology* is usually used to refer to the invention and utilization of material entities, forces, processes, and relations, thus excluding social and moral *inventions*. Representative government, federalism, the initiative and referendum, the Golden Rule, and trial by jury may have been *inventions* but their study hardly comes under the discipline of technology. The line, however, corresponding to that made by anthropologists between material and moral culture, between "a body of artifacts and a system of customs" (25) is difficult to draw. Things are seen

369

and made because they are valued, and values are recognized and accepted because they are illustrated by things and acts.

Elections would usually be considered part of the moral rather than the material culture. The ballot and voting machines are, however, part of the material culture even though party platforms and propaganda, figuring in elections, are part of the moral culture. The printing press, telegraph, telephone, radio, cinema, and television are part of the material culture, while the fine arts, soap operas, law, politics, history, philosophy, religion, magic, and perhaps science are part of the moral culture. Certainly the telescope and microscope, the galvanometer, Gothic cathedrals, incense pots, and priestly vestments, important as they are in the development of science and religion, are part of the material culture but the latter in their symbolic roles come also within the moral culture.

Symbol systems are especially difficult to classify. A symbol is any object, form, or event with a meaning beyond itself. Language—sometimes distinguished by linguists from *culture* (43)—writing and systems of enumeration, mathematics, and symbolic logic may be classified as technology and part of the material culture. They serve primarily as instruments of communication and reasoning, but they also establish the concepts, ideas, ideologies, and normative systems which shape beliefs, behavior, and values, and thus seem part of the moral culture. They are, however, concerned with the relatively fixed and precisely defined meanings of symbols, susceptible of combination and communication, while political, legal, moral, and religious ideologies are concerned with the vague but evocative meanings to which the manipulation of symbols is instrumental (25). Science as a logical system based upon operational definitions and useful for prediction and control may seem part of the material culture even though it utilizes *constructs, conveniences,* or *fictions* incapable of direct observation (38, 56), yet it undoubtedly influences values and, like language, can be considered part of the moral culture (8a, 11a).

Combination and utilization of *symbolic* meanings, especially affective, sentimentalized, and normative meanings, constitute the moral culture while combination of *symbols themselves,* as marks or sounds of precise form with clear significations, constitute part of the material culture, though less clearly so than combinations and utilizations of mineral, vegetable, and animal products; of such forces as wind, waterfalls, electricity; of such processes as the succession of day and night, the seasons, the ebb and flow of the tide; of such relations as space, time, and mass. While the line between technology and ethics, between instruments and values, between the material and the moral culture cannot be precisely defined in general terms, because it differs among different cultures and in different situations, yet for a particular culture at a given moment the distinction is usually clear to the participants in the culture.

The process of technological change may be divided into stages of invention, development, engineering, and utilization (64).

Invention can be dated in time and located in space though not infrequently the same invention is made independently at approximately the same time by different persons in different places. This circumstance is cited as evidence of the social character of inventions (17). The final combination, called the invention, is a consequence of a long process, by which previous inventions or the accumulation of knowledge creates the material conditions making the final combination possible and by which the development of culture and society creates a widespread sense of need for such an invention. Inventions are a combination of technical possibility and social demand. Whenever these factors converge the invention will probably be made although the precise time and place may be determined by individual genius. Thus the airplane could not be invented until the invention of the internal combustion engine had assured a sufficiently light source of power, nor was it likely to be invented until the progress of rail and motor transportation had developed a widespread demand for even more rapid transportation. The demand for flying machines suggested by observation of birds has, however, been potential in all civilizations as indicated by the occasional discussions of the subject to be found in the literature of ancient China, ancient Greece, and the Renaissance (63). It is also true that inventions are sometimes made before there is a social demand in which case they may lie fallow for years. The opposition of vested interests in established technologies may also contribute to this result (34).

Invention, involving artificial combination, is usually distinguished from discovery of natural situations or combinations, but the two conceptions converge. Should it be said that Uranium 235 and its properties were discovered while Plutonium, an element that does not exist in nature, was invented? In both cases elaborate manipulation was necessary to isolate and test the properties of the entity. This might deserve the name of *invention*. It would usually be said that Newton *invented* (contemporaneously with Leibnitz) the differential calculus but that he *discovered* the law of gravitation. Yet the somewhat artificial character of the latter is indicated by the different system *invented* or *discovered* by Einstein two centuries later. For human purposes the distinction between discovery and invention is usually not important. Science and technology develop together, each assisting the other though the motivation of scientists may tend to be curiosity and of inventors utility. Even this distinction, however, is by no means always true (51). The invention of the mariner's compass and the discovery of America were both parts of a social process. Increasingly philosophers of science recognize the creativity of scientific *discovery* (3, 38).

Whatever the social background, invention itself is a psychological process, whereby the inventor synthesizes hitherto separated elements in a new combination, usually seeing the combination as a whole or *gestalt* in a sudden inspiration (41, 57).

In the process of development, involving experiment with models, elimination of *bugs,* and the utilization of appropriate materials and designs to create a workable mechanism or product, the social aspect becomes more prominent. The inventor may have to get financial support, impossible unless there is a potential demand for the invention, and he has to draw on the existing state of the arts to perfect the device (17, 64). Governments often initiate or support this process especially in respect to military inventions (2, 7, 10, 47).

In the engineering stage, social aspects are even more to the front. Economic problems of reducing the costs of production and improving the efficiency of operation proceed with continued benefit of the criticism which arises as the invention begins to be used whether in industry or war.

The engineering stage, in fact, proceeds contemporaneously with the utilization stage, involving advertising, marketing, and extending the use of the invention or, in case of military inventions, testing in actual hostilities (23, 64). Cultures are very variable in their acceptance of new inventions. Closely integrated cultures, guided by custom, like that of most primitive peoples, are conservative and will not accept inventions not clearly perceivable as improvements on existing aspects of the culture, while more loosely integrated cultures, guided by opinion, are more liberal in their acceptance of technological innovations. It is in fact, such a predisposition toward innovation that distinguishes progressive civilizations from customary cultures (21, 37, 62).

In each successive stage, economic and social considerations become more important—personality and psychic considerations, less important.

Once an invention begins to be used on a considerable scale, the problem of adapting other elements of culture and society to it must be faced. The considerable duration of the development and engineering process, in fact, makes possible social preparation to ease the impact of an invention, widespread use of which can be foreseen from a study of the trend of these processes (33, 34). Inventions have social consequences as well as social causes. The more closely integrated and customary is a culture, the more radical is the effect on its structure of a new technology likely to be. The loosely organized democratic countries of the West assimilate new inventions and techniques easily but even with them, the changes may be more widespread and painful than generally thought. All phases of Western civilization, its economy, politics, and even ethics and religion have doubtlessly been greatly affected by such recent inventions as the airplane, the cinema, radio, television, and the atomic bomb (8, 18, 27, 33, 34, 35, 36, 42, 45, 52, 63). These changes, however, are not as profound as those which concern administrators of technical aid to underdeveloped countries. It has been increasingly recognized that these countries must usually undergo considerable social and cultural changes before they will accept more advanced technologies, and that even more significant changes will be consequent upon the extensive utilization of the new technologies. Such administrators are more and more leaning upon the insight of anthropologists to inform them both of the conditions and the probable consequences of the introduction of new techniques in such countries (21, 28).

ASSUMPTIONS

Students of technology have usually made the following assumptions.

1. Technology is an integral aspect of culture. The group's culture, both moral and material, influence its capacity to invent and to utilize technological innovations and the introduction of technological innovations will effect changes in the entire culture.

2. Technology tends to diffuse among similar cultures, and among the nations of modern civilization this diffusion has been rapid. No modern nation can be expected long to remain without any efficient technology which is employed anywhere.

3. Technological progress is an irreversible process within the life of a civilization, and for the history of mankind as a whole.

4. Technological progress tends to accelerate. Each invention increases the possible combinations of ideas thus increasing the probability of more inventions.

These assumptions, though commonly made, are in varying degrees controversial. Each will, therefore, be commented on.

1. **Technology influences values.** Though anthropologists usually divide culture into material and moral aspects, they recognize that these aspects are separated by no sharp line, and that each influences the other. Philosophical historians have made a similar distinction among the aspects of civilization. They have, however, often recognized that among primitive peoples the economic technology has a determining influence on the general level of culture (53). Thus peoples limited to a collecting economy, using only wood and stone implements, are markedly different from those utilizing the technology of agriculture, of animal husbandry, and of metallurgy. Furthermore, the general cultural characteristics of agriculturalists, of pastoral nomads, and of fabricators in copper, in bronze, and in iron differ from one another. Cultural ethnologists and archeologists tend to distinguish groups and periods by the presence or absence of certain technological characteristics (20). The techniques of writing and of mass communication have been regarded as of unusual importance, marking major stages of cultural progress (43, 52, 62). Techniques

in the field of transportation, the use of the horse, the canoe, the sailing vessel, the compass, the steamboat, railroad, motor car, and airplane have also been significant (37). Inventions of basic sources of energy beyond those of human muscle—draft animals, water and windmills, steam and internal combustion engines, hydro-electric power—have fundamentally influenced civilization. Lewis Mumford divides the progress of civilization into the eo-technic age, using wooden construction, wind and water power; the paleo-technic age, using iron and steel construction and steam power; and the neo-technic age, using aluminum and alloys in construction, internal combustion engines and hydro-electric power (29).

In line with these conclusions, Karl Marx thought that technology was of great influence in shaping the form of economy. The latter established a *base* which determined the religious, political, artistic, moral, and ideological *super-structure* of the society (26). Thus Marx reversed Hegel who thought the idea of a civilization determined its basic institutions and that this idea developed technologies to realize itself. While Marx tended to a materialistic and Hegel to an idealistic determinism, both recognized a dialectic between conditions and values, between technology and ethics. While these formulations raise logical questions (31), there is ample evidence of reciprocal influences between the material and moral aspects of a culture.

Anthropologists and ethnologists usually recognize the possibility in all cultures of inventions and of technological borrowing. Cultural change through the reciprocal action of the *base* and the *super-structure*, the resources and technology on the one hand and the ideas and values on the other, appears to be always possible though the probability varies greatly among different cultures.

Historians have sought to trace the reciprocal relationship between war, technology, and morals. War appears to stimulate technological development but to hamper progress in the basic sciences from which new technologies might grow. Technological progress may develop economic surpluses stimulating war and it may also create conditions favorable to peace and moral progress. The moral situation influences the character, both of war and of inventions. The relations among these aspects of culture appear to be extremely complex permitting of no easy generalizations (16, 30). It has been suggested that the acceleration of technological change with the progress of civilization augments its influence as compared with that of traditional value systems (32). It seems probable, however, that technological progress decreases the *determinative* influence of technology. Primitive peoples, who invent or borrow new technologies only slowly and with difficulty, have their entire culture in considerable measures determined by the technological base, whereas civilized peoples, who invent and borrow easily and rapidly, are able in greater measure to retain their values and utilize new technologies to implement them (53, 62). As the process of civilization marks the triumph of the human spirit over conditions of geography and population, so it also marks its triumph over technology. While modern critics have deplored the enslavement of man by his inventions and technologies, it would appear that this enslavement is less than among primitive peoples. Modern man uses technologies to achieve his values whereas primitive man has a technology which severely limits the values which he can achieve, or even think about (54).

Sociologists have pointed to the concealed and delayed influence which technological inventions or introductions may have, even among civilized peoples. Initially a new technology affects consumption and production habits, but later derivative effects may emerge, sometimes strengthened by the converging influences of other inventions (33, 35). Thus utilization of the cotton gin in the early nineteenth century cheapened cotton and increased cotton production in the South and the value of slave labor. This, along with the increasing demand of British textile mills, the specialization of southern agriculture in cotton, and the expansion of cotton growing to the West, increased the differential between the North and the South in economy, culture, and political ideas. This divergence of interest resulted in the state's rights movement in the South, augmented by the centralizing tendencies of the federal government and the Supreme Court, and eventuated in the Civil War after the South became convinced that time was deteriorating its power position. Thus invention of the cotton gin had a profound influence on American history, politics, and culture. While other factors influenced the course of events, the invention and use of the cotton gin was a factor of major importance (36).

Anthropologists and colonial administrators cite many illustrations of the differing ease with which primitive peoples accept technological innovations such as guns, plows, horses, and vaccination. Each people selects easily inventions that fit into the tribal pattern of values and practices, but rejects those that are wholly novel (39, 61, 62). Progress in civilization, as usually understood, implies greater willingness to accept and use technological improvements. Similarly there is evidence of the very different effect which technological introductions have upon different cultures. Some cultures may be disintegrated by the effort to absorb new inventions thus accounting for their reluctance to consider them. Modern civilizations, on the other hand, absorb new technologies with ease, although the consequences upon all aspects of the culture may, in the long run, be profound (33, 34, 35, 36, 63).

The point of this assumption is that technologies are not superficial devices from which all cultures can benefit and which may originate anywhere and diffuse easily and rapidly. On the contrary, technologies are related to the culture as a whole and the origin, diffusion, and influence of a particular invention cannot be understood except in terms of the total culture which originated or utilizes it. Scientists and inventors often assume that their achievements are morally neutral. While it is true that an invention can usually be employed either to forward or to frustrate the values of any culture, some inventions are more likely to do the one and some the other. An unusual number of scientists were aroused to this understanding during World War II. Some felt that the development of nuclear fission and atomic weapons was unethical. They feared that if such weapons existed, they would be used and, in the immature state of politics, that use would be dangerously destructive and might set back the progress of civilization or even destroy civilization altogether (5, 8, 27, 63). It is clear that to assume the reciprocal influence of the technical and moral aspects of culture is to deny the moral neutrality of technology. Many social scientists attribute the disturbed state of international relations today to the lag of social science and ethics behind physical science and technology (36). That position implies that technology is not ethically neutral. As a discipline, technology cannot ignore the effect of its development upon ethical standards and values. One of its tasks is to analyze both the immediate and the ultimate consequences upon civilization as a whole of technological progress (63).

This line of thought suggests reflection on the assumption, which has been implicit in Western civilization during the past few centuries, that all technological progress is desirable. This assumption developed from experience with the conveniences which science and technology made available. This experience, however, promoted certain beliefs which reacted to strengthen this assumption. Among those beliefs were the moral neutrality of technology and the identification of power with goodness. The latter was manifested in the notion of jural positivism identifying law with effective sanction and right with might, and in the notion of rationalism identifying knowledge with virtue. Knowledge, it was thought, increases both power and virtue, and the latter were identified. While these ideas were developed in ancient Greece, they have distinguished modern civilization from most others (38). In general, both primitive cultures and historic civilizations have spent more energy in suppressing science and invention than in encouraging them, and in fact in the early stages of modern civilization science faced new censorships imposed by both church and state (46). Cultures based on custom or conscience have feared new knowledge and new technologies. Histories of the warfare of religion and science have been often written (13, 59). Primitive peoples, scholastic civilizations, and totalitarian states are usually inhospitable to the freedom essential for progress in science and invention, and frequently seek to control both (44). The assumption that science and invention are necessarily good, though given some support in Periclean Greece, in Hellenistic Alexandria, and in the Caliphates of Bagdad and Cordoba, was not widely accepted until the work of Bacon,

Galileo, Descartes, Newton, the encyclopedists, and the economists founded the very idea of progress and civilization upon this assumption (13, 44, 59).

This assumption is today challenged by the conception of cultural lag, which asserts that one aspect of a culture may develop out of harmony with others (32). Consequently the good society must prevent any aspect, even science and technology, from developing out of step with other aspects. If it is acknowledged that inventions are not necessarily ethically neutral, it cannot be said that any and all inventions and any and all directions of technological progress are inherently desirable. Here again, the discipline of technology is faced, not with an assumption, but with a problem. What inventions are good? Where? When? How can society adapt itself to them? The problem of analyzing the probable consequences of technological inventions cannot be evaded (33, 34).

2. **Diffusion.** The second assumption of the discipline of technology is related to the first. Technologies, adding to man's power over nature, tend to be utilized beyond the point of origin, but they will be adopted soonest by cultures sufficiently similar to that of origin to avoid serious inhibitions. Among primitive peoples, neighboring cultures are both most similar and most accessible. Consequently, the *age and area* theory originally applied to the geographic distribution of plants and animals was applied to culture traits. The origin of a technique was located at the center of the area of distribution. Use of a technique was supposed to have moved outward from that center, in all directions, the radius traveled indicating roughly the length of time since its invention (61). Among civilized peoples equipped with more efficient means of communication and transport, techniques diffuse more widely, rapidly, and irregularly, and, furthermore, parallel invention is more probable. Thus among modern nations all techniques rapidly become universal in spite of efforts to control by secrecy or by preferences in exchange of information. It was not to be expected that the Soviet Union would long be unacquainted with the production of atomic bombs (2, 27). This factor tends to eliminate technological differences which in the past have sometimes persisted for long periods of time, permitting of imperial rule by the technologically more advanced nations over the lesser. Such differentials, though they still exist, tend to disappear. In fact in the West, principles of democracy and human rights, as well as pressures of political rivalry, have made the elimination of such differentials major goals of policy. The technical aid programs of the United States and the United Nations seek to eliminate technological differentials as rapidly as possible (21).

3. **Irreversibility.** The history of science and technology unlike that of politics and religion has been cumulative and continuous. Inventions once made are not forgotten. Mankind is saddled with them. It is difficult to

see how man can rid himself of the atomic bomb or the airplane, much as some persons may deplore the consequences of these inventions. From the technological point of view, human history can be written as a continuous progress in which inventions are cumulative, augmenting man's control over nature (44). This is in marked contrast to histories written from the aesthetic, moral, political, economic, or population points of view which are marked by oscillation, in the rise and fall of nations and civilizations (54, 62). These oscillations, have, it is true, sometimes led to technological declines for considerable periods in considerable areas of the world. European technology in the Dark Ages was behind that of Antiquity, as the Aztec technology of Mexico was behind that of the Mayas. Erroneous beliefs and mistaken observations seem at times to have become so embedded in even the most advanced civilizations that they obliterated knowledge and techniques generally known by more primitive peoples (49a). These declines, however, were limited in time, space, or importance. Very rarely have significant inventions or practical arts been entirely lost to mankind. This assumption, justified by the past, may be problematic for the future. The character of modern war, both in its destructiveness and probable universality, and the complexity of the science and the skills on which modern technology rests, makes it more probable than at any previous period of history that war may destroy the accumulated technology of millennia throughout the entire world and reduce the human survivors, if there are any, to primitive conditions. Such a disaster was contemplated by some technological commentators upon the atomic bomb (27), but further consideration seems to have moderated this pessimism (9).

4. **Acceleration.** While technological progress has been more rapid in some areas, and some periods than in others, taking mankind as a whole, its progress has accelerated. Henry Adams thought he detected a tendency for history to move with increasing rapidity (1). Doubtless the superior knowledge of, and interest in, history as it becomes more recent, better known, and more important to the present, in part accounts for this effect. Yet the history of technology suggests that there has been a real acceleration in the rate of change. Important inventions appear more frequently and more patents are granted year by year. Such an acceleration is to be expected from the steady increase in the number of new combinations possible as the number of elementary devices increases. Primitive man could not make many new combinations with the few simple implements and ideas which he had. Modern man has much raw material for invention and his science enables him to make invention a profession. There is no evidence for the occasional suggestion that the possibilities of invention will eventually be exhausted and that the technological progress which has characterized the nineteenth and twentieth centuries will come to an end. Quite the opposite. Unless civilization

destroys itself by war, continued technological progress may be expected and the rate of progress can be expected to accelerate (34).

ANALYSIS

Assuming the reciprocal influence of technology and other aspects of culture upon each other, the rapid diffusion of technologies among modern nations, and the irreversible and accelerating trend of technological progress in the community of nations, what is the significance of technology to contemporary international relations? One significance can be deduced directly from these assumptions, namely that the world is likely to continue to shrink and, as a consequence, to become increasingly susceptible both to anxieties and to central control. International relations is likely to continue at a high level of tension and measures of international regulation and control to become increasingly practical. The condition of increasing tension and increasing control may in fact be considered a general characteristic of progress from primitive societies guided by custom to civilized societies guided by opinion.

High tension is often regarded as a pathological condition to be eliminated, and undoubtedly excessive tension is likely to produce war which, under modern conditions, is antithetic to civilization. On the other hand, very low tension manifests a condition of lethargy and stagnation also opposed to civilization. As high pressure in a boiler, if controlled and directed, can produce work of human value, so high tension in a society controlled and directed to the realization of human values produces social progress. High tension may cause either destructive war or progressive civilization. Which one it actually produces depends upon the magnitude of the tensions in relation to the efficacy and direction of the controls. Tension implies stored-up energy which permits human choice in respect to the circumstances and consequences of its release (62, 63).

Social tension like electrical tension seems to vary as the product of energy and resistance. Social control and direction, through institutions, laws, and organizations, offers resistance to the dissipation of social energy. If this energy is great, as it is in an expanding economy producing surpluses of capital goods, and if society conserves, channels, and directs this energy, preventing its rapid dissipation, high tension will result. If the energy increases, the danger of war or other social break-down will increase, unless the efficacy of social direction reduces resistance by rapidly expending this energy in useful social activity (63).

In international relations, tension occurs on frontiers between nations and increases in proportion to the increase of energy of the nations at each side of the frontier and to the degree of incompatibility of the direction of control exerted by each. W. F. Ogburn has suggested that international tension develops because of the rigidity of political and administrative frontiers and the consequent lag in adjustment to changing conditions. Among such conditions is the pressure of each state on the common frontier. Under the influence of inventions, augmenting wealth and population, states go through stages of optimism, confidence, and aggressiveness, putting ever more pressure upon obstacles to expansion. A similar phenomenon is to be observed in urban centers which develop suburban settlements and trading areas vastly greater than their legal limits. Sovereign states meet greater political obstruction to expansion and seek to conquer territory or subject smaller neighbors to a satellite position (36).

International tensions can be relieved by international or world controls utilizing much of the energy of all nations to promote parallel or common purposes. International organizations or federations may substitute, for struggle over conflicting imperial claims, co-operation across political boundaries to promote a more expanded life for all (36).

Technological progress by increasing human control of nature and augmenting the power of nations, and by shrinking the world and accelerating history, increases international contacts and the probability of inconsistent policies. Consequently it increases both energies and resistances in the community of nations, and higher international tensions can be expected. On the other hand, closer contacts, greater possibilities of interaction between governments and peoples, and the tendency for attitudes to become more favorable to peace, as war becomes more destructive, creates the possibility of such regulation and control as to settle controversies and to direct energies to common purposes. Thus in the international field, technological advance has extraordinary potentialities, both for war and for peace (63, 64).

In considering in more detail the effects of technological advance on international relations, attention may be given to the effects of such advance on the state, on the system of states, on the world's economy, and on the world's polity.

Technological progress and the state. There can be no doubt but that technological progress tends to make states larger in area and population. When the fastest communication was by courier, and the fastest transport was on human backs, man generally lived in small groups of a few score persons and in a few hundred square miles of territory, although in the civilizations of Mexico, these limits were considerably transcended. The use of the horse, the sailing ship, the steam ship, the railroad, and the airplane have increased the capacity of a political center to exercise effective control over increasing areas and populations. Efforts have been made to correlate these inventions with the largest land and maritime empires under each, and to estimate the maximum size of state possible under each. The great horse empires of Kubla Khan and Russia ruled over seven million square miles; the great sailing ship empires of Spain and Britain were even larger. The building of railroad and steam ship empires in the nineteenth century encountered greater resistances but the average size of states was larger than in the earlier periods. The air protected systems of the Soviet Union and the United States in the post-war period have been of unparalleled size, each encompassing nearly half of the world. With the use of airplanes and telecommunications, a world political union has for the first time become feasible. While the possibility for expansion of the area of political rule, inherent in a given technology, has not always been realized, the tendency of invention has been to increase the average size of states and to diminish their number (19, 36).

Furthermore, technological progress has increased the centralization and solidarity of states. With telecommunication, diplomats can keep in immediate touch with the foreign office, and foreign policy-making can be centralized in governments. The policy of a government in each section of the world can be correlated with that in others. Political, economic, social, and cultural factors throughout the world can be correlated to facilitate the choice of feasible policies, and policy can be administered on the military, economic, propaganda, and diplomatic fronts to achieve the policy chosen. Furthermore, technological advance in mass communication and rapid transportation of military equipment has greatly decreased the feasibility of domestic revolt and greatly increased the effectiveness of domestic propaganda and the dependence of the people on the government, thus making possible greater national solidarity and unity in the conduct of foreign and domestic policies.

Finally the invention of new sources of energy and new methods of production and of population control have made possible increase in the level and standards of living and great increases in social energy.

States of greater size, greater centralization, and greater energy tend to be more optimistic, more confident, and more aggressive. They feel more self-sufficient, more powerful, and more sovereign. While the relations of states may in fact render these feelings somewhat unrealistic, there seems to be no doubt but that the governments and peoples, especially when united by democratic participation, tend to regard the national will as capable of realization and to place high value on national independence and sovereignty. Technological advance tends to make states powerful and dangerous (36).

Technological progress and the state system. Technological progress may change the power position of states with relative rapidity. Development of the airplane greatly reduced the power position of Great Britain, dependent on sea communications and invulnerable to attack so long as it maintained a dominant navy, and greatly increased that of Russia and United States, with larger areas, with less vulnerability to air attack, and with less dependence on sea communication. The most superficial view of history indicates a shift of world power from the river empires of the

Middle and Far East based on secure agriculture and the horse, to the Mediterranean empires of Crete, Phoenecia, Greece, and Rome based on trade and disciplined armies. In the Middle Ages centers of power moved to the agricultural areas of northern Europe, western Asia, India, and China, respectively dominated by centralized military empires, such as those of the Carolingians, the Abbassides, the Guptas, and the Tangs. In the Renaissance Spain, Portugal, France, Netherlands, and Britain, profiting by discoveries made possible by better ships and the mariner's compass, established vast overseas empires, linking all parts of the world. The use of gun powder and the printing press increased the power of governments over feudal lords, developed solidarities of national sentiment, and permitted Europe, which developed these techniques most extensively, to dominate the modern world. Great Britain's coal and iron complex gave that country the opportunity to initiate the industrial revolution, to maintain the balance of power in Europe, and to dominate the non-European world in the nineteenth century. With the diffusion of the inventions involving the industrial revolution, other coal and iron producing areas—Germany, the United States, Japan, and Russia—developed in relative power, and with the rise of the airplane to major military importance during World War II the United States and Russia achieved dominant positions (36).

In addition to influencing historical changes in the general location of power and of the relative power position of different states, the progress of invention has tended to magnify the difference between great and small states and to decrease the defensibility of all states. Only states with large populations and industry can produce the equipment of modern war. The smaller the state in area and, therefore, in concentration of its population and resources, the more vulnerable it is to air attack (35, 63).

The progress of technology has a general tendency to improve the relative position of the offensive in war as compared with the defensive, and, therefore, to increase the vulnerability of all states to attack and conquest. Although history indicates ups and downs, the general tendency has been to make the defense of territory less easy. There have been periods of little technological progress when the defensive gained an advantage, as in the middle ages when feudal castles were invulnerable to attack and could be taken only by starvation or treason. Europe as a consequence was divided into thousands of virtually sovereign domains. The defensive seems also to have gained a temporary advantage in the late nineteenth and earlier twentieth centuries when machine-gun-lined trenches were relatively invulnerable, wars could be won only by attrition, and self-determination movements broke up empires and increased the number of states in Europe. In other periods, however, such as that of Roman expansion with invention of the legion, and that of the expansion of modern states and empires through the use of guns, the offensive gained an advantage. States have become larger and their number has diminished (62).

It is clear that long experience with an unchanging military technology tends to improve the position of the defense. The offense depends upon surprise. In time the appropriate defense for all possible offensives will become known provided the technology does not change, but on the other hand, new inventions permit tacticians and strategists to invent new surprises and, therefore, tend to favor the offensive.

But, more specifically, the tendency of military invention especially in recent times has been to increase the striking power and mobility of weapons and thus to give an advantage to the offensive. The destructive power of weapons has increased more rapidly than the cost of making them, and their mobility has increased more rapidly than their vulnerability. With sword and javelin warfare, it in general cost a man to kill a man. With flintlock and rifle warfare, once the enemy was routed, his losses would be considerably greater than those of the victor. With the use of ordinary bombs dropped from the air destruction could be five to ten times the cost of the planes, bombs, and men lost by the offensive. With atomic bombs, this figure may be multiplied by fifty or a hundred. It may be possible to destroy a thousand man hours of labor to every one expended in preparing and launching the attack (27, 63). The extensive industrialization of war has, it is true, tremendously increased the cost of killing a man of the enemy, from perhaps 75 cents in Caesar's time to over $50,000 in World War II, but a state able to meet the vast costs of modern weapons can impose losses upon its enemy of far greater magnitude.

The tank, the Snorkel submarine, and the jet plane with hydrogen bombs have qualities of mobility, protection, and striking power unparalleled in the history of war. As a consequence the enemy's fear of reprisals, rather than the effectiveness of defensive weapons or fortifications, has become the only means of security in war for either soldier or civilian. While there are technologists who optimistically anticipate defenses against air-borne atomic attacks by systems of radar warnings and defense planes surrounding the state (9), statesmen, who appraise the costs and effectiveness of such systems after considering the length of frontiers and the speed and height of attacking squadrons of jet planes, do not share this optimism (27, 36). These conditions have not only increased the vulnerability of all states, and the general costs of war, but they have also increased the relative power position of large states compared with small states and the military advantage of the state which initiates the war. Aggressive or preventive war, while deterred by costs and risks unparalleled in the history of war, is stimulated by the strategic advantages of the initiative (62).

All of these factors decrease the stability of the balance of power.

There is, therefore, a paradox; the states feel more powerful, independent, and sovereign, but in fact the balance of power shifts more rapidly. All are more vulnerable to attack, the consequences of war are more serious for civilization, and the ultimate results are more problematic. While states feel more sovereign, they are, in fact, less so. A lurking political insecurity, because of the instability of the power equilibrium, accompanies the sense of national sovereignty and confidence as technology progresses.

World economy and technology. From the point of view of the masses, the progress of invention increases the prospect of higher levels of living. Inventions in agriculture and industry increase man's control of nature, and inventions in birth control, medicine, and sanitation increase his control of population. The food-population ratio can, therefore, be regulated and all can be more prosperous provided reasonable conservation of resources is practiced. This adds to the power and optimism of the nation which makes use of these inventions, but much of the gain is taken away by the insecurities which derive from a less stable balance of power and the need for expensive military preparation. This may lead to greater understanding of the value for human welfare of international co-operation to utilize inventions in man's struggle against nature. Technology and economy in combination tend to produce a cosmopolitan society characterized by productive specialization, extensive trade, population control, and high living standards. But the personal insecurities engendered by such an impersonal society, because of its tendency to disintegrate primary groups and to isolate the individual, present a problem for sociology and social psychology.

World government and technology. The sense of political insecurity deriving from the rapid changing of power position, the general vulnerability to attack, and the advantage of the offensive in war, together with appreciation of the advantages of world wide economic and social co-operation, increase, as technology advances, the vigor of movements for universal organization to achieve peace. Such movements, are, however, combatted by the self-confidence of national states in their sovereignty and the national sentiments of their people, by the personal insecurity of individuals inducing them to cherish local and national attachments in preference to the anonymity of a cosmopolitan society, and by the political insecurity of the national states inducing them to prepare for defense against war which seems inevitable, thus creating the condition which makes it probable. Each government appears to be faced by two alternatives. It may attempt to augment its power position to prevent attack or to win if war comes, but the consequence will be to increase tensions and to render the power equilibrium even less stable. It may, on the other hand, rely on international co-operation and international organization, acknowledging its dependence on the world community, and seeking to develop collective security, but the consequence may be that other states, by refusing to co-operate, will prevent the development of collective security, and will augment their relative power positions enabling them to launch successful attacks.

Technological advance tends to lead to the dilemma of one world or none. Until there is a sufficiently general and simultaneous will to make international organization work *one world* can give little security. But so long as each state looks to itself alone for defense, no state will enjoy security in a technologically united world. Technological advance has left man with the necessity of understanding himself in society, as well as he understands nature and its control, if he is to solve his political problems (27, 36, 63).

CRITICISM

Technological change has undoubtedly been a major factor in history. Inventions mark the major points of change in the history of man. From the point of view of international relations, inventions in the fields of communication (language, writing, printing, telecommunication), transport (wheels, sailing ships, steam ships, railroads, automobiles, airplanes), war (bow-and-arrow, gun powder, high explosives, atomic bomb), medicine (germ theory, sanitary surgery, anesthetics, vaccination, inoculation, antibiotics) and food preparation and preservation (fire, canning, refrigeration, vitamins) have been of major importance. Back of them have been inventions in power sources (draft animals, wind and watermills, steam engines, electric generators and motors, internal combustion engines, diesel engines), agriculture (plant and animal breeding, genetics, fertilization, plows, reapers, harvesters), textiles (spinning and weaving machinery), metal work (smelting, metallurgy, machine tools, rolling mills) and construction (adobe, bricks, stone cutting, structural steel, skyscrapers, road building, bridges, wharfs) (55).

Taking mankind as a whole, there has been an irreversible movement of technological progress. Techniques once invented have seldom been wholly lost although they may have been lost in local areas. While nations and civilizations have risen and fallen and dominant centers of power and of civilization have moved from one place to another, man as a whole has steadily increased his capacity to control nature and to dominate time and space. This has resulted in a general tendency toward closer contacts among peoples; toward greater vulnerability of all to military, economic, and propaganda attacks; toward more trade and greater dependence of each people upon distant groups for its economy, culture, and security; toward larger and fewer political groups; toward greater similarities of culture among the major groups; toward acceleration of technological, institutional, and cultural change; toward more guidance by opinion, less by instinct, custom, and conscience; and toward greater intergroup co-operation and more capacity for general controls; in short, toward a shrinking of the world and an acceleration of history.

International relations have changed. They began with occasional war-like or ceremonial relations with immediate neighbors by each of tens of thousands of small, isolated, culturally distinct, custom guided, environment controlled, relatively static and immobile tribes. These relations involved relatively little tension, little foresight, and little general co-operation. Today each of a small and diminishing number of large, interdependent, culturally similar, opinion guided, value controlled, progressive and mobile states are in continuous and vital relationships of opposition and co-operation with all other states of the world. These relations involve high tension, continuous foresight and preparation, and increasing efforts to develop general regulations and controls.

It is tempting to consider technology, geography, and population as the master sciences of international relations. Knowledge of these disciplines, it is suggested, will lead to such regulation of technology and population, utilizing geographical conditions and resources as to establish the material foundations of a universal society from which will develop economic, political, communication, and educational systems, religions, and the other moral aspects of culture. Such a one way relation, as suggested by some interpretations of Marxian materialism, seems not to exist. The immaterial superstructure influences changes in technology and population, and in the significance of geography. The influence on human culture as a whole of psychological, sociological, and ethical conditions has probably increased with the progress of technology and the increase of the world's population. The relations of primitive tribes were more determined by the conditions of environment, population, and technology than are the relations of modern nations. Possibilities of control by ethical standards are today greater than ever before. Consequently, the nature of such standards and their functioning in human personalities and societies is of major importance in the study of contemporary international relations.

The discipline of technology, including study of the circumstances and conditions influencing the direction and rate of technological invention and diffusion, and the consequences of such changes on national character and policies and on the development of international institutions and organizations, is an important aspect of the discipline of international relations, but it is not likely that it can provide precise generalizations by which the future of international relations can be estimated.

REFERENCES

The literature on the mechanical and industrial aspects of technology is very great, that on its social consequences much less. A number of societies bring together technicians, industrialists, historians, and social scientists to discuss the history and prospects of technology with some attention to its social consequences. Of these the Franklin Institute of Philadelphia (*Journal*, Annual, 1826–) and the Newcomen Society of London (*Transactions*, Annual, 1920–) with an American Branch (*Addresses*, New York, 1923–) are outstanding. The Reports on *Recent Social Trends in the United States* prepared under the auspices of President Hoover's Committee on Social Trends (W. F. Ogburn, ed., 1933) and on *Technological Trends and National Policy* prepared under the auspices of the National Resources Committee (W. F. Ogburn, ed., 1937) include discussions of the most important social effects of technological change.

1. ADAMS, Henry, "Letter to History Teachers" in *The Degradation of Democratic Dogma* (New York, Macmillan, 1919).
2. BAXTER, James Phinney, III, *Scientists Against Time* (Boston, Little Brown, 1946).
3. BERGSON, Henri, *Creative Evolution* (New York, Holt, 1911).
4. BLOCH, Ivan, *The Future of War* (Boston, World Peace Foundation, 1914).
5. BRADLEY, David, *No Place to Hide* (Boston, Little, Brown, 1948).
6. BRINKMAN, Carl, "Invention," *Encyclopædia of the Social Sciences.*
7. BRODIE, Bernard, *Sea Power in the Machine Age* (Princeton, Princeton University Press, 1939).
8. ———, ed., *The Absolute Weapon* (New York, Harcourt, 1946).
8a. BRYSON, Lyman, FINKELSTEIN, Louis, MacIVER, R. M., and McKEON, R., *Symbols and Values*, Thirteenth and Fourteenth Symposia on Science, Philosophy and Religion (New York, Harper, 1954).
9. BUSH, Vannevar, *Modern Arms and Free Men* (New York, Simon & Schuster, 1949).
10. ———, *Science, The Endless Frontier*, A Report to the President (Washington, Government Printing Office, 1945).
11. ———, *Endless Horizons*, Washington, Public Affairs Press, 1946.
11a. CASSIRER, Ernst, *An Essay on Man*, 1944 (New York, Doubleday, 1953).
12. CROWTHER, J. G., and WHIDDINGTON, P., *Science at War* (New York, Philosophical Library, 1950).
13. DRAPER, J. W., *History of the Conflict Between Religion and Science* (New York, Appleton, 1875).
14. EARLE, Edward Mead, "The Influence of Air Power upon History," *Yale Review*, vol. 35 (1946), pp. 577-593.
15. FULLER, Major General J. F. C., *The Reformation of War* (New York, Dutton, 1923).
16. ———, *Armament and History* (New York, Scribner, 1945).
17. GILFILLAN, S. C., *The Sociology of Invention* (Chicago, Follett, 1935).
18. ———, "The Sociological Consequences of Technological Progress," *Current Sociology*, International Sociological Association (1954); see also Ogburn, ed., *Technological Trends and National Policy*.
19. HART, Hornell, *The Logistic Growth of Political Areas, Social Forces*, Vol. 26 (1948), pp. 397 ff; see also Ogburn, ed., *Technology and International Relations*.

20. HOBHOUSE, L. T., WHEELER, G. C., and GINSBURG, M., *The Material Culture and Social Institutions of the Simpler Peoples* (London, Chapman and Hall, 1915).

21. HOSELITZ, Bert F., ed., *The Progress of Underdeveloped Areas*, Harris Institute Lectures (Chicago, University of Chicago Press, 1952).

22. LAUFER, Berthold, *The Prehistory of Aviation*, Field Museum, Anthropological Series, Vol. 18 (Chicago, 1928).

23. LEDERER, Emil, "Technology," *Encyclopædia of the Social Sciences.*

24. LERNER, Daniel, and LASSWELL, H. D., *The Policy Sciences* (Stanford, Stanford University Press, 1951).

25. MALINOWSKI, Bronislaw, "Culture," *Encyclopædia of the Social Sciences.*

26. MARX, Karl, and ENGELS, Friedrich, *Manifesto of the Communist Party,* 1848 (New York, Rand School, 1919).

27. MASTERS, Dexter, and WAY, Katherine, eds., *One World or None* (New York, McGraw-Hill, 1946).

28. MEAD, Margaret, ed., *Cultural Patterns and Technical Change* (Paris, UNESCO, 1953).

29. MUMFORD, Lewis, *Technics and Civilization* (New York, Harcourt, 1934).

30. NEF, John U., *War and Human Progress* (Cambridge, Harvard University Press, 1950).

31. NORTHROP, F. S. C., *The Taming of the Nations, A Study of the Cultural Base of International Policy* (New York, Macmillan, 1952).

32. OGBURN, W. F., *Social Change with Respect to Culture and Original Nature,* 1922 (New York, Viking, 1928).

33. ———, ed., *Recent Social Trends in the United States* (New York, McGraw-Hill, 1933), 2 vols.

34. ———, ed., *Technological Trends and National Policy*, Report to Subcommittee on Technology of the National Resources Committee (Washington, Government Printing Office, 1937).

35. ———, *The Social Effects of Aviation* (Boston, Houghton Mifflin, 1946).

36. ———, ed., *Technology and International Relations*, Harris Institute Lectures (Chicago, University of Chicago Press, 1949).

37. PEAKE, Harold J., and FLEURE, Herbert J., *The Corridors of Time* (New Haven, Yale University Press, 1927-1936), 9 vols.

38. PEARSON, Karl, *The Grammar of Science*, 2nd ed. (London, Black, 1900).

39. PITT-RIVERS, Lieut-Gen. A. Lane-Fox, *The Evolution of Culture and Other Essays* (Oxford, Clarendon Press, 1906).

40. PUTNAM, Palmer, *Energy in the Future* (New York, Van Nostrand, 1953).

41. ROSSMAN, J., *The Psychology of the Inventor* (Washington, Inventor's Pub. Co., 1931).

42. SALTER, J. Arthur, *Modern Mechanization and Its Effects on the Structure of Society* (London, Oxford University Press, 1933).

43. SAPIR, Edward, *Language, An Introduction to the Study of Speech* (New York, Harcourt, 1921).

44. SARTON, George, *Introduction to the History of Science* (Washington, Carnegie Institution, 1927, 1931), 3 vols.

45. SCHURR, S. H., and MARSCHAK, Jacob, *Economic Aspects of Atomic Power* (Princeton, Princeton University Press, 1950).

46. SIEBERT, Fred S., *Freedom of the Press in England, 1476-1776, The Rise and Decline of Government Controls* (Urbana, University of Illinois Press, 1952).

47. SMYTH, Henry de Wolf, *Atomic Energy for Military Purposes* (Princeton, Princeton University Press, 1945).

48. SPAULDING, O. L., NICKERSON, H., and WRIGHT, J. W., *Warfare: A Study of Military Methods from the Earliest Times* (London, Harrop, 1924).
49. STALEY, Eugene, *World Economy in Transition* (New York, Council on Foreign Relations, 1939).
49a. STEFANSSON, Vilhjalmur, *Adventures in Error* (New York, McBridge, 1936).
50. STONE, Marshall, "Science and Statecraft," *Science,* Vol. 105 (May, 1947), pp. 507 ff.
51. TAUSSIG, Frank W., *Inventors and Money Makers: Lectures on Some Relations Between Economics and Psychology* (New York, Macmillan, 1915).
52. TAYLOR, George Rogers, *The Transportation Revolution: Industry, 1815-1860* (New York, Rinehart, 1951).
53. THOMAS, Franklin, *The Environmental Basis of Society, A Study in the History of Sociological Theory* (New York, Century, 1925).
54. TOYNBEE, Arnold, *A Study of History* (London, Oxford University Press, 1934, 1939, 1954), 10 vols.
55. USHER, Abbott Payson, *A History of Mechanical Inventions*, rev. ed. (Cambridge, Harvard University Press, 1954).
56. VAIHINGER, H., *The Philosophy of "As If," A System of the Theoretical, Practical and Religious Fictions of Mankind,* trans. by C. K. Ogden, 2nd ed. (London, Kegan Paul, 1935).
57. VEBLEN, Thorstein, *The Instinct of Workmanship and the State of the Industrial Arts,* 1914 (New York, 1918).
58. VINER, Jacob, and others, "Symposium on Atomic Energy and Its Implications," American Philosophical Society, *Proceedings,* Vol. 90 (1946), pp. 1 ff.
59. WHITE, Andrew D., *A History of the Warfare of Science with Theology in Christendom* (New York, Appleton, 1896).
60. WIENER, Norbert, *Cybernetics, or Control and Communication in the Animal and Machine* (New York, Wiley, 1948).
61. WISSLER, Clark, *The Relation of Nature to Man in Aboriginal America* (New York, Oxford University Press, 1926).
62. WRIGHT, Quincy, *A Study of War* (Chicago, University of Chicago Press, 1942), pp. 40, 46-48, 80-88, 144-151, 168, 291-328, 383-385, 426-429, 501, 508, 575-590, 606-608, 613, 666-676, 714, 792-797, 805, 810, 857, 1228, 1241-1246, 1291-1293.
63. ———, *Problems of Stability and Progress in International Relations* (Berkeley, University of California Press, 1954).
64. WRIGHT, Theodore P., *Aviation's Place in Civilization,* Wilbur Wright Memorial Lecture, Royal Aeronautical Society (London, May 31, 1945).

The Sociology of
International Relations

DEFINITION

THE SOCIOLOGY of international relations is the science relating human
groups with one another and with the supergroups in which they participate. It includes also the art of uniting groups into supergroups, and
of maintaining and developing the latter. It has a close relationship to the
history and the philosophy of international relations, dealing respectively
with the actual course of intergroup co-operation and opposition in time,
and with the values which have united and divided groups.

The sociology is closely related to the psychology of international relations because a group is at the same time a social and a psychic phenomenon. It exists as a social entity with observable processes and institutions
of intra- and intergroup communication, of cultural maintenance and
transmission, of co-operation to achieve group ends, and of organization
to promote group unity and to facilitate group action. A group also exists
as a psychic phenomenon in patterns of thought and action in the minds
of individuals discoverable by the introspection of its members or by
observation of their behavior. Such patterns permit members to recognize
and identify the group and its agencies, to anticipate appropriate behavior of other members in given situations, to understand certain symbols and conventions, and to maintain certain opinions and attitudes
shared with other members (132). The attitudes of non-members in contact with a group may be no less important in defining it than those of
its members.

There have been controversies in the past as to the priority of the individual or of the group, of man or the state (109), but modern social psychologists, reverting to Aristotle's conception that man is a political or social animal, usually assume the continuous interaction of individuals and groups (21, 118). Men are found only in groups. Individuals do not manifest human characteristics apart from group experience and obviously groups do not exist without the individuals that compose them. Sociology and psychology, therefore, are not to be distinguished by the assertion that one deals with groups, the other with individuals, but rather as different approaches to the problem of human behavior—the one through study of the groups, organizations, communities, societies, institutions, cultures, social values, and ideologies which reflect human personality and influence human behavior, and the other through study of the biological inheritance, physiological characteristics, psychic mechanisms, and specific attitudes, and opinions which form personality, explain its functioning in group life, and modify societies and cultures.

These two approaches, converging in the disciplines of psychological sociology and social psychology, may constitute the fundamental, but still imperfectly developed, bases for a discipline of international relations, as indeed, of all the other social disciplines. Social behavior cannot be explained if either the cultural background or the individual attitudes involved in a situation are neglected (118).

Sociology has roots in antiquity and the renaissance. Plato, Aristotle, Machiavelli, Bodin, Vico, and Montesquieu wrote on human and social behavior and its adaptation to the environment. As a discipline, however, sociology hardly emerged until the nineteenth century when the speculations of political philosophers, philosophers of history, and philosophers of science, and the activities of practical reformers were synthesized in the comprehensive systems of Auguste Comte (20), Herbert Spencer (109), and Lester Ward (125). These and other writers sought to apply the methods of natural science to the study of human society, but even those trained in scientific observation like Lester Ward, a paleo-botanist, and L. H. Morgan (75), an ethnologist, based their sociological theories in large measure upon assumptions about human nature confirmed only by introspection. The broad systems of these writers dealt with, and often centered upon, international relations. The problem of co-operation within groups and conflict between them as exemplified in the relations of states naturally attracted attention because states were the dominant groups at the time they wrote. Different writers gave different emphasis to these two aspects of group activity, and to the significance of different types of groups in the process of social evolution, social dynamics, social progress, social adaptation, or social change. All of these terms were utilized by the early sociologists, most of whom were influenced by the concept of organic evolution (16).

Comte thought the significant conflict was between the party of order and conservatism desiring to maintain the existing social equilibrium and the party of progress and liberalism desiring to improve that situation, but he was confident that with advance in sociological knowledge the objectives of these opposing parties could be synthesized in a higher co-operation (20). Karl Marx thought the significant conflict was between economic classes, the exploiters and the exploited in the production process, and that progress in technology and social awareness making a particular economic organization obsolete would lead to revolutionary action by the exploited, resulting in a new economic and social order (70).

Herbert Spencer envisaged the major conflict as that between the individual, whose character was shaped by the traditions of an earlier state of society, and society itself, especially as organized in the state which could only function satisfactorily if man's character was adapted to its needs. Like Comte, he hoped this conflict would be resolved by broader understanding of the ethical principles applicable to contemporary society, but he insisted that this understanding could be effective only if founded upon knowledge acquired by free individuals. He had less confidence than Comte in the active initiative of organized society, and his individualism was at the opposite end of the spectrum from the socialism of Marx (109, 110). Lester Ward, with characteristic American belief in education, gave greater weight than did Spencer to social planning, although the basic conflict he envisaged, similar to that of Spencer, was between the utilitarian disposition of man to adapt himself to social conditions in order to maximize happiness through social planning, and the instinctive urges for food and sex which if unrestrained would lead to antisocial action (125). Both Spencer and Ward recognized the conflict between territorially defined groups, usually called *races, nations,* or *states,* but they distinguished the *militaristic* states, governed by traditional and *irrational* motives, from the *industrial* states, governed by utilitarian and *rational* motives. They were convinced that the latter would prevail and war would disappear as man's understanding increased through education. Both of these writers regarded the process of increasing social integration as *natural* and in accord with the general movement of evolution from incoherent homogeneity to coherent heterogeneity, thus putting themselves in opposition to the second law of thermo-dynamics which holds that entropy tends to a maximum, or, in other words, that stability is increased by the disintegration of structures into *incoherent homogeneity.* Spencer indeed gave a certain recognition to these opposite tendencies by assuming that in course of time evolution would end and the process of disintegration would begin. But these oscillations, in the order of billions of years, were not of importance in the present stage of cosmic history in which more complex organizations of matter, life, and society were evolving (16).

All of the writers which have been mentioned conceived of the primary social conflict as within rather than between nations. They believed that conflicts between parties, classes, or opinions, or conflicts between the individual and society created conditions which generated conflict between states. It remained for Gumplowitz (32) and to a lesser extent his disciple Ratzenhoffer (96) to give primary emphasis to international conflicts. The former, regarding the state as an organism and applying the Darwinian hypothesis of struggle for existence and survival of the fittest, concluded that international strife was inevitable, and that this strife determined the internal structure of a society and the character of the individuals which composed it. He pessimistically concluded that nations would persist in policies of power and expansion, bringing them into conflict with other nations. Through such conflict the victor might progress toward achievement of its ideals, but no general progress was to be expected only relatively frequent oscillations. This extreme social Darwinism was undoubtedly influenced by, as it in turn influenced, the political theory and practice of states, during the late nineteenth and twentieth centuries, especially those of Germany (42).

The Hegelian and Marxian theories of group conflict and co-operation foresaw continuous social progress, through the dialectic of thesis, antithesis and synthesis, rather than through the Darwinian theory of struggle, elimination and survival of the fittest. They thus gave some support to the theses of sociologists such as the anarchist Kropotkin (41) and the internationalist Novicov (80), that co-operation was a more significant feature of social (as distinct from organic) evolution than conflict. The relation between co-operation and conflict in social organization and change was given a new emphasis by Georg Simmel who held that both processes necessarily coexisted in all groups even primary groups (102, 111). He thus brought intragroup and intergroup relations into the same category. Intergroup relations can be interpreted as the internal relations of a supergroup within which the element of opposition among the member groups is relatively great and that of co-operation among them is relatively small (132).

While the great sociological systems of the nineteenth century developed useful concepts and classifications, they did not stimulate detailed and relevant observation, or methods permitting quantification. It was not until the early twentieth century that sociology began to move from a philosophy to a science. At that time W. I. Thomas' study of the Polish peasant (118), the accumulating observations of numerous field anthropologists (31, 75, 121), and the extensive applications of statistical method to social phenomena (97) gave sociology an empirical basis and a method for quantitative comparison of forces and relations. The utilization of psychological analysis, emphasized by Lester Ward, was stimulated by the investigations of Freud and the techniques of Thurstone and others for measuring attitudes and opinions, giving rise to the disciplines of psychological sociology and social psychology.

With this new scientific orientation, however, sociology tended to concentrate on methodology; on group processes, forces, and relations for the study of which statistics were available; on the detailed study of relatively small and simple groups; and on particular processes in the life of complex groups, such as the family, urban life, rural life, and delinquency, not within the direct orbit of other recognized social disciplines. Since international relations presents peculiar difficulties either for direct observation or for statistical or psychological analysis, it tended to be neglected. Few twentieth century sociologists have devoted specialized attention to this field. A list of twenty-nine specialized fields of sociology published in 1924 did not include the sociology of international relations although some works in this field were included in the bibliographies on *political sociology* and *the sociology of economic relations* (11).

The sociology of international relations sets the concrete problems of relations among contemporary states in the broad context of relations between any human groups. Such groups are of many kinds. They may be distinguished by relative size ranging from the family of two or three people to the human race of over two billion; by relative permanence ranging from the casual street crowd to the state or civilization which may last for millennia; by degree of solidarity and integration ranging from the casual, unorganized meeting whose members manifest more opposition than unity, to nations and states integrated by elaborate systems of communication and organization and unified by cultural traits and social, economic and political purposes shared by all the members; and by degree of artificiality ranging from natural, unplanned groups such as the family, tribe, and village (*Gemeinschaft*) to the consciously planned commercial corporation, international union, and voluntary association (*Gesellschaft*) (120). Groups may also be distinguished by degree of comprehensiveness ranging from the diplomatic conference to discuss a very limited agenda to the government of a state with powers of life and death over its members and capacity to bring the activities and interests of all subgroups and individuals within its direction; by degree of participation ranging from the autocratic group identified in opinion, policy, and action with the ruler to the democratic group in which the opinion of all the members contributes to a public opinion controlling the group's form, policy, and behavior; and by degree of mobility ranging from the political state fixed to a territory with definite boundaries and with constitution and laws not easily nor frequently altered to a group of travelers moving through the world by air with plans subject to easy and rapid change. The distinction of groups according to their degree of complexity is considered of major importance by many. This ranges from the primary group of family, clan, or village in which all members of the group meet face to face and feel secure because of confidence in the solidarity of the group and its support of its members in all emergencies, through secondary groups bringing primary groups together, to tertiary, quaternary, or even higher degrees of organization, including numerous cross-sectioning, functional groups such as are found in contemporary, national, and international societies. Such complexity is believed by some to disintegrate the primary groups, to isolate the individual to a condition of *anomie*, and to reduce his sense of security (27, 37). In such complex groups, however, the relations of super groups with subgroups, of both with functional groups, and of all with the ultimate individuals, may be very varied, and the consequences upon the individual may be equally varied.

Many other criteria for classifying groups could be devised, but from the point of view of the sociology of international relations, the most important distinctions are probably those concerning degree of complexity and degree of participation. While modern sociologists in general, and particularly the anthropologists and psychological sociologists, have been especially interested in primary groups, the sociology of international relations is more concerned with extremely complex groups, although *artificial* primary groups, such as the diplomatic conference and the international council and assembly, have been increasingly important in international affairs. The nation-state is itself a complex group composed of numerous families, villages, cities, counties, provinces, churches, corporations, associations, parties, pressure groups, and so forth. It tends, however, to develop a highly integrated system of internal communication and organization and a high degree of solidarity of culture and opinion. Thus it becomes a primary focus of loyalty among its members and dominates over all the subgroups within it. The nation-state, therefore, may be regarded as a primary group if that term is used in a broad sense. International organizations and diplomatic systems composed of states may in the same sense be regarded as secondary groups.

Political scientists and international lawyers usually assume this situation and regard the world's structure as a relatively simple one, involving only nation-states and the family of nations. The sociologist, however, recognizes the tremendous complexity of the situation, because of the complexity of the nation-state itself, and the existence of numerous other groups both regional and functional. Furthermore, if to simplify, they treat the relationship of the nation-states to the family of nations in abstraction, they treat it as an example of the relation of groups to parallel and supergroups observable in numerous other situations. They recognize that the modern period of world history dominated by nation-states and international organizations is not the necessary condition of a universal society. It is, in fact, sharply distinguished from the European middle ages in which a hierarchy of political groups, primary, secondary, tertiary, quaternary, and more, pyramided up from families, villages, and manors, through various degrees of feudal lordship to kingdoms, themselves subordinate to the theoretically universal empire. Furthermore, the power of these political groups was paralleled by the power of religious groups similarly pyramiding up to the Pope representing the Universal Church. The almost sovereign powers of commercial leagues composed of widely separated cities further complicated the situation in the later middle ages. Primary groups of family and village dominated as they have in China and most of Asia until very recent times (37).

The sociologist of international relations, differing from other sociologists, is especially interested in groups which, like states, are relatively large, relatively permanent, relatively solid, relatively natural, relatively comprehensive, and relatively immobile, though the effects of variations of these characteristics is of interest. Nation-states in fact exhibit a wide range of variation in all of these characteristics.

Sociologists distinguish *social entities* existing in time and space, of which groups are the most important; from *social processes* or typical sequences by which social stability is maintained or social adaptation takes place; from *social forces* conceived as outside of social entities and social processes but causing adaptive or destructive changes within or among them; and from *social relations* expressed by abstract formulae indicating the influence of change in one variable upon change in another (132).

Typical entities, processes, forces, and relations are expressed by sociological terms which usually signify complex variables. Thus social entities include such variables as personality, culture, community, society, association, organization, institution. Social processes include such variables as interaction, diffusion, assimilation, opposition, competition, conflict, accommodation, collective behavior, integration, differentiation, unrest, co-operation, social control, government, politics, administration, education, propaganda. Social forces include such variables as social pressure, attitude, interest, opinion, value symbol, and action. Finally, social relations include such variables as social distance, social status, cultural lag, social contact, social isolation, social solidarity, social hierarchy. War, for example, may be treated as a species of conflict which is itself a species of opposition, and that a species of social process contrasted with co-operation. This terminology may suggest that conflict is an entity which is either present or absent in a given situation but the sociologist treats it as a variable which exists in greater or less degree in most situations. Both opposition and co-operation, though analytically opposed, are, as Simmel pointed out, to be expected to co-exist in some degree in all situations. Even active belligerents occasionally co-operate through cartels for the exchange of prisoners of war or for mutual observance of the laws of war (132, 134).

Somewhat parallel to the distinctions between entities, processes, forces, and relations is that between social structure, social function, social change, and social analysis, often appearing as the basic divisions in text books on sociology.

Discussions of social structure describe such complex entities as a society or a community in terms of the component and constituent groups or other entities of which it is composed much as anatomy describes the body in terms of its bones, organs, systems, and other parts. Some sociologists instead of considering the elements of social structure as groups, consider them as institutions which formalize expectations, roles, and functions (89, 102).

Social function refers to typical processes within a social structure, with the motivation of such processes in a given situation, with their service to the stability or adaptation of the structure, and with the mechanisms of social control. It is related to the study of social structure much as is physiology to anatomy.

Social change deals with the external influences, sometimes called social forces, such as inventions, population movements, cultural diffusion, political conquest, ideological propaganda tending to change social structures, often utilizing such typical processes as competition, conflict, accommodation, assimilation, and cultural lag. The social psychologists pay especial attention to the interaction of group values and individual attitudes toward them in explaining social change (118). Social change deals with the dynamics of society, whether the process is gradual or revolutionary, while social structure and social function deal with its statics.

Social analysis seeks to define a society or social situation in terms of relationships among operationally defined variables and constants, such as distances, energies, tensions, resistances, within a given system. Many sociologists, while recognizing the ultimate importance of such an analysis, similar to that customarily employed by physical scientists, believe that sociology will for a long time have to content itself with the type of structural-functional analysis characteristic of much of biology (89).

Sociologists who have dealt with international relations have approached the subject from many angles, including approaches characteristic of other disciplines. Thus sociologists have studied the international consequences of environmental differences, of population movements and migrations, and of new inventions and introduced technologies, but these studies are also within the fields of international economics, geography, demography, and technology. Sociologists have also studied public opinion, semantics, and propaganda. These studies have special relevance to international affairs and are dealt with in the specialized discipline of international communication. The study of attitudes, of personality in relation to culture, of group dynamics, and of education are also sociological subjects, but have been more commonly approached from the psychological point of view and, as applied to international affairs, constitute much of the disciplines of international education and the psychology of international relations.

The sociology of international relations, like sociology in general, has suffered attrition through the development of certain of its aspects into independent disciplines. As has been the case with philosophy and history, there has been controversy whether sociology should be regarded as the most general social discipline treating social phenomena as a science, or as itself a specialized discipline approaching social phenomena and problems from the concept or the group and the institution. This conception would differentiate sociology from social psychology emphasizing individual social behavior, from social ethics emphasizing social ideologies, and from demography emphasizing social conditions. There has in fact been a tendency to distinguish the *social sciences* (sociology, economics, political science) from the *behavorial sciences* (social psychology, cultural anthropology), the *policy sciences* (politics, administration, communication, education, ethics, technology), and the *demographic sciences* (population, social geography), but most of the social disciplines actually utilize more than one of these points of view (48).

ASSUMPTIONS

Sociologists usually assume (*a*) that human beings exist only in groups characterized by more or less communication among the members, by more or less common culture, by more or less co-operation to maintain common values or to achieve common goals, and by a more or less centralized organization of the group as a whole; (*b*) that groups originate through the interaction of individuals with one another producing relations of co-operation and opposition, that they develop through the interaction of individuals with *in-groups* in which co-operation predominates and with *out-groups* with which opposition predominates, but that the complex of interactions produces relations of opposition, as well as of co-operation, within every group; (*c*) that the socially significant behavior patterns of individuals are a consequence not of heredity but of their participation in group life, culture, and institutions; and (*d*) that group characteristics handed down by tradition and stabilized by institutions are continually modified through the influence of leaders, of migrants from other groups, of invented and imported ideas and techniques, and of random variations in the attitudes of members.

The sociologist of international relations in addition to these propositions usually makes the following more concrete assumptions. (*a*) Sovereign states like all other groups are continually changing through the influence of new technological and demographic conditions, of the attitudes of leaders and of the opinions of other groups, subordinate, co-ordinate, and superordinate.

(b) The present situation, in which sovereign states are the dominant groups demanding and receiving the primary loyalty of individuals, and international organizations are secondary groups inferior in power, is a historical, not a necessary, situation.

(c) Opposition to the *out-group* has been the most important, but not the only, means for maintaining the identity of large *in-groups*, and for integrating supergroups. International groups, consequently, tend to be merely political and unstable, but they may become social and institutional.

(d) Modern inventions have tended to shrink distances between all parts of the world; to increase the vulnerability of all groups to military, economic, and propaganda attacks; to increase the destructiveness of such attacks; to accelerate rates of cultural diffusion and social change; and also to accentuate the tendency to maintain existing groups and structures threatened by social change. On the one hand is a tendency toward increasing solidarity, integration, and co-operation of more comprehensive groups, regional or universal, and on the other hand, a tendency toward greater loyalties to, and greater animosities and tensions among, the established groups, especially the national states.

The striking feature of these assumptions is that they set few limits to the possibilities for reconstructing world society. Sociologists do not assume the inevitability of any institution nor of a *human nature* which is implacably aggressive, implacably irrational, or implacably incorrigible. Institutions are the consequence of historic contingencies and they change as men plan and history proceeds. Human behavior, while based upon the biological character of man, is a consequence, so far as international relations is concerned, of technological, cultural, and institutional conditioning.

Sociologists do not attribute a necessary or persistent nature to any particular type of group such as the sovereign state. The character of sovereign states in general, or of particular states, or of systems of states are the consequence, not of abstract definition, but of continually changing conditions of technology, organization, external relations, and opinion. Sociologists particularly emphasize that the existence of groups, their solidarity, power, policy, and action depend in no small measure upon the public opinion of their members which continually gnaws away at beliefs, value systems, and institutions, and is continually modified by inventions, propaganda, new technologies, and changes in international relations. While instinct may in large measure guide the behavior of animals, custom that of primitive man, and conscience that of men in earlier civilizations, opinion becomes increasingly the guide as communication increases the contact and interdependence of groups of diverse culture (100).

Public opinion is notably fluid and yet in the modern world it is the foundation upon which many of the generalizations in the fields of international politics, international organization, international law, and international economics are based. The institutions, value systems, loyalties, ideologies, and group interests which these disciplines assume would vanish if public opinion ceased to support them. The sociologist of international relations is in a better position to appreciate the quicksand upon which these disciplines are founded than are the students of these disciplines themselves.

The sociologist of international relations, therefore, aware of the variety among primitive peoples, historic civilizations, and modern nations, and the mutability of public opinion, is ready to examine sympathetically, but critically, the possibilities of all proposals of international reform. They realize the possibility of change but at the same time, aware of the tenacity of some institutions, cultures, and attitudes, they are skeptical of the feasibility of proposals for sudden change based only on rational grounds. Aware of the interrelationships of institutions, culture traits, and social stability, they are cautious, and insist upon examination of the more remote, as well as the immediate, consequences of proposals. The modern sociologist, aware of the reason both for the conservatism of Edmund Burke and the radicalism of Jean-Jacques Rousseau, is anxious not to throw the baby of present happiness out with the bath of obsolete practices, or to destroy individual personality by subordinating it to the perfect functioning of the great Leviathan. He can be an *idealistic-realist* and a *realistic-idealist* at the same time (132, 133).

The biological character of man, the density and distribution of population, the physical resources of the world, the existing technologies for their exploitation, and the requirements of group life set limits to the possibilities of social and political organization. But these limits are wide and within them all is flux. Given time and wise leadership, history may realize forms of world society which today are only speculations of philosophy (47, 48, 49, 65, 72, 79).

ANALYSIS

While sociology and anthropology have sought more than the other social sciences to follow the methods of natural science, to emancipate themselves from practical needs of the moment, and to develop generalizations of predictive value, sociologists and anthropologists perhaps tend to be more cautious than other social scientists in venturing upon definite predictions. The breadth of their assumptions permit a wide range of possibilities for the future and the breadth of their experience manifests the variability of social forms and behaviors (71). They are aware that what generalizations can be made are contingent upon many variables which have not been and perhaps cannot be analyzed and, therefore, may not be valid under cultural and social conditions different from those in which the observations were made on which the generalization is based (118). Political scientists may make predictions on the assumption that sovereign states will always be what they have recently been. Economists may make predictions on the assumption that the economic man and the market in which he functions will again become what they were in the nineteenth century. But the sociologist has avoided such narrow assumptions. If he predicts at all, he has to predict, not what would have happened if his assumptions had remained valid, but what will actually happen, or what will happen under precisely defined conditions.

The earlier sociologists who sought to make long-range predictions in the international field were usually either rational humanists, like Comte, Spencer, and Ward, who assumed that man had certain permanent needs and would eventually arrange his affairs to maximize their realization, or biological determinists, like Gumplowitz and Ratzenhoffer, who assumed that men and groups would always utilize the means that tradition and circumstances had placed in their hands to achieve their fundamental wants with little regard for long-run consequences or the interests of other human beings. The first type tended to be *idealistic* philosophers, the second type *realistic* historians. Between them are the modern sociologists, who recognize that men are guided by both needs and desires, by both long-run and short-run considerations. They refuse to oversimplify either *human nature* or *group interests* and find that most human situations are influenced in varying degrees by both egoism and altruism, both individual attitudes and group opinions, both *inner directives* and *other directives*, both drives and ideals, both custom and conscience, both traditions of the past and opportunities of the future. They are often baffled by the complexity of the world situation, refuse to deal with it comprehensively, and content themselves with the detailed description of primitive tribes, civilized towns, or particular professions or classes; with the elaboration of definitions, concepts, and methodologies; or with advising on practical subjects like crime, poverty, prostitution, race prejudice, or war. These studies have all contributed to the development of sociology and some of them, such as studies of the sociology of war (25, 107, 108, 132), race prejudice (53, 77), migration (30), and invention (84, 134), have contributed to the sociology of international relations. There have not, however, been any adequate analyses of the latter subject as a whole. It is not yet a discipline distinct from sociology in general.

As already noted, sociologists have often divided their subject into the study of social structure, social function, social change, and social analysis, respectively emphasizing the more precise concepts of social entity, social process, social force, and social relation. The characteristic approaches of the emerging discipline of the sociology of international relations have been similar, but with slightly different emphasis because of the great practical importance in international affairs of distinguishing the factors making, on the one hand, for peace and stability and on the other for war and change. The terms *international typology, international statics, international dynamics,* and *international analysis* may be suggested. In all of these approaches, the sociologist of international relations co-operates, not only with the sociologists and the social psychologists, but also with the cultural anthropologists, who, through familiarity with primitive peoples, can observe social structures and processes on a small scale and can infer functional and dynamic relationships through comparison of many diverse groups. Also suggestive in all of these aspects of the sociology of international relations is the work of the ecologists. With an even broader base in the behavior patterns of all biological forms, they are able to apply to intergroup relations the physiologists conception of *homeostasis* or self-regulated maintenance of life conditions, continuously self-corrected to approach an optimum stability (29). Human ecology, predominantly influenced by cultural conditions, cannot be treated by the same methods as animal ecology, determined by natural conditions (62, 87).

International typology. The study of international structure involves the classification of groups in accordance with the types to which they tend to conform, and description of the entities of which they are composed. States, nationalities, minorities, elites, governments, international organizations, and other entities entering into international relations have been thus classified and typified (49, 112, 135). Nineteenth century sociologists often distinguished between industrial and military states (110); while political scientists distinguished great powers and smaller powers. Others have distinguished young, adolescent, and old states; democratic and autocratic states; maritime and terrestrial states; industrial and agricultural states; traditional and progressive states; efficient and inefficient states. Efforts have been made to relate typical foreign policies to each of these types (132). Actual states, however, have such varied characteristics and are so suspectible to change, that they do not easily fall into any typology. While the first two of the categories noted have been of importance in studies of international politics, in most cases policy cannot be closely correlated with any one characteristic. Such categories may be useful if treated as abstract variables which may be possessed by any state in some degree. Thus treated, the study of structure and typology merges into that of function and relations.

The typology of nationalities, minorities, and elites has been of some significance and has contributed to the understanding of particular situations (80, 112, 130, 135). Less attention has been given by sociologists to the typology of international organizations, alliances, and regional arrangements (18, 49) though recent studies of the typology of organizations by economists and administrators (5, 24, 103) as well as by sociologists (50, 73, 74) have greatly improved on the classifications of governments familiar to political scientists since the time of Aristotle. In general it may be said that the method of typology has not yet proved particularly useful in the study of international relations. The entities primarily involved are so few in number, so variable in character, and so great in extent that each tends to be *sui generis* and classification is difficult (79).

A more sophisticated approach to the study of international structure might seek to analyze the entire institutional structure of the world with reference to the functional relevance of each part to the whole as does the anatomist for the human body, though the *structures* with which the latter deals are much more tangible. Such an analysis, taking account of all the official and unofficial international organizations, as well as the institutions of state, church, education, industry, and commerce, might if treated historically indicate the processes of adaptation, self-correction, obsolescence and elimination, maintaining, or failing to maintain, stability (49). If treated synthetically, utilizing recent theories of organization, administration and planning, such studies might appraise this structure in accordance with defined human values and suggest practical action (24).

International statics. The study of social processes in relation to social functions has been central in most sociological treatises. As the physiologist recognizes the interdependence of, and need of balance among, many organic processes—digestion, circulation, heat regulation—to maintain a healthy organism (17), so the sociologist recognizes the need for equilibrium among many social processes—conflict, accommodation, co-operation—to maintain a healthy society. But because these processes are creations of language and culture rather than of matter and motion, they are difficult to identify and classify. Such words as *conflict, competition, accommodation, co-operation, progress, diffusion, assimilation, integration,* and *differentiation* occur in the discussion of many situations. Conflict, for instance, takes place in street brawls, in strikes, in insurrections, in revolutions, and in wars. Some light can be thrown on the latter by understanding the genesis, development, and termination of other types of conflict. Each type of conflict has its peculiar characteristics, but knowledge of the genera contributes to knowledge of the species and of the particular case (104, 132, 134). More importance, for the study of international statics, may be attributed to the analysis of other terms pointing to processes of peaceful adjustment, such as adjudication, administration, conciliation, and negotiation (24, 132).

Determination of the influence of different social processes in producing stability or change is of great importance in international relations. International politics has paid particular attention to the balance of power but this particular equilibrating process has proved to be of increasingly dubious efficiency as the cost of war and its probable destructiveness, even to the victor, have increased. Sociologists of international relations may, by more extensive analysis of the processes of the world community, discover regulatory procedures of more anticipatory and less drastic character than those traditionally relied upon by the power politicians. Various measurements of international relations may contribute to this end (134).

Of particular importance to international relations is the study of the process by which geographically related groups have become assimilated into a supergroup. This process has been observed among primitive peoples in which clans become absorbed into tribes and tribes into nations and federations. It has also been observed in the history of modern federations in which loyalties have moved from the state to the union. Sometimes such movements defeat themselves by the very rapidity of their initial success. The progress of federation if too rapid may stimulate countermovements in which traditional groups resist the process of assimilation and may frustrate it by revolt or withdrawal. The over-rapid progress in developing more comprehensive social units may lead to civil war as in the case of the United States. It is important, in developing world organization, to attempt to analyze the process, to measure the speed with which it can safely proceed, and, if possible, to regulate the rate of change (122, 133, 134).

Sociologists have examined the processes of communication, standardization, co-operation, and organization with this end in view. Increasingly abundant communication tends to develop greater cultural standardization within the supergroup. Increase in common values tends to develop more widespread co-operation to realize these values and this is facilitated by more efficient organization. Communication may, however, be resisted through the erection of artificial barriers when its corroding influence on local culture is observed. Organization to extend communication, to maintain common standards, and to facilitate co-operation in larger areas may present a focus for attack by local areas that do not as yet share the prevailing cultural standards. Measurement of the rate of change of these processes might facilitate the application of measures to maintain dynamic stability (84, 133, 134).

Closely related to these social and economic processes are the political processes of propaganda, law enforcement, public administration, and politics by which communication, standardization, co-operation, and organization are respectively facilitated. These are the methods by which groups have been built but their study comes rather in the orbit of political science than of sociology. Because violence may be the most rapid means for influencing dissident opinions to conform and to permit law and organization to progress in the larger sphere, the process of integrating states into superstates has seldom been free from war. Union against a common enemy or union under a powerful empire have been more common than voluntary federation to realize the benefits of peaceful co-operation (132).

International dynamics. While many sociologists have accounted for social change by the operation of *social forces*, there is considerable difference in the interpretation of this term. Technological inventions, discoveries of new resources, dynamic personalities, new ideologies and religions, concentrations of political power, changes in population and wealth may produce far-reaching social effects (82, 83). Sociologists have studied such effects and have sought to predict consequences expected from particular inventions such as the airplane and the atomic bomb, from the introduction of new technologies into underdeveloped areas; from the progress of literacy in particular areas; from the propaganda of new ideologies; and from the differential growth of population. Such studies have attempted to analyze different, but interdependent, aspects of a culture or civilization—the technology, the ideology or value system, the political and legal system, the economic system, the social organization, and so forth—and to estimate disturbing effects of the lag of one aspect behind another (82). They have also attempted to identify the type of influence most likely to initiate a process of social change (84).

The classes of historic events, personalities, or movements just discussed, while susceptible of sociological study, have sometimes been considered not as elementary *social forces* but as complexes of social forces, reserving the latter term, as did Lester Ward who stimulated their study in the nineteenth century, to psychic characteristics such as inventiveness, the scientific spirit, progressiveness, aggressiveness, managerial capacity, political judgment, procreativeness, educatability, inquisitiveness (125). The social psychologists identify individual attitudes and public opinions diverging from established social values and cultural standards as *social forces* (118), while the psychoanalysts emphasize the dynamic influence of individual drives of sex and dominance operating through such mechanisms as ambivalence, repression, displacement, projection, and identification, and conditioned by social experience. Such human characteristics may exist in greater or less degree in a given population, situation, or personality, and are thus, at least theoretically, measurable. The analysis of organic drives, such as sex, food, self-preservation, and dominance (132), and of human wishes such as security, recognition, intimacy, and adventure (118), or survival, order, belonging, and security (95), and the measurement of concrete attitudes and opinions in a given community may provide the best approach to the study of social forces. This study has been particularly developed by social psychologists to be considered in the next chapter.

A distinction may, however, be made between individual drives, motivations, psychic mechanisms, and attitudes—primarily a psychological study—and social opinions, policies, goals, and values—primarily a sociological study (118). The former refers to patterns or dispositions of individual minds while the latter refer to ideas, proposals, or objectives which are communicated from one person to another and thus function as social norms or standards. An opinion has been defined as an expressed attitude, though the expression may, intentionally or unintentionally, diverge from the attitude. Social policy or action cannot proceed far on the basis of undisclosed attitudes, though attitudes and opinions reciprocally influence each other and the attitudes of leaders may have a major influence on public opinion (132, 133, 134).

The study of opinion as effecting international relations lies in the field of international communication, while the study of attitude is an important aspect of international education.

International analysis. The analysis of relations, especially of quantitative relations, among operationally defined variables and constants, is the final step in the development of a science. The sociology of international relations has made beginnings in this form of analysis.

Investigators with a sociological orientation have analyzed economic, administrative and communication systems; have subjected such concepts as organization, administration, competition, monopoly, monopsony, oligopoly, rational behavior, optimal communications, and games to measurable terms; have devised models exhibiting the operation of such systems; and have treated the relations involved mathematically (24, 48, 103). These studies, referred to in the chapters on economics and communications, may prove of great value in the study of international relations.

The concepts of *menace* and *defense* in international politics may be measured in terms of the rate of change in armament budgets, and the relation of these variables to armament races, international tension, and war may be estimated if such factors as political grievances, economic disadvantages of armament costs, and economic advantages of trade with a rival are treated as parameters (98). The statistical analysis of the frequency distribution of *lethal quarrels* (measured by number killed from 10^0 in murders to 10^7 in world wars) in different places and different periods of history may throw light on the causes and consequences of interpersonal and intergroup hostilities (99).

The concept of *distance*, springing from the simple idea of space, may be extended by analogy to many types of relations between two social entities. The technological distance between two states, for example, refers to the ease of communication and transport between them, and strategic distance refers to the ease of military attack by one on the other. Legal and ideological distances refer respectively to the degree in which each group recognizes the legal equality of the other, and the degree in which the intellectual processes of each is comprehensible by the other.

Social and political distances refer respectively to the degree in which the two groups have similar social institutions and to the degree in which they participate in a unified political system. Psychological and war-expectancy distances refer respectively to the degree of friendliness or hostility between two groups and to the degree in which they anticipate peace or war in their relations. These distances may be roughly measured by the method of comparative judgment. Analysis of the relation of these variables to one another has proved of some value in determining the probability of war between pairs of states (132, 134).

Study of the rigidity of social structures measured by their resistance to change; study of the rate of accumulation of social energy measured by the rate of capital growth; and study of the fluctuation of social tensions measured by analysis of the press and other media of public opinion might provide a basis for establishing the relation between these apparently dependent variables. It has been suggested that this relation may be analogous to that of resistance, current strength, and electromotive force in an electrical system ($E = CR$). Such measurements and the understanding of such relations might provide useful guides for operating regulatory devices designed to control intergroup violence (134).

The study of social tensions at once raises the problem, examined theoretically by nineteenth-century sociologists, of the relation of international to intranational tensions, and of the latter to tensions among subgroups, and eventually to tensions within the minds of the individuals who constitute the nation. Study of the process by which tensions in the minds of the individuals often arising from ambivalence and repression may extend themselves through mechanisms of identification, projection, and displacement to international tensions, brings sociology into close contact with social psychology. The in-group out-group relationship, familiar to sociologists, deals with an aspect of the psychological processes of identification, displacement, and projection (101, 134).

Scientific study of the influence on international relations of the use of regulatory devices such as armament building, negotiation, adjudication, propaganda, education, and economic controls might proceed through operational research and the results, combined with indices of the changing state of distances and tensions, suggested in earlier paragraphs, might provide international organizations and peace-loving governments a basis for successful regulation in the interest of stability. The Central Banks of the leading countries and the International Monetary Fund have utilized regulatory methods such as changes in discount rates, loans, and the regulation of exchange ratios to maintain economic stability. In this task they have been guided by typical series of monetary, commercial, population, and income statistics. Social agencies have utilized factual surveys in regulating the relations of immigrant, racial and nationality groups in large American cities (3). International political regulation, while more difficult, might profit by better knowledge of the effect of regulatory activity and better indices of the fluctuations of distances, opinions, tensions, and relative power than have heretofore been available (134).

The relation of stability in the existing state of culture to legal regulation is a field in which the sociology of international relations comes into close contact with the disciplines of international law and international organization (129). The United Nations has for one of its purposes "to establish conditions under which justice and respect for the obligations arising from treaties and other sources of international law can be maintained." While international politics and international organization can contribute to creating such conditions, the sociology of international relations by studies measuring fluctuations of the kind referred to in the preceding paragraph, may also contribute to these conditions (134).

CRITICISM

Sociology and social psychology may become the basic disciplines in the study of international relations. Sociology, which deals with the normative and institutionalized aspects of human behavior, might criticize and correct the disciplines of international organization and international law, both of which rest upon certain assumptions concerning the institutional structure of the world community. Social psychology might similarly criticize and correct the disciplines of international politics and international economics, the assumptions of which concern human attitudes and motivations rather than social norms and institutions, although the two are always related.

Sociology is, however, only on the threshold of providing methods and conclusions directly relevant to international relations. Within this field the problems of accurate observation, comparison and analysis, and of verifying conclusions, present greater difficulties than in the fields of primitive societies, of family and local institutions, and of formalized structures, such as law, medicine, administration, and religion. Because of the uniqueness of international situations, and the large areas and long periods of time involved in the functioning of international processes, analysis and measurement is particularly necessary. A forester has to have more complicated methods of analysis and measurement than does a gardener, a geologist than a surveyor, an architect than a toy-maker. The specialized discipline of international communication involving refined analysis of the impact of symbols and the measurement of opinion may therefore be of particular value in applying the concepts of sociology to the field of international relations.

In spite of their undeveloped character, sociological concepts have contributed to moderating the rigidities of the assumptions and concepts which have dominated both the theory and the practice of international relations, and to disclosing the relativity of the entities and processes involved. It has served to remove some of the distortions from the spectacles through which scholars and statesmen, versed in the prevailing culture of sovereign national states, have viewed the international scene. The study of social psychology may remove more of these distortions. It is not to be expected, however, that the distortions can be removed from the spectacles of the general public until these disciplines have developed more persuasive methods of observation, analysis, measurement, and demonstration. Nor is it certain that the removal of all these distortions is desirable.

Commitment to group values is a condition of social life and such commitment implies a bias in interpreting social processes and social functions. The sociological problem, therefore, involves the maintenance of balance between scientific analysis and ethical commitment. The sociologist of international relations must be a citizen as well as a scientist. He must appreciate that an objectivity which eliminates all sense of values from the minds of man may go far toward eliminating all groups and institutions and, in fact, the very conditions which make possible the existence of man as a social animal. While the sociologist, as scientist, may understand the relativity of all values, as a citizen, he must consider the influence which such skepticism might have if generally accepted by the public. Among numerous generalizations, many of doubtful validity and doubtful social effect, Pareto observed, "the fewer the scientific problems one considers and the greater the skill with which one evades and conceals them, the better one's talk will be as regards the effectiveness of its derivatives.... The compositions that best serve for purposes of persuasion, for arousing sentiments and urging people along a given line of conduct, are combinations of the categories above (ideals, myths, derivatives) because the human mind requires the ideal and the real in varying dosages" (85).

It is not necessary to endorse Pareto's distinction between derivatives (social ideologies and institutions) and residues (human motivations and dispositions) to agree with him that the solution of practical problems of social stabilization and control may not be facilitated and may even be hampered by an objectivity which undermines existing institutions. The scientist of human behavior must be on guard in spreading his pearls, lest imperfect understanding should destroy institutions which, as a citizen, he is committed to preserve.

Propositions of social science differ from those of natural science in that their public communication may modify the properties and relations of the entities with which they deal. While natural scientists are faced by the problem—the physician must adhere to the Hippocratic oath and regard the health of his patient as an absolute good, and the physicist may hesitate to give immature politicians dangerous weapons to play with—

social scientists face the problem more continuously. The sociology of international relations must continually relate the problem of values to that of institutional processes. The study of international ethics, which is a philosophical as well as scientific study of values, will be considered in a later chapter.

REFERENCES

1. ALIHAN, Milla Aissa, *Social Ecology, a Critical Analysis* (New York, Columbia University Press, 1938).
2. ALMOND, Gabriel A., *The American People and Foreign Policy* (New York, Harcourt, 1950).
3. ANGELL, Robert, "Integration of Nationalities in Cities," *American Journal of Sociology* (July, 1951).
4. BAGEHOT, Walter, *Physics and Politics* (London, Kegan Paul, 1903).
5. BARNARD, Chester I., *The Function of the Executive* (Cambridge, Harvard University Press, 1936).
6. BARNES, Harry Elmer, ed., *The History and Prospects of the Social Sciences* (New York, Knopf, 1925).
7. ———, *An Introduction to the History of Sociology* (Chicago, University of Chicago Press, 1948).
8. ———, *A Survey of Western Civilization* (New York, Crowell, 1947).
9. BENEDICT, Ruth, *The Chrysanthemum and the Sword, Patterns of Japanese Culture* (Boston, Houghton Mifflin, 1946).
10. BENTLEY, Arthur, *The Process of Government* (Chicago, University of Chicago Press, 1908).
11. BERNARD, L. L., ed., *The Fields and Methods of Sociology* (New York, Holt, 1934).
12. ——— and BERNARD, Jessie, *Origins of American Sociology* (New York, Crowell, 1943).
13. BOAS, Franz, and others, *General Anthropology* (Boston, Heath, 1938).
14. BOGARDUS, Emory S., *Development of Social Thought*, 2nd ed. (New York, Longmans, 1947).
15. ———, *Sociology*, 3rd ed. (New York, Macmillan, 1949).
16. BRISTOL, Lucius Moody, *Social Adaptation* (Cambridge, Harvard University Press, 1915).
17. CANNON, Walter, *The Wisdom of the Body* (New York, Norton, 1932).
18. CHILDE, V. Gordon, *Social Evolution* (New York, Schuman, 1951).
19. Commission to Study the Organization of Peace, *Regional Arrangements for Security and the United Nations*, Eighth Report and Papers Presented to the Commission (New York, June, 1953).
20. COMTE, Auguste, *The Positive Philosophy* (1830-1842), trans. by Harriet Martineau, 3rd ed. (London, 1893), 2 vols.
21. COOLEY, Charles Horton, *Human Nature and the Social Order* (New York, Scribner, 1902).
22. ———, *Social Organization, A Study of the Larger Mind* (New York, Scribner, 1909).
23. ———, *Social Process* (New York, Scribner, 1918).
24. DAHL, Robert and LINDBLOM, Charles E., *Politics, Economics and Welfare* (New York, Harper, 1953).

25. DAVIE, M. R., *The Evolution of War* (New Haven, Yale University Press, 1929).
26. DURKHEIM, Emile, *The Rules of Sociological Method* (Glencoe, Ill., Free Press, 1951).
27. ———, *The Division of Labor in Society* (Glencoe, Ill., Free Press, 1951).
28. EDWARDS, Lyford P., *The Natural History of Revolution* (Chicago, University of Chicago Press, 1927).
29. EMERSON, Alfred E., "The Biological Bases of Social Co-operation," *Illinois Academy of Science, Transactions*, Vol. 39 (1946), pp. 9 ff.
30. FERENCZI, Imre and WILLCOX, Walter F., eds., *International Migration* (New York, National Bureau of Economic Research, 1929), 2 vols.
31. FRAZER, Sir James G., *The Golden Bough, a Study in Magic and Religion*, 1 vol. ed. (New York, Macmillan, 1927).
32. GUMPLOWITZ, Ludwig, *Der Rassenkampf* (1883); (Innsbruck, 1909).
33. GURVITCH, Georges and MOORE, Wilber E., *Twentieth Century Sociology* (New York, Philosophical Library, 1950).
34. HECKER, Julius F., *Russian Sociology* (New York, Columbia University Press, 1915).
35. HERSKOVITS, Melville J., *Man and His Works* (New York, Knopf, 1948).
36. HOBHOUSE, Leonard T., WHEELER, G. C., and GINSBURG, M., *The Material Culture and Social Institutions of the Simpler Peoples* (London, Chapman and Hall, 1915).
37. HSU, Francis L. K., *American and Chinese, Two Ways of Life* (New York, Schuman, 1953).
38. KLUCKHOHN, Clyde, *Mirror for Men* (New York, McGraw-Hill, 1949).
39. KROEBER, A. L., *The Nature of Culture* (Chicago, University of Chicago Press, 1952).
40. ———, ed., *Anthropolgy Today: an Encyclopædic Inventory* (Chicago, University of Chicago Press, 1953); see also Tax, Sol, and others.
41. KROPOTKIN, P., *Mutual Aid, A Factor of Evolution* (New York, Knopf, 1925).
42. LANGER, William L., *The Diplomacy of Imperialism, 1890-1902* (New York, Knopf, 1935).
43. LASSWELL, Harold D., *The Analysis of Political Behavior: an Empirical Approach* (London, Kegan Paul, 1948).
44. LEBON, Gustav, *The Crowd: A Study of the Popular Mind* (London, Macmillan, 1896); new ed. (1947).
45. LEHMAN, W. C., *Adam Ferguson and the Beginnings of Modern Sociology* (New York, Columbia Press, 1930).
46. LEIGHTON, Alexander H., *The Governing of Men* (Princeton, Princeton University Press, 1945).
47. ———, *Human Relations in a Changing World* (New York, Dutton, 1949).
48. LERNER, Daniel, and LASSWELL, H. D., *The Policy Sciences, Recent Developments in Scope and Methods* (Stanford, Stanford University Press, 1951).
49. LEVI, Werner, *Fundamentals of World Organization* (Minneapolis, University of Minnesota Press, 1950).
50. LEVY, Marion, *The Structure of Society* (Princeton, Princeton University Press, 1952).
51. LICHTENBERGER, James P., *Development of Social Theory* (New York, Century, 1923).
52. LINTON, Ralph, *The Tree of Culture* (New York, Knopf, 1953).

53. LOCKE, Allain and STERN, Bernhard J., *When Peoples Meet: A Study in Race and Cultural Contacts* (New York, Progressive Education Association, 1942).
54. LOWIE, Robert H., *The History of Ethnological Theory* (New York, Rinehart, 1937).
55. ———, *An Introduction to Cultural Anthropology* (New York, Rinehart, 1940).
56. ———, *Social Organization* (New York, Rinehart, 1948).
57. LUNDBERG, George A., *Foundations of Sociology* (New York, Macmillan, 1939).
58. LYND, Robert S., *Knowledge for What?* (Princeton, Princeton University Press, 1939).
59. MACIVER, Robert M., "Sociology," *Encyclopædia of the Social Sciences.*
60. ———, *The Web of Government* (New York, Macmillan, 1946).
61. ——— and PAGE, C. H., *Society: An Introductory Analysis* (New York, Rinehart, 1949).
62. MACKENZIE, Roderick, "Ecology, Human," *Encyclopædia of the Social Sciences.*
63. MACLEOD, W. C., *The Origin and History of Politics* (New York, Wiley, 1931).
64. MALINOWSKI, Bronislaw, *Magic, Science and Religion,* introduction by Robert Redfield (Boston, Beacon Press, 1948).
65. MANNHEIM, Karl, *Ideology and Utopia* (New York, Harcourt, 1936).
66. ———, *Freedom, Power and Democratic Planning* (New York, Oxford University Press, 1950).
67. ———, *Essays on the Sociology of Knowledge* (New York, Oxford University Press, 1953).
68. MARETT, R. R., *Psychology and Folklore* (London, Methuen, 1920).
69. ———, *Sacraments of Simple Folk* (Oxford, Clarendon Press, 1933).
70. MARX, Karl, and ENGELS, Friedrich, *Manifesto of the Communist Party,* 1848 (New York, Rand School, 1919).
71. MEAD, Margaret, *Co-operation and Competition Among Primitive People* (1937); (New York, McGraw-Hill, 1951).
72. ———, *And Keep Your Powder Dry* (New York, Morrow, 1942).
73. MERTON, Robert K., *Social Theory and Social Structure* (Glencoe, Ill., Free Press, 1951).
74. ———, ed., *Reader in Bureaucracy* (Glencoe, Ill., Free Press, 1951).
75. MORGAN, Lewis H., *Ancient Society* (1877); (Chicago, Kerr, n.d.).
76. MÜLLER-LYER, F., *The History of Social Development* (New York, Knopf, 1921).
77. MYRDAL, Gunnar, *An American Dilemma* (New York, Harper, 1944), 2 vols.
78. ———, *The Relation Between Social Theory and Social Policy* (London, British Sociological Association, 1953).
79. NORTHROP, F. S. C., *The Taming of the Nations* (New York, Macmillan, 1952).
80. NOVICOV, Jacques, *Les Luttes entre Sociétés Humaines et leur phases successives* (Paris, 1893); 2nd ed. (1896).
81. ODUM, Howard W., *Understanding Society: The Principles of Dynamic Sociology* (New York, Macmillan, 1947).
82. OGBURN, William F., *Social Change with Respect to Culture and Original Nature* (1922); New York, Viking, 1928).

83. OGBURN, William F., and NIMKOFF, M. F., *Sociology* (Boston, Houghton Mifflin, 1940).
84. ——, ed., *Technology and International Relations*, Harris Institute Lectures (Chicago, University of Chicago Press, 1949).
85. PARETO, Vilfredo, *The Mind and Society* (New York, Harcourt, 1935), 4 vols.
86. PARK, Robert E., and BURGESS, Ernest, *Introduction to the Science of Sociology* (Chicago, University of Chicago Press, 1921).
87. ——, *Human Communities* (Glencoe, Ill., Free Press, 1952).
88. PARSONS, Talcott, "Society," *Encyclopædia of the Social Sciences*.
89. ——, *Essays in Sociological Theory* (Glencoe, Ill., Free Press, 1949).
90. ——, *The Structure of Social Action* (Glencoe, Ill., Free Press, 1950).
91. ——, *The Social System* (Glencoe, Ill., Free Press, 1951).
92. —— and SHILS, Edward, eds., *Toward a General Theory of Action* (Cambridge, Harvard University Press, 1951).
93. PETTEE, G. S., *The Process of Revolution* (New York, Harper, 1938).
94. PITT-RIVERS, G. H., *The Clash of Cultures and Contact of Races* (London, Routledge, 1927).
95. RAPAPORT, Anatol, *Operational Philosophy* (New York, Harper, 1953).
96. RATZEHNOFFER, Gustav, *Die Sociologische Erkenntnis* (Leipsic, 1898); summarized in A. W. Small, *General Sociology* (Chicago, University of Chicago Press, 1905).
97. RICE, Stuart A., *Quantitative Methods in Politics* (New York, Knopf, 1928).
98. RICHARDSON, Lewis F., "Generalized Foreign Politics," *British Journal of Psychology*, Monograph Supplement, Vol. 23 (Cambridge, 1939).
99. ——, "Variation of the Frequency of Fatal Quarrels with Magnitude," *Journal of the American Statistical Association*, Vol. 43 (December, 1948), pp. 523-546.
100. RIESMAN, David, in collaboration with DENNEY, Reuel, and GLAZER, Nathan, *The Lonely Crowd, A Study of the Changing American Character* (New Haven, Yale University Press, 1950).
101. SHERIF, Muzafer and Carolyn W., *Group Harmony and Tension* (New York, Harper, 1953).
102. SIMMEL, Georg, *Sociology*, trans. by Kurt H. Wolff (Glencoe, Ill., Free Press, 1950).
103. SIMON, Herbert A., SMITHBURG, D. D., and THOMPSON, V. A., *Public Administration* (New York, Knopf, 1950).
104. SINGER, Kurt, *The Idea of Conflict* (Melbourne, University Press, 1949).
105. SMALL, Albion W., *General Sociology* (Chicago, University of Chicago Press, 1905).
106. SOROKIN, Pitirim, *Contemporary Sociological Theories* (New York, Harper, 1928).
107. ——, *Social and Cultural Dynamics* (New York, American Book Co., 1937), 4 vols.
108. SPEIER, Hans, *Social Order and the Risk of War, Papers in Political Sociology* (New York, Stewart, 1952).
109. SPENCER, Herbert, *Social Statics or the Conditions Essential to Human Happiness Specified and the First of Them Developed* (1851) (New York, Appleton, 1865).
110. ——, *Principles of Sociology*, 3rd ed. (New York, Appleton, 1925), 3 vols.

111. SPYKMAN, Nicholas J., *The Social Theory of Georg Simmel* (Chicago, University of Chicago Press, 1925).

112. SULZBACH, Walter, *National Consciousness, a Dissection of Fundamental Fallacies* (Washington, Public Affairs Press, 1943).

113. SUMNER, William Graham, *Folkways* (Boston, Ginn, 1906).

114. ———, and KELLER, A. G., *The Science of Society* (New Haven, Yale University Press, 1927, 1928), 4 vols.

115. TARDE, Gabriel, *The Laws of Imitation*, trans. by Elsie Clews Parsons (New York, Holt, 1903).

116. TAX, Sol., and others, eds., *An Appraisal of "Anthropology Today"* (Chicago, University of Chicago Press, 1953); see Kroeber, A. L.

117. THOMAS, William I., *Source Book of Social Origins* (Chicago, University of Chicago Press, 1907).

118. ———, and ZNANIECKI, Florian, *The Polish Peasant in Europe and America* (1919); (New York, Knopf, 1927), 5 vols.

119. TOMASIC, Denko, *Personality and Culture in Eastern European Politics* (New York, Stewart, 1948).

120. TONNIES, Ferdinand, *Gemeinschaft und Gesellschaft* (Leipsic, 1887); 3rd ed. (Berlin, 1926).

121. TYLOR, Edward B., *Primitive Culture, Researches into the Development of Mythology, Philosophy, Religion, Arts and Custom* (London, Murray, 1871), 2 vols.

122. VANWAGENEN, Richard, *Research in the International Organizational Field* (Princeton, Center for Research in World Political Institutions, 1952).

123. WALLAS, Graham, *The Great Society, a Psychological Analysis* (New York, Macmillan, 1917).

124. ———, *Social Judgment* (London, 1934).

125. WARD, Lester F., *Dynamic Sociology, or Applied Social Science*, 1883 (New York, Appleton, 1926), 2 vols.

126. WEBER, Max, *The Theory of Social and Economic Organization*, trans. by A. M. Henderson and Talcott Parsons (New York, Oxford University Press, 1947).

127. ———, *Essays in Sociology*, trans. by H. H. Gerth and C. W. Mills (New York, Oxford University Press, 1946).

128. ———, *The Methodology of the Social Sciences* (Glencoe, Ill., Free Press, 1949).

129. WEST, Ranyard, *Conscience and Society, A Study of the Psychological Prerequisites of Law and Order* (New York, Emerson, 1945).

130. WIRTH, Louis, "Types of Nationalism," *American Journal of Sociology*, Vol. 41 (May, 1936), pp. 723-737.

131. WISSLER, Clark, *Man and Culture* (New York, Crowell, 1923).

132. WRIGHT, Quincy, *A Study of War* (Chicago, University of Chicago Press, 1942), pp. 45-56, 53-74, 249-272, 372-405, 471-478, 496-500, 527-565, 571-590, 705, 955-1042, 1079-1117, 1231-1233, 1250-1252, 1299-1309, 1326-1352, 1355-1364, 1432-1444, 1448-1453, 1456-1465, 1472-1497.

133. ———, ed., *The World Community*, Harris Institute Lectures (Chicago, University of Chicago Press, 1948).

134. ———, *Problems of Stability and Progress in International Relations* (Berkeley, University of California Press, 1954).

135. ZNANIECKI, Florian, *Modern Nationalities, A Sociological Study* (Urbana, University of Illinois Press, 1952).

The Psychology of
International Relations

DEFINITION

THE PSYCHOLOGY of international relations is the science relating the individual, as citizen of a state, to other states and their citizens and to international organizations, and the art of modifying those relations. In a wider sense it is the science relating the individual, as member of any group, to other groups and their members, and to supergroups and the art of modifying those relations.

The psychology is distinguished from the sociology of international relations in that it approaches the problem of international relations from the point of view of the individual rather than of the group. The psychology of international relations, which has hardly emerged as a distinct discipline, is an aspect of the discipline of social psychology. The latter, in turn, is that aspect of general psychology which studies the human mind, personality, and behavior on the assumption that the individual is a social animal—a participant in, and, in considerable measure, a product of, group life. Social psychology thus excludes the biological and physiological points of view which treat the individual as an organism. On the other hand, social psychology is distinguished from psychological sociology in that the latter, while dealing with the psychological foundations of society, proceeds from the point of view of the group and is, therefore, an aspect of sociology.

The psychology of international relations has been treated as a science and, together with the sociology of international relations, has been regarded as the master science of international relations. Some would say that since the foundations of sociology are psychological, the psychology of international relations is even more fundamental than the sociology of international relations.

Primary and secondary groups. The individual is in modern civilization a member of many groups—family, village, church, state, nation, and so forth. The groups in which he directly participates may be called *primary groups* in a sense enlarging the meaning of that term beyond the small face-to-face groups often intended by it. Social psychology has been in considerable measure concerned with the effect of the interaction of the individual with other members of face-to-face groups. Primitive peoples and children have few other contacts and the influence of these contacts is doubtless of major importance in shaping the personality of everyone. The modern adult, however, participates directly in many groups—religious, political, social and professional—very few members of which he ever meets. He is, however, in direct contact with officials, representatives, and institutions of these groups. In a wide sense of the term, therefore, these groups may be called *primary groups* in respect to their members, in distinction from subgroups of these groups, parallel groups, and supergroups with which the individual has contacts only indirectly through his primary group. A person may live in a family, belong to a neighborhood club, own stock in the X Corporation, be a citizen of Chicago, of Illinois, and of the United States, and a member of the Republican party, the American Economic Association, the American Association of University Professors, the Presbyterian Church, and the American Legion. These are all primary groups in the wide sense, though in the narrow sense that would be true only of the first two. He may, however, participate in meetings of stockholders, citizens, or members of these various groups, and such meetings would in the narrow sense be primary groups.

He also, however, has indirect contacts with subgroups of the United States such as New York and Indiana, with parallel groups, such as the United Kingdom, France, the Democratic party, the Congregational Church, and the American Federation of Labor, and with super or *secondary* groups such as the United Nations, UNESCO, the National Council of Churches, the International Economic Association, and so forth. He is likely to make occasional direct contacts with members of these groups. It is these relations that constitute the subject matter of the psychology of international relations.

A typical instance of such relations is to be found in the modern state system. The nation-state is the dominant, primary group of most individuals, but these are related to one another in international organizations which constitute *secondary* groups. Each individual has relations to sovereign states other than his own, to their nationals and governments, and to international organizations and their officials, directly through contact with foreigners or foreign or international officials, indirectly through the contacts of representatives of his state in conducting foreign policy or dealing with international and supranational organizations, and symbolically through educational and informational media.

Individual and group. Different schools of social psychology have been influenced by preconceptions emphasizing the similarities of individuals or their differences; emphasizing the influence of inherited nature or of acquired nurture; emphasizing the influence of culture on personality or of personality on culture; emphasizing the irrational and unconscious aspects of personality or its rational and conscious aspects; emphasizing the influence of primary group experience, especially that of infancy, or the continuing influence of communication and group experience.

The present tendency of social psychologists is to avoid such dichotomies and to envisage the individual at any stage of his existence as a consequence of the interaction of the individual's distinctive physiological and psychological characteristics and the universal aspects of human nature, of his inheritance and his experience, of his personality and the culture in which he participates, of his unconscious drives and his conscious intentions and purposes, and of his primary group contacts and his contacts with other groups. The personality (the ego) is conceived as a system of action composed of drives, needs, and dispositions (the id) urging action on suitable stimuli, but usually hesitating among alternative actions and eventually choosing one on the basis of evaluative standards acquired from cultural and social experience (the superego).

The extreme complexity and the continuous malleability of the individual, the influence on his behavior, not only of his general personality, but of his interpretation of the particular situation and of the initial reaction of others to his behavior in that situation, makes social psychology a subject in which successful generalization is difficult. The psychology of international relations is the most illusive aspect of this subject. The indirect influence of individual personality patterns upon parallel groups and supergroups affected by the individual's role and status, by primary group representatives, by international institutions, and by the distortions of the media of education and information, is especially difficult to trace. No less difficult is it to trace the influence of these more remote groups upon the individual's personality, motives, and behavior. War and peace may be made in the minds of men, but the process by which the state of mind of a particular individual influences and is influenced by international war or peace, and the measurement of the factors involved in that influence presents a problem of extreme complexity (21).

Processes of education and communication exert a major influence upon the individual's attitudes toward groups, particularly groups other than the face-to-face groups, such as his family, village, or local club, in which he participates. In the case of groups of which he is not a member at all, those with which the psychology of international relations is primarily concerned, his attitudes are almost entirely shaped, unless he travels a great deal, by symbolic representations acquired through these processes. The psychology of international relations provides the basis for the practical disciplines of international education and international communications, though the latter, which includes the use of mass media for influencing public opinion, is equally dependent upon the sociology of international relations.

The development of psychology. Psychology began in antiquity with philosophical introspection concerning human motivation and philosophical classification of human personalities. Natural inequality, urged by Aristotle, contested with natural equality, urged by the Stoics and Christians. It developed in discussions by Descartes, Leibnitz, Hobbes, and Locke in the seventeenth century, and by Berkeley, Hume, Wolff, Herbart, Hartley, and Bentham in the eighteenth century. These discussions were especially concerned with the role in knowledge of innate qualities and of acquired experience, and with the role in judgment and action of reason and of association. The conclusions of these writers were influenced by their attitudes on the philosophical problem of the relation of mind to body and to reality, and on the ethical problem of the relation of motivation and intention to utility and consequences. Kant summarized these discussions by distinguishing the fixed forms or categories of the mind from the varying substances or impressions received from the world, the impact of one on the other constituting experience. Experience guiding "pure reason" to knowledge of phenomena was contrasted with the "categorical imperative" which reconciled individual freedom with universal law and guided "practical reason" in the noumenal world of ends and action.

Psychology, however, hardly became a scientific discipline until the concept of distinct mental faculties lead in the early nineteenth century to efforts by Gall and others to describe such faculties as static entities in the mind closely related to the anatomical structure of the brain. The basic faculties of sensation, intuition, volition, and reason were recognized and subdivided. Sensation or immediate experience of the outside world was related to memory, perception, and conception. Intuition or immediate experience of the inside world was related to feeling, emotion, and evaluation. Volition or experience in choosing, deciding, and acting was related to attention, judgment, and motivation. Finally, reason or the experience of thinking was related to analysis, synthesis, and formulation (11, 33).

Dynamic psychology, which diverted interest from entities to processes and forces, began with the associational school of Bain in the mid-nineteenth century. This school equated mental processes to habits or paths developed by repetition and association. The conditioned-reflex school initiated by Pavlov in the twentieth century emphasized the sensory-motor circuit from stimulus to action, and studied the possibility of conditioning the personality through continuous substitution of different stimuli, especially symbolic representations, to activate the same motor response. These ideas were developed by the "behaviorists," led by Watson, who sought to eliminate introspective evidence from psychology. The "psychoanalysts" (Freud, Jung, Adler), the "gestaltists" (Ehrenfels, Köhler, Koffka), and the "group dynamists" (Lewin) emphasized the complexity of the mental processes and mechanisms which result from the experience of the individual and influence his instinct (i.e., his inherited impulse to respond to a given stimulus in a given way). As the personality matures, the mental processes and mechanisms moderate the individual's response to "wishes" by appreciation of the "realities" of the situation as a whole. The sensory-motor circuit, manifested by the instinctive behavior of animals and the spontaneous responses of infants, was found to be so complicated by the adult's "conditioning," especially his cultural and social conditioning, that the response to a given stimulus could not be predicted without an understanding of his total personality at the time. This understanding could hardly be obtained without knowledge of the individual's entire personal experience up to that date. The psychoanalysts described this personality in terms of the individual's experiences of frustration, satisfaction, and ambivalence, especially during infancy, developing habits of repression, displacement, projection, sublimation, and so forth. The Gestaltists and group dynamists described personality in terms of the individual's interpretation of the total situation with which he was confronted at a given moment or during a period of time—his "life-space," with its pattern of goals, obstacles, and paths, defining the position of his wishes in this often distorted interpretation of external reality. Group discussion, agreement, and action were interpreted in terms of the congruity or incongruity of the "life spaces," or views of the situation, of the members of the group (33, 35, 47).

The dynamic psychologists, while discussing the processes of mental life and the observable behavior consequent upon these processes, were interested in the forces which gave vigor and direction to the impulse which traveled from stimulus to action through the mazes of the mind. Philosophical psychologists described the roles of innate ideas and of experience. Utilitarians assumed the dominance of rational and planned action relating means to the end of maximizing pleasure and minimizing pain. Both were attacked by the impulse school which detected irrational urges of fear, sympathy, dominance, imitation, suggestability, gregariousness, acquisitiveness, and so forth, hampering clear definition and evaluation of goals, biasing the selection and application of means, and distracting attention from such ends and means as might have been chosen. The latter line of thought was pursued by studies of instinct stimulated by comparison of man with other animals. Various lists of instinctive patterns were described by McDougal, Thorndike, and others (31, 52, 74). The tendency was, however, to emphasize the great malleability of inherited reflexes and instincts in man, and to use words such as *drive, wish, disposition,* or *motivation* which recognized that the response of the adult was in large measure the result of the extensive conditioning of original impulses by experience (73, 80). The tendency was to reduce these original drives to a small number, characteristic of all living things, such as the urges of hunger, sex, self-preservation, and dominance (83). These drives manifested themselves in different ways according to the individual's experience in a particular family, society, and culture. Nevertheless, these urges to action were the central feature of the mind without which mental structures and processes lost meaning (1, 25).

The final stage of psychological study has been the effort to define mental processes and forces in the form of quantitative variables susceptible of measurement, the relationship of which may facilitate the explanation, prediction, and control of behavior. For this purpose the biological term *instinct,* the juridical term *interest,* the literary terms *wish, motive,* and *purpose* have proved less useful than the term *attitude* defined as the behavior pattern of a personality with reference to a particular event, situation, condition, or symbol (73, 75). This term does not raise the issue between innate and acquired tendencies, but assumes that at a given moment an individual has an attitude toward anything that attracts his attention—an event, a word, a work of art, a philosophical or social concept, a condition of culture, a personality, a society, or a policy —and that this attitude can be measured, theoretically and to some extent practically, in four dimensions— (*a*) direction: the attitude is favorable or unfavorable to its object; (*b*) intensity: the attitude has a position on a scale from very favorable to very unfavorable; (*c*) continuity: the attitude is persistent in time or variable; and (*d*) homogeneity or rationality: the attitude has various degrees of consistency with the individual's other attitudes and with his personality as a whole (75, 76, 83).

Attitude and opinion. The psychological concept of *attitude,* a function of the individual mind, has been distinguished from the sociological concept of *opinion,* a function of communication within a group. Opinion has been defined as the expression of an attitude, but the expression inevitably differs from the attitude, not only because the individual expressing an opinion may wish to conceal his attitudes or to mislead others, but because others may misinterpret the expression. Expressions of opinion, whether verbally, by writing, by ballot, or by artistic or symbolic representation, have important sociological effects. Democratic government has, in fact, been regarded as a system for realizing, in law and practice, *public opinion* defined as the opinion on controversial issues held by a majority of the members of a public and acquiesced in by substantially all. Public opinion in a given community, in reference to a given symbol or policy can be measured, as can the attitude of individuals, in the dimensions of direction, intensity, continuity, and homogeneity. But the measurement is accomplished by statistical analysis of the expressions of opinion by all, or by a representative sample, of a *public* which consists of many individuals interested in the symbol or policy in question. Conditions of group tradition, suggestion, leadership, and crowd interaction may develop a public opinion, perhaps leading to group action, which is contrary to the attitudes of most or perhaps all of the members of the group (46, 78, 85).

It may be that the difference between attitudes, constituting units of psychological study, and opinions, constituting units of sociological study, can best characterize the difference between the disciplines of psychology and sociology. Attitudes are especially influenced by the system of education, opinions by the system of communication, especially mass communication. The two cannot be regarded as independent variables because an individual's attitude toward an object often influences his opinion (he may say what he means), and his opinion often influences his attitude (he may come to believe what he says), yet there is a high probability of error in inferring one from the other. This becomes clear if one considers the great differences frequently found between the private letters and the public utterances of politicians and statesmen in any society, and between the statements of refugees from totalitarian states and of the same persons while resident within them. The state of public opinion influences the opinions and may influence the attitudes of each member of that public, and the attitudes of each member may be reflected in their expressions of opinion and thus influence public opinion, but these reciprocal influences vary greatly in character in different societies. Public opinion may be more or less coercive; individual opinion may be more or less free. It is clear that the attitudes of individuals and the state of public opinion do reciprocally influence one another, but the relation is circuitous and indirect, and one cannot be measured by the other. Public opinion is not a safe index of the attitudes of the members of a public, and the measurement of the attitudes of the members of a public is not a safe guide to public opinion.

The group, guided by public opinion, exists, therefore, in some degree as an entity distinct from its members, and they exist in some degree as entities distinct from the group. Interaction of group members with one another and with the group as a whole influences the character of both group and individuals, but it does not result in their complete integration. They remain distinct *systems of action*. Measurement of the divergencies of private attitude and public opinion in a given group may provide a valuable guide for estimating both sociological and psychological trends. Great divergence may lead to such group crises as revolution or war, or to such individual crises as neurosis or suicide. Stability and satisfaction in individual and group life may be a consequence of close parallelism between the two (83).

Schools of social psychology. Social psychology began to develop as a distinct discipline in the late nineteenth century as a result of the convergence of the psychological interest of certain sociologists (Tarde, Durkheim, Ward, Cooley, Thomas, and LeBon), cultural anthropologists (Boas, Goldenweiser, Lowie, and Wissler), and political scientists (Bagehot and Wallas) with the social interest of certain psychologists (Wundt, James, Dewey, Mead, Baldwin, McDougal, Thorndike, Watson, and Freud). But as noted, the convergence has not resulted in complete identity of points of view. Psychological sociology, which attributes some sort of priority to the group or culture, can still be distinguished from social psychology which regards the individual as the basic object of study. A few of the sociologists like Thomas (73) and Cooley (17) may belong in the latter category and some of the psychologists like Wundt, who was equally an anthropologist, belong in the category of psychological sociologists (2).

Among the psychological sociologists are folk psychologists (Wundt, Durkheim) and crowd psychologists (LeBon), while the social psychologists include personality analysts (Freud), behaviorists (Watson, Pavlov), and psychological measurers (Thorndike, Thurstone). Social interactionists (Dewey, Thomas, Mead, Simmel) including the Gestaltists (Koffka) and group dynamists (Lewin) have perhaps established the most perfect balance between the two points of view (83). To them society and history are neither the result of natural development under the influence of blind social forces as affirmed by the evolutionary anthropologists, nor the result of conscious planning by individuals to achieve goals or values as affirmed by the functional anthropologists. Rather society and history are the result of conversations or dialectics. Individuals interacting upon one another and upon the environment produce groups, societies and cultures, which in turn interact upon one another and upon individuals producing histories.

The basic problem of social psychology from this point of view is to trace the mechanism of this interaction. It begins in contact, conflict, and interaction between inconsistent impulses in the individual mind, and develops in contact, conflict, and interaction between individuals and groups. The description of the socio-psychological processes, the identification and measurement of socio-psychological variables, and the discovery of persistent relationships among them have become the main interest of the social psychologists (17, 36, 54, 65, 69, 73, 77).

ASSUMPTIONS

Social psychologists usually make the following assumptions: (*a*) The individual's behavior is a consequence of his *state of mind* at the moment, intervening between stimulus and reaction. This *state of mind* is a continually changing pattern of sense impressions, feelings, perceptions, memories, ideas, values, and attitudes, different aspects of which successively come within the focus of attention. It includes predispositions or background drives, dispositions, and wishes, often in considerable measure unconscious, and always the consequence of the conditioning, through experience, of inherited impulses. It also includes the individual's current information, and his interpretation of that information and of the situation with which he is confronted at the moment. This interpretation is influenced as much by the predispositions through which his sensory and instinctive impressions are screened as by the *actual facts* of the situation as it would appear to a wholly unbiased observer.

(*b*) The innate or instinctive drives of human beings are extremely malleable and while there are hereditary differences in their relative intensity among individuals the average is substantially the same in all races, nations, classes, or other large groups of human beings. Consequently the great differences in the socially significant behavior patterns of adults of different groups are the consequence not of heredity but of the conditioning of original drives through experience in the group and the culture.

(*c*) Certain infantile experiences are similar in all cultures and similarly condition human biological drives, thus creating a *human nature* consisting of basic wishes and reaction patterns common to all persons in all cultures, but, (*d*) a large part of adult behavior results from choices on the basis of abstract criteria derived from language, conceptual systems, value systems, and typical motivations and situational appraisals. These are the consequence of a particular culture or particular institutions, modified by the particular experience of the individual. Most behavior significant for intergroup relations can only be understood through understanding of this sort of conditioning.

The psychology of international relations deals with situations in which the individuals concerned have been subjected to such varied cultural, social, and institutional conditioning that the attitudes, opinions, and values which influence their decisions are very diverse. Their behavior cannot be related to any universal conditions except *human nature* and this is relatively unimportant in accounting for most behavior in this field. Therefore, in addition to the general assumptions of social psychology, the psychology of international relations makes the following assumptions:

a. The relations between groups are a function of the atmosphere of public opinion within each of these groups and within the supergroups of which they are members. That atmosphere is influenced, among other factors, by the *attitudes* of the members of the group with respect to parallel and supergroups and by the great instability of those attitudes.

b. Individual attitudes are formed through the complex mechanisms of *interaction* among personalities in a social situation and the field of interaction continually expands with progress in the technology of communications. The objects of interest and attention, significant for international relations, and predominant in individual minds and in the atmosphere of public opinion, are, therefore, relatively changeable and unpredictable, and increasingly so as technology progresses.

c. Conflict among attitudes gives rise to *tensions* in the individual mind and these give rise to social and intergroup tensions, with the result that each group finds itself in relations of opposition with some groups and of co-operation with others.

d. The opinion, policy, and action of groups, and the relations of groups with one another and with supergroups, are greatly influenced by the personality and attitudes of *leaders* and elites, and by the vocabulary with which they express themselves.

These assumptions can be summarized in the formula of UNESCO's constitution: "Since wars begin in the minds of men, it is in the minds of men that the defenses of peace must be constructed" (21).

They provide a basis for examining and criticizing the assumptions of international politics, international law, and most of the other special disciplines of international relations. The character of a mechanism or other material object can be viewed as a function of its gross, physical properties. It can also be viewed as a function of its human utility. But it may also be viewed as a function of matter and energy in a field, or even as a function of a particular patterning of molecules, atoms, and subatomic entities in time and space. The latter points of view can indicate the conditions under which it can operate or even exist as a mechanism or a utility. A stove or an internal combustion engine, for example, can operate only within a certain range of temperature and pressure. Similarly, the psychology of international relations makes it possible to view the character, and even the existence, of states, nations, and international organizations as a function of the attitudes, interests, mechanisms, and tensions of individual minds, and permits examination of the conditions of culture and public opinion in which particular institutions can function. Practically the psychologist of international relations assumes that action in the realms of education, communication, technology, and other processes of cultural change can recondition the individual mind, and modify the conditions of culture and opinion which have been assumed in the past and in this way change the character of international relations.

While under familiar conditions the assumptions of the cook or mechanic about the properties of stoves or engines are adequate, under extreme conditions found on high mountains, in the Arctic, or in the stratosphere they are not. The rapid and radical changes in the conditions of opinion, education, communication, technology, and war may today make it urgent to subject the assumptions of the traditional disciplines of international relations to psychological criticism.

ANALYSIS

The four assumptions of the psychology of international relations concerning attitudes, interaction, tension, and leadership have each stimulated an analysis of international relations.

Attitudes. It may be possible to measure attitudes, but the problem is much more difficult than that of measuring opinions. The method developed by Thurstone (75) involves the preparation of schedules of statements, each of which has been pretested to determine its significance with reference to a given symbol or policy. By marking the schedule, indicating acceptance or rejection of, or indifference toward, each statement, the individual unwittingly indicates his attitude toward the symbol or policy. By averaging, this attitude can be located on a scale extending from very favorable, through neutral, to very unfavorable. The value of each statement is originally determined by utilization of the method of comparative judgment. A number of judges distribute many statements in the position they deem appropriate on such a scale. Only those statements are used on which the judges in large measure agree. The significance of other statements are considered uncertain.

This method eliminates in considerable degree the conscious or unconscious warping which is likely if the individual is asked to state his attitude toward a given symbol directly to an interviewer or on a questionnaire. The method is sufficiently refined to permit study of the effect on a particular attitude of educational or communication activity, such as reading a book or viewing a moving picture. By repetition at intervals, it is possible by this method to determine all dimensions of an attitude—direction, intensity, continuity, and homogeneity (83).

The prolonged interview of the psychoanalyst may penetrate even more deeply into the individual's attitudes and their interrelationships, but that method is so expensive and time-consuming as to preclude application to any adequate sample of a considerable population (44).

Attitudes may be regarded as the basic element of psychic character in somewhat the same way as genes may be regarded as the basic element of biological character, although they differ in being much less stable. As the interests of biologists have moved from a study and classification of animals as a whole to a study of genes, their arrangement in the cell, their mutation and combination, so as to produce a great variety of animal species, so the interests of the social psychologist may move from a study of the personality as a whole to the study of attitudes, their formation and dissemination, and the effect of their combination in a given personality in producing tensions, opinions, and behavior.

By application of the methods discussed to a suitable sample of a population, it may be possible to determine the statistical distribution in that population of attitudes measured in all of their dimensions toward such symbols as the names of other states, of international organizations, and of international processes like war, diplomacy, conciliation, and consultation. Correlation of this distribution with the social and political status of the persons that hold them and with the current state of public opinion concerning the same and other symbols may provide materials useful for predicting and regulating international relations (66, 83, 85). Such data might be of particular importance in determining the appropriate direction and probable effect of activities in the fields of international education and international communication. It must be recognized, however, that the effort to analyze mental states or personalities into combinations of attitudes may prove no more fruitful than was Condillac's effort to analyze them into discrete sensations. Attitudes may be fleeting nexuses of feeling, sensation, memory, perception, and conception taking color from the *gestalt* (41, 42) or situation as a whole (47, 73) and from the total personality (67), with insufficient coherence or stability to make them measurable or comparable. Study of the process of interaction may, therefore, prove more fruitful.

Interaction. In studying the mechanisms of interaction, social psychologists have increasingly emphasized the active role of the mind. The mind is not a slate on which experience writes, as suggested by Locke, nor is it a filing system in which experience is classified as suggested by Kant. It is rather a complex and active agent that selects, dissects, and disposes of experience as a cat deals with a mouse (30). The tendency has been to place the situs of interaction within each mind.

Some of the earlier sociologists like Gumplowitz, emphasizing the determinism of the individual by the group, assumed that the relations of groups were fundamental. If two groups were hostile, this hostility would be transmitted to their members. Group interests, he thought, determined individual attitudes. Other sociologists like Spencer, Ward, and Cooley (17), regarded the relation of individuals to the group, especially to the primary group of which they are members, as the dominant influence in shaping personality. The culture and institutions to which he is subjected, they thought, condition the personality of the growing child. On the other hand, they recognized that the personality of leaders might modify the culture. The interaction of group and individual, therefore, determines the personality of individuals and the culture of the group. The social interactionists, like Thomas, gave primary emphasis to the interaction of individuals upon one another in a social situation. Through this interaction, opinion, culture, and groups are formed. Not interaction among groups, nor interaction between individuals and groups, but interaction among individuals determines groups, cultures, intergroup relations, and institutions.

This emphasis led the social psychologists to examine the precise mechanism by which one individual interacts with another. William James had emphasized the concept of the *objective ego* and the *social self* by which the individual identified the things, persons, and groups with which he was most closely associated as part of himself (31). Dewey in describing the learning process emphasized the active role of the learner. A student, he thought, does not learn except through doing, through perceiving the relation of experience to his interests and actively incorporating this experience in his personality (18). Mead explained the process of interaction in detail. *A*'s response to *B*'s word or gesture is determined by *A*'s preconception of *B* in terms of *A*'s own personality. If *A* and *B* have developed in the same primary group, this interpretation may be fairly accurate, but if they come from very diverse groups or cultures, it will usually be erroneous. If *B* disappoints *A*'s preconception, *A* is faced by the problem of reconciling his preconception with the actual behavior of *B*. He may reorient his conception of *B* and interaction can proceed, or he may regard *B* as impossible and hostile, as he is likely to do if *B* comes from a very different cultural group (54). The traditional hostility of the average man to the alien and to foreign countries is influenced by this phenomenon though it may be accentuated by the sociological function of the hostile out-group in integrating the in-group, and by the particular political situation of hostility or alliance (22).

With this explanation real interaction between *A* and *B* is on the one hand in *A*'s mind between his concept of his own personality and his concept of the relation of *B*'s personality to it, and on the other hand in *B*'s mind between *B*'s concept of his own personality and *B*'s concept of the relation of *A*'s personality to *B*. The psychic relations are therefore primarily relations between elements of a single personality, only indirectly between different personalities, and even more indirectly between a group and persons, or between different groups.

This point of view emphasizes the significance of the *looking-glass self* referred to by Cooley. In every conversation, he suggested, there are at least six persons: *A* and *B*, *A*'s concept of *B*, *B*'s concept of *A*, *A*'s interpretation of *B*'s concept of *A*, and *B*'s interpretation of *A*'s concept of *B*. The process may go on to greater subtleties such as *A*'s interpretation of *B*'s interpretation of *A*'s concept of *B*, *ad infinitum* (17).

The psychoanalysts have interpreted interaction in terms of fixed mechanisms of the mind for disposing of experience. Unpleasant experiences may be *repressed* from consciousness but continue in the unconscious. The attitudes of others may be interpreted by *projection* upon them of one's own attitude toward them. Since *A* feels aggressive against *B*, he interprets *B*'s behavior as manifestation of aggression toward *A*. *Ambivalent* feelings toward another may be relieved by *displacement* of the unacceptable feeling upon a *scapegoat*. A child loves his mother as a source of his indulgences but hates her because she disciplines him. He may then displace his hatred upon someone else. A man may hate his employer but expediency suggests he suppress this feeling, perhaps displacing it upon another worker, or a subordinate chosen as a scapegoat (20, 22). Sir James Frazer has drawn attention to the importance of the phenomenon of the scapegoat in many primitive societies (24), and the sociologists do so in pointing to the function of the hostile *out-group* in maintaining the solidarity of the *in-group*.

Freud located the dynamics of human behavior in basic *wishes* of which at first he considered sex all-important. The attitudes toward others, he thought, were determined by their relation to these wishes as distorted by the psychic mechanisms and somewhat influenced by the *reality* principle through which the individual learns that the world and society has an objective character to which he must adjust his wishes (25).

The Gestaltists Köhler (42), and Koffka (41) have emphasized the significance of the individual's view of the whole in interpreting its elements. Thomas had given a similar emphasis with his conception of the *situation* as a whole. Kurt Lewin elaborated the concept of the individual's *life-space*—the simple picture of the situation with its goals, obstacles, and paths—which explains his behavior and his interpretation of the attitudes and the personalities of others in the picture. He pointed out that individuals do not act on the basis of the *reality* of the situation, but on the basis of their interpretation of that reality, usually distorted by their cultural preconceptions, as well as by individual deficiencies of sight, hearing, understanding, language, and prejudices arising from personal experience. One can picture each individual as acting on the basis of a world seen through spectacles which grossly distort it. Beliefs, value systems, opinions, and personal wishes, the idols of the tribe, the market place, the theater, and the forum discussed by Bacon, all conspire to distort the lenses through which the individual sees the world and interprets the situations with which he is faced. His behavior cannot be understood unless these distortions are taken into consideration.

This concept is particularly applicable to international relations because most people get their ideas about other nations from information which comes through the bottleneck of a few journalists or interested propagandists, and which they interpret with the aid of slight recollections of school geography and history. The role of other nations in the life-space is, therefore, likely to be extraordinarily distorted.

The problem of education and communication in a democracy can, from this point of view, be interpreted as that of conforming the life-space of the individual, on the basis of which he thinks, talks, votes, and acts, to the situation as it *really* is. Since no one is free from these distortions, and since commitments to values and institutions and to social and individual life, implies selection and discrimination, and, therefore, some distortion, that *reality* is not easy to describe. It may in fact be best conceived as the generalized consequence of human evolution and interaction rather than as a mechanism which exists independently of minds (3, 16, 60, 86).

Detailed examination of the process of interaction indicates the great importance of face-to-face relations in determining personality, attitudes, and action, and the importance of founding those relations upon as objective a reality as is possible. Consequently attention should be given to the extraordinary influence which distortion, flowing from stereotypes, misinformation, interested propaganda, party politics, political activities, and gusts of opinion, can have upon international relations. In this field, face-to-face relations are relatively unimportant, and there is no direct access to objective *reality*. The attitudes influential in international relations are likely to be remote from any scientific analysis of *reality*. International relations is, therefore, in large measure relations between fantastic beliefs about nations not between actual nations, and is regulated by fantastic beliefs about the effect of acts and procedures not by the real effects. As one analyst put it, statesmen often turn the rudder of the ship of state the wrong way to reach the desired port (63).

Tension. It is common to say that tension between two countries is increasing or decreasing or that there is more tension in this situation than in that. The problem of measuring the degree of tension in an individual mind, among subgroups within a society, or between societies is, however, one of great difficulty. Methods for measuring the intensity of attitudes and opinions through schedules or questionnaires, and content analysis of the press and other published documents, has contributed to the solution of this problem.

The concept of psychic or social tension has developed by analogy from the concept of physical tension as in a stretched rope or overladen beam, or from the concept of tension in an electrical or a hydraulic system. In such systems tension or the rate of flow varies as resistance, or the rate of change of constriction of flow multiplied by energy, or the rate of change of quantity of flow. It has been suggested that, similarly, social tension may vary as the product of social resistance (perhaps measured by the rigidity of social institutions), and social energy (perhaps measured by the rate of capital accumulation) (83, 85).

Social tension has been defined as a condition of inconsistency among initiatives within a personality or group, and it has been recognized that this condition is essential to choice and progress. Excess of tension, however, leads to revolution in, or war between, societies, or to neuroses in, or suicide by, individuals. Because tension refers to a quantity, either too little or too much of which may be undesirable, it is particularly important that it be measured. UNESCO has initiated a research on international tensions which, however, has sought to explain the situations leading to tensions rather than to measure the amount of tension in given situations (13, 39).

Social psychologists have attached great importance to the mechanisms of repression, ambivalence, and frustration in accounting for the amount of tension in an individual, and to the mechanisms of displacement and projection upon a scapegoat in accounting for the conversion of individual tensions to intergroup and international tensions and eventually tensions between the two halves of a bipolar world (20, 22, 85). As the group with which the individual is associated expands, he must find a target or scapegoat for his aggressions in a more and more distant *out-group*. Thus the process tends toward a bilateralization of group hostility, but political friendships and hostilities may fluctuate. Politicians recognize that either alternative may on occasion be useful in the formula "fight them or join them." The Republicans fight the Democrats to increase their unity and power within the state, but, if international politics require, they may join with the Democrats to unite the country against a dangerous rival, and later they may join this rival when a third state becomes even more menacing. A complete unification can result only if the scapegoat is sublimated in the form, not of an out-group of similar character, but as a general enemy of man such as poverty, disease, or war itself (32). The management of co-operation and opposition so as to keep tensions within proper bounds is a major art of leadership especially in international politics.

Leadership. Social psychologists have recognized the significance of the leader and *the elite* in group formation and in determining group policies. While the state of opinion in the group exerts influence on the type of personality likely to achieve leadership, a leader once recognized can greatly influence the group policy, institutions, and culture. The psychological study of leadership has therefore assumed importance especially in political science. Social psychologists recognize that no particular type of personality is universally qualified for leadership. A great variety of different types have achieved leadership, but different types exercise leadership in a different way, and with different results for intergroup relations. For example, the type that seeks leadership to compensate for a frustrating experience or an inferiority complex is, if successful, likely to pursue aggressive policies. Conditions of high tension, a rigid hierarchical order, and economic frustration may throw such leaders to the top, thus initiating a vicious circle in which groups and leaders react to increase tensions, displace aggressions upon an external scapegoat, and integrate the group about an aggressive policy useful for manifesting group sentiment and keeping the leader in office. Out of such conditions war is likely to develop. On the other hand, the type that seeks leadership to forward social ideals and to express a broad social sympathy is likely to pursue a co-operative policy. Conditions of moderate tension, democratic order, and economic progress may throw such leaders to the top, thus initiating a cumulative movement toward broadening co-operation, reduction of tension, and integration of the group about policies of peaceful prosperity and progress. Such conditions may initiate long periods of comparative tranquillity and international intercourse throughout the world (44). Different types of leadership develop simultaneously in different nations but they tend to react upon one another thus producing oscillations of general war and general peace in the community of nations (83).

Individual leaders can seldom function except with support of a leadership group known as the elite. This group goes beyond those occupying formal positions of power. It may be characterized by a predominant type of personality and by a particular vocabulary or ideology justifying its position. Revolution usually signifies a change of both the personnel of the elite and the vocabulary of social and political authority. The quantitative and qualitative study of both these aspects of the elite promise to throw light upon the dynamics of social change (66).

The changing character of leaders, of elites, and of the prevailing personality and character types in a society have been related to such phenomena as technological change (Ogburn), population change (Riesman), ideological change (Toynbee), changes in social and economic structure (Marx) and changes in the general rate of social change (Lasswell). Such studies, however, fall in the field of sociology rather than of psychology.

CRITICISM

The psychology of international relations has sometimes been considered the basic discipline in the field. Social psychology, however, is a young discipline only emerging in the twentieth century. The analysis which it provides has led to some usable conceptual systems but quantification has only begun. The study of attitudes, of interaction, of tensions, and of leadership undoubtedly have much to contribute to the development of the science of international relations particularly through the influence such studies may have on the practical disciplines of international education and international communications.

The psychology of international relations may also serve as a basis for criticizing other practical disciplines in the field such as international politics and international law. These disciplines assume that nations are institutions that act as units and that international relations can, therefore, be sufficiently understood by a study of intergovernmental relations. Governments, it is true, often make it an object of policy to realize these assumptions by monopolizing control of foreign relations. They seek to accomplish this by increasing their domestic power and erecting barriers to communication, trade, and travel across their frontiers. Such a policy is assisted by developing a distinctive language, culture, and legal system and distinctive institutions so that the mind of the individual citizen will not be affected by foreign influences and will not influence foreign opinion, policy, or action except indirectly through his government. If such methods are carried to an extreme, the citizen can know what goes on abroad only as his government informs him, he can be aware only of his government's interpretation of these events, and he can exert influence only through bringing domestic pressures on his government.

In proportion as such a policy is successful, nations tend to resemble organisms. An organism reacts to other organisms and to the environment as a unit co-ordinated through the central nervous system. The cells of which the organism is composed are not influenced directly by outside events with exception of the cells of the sensory organs and other cells accidentally damaged by blows, poisons, or bacteria. In general, the cells develop within a protected environment with even temperature, regular supply of food through the blood stream, and the stimuli of the nervous and endocrine systems. Even in studying an organism, however, the psychologist, who deals with its behavior as a whole, cannot ignore physiology which deals with the relation of cells and organs within the body and their influence upon and response to stimuli by the central nervous system.

Thus, even if "Iron Curtain" policies were able to create isolated publics within each state, psychological analysis would be necessary to explain the influence of the individuals that constitute those publics upon government foreign policy and the influence of governments upon their citizens insofar as the attitudes of the latter are important in formulating and conducting foreign policy. If to the "Iron Curtain" is added the "garrison-prison state," subjecting the population to the government, the latter influence may be minimized. The ruler becomes the state.

However, in the modern age of electrical communication, economic interdependence, and general vulnerability to aerial attack, such a complete isolation and subjugation of any public is not possible. Citizens of a nation are not like cells of an organism. They have many contacts, direct, indirect, and symbolic with persons, conditions, and ideas in foreign countries. While it is the object of some national governments to minimize these contacts, it is the object of other national governments and of international organizations to maximize them by programs of exchange of persons, international communication, international education, technical assistance, and freer international trade.

International relations cannot, therefore, be confined to intergovernmental relations and conclusions based on the assumption that they can fail to provide an adequate foundation for prediction and control. The minds of the individuals who constitute the world's population, the influences that affect them, and the influences they exert, both domestic and foreign, must be taken into account by examining their minds. The psychology of international relations provides necessary correctives to the more formal disciplines of international relations, but it must itself lean to some extent upon the sociology of international relations. The behavior and social character of the individual is not autonomous but is influenced by the evolution of human culture and human societies. Personality and culture meet (67, 68).

Among animals, behavior and character is dominated by inherited instincts. The family, community, association, or other animal group functions because the *instincts* of each animal direct appropriate social behavior. Among primitive peoples individual behavior and character is largely dominated by custom transmitted by tradition and conditioning inherited impulses. Clans, tribes, societies, age groups, and villages function as they do because their customs, folkways, and mores direct appropriate social behavior by the members. Among civilized peoples individual behavior and character is dominated by conscience, or principles and ideologies, discriminating values learned in childhood from parents and elders, supported by practice and institutions of religion, law and government, defining situations and guiding choices. Groups function as they do by virtue of such principles, ideologies, and rules sanctioned by institutions which both create and rest upon the individual conscience.

In modern times, however, the expansion of means of communication subjects many persons to influences from diverse cultures, nations, and peoples. Furthermore the rapidity of invention and the radical change of techniques and other conditions during a single lifetime augments the influence of current opinion upon individual behavior. While custom and conscience continues to play a role, people tend to be *other directed* rather than *inner directed* (62).

This analysis does not imply that these differences in the source of human motivations necessarily evolve in definite sequence. *Inner-directed* and *other-directed* individuals and groups may exist in close proximity and a group may under certain circumstances, move from predominant *other direction* to predominant *inner direction*. The conditions of a shrinking and rapidly changing world and the tendency of populations to reach a condition of stability with low birth rate, low death rate, and high living standards, especially notable in the United States and Western Europe, tends, however, to supersede the rule of instinct, custom, and conscience by that of opinion.

Under these conditions communication, influencing opinions, is no less important than education, influencing attitudes. Among instinct-directed animals biology may be the master study of intergroup relations and among custom-directed primitive peoples, anthropology. Among conscience-directed civilized peoples and opinion-directed modern groups, psychology and sociology appear to be of predominant and equal importance.

REFERENCES

1. ALEXANDER, Franz, *Our Age of Unreason,* rev. ed. (Philadelphia, Lippincott, 1951).

2. BARNES, Harry Elmer, ed., *The History and Prospects of the Social Sciences* (New York, Knopf, 1925).

3. BERGSON, Henri, *Creative Evolution,* trans. by A. Mitchell (New York, Holt, 1911).

4. BERNARD, L. L., "Attitudes," *Encyclopædia of the Social Sciences.*

5. ——, "Instincts," *ibid.*

6. ——, "Social Psychology," *ibid.*

7. BLOCH, Herbert A., *The Concept of Our Changing Loyalties, An Introductory Study into the Nature of the Social Individual* (New York, Columbia University Press, 1934).

8. BOAS, Franz, *The Mind of Primitive Man* (1929); (New York, Macmillan, 1938).

9. BRITT, Stewart H., *Social Psychology of Modern Life* (New York, Rinehart, 1949).

10. ——, *Selected Readings in Social Psychology* (New York, Rinehart, 1950).

11. BRUNSWIK, Egon, "The Conceptual Framework of Psychology," *International Encyclopedia of Unified Science* (Chicago, University of Chicago Press, 1952), Vol. 1, No. 10.

12. BURGESS, Ernest, ed., "Personality and the Group," *Proceedings,* American Sociological Society (1927).

13. CANTRIL, Hadley, ed., *Tensions That Cause War* (Urbana, University of Illinois Press, 1951).

14. CATTELL, R. B., *Personality Study* (New York, Longmans, 1950).

15. CARTWRIGHT, Dorwin, and ZANDER, Alvin, eds., *Group Dynamics, Research and Theory* (Row, Peterson, Evanston, Ill., 1953).

16. CLIFFORD, W. K., *Lectures and Essays* (London, Macmillan, 1879), 2 vols.

17. COOLEY, Charles Horton, *Human Nature and the Social Order* (New York, Scribner, 1902).

18. DEWEY, John, *Experience and Education* (New York, Macmillan, 1938).

19. ——, "Human Nature," *Encyclopædia of the Social Sciences.*

20. DOLLARD, John, and others, *Frustration and Aggression* (New Haven, Yale University Press, 1939).

21. DUNN, Frederick S., *War in the Minds of Men* (New York, Council on Foreign Relations, 1950).

22. DURBIN, E. F., and BOWLBY, John, *Personal Aggressiveness and War* (New York, Columbia University Press, 1939).

23. EYSENCK, H. J., *The Scientific Study of Personality* (New York, Macmillan, 1952).

24. FRAZER, Sir James, *The Golden Bough, a Study in Magic and Religion* (New York, Macmillan, 1927), 1 vol. ed.

25. FREUD, Sigmund, *Collected Papers*, trans. by Joan Riviere and others (New York, International Psycho-analytical Press, 1924-1925), 4 vols.

26. ——— and EINSTEIN, Albert, "Why War?" *Open Letters* (Paris, International Institute of Intellectual Co-operation, 1933).

27. FROMM, Erich, *Escape from Freedom* (New York, Rinehart, 1941).

28. GLOVER, E., *War, Sadism, and Pacifism* (London, Allen and Unwin, 1947).

29. HALL, J. K., ed., *One Hundred Years of American Psychiatry* (New York, Columbia University Press, for American Psychiatric Association, 1944).

30. HAYEK, F. A., *The Sensory Order* (Chicago, University of Chicago Press, 1952).

31. JAMES, William, *Principles of Psychology* (New York, Holt, 1890), 2 vols.

32. ———, "The Moral Equivalent of War," in *Memories and Studies* (New York, Longmans, 1912).

33. JASTROW, Joseph, "Psychology," *Encyclopædia of the Social Sciences*.

34. JOAD, C. E. M., *How Our Minds Work* (New York, Philosophical Library, 1950).

35. KALLEN, Horace, "Psychoanalysis," *Encyclopædia of the Social Sciences*.

36. KARDINER, Abram, *The Individual and Society* (New York, Columbia University Press, 1939).

37. ———, *The Psychological Frontiers of Society* (New York, Columbia University Press, 1945).

38. KISKER, George W., *World Tension, The Psychopathology of International Relations* (New York, Prentice-Hall, 1951).

39. KLINEBERG, Otto, *Tensions Affecting International Understanding, A Survey of Research* (New York, Social Science Research Council, 1950).

40. KLUCKHOHN, Clyde, and MURRAY, Henry A., *Personality in Nature, Society and Culture* (New York, Knopf, 1952).

41. KOFFKA, K., "Gestalt," *Encyclopædia of the Social Sciences*.

42. KÖHLER, W., *Gestalt Psychology* (New York, Liveright, 1947).

43. LASSWELL, Harold D., *World Politics and Personal Insecurity* (New York, McGraw-Hill, 1935); see also Rothwell, C. E., ed.

44. ———, *Political Writings* (includes "Psychopathology and Politics," 1930; "Politics, Who Gets What? When? How?" 1936; "Democratic Character," 1941 (Glencoe, Free Press, 1951).

45. ———, *Analysis of Political Behavior: An Empirical Approach* (International Library of Sociology and Social Reconstruction, Oxford University Press, 1947).

46. LEBON, Gustav, *The Psychology of Peoples* (London, Fisher, Unwin, 1899).

47. LEWIN, Kurt, *A Dynamic Theory of Personality* (New York, McGraw-Hill, 1935).

48. ———, *Resolving Social Conflicts* (New York, Harper, 1948).

49. ———, *Field Theory in Social Science, Selected Theoretical Papers* (New York, Harper, 1951).

50. LINTON, Ralph, *The Cultural Background of Personality* (New York, Appleton-Century-Crofts, 1945).

51. ———, ed., *The Science of Man in the World Crisis* (New York, Columbia University Press, 1945).

52. McDOUGAL, William, *An Introduction to Social Psychology*, 15th ed. (Boston, Luce, 1923).

53. MAY, Mark A., *A Social Psychology of War and Peace*, Institute of Human Relations (New Haven, Yale University Press, 1943).

54. MEAD, George Herbert, *The Philosophy of the Present* (Chicago, University of Chicago Press, 1932).

55. MILLER, Emanuel, ed., *The Neuroses of War* (New York, Macmillan, 1940).

56. MURCHISON, Carl, *Psychologies of 1930* (Worcester, Clark University Press, 1930).

57. MURPHY, Gardiner, ed., *Human Nature and Enduring Peace* (Boston, Houghton Mifflin, 1945).

58. MYRDAL, Gunnar, "Some Psychological Impediments to International Cooperation," Supplement No. 6, to *Journal of Social Issues* (New York, 1933).

59. PEAR, T. H., ed., *Psychological Factors in Peace and War* (New York, Philosophical Library, 1950).

60. PEARSON, Karl, *Grammar of Science* (1892); 2nd ed. (London, Black, 1900).

61. RICE, S. A., *Methods in the Social Sciences* (Chicago, University of Chicago Press, 1931).

62. RIESMAN, David, in collaboration with DENNEY, Reuel, and GLAZER, Nathan, *The Lonely Crowd, a Study of the Changing American Character* (New Haven, Yale University Press, 1950).

63. RICHARDSON, Lewis F., "Generalized Foreign Politics," *British Journal of Psychology*, Monograph Supplement, Vol. 23 (Cambridge, 1939).

64. RIEZLER, Kurt, *Man: Mutable and Immutable* (Chicago, Regnery, 1952).

65. ROHRER, John H., and SHERIF, Muzafer, eds., *Social Psychology at the Crossroad* (New York, Harper, 1951).

66. ROTHWELL, C. Easton, ed., *Radir Project* (Revolution and the Development of International Relations) a series of comparative studies of élites, symbols, and countries by H. D. Lasswell, Ithiel deSola Pool, Daniel Lerner, and others (Stanford, Stanford University Press, 1951—).

67. SAPIR, Edward, "Personality," *Encyclopædia of the Social Sciences.*

68. SARGENT, S. Stansfeld, and SMITH, Marian W., eds., *Culture and Personality* (New York, Viking Fund, 1949).

69. SKINNER, B. F., *Science and Human Behavior* (New York, Macmillan, 1953).

70. STANTON, Alfred H., and PERRY, Stewart E., eds., *Personality and Political Crisis* (Glencoe, Ill., Free Press, 1951).

71. STOUFFER, Samuel A., *Studies in Social Psychology in World War II* (Princeton, Princeton University Press, 1949-1950), 4 vols.

72. STRATTON, George Malcolm, *Social Psychology of International Conduct* (New York, Appleton, 1929).

73. THOMAS, William I., and ZNANIECKI, Florian, *The Polish Peasant in Europe and America* (1918); (New York, Knopf, 1927), 5 vols.

74. THORNDIKE, E. L., *Human Nature and the Social Order* (New York, Macmillan, 1940).

75. THURSTONE, L. L., and CHAVE, E. J., *The Measurement of Attitude, A Psychophysical Method and Some Experiments with a Scale of Measuring Attitude Toward the Church* (Chicago, University of Chicago Press, 1929).

76. ——, *The Vectors of Mind* (Chicago, University of Chicago Press, 1935).

77. ——, ed., *Applications of Psychology: Essays to Honor Walter V. Bingham* (New York, Harper, 1952).

78. WAELDER, Robert, "The Psychological Aspects of War and Peace," *Geneva Studies*, Vol. 10, No. 2 (May, 1939).
79. WALLAS, Graham, *Human Nature in Politics*, 3rd ed. (London, Constable, 1920).
80. ———, *The Great Society* (New York, Macmillan, 1917).
81. WEST, Ranyard, *Psychology and World Order* (New York, Penguin, 1945).
82. ———, *Conscience and Society, A Study of the Psychological Prerequisites of Law and Order* (London, Methuen, 1942).
83. WRIGHT, Quincy, *A Study of War* (Chicago, University of Chicago Press, 1942), pp. 42-45, 74-80, 131-144, 272-290, 479-496, 519-526, 703-704, 714, 1198-1224, 1234-1235, 1288-1291, 1382-1388.
84. ———, ed., *The World Community* (Chicago, University of Chicago Press, 1948).
85. ———, *Problems of Stability and Progress in International Relations* (Berkeley, University of California Press, 1954).
86. WRIGHT, Sewall, "Genes and Organism," *American Naturalist*, Vol. 87 (January, 1953), pp. 5 ff.
87. YOUNG, Kimball, *Social Psychology*, 2nd ed. (New York, Appleton-Century-Crofts, 1944).

International Ethics

DEFINITION

International ethics is here defined as the science relating the standards and values which individuals, governments, and international organizations believe they ought to observe in their decisions intended to influence international relations. It also includes philosophical analyses and evaluations of alternative principles of international relations; practical rules for formulating, interpreting, and applying standards and values in the conduct of international relations; and historical studies contributing to this science, philosophy, and art.

International ethics is a branch of general ethics, but it has been treated as a distinct discipline because of the belief expressed by writers on international politics in various civilizations, such as Kautilya, Prince Shang, and Machiavelli, that its standards are inevitably and radically different from those of other branches of ethics. The difference has been asserted to flow from the lack of a universal society or culture establishing standards valid for the nations. Sovereign princes or nations have been described as in a "state of nature" with reference to one another, and it is said that ethical principles which flow from participation in a common society and culture are, therefore, inapplicable to them. Some writers, like Hobbes, found that in such a "state of nature," observance of no general standards could be anticipated, however desirable such observance might be, and therefore a state of war of each against all could be expected. Others like John Locke were less pessimistic and anticipated that some principles of "natural law" would be observed because of self-interest. However, both of these schools of thought agreed that only with the formation of social institutions by the "social contract" could there be much reliance on observance of principles either of law or of ethics.

This position has been attacked on three grounds. First, it has been asserted that ethical principles flow from sources broader than particular societies and cultures and exist wherever choices are made. Consequently, there must be principles of international ethics discoverable by careful observation of practice. Second, it has been suggested that whenever personalities or social groups are in contact, there is some interaction; consequently, there must be at least a rudimentary international society and at least rudimentary international ethical principles. In the third place, it is suggested that the ethical standards observed within each culture or society differ from those observed in others, and consequently international ethics differs only in degree, not in kind, from the ethical principles observed among individuals in particular national, religious, tribal, or other societies.

Consideration of the special character of international ethics involves some consideration of ethics in general. Ethics, as the discipline dealing with the norms of human conduct, is concerned with the problem of evaluation necessarily involved in the making of choices and decisions. Sociologists and psychologists have suggested that "systems of action," including both individuals and social systems, face certain necessary alternatives in acting. Talcott Parsons, for example, has suggested five such basic alternatives or "pattern variables" (100). The discipline of ethics indicates the circumstances under which such alternatives are presented, how people choose among them, why they make the choices they do, and what choices they ought to make. This suggests that the subject matter of *ethics* enters into all the social sciences since they all have to do with human choices. If treated by anthropologists, sociologists, or social psychologists such words as *habits, folkways, mores,* and *culture* will be used, and if treated by historians, *institutions, traditions, customs, conventions, fashions, etiquette,* and *law.* The terms *morals, moral conduct,* and *social control* are also closely associated with ethics indicating the content, the social and personal objectives, and the sanction of its rules, while *religion* has been variously considered a manifestation and a rationalization of the personal, social, or cosmic meaning of human conduct. Each of these terms has distinct shades of meaning, as indicated by the article devoted to each in the *Encyclopædia of the Social Sciences,* but all indicate norms of human choice which constitute the subject matter of ethics.

Ethics is usually treated as a philosophy, rather than as a science. It is said to be a normative discipline, dealing with *values,* the subject of philosophy, rather than with *facts,* the subject of science. Facts, said to exist in time and space, are contrasted with values, said to exist only in a culture, an ideology, an ideal or other belief. However, the adherents of a particular belief are located in time and space and consequently values, if considered functions of a particular belief, are questions of *fact*. The circumstances, the methods, and the purposes of choice-making in particular times and places can be investigated by science. Anthropologists and sociologists continually make the observation that in such and such a tribe or community, such and such values are recognized, and that they influence behavior in such and such a way. In this sense, values are as much a matter of *fact* as are mountains or rivers.

This can hardly be denied, but it is said, the essence of the problem of values is not what values exist here or there, but what values should I or the group I am interested in apply here and now? The issue is not, what values people around me are applying? or what values I will probably apply?, but, what values *ought* I to apply? The *ought* is said to differentiate values from facts (102).

Even here the two are related. The values and other norms which a person decides by *free will* he ought to apply, may become so internalized in his character that there is a high probability he will apply them in future situations. The norms thus become predictive formulae of high reliability. It becomes a *fact* in the individual's behavior pattern. So also, a society may incorporate an accepted norm in its law, and sanction the law by such effective procedures that it is generally observed. The *ought*, in such circumstances, has become a *fact* of general behavior in that community. This happens less formally in the development of cultures, but no less effectively. The norms established in the culture are regularly observed in the practice of the peoples, institutions, and social systems guided by it.

Thus norms can be facts. Also facts may be dependent upon norms. Behavior, as has been noted, insofar as it is dependent on choice, is dependent on norms. Both creation and criticism of art and literature involve evaluation. Logicians and mathematicians apply norms to determine the validity of inferences. Even the determination of past facts may depend on norms. There is a law of evidence, applied in legal procedures, in order to determine what happened. Historians and scientists apply norms, known as historical or scientific method, to determine facts (100). It appears therefore that values are involved in determining, not only the good, the true, and the beautiful, but also the real. Descriptions of fact (perceptions) are dependent on values no less than are decisions of action (conations), understanding of relations (cognitions), and expressions of feeling (appreciations). History, philosophy, science, and art all involve evaluation. Clyde Kluckhohn has defined a value as "a conception, explicit or implicit, distinctive of an individual or characteristic of a group, of the desirable, which influences the selection from available modes, means and ends of action." He emphasizes that as a "conception," it lies in the *cognitive* realm, as indicative of the "desirable" it lies in the *appreciative* realm, and as "influencing selection" it lies in the *conative* realm. He might have added that as "distinctive of an individual or characteristic of a group" it lies in the perceptive realm (100).

Values and facts are interrelated, but the problem of evaluation, for purposes of selection, appears to be different from that of fact-determination. The former involves the weighing of considerations and the making of practical judgments while the latter involves observation of phenomena and detection of relations among them. Evaluation looks toward action rather than knowledge, and lies in the realms of philosophy and art. Both decision-making and action, however, require knowledge of facts as well as commitment to values. The actor cannot rationally commit himself to a value without some knowledge of the social consequences of its realization, and of the means for realizing it, in the situation. This knowledge may indicate facts inducing modification of the commitment. The ethical decision-maker therefore seeks to discover the values and the facts most relevant to the situation with which he is faced and to combine them in a decision of maximum value and minimum evil. His experience develops the art of ethics. The theorist relates the experience of decision-makers with the consequences of their decisions in many past situations to create a science of ethics. But to analyze these experiences he must distinguish values and facts.

How are values to be determined? Are they products of caprice, custom, necessity, or rational choice? There appear to have been four distinct approaches—the psychological, the sociological, the scientific, and the philosophical. These, respectively, refer values to human nature, to social custom, to physical nature, and to rational analysis and synthesis. They are respectively related to the usually accepted classes of legal sources suggested in the statute of the International Court of Justice (Art. 38)— agreement, custom, authority, and reason. They may also have some parallelism to the factors which Machiavelli, following an ancient Greek tradition, found to condition the decisions of statesmen—*fortuna, occasione, necessita,* and *virtu* (110), and to Santayana's interpretation of the philosophies respectively of Goethe, Shakespeare, Lucretius, and Dante (118).

The *psychological* point of view starts with the propositions that happiness is good, and what contributes to it can be discovered by introspection. Each person knows what he sees, what he feels, what he wants, and what he thinks, and whether these experiences make him happy or unhappy (46). Each is the final judge of the real, the good, the beautiful, and the true, so far as his own happiness is concerned. Values thus tend to be equated with attitudes. Tolman, a psychologist, so equates them (100). They are merely generalized expressions of desire (122). It is, however, recognized that inconsistencies will arise in a society. Consequently, formulae are devised to deal with them; for example, "the greatest good of the greatest number," which assumes the equality of men and of desires (utilitarianism), or "to each according to his needs, from each according to his capacity," which assumes inequality of capacities and of desires (communism). Such formulae distinguish the *desirable* from the *desired*. The desirable is determined by social systems applying such formulae through social procedures, such as the free market or social planning. These procedures establish objective values in the society (64).

The psychological conception of values developed among the Sophists in Greece and was accepted by Hobbes and the British epistemologists, by Bentham and the British utilitarians, by Marx and the socialists, and by the modern attitude-measurers. However, insofar as they recognize the social function of reconciling conflicting subjective values, resulting in the establishment of objective values, these writers moved toward the sociological point of view. Even the marginal utility economists, who emphasized the role of subjective values in determining objective economic values, actually attributed controlling influence to such social institutions as the market and the price system.

The *sociological* point of view starts with the proposition that what everybody says is good must be good. *Vox populi, vox dei.* The good is determined by custom, opinion, tradition, or culture. Each society establishes through its own culture what is real, what is beautiful, what is good, and what is true. Values are aspects of culture; they are generalized expressions of the experience of the persons and organizations of a society in making choices. Choices are determined by cultural patterns, acquired by persons, and implicit in institutions. A problem arises, however, when contact occurs between different cultures or when changes of conditions render traditional values obviously unworkable. Such circumstances induce criticism of the values established by the culture from sources broader than the culture itself. Local positive law is criticized by appeal to universal principles of *justice* or *natural law*. Local ethical standards are criticized by universal standards derived from comparison, introspection, or revelation. Traditional perceptions of reality are criticized by universal standards of evidence and of observation derived from science. Local standards of beauty also become subjected to aesthetic and literary criticism, based on broader considerations. This criticism of local by universal values may be based on conceptions either of necessity or of reason leading to the scientific and the philosophical approaches to value.

The sociological or cultural theory of values has been adhered to by conservatives in all periods. It is undoubtedly the basis of most choices. This has been emphasized by modern anthropologists, who sometimes assert an extreme relativism denying any criteria of values apart from the prescriptions of a particular culture, valid only for that culture (139, 144). Efforts to rationalize and universalize traditional values, even when faced by demands for change, are to be found in some cultural systems, such as those of Judaism and Confucianism. The problem of gradually modifying a system of traditional values, regarded by many as the very essence of a culture, a nationality, or a civilization, when that system is faced by new contacts or conditions rendering it unworkable, is a major problem of society. Failure to meet such challenges has often resulted in the collapse of a civilization (127, 143). Such disasters can hardly be avoided unless methods are applied for criticizing and reforming existing values. This problem of *self-correction* was solved in the field of law, according to Sir Henry Maine, by the techniques of *fictions*, of *natural law*, and of *legislation* in successive periods in both ancient Rome and modern Britain. Adjustments of basic cultural patterns to new conditions have, however, seldom been made without much violence, as exhibited, for example, in the aesthetic, religious, scientific, and political criticism of the culture of medieval European Christendom at the time of the Renaissance and the Reformation.

The *scientific* point of view concerning values starts with the proposition that what is necessary must be accepted. If something is bound to happen, no theory of values can or should stand out against it. Copernicus' theory was used to criticize the anthropocentric universe of the Middle Ages. Darwin's theory was invoked to criticize ethical theories that ignored the process of *natural selection*. Freud's exposition of human motivation as it actually operates weakened the foundations of some traditional moral values. In the field of politics, Machiavelli's analysis was thought to demonstrate that power would inevitably triumph over morality, that might would make right. This *demonstration* influenced the behavior of princes, though modern sociologists and political scientists have shown that these two categories are, in fact, interdependent. Right may influence might (91, 125).

The attack on traditional values by *science* has often been made under the banner of *realism* versus *idealism*—ideal values must, it is said, give way to reality. Scientific formulae, based on biology, have been invoked to demonstrate inevitabilities in the future of social organization, and formulae have also been based on the conditions of geography, of technology, and of population, demonstrating that societies *must* adapt their values to these conditions or cease to exist.

Modern sociology has tended to be skeptical about allegedly scientific formulae which assert categorically that such and such values must be abandoned, or that such and such values must be adopted. The world of sense and the world of values are related in a more intricate manner than such formulae suggest. Values have a certain flexibility. They are usually susceptible of interpretations which would adjust them to the world as science sees it. The world, as science sees it, also has a certain flexibility (101). The scientist may see it as he does because of the values and standards often implicit in language by which he observes and interprets, and philosophers or even scientists themselves may extend scientific generalizations into fields to which the data do not apply. Conflicts between science and value do, however, occur. There doubtless are cultures which, in the modern world of widespread international contact, must abandon many of their values or perish. Usually, however, the problem is one of reinterpretation, rather than one of abandonment. It is premature to say that the values of nationalism are incompatible with the scientific knowledge of nuclear fission, radio communication, and aviation, or that the values of internationalism are incompatible with the scientific knowledge of organic evolution or human nature. It is safer to suggest reconsideration of the meaning of these values in the light of the conditions which science has established. Such reconsideration and adjustment has been considered a task transcending science. The weighing of values and conditions is said to be the task of philosophy, which alone can serve as a self-corrective device of cultures and value systems. This issue depends upon the definitions of science and philosophy. It may be that at this point they converge (39, 107).

The *philosophic* point of view starts from the proposition that you cannot have your cake and eat it. Knowledge, as Socrates said, is virtue, and knowledge includes acquaintance with values as well as with conditions. It is to be found by the dialectical process of discovering inconsistencies and seeking to resolve them in higher generalizations. Philosophy is, therefore, synthetic as well as analytic. It understands the importance in the establishment of values of individual desires and attitudes, of social customs and opinions, and of the conditions growing from advancing scientific knowledge and technology. It also understands the role of logic and the technique of resolving inconsistencies and contradictions. The philosophic process takes form in the emergence of ideologies, often the creations of genius, stating new religions or social philosophies, usually with sufficient ambiguity to admit of much interpretation. The influence of these ideologies may come through sponsorship by revolutionary parties or conquering nations, or through the gradual modification of opinion by communication and education. Such ideologies may emphasize new formulations of values, they may emphasize new processes for interpreting values, or they may emphasize new relations between accepted values (45, 79). The problem of international ethics in the modern shrinking world is therefore to be solved by philosophic effort to achieve such syntheses. The scientists do not consider such efforts outside their interest, which includes both "analysis and synthesis of knowledge" and the integration of science and philosophy. "The real meaning of these (most abstract) generalizations can be found within science if we include also the social sciences in the system of science. The idea of a super-science called philosophy or metaphysics arises only if we mean by 'science' some special science instead of the system of all the sciences" (39).

ASSUMPTIONS

The discipline of international ethics is based on the following assumptions:

1. The value systems of the principal nations of the world differ, and are, in varying degree, inconsistent with one another. The variations in the degree of difference tend to group the nations into blocs of considerable cultural similarity. There is an Atlantic group with Graeco-Roman-Christian civilization, divided into a southern European, predominantly Catholic group; a northern European, predominantly Protestant group; a central European group largely outside the area of the ancient Roman Empire of mixed Protestant and Catholic religion; an English-speaking group, predominantly Protestant; and a Latin-American group, predominantly Catholic. There is a Eurasian group, with a developing Communist culture, divided into a Slavic group based on a Byzantine orthodox culture and a Far Eastern group, based on a Buddhist-Confucian culture. There is a Middle Eastern group of Moslem culture, divided into an Arab group and a Turko-Iranian group. There is a South Asian group, divided into an area of Hindu culture in the center, and areas of Buddhist and Moslem culture on the periphery. There is a Far Eastern-Pacific group, divided into areas in which Confucian, Buddhist, or Christian cultures have been superseding primitive cultures. Finally there is an African group, divided into areas in which Moslem or Christian culture have been superseding primitive cultures (21, 98).

2. The conditions of the modern world by increasing the contacts between persons and social systems guided by divergent value systems have developed these inconsistencies into conflicts of interest, of more or less intensity. There seem to be three basic factors in this condition. First is the vulnerability of each nation to military, economic, and propaganda attack from any part of the world, because of recent inventions, such as the airplane, the radio and the atomic bomb, and the economic interdependence of the nations. The latter has developed from the ease of transport, the industrial revolution, and the unequal distribution of raw materials, industrial plants, and markets throughout the world. The second factor is the continuous cultural interchange between peoples across national lines, varying greatly in abundance and in the degree of social interaction, according to the similarity of cultural backgrounds and the effectiveness of political obstructions. The third factor is the division of the world into sovereign states constituting the predominant social systems of action, each seeking to maintain, to defend, and in varying degree

to expand its culture. Each fears encroachments by another, proportionate to the degree of cultural difference, of aggressiveness, and of capacity to launch a successful attack attributed to it. Attacks may be anticipated immediately or in the long run, and by psychological, economic, or military methods. Expectation of immediate military attack induces the greatest degree of anxiety (145).

3. These contacts have resulted in the emergence of an embryonic, universal culture and of institutions and organizations for its interpretation and application, seeking to resolve inconsistencies and conflicts. The evidence for the existence of such a universal culture is to be found in four bodies of data. First, the increasing diffusion throughout the world of technical processes, types of consumption goods, skills, art forms, ideologies, and other aspects of each of the major cultures. Second, the convergence of the laws, opinions, and attitudes influencing peoples, manifested by discussions in the mass media, literature, and art of each of the principal nations and the formal agreements among them concerning the values asserted in the United Nations Charter and other international instruments. Third, the development of numerous international and transnational institutions and organizations, many of universal scope, to maintain generally accepted values, to promote generally accepted goals, and to resolve inconsistencies and conflicts of world importance. In the fourth place, philosophers of all the leading cultures have attempted to formulate the basic values and processes of the emerging universal culture (57, 98, 106, 109, 143).

4. Social observation and analysis indicate that value systems can be synthesized, and that philosophic insight and analysis can develop and continually reinterpret universal values to facilitate such synthesis. Anthropology and history bear witness to the frequent synthesis of cultures and integration of groups into more comprehensive cultures and groups, as well as a reverse process of differentiation and disintegration. On the whole, the processes of integration, accommodation, and assimilation have dominated in human history. Man has always participated in groups, but, as history has advanced, these groups have become larger in area and more complex in structure. Instead of thousands of independent, small, and distinctive tribes, there are today only some seventy nations, and these are so grouped as to tend toward five or six great regions. The studies of the sociological processes of interaction, of accommodation, and of assimilation indicate the mechanisms of these changes. Furthermore, analyses of systems of action indicate that pattern variables and values guide choice and action, that the number of value systems, resulting from the combinations of one or the other alternative in the pattern variables, is not unlimited, and that consequently it may be possible to determine the basic points of similarity or difference in value systems (98, 100). Such a determination may suggest the points to which efforts at

philosophical and practical synthesis should be directed. Northrop, for example, believes that there is a basic difference between the philosophy and practice of the Orient based on aesthetic intuition and those of the Occident based on conceptual postulates and that this difference can be bridged by recognition of "epistemic correlations" between the immediately sensed and the logically inferred elements of reality. He also anticipates that this synthesis may provide a bridge between the conflicting theories of the west, of which he distinguishes Aristotelian-Thomistic-Catholicism; Newtonian-Lockian-democratic-empiricism; Kantian-Hegelian-Germanic-idealism; and Marxist-Leninist-Communist-dialectical-materialism.

The first and second of these assumptions are assertions of fact, which can hardly be doubted. The third and fourth are assertions both of fact and value, which are controversial, but which manifest a reasonable faith that the problem of formulating and realizing international ethical standards is soluble.

For those who assert the impossibility of peaceful reconciliation of values or of peaceful coexistence of diverse value systems, there is no problem of international ethics. Such beliefs deny the possibility of such a general integration of values that institutions to maintain international peace and security can function. If international ethics is believed to be an unrealizable ideal, it presents no problems.

A discipline of international ethics, like any other ethical discipline, must be based on assumptions, both of fact and of faith. The assumption of an inevitable and unbridgeable inconsistency between ethics and policy, between right and expediency, is a denial of this faith. Such a denial is sometimes stated in terms of an absolute ethic, binding on individual relations everywhere, but inapplicable to international politics. At other times, it is stated in terms of the absolute applicability of each national ethical system to both individual conduct and national policy, and the irreconcilability of these different systems by any universal standards because each is the consequence of unique geographic, historic, and cultural conditions. These two points of view are sometimes combined by asserting the absoluteness and the eventual universality of the national ethical system. The first of these points of view, commonly associated with Machiavelli, says that a statesman must separate his representative capacity in which he acts only from expediency, from his personal capacity in which he ought to follow universal ethical principles (93). The second point of view, to be found in the memoirs of most contemporary statesmen of the democracies, says the statesman must follow his national culture which defines the national interest, that this will lead to conflicts with statesmen from other nations with other cultures, and that while temporary compromises may be made, "principles" of the national ethics must not be sacrificed. The third point of view says the statesman must actively strive to impose the national ethical system on others or, if that is not at the moment practical, to shield its purity until the opportunity arises. This faith, illustrated by some self-righteous American isolationists, often with roots in literalist Protestant sects (112), approaches the religious, racial, or ideological imperialism of an Urban II, a Philip II, a Hitler, or a Stalin.

None of these antinomies seems necessary. Ethics and expediency are separated by no such sharp lines. Ethics is long-run expediency, and expediency is short-run ethics. Absolutistic theories of ethics are not adapted to a world of increasing contact among diverse cultures, nor are they supported by history or philosophy. If applied vigorously, they have induced persecution and war; and if they have endured, their "absoluteness" has been abandoned by the process of adaptive interpretation. If examined critically, their assumptions prove unnecessary and their conclusions unconvincing. Ethical systems which differ because they have arisen under different conditions are never insusceptible of adjustment, if the common elements flowing from a universal human nature are understood. The difficulty lies in the positing of absolutes, which are unnecessary, but which tend to be assumed, because of the characteristics of language and of traditional philosophies and theologies, and because of the utility of firm commitment to values in certain situations of social life. Such situations are characteristic of primitive societies and of the family, the church, and the army in modern life. Understanding of the general diversity of value patterns which have been applied in different periods, in different areas, and in different situations may contribute to eliminating these unnecessary antinomies.

ANALYSIS

The analysis of international ethics concerns: (a) the general characteristics of a system capable of becoming universal under present conditions, (b) the forces which may be invoked to effect such an internalization of the principles of that system that they will be realized in actual behavior, (c) the process of interpreting and applying those principles for the solution of practical international problems, and (d) the relations of the international to national ethical systems which might permit and assure continual self-criticism and self-correction adapting international ethical principles to new conditions.

Standards of international ethics. Cultural anthropologists, aware of the great variety of value systems which have functioned in different societies and cultures have usually been skeptical of efforts to establish ethical systems of universal applicability. They suggest that while values vary in their comprehensiveness absolute universality or eternity can be ascribed to none. Common opinion, however, tends to assume that values, if not good for all situations, past, present, and future, are good for nothing. Korzybski and his school of general semantics attributes the tendency of people, especially those of western culture, to demand absolute values, to the error of Aristotelian logic, subtly injected into their languages, inducing them to identify words with things, to assume that members of a class are identical, and to attribute reality to logical deductions from general propositions (50, 65, 98, 107).

However, though rejecting all absolute values, it is not necessary to follow the relativity of some anthropologists who regard each culture as a unique organization of values incapable of being evaluated (139). While no values or value systems are perfect some may be better than others. It may be possible to criticize all, but by what criteria?

Sources of universal values. The psychological, scientific, philosophical, and sociological schools of general ethics have respectively based values on desire, necessity, reason, and custom. Universal values have been drawn from each of these sources.

Desires have been attributed to biological needs of the organism. Needs to survive, to belong to a group, to create order, and to feel secure for the future have been invoked (107) as have basic drives of food and activity, sex and society, dominance and independence, and defense and territory (143). W. I. Thomas emphasized four basic wishes—adventure, intimacy, recognition, and security. Satisfaction of these needs, drives or wishes has been considered a value applicable to all mankind.

Necessity has been identified with the acknowledgment of superior power, but power is defined in many ways. Scientists have tended to identify power with knowledge, and knowledge with communication (107). Thus to appraise the survival prospects of a value system in the long run the general semanticists ask "to what extent does it permit or encourage the free exchange of communication and the fullest transmission into the future of usable knowledge of the past, so that knowledge increases in accuracy and predictive value as time goes on?" (50). "The circulation of information," according to the science of cybernetics, "is central to social order, since for human beings 'to live effectively is to live with adequate information'" (141). To the same effect the Supreme Court of the United States has held that freedom of speech and press, because they are essential for constitutional democracy, have a "preferred position" over all other constitutional guarantees and over all legislative powers (105). In other words, value systems are to be valued by their practical effectiveness in maximizing communications. Such practical effectiveness is unlikely, in the varied situations with which people are confronted, unless the system accepts the relativity to time, space, and circumstances of the meaning of all general terms and propositions. Such relativity may moderate the prejudice, inflexibility, dogmatism, and reliance on word magic which has, in general experience, proved hostile to effective communication and to sane social behavior (50). To escape their own criticism of absolute ethical systems, the semanticists suggest that standards designed to protect the dignity of man, the diversity of nations, and the stability and progress of the world should be confined to a general injunction to avoid choices which, in a given situation, appear to militate against free communication (107, 140).

Philosophers applying reason have reached similar conclusions. The principles attributed by writers as different as Grotius and Hobbes to *natural law* gave prominence to good faith in the observance of promises, and some modern jurists have suggested that observance of agreements is the basic norm of international law (62). Failure to observe this standard undoubtedly militates against communication and stultifies the settlement of differences by rational argument, reducing relations to hot or cold war. Philosophers of many civilizations have sought to elaborate systems of *natural law* from such general propositions, while jurists have sought the same end through comparing actual systems of law and ethics, and organizing their common elements into a universal system. The Roman jurists called such a system the *jus gentium* or law of nations and it was found to differ more in method of discovery than in content from the *jus naturale* or law of nature deduced from ethical postulates. Both the deductive and the comparative methods, as well as the method of diplomatic negotiation, have been utilized in elaborating the conception of "Human Rights and Fundamental Freedoms" accepted in the United Nations Charter. The Universal Declaration of Human Rights which emerged in 1948, rather as a guide to achievement than as a rule of law, has commanded general support among statesmen, though the philosophers differ in the postulates which could support it and the jurists differ in their interpretation of its provisions (70, 86). Philosophers have, however, suggested that fundamental analysis of the various ethical systems will disclose possibilities of reconciliation (98, 99).

Cultural anthropologists, semanticists, and lawyers appreciate that formal principles developed by the methods just discussed are likely to be neither convincing nor effective unless the persons and groups among which they are to function participate in some degree in a common culture giving the terms a common meaning both intellectual and emotional (85). Custom is the basis of culture, and the *positivist*, differing from the *naturalist*, school of international law has attributed international obligation to custom (62). The system of international law, whether based on custom, consent, the requirements of international order, or the requirements of state independence, formulates norms of state conduct, observance of which is considered an ethical as well as a legal duty. This duty, however, applies primarily to governments rather than to individuals. Is there evidence of a universal culture capable of supporting international law?

A universal culture. In an earlier work the present writer suggested that a universal culture began to develop in the late fifteenth century after the discoveries and the Renaissance had brought remote civilizations into continuous contact with one another, and that it had been developing certain general ethical standards characterized as belief in humanity, in liberty, in science, and in tolerance (143). This culture of humanism, liberalism, pragmatism, and relativism suggests standards by which freedom of communication and other human rights, as well as national rights, might be justified and interpreted.

Humanism asserts that the source of values is human insight, particularly the insight that every man is an end, that institutions and arts exist for man, and that every member and section of the human race is worthy of consideration in social planning and action. . . . *Liberalism* asserts that every individual should have an opportunity to develop his own personality. . . . Men like certainty, security and direction, but throughout most of modern history they have tended to insist even more on freedom and the opportunity to make up their own minds. . . . *Pragmatism,* which means the general application of scientific method, diverts men from the quest for certainty, by denying that certainty is possible. It asserts that the only test we have for judging the truth of any proposition is confirmation by experience of its concrete consequences. It assumes that, with the recording of new experiences, every truth will in time be discarded or limited in its scope. . . . *Relativism,* asserting that no experience is real except in relation to a frame of reference has been demolishing what little of certainty pragmatism has left. For relativism, there is no being apart from our knowledge about it, and that knowledge always proceeds from postulates that are themselves continually changing. It thus leaves the entire field of philosophy to pragmatism and cultivates an attitude of tolerance (143).

This developing system of thought was called *modernism* because continuous adaptation to changing conditions, which is its essence, would keep it always up to date. It resembles the *Maitreyism* devised by Charles Morris to synthesize the attitudes encouraged by the great religions of the past (94), and the *evolutionary scientific humanism* expounded by Julian Huxley, the first Director-general as a possible philosophy for UNESCO (55). Because of opposition from both Catholics and Communists and a feeling that any formulation would be premature, this statement proved unacceptable to the UNESCO Conference, though it seemed to synthesize the actual statements of purpose in the Constitution of that organization. Recognizing the "unsatisfactory connotations" of "humanism," Mr. Huxley later suggested the term *transhumanism* as better expressing "the idea of humanity attempting to overcome its limitations and to arrive at fuller fruition" and "the realization that both individual and social development are processes of self-transformation." He thought "the truth of the transhumanist approach and its central conception greater and more universal than any previous truth" and "if so, bound in the long run to supersede lesser, more partial or more distorted truths." He suggested that:

Various elements in other previous systems could and should obviously be taken over by the new system of thought, and made over in its new pattern. There is the equal worth or intrinsic value of all human beings, taken over from Christianity and Western democracy; the importance of the individual, from the post-Renaissance era; the importance of liberty from the post-Revolutionary era; the scientific method of objective testing and the principle of limited certitude, from the last three centuries of natural science; the importance of quantity thinking, from technology and precision control; the application of the evolutionary or historical idea to society, from Hegel and Marx; the value of variety, both for individuals and for cultures, from social anthropology; the idea of what we may call external adventure—activism, exploration, control of nature—from the Renaissance and natural science, from technology and sport, and from the underlying philosophy of Marxism; but also the correlative of this, on the other side of the basic split, the idea of internal adventure—contemplation, self-discipline, and control of oneself—from the poets, artists, philosophers, and mystics of all continents. Then we are very much in need of taking over the ideas of wholeness and harmony, largely from Oriental thought; and, of course, the idea of order, law, and the necessary hierarchy of authority from various sources in past history (56).

These expositions of the developing universal culture appear to accept the ethical or conative value of human welfare, the appreciative or aesthetic value of individual personality, the rational or intellectual value of scientific method, and the observational or perceptive value of toleration, derived, respectively, from reason, desire, necessity, and custom. This culture, therefore, synthesizes the philosophic, psychological, scientific, and sociological points of view in regard to the sources of values.

In his earlier work, the present writer commented:

Humanism, liberalism, pragmatism and relativism are becoming the faith of the contemporary world civilization, and, viewing their long-run effect, it seems that conditions are not unfavorable to an even more intensive and extensive acceptance of these attitudes, though it is the essence of pragmatism and science, of relativism and toleration, to acknowledge the possibility that these or any other attitudes will eventually change. It is also to be noted that these attitudes constitute frames of reference of the broadest type. Their general acceptance is not incompatible with a wide variety of laws, customs, and institutions in different parts of the world and among different social groups. General acceptance of these attitudes would not provide a basis for predicting the forms of world-civilization in any concrete detail, although it might suggest some of its broadest outlines (143).

Pattern variables. These criteria for determining the good, the beautiful, the true, and the real in international ethics may be related to the basic *pattern variables* or alternatives of choice developed by the sociological analysis of systems of action initiated by Talcott Parsons (100). According to this analysis, in deciding upon action, a personality or social system must make a succession of choices which at an appropriate level of generalization can be reduced to five alternatives or pattern variables:

1. Shall action in a given situation be based on impulse or on deliberate thought (affectivity-affective neutrality)?

2. Shall it be based on self-interest or on considerations of social responsibility (self-orientation—collective-orientation)?

3. Shall it be based on universal standards or on standards applicable only to a particular group or situation (universalism-particularism)?

4. Shall it be based on standards which classify the other people involved by general qualities ascribed to them or by their achievements relevant to the situation (ascription-achievement)?

5. Shall it be based on a particular interest of the actor (ego) in the other person concerned (alter) or on a general interest of ego in alter (specificity-diffuseness)?

This scheme suggests that in dealing with the Soviet government, for example, American statesmen must first decide whether to act impulsively or reflectively. If they decide to reflect, they must then decide whether to consider only American self-interest or general standards of the community of nations. In either case, it would be necessary to decide whether to deal with the Soviet Union in a way to contribute to a permanent and general improvement of the situation, or in a way to best meet the immediate problem by satisfying the most pressing demands of citizens and others. It would also be necessary to decide whether to be guided by consideration of certain general qualities ascribed to the Soviet Union, such as *Communism* or *dictatorship,* or to be guided by its behavior relevant to the particular situation, such as its record in negotiations and treaty observance. Finally, it would be necessary to consider whether to deal with the Soviet Union in a limited way, discussing only one interest at a time, or, in a general way on the assumption that the United States has a general interest in the Soviet Union because of common membership in the family of nations. These decisions involve evaluation—whether of an appreciative, ethical, cognitive, or perceptive character—and suggest that in international relations, ethics and evaluation are relevant, and that some criteria will inevitably be applied consciously or unconsciously.

Parsons and others consider this particular list of alternatives both necessary and complete and they further consider them alternatives permitting of no compromise. These characteristics are perhaps stated too absolutely. It would seem that frequently actors do attempt to compromise between these alternatives as by deliberating some, but not much, before choosing. They also frequently interpret or rationalize self-interest in terms of social responsibility, and seek to justify racial, national, religious, or other prejudices in terms of achievements relevant to the situation. Efforts to construct a rigid system of alternatives seems, therefore, subject to the same criticism that has been leveled against efforts to construct a rigid system of values for selecting between such alternatives.

Korzybski's prescriptions for avoiding the absolutistic Aristotelian orientation may suggest how an ethical system may avoid both absolute values and absolute pattern variables (50, 65). His caution against the identification of words with things, suggests that neither impulses nor thoughts are identical with the words that symbolize them, though both are influenced by language. Consequently, actions based on one or the other differ in degree rather than in kind. If care is taken, as urged by the *non-Aristotelians*, to hyphenate words which bring together linguistically discrete concepts, it may be seen that self-interest and social responsibility are not necessary alternatives but that *egoistic-altruistic* interests influence most decisions. If care is taken to limit the validity of general terms to specific dates and circumstances, the distinction between *universal* and *particular* standards will be seen to be relative. So also if all general terms are *indexed* to suggest that each of the instances denoted by a term has its own peculiarities, it will be clear that differences between *ascriptive* and *achievement* characterizations are relative. Finally if general terms of social science are put in quotation marks, as the non-Aristotelians advise, it will be suggested that they probably have connotations of metaphysical or affective character and consequently that the difference between *specific* and *diffuse* interests are differences of degree, not of kind. In short, application of semantic tests suggests that Parson's system of *pattern variables* does not exclude the possibility that criteria may be discovered and applied in particular situations which neither accept nor reject either horn of the five dilemmas postulated.

However, there is a difference between criteria of choice and alternatives (or continua) soliciting choice, although the two are related. The circumstances affecting choice may be infinitely diverse, but the process of choice may be, in a measure, determined by the necessary structure of a *system of action*. It may therefore be possible to make a general description of that process, verifiable by the scientific methods of observation and analysis. Parsons and his colleagues have attempted to do this. In the same way scientific jurists, while recognizing that there may be an infinite variety of legal systems, assume that there are some necessary alternatives faced by courts in the process of administering justice. For example, they must decide whether to apply law or to act at discretion in accepting jurisdiction, in receiving evidence, in listening to argument, and in giving judgment. The decisions taken on these matters will determine whether the court is of judicial, quasijudicial, administrative, or legislative character. However, the character of courts determined by this process affects the character and pervasiveness of the law which feeds back to influence the character of the courts. More generally, it can be said that in systems of action the character of the process of choosing affects the character of the choices. Consequently if there is a limited system of pattern variables, as Parsons claims, there may be a limited number of possible ethical systems though each system may permit of considerable adaptation to conditions and circumstances.

All possible combinations of Parsons' five alternatives permit of thirty-two (2^5) value systems, but Parsons suggests that many of these possible combinations rarely occur in social systems. While the second alternative (collective or self-orientation of the actor) is applicable to both individuals and organizations, individuals (personalities or systems of "need-disposition") are primarily concerned with the first and last alternatives, while organizations (social systems, or systems of "role-expectation") are primarily concerned with the third and fourth alternatives.

Applying his system, Parsons concludes that the cultural ideal of the United States tends to choose in accord with universal or intellectual standards and to apply them to the achievement of the person evaluated rather than to ascriptive categories such as race, color, or national origin. The German and perhaps the Fascist and Soviet cultural ideals, he thinks, also tend to evaluate by universal standards, but to apply them to such ascriptive categories as race, class, ideology, or party membership. The Chinese cultural ideal, prior to the development of Communism in that country, differs, Parsons suggests, from both in that it tends to evaluate by particularistic standards such as the evaluator's family or local community relations, but tends to classify persons, as does the American cultural ideal, by achievement determined, for example, by civil service examinations or scholarship. Determination of the actor's responsibility by particularistic standards which permit discrimination between people on the basis of family relationship tends to conflict with the evaluation of others by achievement standards which seek to avoid such discrimination. This has generated a major subject of research: Did family connections or impartial examinations contribute most in the recruitment of the Chinese civil service at various periods of history (54)? The Latin-American cultural ideal is believed by Parsons to manifest the fourth possible combination among these two alternatives, that is particularistic standards of evaluation as in the Chinese cultural ideal, but ascriptive classification of others, as in the German cultural ideal. These typical systems of evaluation, represented by the accompanying diagram, may be compared with the philosophic analysis of these cultures by Northrop (98).

Classification of others \ Standards of actor	Particularistic	Universalistic
Ascription	Latin-Americans	Germans
Achievement	Chinese	United States

Relativity of value systems. It is believed that a philosophic consideration of all of these alternatives will suggest, as insisted by the semanticists, that different combinations are appropriate to different situations.
This is suggested by the actual variety of value systems in different
cultures and in different contexts in the same culture. It seems likely that
universal ethical standards, while necessary under modern conditions,
function to co-ordinate lesser ethical systems rather than to assimilate
them (99). Most ethical standards are relative to the individual and
organizations that apply them and to the situations and cultures within
which they are applied. Studies by Charles Morris of the preference of
different somatic types for different value systems support this conclusion (94).

Differences in the value systems appropriate to different social roles
become evident if consideration is given to the roles of the individual in
the smallest relatively permanent social system, the family, and in the
most comprehensive social system, the world society. In the former there
are of course differences in the standards applicable by parents and
children, and in the latter in the standards applicable by national and
international statesmen and by private persons, but these differences
seem less important than those which flow from the difference between
the family and the world.

The family involves continuous and intimate contact of all its members.
Consequently each member should react spontaneously, only possible if
patterns are highly internalized; should subordinate self-interest by regard for the whole; should apply different standards to members of the
family from those applied to others; should differentiate among members
of the family because of the clear functional difference of father, mother,
and children; and should manifest a general and diffuse interest in all
the others. In short, the ethics of the family seem to require that the
members make choices on the basis of affectivity, collective orientation,
particularistic standards, ascriptive classifications of, and diffuse interest
in, others. This is the ethics of love and has been influential in the great
religions and in cultures emphasizing the family such as that of Confucian China.

On the other hand, in the world society, the opposite standards of evaluation seem generally appropriate. International ethics would seem to
require the representative of a nation to suppress spontaneity and to
reflect deliberately before making any choice because of the great variety
of considerations likely to be involved and the improbability that internalized patterns of behavior would be applicable. Because of the great
variety of interests and cultures in the human race and the improbability
of any action being satisfactory to everyone, he should give major consideration to the interests of his own state unless explicit responsibilities
require a collective orientation. He should, however, apply universalistic

or intellectual standards calculating the consequences of each possible course of action as broadly as possible and eliminating affective biases toward particular persons or groups. He should be especially careful to classify others involved in a situation by achievement standards in order to avoid unnecessary conflict. The sensitivity of persons to discriminatory treatment, on the bases of race, nationality, language, religion, or other ascriptive characterization, is notorious and has been behind much international conflict. The repudiation of such bases for discrimination has been emphasized in the United Nations Charter and the Universal Declaration of Human Rights as well as in most national constitutions, which govern large numbers of persons of varied characteristics. The failure to observe such cultural ideals in practice has, it is true, been notorious, even in democracies such as the United States, and it has been doubted whether the repudiation of ascriptive discrimination, even though formally recognized in imitation of the democracies, is actually the ideal of either the Latin-American or Soviet cultures. The principle of the equality of man, demanded by democracy in opposition to earlier class and caste systems, means the right of everyone to be judged by standards of achievement rather than by standards of ascription. With the increasing literacy and communication among all sorts of people in the world and the concomitant sensitivity to ascriptive discriminations, it would seem necessary for international ethics to avoid ascriptive standards. It is to be noticed that in the exchange of discourtesies between the western and Soviet worlds during the course of "cold war" each in principle repudiated ascriptive standards for itself and attributed them to the other. For statesmen observance of the international conventions concerning the equality of states is equally important.

International ethics seems also to require that choices be based on a specific rather than a diffuse interest in others. It is impossible for a person to feel the same general interest in, or responsibility for, the two billion people in the world that he feels for members of his family. It is also impossible for a statesman, at least one who expects to hold his job, to feel the same general responsibility for other nations that he feels for his own. The presumption of international ethics must be that the interest in, or the responsibility for, others is that which arises from a specific contract or other particular conditions of a given situation. These interests may become somewhat extended, as for instance, the contemporary American interest in improving the standards of living of underdeveloped peoples under the technical aid programs. The particular situation may justify this relatively diffuse interest, but it is a consequence of that particular situation, and the presumption is against it. International ethics, differing from family ethics, appears, therefore, to call for effective neutrality, self-orientation, universalistic standards, achievement classifications of others, and limitation of interest in them to relations flowing from the specific situation. This is the ethics of reason and has influenced international law, and national legal systems, such as that of the United States, based on territorial sovereignty rather than consanguinity. Its difference from the ethics applicable to the family has troubled believers in absolute ethical standards (93, 97).

It will be observed that the standards of international ethics derived from Parsons' social analysis closely resembles the values of modern civilization which the writer discovered by observation of the historic tendencies of the last four centuries. Humanism implies the application of achievement standards to all members of the human race. Liberalism implies a wide freedom for self-orientation of the actor. Pragmatism implies action guided by scientific or universal standards. Relativism implies that action be guided by the specific peculiarities of the situation. These standards also appear favorable to the broadening of social communication as demanded by the semanticists and to the preservation of societies able to satisfy the biological needs of the individual. International law based on custom and agreement has functioned to maintain order among nations, each with a distinctive culture.

The standards of universal culture have, in considerable measure, been accepted as legal obligations by most of the countries of the world in approving the United Nations Charter, the Universal Declaration of Human Rights, and other recent international instruments. It is clear, however, that even when so accepted they are not necessarily sufficiently internalized in the minds of men, even in their official roles, to make their application in practical situations in any high degree reliable. Furthermore, the meaning of these standards is not clear, as is evident from the effort of different cultures to justify very diverse practices in their terms. Finally, it is by no means clear how these or any other international ethical standards, even if, and perhaps especially if, their meaning is clarified and generally sentimentalized, can be kept from becoming unadapted to changing conditions, as have the standards of past civilizations. It is clear that all human relations cannot be guided by these or any other abstract principles of international ethics. Human nature requires some of the spontaneous, affectionate, collective, particularistic, and diffuse relations characteristic of the family. Some such standards may also be appropriate to the situation presented by religious, social, and some types of professional life. This conclusion has been suggested by comparison of the American and Chinese cultures, respectively emphasizing universal and family relationships (54). The problem of integrating a plurality of standards appropriate to different persons, different groups, and different situations is one of the problems of international ethics. These problems will be considered in the following section.

Forces of international ethics. Ethical values are not reliable unless they are internalized in the personality of the acting individual and institutionalized in the culture of the acting social system. Both imply that the individuals who may in an important degree influence decisions have identified themselves with these values. International ethics, therefore, faces the problem of incorporating the appropriate values in the personality of the individuals who are influential in all countries.

What forces can be utilized for this purpose?

The term *social forces* usually refers to wishes, attitude-patterns, and interests influencing individuals to modify social structures or processes, but here we are concerned with social forces in an opposite sense, that is, with social forces which can modify existing wishes, attitude-patterns, and interests of the individual. We are concerned, in other words, with social direction and control of the learning process. In this sense, four social forces seem available: (*a*) international commitment, (*b*) public opinion, (*c*) national legislation, and (*d*) international education.

While formal commitment by governments to international ethical principles is not enough to assure their application, such commitments as indicated in the chapter on international law may be a force of some importance in influencing national legislation, public opinion, and international education. Unless followed by other methods, however, such commitments may be worse than useless in that they will mislead governments and create within the public a sense of disillusionment in the process of international negotiation and in the value of international law and treaties. Such commitment is at best only a first step in establishing principles of international ethics (31).

A second force arises from the utilization of media of mass communication to incorporate in public discussion the vocabulary of an appropriate international ethical system, and thus to develop a public opinion in all countries favorable to such a system. People have some tendency to believe what they continually say, or hear. While attitudes and cultural patterns do not necessarily conform to opinion, they tend to do so. Public opinion, as pointed out in the chapter on international communication, is a force not only in guiding the immediate policy of governments, but also in influencing the culture and the ethical standards of the people. But here, as in the case of international agreement, more is needed. Opinions generated by mass communication are notoriously unreliable over long periods of time.

A third force develops through the institutionalization of public opinion by national legislation or policy declaration. National law is a more certain guide to national action than either international law or public opinion because it is supported by the sanctions inherent in the national culture, which usually places high ethical value upon the observance of law, as well as by the more positive sanctions of administrative and judicial procedures. Laws can create attitudes. It is this proposition that advocates of world government rely upon in proposing to create international institutions directly binding upon individuals. Such advocates believe that *world law*, emerging from such institutions, will build a universal culture with ethical standards appropriate to a world society. However, as pointed out in the chapter on the conduct of foreign relations and international organization, unless such world institutions already derive authority from the culture of the public to be affected by their pronouncements, it is difficult to see why they would be more influential in internalizing international ethical standards than are the present international institutions.

International education, operating directly on individual minds through national and international agencies, appears to be the force which must mainly be relied upon. This subject has been discussed in an earlier chapter. Such education can proceed by appeals to reason, to sentiment, and to self-interest, with the aim of giving vitality, in the local and national cultures, to appropriate principles of international ethics. The school, the pulpit, and private organizations, can all aid in this task. It is necessary, however, to avoid such an inflexible and vigorous internalization of standards of international ethics as to destroy the flexibility of world society. To suggest this danger seems rather chimerical at the present time, but it will be considered in the next two sections of this chapter.

The process of interpretation. No ethical system can be applied automatically, any more than can a legal system. Seldom is conditioning so explicit in the personality of individuals or in the institutionalization of organizations that the sensory-motor circuit can be completed automatically as it is in reflexes or in the instinctive behavior of animals. Choice always intervenes. Even if action is supposedly spontaneous, the possibility or expediency of deliberation will usually have been considered.

As a result, even if a system of international ethics were generally accepted and widely internalized in the personality of the members of the population in their various roles, the question would arise for a person in a given situation (*a*) are international ethical standards applicable to this situation, and (*b*) if they are, what behavior does international ethics require in this particular situation. These questions are like those faced by a court, in first analyzing the facts to decide whether a given legal principle or rule is applicable and then, if the answer is affirmative, to interpret those principles and rules, and to apply them to the facts in order to give a judgment.

It is assumed that sometimes an individual acts autonomously in accord with his basic drives, attitudes, and *need dispositions,* and that sometimes he acts representatively in accordance with the role assigned to him by a social system. In the first case the person is the actor; in the second the social system is the actor. Actually the individual makes the decision in either case, although when acting in a role, the decision may not be conclusive; he may be just one member of a court, a legislature, or other body which decides by some collective procedure upon action by the social system.

Applicability of international ethics. How can an individual tell whether principles of international ethics are applicable in a situation with which he is faced? In deciding on family purchases, on whether to go to church, on how to vote in a club election, he would hardly be concerned with principles of international ethics. It might be said that if the action will affect international relations, international ethics is applicable. But with the extensive interrelations of peoples and institutions in the present shrinking world most action has some international repercussion, immediate or remote. The individual clearly has less precise criteria for deciding whether principles of international ethics are applicable in a given situation than do officials or courts in deciding whether international law is applicable to a situation, and even there the problem is difficult enough. There have, in fact, been several schools of thought on the latter subject. *International monism* insists that priority should be given to international law in all situations, and holds that rules of municipal law if they conflict with international law are inapplicable in any situation. *National monism,* on the other hand, gives priority to municipal law and leaves the resolution of conflicts to the political processes of negotiation or war. *Dualism,* or *pluralism,* compromising between the two, holds that international law and each system of municipal law is a distinct system on a parity with one another. Consequently, international tribunals or agencies should apply international law and municipal tribunals and agencies should apply municipal law. Conflicts should be decided by the principles that municipal tribunals are final only on *domestic questions,* and that these include only questions which do not involve an international obligation of the state. If these latter principles are considered principles of international law, as they are by international tribunals, *pluralism* comes close to international monism but if they are considered principles of each system of municipal law, as they usually are by national tribunals, *pluralism* implies that international law and municipal law may decide differently. Consequently unless an international tribunal has jurisdiction, conflicts may require political adjustment (62, 143).

Should international ethics provide values of superior importance which should be applied in all situations, overriding conflicting values derived from local cultures or from particular institutions? Such a conclusion would tend to eliminate local cultures and the autonomy of social systems; to deprive world civilization of the variety essential to its continuous development; and to be unsatisfying to human nature developed in local environments and requiring the intimate relations of family, local community, and nationality for self-realization. This solution would appear to be impracticable. Nevertheless, as already suggested, there may be some values, such as those suggested by the words *humanism, liberalism, pragmatism,* and *relativism* so inherent in modern culture that they apply universally. By its nature this universal ethic would protect rather than crush the variety of personality and societies.

It is to be expected that when acting autonomously as a personality, that is, when his culture and institutional relations do not impose a role upon him, the individual will give little thought to international ethics. When he is acting in a social role, as may be the case with anyone travelling abroad or dealing with a foreigner, the account to be taken of international ethics would be determined by that role. The culture or the situation which establishes the role would determine what ethical standards are applicable. Individuals functioning for international organizations should in that role always observe standards of international ethics. Individuals functioning for foreign offices may face conflicts between national and international standards. Legislators, public orators, voting citizens, and travellers are often faced by situations in which international ethical standards should be considered, even though they conflict with other applicable standards. The individual would, in such circumstances, be faced with the problem of weighing the relative importance of the local and universal aspects of the situation and of selecting appropriate ethical values accordingly. In practice such choices would be influenced by the development of international ethical standards, and their internalization in the attitudes of persons. The competition of different standards in the present world of wide and abundant communication is a condition faced by every individual and the destiny of the world, whether toward a uniform world culture, toward conflicting national cultures, or toward a stable balance of the two, may be determined by the results of that competition. The latter type of world— an international world, rather than either a cosmopolitan or a nationalistic world—appears to offer the greatest hope of stability, and consideration of the value of stability might well influence the individual's conscious choice of the system of values to be applied in his various roles.

Interpretation of principles of international ethics. The interpretation and application of standards of international ethics presents problems analogous to those faced by officials in interpreting and applying international law. In this field a distinction has been made, especially in the interpretation of general treaties, between *restrictive interpretation* which presumes that there is no international obligation unless explicitly defined in the instrument and *effective interpretation* which presumes that whatever action is not expressly forbidden and is necessary to achieve the purposes asserted in the instrument is permitted and, if within the general scope of powers, is obligatory. The scope of a state's *domestic jurisdiction* would differ greatly according to which one of these standards is applied to determine its international obligations and the competence of the international organizations of which it is a member (145).

Application by analogy of these different approaches might greatly affect the content of international ethics. Should it be said that values essential to the realization of broad goals which have been widely accepted, such as the maintenance of international peace and security, international co-operation for human welfare, and protection of human rights, are requirements of international ethics? Or should it be said that international ethics requires observance only of values supported by clearly defined rules of international law which have been formally accepted by the participants in a given situation? The latter position would reduce international ethics to a moral duty to support international law. Undoubtedly, in the international field, as in other fields, ethical standards are broader than legal standards. In all situations, there are values which the culture recognizes, but which it does not deem to be susceptible of objective sanction as rules of law. Conversely, there may be values, such as the observance of traffic regulations, which are legally sanctioned, but which are hardly regarded as ethical values except in the general sense that ethics requires law observance.

In dealing with the interpretation and applicability of international ethical standards, the individual will judge, and doubtless his judgment will be determined by the intensity of his loyalty to the world community and its goals and institutions, in comparison with his loyalty to other groups. An individual's loyalty and commitment to a particular organization and his performance of the role assigned by it, should be distinguished from his internalization or sentimentalization of the principles and standards of the culture, ideology, or ethical system within which the organization developed. The two are, however, closely related. Intense loyalty to a particular organization tends to sentimentalize the ethical standards deemed essential to its life and development, and extreme sentimentalization of an ideology or culture tends to create loyalty to the organizations and institutions which maintain it. Thus loyalty to a particular Christian church tends to a sentimentalization of Christian ethics, and conversely, strong attachment to Christian ethics may increase loyalty to the particular church with which an individual is associated, even though that association may have been derived from adventitious circumstances. Similarly, loyalty to the United Nations doubtless tends to the sentimentalization of the standards of international ethics set forth in the charter, and conversely devotion to those standards is likely to increase loyalty to the United Nations, UNESCO, and other international organizations.

In the chapter on the sociology of international relations it was pointed out that parallel groups are continually being integrated into more comprehensive groups through the four processes of contact and communication, cultural synthesis and standardization, co-operation to achieve common goals and objectives, and institutional organization of, and role-determination in, the comprehensive group. These processes can be observed in the development of states, federations, and international organizations from lesser units. The four processes are interdependent. Progress in any one may lead to progress in others, but extreme lags or leads in one process may cause reaction. Thus excessive communication between groups of very diverse cultural standards may lead to *states' rights* or *nationalistic* movements, emphasizing traditional local standards and halting the process of cultural synthesis, co-operation, and superorganization. So also, excessive emphasis upon ethical standards appropriate to the more comprehensive group, upon common goals, or upon superorganization may lead to reaction.

The values of international ethics gain precision, validity, and reliability through their interpretation and application by millions of people, considering their interests, their roles, and their criteria of choice in the many situations with which they are faced. Philosophic formulae and social effort in international communication and international education, as well as the official positions of governments and international organizations, continually influence this development.

Relations among ethical systems. What should be the relation between a universal culture establishing values and principles of international ethics, and the local and national cultures? This subject has already been touched upon in dealing with the characteristics, the supporting forces, and the interpretation and application of international ethics. Here, however, attention will be given to the general characteristics of the relationships which a philosophy of the subject should have in mind. It has already been suggested that internationalism, recognizing the continual coexistence of distinct national and local cultures, each with is appropriate values and ethical system, and also of a universal culture with its appropriate values and ethical system, is to be preferred over either a cosmopolitan culture eliminating local cultures or local cultures struggling for existence without higher principles which permit peaceful adjustment of conflicts (99, 145). This position is believed to be justified by considerations of practicability, human needs, future progress, and flexibility.

Practicability. National cultures are today rigorously institutionalized and powerfully organized. The people of each nationality have numerous internalized patterns inherent in the national language and tradition, which they have learned in youth and which are continually reinforced by the symbols and celebrations of national life. Furthermore, nationalities are in general organized in states which determine national laws and policies and establish governments able to invoke the people's loyalty to national symbols in support of the state, its constitution, and its policies. This situation is a consequence of history, during much of which nations have developed in comparative physical isolation from one another, or in conditions of rivalry which maintain artificial barriers to communication, cultural assimilation, international co-operation, and international organization (90, 143).

The shrinking world has greatly reduced natural barriers, but the force of nationalism has maintained artificial barriers, with the consequence that the embryonic world culture and world institutions uniting the nations have remained feeble.

It has been argued that the continued shrinking of the world, in respect to the time necessary to communicate information and to transport goods or persons from one place to another, will produce more and more international contact and more and more interaction between people of different nationality, strengthening world culture, and that the increasing destructiveness of war and vulnerability of each people to its ravages will tend to strengthen loyalties to, and the efficiency of, international institutions to prevent war. These conditions, it is suggested, will in time establish a cosmopolitan culture and a world state (12, 22).

These tendencies, however, are moderated by the considerable physical differences of different areas of the world. Differences in climate, resources, and access to the sea will always produce differences in population and technology, which, in turn, will lead to differences in economic production, social energy, and group interest. Such differences are still reflected in important cultural differences in different regions within each of the larger national states. In France, for example, Normans, Bretons, and Provençals are each distinctive. Furthermore, differences in language, in religion, and in historical traditions will continue to maintain variations in cultural patterns and resistances to social change, where these differences are of such magnitude as they are between many of the nations (26, 54, 90).

When one considers the tremendous variety in the world in all of these factors, the elimination of national cultures and the development of a dominant cosmopolitan culture seems unlikely even in the distant future. It seems probable that the dominant internalized behavior patterns of people will continue to be national and local. Efforts to create a cosmopolitan world society seem not to be within the realm of practicability, either now or in any foreseeable future. Great ideological efforts, such as those of Christianity, Islam, and Communism, though attempting over many years to synthesize local and national cultural differences in, or to subordinate them to, a universal system of beliefs and values, have registered only qualified successes. It is not to be expected that any system of ethics, such as that discussed in this chapter, will eliminate the vitality of competing value systems in local or functional areas.

Human needs. Furthermore, as pointed out in Chapter 27, men need intimacy and affection, new experiences and adventure, as well as political and economic security and recognition of status. A universal culture might support an ethical system, as well as institutions and technology able to supply the latter needs. It might organize the world against war, famine, disease, and violent economic fluctuations. It might eliminate prejudices and establish a law recognizing the equal status of all persons and assuring them equality of opportunity. Because of the difference of conditions in different areas of the world, it would doubtless be difficult to realize these goals, unless each area enjoyed considerable autonomy, in legislation and administration, but achievement of these goals is at least conceivable.

However, such human needs as affection, new experience, and adventure are perhaps equally important, at least for many people, and can hardly be provided to all peoples, with their varieties of somatic type and of environmental conditions, by any universal culture (54, 94). Different cultures, institutions, and loyalties adapted to different people must be provided, or these human needs will be starved. Families with their own ethics, churches with specialized beliefs, voluntary associations with their peculiar goals, and a wide freedom for each individual to formulate his own fundamental values are needed, as also are geographically defined communities, cities, provinces, nations, and regions, with variations in culture and ethical standards. The tendency of the universal culture and technology of industrialism and trade to crush out these variations has doubtless accounted for some of the revolts, characteristic of the twentieth century, by people seeking less impersonal standards (25, 42). In eastern Europe and Asia, revolt, while demanding better access to the technological proficiency of the West, has demanded even more vigorously emancipation from the economic, political, and cultural "imperialism" of the West, believed to be subversive of the dignity and genius of local customs and values. These two aspects of recent revolutionary movements may be contradictory. Indian nationalism at one stage demanded at the same time return to the spinning wheel and more industrialization. A similar duality is to be observed in the Middle East. Arab tribalism and western technology are both wanted. Soviet culture has vacillated between cosmopolitan Marxism and a mystic Slavism; it has sought "Fordism" and high levels of technology and production, but at the same time commercial and cultural isolation from the "capitalistic" world and opportunities for the peculiar creativeness of the Soviet, Slavic, or even Russian genius (14, 17, 19, 54, 99, 128).

Human nature seems to require a pluralism of cultures and a variety of ethical standards, available to persons in different situations or of different characteristics. It is unlikely that any cosmopolitan culture dominating over lesser cultures could prove satisfactory to the world's population.

Future progress. Apart from its impracticability and its inadequacy, a cosmopolitan culture could hardly provide conditions for self-criticism and self-correction capable of modifying its own standards and adapting them to changes consequent upon changes in climate and terrain, the exhaustion of resources, and new inventions and technologies.

Isolated cultures tend to become static or to break up into differentiated and rival groups. If a culture remains united, its basic values tend to become universally accepted and so to be regarded as the order of nature. Primitive peoples exhibit this characteristic, and the culture of certain civilized peoples like the Chinese, have, in spite of frequent political divisions, manifested this static condition through long periods of history (54).

Criticism emerges from contact with outside cultures or from the competition of divergent sub-cultures within a culture. Individual creativeness becomes impossible where it is subjected to the pressure of a universally accepted culture. Flinders-Petrie concluded from a study of the long history of ancient Egypt that periods of long isolation accounted for periods of stagnant culture, unadaptability to new conditions and vulnerability to invasions (38). Arnold J. Toynbee, while recognizing the autonomy of a "civilization" as an intelligible field of study, has found that in time civilizations become stagnant and disintegrate unless rejuvenated from outside (127).

As indicated, the variety of the world's conditions and the variety of demands made by human nature are likely to perpetuate cultural competition, to provide the stimulus and data for individual creativity, and to sustain persons and groups criticizing the dominant ethical requirements and urging correctives. Institutions and ethical standards valuing freedom of speech, press and opinion encourage such self-criticism (1, 5, 61, 74, 83, 86, 88, 103), but even with such standards incorporated in an international ethical system (70), criticism could hardly flourish without the possibility of observing the operation of a variety of cultural and ethical systems. Socrates, Plato, and Aristotle were able to criticize Athens, because they were acquainted with other Greek cities. The British, the French, and the Japanese have in modern times acquired critical ideas from other nations. Writers in all modern nations have gained new insight into the possibilities of cultural construction from studies of history and anthropology.

The opportunities for self-criticism and self-correction provided by conditions favoring the coexistence and competition of divergent cultures have, it is true, seldom been adequate to preserve civilizations. Forces of inertia have frequently demanded crucifixion of the critics and the masses of the people have often adhered to obsolete cultural and ethical standards, with the result that changes have taken place only through violent conquest or revolutuion (127). A stable world can, it would appear, only be based on the hope that an international culture can be established of such character that it will sustain ethical and legal standards able to moderate the rate of change while at the same time sustaining the variety of cultures, permitting self-criticism and self-correction, and by its very support of freedom to encourage these conditions and processes (20, 82, 145).

Flexibility. The foregoing consideration of the relations between a universal system of international ethics and localized or specialized ethical systems raises the following question: What internal principles may limit the development of an international culture and an international ethical system, so that while regulating the competition of local and national cultures and ethical systems it will not in time destroy them? This problem is faced by all large states and the tendency has been toward either centralization and uniformity or disintegration and war. A federal system continually maintaining a balance between these two tendencies has proved difficult to achieve. The historian Freeman, in his volume published in 1863 entitled, *History of Federal Government from the Foundation of the Achaean League to the Disruption of the United States,* thought such a balance unlikely. Federalism, he said, must be a transitory form of government, because it must "depend for its permanence not on the sentiment but on the reason of its citizens," which is likely to suggest either consolidation or separation when circumstances change (40).

A universal international culture would differ from historic federal cultures in having no hostile culture on its periphery. All different cultures would be within it. The powerful centralizing tendency created by the continued necessity of defense against external aggression would not be present. In fact, the absence of this pressure constitutes the major problem of a universal international culture and ethic, that of sustaining sufficient centralization and cultural uniformity to maintain the rudiments of order. Very wide spread empires or federations have been more likely to break up than to become overcentralized.

However, the steady influence of communication, of military technology, of vulnerabilities and of interdependencies in shrinking the world may, during the course of centuries, augment the forces of centralization and uniformity beyond the danger point. A uniform culture may develop and all people may become so habituated to it that they will regard it as of the order of nature. Such a condition would be likely to render the society so unadaptable that, when eventually it is faced by changing conditions of climate, exhaustion of resources or epidemic disease, the civilization along with the population might go the way of the dinosaurs. The culture itself should, therefore, include philosophic principles guarding against such overcentralization and over-uniformity.

The general concept of an international rather than a cosmopolitan culture and ethic may contribute to this end. States formally designating themselves as federal have been able to resist overcentralization by recognizing the legitimacy of the political and cultural autonomy of the member states more than have states formally designating themselves as unitary, even though in law the differences may not be great.

Furthermore, the content of the international ethical system itself, emphasizing human rights, toleration, and pluralism may contribute to the preservation and functioning of a great variety of cultures and value systems. Any absolutistic ethical system would seem to be unadapted to universal acceptance and also dangerous to civilization, if it should be so accepted.

Finally, overcentralization may be prevented if the universal system is sustained in large measure on the level of opinion, reason, and law rather than on that of attitude, conscience, and custom. Doubtless, if an international ethical system is to be viable, it must to some extent be internalized in the personality of many individuals. Leaders of opinion must have attitudes favorable to the major principles of international ethics, so sentimentalized that it would be difficult for them to depart from these standards even in emergencies. With such leadership, a world opinion may be maintained able to sustain international institutions capable of preventing violence and facilitating international co-operation. In such circumstances, international ethics might remain, for the masses of the people, at the level of opinion, reason, and law, and would not, therefore, offer massive resistance to changes necessitated by new conditions. In such circumstances, the attitudes and sentiments of the masses would be more intimately engaged by the values of national, religious, family, or other groups than by those of the world community.

Such a condition would, as Freeman has pointed out, militate against the power of the world community to perform its functions and against the reliability of its ethical standards. Whatever their convictions, leaders must under democratic conditions conform to the demands of those upon whose suffrage they are dependent. Consequently, it is insisted, an international ethical system cannot be viable unless the masses of mankind have internalized its values. The problem here presented is less theoretical than practical. The intensity with which values have been internalized may vary. International ethical standards should be to some extent internalized among the masses and to a greater extent among the leaders. The degree of internalization which would maintain stability without stultifying the conditions essential for self-criticism, self-correction, and change would involve continual measurement, the application of judgment guided by broad philosophical understanding of the need for balance, and controls through institutions of education and communication.

It has been suggested that human behavior has been dominantly directed in succeeding stages of social development from animals through primitive and civilized man to modern man by instinct, custom, conscience, and opinion. Each successive advance marked by the inventions of language, writing, and printing followed by other means of mass communication has not wholly excluded the earlier forms of direction, but has added new ones, especially relevant to the larger groupings which these successive inventions in the field of communication have permitted. Thus modern man, in his smaller groupings, such as the family, is guided in considerable measure by instinct; in his local communities, churches, and societies, custom still has an important role. In business, government, and numerous personal transactions, conscience, established by education, in the family, school, and church is an important guide. But in legislation, international policy, and the functionings of the international community, opinion is the main guide. Men learn from current observation of the opinion of others, appraise action, and make choices on the basis, not of precise rules, but of the general state of opinion. This analysis suggests that an international ethics should function in large measure on the level of opinion. Its standards should be developed by education and should be supported by rational considerations, thus escaping the extreme and irrational sentimentalization commonly attached to standards acquired in early infancy (11, 112). This becomes possible only if suitable institutions permit the formulation and focusing of predominant opinion on the requirements of international ethics in a particular situation. In this way, the world community and the principles of international ethics may themselves remain flexible and capable of self-criticism, self-correction, and adjustment to new conditions.

CRITICISM

The analysis in this chapter indicates the dominant role of international ethics as a basis for criticizing the assumptions of international politics, international law, and international economics, and for guiding international organization, international education, and international communications. It also suggests that a system of international ethics must itself remain flexible and capable of self-criticism and self-correction. Can a discipline so vague and illusive serve as a master critic of the more precise findings of the subordinate disciplines?

This is one aspect of the general relation of philosophy to science, history, and art. Philosophy, which seeks to orient man and society to their changing environment, is continually being brushed aside by the special sciences able to predict and perhaps control the consequences of concrete action with some degree of precision; by history, which presents examples of concrete actions and their consequences illustrating the cumulative pressure of the past upon the immediate situation of action; and by art, which permits leaders in strategic situations to inject their personalities and ideas into the opinion and action of the moment.

The problem for philosophy is that of the general versus the particular. The function of both the generalist and the specialist is recognized in most fields of human interest—government, business, education, and religion. International ethics must be the product of the most general outlook available to man, balancing the whole with the part, the future with the past, the long-run with the short-run, the desirable with the practical, man with nature. That is the field of the philosophy of science and the science of philosophy (3, 9, 39, 49, 114, 140, 145). Unless man can combine philosophy and science sufficiently to permit these broad considerations to develop international ethical values able to play a practical role in their affairs, the world community can hardly develop a public opinion permitting the peaceful coexistence of many nations, cultures, and personalities and the functioning of international institutions to realize those values.

REFERENCES

In a broad sense the bibliography of international ethics includes the entire bibliography of international relations. All books in the field are concerned with the nature, the consequences or the causes of effective beliefs, dynamic ideas, and other values which influence the policy and action of individuals or groups. The practical disciplines of international relations assume certain values, but their emphasis is upon the means for achieving them. The theoretical disciplines are generally concerned with the values which influence action in different societies, but they emphasize the conditions which account for those values rather than the values themselves. International ethics in a specialized sense is concerned with values themselves and their relation to one another. This list includes some histories of political and ethical theories, some expositions of ethical theories influential in international affairs, and some recent analyses of the concepts of value and valuation in relation to the contemporary international situation and to civilization.

1. ACTON, Lord, *Essays on Freedom and Power* (Boston, Beacon Press, 1948).
2. ANSHON, Ruth Nanda, ed., *Our Emergent Civilization*, Science of Culture Series, Vol. 4 (New York, Harper, 1947).
3. ———, ed., *Moral Principles of Action, the Ethical Imperatives* (New York, Harper, 1953).
4. BARKER, Sir Ernest, *Principles of Social and Political Theory* (New York, Oxford University Press, 1951).

5. BARTH, Alan, *The Loyalty of Free Men* (New York, Viking, 1952).
6. BAUMGARDT, David, *Bentham and the Ethics of Today* (Princeton, Princeton University Press, 1952).
7. BENES, Eduard, *Democracy, Today and Tomorrow* (London, Macmillan, 1939).
8. BENTHAM, Jeremy, *Introduction to the Principles of Morals and Legislation* (1789); (Oxford, Clarendon Press, 1892).
9. BENTLEY, Arthur F., *Relativity in Man and Society* (Bloomington, Ind., Principia Press, 1926).
10. BERLE, Adolf A., *Natural Selection of Political Forces* (Lawrence, University of Kansas Press, 1950).
11. BLANSHARD, Paul, *Communism, Democracy, and Catholic Power* (Boston, Beacon Press, 1951).
12. BORGESE, G. A., *Foundations of the World Republic* (Chicago, University of Chicago Press, 1953).
13. BOUGLÉ, C., *The Evolution of Values*, introduction by Roy Wood Sellars, trans. by Helen S. Sellars (New York, Holt, 1926).
14. BROGAN, D. W., *The Price of Revolution* (New York, Harper, 1952).
15. BRYSON, Lyman, FINKELSTEIN, Louis, and McIVER, R. M., eds., Annual Symposia of Conference on Science, Philosophy and Religion (New York, Harper, 1942—).
16. BURNS, C. Delisle, *Political Ideals: an Essay*, 4th ed. (London, Oxford University Press, 1929).
17. CARR, Edward Hallett, *Nationalism and After* (London, Macmillan, 1945).
18. COHEN, Morris R., *Reason and Law* (Glencoe, Ill., Free Press, 1950).
19. COLE, G. D. H., *World in Transition: A Guide to the Shifting Political and Economic Forces of Our Times* (New York, Oxford University Press, 1949).
20. Commission to Study the Organization of Peace, *The Organization of Peace*, 1st Report, and Papers submitted, International Conciliation (April, 1941).
21. ———, *Regional Arrangement for Security and the United Nations*, 8th Report, and Papers presented to the Commission (New York, June, 1953).
22. COUSINS, Norman, *Who Speaks for Man?* (New York, Macmillan, 1953).
23. DAHL, Robert A., and LINDBLOM, Charles E., *Politics, Economics and Welfare* (New York, Harper, 1953).
24. D'ENTREVE, A. P., *Natural Law* (New York, Longmans, 1951).
25. DeGRAZIA, Alfred, Jr., *Public and Republic* (New York, Knopf, 1951).
26. DEUTSCH, Karl, *Nationalism and Social Communication* (New York, Wiley, 1953).
27. DEWEY, John, and TUFTS, James H., *Ethics* (New York, Holt, 1908).
28. ———, *Logical Conditions of a Scientific Treatment of Morality* (Chicago, University of Chicago Press, 1903).
29. ———, *Human Nature and Conduct* (New York, Holt, 1922).
30. ———, *Reconstruction in Philosophy* (New York, Holt, 1920).
31. ———, "Ethics and International Relations," *Foreign Affairs*, Vol. 1 (March, 1923), pp. 85-95.
32. ———, *Freedom and Culture* (New York, Putnams, 1939).
33. DURKHEIM, Emile, *The Elementary Forms of the Religious Life, A Study in Religious Sociology*, trans. by J. W. Swain (London, Allen and Unwin, 1915).

34. EASTON, David, *The Political System, An Inquiry into the State of Political Science* (New York, Knopf, 1952).

35. EBENSTEIN, William, *Great Political Thinkers, Plato to the Present* (New York, Rinehart, 1951).

36. ———, *Man and the State: Modern Political Ideas* (New York, Rinehart, 1947).

37. EINSTEIN, Albert, and FREUD, Sigmund, *Why War? An Exchange of Letters, July 30, 1932* (Paris, International Institute of Intellectual Co-operation, 1933).

38. FLINDERS-PETRIE, W. M., *The Revolutions of Civilization*, 3rd ed. (London, Harper, 1922).

39. FRANK, Philipp, ed., "Contributions to the Analysis and Synthesis of Knowledge," *Proceedings*, American Academy of Arts and Sciences, published in co-operation with Institute for the Unity of Science, Vol. 80, No. 1 (July, 1951).

40. FREEMAN, Edward A., *History of Federal Government*, 2nd ed. (London, Macmillan, 1893).

41. FREUD, Sigmund, *Civilization and Its Discontents*, trans. by Joan Riviere (London, 1930); see also Einstein, A., and Freud, S.

42. FROMM, Erich, *Man for Himself: an Inquiry into the Psychology of Ethics* (New York, Rinehart, 1947).

43. FUNG, Yu-lin, *A History of Chinese Philosophy* (1934), trans. by Derk Bodde (Princeton, Princeton University Press, 1952, 1953), 2 vols.

44. GOLLANCZ, Victor, *Our Threatened Values* (Chicago, Regnery, 1952).

45. GOLOB, Eugene O., *The Isms, a History and Evaluation* (New York, Harper, 1954).

46. GIVLER, R. C., *The Ethics of Hercules, a Study of Man's Body as the Sole Determinant of Ethical Values* (New York, Knopf, 1924).

47. GROSS, Feliks, ed., *European Ideologies*, introduction by R. M. McIver (New York, Philosophical Library, 1948).

48. HALL, Everett W., *What Is Value? An Essay in Philosophical Analysis* (New York, Library of Psychology, Philosophy and Scientific Method, 1952).

49. HARTSHORNE, Charles, *Reality as Social Process* (Glencoe, Ill., Free Press, 1952).

50. HAYAKAWA, S. I., "Semantics, General Semantics," *Encyclopædia Britannica;* "Ten Eventful Years," 1947; also in *ETC*, Vol. 9 (Summer, 1952), pp. 243-257.

51. HAYEK, F. A., *The Sensory Order* (Chicago, University of Chicago Press, 1952).

52. HIMMELFARB, Gertrude, *Lord Acton: A Study in Conscience and Politics* (Chicago, University of Chicago Press, 1952).

53. HOBHOUSE, L. T., *Morals in Evolution: A Study of Comparative Ethics* (1906); 5th ed. (New York, Holt, n.d.).

54. HSU, Francis, *American and Chinese, Two Ways of Life* (New York, Schuman, 1953).

55. HUXLEY, Julian, *UNESCO: Its Purpose and Its Philosophy* (Washington, Public Affairs Press, 1948).

56. ———, *Knowledge, Morality and Destiny* (Washington, William Alanson White Psychiatric Foundation, 1951).

57. HUXLEY, T. H., and Julian, *Touchstone for Ethics* (New York, Harper, 1947).

58. JURJI, Edward J., ed., *Great Religions of the Modern World* (Princeton, Princeton University Press, 1946).

59. KALLEN, Horace M., "Morals," *Encyclopædia of the Social Sciences.*

60. ———, *Why Religion?* (New York, Liveright, 1927).

61. ———, *Individualism: An American Way of Life* (New York, Liveright, 1933).

62. KELSEN, Hans, *Principles of International Law* (New York, Rinehart, 1952).

63. KIRCHWEY, Freda, ed., *Our Changing Morality* (New York, Boni, 1924).

64. KNIGHT, Frank, "Value and Price," *Encyclopædia of the Social Sciences.*

65. KORZYBSKI, Alfred, *Science and Sanity* (1933); 3rd ed. (Lakeville, Conn., Institute of General Semantics, 1948).

66. KRAUS, Herbert, *La Morale internationale*, (1925), trans. (Paris, Hague Academy of International Law, 1928), Vol. 16, pp. 385-539.

67. LAMONT, Corliss, *Humanism, a Philosophy* (New York, Philosophical Library, 1950).

68. LASSWELL, Harold D., *National Security and Individual Freedom* (New York, McGraw-Hill, 1950).

69. ———, "Morale," *Encyclopædia of the Social Sciences.*

70. LAUTERPACHT, Hersch, *International Law and Human Rights* (London, Stevens, 1950).

71. LAVES, Walter H. C., ed., *The Foundations of a More Stable World Order,* Harris Institute Lectures (Chicago, University of Chicago Press, 1941).

72. LÉVY-BRUHL, Lucien, *Ethics and Moral Science*, trans. by Elizabeth Lee (London, Constable, 1905).

73. LEY, Wayne A. R., *Ethics for Policy Decision: The Art of Asking Deliberative Questions* (New York, Prentice-Hall, 1952).

74. LILIENTHAL, David E., *This I Do Believe* (New York, Harper, 1949).

75. LINDSAY, A. D., *The Modern Democratic State* (New York, Oxford University Press, 1947).

76. LIPPMANN, Walter, *A Preface to Morals* (New York, Macmillan, 1929).

77. ———, *The Good Society* (Boston, Little, Brown, 1937).

78. LOOS, A. William, *Religious Faith and World Culture* (New York, Prentice Hall, 1951).

79. LOWENSTEIN, Karl, ed., "The Role of Ideologies in Political Change," Symposium, International Political Science Association, The Hague, 1952, *International Social Science Bulletin,* UNESCO, Vol. 5 (1953), pp. 51-74.

80. LUNDBERG, George A., *Can Science Save Us?* (New York, Longmans, 1947).

81. McIVER, R. M., ed., *Great Expressions of Human Rights* (New York, Harper, 1950).

82. ———, ed., *Conflict of Loyalties* (New York, Harper, 1952).

83. McKEON, Richard, and ROKKAN, Stein, eds., *Democracy in a World of Tension*, a symposium prepared by UNESCO (Chicago, University of Chicago Press, 1951).

84. MAINE, Sir Henry Sumner, *Ancient Law, Its Connection with the Early History of Society and Its Relation to Modern Ideas* (1861); 10th ed. (London, 1884).

85. MALINOWSKI, Bronislaw, "Culture," *Encyclopædia of the Social Sciences.*

86. MARITAIN, Jacques, *Human Rights, Comments and Interpretations,* a symposium edited by UNESCO (London, Allan Wingate, 1949).

87. MEAD, Margaret, *And Keep Your Powder Dry* (New York, Morrow, 1942).

88. MEIKLEJOHN, Alexander, *Free Speech: and Its Relation to Self Government* (New York, Harper, 1948).

89. MERRIAM, Charles E., and BARNES, Harry Elmer, eds., *A History of Political Theories, Recent Times* (New York, Macmillan, 1924).

90. ———, *The Making of Citizens* (Chicago, University of Chicago Press, 1931).

91. ———, *The New Democracy and the New Despotism* (New York, McGraw-Hill, 1939).

92. MOORE, G. E., *Ethics*, Home University Library (New York, Oxford University Press, 1912).

93. MORGENTHAU, Hans, *Scientific Man vs. Power Politics* (Chicago, University of Chicago Press, 1946).

94. MORRIS, Charles, *Paths of Life, Preface to a World Religion* (New York, Harper, 1942).

95. MUMFORD, Lewis, *The Story of Utopias* (New York, Boni and Liveright, 1922).

96. ———, *The Conduct of Life* (New York, Harcourt, 1951).

97. NIEBUHR, Reinhold, *Moral Man and Immoral Society, A Study in Ethics and Politics* (New York, Scribner, 1932).

98. NORTHROP, F. S. C., *The Meeting of East and West* (New York, Macmillan, 1946).

99. ———, *The Taming of the Nations, A Study of the Cultural Basis of International Politics* (New York, Macmillan, 1952).

100. PARSONS, Talcott, and SHILS, Edward, eds., *Toward a General Theory of Action* (Cambridge, Harvard University Press, 1951).

101. PEARSON, Karl, *The Grammar of Science*, 2nd ed. (London, Black, 1900).

102. PERRY, Ralph Barton, *General Theory of Values* (Cambridge, Harvard University Press, 1954).

103. POPPER, Karl R., *The Open Society and Its Enemies* (Princeton, Princeton University Press, 1950), 2 vols.

104. PRIBRAM, Karl, *Conflicting Patterns of Thought* (Washington, Public Affairs Press, 1949).

105. PRITCHETT, C. Herman, *Civil Liberties and the Vinson Court* (Chicago, University of Chicago Press, 1954).

106. RADHAKRISHNAN, Sarvepalli, and others, eds., *History of Philosophy, Eastern and Western*, sponsored by the Ministry of Education, Government of India (London, Allen and Unwin, 1952), Vol. 1.

107. RAPAPORT, Anatol, *Operational Philosophy, Integrating Knowledge and Action* (New York, Harper, 1953).

108. RAPPARD, W. E., *The Crisis of Democracy*, Harris Institute Lectures (Chicago, University of Chicago Press, 1938).

109. REDFIELD, Robert, "The Primitive World View," *Proceedings, American Philosophical Society*, Vol. 96 (February, 1952), pp. 30 ff.

110. RIEZLER, Kurt, "Political Decisions in Modern Society," *Ethics*, Vol. 64 (January, 1954), Part II.

111. Ross, Edward A., *Social Control* (New York, Macmillan, 1901).

112. ROY, Ralph Lord, *Apostles of Discord, A Study of Organized Bigotry and Disruption on the Fringes of Protestantism* (Boston, Beacon Press, 1953).

113. RUNES, Dagobert D., *Twentieth Century Philosophy, Living Schools of Thought* (New York, Philosophical Library, 1943).

114. RUSSELL, Bertrand, *Religion and Science,* Home University Library (Oxford University Press, 1935).

115. ———, *The Impact of Science on Society* (New York, Simon & Schuster, 1953).

116. RUSSELL, Mrs. Charles E. B. (Lilian M.), *The Path to Reconstruction: a Brief Introduction to Albert Schweitzer's Philosophy of Civilization* (London, Black, 1941).

117. RUSSELL, Frank, *Theories of International Relations* (New York, Appleton-Century-Crofts, 1936).

118. SANTAYANA, George, *Three Philosophical Poets* (Cambridge, Harvard University Press, 1910).

119. SAPIR, Edward, "Custom," *Encyclopædia of the Social Sciences.*

120. SCHUMAN, Frederick L., *The Commonwealth of Man* (New York, Knopf, 1953).

121. SIMON, Yves, *Philosophy of Democratic Government* (Chicago, University of Chicago Press, 1951).

122. SMITH, R. Elburton, "Value Judgment and the Social Sciences," *Bulletin,* American Association of University Professors, Vol. 35, p. 628.

123. SMITH, T. V., "Ethics," *Encyclopædia of the Social Sciences.*

124. STOUFFER, Samuel I., *Studies in Social Psychology in World War II* (Princeton, Princeton University Press, 1949, 1950), 4 vols.

125. STRAUSS, Leo, *Natural Right and History* (Chicago, University of Chicago Press, 1953).

126. SUMNER, William Graham, *Folkways* (Boston, Ginn, 1907).

127. TOYNBEE, Arnold J., *A Study of History* (New York, Oxford University Press, 1934, 1939, 1954), 10 vols.

128. ———, *The World and the West* (New York, Oxford University Press, 1953).

129. UNESCO, see 79, 83, 86.

130. VEBLEN, Thorstein, *The Theory of the Leisure Class* (New York, Macmillan, 1899).

131. VIVAS, Elisea, *The Moral Life and the Ethical Life* (Chicago, University of Chicago Press, 1951).

132. VOEGELIN, Eric, *The New Science of Politics* (Chicago, University of Chicago Press, 1952).

133. WALLAS, Graham, *The Great Society* (New York, Macmillan, 1917).

134. WARNER, W. Lloyd, *Democracy in Jonesville: A Study in Quality and Inequality* (New York, Harper, 1949).

135. WATTS, Alan W., *The Wisdom of Insecurity* (New York, Pantheon, 1952).

136. WEBER, Max, *The Protestant Ethic and the Spirit of Capitalism,* trans. by Talcott Parsons, Foreword by R. H. Tawney (London, Allen and Unwin, 1930).

137. WEST, Herbert F., *Rebel Thought* (Boston, Beacon Press, 1953).

138. WEST, Ranyard, *Conscience and Society, A Study of the Psychological Prerequisites of Law and Order* (London, Methuen, 1942).

139. WESTERMARCK, E. A., *Ethical Relativity* (London, Kegan Paul, 1932).

140. WHITEHEAD, Alfred North, *Science and the Modern World* (New York, Pelican, 1948).

141. WIENER, Norbert, *Cybernetics, or Control and Communication in the Animal and Machine* (New York, Wiley, 1948).

142. WILD, John, *Plato's Modern Enemies and the Theory of Natural Law* (Chicago, University of Chicago Press, 1953).

143. WRIGHT, Quincy, *A Study of War* (Chicago, University of Chicago Press, 1942), pp. 48-52, 88-100, 103-112, 152-165, 169-196, 202-204, 329-356, 368-370, 397-405, 429-437, 508-518, 615-624, 705-706, 814-818, 833-848, 972-975, 1009-1011, 1025-1049, 1079-1117, 1200-1224, 1235-1239, 1246-1256, 1299-1309, 1326-1352, 1448-1465, 1493-1497.
144. ———, ed., *The World Community*, Harris Institute Lectures (Chicago, University of Chicago Press, 1948).
145. ———, *Problems of Stability and Progress in International Relations* (Berkeley, University of California Press, 1954).

Toward a Unified Discipline of International Relations

Conceptions of
International Relations

INTERNATIONAL RELATIONS, as a discipline contributing to the understanding, prediction, evaluation, and control of the relations among states
and of the conditions of the world community, is at the same time a
history, a science, a philosophy, and an art.

This discipline is beginning to emerge in efforts to analyze and to synthesize numerous disciplines which have sought to guide practical activities in the international field or to develop general theories concerning
that field from particular kinds of data or from particular points of view.
This effort has been hampered by the comprehensiveness and complexity
of the subject and the lack of consensus upon unifying concepts. International relations may be influenced by anything that concerns man—his
impulses, attitudes, opinions and actions, and his technologies, cultures,
associations, and organizations. International relations may also be influenced by anything that concerns the world—the distribution of its land
masses, climates, resources, and industries, and the character of its
peoples, nations, states, and governments. An effort to synthesize the
studies important for international relations, therefore, appears to approach the ambitious task of synthesizing all the disciplines—humanistic,
social, and natural.

The effort to unify the study of international relations resembles the
effort to unify all knowledge. Such an effort, undertaken by the American
Academy of Arts and Sciences and the Institute for Unity of Science, was
thought to involve two tasks—"the logical analysis" and "the speculative
synthesis" of knowledge, which though often contrasted in fact "comple-

ment one another and are fundamentally one and the same" (15). According to Philipp Frank,

By analyzing knowledge, we find the elementary operations of which our scientific knowledge consists. But we recognize that these elementary operations are essentially the same ones in all fields of science and learning. They can serve as the building stones for the syntheses and integration of our knowledge in all fields. This means the construction of a picture of the world which is speculative, in the sense that atomic physics is speculative. But it is analytical in the sense that the sciences of mechanics or genetics or economics are analytical.

This analysis and synthesis of knowledge, when applied to both the sciences and the humanities, suggest "the focal importance of the integration between science and philosophy" (15).

Frank suggests that analysis of the individual disciplines can proceed from the logical or from the semantical points of view—that is, from the points of view of "internal coherence" of the discipline, or from that of its "meaning in the world of our experience." These "internal" problems, however, cannot be solved in themselves. The "external" problem has to be considered "whether a certain formal system, as a whole, with the addition of a semantical interpretation, is useful for the orientation of man in the world of experience." Science has to be considered "a human enterprise by which man tries to adapt himself to the external world." The "pragmatic" and "expressive" points of view of practice and history have to be added to the logical and semantic points of view of philosophy and science.

This conclusion, arrived at from an effort inspired by science to synthesize all the disciplines dealing with nature and man may be compared to the conclusion arrived at from a similar effort, inspired by religion. Albert Schweitzer, after reviewing the evolution of religious, metaphysical, and ethical theories, each seeking to rationalize introspections through developing the conceptions of the world which those introspections seemed to demand, concludes:

But it so happens that the conception of the world which ethics can invoke is the result of the interpretation of the very world to which ethics has offered and still offers, itself. It attributes to the universal will qualities and intentions which give satisfaction to its own way of feeling and of judging. But in the course of the nineteenth century the research which allowed itself to be guided solely by concern for the truth was bound to surrender to the evidence that ethics can expect nothing from a true knowledge of the world. The progress of science consists in an increasingly precise observation of the processes of nature. These allow us to harness the energies manifesting themselves in the universe to our own use. But they oblige us at the same time increasingly to give up any attempt to understand its intentions. The world offers us the disconcerting spectacle of the will to life in conflict with itself. One existence maintains itself at the expense of another.

Thus ethics has been obliged to accept an unethical world. It cannot prove its theses by science or history and so, to avoid skepticism, must depend on its own methods. "Having arrived at the knowledge that its fundamental principle is devotion, it becomes fully conscious of itself and thereby becomes autonomous." Devotion to the good must, he thinks, accept as the good "the immediate datum of our consciousness."

I am life which wants to live surrounded by life which wants to live. Being will-to-live, I feel the obligation to respect all will-to-live about me as equal to my own. The fundamental idea of good is thus that it consists in preserving life, in favoring it, in wanting to bring it to its highest value, and evil consists in destroying life, doing it injury, hindering its development.

Since life actually involves destruction of life, ethical conduct requires a continuous balancing of good and evil. "The term 'respect for life' is (therefore) broader, and because of this more colorless, than that of love. It bears the same energies within it ... and is more complete because it includes (in addition to our compassion for others) our obligation toward ourselves, our dignity and sincerity ... renouncing every kind of dissimulation (such as distorting the world to justify our faith)" (38).

Schweitzer's ethics emphasizes that guidance of action by the "principle of respect for life," implies the use of science to judge the consequences of the alternatives offered in a given situation, permitting choice of the better, in the knowledge that each involves some sacrifice as well as some advancement of life. The objective knowledge derived from science and history has to be added to the ethical intuitions of philosophy and art if the mystery of life is to have meaning and to provide guidance for each of us. The dualism in the sources of science and philosophy are therefore synthesized in the continuous process of choice and action. Science and history seek a universal synthesis in a theory of the whole (15, 30); philosophy and art seek such a synthesis in the immediate experience of the act (27, 38).

In considering the definition, assumptions, and methods of analysis of each of the disciplines which have been discussed in this book because they were considered most relevant to the study of international relations, it is hoped that "the internal coherence" and "meaning in the world of experience" of these disciplines may have been sufficiently suggested to encourage more precise studies of the logic and language of each, perhaps utilizing the developing disciplines of logical positivism (24) and semantics (35), and also to encourage more mature reflection on the meaning and role of each, utilizing our intuitions of life and our consciousness of choice. An effort has also been made to suggest the historical importance and present utility of each of these disciplines. But, as Frank suggests, understanding of the position and the significance of each of these disciplines in a unified discipline of international relations would be facilitated by "the construction of a picture of the world," even though that picture may be speculative, subject to change as knowledge advances, and incapable of completely reconciling the scientific, philosophic, and other approaches to the subject.

Such pictures have guided thought in all cultures and at all periods of history. Every culture or civilization has its *Weltanschauung*, greatly influencing, though not absolutely determining, the *Weltanschauung* of the individuals which compose it. Imaginative universes, synthesizing primitive myths, have given way to ideal universes necessary to support religious and ethical values, and these have given way to real universes consistent with observation and reason. The limited, geocentric, anthropocentric, teleological universe of Aquinas and Dante gave way to the infinite, continuous, mathematical, natural universe of Galileo and Newton, and that in turn is giving way to the relative and uncertain universe of Einstein, Planck, and Heisenberg. Historians of science have pointed out that comprehensive pictures or "conceptual systems" have usually guided particular scientific advances and particular disciplines (7, 10). A unified discipline of international relations implies a generally accepted conception of the human world (11, 22).

The pictures of the world actually influential among civilized peoples have usually resulted from the interplay of science, demonstrating that one picture fits the facts of observation more accurately and economically than another; of social authority, convinced that one picture will encourage more desirable human conduct than another; of culture, providing myths and traditions appealing to the imagination of the people; and of human nature seeking escape from the vague, ominous, menacing, conspiratorial character which the world presents to ignorant man especially in times of disaster, violence, and rapid social change. Men seek a clear picture of the world that can provide a basis of policy and action, and an escape from the dread of a world of vague ghosts, conspiracies, and terror which phantasy anxiety and self-interested politicians or priests can easily create. Whether or not they contribute to this anxiety, such leaders often provide a picture which will both satisfy this popular demand and serve their own interests. Science may permit some choice of alternative pictures, authority may be able to interpret a picture which scientific evidence requires it to accept in order to support the value system it desires, myths are susceptible of symbolic interpretation, and any clear picture is better than the awful unknown. Consequently, inconsistencies among the pictures springing from these different sources are seldom wholly insoluble, but the process of conflict and accommodation among them is a continuous and significant aspect of history. Every discipline has both a philosophical and a scientific aspect (10) and the picture of the world on which it rests may also retain elements which are merely traditional or imaginative. Such *conceptions* or mental images which vary from person to person may be objectified by elaboration with actual or imaginary details into histories and Utopias capable of influencing belief and action (30a, 30b). They may also be objectified by precise definition, eliminating nonessentials and establishing *concepts* of abstract, invariable, communicable form capable of logical analysis and development into scholarly disciplines.

Let us consider some of the conceptions of the world that have been influential.

The world as plan. Many people have conceived the world as an immutable plan or idea determining the origin and the destiny of the human race, and, in a rough way, the process between this first and final cause. Some, like the author of the Book of Genesis have attributed this plan to God, who conceived it in order to realize in time his foreordained destiny for man.

Others have attributed it to *history*. They have conceived history as the demonstration of right and wrong by the consequences of behavior, as the evolution of civilization through inevitable stages or oscillations, or as the realization of right and justice through the continuous synthesis of contradictory ideas. The widespread belief in the eventual triumph of the "right" and of the "inevitable progress" of civilization, which has characterized most western peoples from the seventeenth to the twentieth centuries, exemplifies this conception of the world. History to Hegel, Marx, and Acton was philosophy in action. Actually, however, philosophers of history have been as varied and unconvincing in their interpretations as have theologians.

Still others have attributed a universal plan to *nature*. They have assumed that men and societies have necessary and immutable characteristics which establish a *natural law* which can be discovered by introspection and observation, and can be formulated into a logical system describing how men and nations behave. But does this *law of nature* describe how they *will* inevitably behave thus permitting prediction, or how they *ought* to behave thus providing a guide to conduct which might be disregarded? Hobbes distinguished these two meanings, attributing to *natural right* the inherent properties or self-regarding impulses of man in a state of nature, and to *natural law* the norms, observance of which is essential for social order including such rules as good faith in the observance of agreements. Other writers were less clear in making this distinction and often differed in interpretation according to the source from which *natural law* was discovered. If from introspection, as was usual until recent times in a psychology which differentiated mind accessible only to introspection from matter accessible to observation, *natural law* appeared to be a moral law because it would seem to the introspector that he had freedom to choose among the motives he discovered in his mind. If, on the other hand, *natural law* was derived from observation of others, as

Hobbes derived his *natural rights* of man in a *state of nature* and as Newton derived his laws of physics, then it would appear absolute in proportion as all observations conformed to the law (20). As the objective study of psychology, economics, sociology, politics, geography, demography, and technology has developed, there have been efforts to formulate *natural laws* concerning the incidence, course and effects of wars, revolutions, foreign policies, treaties, and other phenomena of international relations. These *laws* have sometimes been based on theories of human motivation, of state policy, or of environmental conditions deemed to be immutable and historically verifiable, and have been invoked to establish *realistic* ideologies of international politics contrasted with the *idealistic* ideologies which attribute only a moral character to *natural law* (18).

A thoroughgoing attempt to conceive the world as a plan was made by Thomas Aquinas in the thirteenth century. He, however, found it necessary to distinguish *eternal law* (absolute law binding even God, but relevant to nature rather than to man), from *divine law* (moral law revealed in the Bible), from *natural law* (moral law discovered by human introspection), and from *civil law* (positive law of states which ought to conform to divine and natural law), thus greatly reducing the rigidity of the plan. The world to Aquinas, as to most men of the middle ages, was a plan, but a moral plan in which there was much freedom of choice.

The conception of the world as a plan was in harmony with the theology and philosophy of the Middle Ages, the Renaissance and the Enlightenment, and even of the science of the latter periods. Christian faith seemed to require acceptance of this conception because at Genesis God created the universe out of nothing to which he would return it on the day of judgment (4). The philosophy of Plato, and in lesser degree that of Aristotle, taught that *ideas* rather than observation determine *reality* and *truth*. Aristotle, it is true, was interested in observing facts of both the natural and the human worlds, but his syllogistic method of reasoning relied upon the validity of universal ideas. Descartes' philosophy, identifying certainty with clarity of thought and reason with logic, implied that the universe must be rational. It must be deducible from reason because otherwise there could be no certainty that it existed at all. Scientific thought, in spite of Bacon's empiricism, generally accepted Descartes' rationalism until the nineteenth century, and seemed to be supported in doing so by astronomy and physics as formulated in Newton's *Principia*. These sciences seemed to demonstrate that the actual order of the universe conformed to a logical system derived by mind from a few assumptions.

To these introspective and observational demonstrations were added those of expediency. Hobbes, while failing to find a natural order among men, but rather a war of all against all, believed that human reason demonstrated the expediency of order if the human desire for peace and security was to be realized. He also believed he had demonstrated the contingency of that order upon the observance of rules of *natural law* deducible by reason and the contingency of that observance upon the establishment of civil authority. Reason, therefore, would in time lead man from a disordered state of nature to the ordered state of society. Potentially, if not actually, the human world was ordered by *natural law* maintained by human authority (20). Dante's conclusion, that human order required a universal emperor to settle all disputes and that, therefore, such a universal authority would eventually be established, was similar, although the specific arguments were different (12). The same conclusions have been reached by recent advocates of world government though they differ as to whether the advancing understanding by man of the necessary implications of reason would achieve the goal they desire in a decade or in five centuries (1, 5, 37, 42). A plan based on expediency, however, is not an explanation of the world but a means for its control, not a law of God, history, or nature but an hypothesis constructed for human use.

The more the method of science has been utilized, the less the world has been envisaged as a reliable plan. Theories of economic, geographic, and demographic determinism have not withstood scientific criticism. Modern psychology, sociology, economics, and politics assume a high degree of choice in human and group behavior. Decision-making, influenced by many factors, rather than inevitable behavior in response to instincts, drives, or conditioned reflexes, is today at the center of these studies (13, 27, 32). Historical determinism has been condemned as *historicism* by some philosophers (41), historians (34), and social scientists (13, 19). Its alleged necessity they find is qualified by much contingency and choice. As the conception that the physical universe conforms to the plan written out in Newton's *Principia* has receded before the relativity of Einstein and the uncertainty of Heisenberg, so the conception that the human world is a plan, whether revealed by God, by history, or by nature, has receded before the modern social sciences. These sciences, doubtless will continue their quest for a conceptual system that is as simple, as general, as reliable, and as valid as possible—that is the nature of science—but they seek an objective concept rather than a subjective conception, and they tend to form concepts which do not imply that the world of man can be fitted to any foreordained plan (13).

The world as equilibrium. Many have conceived the world as an equilibrium, the stability of which varies in time. This equilibrium results from the force, driving each geographically defined state to expand and increase in power faced by the force driving each to preserve itself. The concept, popular in the seventeenth century, of balance between the force of inertia driving the heavenly bodies to continue their existing motions in a straight line and the force of gravitation driving them to move together was applied to states driven by the opposing forces variously called dominance and self-preservation, aggression and defense, imperialism and the *status quo* (29).

Even before Kepler, Galileo, and Newton had utilized the conception of equilibrium to explain the system of the universe, it had been utilized to explain the system of states. Lord Shang in ancient China, Kautilya in ancient India, Polybius in ancient Rome, and Machiavelli in sixteenth century Italy called attention to the tendency of states to gang up against the most powerful of their number, thus preventing universal conquest and preserving an equilibrium of power. Even biology, which dominated political thought after evolution had become established in the nineteenth century, led some writers to the conception of equilibrium. The stable conditions of temperature, salinity, and pressure within the organism, permitting it to function, were attributed to balances between opposing forces establishing a homeostacy or self-corrective system (8, 14). Obviously the meaning of equilibrium varies greatly in accordance with the source of the conception. Mechanical, historical, and biological analogies imply very different degrees of complexity (44).

Usually as applied to the world, adherents of this conception have had in mind a simple mechanical system like an apothecary's balance, each of the two major rivals at any moment, occupying one of the pans, the lesser powers shifting their weight by alliances from one pan to the other in order to maintain equilibrium. Sometimes a more complicated system involving all the great powers has been in mind. Calculation of the aggressive and resisting power of each and the distances and barriers which separated them might sufficiently determine the stability of the system and, in case of disturbance, indicate the points at which force should be applied or resisting forces co-ordinated to restore equilibrium. Writers on power politics have usually thought that social, moral, and ideological factors might be safely disregarded (16, 29).

Some writers, however, influenced particularly by the biological analogy have considered it necessary to scrutinize all of the complicating factors. They have conceived the world, as an equilibrium among numerous decision-makers, representing not only great powers but also lesser powers, regional arrangements, international organizations, unofficial groups, and even individuals, each influenced by numerous forces, both material and moral, both military and organizational, both international and domestic. Such a complication of the conception of equilibrium pulls it away from the analogy of a physical system toward that of a political system with checks and balances as exhibited in the United States Constitution, or even toward that of an administrative organization or a biological organism (44). Thus the conception of the world as a balance of power merges into the conception of the world as an organization.

The world as organization. This conception, natural to observers of political or social groups, and developed by such Medieval and Renaissance writers as Marsilius of Padua and Johannes Althusius, was emphasized by the biological and evolutionary point of view, current in the late nineteenth century. There was, however, doubt whether the analogy was to the ecological community, the animal species, the animal organism, or the animal association. Was the totality of men and nations comparable to the varied organic inhabitants of an area, each occupying its niche; to the biologically similar members of an organic species; to the structurally and functionally differentiated cells of an organism; or to the structually similar, but functionally specialized members of an insect colony or of a herd or association of mammals or birds? Was the emphasis upon geographical specialization, upon biological similarity, upon organic unity, or upon functional organization and evolutionary change (44)? Some biologists have tried to bring all of these conceptions together in the idea of homeostasis, a conception of equilibrium which is so dynamic and self-correcting as to come rather under the conception of organization (14).

Some social scientists have conceived the world as a human population, continually varying in numbers, in distribution, in grouping, and in the patterns of behavior of both the individuals and the groups. The Darwinian conception of struggle for existence and survival of the fittest was applied rather indiscriminately to individuals and groups, explaining, and sometimes attempting to justify, extreme methods of economic competition or political conflict (17). Studies of population change, land utilization, technological invention, and economic activity have been made to explain the order of the world, motivated ultimately by biological urges adapting men and groups to the physical and social environment.

Others with a biological point of view, have emphasized less the relation of human groups to one another and to the environment, than the unity of the human species as a whole in relation to other organic forms. Mankind, they said, is the proper study for man. This notion encouraged by observations of co-operation among animals of the same species (6, 23) led to conceptions of humanism and cosmopolitanism supported by belief in the universal sentiment of human sympathy. This point of view encouraged respect for human rights, assumption of responsibilities of world citizenship, and establishment of a commonwealth of man to maintain this responsibility and to maximize enjoyment of these rights (37).

Others among the biologically inspired have emphasized the similarity between all organic forms, including man, and their difference from the inorganic environment. They have conceived the world as a great organism including all organic life, and the utilizable aspects of the inorganic environment, enduring in time under the persistent urges of protoplasm to eat, to reproduce, to dominate, and to explore in order that each urge may be realized so far as is compatible with the equal realization of the others. Man, they said, can only be explained as an organism and the introduction of supernatural or nonnatural concepts violates the scientific principal of parsimony, at least until these concepts have proved inadequate (39). This conception has encouraged researches in the relation of morphological structure to function in different organic forms (9) and in the relation of morphological characteristics to behavior (39) and values (30). Some philosophers like Schaeffle have drawn out in great detail the analogy of societies to organisms (6), and others like Fechner have conceived the whole world as an organism (21), relying upon mystical insight rather than objective evidence, thus approaching the position of those who conceive the world as a spiritual community. Historians with a biological point of view, like H. G. Wells, have interpreted human history as a phase of organic evolution, guided, not by persistent ideas but by efforts of the human organism and human societies better to adapt themselves to the environment, natural and social, utilizing the arts of communication, invention, organization, and war for this purpose.

Many of the biologically minded, however, have compared the world of man not to an animal organism but to an animal association, particularly to colonial insects, emphasizing the role of the self-regarding drives of the individual to the solidarity and functioning of the whole (2, 26, 40). The variety of animal associations, it was thought, could provide the basis for identifying typical forms of organization and for evaluating their efficiency. Most psychologists and sociologists, however, while recognizing the biological basis of mind and society, have insisted that human communication, utilizing symbols for abstract ideas, has introduced an element in human behavior which is *social* and not merely *biological*. Spencer suggested that the *super organic* differentiates man from the apes, and human societies from social insects. Men and societies utilize abstract ideas, values, and pattern variables to make choices, thus giving an indeterminate character to their decisions, different in kind from the instincts or habits guiding animal behavior. Biologists may object to having these *wild cards* introduced into the game (39), but sociologists and psychologists insist they are there and cannot be eliminated (30).

Most of those who have conceived the world as an organization have expressly or tacitly accepted this distinction. They have treated biological materials and generalizations as the biologists have treated chemistry and physics in their discipline, that is, as antecedent in time, as elementary in explanation, and as suggestive by analogy, but not as sufficient. They have conceived of the human world as a social organization rather than as a biocenosis, an organic species, an organism, or an animal association and have considered the history of diplomatic systems, international unions, the League of Nations, and the United Nations as evidence of the evolution of that organization.

The world as community. Many have conceived the world as a potential, spiritual or mystical community in which men feel themselves to be brothers with a common origin and a common destiny, and behave with mutual consideration and love, thus establishing a universal harmony. This conception, inherent in the universal religions, and elaborated in the writings of many saints, mystics, and humanitarians, has been rationalized in theologies and ideologies, and efforts have been made to justify it by biological and historical studies. It therefore merges into the conceptions of the world as idea and as organization, but differs from both in its emotional and spiritual emphasis (38).

The world as field. It requires considerable intellectual sophistication to conceive the world as a field of conditions, values, ideals, and attitudes, in continuous flux, but at any point and moment exerting influence upon the actions of individuals, associations, and nations. But is this field one of nature, of custom, of ethics, or of opinion? Is it constituted by the relations of human individuals and groups, of human interests and policies, of human personalities and cultures, of human organizations and institutions, of human instincts and drives, of human habits and customs, of human values and consciences, or of human attitudes and opinions? Some of these factors may best account for human behavior at some times and places and others at other times and places.

Some have interpreted the field as a system of law defining the relations of the persons which together compose the world. The *naturalists* have attributed this law to the *nature* of man and society and the *positivists* have attributed it to convention and custom. The first conceive the world as idea, but the latter conceive it as a changing field of rights and duties, powers and responsibilities, which influences but does not determine all decisions. The international *monists* regard the field of law as universal and integrated, thus having the character of a universal moral ideology, which is imperfectly sanctioned and which, therefore, may often be violated. The *dualists* and *pluralists*, on the other hand, look upon international law and the national law of states as distinct systems. Consequently the behavior of individuals and governments in domestic matters is, in principle, influenced by legal fields which differ from one another and from the legal field which influences the behaviors of states in international relations. In domestic matters, individuals and governments are influenced by international law, according to this theory, only so far as that law has been incorporated into national law by a general or specific act of the particular state (28).

Others have interpreted the field politically as composed of interest groups in a continuous flux of oppositions and coalitions to survive and achieve their ends (3). Some political scientists have criticized the atomism of this picture, and have conceived the world as a field of values, purposes, and policies, organized in parties, each claiming to represent the common element in the members of the public, or the general welfare (36). Interest groups may be defined geographically or functionally, they may be defined economically or politically, and they may be dominated by special interests or by common interests, but in any case this conception approaches that of the world as equilibrium.

Other conceptions of the field of international relations look behind both legal formulations and political structures, and conceive the world as a field of continually varying interests, attitudes, opinions, and values in which every local area is always changing in respect to the symbols commanding attention, in respect to the elites or leaders interpreting these symbols, in respect to the direction, intensity, homogeneity, and continuity of opinions and attitudes concerning each symbol, and in respect to the relative influence of value systems and ideologies. The characteristics, however, of every point in the field at every moment are influenced by the field as a whole. Knowledge of all these aspects of the field would assist in explaining or even in predicting decisions and actions of persons or organizations within it. This point of view, characteristic of cultural anthropologists, of social psychologists, and of practitioners of the arts of communication and education, encourages efforts to measure these variables, and to explore hypotheses concerning their causation, their consequences, and their co-ordination at any point in time and space (25, 33, 43).

Influence of different conceptions of the world. While these different conceptions of the world suggest different directions of study and different values, none of them has been formulated with sufficient precision to become the bases for detailed deductions of consequences in operative terms susceptible of verification. Their propaganda may, however, have contributed to the willingness of peoples to accept a particular policy. The imperial policies of a Louis XIV or a Napoleon required that the people have a conception of the world different from that required to maintain the power-balancing policy of a William Pitt or a Metternich or from that required to maintain the organizational policy of a Woodrow Wilson or a Franklin D. Roosevelt. If a policy were to be formulated by the authors of *Recent Social Trends in the United States* or the Radir Project, it could hardly be maintained without wide acceptance of a different conception of the world, perhaps a field conception. *Recent Social Trends* proposed that policy should be guided by the *fundamental principles* that:

Social problems are products of change, and that social changes are interrelated. Hence, a change in one part of the social structure will affect other parts connected with it. But the effects do not always follow immediately—an induced change may lag years behind the original precipitating change. These varying delays among correlated changes often mean maladjustment. They may arise from vested interests resisting change in self defense, from the difficulty with which men readjust familiar ideas or ideals, or from various obstacles which obstruct the transmission of impulses from man to man. These interrelated changes which are going forward in such bewildering variety and at such varying speeds threaten grave dangers with one hand, while with the other hand they hold out the promise of further betterment to mankind. The object of any conscious control over the process is to secure a better adjustment between inherited nature and culture. The means of social control is social discovery and the wider adoption of new knowledge (31).

The Radir Project emphasized as a means "of improving judgments of the future" such special tools as the "developmental construct" which "characterizes a possible sequence of events running from a selected cross section of the past to a cross section of the future." Such a construct was not designed to "arbitrate among metaphysical or theological beliefs" but rather "to work with conceptions of human affairs which are both tentative and amenable to revision in the light of empirical inquiry" (25). After reviewing various "models" in the mind of past policy-makers and thinkers on world affairs, the introducer of one of these volumes said the model envisaged by the Radir study:

envisages the human world as a complex of innumerable variables in more or less dependent relationship. The temporal changes of some of these variables can be measured, but in other cases, measurement is extremely difficult if not impossible. Some of these variables can be manipulated by human actions, some cannot. Some function directly in international relations, some do not. The problem of prediction and control in international relations is, therefore, to discover variables which can be measured; to determine their correlation with, or degree of dependence upon, variables that can be manipulated; and in turn the degree of dependence of those upon variables that are functionally important (33).

The different types of world structure, though they often spring from different conceptions of the world, may merge into one another. A world empire, as its ideology becomes less rigid and its authority less centralized, may adjust itself to differences of opinion among its subjects and may merge into a federation or an international organization. If, on the other hand, its peoples acquire a common culture and common sentiments, it may merge into a universal spiritual community, ready to divide into competing groups if heresy develops. So also a balance of power, if it becomes complicated and stable, may assume the aspects of an international organization and if it becomes simple and unstable, reducing the number of elements in equilibrium, it may become an empire through universal conquest by one. The dominant picture in the European mind moved from universal empire centered in Rome to the community of Christendom in the Middle Ages and then to a balance of power, now tending toward international organization, but at all times there have been opposing views (44). The five conceptions envisaging the world as a plan, an equilibrium, an organization, a spiritual community, and a field have competed with one another. Each has tended to induce different structural forms in the family of nations, different behaviors by peoples and governments, different policies by statesmen and politicians, and different lines of research by scholars and students.

Each conception of the world has also been reflected in different conceptions of the groups and of the individuals within it. The major groups, into which mankind is today divided and whose relations constitute *international relations,* have been variously designated *states, governments, nations,* and *peoples,* and individuals have been variously treated as *characters, decision-makers, personalities,* and *men.* If the world is conceived as a plan, the major groups have tended to be conceived humanistically as *states,* and individuals as *characters* which acquire their roles from the plans or ideas of the state or the world with which they are identified. If the world is conceived as a balance of power, the major groups have tended to be conceived politically as *governments,* organizing and controlling power and the individuals as *decision-makers* contributing to the power of these governments. If the world is conceived as an organization, the major groups have tended to be conceived sociologically as *nations* and the individuals as *personalities* reflecting the culture in which they developed. If the world is conceived as a *spiritual community* the major groups have tended to be conceived psychologically as *peoples* and the individuals as *men* and women aware of common feelings and common aspirations. Elsewhere the writer has discussed the implications of the legal, military, sociological, and psychological points of view in respect to war, to some extent reflecting respectively the first four of these conceptions of international relations. Each of these points of view, it is noted, could be treated as a deterministic system, permitting prediction or as a voluntaristic system permitting choice and control (44). The conception of the world as a field is perhaps best adapted to a synthesis of the other conceptions of the world, the group, and the individual.

These five conceptions of the world have influenced the formulation of research problems and the nature of the sources to be examined. The study of plans and ideologies, their formulation, and their realization in literature and art has dominated in the *humanistic sciences.* The study of government and power relations is the subject of the *political sciences,* that of organization and society is the subject of the *social sciences,* while the study of fields of population, culture, and opinion has been the subject of what is called from the deterministic point of view, the *behavioral sciences* and from the voluntaristic point of view the *policy sciences.* The study of the spiritual community of man has been the subject of religion and ethics.

Doubtless these different views of the nature of the world, of groups, of man, and of the sciences for studying them are interrelated. It is suggested, however, that the conception of the world, the *Weltanschauung* accepted by an individual or a group, is likely to control also conceptions of lesser groups of individuals, and of appropriate methods of study. The whole sets the pattern for the parts.

What conception of the world is most suitable for a discipline of international relations? Are there criteria by which such conceptions can be *evaluated?* Even if it is the essence of international relations that incompatible conceptions of the world struggle for realization, still one conception of the process as a whole may be better than another. The criteria for deciding which is better would seem to depend on the one hand upon the nature of knowledge and on the other upon the functions of the discipline. The discipline should be both true and valuable, or, using the terminology suggested in Chapter 3, it should be true both objectively and subjectively in the sense that its propositions are on the one hand convincing and correct, and on the other effective and persuasive. As has been noticed, one of these characteristics has often been exaggerated at the expense of the other. Political and other authorities have inculcated doctrines believed to be valuable or useful without regard to their objective truth, and science has developed theories believed to be objectively true without regard to their social consequences. Doubtless utility is more important in the applied sciences and objective truth in the pure sciences, but neither can be neglected in a general discipline such as international relations, aiming to be at the same time a science, a philosophy, a history, and an art. The criteria for determining the truth of such a discipline will be discussed in the next chapter and its value in the final chapter.

REFERENCES

1. ADLER, Mortimer, *How to Think About War and Peace* (New York, Simon and Schuster, 1944).
2. ALLEE, Warder, *The Social Life of Animals* (New York, Norton, 1938).
3. BENTLEY, Arthur F., *The Process of Government, A Study of Social Pressures* (Chicago, University of Chicago Press, 1908).
4. BOAS, George, "A Fourteenth Century Cosmology," *Proceedings, American Philosophical Society,* Vol. 98 (February 15, 1954), pp. 50 ff.
5. BORGESE, G. A., *Foundations of the World Republic* (Chicago, University of Chicago Press, 1953).
6. BRISTOL, L. M., *Social Adaptation* (Cambridge, Harvard University Press, 1915).
7. BUTTERFIELD, H., *Origins of Modern Science, 1300-1800* (London, 1950).
8. CANNON, Walter, *The Wisdom of the Body* (New York, Norton, 1932).
9. CHILDS, Charles M., *Physiological Foundations of Behavior* (New York, Holt, 1924).
10. CONANT, James Bryant, *Science and Common Sense* (New Haven, Yale University Press, 1951).
11. CORBETT, P. E., *Post-War Worlds,* Institute of Pacific Relations, Inquiry Series (New York, Rinehart, 1942).
12. DANTE, *De Monarchia,* ed. by Aurelia Henry (Boston, Houghton Mifflin, 1914).

13. EASTON, David, *The Political System, an Inquiry into the State of Political Science* (New York, Knopf, 1952).

14. EMERSON, Alfred E., "Dynamic Homeostasis, a Unifying Principle in Organic, Social and Ethical Evolution," *The Scientific Monthly*, Vol. 78 (February, 1954), pp. 67 ff.

15. FRANK, Philipp, ed., "Contributions to the Analysis and Synthesis of Knowledge," *Proceedings, American Academy of Arts and Sciences*, in cooperation with the Institute for the Unity of Science, Boston, Vol. 80, No. 1 (July, 1951).

16. FRIEDRICH, Carl J., *Foreign Policy in the Making* (New York, Norton, 1938).

17. GUMPLOWITZ, Ludwig, *Der Rassenkampf* (Innsbruck, 1909).

18. HERZ, John, *Political Realism and Political Idealism, A Study in Theories and Realities* (Chicago, University of Chicago Press, 1951).

19. HAYEK, F. A., *The Counter Revolution of Science* (Glencoe, Ill., Free Press, 1952).

20. HOBBES, Thomas, *Leviathan* (1651).

21. JAMES, William, *A Pluralistic Universe* (London, Longmans, 1912).

22. KOHN, Hans, *World Order in Historical Perspective* (Cambridge, Harvard University Press, 1942).

23. KROPOTKIN, P., *Mutual Aid, a Factor of Evolution* (New York, Knopf, 1925).

24. LANGER, Suzanne K., *An Introduction to Symbolic Logic*, 2nd ed. (New York, Dover, 1953).

25. LASSWELL, Harold D., *The World Revolution of Our Time*, Radir Project Study (Stanford, Stanford University Press, 1952).

26. MANDEVILLE, Bernard de, *The Fable of the Bees, or Private Vices, Public Benefits* (1714); 4th ed. (London, 1925).

27. MEAD, George Herbert, *The Philosophy of the Present* (Chicago, University of Chicago Press, 1932).

28. MASTERS, Ruth B., *International Law in National Courts* (New York, Columbia University Press, 1932).

29. MORGENTHAU, Hans J., *Politics Among Nations* (New York, Knopf, 1948).

30. MORRIS, Charles, *The Science of Man and Unified Science*, in Frank, ed., above, pp. 37 ff.

30a. MUMFORD, Lewis, *The Story of Utopias* (New York, Boni and Liveright, 1922).

30b. NEGLEY, Glenn and PATRICK, J. Max, *The Quest for Utopia, an Anthology of Imaginary Societies* (New York, Schuman, 1952).

31. OGBURN, W. F., ed., *Recent Social Trends in the United States* (New York, McGraw-Hill, 1933, 2 vols.).

32. PARSONS, Talcott, and SHILS, Edward A., eds., *Toward a General Theory of Action* (Cambridge, Harvard University Press, 1951).

33. POOL, Ithiel de Sola, *Symbols of Internationalism*, Introduction by Quincy Wright (Stanford, Stanford University Press, 1951), part of the Radir Project, C. Easton Rothwell, ed., H. D. Lasswell, Daniel Lerner, and others, contributors.

34. POPPER, K. R., *The Open Society and Its Enemies*, rev. ed. (Princeton, Princeton University Press, 1950).

35. RAPAPORT, Anatol, *Operational Philosophy* (New York, Harper, 1913).

36. SCHATTSCHNEIDER, E. E., "Political Parties and Public Interest," in *Ethical Standards in American Public Life*, C. N. Callender and J. C. Chadwick,

eds., *Annals*, American Academy of Political and Social Science, Philadelphia, Vol. 280 (March, 1952), pp. 18 ff.

37. SCHUMAN, Frederick L., *The Commonwealth of Man* (New York, Knopf, 1952).

38. SCHWEITZER, Albert, "The Problem of Ethics for Twentieth Century Man," *Saturday Review* (June 13, 1953), pp. 9-11, 46-48.

39. SHELDON, W. H., "Integration in the Biological and Social Sciences," in Frank, ed., above, pp. 31 ff.

40. SMITH, Adam, *An Inquiry into the Nature and Cause of the Wealth of Nations* (1776); Cannon, ed. (London, Methuen, 1904).

41. STRAUSS, Leo, *Natural Rights and History* (Chicago, University of Chicago Press, 1953).

42. STREIT, Clarence, *Union Now* (New York, Harper, 1930).

43. THURSTONE, L. L., "The Prediction of Choice," *Psychometrika*, Vol. 10 (December, 1945), pp. 237 ff.

44. WRIGHT, Quincy, *A Study of War* (Chicago, University of Chicago Press, 1942), pp. 509, 747, 965 ff., 1227, 1235.

Approaches to a Discipline of International Relations

IF A DISCIPLINE of international relations is to expand human knowledge it must be semantically and logically true, that is, using the terminology suggested in Chapter 3, its propositions must be convincing and correct. Such a discipline should also be as brief as possible, conforming to the principle of not unnecessarily multiplying essences or definitions. While the social consequences of action based on its conclusions should be acceptable, this consideration, would be unimportant if its form is adapted only to research workers, not to the public. A discipline in that form need not indulge in Plato's "noble lies," in Machiavellian deceptions, in the propaganda art of persuading by half truths, or in the philosophical prudence of not spreading pearls before swine (10). The influence of the discipline on research workers themselves is, however, an important consideration. The following criteria will therefore be applied in this chapter in considering the form, content, and method of such a discipline. Its generalizations (a) should not be contradicted by any observations, (b) should be logically consistent with one another, (c) should be as parsimonious in assumptions as is compatible with comprehensive treatment of the subject, (d) should be so presented as not to discourage belief in, and observance of, the best values, and (e) should be so arranged as to stimulate its own self-correction and continuous improvement.

Conformity to the first of these requirements may be tested by the application of appropriate scientific and historical techniques. Terms should be clearly defined and inferences made from propositions relating them should be confirmed by experiments, observations, or historical sources.

Conformity to the second requirement may be tested by the application of logical and mathematical analyses. Is the meaning of the terms used unambiguous? Are the propositions related to one another by proper inference?

Conformity to the third requirement is not susceptible of precise determination. It depends on an aesthetic judgment of harmony and proportionality. Occam's injunction against the multiplication of essences has to be balanced against a sense of the proper scope of the discipline. Science seeks to comprehend all knowledge with a minimum of assumption and definition, but the vastness of knowledge and the difficulty of integrating all its aspects requires that it be broken up into disciplines, each of which has a unity resulting from the completeness and elegance with which it covers an easily defined subject matter by deduction from a minimum number of terms and assumptions (parameters). As the number of parameters increases in proportion to the number of conclusions, the discipline becomes inductive (22), but unless there are more conclusions than parameters there is no science (42).

Conformity to the fourth requirement is certain to be controversial. It depends upon practical judgment of the consequences upon political behavior of knowledge of the discipline and upon the philosophy by which these consequences are evaluated. What values did the makers of the discipline believe in? Have these values influenced the form or content of the discipline? What values ought to be realized at the present time? What is the relation of these values to one another? What behavior in different situations accords with these values? What behavior is likely to result among different people from understanding the discipline? Natural scientists have usually regarded the consideration of such questions as irrelevant or even harmful. They have considered that a discipline if real, true, and beautiful, according to the first three tests, is bound to be good for man and society; that the only good which science can consider is the advancement of itself as suggested by the fifth test; or that goodness is a matter too difficult or dangerous for them and that they should be content to follow the opinions of others with social authority and responsibility. This position has probably contributed to the advancement of natural science during the past few centuries by eliminating subjective biases from scientific observation and inference (19). It has become so widely accepted that government censorship of pure science in the alleged interest of morals or social values has been generally repudiated, outside of the Soviet orbit, except for reasons of national security. These propositions are, however, less widely accepted in the case of the social sciences. Social and even legal pressures in most countries qualify freedom in the public exposition of social theories deemed by prevailing opinion to support beliefs dangerous to values of the particular society. Since in the social field, the relation of scientific theories to social beliefs and behavior is much closer than in the physical and biological fields, the social disciplines can not ignore the problem (47). However, these questions clearly cannot be answered by objective methods of observation or logic but only by knowledge of the audience to which the discipline will be communicated, of the method and form of that communication, of the state of affairs in the world at the time, and other matters hardly susceptible of general analysis. The observance of this requirement is less a function of the discipline itself, than of the time, place, method, and manner of its communication.

Conformity to the fifth requirement can hardly be appraised without acquaintance with scientists and scholars in the field permitting judgment of the probable influence upon their scholarly activities of understanding the discipline. What flaws in the discipline are likely to attract attention? What proportion of its propositions are insufficiently supported? Are scholars likely to be incited to remedy these flaws and to seek new data to support these propositions? This practical influence of a discipline upon scientific research is regarded by James B. Conant and others as its most significant value (8). Yet the effect of a discipline in stimulating scientific work, and thus in correcting itself, is not easily susceptible of general investigation by fact or logic. Determination of this effect depends upon knowledge about particular scholars and their situations and interests at the moment, and about the availability of materials, the state of opinion in the world, and other factors concerning the circumstances under which the discipline is utilized by particular persons. It may be, however, that some general characteristics of a discipline qualify it to meet this requirement. For example, if most of the propositions appear to conform to the first two of these requirements, then the attention which the discipline focuses upon a few propositions which do not so conform is likely to stimulate scientific activity. This would not be the case if most of the propositions were vaguely stated or inadequately supported. If the discipline has an aesthetic quality appealing to the sentiments, it may attract defenders anxious to eliminate weaknesses by discovering new evidences and new inferences. Furthermore, if inferences from the discipline either obviously support or obviously attack existing social theories, sentiments, values, and practices, it will stimulate investigation more than if it is neutral in this regard. It seems probable, therefore, that in proportion as a discipline conforms to the first three of these requirements it will conform to the fifth.

It appears that conformity to only the first two requirements (reality and truth) can be examined in precise and general terms, but such an examination is possible only after the discipline has been formulated.

Since a discipline of international relations has not yet been formulated, all that can be done at this point is to discuss the methods which might be used to construct it with the greatest hope of meeting these tests. Such an effort might start empirically with the facts of international relations, and then proceed to classify, analyze, and relate them; or it might start hypothetically with a general concept or model, and then seek to confirm deductions from this concept by reference to the facts.

THE EMPIRICAL APPROACH

The empirical approach should proceed from a detailed observation of the conditions of international relations, at present and in the past, but since any occurrence of history or contemporary life may be relevant, this task would be impracticable without establishing some preliminary criteria of relevance. The general concepts or models to be discussed in the next section may provide such criteria, but each of the existing disciplines of international relations also attempts to do so. These disciplines may in some cases rest upon unconvincing definitions and assumptions and may sometimes utilize incorrect methods of inference, but an attempt to synthesize them by classification and analysis may be illuminating. This task should be more manageable than that of synthesizing the raw data. If such a synthesis were accomplished it would of course be necessary to check deductions from the general concepts that emerged by direct reference to the facts of international life.

The sixteen disciplines discussed in Parts III and IV of this book have been divided into ten which emphasize practical analysis and six which emphasize theoretical analysis. It has been pointed out that this distinction cannot be maintained rigorously. Some of the practical or *applied* disciplines such as international economics and international law have developed much pure theory. All of these disciplines, however, grew from professional interests in fields of international activity rather than from disinterested curiosity or love of knowledge. On the other hand, practical interests have not always been wanting among students of the *pure,* disinterested, or theoretical disciplines. Geography and demography have, for example, much direct practical utility. In general, however, the writers in the theoretical disciplines have been less influenced by value considerations. Even international ethics, which deals with values, has often been treated objectively, seeking standards apart from the writer's preferences or cultural tradition.

These disciplines can also be classified into ten disciplines which are relatively abstract and deductive, and six which are relatively concrete and descriptive. This distinction again is relative. The art of war, for example, has led to abstract thinking, as by Clausewitz, but on the whole it has kept close to concrete facts of military history, geography, and technology. Political geography has also led to abstract theorizing by some scholars such as Ellsworth Huntington and Griffith Taylor, but on the whole geographers have kept close to earth. The result of combining these two principles of classification is to distinguish four types of discipline.

A CLASSIFICATION OF THE DISCIPLINES OF INTERNATIONAL RELATIONS

	Theoretical	*Applied*
Abstract	Sciences Psychology Sociology Ethics	Philosophies Politics Colonial government Organization Law Economics Communications Education
Concrete	Histories Geography Demography Technology	Arts Art of war Art of diplomacy Conduct of foreign relations

In the definitions of these disciplines suggested in Parts III and IV of this book the "theoretical" disciplines are characterized as *sciences*, though the more concrete ones, being largely descriptive, might have been characterized as *histories* in the sense of *natural history*. The *applied* disciplines are, on the other hand, characterized as *arts* though the more abstract might have been characterized as *philosophies*. The distinctions made between a science, a philosophy, a history, and an art in the second part of this book will assist in characterizing each of these four classes of disciplines, although, as noted, most of them actually treat their subject matter from all four of these points of view.

The assumptions stated for each discipline seek to describe the objective facts which the majority of writers on the subject have taken for granted. Very often, however, assumptions have also been made in regard to values. Each of the applied disciplines assumes the validity of certain values and is oriented about them. This indeed is what makes them *applied* disciplines. The discipline of medicine, for example, assumes that health is good and the discipline of law assumes that justice is good. Similarly the discipline of international politics has usually assumed that the independence of the state is good, the art of war that victory is good, the art of diplomacy that the interests of the state are good, and the conduct of foreign relations that efficiency abroad and democracy at home are good. Colonial government has assumed that the development of colonies is good, international organization that co-operation among nations is good, international law that justice among nations is good, international economics that prosperity is good, while international communications and international education regard increased understanding by the people of each nation about the others as good. In some cases these values may be controversial. For example, the art of war may be valued, as it was by Thomas Aquinas, because of the contribution it may make to justice. International economics may be valued, as it was by some of the mercantilists, because of the contribution it may make to the power position of the state. International law and international communications may be valued because of the contribution they may make to the maintenance of the state's independence. These illustrations make it clear that there is not complete agreement on the values about which the applied disciplines should be oriented, even though it is generally conceded that they ought to be oriented about some value or values. International law was said by Sir James Lorimer to attribute equal value to national independence and cosmopolitan co-operation, its essence consisting in the maintenance of a balance between the realization of these conflicting values (26). In similar manner, international politics has been considered by some to strive for a balance between the values of national power and of international peace (27).

Still other values have often been assumed in some of these disciplines. For example, the aesthetic values of restraint and harmony have sometimes influenced writers on the arts of diplomacy and war. Such writers have sometimes qualified conduct in these fields, not only as *effective* to achieve its ostensible ends, but also as *justly* or *properly* conducted, thus implying an aesthetic or a moral valuation by a community which includes both of the disputing states (14). Writers of serious disciplines are generally assumed to value objective *truth*, and ordinarily its demonstration is the object of the exposition. Sometimes, however, the truth of controversial propositions is assumed. For example, among the assumptions of international politics, is the proposition that the "only reliable means available to maintain national independence is self-help supported by military power and alliances." The truth of this proposition has been doubted, yet writers on international politics commonly assume it without argument.

While the assumptions of each discipline are here stated as objective facts or as axiomatic truths, thus attributing scientific meaning to the discipline, in the case of the applied disciplines moral or aesthetic values are implied by the definitions of the disciplines, thus giving them the character of philosophies or arts.

Anything may be assumed as a basis for the logical development of a discipline, but the meaning of the results depends upon the meaning attributed to the assumptions. If the assumptions are intended to be facts uniformly observed or truths which are axiomatic, the discipline, if logically developed, becomes a science formulating the conditions of the world within the time and space postulated. If some of the propositions which are assumed are not true, no refinement of logic can make conclusions drawn from them true. Similarly, if certain moral or aesthetic values are assumed, the resulting philosophy cannot demonstrate the superiority of these values. If a discipline mixes assumptions of fact and of value without discrimination its meaning may be obscure. For example, the first two assumptions of international politics are said to be: "Sovereign, territorial states with conflicting policies exist in contact with one another," and "the major value of each is its own continuous independent existence." These are stated as facts, but writers on international politics who make these assumptions, sometimes treat them as moral values. They sometimes assume that "sovereign territorial states with conflicting policies *ought to* exist in contact with one another," and that "the major value of each state *ought to be* continuous independent existence." In either case the meaning of the assumptions, and so of the discipline, is clear, but sometimes these two assumptions are treated as both fact and value, thus making the meaning of the discipline obscure. They are used at one point to infer how states can be expected to act in given circumstances, and on another occasion to infer how they ought to act. "National interest" often used as a short expression for these two assumptions is sometimes treated as both a sufficient explanation and a desirable goal of state behavior.

Scrutiny of the assumptions of the sixteen disciplines here considered indicates that those of the applied disciplines are usually simpler but more controversial than those of the theoretical disciplines. This suggests that the applied disciplines should be parts of more fundamental disciplines capable of criticizing these assumptions and defining the orbit of their applicability. The theoretical disciplines with less controversial assumptions may serve this purpose but the somewhat complicated character of the assumptions in some of the latter indicates that the disciplines are far from being well developed. There is in most cases controversy about what assumptions will best fulfill such requirements as parsimony of assumptions, elegance of demonstration, and utility of operation. The variety of approaches to the discipline of psychology is particularly notable (5). The assumptions selected in the discussion of this discipline, as indeed, of all the abstract, theoretical disciplines, are of an eclectic character.

How may these disciplines be best ordered for the purpose of developing a general discipline of international relations of the widest possible applicability? I believe that the psychology of international relations and political geography should be placed at the center. International relations has to do with man and the physical world. These are the least changing aspects of the field.

The characteristics of some human individual account for every decision and action of importance in international relations, if all aspects of the individual are considered. At a given moment, an individual is an *organism* with inherited traits and capacities; a *personality* with habits, attitudes, and values derived from the culture in which he was born and lives; a *character* with opinions and patterns of behavior derived from the role he occupies in the society and in its institutions; and a *decision-maker* choosing among alternative courses of action on the basis of abstract criteria influenced by his drives, his culture, and his role. The decisions and actions of all human beings together, whether motivated by necessity, custom, caprice, or reason, ultimately account for the fluctuations of population, of technology, and of prosperity; the development of groups, policies, and conflicts; the enunciation and spread of ideologies, opinions, and movements; and the rise and fall of nations and civilizations. Apart from physical catastrophe or environmental change beyond human control, these constitute the phenomena with which international relations is concerned.

The significance of the human being in international relations cannot, however, be understood without locating him on the map. The world, with its variations of climate, of land and sea, and of resources of mine, soil, and river; with its natural and artificial barriers, passageways, and political boundaries; with its distribution of population, cities, industries, legal systems, cultures, ideologies, and religions, and with its occasional catastrophes of storm, flood, dessication, and pestilence, is the scene of international relations. Human capacities and behavior can only be understood if their environment on the physical, economic, cultural, and political map of the world is understood. The union of these two disciplines, the one tending to be abstract and universal, the other tending to be concrete and local, may provide the master science of international relations.

Derived from, but at the same time qualifying, these two disciplines are the other theoretical sciences. Demography and technology add to the conclusions of geography by explaining the changing significance to man of the earth's features and resources. These three disciplines analyze the material conditions of international relations in space and describe the succession of these conditions in time, thus constituting a history. Sociology and ethics are related in the same way to psychology. These three abstract disciplines analyze the human basis of international relations, and, utilizing the material of the three concrete disciplines, provide the fundamental theory for a discipline of international relations.

Derived from these six theoretical disciplines are seven philosophical disciplines or applied sciences based on assumptions which can presumably be justified from the conclusions of the theoretical disciplines. International politics appears to be most closely related to ethics, technology,

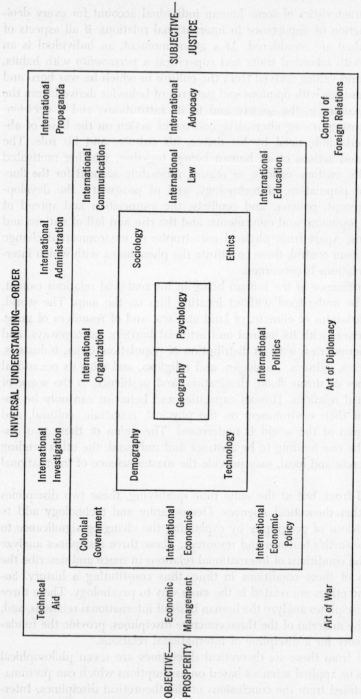

RELATIONS AMONG THE DISCIPLINES CONCERNED WITH INTERNATIONAL RELATIONS

and geography; international organization to sociology, demography, and psychology; international law to ethics, sociology, and psychology; and international economics to technology, demography, and geography. An applied science of international economic policy, more closely related to international politics, might be differentiated from the latter. The relations of these disciplines and of international communication, international education, and colonial government are indicated on the diagram on page 506.

Derived from the applied sciences are the arts most immediately connected with the practical conduct of international relations at the present time, the arts of diplomacy and war, and the control of foreign relations. To those may be added the arts of international advocacy, propaganda, administration, investigation, technical aid, and economic management, not separately discussed in this book, but of increasing importance. The assumptions of these arts should be justified by the conclusions of the applied sciences to which they are most closely related.

This diagram, indicating the relation of these disciplines to one another, is designed to be suggestive rather than conclusive. The disciplines at the center are the most theoretical and those at the periphery the most practical. Those at the right hand side of the diagram are oriented to subjective factors and feelings, and those at the left to objective factors and observations, as indicated by the difference between psychology and geography. The arts at the right, therefore, tend to aim at justice and those at the left at prosperity. The disciplines at the top are oriented to universal understanding and those at the bottom to particular action as indicated by the disinterested character of sociology and demography compared to the practical character of technology and the ethics. The arts at the top, therefore, tend to aim at order and those at the bottom at power.

Other disciplines might have been included, most of the disciplines have some aspects not consistent with their position in the diagram, and the diagram does not indicate all of the relations which exist. A three dimensional diagram would have been more comprehensive. This scheme is not intended to provide the basis for a unified discipline of international relations, but it is presented to suggest how such a discipline might be developed by relating the assumptions of the more practical arts and sciences to the conclusions of the theoretical sciences.

Such a discipline if constructed should be tested by the criteria suggested at the beginning of this chapter. By giving central weight to the concrete disciplines of geography, demography, and technology, it would keep close to the observable facts which appear to be most relevant to international relations in the large, and by giving similar weight to the more abstract disciplines of psychology, sociology, and ethics, it would keep close to the facts relevant to international relations in the small. In the large, international relations is concerned with the world as a changing complex of physical, technological, and demographic conditions which set limits to the policies, decisions, and actions of governments. In the small it is concerned with the action of a foreign policy decision-maker, with the interactions of two or more representatives of different groups dealing with a controversy or co-operating to achieve a common goal, or with the behavior of a mediator, a commission, or a tribunal similarly engaged. Both the macrocosm and the microcosm must be kept in mind.

To establish a discipline bringing the six theoretical sciences, using different technical terms and different methods, into a logically consistent structure is a monumental task, which seems unlikely to be accomplished unless some general hypothesis, conceptual system, or model is assumed in advance. Alternative conceptual systems which seem available will be discussed in the next section.

The problem of logically relating the applied sciences and the arts of international relations to such a pure science, once it is constructed, should prove less difficult. The problem would be to reformulate the definitions and assumptions of the applied disciplines and arts so that they conform to the language and the conclusions of the pure science, and at the same time to the values which each of the applied sciences and arts seeks to realize.

To make a discipline of international relations conform to the criterion of parsimony would require discrimination in the formulation of definitions and the selection of assumptions. It must be emphasized that the construction of a discipline is a work of art. The facts of observation, the rules of logic, and the scope of the discipline, while restrictive, leave the creator considerable freedom in defining terms, selecting assumptions, and ordering propositions so as to maximize the effectiveness of the discipline and to minimize its verbiage.

Determination of the degree of conformity of a discipline of international relations to the fourth criteria stated at the beginning of this chapter, that of supporting the best values, is complicated by the controversial character of the relevant values. Some of the assumptions deemed necessary to support the values inherent in a particular applied science or art of international relations might prove incapable of reconciliation with the results of the pure science. The advocates of these values would in that case be likely to regard publication of such a pure science as inexpedient or even as subversive. Others would probably urge reconsideration of the values in question or of the assumptions thought necessary to support them. A valid science of international relations might cause as much agitation among advocates of some current values, as did the physical sciences of Copernicus, Galileo, and Descartes among the advocates of certain values of their period. It remains to be seen whether the creator of such a discipline of international relations will be as hesitant to publish as was Descartes when he:

Learned that persons to whom I greatly defer, and whose authority over my actions is hardly less influential than is my own reason over my thoughts, had condemned a certain doctrine in physics, published a short time previously by another individual (Galileo) to which I will not say that I adhered, but only that, previously to their censure, I had observed in it nothing which I could imagine to be prejudicial either to religion or to the state, and nothing, therefore, which would have prevented me from giving expression to it in writing, if reason had persuaded me of its truth (10).

Descartes' exposition of his reasons, first for deferring publication for three years and finally for publishing, constitutes an illuminating reflection by a mind of unusual clarity on the relations between scientific integrity and moral responsibility.

Whether a discipline formed by this empirical method would conform to the fifth criteria, that of stimulating further scientific research, can hardly be judged in advance. Such stimulation has often resulted from the formulation of a conceptual system suggesting logical deductions and new observations or experiments. Mere classifications of facts have proved less stimulating.

THE CONCEPTUAL APPROACH

In the preceding chapter have been set forth five conceptions of the world which have been influential at different periods, in different countries, and in the minds of different persons. None of these conceptions has yet been developed into a unified discipline applicable to all situations and problems of international relations. International law has been developed by the *naturalists* from the conception of the world as a plan or rational idea, international politics from the conception of the world as equilibrium, international organization from the conception of the world as organization, and pacifism from the conception of the world as spiritual community. Political geography, the sociology of international relations and international communications have usually conceived the world as a field. It is possible that each of these five points of view might be broadened and formalized so as to integrate many if not all of the relevant disciplines. This has not been done and until such efforts have been made it will not be possible to determine which point of view is most satisfactory.

Some preliminary explorations are, however, possible. How might these conceptions be formalized and tested? An objective *concept* as distinct from a subjective *conception*, must be represented by a word, a model, a form, a symbol or other sign so defined that its application or meaning can be identically interpreted by any one (22). The word *tree* is an objective concept if it is so defined that all people will reach the same conclusion in designating an object as a tree or not a tree. Logical positivists (32) and general semanticists (15) seem to agree that such definitions must ultimately be operational, that is, they must consist of instructions for doing or observing. The term *tree* can never be meaningfully defined to persons who have never seen a tree, or a picture of a tree, or the elements —trunk, branches, leaves—of which a tree is composed. Consequently the definition of a tree ultimately must consist of instructions on where to go to see one, or a picture of one, or how to combine elements with which the person is familiar to make a tree. "Knowledge of acquaintance," linking symbols with experience, must precede "knowledge about," linking symbols with symbols. In the terminology suggested in Chapter 3 an informational proposition to be convincing must rest on definitions referring to "knowledge of acquaintance," but a formulating proposition may be correct which rests only on definitions referring to "knowledge about."

In this section the possibility will be considered of formulating the conceptions of the world discussed in Chapter 30 as objective concepts, and of applying to these concepts the criteria suggested at the beginning of this chapter.

The world as plan. A plan is a form, order, design, or idea to which phenomena, with all their variety and change, persistently conform. It may be transcendent above or immanent within the phenomena. A concept of the world as a plan implies that the world can be formulated in a few postulates, whether as goals or as conditions, and that its past, present, and future can be deduced by logic from those assumptions. Put otherwise, the world is conceived as an entity the essential properties of which persist.

This concept of the world has dominated western thought inspired by Greek philosophy, Christian theology, and Renaissance rationalism. All assumed that the universe was rational and that rationality is a function of mind. Theists held that it existed in the mind of God before creation; humanists that it existed in the mind of man endowed by God or nature with reason; and pantheists that it existed in itself, that the universe was both mind and matter.

To explain why western man has tended to conceive his world as a plan, idea, or entity is not to demonstrate that this conception can be formulated as a concept susceptible of verification or, if it can, that relations deduced from it would prove valid or valuable. There have always been empiricists, atomists, nominalists, and pluralists who have questioned this conception, and modern science, with its ideas of evolution, of relativity, and of uncertainty, has moved away from it.

Many international lawyers and international moralists have, however, attempted such formulations in terms of more or less precision and in systems more or less logically articulated. Assuming, therefore, that a precise plan of the world can be formulated, how would a discipline of international relations based on it be likely to pass the five tests suggested at the beginning of this chapter?

A discipline constructed upon such a concept could pass the test of internal consistency, but, in proportion as it did so, it would probably fail in the test of observation. The systems of natural law developed by Pufendorf and Wolff and the systems of history developed by Hegel and Marx exhibited a measure of logical articulation but they have not proved of great value for predicting or controlling the future, or for explaining the past. The *determinism* or *historicism* inherent in the concept of the world as a plan seems unadapted to the degree of freedom and unpredictability which both observation and introspection disclose in human affairs. It seems improbable that the destiny of the world was inherent in its origin, that every situation of the world determines that which follows, and that choice either is an illusion or is determined by criteria which are themselves determined by the past. In any case the complexity of the relations of causes, including as they do ideal ends or values, is such as to make highly improbable any formula of absolute prediction. Propositions useful for prediction and control can only state probabilities with considerable margins of error, not logical inferences from absolute principles, propositions, or formulae. The past, present, and future of man and the world does not seem to be an entity, the total configuration of which is determined and only wants to be discovered.

While the principle of parsimony urges continuous effort to reduce a discipline of international relations to a logical system developed from precise postulates, the intransigence of the materials makes it unlikely that this can be done, consistently with observations, unless assumptions are greatly multiplied—this in fact is the meaning of the present division of international relations into many disciplines, each with its own body of definitions and assumptions. Biology, when conceived as an absolute idea of creation in the mind of God assumed that each of the innumerable species of plants and animals was a distinct concept or essence. The concept of organic evolution made it possible to demonstrate the natural origin of species, thus greatly reducing the number of essences in the discipline. Subsequently the concept of the organic world as a statistical field in which species, defined as differential gene frequencies, are subjected to certain measurable pressures for change, has further reduced the assumptions of biology. It appears quite probable that parsimony in the assumptions of the discipline of international relations can be achieved through conceiving the world as something other than a plan or idea.

The practical effect of concepts of the world as plan depend upon the assumption made concerning the source of the plan. If the plan is attributed to God, whose mind is inaccessible to the average man, a mundane interpreter is necessary and that interpreter must have authority to induce acceptance of his revelation, to eliminate inconsistencies certain to arise from individual interpretations of holy writ, and to settle secular controversies. This argument was vigorously set forth in the early fourteenth century by Dante (9), speaking for the cause of the Emperor, and by Pope Boniface VIII speaking for his own cause. Thus interpreted, the universal plan rests on faith in the interpreter rather than on the reason of the average man, and has proved of little use as a basis for harmony among peoples who enjoy freedom of expression and a high degree of control over their governments. This conception of the world has, therefore, been best adapted to absolutistic governments in a position to control the opinion of the people subject to them—to popes, emperors, kings ruling by divine right, or dictators ruling by right of power. If the plan or idea is attributed to history, accessible by suitable reading, or to nature, accessible to the average man through introspection or observation, it need not be inconsistent with democracy, but interpretations of the plan will be so numerous and varied as to be useless for prediction or control.

Any concept of the world as plan implies that the future is predestined or predetermined and tends to promote belief either in fatalism destructive of human effort or in dogmatism calling for conversion or destruction of the infidel, heretic, or deviationist. For this reason, *rationalism* in respect to human affairs has tended to support absolutism in government, whether of the nation, of the world, or of the universe. This was indicated by the prevalence of benevolent despotism, cosmopolitan imperialism, and universal deism in the thought of the European *Enlightenment*. If the plan is to be effective, whatever its source, it must be interpreted by a determinate authority. Such an authority was demanded, not only by monarchists and imperialists but also by rationalists such as Bodin, Hobbes, and Rousseau, giving rise to the concept of *sovereignty*. Rationalism, it is true, in basing knowledge and authority on human reason and agreement, rather than on supernatural revelation or social tradition, inspired the constitutional democracy of Locke, Montesquieu, and Jefferson, but these writers, proceeding from empirical philosophies, construed *natural law* in human affairs as modern scientists construe it in nonhuman affairs. They did not consider it an absolute system but a tentative formulation of human experience to be continually reinterpreted in the light of changing circumstances (25). It could not be relied upon to protect the *natural rights* of man if its interpretation were left to individual judgment, to an absolute ruler, or even to a court guided by an absolute law. In this spirit it has been said that the task of the Supreme Court of the United States is to "balance the conflicting claims of liberty and authority" in a "pluralistic society," and, avoiding the "tyranny of labels" to judge cases "in a framework of circumstances rather than of concepts"

(31). The theory and practice of constitutional and democratic government has developed less from the concept that the state is a plan than from the concept that it is an equilibrium or an organization. Concepts of the world as a plan seem to have supported values of absolutism rather than of democracy.

Have concepts of this kind contributed to the development of a discipline of international relations? During the seventeenth and eighteenth centuries, while rational concepts of the universe were stimulating research in the physical sciences, rational concepts of the human world were encouraging research in the social sciences, including international relations. This research was, however, less fruitful in the case of international relations than in that of astronomy or physics. In this field, the greatest triumphs of the rationalist approach were probably in the international law of Grotius and the international economics of Adam Smith. In both, however, concepts of a rational order were influenced by, if not subordinated to, concepts of equilibrium and organization.

It is doubtless true that the effort of science to develop disciplines which conform both to observation and logic will be encouraged if scientists believe that a logical order is inherent in phenomena. A person convinced that the field of his interest is a chaos is not likely to devote himself wholeheartedly to discovering its order. Nevertheless modern scientists, inspired by the idea that order is less an inherent characteristic of all phenomena than a characteristic which may be successfully imputed to some ranges of phenomena by looking at them or manipulating them in the right way, have been no less active than those of the age of rationalism (29). If science is to invent rather than to discover order, to many its lure may be even greater. In fact the most productive social scientists, even of the Enlightenment, attributed social order to artificial agreements, institutions and laws. The *social contract* converted the chaotic state of nature to the order of society.

We may conclude that a concept of the world as a plan may encourage research, but it will be research in the logical development of ideas rather than in the broadening of empirical knowledge. So far as ideas are related by logic, they are likely in this field to resist testing by observation or practice. Perhaps no better illustration can be found than in studying the casuistry of organizations professing rigid ideologies in reconciling their behavior with their doctrines.

Actually, when conceptions of the world as plan have functioned, they have done so as *developmental constructs* or affective hypotheses, rather than as scientific concepts (23). In this sense they have expressed a possible future of the world which if sufficiently accepted may eventually be realized. They are designed as guides to education, propaganda, evaluation, and conduct, and, far from assuming determinism, they have assumed that the future of the world is to be made by human belief and activity. Their frequent insistence upon the inevitability of realization, whether through a foreordained theological plan or an inherent order of natural justice or historical determinism, should thus be interpreted, not as asserting that the idea has absolute validity, but as asserting its possibility and its utility in influencing human beliefs. Men find it easy to believe and to adapt their behavior to what they are convinced is inevitable. Thus the arts of propaganda recognize that half the battle is won if people can be convinced that realization of the desired end is certain. The certainty of victory of our side and defeat of the enemy is the universal slogan in wars and election campaigns. A *scientific concept* and a *developmental construct* differ in that the latter urges continuous reappraisal of the probability and the desirability of realization and so accepts the *inevitability of realization* in a highly pragmatic sense. The construct continually reconstructs itself. A conception of the world, elaborated and continually re-elaborated as a developmental construct is, therefore, more suitable as the foundation for a discipline of international relations than is an absolute idea, but such a construct approaches the conception of the world as equilibrium or as organization.

The world as equilibrium. An equilibrium is a relationship among the forces operating upon or within an entity or group of entities so that the whole manifests in some degree some form of stability. The whole lacks the logical structure of a plan or the functional structure of an organization, and its stability is explained not by its principles but by the properties of its parts, the relations among them, and the forces influencing them. A concept of the world as equilibrium implies that the forces influencing, and the distances separating, the collective systems of action which are its major components can be roughly measured and from these measurements probable changes in the world can be inferred and perhaps regulated. Such a concept can at best yield a degree of probability in prediction and control not the certainty which would be possible if the world were a rational plan or idea.

Concepts of the world as equilibrium have inspired many scientific observers. The classical atomists—Democritus, Lucretius, and the Epicureans—conceived the entities of nature as equilibria manifesting varying degrees of stability among the atoms moving in the void. The mathematical precision of Newton's system supported a concept of the world as a plan, but he attributed the motion of the planets to an equilibrium among heavenly bodies moving in space under control of the centrifugal force of inertia and the centripetal force of gravitation. Concepts of equilibrium have been applied by ecologists to the organic population of an area, by physiologists to the system of the body, and by sociologists and anthropologists to cultures and societies. A concept of balance of power among states and of checks and balances among the organs of constitutional governments and international organizations have been utilized by political scientists.

Scientists tend to see all entities or conditions which are relatively permanent as the consequence of some sort of equilibrium among forces inherent in their structure and the relation of their parts. By opposing one another, these forces create for a time a stalemate in the general process of change. Scientists have characterized equilibria, not only as stable or unstable, but also as static, dynamic, oscillating, or adaptive (45). A mass of material is available to support concepts of the order of both nature and man as complicated, interrelated equilibria of equilibria. How would a discipline of international relations based on such a concept meet the tests?

It would probably be easier to reconcile such a discipline with observation than with logic. Concepts of equilibrium do not lend themselves to precise logical deduction but have to rest on the calculation of probabilities.

From the point of view of parsimony, concepts of the world as equilibrium appear to have advantages. Such concepts were given precise meaning in the physical sciences where forces could be accurately measured and their parameters defined. There they served to unify varied phenomena. Efforts to develop such concepts in the social sciences have been less fruitful. The conception of equilibrium has, it is true, been interpreted with sufficient breadth and flexibility to embrace much of the field of international relations, but its flexibility and wealth of connotations has encouraged ambiguity of meaning and vagueness of inference. The balance of power has tended to become a historical or political principle, giving a literary unity to large bodies of material or a popular unity to various policies, rather than to develop scientific concepts providing the basis for a precise discipline useful for prediction or control. Only as methods are devised for measuring the forces whose equilibrium makes for stability, and defining operationally the conditions effecting them, can scientific concepts be formulated and a discipline developed from them. Some efforts have been made to this end (13, 27, 45, 47).

From the point of view of values, the conception of equilibrium gains support from Aristotle's ethics. Although "the philosopher's" logical method tended toward ideological absolutes, in practical affairs he emphasized the virtue of the *via media* or the policy of balance. Practical moralists have often argued in the manner of Aristotle that extremes are presumptively bad and moderation is good. In politics particularly it has been urged that compromise is the highest value. This moral position suggests that the world itself is an equilibrium of values and that political action should seek to maintain the coexistence of, and balance among, divergent value systems and the power systems sustaining them.

The concept of *practical judgment* resulting from *sufficient reason* derived from a balancing of considerations for and against a course of action has been supported by philosophical idealists like Descartes. "In relation to practice," he wrote, "it is sometimes necessary to adopt, as if above doubt, opinions which we discern to be highly uncertain" (10). "Every year if not every day we have to wager our salvation upon some prophecy based upon imperfect knowledge," said Justice Holmes (17). In making practical decisions of policy statesmen balance and weigh alternatives unless necessity leaves only one course. Even though in public they may assert allegiance to principles, they seldom make decisions by abstract reasoning. They think practically rather than *theoretically*. If it is indeed wise to balance considerations in arriving at practical decisions and actions, this might be because we are ignorant and the average of errors will approach the truth, but it may also be because the world is an equilibrium which can only be maintained by weighing the consequences of alternative actions. This method has been urged as especially appropriate in the study of foreign policy and international politics (4).

It has already been noticed that many seekers after stability in government think it more likely to be found by balancing developing opinions and forces in a constitutional system than by establishing an ultimate authority capable of solving all disputes. Similarly, advocates of diplomatic action to maximize the stability of the balance of power like David Hume (18) and George Kennan (21) have opposed the advocates of more centralized world federation like the Abbé St. Pierre (36) and Giuseppe Borgese (3).

Concepts of equilibrium support values of moderation rather than of reform. They appeal to the Edmund Burkes seeking stability rather than the Jean Jacques Rousseaus seeking progress. Studies of international relations based on such concepts have been no more vulnerable to moral protest than those based on a particular idea or plan, even though ardent advocates of ideologies of opposing types—radical and reactionary, democratic and autocratic, pacifistic and militaristic, internationalist and nationalist—have often attacked them as lacking in *idealism* or *realism* or both.

Concepts of the world as equilibrium have stimulated much research in international relations. These researches include analyses and measurements of the factors of national power and of the conditions leading to the rise and fall of a state's power position. They also include measurements of the various aspects of distance between states, analyses of the relations of these distances to the balance of power, and determination of the factors leading to the deterioration or progress of balance of power systems. Constructive studies have been made of methods for stabilizing the equilibrium of the world by such means as increasing the number of power centers, grouping states in regions, organizing them in international institutions, and developing opinions and parties across state boundaries in order to make the equilibrium more complicated and more stable (27, 45, 47). A discipline which has produced such results, even though lacking the stimulus of precise logic, seems well adapted to encouraging research and continually improving itself.

In summary, it may be said that concepts of the world as equilibrium, in the simple form usually set forth, conform to observations in certain periods and places of world history but do not conform to all history. No such concept has provided the basis for a universally applicable discipline of international relations. Such a concept cannot in itself explain the process of transition from a world of equilibrium to a world of empire, of international organization or of something else, nor can it suggest practical policies for preventing, for effecting, or for regulating such a transition. General acceptance of a discipline based on the concept of equilibrium may in fact impede thought on the possibilities of fundamental change.

Concepts of world equilibrium, if formulated in terms broad enough to permit of general applicability, have been so lacking in clarity as to make logical inference of their consequences and tendencies difficult if not impossible. What are the entities whose opposition is deemed to maintain the equilibrium? How is the power of each to be measured? Does power refer to a desirable goal or to an inherent property of these entities? Does power include moral as well as material factors? Does equilibrium refer to a condition of stability changing only gradually, or does it permit of oscillations of great duration and amplitude? If these questions are answered with due consideration of all relevant factors in a variety of historical times and places, the concept becomes so vague that it cannot be tested by objective observation or historical records, or else it becomes so complicated as to approach the concepts of the world as an organization or as a field.

The world as an organization. An organization is a structure or process composed of parts related, interacting, or functioning in subordination to the whole. In social organizations the whole is characterized by purposes, and by controls of the organisms, persons, or suborganizations which constitute its parts, so that it can adapt itself to changing conditions, make decisions, and achieve its goals. In proportion as the subordination of parts to whole become instinctive and extreme, a social organization approaches a biological organism as in the case of social insects. A social organization differs from a social plan in that it has structure and adaptability, and from a social equilibrium in that the whole dominates over the parts. The parts are related logically in a plan, mechanically in an equilibrium, and functionally in an organization. The concept of organization is, however, less precise than that of plan or that of equilibrium. A social group may be organized much or little, and opinions may differ on whether it is organized at all. A concept of the world as organization implies that the structure and processes of mankind as a whole can be so described that purposes and controls can be in a measure inferred.

Concepts of the world as an organization have been supported by observations of phenomena in both the organic and social realms. Differentiation of function, parts functioning in the interests of the whole, central directives, levels of initiative, hierarchies of authority, and complex systems of communication are the essence of biological organisms and of social organizations. Differences in the complexity of organizations and in the adequacy of their adaptation to the environment are familiar notions influenced by the theory of evolution, which according to Herbert Spencer, is "an integration of matter and concomitant dissipation of motion; during which the matter passes from an indefinite, incoherent homogeneity to definite, coherent heterogeneity" (40). The world has logical, physical, and human aspects, respectively lying in the realms of ideas, mechanisms, and societies. Those who conceive it as an organization apply biological and social concepts to the physical and to the logical, as well as to the human, world, those who conceive it as an equilibrium apply mechanical concepts to all three, while those who conceive it as a plan apply logical concepts to all three.

Philosophers have utilized the concept of organization in their theoretical systematizations of knowledge. Practitioners have utilized it in their arrangements for effecting collective adjustments and decisions, and for co-ordinating decision-makers with one another and with their advisors (6). Social scientists have written of the organization of thought, of will, and of happiness in the great society to better meet its problems (44). Monists, whether pantheistic or materialistic, rejecting the dualism of mind and matter and the pluralism of opposing forces and initiatives, have conceived the universe as one mind-in-matter, one god-immanent-in-all, or one-in-many, as did Spinoza and Leibnitz in the seventeenth century, and Fechner, Haeckel, and Ostwald in the nineteenth century. Such conceptions tend to merge into the mystical or spiritual view of the world. The concept of the world as organization may thus be viewed as an effort to synthesize the mechanical and the spiritual conceptions.

In the nineteenth and twentieth centuries both writers and statesmen seeking for stability in world affairs increasingly applied the concept of organizing varied interests to solve problems, in contrast to the medieval tendency to establish authority in order to realize an idea, and the eighteenth century tendency to balance power in the interest of stability. The International Unions, the League of Nations, the United Nations, and the Specialized Agencies manifested this tendency which had come to dominate thought about states and other groups. After organic evolution became the vogue, following the publication of Darwin's work, political entities have been thought of as organizations or even as organisms rather than as systems of checks and balances or realizations of plans or ideas. Modern sociology developed from that conception and modern political science has paid much attention to it. How would a discipline based on this conception meet the tests?

General social disciplines based on concepts of organization have tended to assume the form of descriptive and historical analyses, as did Spencer's Synthetic Philosophy and the sociological philosophies of Comte and Ward. Facts have been fitted into an organizational framework, but concepts of organization have lacked operative and measurable qualities, permitting of precise inference and verification by experiment or observation. Disciplines developed from such concepts have failed to meet the tests of precise logic and observation which might make them useful for prediction and control. Recent studies in communication and administration have sought to remedy this defect (39). Detailed studies of administrative, legal, and political arrangements and procedures have thrown important light, both theoretical and practical, on the conditions of effectiveness in the processes of dispute settlement and decision-making. Such studies may in time be integrated into a general discipline of international relations from the organizational point of view (41, 44).

The test of parsimony has been met by general studies of the world or the universe conceived as an evolving organization. The comprehensiveness, unity, and comprehensibility of the works of Comte, Spencer, and Ward brought admiration from many and inspiration to some, but utilization by few. They were works of philosophical art rather than of pure or applied science. On the other hand the empirical studies of administrative, legal, and political processes and organizations have not yet been unified by general concepts, though progress in this direction has been made by students of political science, public administration, law, and economics (39).

The concept of organization has value implications. It has led some to identify body and mind and has been thought by some to oppose freedom of the will. This conclusion, which might be justified if the term *organism* were applied to the world, may be avoided if the term *organization*, not incompatible with certain meanings of dualism, is employed. Concepts of organization suggest greater freedom in developing suitable adjustment of man to his environment than do concepts of equilibrium. The issue of socialism v. individualism, depends on the degree of centralization of organization, not on the concept of organization itself.

Concepts of international organization proved stimulating to research in the nineteenth century. Empirical studies of the procedures of negotiation, mediation, conciliation, arbitration, and adjudication were suggested, as were studies of the history, structure, scope, functions, and processes of regional and universal international organizations. Philosophical studies were suggested of the meaning, conditions, and processes of social evolution and progress as applied to the world community and international organizations. Each nation, guided by the interests, inherent in its structure and origin, interacts with others and with the environment thus evolving international organizations. Nations also co-operate consciously to realize common values and purposes under the objective conditions with which they are confronted, thus progressing to higher forms of organization.

Concepts of international organization have recently inspired studies of the processes of negotiation and conference, utilizing the psychological insights developed by the disciplines of *psychoanalysis* and *group dynamics*. The simplest case of two diplomats negotiating, each operating as representatives of their nations with varying degrees of freedom and instruction, might be studied utilizing the concept of interaction between the negotiators and giving due consideration to the personality and role of each. The study of such a simple negotiation could be complicated by considering multilateral conferences and studying the influence of numerous conditions of documentary preparation, interpretation, international tension, third party pressures, and so forth (43). Detailed examination of the history and functioning of international organizations and conferences have been made from this point of view. The comparison and analysis, of types and processes of international organization, bilateral and multilateral; political, legal, and administrative; centralized and decentralized; institutionalized and *ad hoc*, present a vast field of study which can be and has been explored from this point of view.

Concepts of organization applied to the world have probably produced more research in the field of international relations than any other concept, in the twentieth century. Whether a discipline based on such a concept would be more fruitful than one based on a concept of equilibrium is uncertain. Each type has flourished in favorable atmospheres of opinion, organizational studies in periods of optimism, equilibrium studies in periods of pessimism.

To summarize, concepts of the world as organization are limited in applicability unless the term *organization* is defined sufficiently broadly to include not only governments, federations, confederations, and international unions, and their processes, but also political systems organized only by diplomacy, cultural uniformities maintained only by custom, and spiritual unions maintained by propaganda. If the term is narrowly defined it may serve as a developmental construct, useful in education and propaganda to direct attention to, and build opinion about, one potentiality of the future which may, by these means, eventually become susceptible of verification. In the broad sense concepts of equilibrium and organization merge into one another and also into concepts of community.

The world as a spiritual community. A spiritual community is a group, the members of which are harmoniously united by common attitudes and sentiments. Concepts of such a community have lacked the precision of a plan, the measurability of an equilibrium, or the describability of an organization. They have hardly been concepts at all but vague and mystical conceptions. Conceptions of the world as a spiritual community, in which all persons will come to love one another and to co-operate for common goals manifesting their common humanity and their common values, have been developed by medieval Christendom, medieval Islam, and modern communism. Such a mystical cosmopolitanism has inspired all universal religions of the spirit. Theologies have sought to crystallize such vague conceptions into ideologies, and ecclesiastical organizations have sought to give them practical meaning. Such a conception figured in the thinking of Socrates, Buddha, and Jesus and in Hinduism, Stoicism, and the *Enlightenment* of modern Europe. Pacifists and humanitarians inspired by this conception have appeared in all lands and in all periods of history, but particularly in periods following great wars and revolutionary disturbances (45). The modern movement for a universal commonwealth of man springs from this conception rather than from the more structural conception of international organization (3, 38).

Evidence for this conception is introspective rather than observational. To some people it is self-evident that mankind is a spiritual community. The realization of this sentiment depends on universal conversion to that state of mind. The *brotherhood of man* preached by the *universal* religions appears to be given only lip service by many who profess it. Among most peoples loyalty to lesser groups, to a particular religion, culture, or nation takes precedence over loyalty to the human race or to the world community (6a).

Some administrators of international organizations believe that a sentiment of world community can only become universal as a consequence of world organization. The first conception of universal religion may have been developed by the Pharaoh Ikhnaton after his empire had organized much of the middle east and may then have been transmitted from Egypt to the Jews by Moses, and in time to the other universal religions (38). Others think that international organization cannot be effective until a widespread sentiment of world community and world citizenship has developed (6a, 20). It may be that the sentiment of community and the structure of organization are interdependent. People have been welded into nations by strong governments and governments have functioned most effectively when their subjects had the potentiality of common nationality. Large-scale anarchies where people behave harmoniously because of sentiment are more familiar in literature than in history. Yet the conceptions of community and organization can be separated. Judaism existed for millennia as a community of the spirit with its members dispersed and divided among many states. On the other hand, the British Empire existed for centuries as an organization ruling peoples of different religion, culture, and nationality with little sense of community.

The conception of the world as a community of the spirit cannot be formulated as a scientific concept and is difficult to justify by objective observation. Such conceptions have rested on faith springing from mystic insight or from confidence in the revelations or insights of leaders. The will to believe, stimulated by the beauty of the vision, by its social value if realized, and by its spiritual value to the believer has accounted for the certainty of the faithful, rather than any conformity of the vision to present or past conditions of mankind.

Some cosmopolitans of the eighteenth century believed that *natural man* lived in a paradise controlled by sentiment rather than by authority, and a few anthropologists believe that before civilization had introduced property and class differentiations, war and strife were unknown. They point to the present behavior of the friendly Andamans, the Greenland Eskimos, and a few other isolated peoples (30), but these illustrations have been far from convincing, and it is safe to say that the world community has disclosed as much of strife as of harmony in history (45).

This conception is difficult to test by standards of internal consistency. The terms in which it has been expressed aim at persuasion, incitement, self-expression, or inspiration, rather than at information or formulation. Efforts to state the universal religions in logical form have converted them from spiritual visions to dogmatic theologies. The Bhagavadgita seems to reconcile participation in actual war with spiritual peace and to recommend training in the Karmayoga which will cultivate indifference to all things of the world including the suffering of the self and others. The Sermon on the Mount seems to reconcile the peace of the Kingdom of God with the strife of the world by urging the faithful to renounce violence and to endure martyrdom in the faith. Such expositions are addressed to the individual pointing ways to spiritual conversion adequate to meet fate with equanimity and can be deemed conceptions of the world only because of the implication that when all souls are thus converted harmony will prevail. Logical analysis of neither the ideas nor the words is applicable to these expositions. No deduction from what is known of human nature and human motivations supports the anticipation of harmony among all men, any more than what is known of biology supports the anticipation that the lion will peacefully lie down with the lamb. Such deductions suggest that the coexistence of love and hate, of co-operation and opposition, are to be expected in human relations, however much the forms of their expression may be modified by education and social arrangements. Efforts to apply to this conception tests of objective observation and logic misinterpret its intention.

This conception of the world may be both economical in its assumptions—love is enough—and valuable in its effects. To the individual it may bring the peace that passeth understanding. Its intention whether manifested by spiritual religion, by mysticism, or by poetry and the fine arts is not to explain man or the world but to create values and to inspire belief (45). Whether the values created and the beliefs inspired by any particular manifestation of this conception are indeed the best for all mankind can only be tested by faith or by subsequent experience. The faithful of different revelations have clung to their visions and have often rationalized and organized them, and fought one another, each seeking to promote the triumph of his own. None has been universally realized in human history. Introspection and history may in time tell a different story, but in the meantime, more objective approaches will continue to be utilized to ameliorate human conditions.

This conception may seriously affect existing social values such as the solidarity of the nation-states. If the population of certain states accepted sentiments putting world loyalty first, they might make the state an easy victim of neighbors whose citizens were not so affected. The problem of Christian pacifism faced Rome when attacked by barbarians, and the church led by Augustine reinterpreted its doctrine. It accepted the civic obligation of Christians to defend the empire, which had become formally Christian, in "just wars." As Rome approached a *universal state*, it was easier for the Church to reconcile loyalty to mankind with loyalty to the state than has been the case with Christian citizens of modern nations (7, 45). Within the latter only a few relatively small sects are prepared to put pacifism ahead of civic loyalty. The concept of a world community is not likely to make for peace unless it is accepted simultaneously by the vast majority of peoples in all sections of the world, or unless an effective universal organization is developed within whose protection it may exist.

This conception has been less fruitful in encouraging research than in inciting practical activity to make converts. Some sociological and psychological research has, however, sought to formulate the kinds of information and attitude which would inspire acceptance of the conception of a world community (46). Some research on methods of mediation, conciliation, and conference have been inspired by active pacifists. Research in the fields of education and communication have examined the methods which might create sentiments of world citizenship. Undoubtedly such research is hampered by the prevailing sentiment of nationalism which often regards efforts to convert people to world citizenship as subversive. Universal religions, whatever their theory, hesitate to engage in activities that would encourage universal loyalties above that of the state.

The concept of the world as a spiritual community may be self-corrective. The various interpretations of the way by which the individual may control the conflicts of his biological urges with the attitudes conducive to a spiritual world community, of the old Adam with the Kingdom of God, of the id with the super-ego, may correct one another as experience with each increases. Is the way of the Upanishads, of Moses, of Confucius, of Gautama, of Socrates, of Jesus, of Mohammad, or of Marx most effective? Perhaps one is best adapted to certain conditions of society and to certain types of man, and another to other conditions and types (28)? Perhaps there are similarities in all these ways that rest on characteristics of human nature common to all man? Perhaps experience will develop ways better than any which have so far been revealed or practiced to achieve desired attitudes? It can be said that for many persons the spiritual approach to conduct and to a point of view above the world has been successful in the life of the individual. It cannot be said that the spiritual way will forever fail in its effort to create a universal and harmonious commonwealth of man. It does not appear, however, that this conception can serve as the foundation for a scientific discipline of international relations.

To summarize the concept of the world as a spiritual community can hardly be defined in terms which make possible either historical testing or logical inference. Its very vagueness, however, may add to its merit as a developmental construct useful for guiding individual behavior. Such sentiments as the brotherhood of man, universal spiritual harmony, a classless society, a good neighbor to everyone, are universally attractive, because susceptible to interpretation by everyone according to his inclination but so vague as to be hardly useful as developmental constructs for social policy. Their significance is in the realm of individual self-control and adaptation. As guides to group policy or action they have little utility and are concepts upon which a scientific discipline could hardly be formed that would conform to the criteria suggested.

The world as field. A field is a system defined by time and space or by analytical co-ordinates, and by the properties, relations, and movements of the entities within it. The concept assumes that the characteristics of the field and of the entities within it reciprocally influence one another. Description of the field therefore provides a basis for explaining the past and in a measure predicting the future of these entities. While more complex and more resistant to logical formulation than the concepts of plan and equilibrium, this concept is more susceptible of objective description and logical analysis than are the concepts of organization and community. Furthermore, it is applicable to all situations. While situations frequently manifest spiritual community, organization, equilibrium or even logical structure only potentially if at all, every situation can be conceived as a field by the postulation of suitable co-ordinates.

After Europeans in the fifteenth and sixteenth centuries had explored new continents, disclosing peoples whose manners and customs were unfamiliar, they began to conceive the world as a field of human opportunity rather than as a plan of God. Writers like Montaigne and Montesquieu, reading reports of travellers and geographers, were more impressed by the variety and unexpectedness of human societies than by their conformity to an idea or plan. With this expanded view of the human race they found it difficult to think of mankind even potentially as either a universal organization or a universal spiritual community. As has usually been true of historians and geographers since the time of Herodotus, they emphasized the unique and the curious.

The inductive philosophy of Bacon and the inductive psychology of Hobbes as developed by Locke and Hume encouraged empiricism, repudiated certainty, and paved the way for the pluralism of American pragmatism, and the emancipation of science from the rationalism of Descartes. Bacon broke from medieval rationalism by urging the practical value of observing nature, and subsequently, science, however much it may have profited by the method of deduction from universal concepts, has contributed more to man's mastery of nature by giving observation priority over logic. To the philosophical empiricists, the world was a field in which man and society might behave in ways which no reason could have foretold. Science was more concerned with statistical correlations and degrees of probability than with causal relations demonstrated by pure reason (29).

This has been no less true in the social than in the natural sciences. Field surveys of social conditions, of economic resources, and of public opinion have proved more useful than theories deduced from premises about human nature. Modern legislation and public policy is based upon statistical surveys and factual reports rather than upon deductions from natural law or universal principles of justice (35).

The concept of the world as a field begins with faith in the existence of time and space, within which things exist and events occur. If the Book of Genesis was the Bible of the world as idea, Euclid's geometry was the Bible of the world as field. Changing concepts of the nature of time and space have not modified the scientific faith in their reality in spite of Kant's criticism. Einstein's four dimensional curved time-space may differ from Euclid's three dimensional space, but they are both real fields.

Modern astronomy and physics with improved instruments of observation have conceived the physical universe as a field, full of irregularities, the total configuration of which at any moment influences what happens in any part. The ecologists picture distinctive biological environments as fields in which competition and symbiosis develop order among the various species of plants and animals, accommodating each to a particular niche. Modern social ecologists and geographers similarly picture the relations of the physical and social environment to the forms, functions, and changes of institutions and societies. Students of communication have considered populations as fields within which individuals are connected by communication networks manifesting varying degrees of complexity and discontinuity, engendering groups, opinions, policies, and decision-making structures (11, 23).

Scientists have utilized field concepts to locate entities and exhibit their relationships and changes not only in respect to time and space, but also in respect to other significant variables selected as analytical co-ordinates. Modern anthropologists consider each culture as a field constituted by a complex of symbols, values, ideas, and practices interpreting the environment and reflected, somewhat imperfectly, in the attitudes, opinions, and behavior of the people (37). Sociologists have conceived a community or a society as a field defined by structural and functional co-ordinates determining values, procedures, and roles (45). Dynamic psychologists treat the mind as a field or *life space* reflecting, with distortions due to peculiarities of culture and personality, the situation which faces the individual, and locating the goals, obstacles, and alternative courses which he envisages at the moment (24). Geneticists have conceived the factors responsible for organic evolution as the co-ordinates of an analytical field. Every species has a position in this field determined by the average gene frequencies of its members and by the pressures of variation, mutation, hybridization, selection, drift, and other factors tending to modify these frequencies. The contours of this field indicate the relative environmental adaptability of a particular gene frequency. The more abundant species will presumably be located at the higher elevations. The distance between two peaks and the height of the saddle between indicates the probability that parts of a species located near one will so change in gene frequency under the pressures bearing upon it as to become a new species able to exploit the opportunities of the higher peak (48).

Scientific thought has tended to move away from the dualistic conception that the world is an idea, and the monistic conceptions that it is an organization or a community, to the pluralistic conceptions that it is an equilibrium (homeostasis) or a field. Its characteristics are to be found by exploration rather than by deduction or insight.

A discipline of international relations developed from the concept that the world is a field could more easily meet the test of conformity to observation than that of conformity to logic. Sociologists who have proceeded from the field concept of ecology have been criticized for lack of precision in their terminology and concepts (2). It has always taken time to develop logical systems that meet the test of conformity to accurate observation of the varied conditions and behaviors of nature. It took millennia before a logically consistent system was found which could be confirmed by observation of planetary motions. It is to be expected that it will take even longer to develop a system with even a modicum of logical rigor that conforms even in moderate degree to the more complicated human activity observed in the world and recorded by history.

The same conditions make it difficult for a discipline of international relations developed from field concepts to pass the tests of parsimony and elegance. Such a discipline tends to be merely descriptive or finds it necessary to invent new concepts for every area of study. The human desire for adventure and novelty may be satisfied, but the equally human desire for simplicity, harmony, and unity is balked by the untamed wilderness of the world as presented by such concepts. Only by an active imagination disciplined by the higher mathematics can order be imposed upon the wilderness.

Concepts of the world as a field of law and opinion tend to induce acceptance of a political system of freedom and democracy in which everyone can entertain and express values and opinions with the hope that the more suitable will survive and spread. This was said by Justice Holmes to be the theory of the United States Constitution (17) and it has been espoused by students of semantics. "Cultural institutions or evaluative habits," writes Hayakawa, "which inhibit communication or cause communication to miscarry are subversive of the cultural process" (15). The issue of freedom of communication has separated the United States from the Soviet Union by a wide gulf. The semanticists believe such gulfs might more easily be bridged if the language and logic of Aristotle defining reality by immutable concepts were superseded by those of Korzybski limiting the validity of all definitions to a particular time and place (15).

Concepts of the world as plan induce centralized empire, those of the world as equilibrium a decentralized balance of power, those of the world as organization a complicated world federation and those of the world as spiritual community a universal commonwealth of men. Concepts of the world as a field tend toward a system of regulation of maximum flexibility, guided by information of maximum comprehensiveness, to realize values of maximum acceptability, by methods of maximum efficiency. What these maxima might be could be determined only by quantification of the variables involved (47). Social psychologists have noticed that the rising generation in a shrinking, complicated, and changing world has tended to be guided by the opinion of the *peer-group* rather than by a *conscience* fixed by early education (33). Sociologists have pointed out that opinion, with its tides and currents, has changed from an object of scorn to a final court of appeal in political life (12). Such views rest upon a concept of the world as a field of changing opinion.

Applied to practical affairs, this concept probably supports liberty rather than order, democracy rather than absolutism, decentralization rather than centralization. Does it support war or peace? If the world is a field permitting indefinite possibilities of human action and behavior under different conditions there is nothing to inhibit freedom in politics and business. While some believe that unity of ideas, of organization, or of sentiment is necessary for peace, others point out that the efforts to realize such unities beyond the possibilities of the situation induce war, and that peace can only be found by general acceptance of the need for continuous accommodation to the differences actually characteristic of the field. The discovery of America, emancipated European man from the closed society of the Middle Ages, encouraged him to view the world as a field for investigation and exploration, and induced him to establish open societies putting freedom and opportunity ahead of order and law.

The concept of the world as a field has promoted much social science research. Geography, demography, technology, and anthropology have arisen from the curiosity of explorers and from their effort to give some order to the varied phenomena they found in different parts of the world. Systematic surveys in all fields—social, economic, political, and cultural— have been analyzed by statistical as well as by less refined methods, and have led to generalizations about the probabilities of such phenomena as violence, revolution and war, and to proposals of preventive and remedial action (23, 35, 45).

It cannot be said that the values supported by field concepts are less suitable guides for human action than those supported by other concepts, nor can it be said that field concepts would be less stimulating to fruitful research than any of the other concepts. Scientists have disputed on whether Bacon or Descartes gave the greater impetus to science. Both methods have doubtless been of importance. Science cannot progress without both induction and deduction. It cannot be said that curiosity and the expectation of variety is any less stimulating to mental activity than reflection and the expectation of rationality.

REFERENCES

1. ADLER, Mortimer, *How to Think About War and Peace* (New York, Simon and Schuster, 1944).
2. ALIHAN, Milla Aissa, *Social Ecology, a Critical Analysis* (New York, Columbia University Press, 1938).
3. BORGESE, G. A., *Foundations of the World Republic* (Chicago, University of Chicago Press, 1953).
4. Brookings Institution, *Major Problems of United States Foreign Policy, 1952-1953* (Washington, 1953).
5. BRUNSWIK, Egon, "The Conceptual Framework of Psychology," *International Encyclopedia of Unified Science*, Vol. 1, No. 10 (Chicago, University of Chicago Press, 1952).
6. BRYSON, Lyman, *The Communication of Ideas* (New York, Harper, 1948).
6a. BURROW, Trigant, *Science and Man's Behavior, the Contribution of Phylobiology* (New York, Philosophical Library, 1953).
7. CADOUX, C. J., *The Early Christian Attitude to War* (London, Headley, 1919).

8. CONANT, James B., *Science and Common Sense* (New Haven, Yale University Press, 1951).

9. DANTE, *De Monarchia*, Aurelia Henry, ed. (Boston, Houghton Mifflin, 1904).

10. DESCARTES, René, *Discourse on Method* (1637), Part VI.

11. DEUTSCH, Karl W., *Political Community at the International Level, Problems of, Definition and Measurement* (New York, Doubleday, 1954).

12. FARIS, Ellsworth, "Of Psychological Elements," *American Journal of Sociology*, Vol. 52 (September, 1936), p. 174.

13. FRIEDRICH, Karl J., *Foreign Policy in the Making* (New York, Norton, 1938).

14. GENTILI, Alberico, *De Jure Belli*, Libri Tres, English trans. by Rolfe (Washington, Carnegie Endowment for International Peace, 1933), Book I, Chap. 2.

15. HAYAKAWA, S. I., "Semantics, General," *Encyclopædia Britannica;* "Ten Eventful Years," 1947; also in *ETC*, Vol. 9 (Summer, 1952), pp. 243-257.

16. HOBBES, Thomas, *Leviathan* (1651).

17. HOLMES, Oliver Wendell, Jr., dissent in *Abrams v. U.S.*, 1919 (250 U.S. 616).

18. HUME, David, "Of the Balance of Power," *Philosophical Works*, Vol. 3 (Boston, 1854), pp. 364 ff.

19. HUXLEY, Julian, *Knowledge, Morality and Destiny* (Washington, William Alanson White Psychiatric Foundation, 1951).

20. International Congress on Mental Health, statement by International Preparatory Commission (London, August, 1948). See also World Federation of Mental Health, *Bulletin* (London, 1949).

21. KENNAN, George, *American Diplomacy, 1900-1950* (Chicago, University of Chicago Press, 1951).

22. LANGER, Suzanne, *An Introduction to Symbolic Logic*, 2nd ed. (New York, Dover Publications, 1953).

23. LASSWELL, Harold D., *The World Revolution of Our Time*, Radir Study (Stanford, Stanford University Press, 1951).

24. LEWIN, Kurt, *A Dynamic Theory of Personality* (New York, McGraw-Hill, 1935).

25. LOCKE, John, *Two Treatises of Government* (1690).

26. LORIMER, James, *Institutes of the Law of Nations* (Edinburgh, Blackwood, 1883), Vol. 1, pp. 9 ff.

27. MORGENTHAU, Hans J., *Politics Among Nations, the Struggle for Power and Peace*, 2nd ed. (New York, Knopf, 1954), p. 20.

28. MORRIS, Charles, *Paths of Life, Preface to a World Religion* (New York, Harper, 1942).

29. PEARSON, Karl, *The Grammar of Science* (London, Black, 1900).

30. PERRY, W. J., *The Growth of Civilization* (New York, Dutton, 1923).

31. PRITCHETT, C. Herman, *Civil Liberties and the Vinson Court* (Chicago, University of Chicago Press, 1954).

32. RAPAPORT, Anatole, *Operational Philosophy* (New York, Harper, 1953).

33. RIESMAN, David, in collaboration with DENNY, Reuel, and GLAZIER, Nathan, *The Lonely Crowd, A Study of the Changing American Character* (New Haven, Yale University Press, 1950).

34. ROUSSEAU, Jean Jacques, *The Social Contract* (1763).

35. Russell Sage Foundation, *A Bibliography of Social Surveys; Reports of fact-finding studies made as a basis for social action, arranged by subjects and localities,* Reports to January 1, 1928, by Allen Eaton and Shelby M. Harrison (New York, Russell Sage Foundation, 1930).

36. SAINT PIERRE, Abbé Charles Irenee Castel de, *Projet pour rendu la paix perpetuelle en Europe* (Utrecht, 1713-1717), 3 vols.

37. SARGENT, S. Stanfeld, and SMITH, Marian W., eds., *Culture and Personality* (New York, Viking Fund, 1949).

38. SCHUMAN, Frederick L., *The Commonwealth of Man* (New York, Knopf, 1952).

39. SIMON, Herbert A., "A Comparison of Organization Theories," *The Review of Economic Studies,* Vol. 20, No. 51 (1952-1953).

40. SPENCER, Herbert, *First Principles* (1862); (New York, Appleton, 1879). Chap. 17, p. 396.

41. STREIT, Clarence, *Union Now* (New York, Harper, 1939).

42. THURSTONE, L. L., *The Vectors of Mind* (Chicago, University of Chicago Press, 1935).

43. UNESCO, *The Technique of International Conferences,* a Progress Report on Research Problems and Methods (Paris, UNESCO, 1951).

44. WALLAS, Graham, *The Great Society* (New York, Macmillan, 1917).

45. WRIGHT, Quincy, *A Study of War* (Chicago, University of Chicago Press, 1942), pp. 158, 387 ff., 471 ff., 743 ff., 747, 1079 ff., 1302.

46. ———, ed., *The World Community* (Chicago, University of Chicago Press, 1948).

47. ———, *Problems of Stability and Progress in International Relations* (Berkeley, University of California Press, 1954).

48. WRIGHT, Sewall, "Evolution, Organic," *Encyclopædia Britannica.*

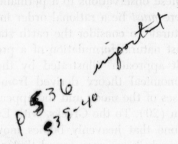

CHAPTER
32

The Form of a Discipline of International Relations

IT MAY BE that a discipline of international relations could be developed and its parts integrated on the basis of any one of the conceptions of the world which have been discussed. The actual trend of modern thought has been to abandon the conception of the world as plan, to assign the world as spiritual community to realms other than that of science, and to utilize in international relations the conceptions of the world as equilibrium, as organization, or as field. The last conception has the advantage of being applicable to all situations of international relations. Furthermore it may facilitate synthesis of what is valid or useful in the others.

THE EVOLUTION OF WORLD CONCEPTS

The history of the discipline of international relations suggests that different conceptions of the world are appropriate in different stages of its development. The more developed disciplines such as astronomy, physics, chemistry, biology, and psychology have employed different conceptions of their subject matter at different stages of their history. The concepts of *entity,* of *force,* of *process,* and of *relation* have tended respectively to be emphasized in successive stages in the history of each of these disciplines and each emphasis has given the discipline a different conception of its subject matter as a whole (34).

Astronomy began with observations of *entities*—the sun, moon, and planets and of their motions among the fixed stars—and the application

531

of reason to fit these observations to a permanent form or order. It was assumed that there *must* be a rational order in creation and in such an order it was "natural" to consider the earth stable. It has been pointed out that "the most natural formulation of a problem usually constitutes the most difficult approach" illustrated by the extreme complexity of Babylonian astronomical theory derived from the most obvious phenomena, the phases of the moon and the appearance of heavenly bodies above the horizon (20). To the Greeks, with Euclidian geometry, it was "natural" to assume that heavenly bodies moved around the earth in perfect circles though it was soon found that *epicycles* around points in the *cycles* had to be conceived to account for the observations (Ptolemy). More accurate observations suggested that the sun was stable and in the center and that the planets moved in elliptical orbits around it. These motions, it was found, could be accounted for by the balance of opposing *forces* of inertia and gravitation acting upon bodies in a frictionless space (Copernicus, Kepler, Newton). Subsequently the identification of the fixed stars as suns of different size, brightness, and color suggested a *process* of change in the physical character and motions of the heavenly bodies. At first this process was accounted for by the tendency of an originally diffuse distribution of matter in nebulae to concentrate under the influence of gravitational forces (Kant, Laplace). Later observations of displacement of spectral lines in distant galaxies and of the distribution of heavenly bodies made possible estimates of their ages and suggested an original concentration of matter and a process of continuous expansion and differentiation into numerous galaxies, each with billions of stars, some of them surrounded by satellites (Jeans, Eddington). Further analysis utilizing modern physical theories and observations with more powerful telescopes has led astronomers to conceive the universe as a field of *relations* in which magnetic, electrical, optical, and gravitational tensions at every point in time and space are a function of tensions at all other points, the whole influencing the evolution and changes of matter and motion. The universe may be infinite or it may be finite and expanding. The field cannot be defined by any absolute co-ordinates. Consequently all observations and calculations have to be relative to the time and place where made (Clerk-Maxwell, Einstein).

Physics was first guided by the "natural" idea that tangible *entities* rest or move toward the center of the earth unless a *force*, like that of a horse pulling a cart, is continually exerted upon them, and that space is always full because "nature abhors a vacuum" (Aristotle). Consideration of moving bodies like arrows and projectiles gradually developed the concept of *impetus*, or a *force* imparted to a body and continuing to move it for some time (Buridan), leading to the concepts of inertia, gravitation, and friction defined in terms of time, space, mass, and texture to account for the rest or motion of objects (Galileo, Newton). A "sea of air" exerting continuous but variable pressure around the earth (Torricelli, Boyle) and conveying sound waves, and an "ether" conveying optical and electrical waves in space were then conceived to account for *processes* of change, and for the impact of matter upon the senses. Finally time and space have been conceived as a four dimensional field defining and defined by the *relations* of matter and energy and of the electrons, protons, neutrons and photons which are the ultimate constituents of "matter-energy" (Clerk-Maxwell, Einstein, Rutherford, Planck, Bohr, Heisenberg) (5, 6).

Chemistry was first guided by the "natural" idea that earth, water, air, and fire were qualitative essences of every material *entity*, their proportions determining its properties (Greeks, alchemists). "Phlogiston," a substance or *force* was invented in early modern times to account for the transformation of matter in gradual oxidation, burning, or explosion. Tangible "atoms" combining according to their affinities in definite numbers to form tangible "molecules" were conceived as the elements of matter, their combinations accounting for the *processes* of chemical change (Lavoisier, Dalton). The *relations* of intra-atomic entities is now conceived as the basis of all matter and energy bringing chemistry and physics together (Rutherford) (6).

Biology began with the classification of biological *entities*—animals and plants—assuming that each species was immutable and independently created in accord with God's idea manifested by an apparently "natural" classification (Aristotle, Linaeus, Cuvier). The distinction between homology (similarity in origin) and analogy (similarity in function) inherent in this "natural" classification, led to the idea of evolution, verified by the paleontological record, by the geographical distribution of varieties and species, and by the practices of breeders of domestic animals. The *forces* of self-preservation and sexual attraction were invoked to account for selection and evolution in nature (Darwin). Studies of cytology, morphology, and ecology exhibiting the *processes* of life, the functioning of parts in the service of the whole, and the adaptation of the whole to its environment then became prominent. Finally the study of the *relation* of genes, whose combinations determine organic forms, forces, and processes in cells and in populations, made possible more precise explanations of organic evolution by establishing statistical relationships in a field. This facilitated prediction of the results of breeding and control of plant and animal types for human purposes (Mendel, Morgan, Fisher, S. Wright) (40).

Psychology began with a concept of mind as an *entity* with properties distinguishing it from matter and discoverable only by introspection (Aristotle, Descartes). The *forces* of sensation, linking mind to matter, and of association, uniting sensations into perceptions and conceptions, were more susceptible of objective observation and educational utilization (Hobbes, Locke, Hume). The *process* of stimulus and response governed by conditioned reflexes was utilized to account for observed behavior (Pavlov, Watson). The *relations* of complex mechanisms of the personality, involving conflict and choice within the field of the conscious or unconscious mind were analyzed by procedures involving introspection and observation to account for the interpretation of situations and for action (Freud, Lewin) (3).

In a manner similar to these disciplines, the subject matter of the social sciences—economics, political science, sociology, and anthropology— seems to have changed in successive periods from entities and forces to processes and relations, and these changes have induced changes in the conception of the world from an idea or an equilibrium to an organization or a field. Analysis of the materials in Chapters 4, 5, and 6 suggest such a development in the study of international relations.

This study was first concerned with the characteristics of social *entities* —individuals, groups, nations, and mankind as a whole, especially as manifested in law and history. The writers often hoped to discover the plan or idea of God, of nature, or of history in the belief that it would prove the key to conduct and to comprehension of the destiny of these entities.

Later studies of the arts of war and international politics dealt with the *forces* utilized by governments and other entities to maintain order or promote policy and the factors disturbing balance among them. Impersonal forces such as nationalism, imperialism, and militarism; religious, political, and economic interests; and pressures of population, technology, and ideology were also invoked to account for changes from periods of peace and order to periods of war and disorder.

More recently much study has been devoted to international organization, international economics, and the *processes* by which states, alliances, international organizations, empires, and other entities function with varying effectiveness to achieve human ends. The establishment of many international organizations during the last century, the use of new types of international procedure, and the availability of more materials on the traditional processes of diplomacy and conference have offered increasing opportunities for study from this point of view. The most recent tendency has been to analyze the *relations* between states by locating them in a multidimensional field defined by geographical and analytical co-ordinates. Quantitative variables, susceptible of measurement and of mathematical analysis, have been sought. The application of psychology, sociology, communications, and geography to international relations has made possible this development.

At all times many persons have rejected the methods of observation and logical analysis, whether applied to entities, forces, processes, or relations and have insisted that human affairs are different from the order of nature and must be studied by introspection or by attention to the insights of prophets and seers. Knowledge of the human spirit, to be obtained by self-discipline, they have considered the way to individual and social progress. Many people are guided by a faith springing from this hypothesis and the existence of such faiths influences human affairs, particularly international affairs. Attitudes and sentiments may transform the entities, modify the forces, and change the processes with which international relations is concerned. No method of study can ignore these subjective factors. Such sentiments can, however, be treated objectively as forces measured by their observable effects and a discipline, which seeks to test propositions by their conformity to observation and logic, can deal with sentiments only in this way.

In this respect, however, the social sciences may differ from the natural sciences. Individuals and organizations with whose acts the social sciences, and particularly international relations, are concerned, do not necessarily conform their acts to any conditions or formulae which past observation and principles of logic might disclose. Each acts according to its *interpretation* of the conditions, situations, and problems with which it is faced and this interpretation may result in action which is creative or capricious in the sense that it depends in large measure on subjective phenomena which cannot be examined by the observational and logical methods appropriate to the natural sciences. Such phenomena can only be examined through contact with the minds of the actors involved and this is possible only through communication utilizing language and other symbols (10, 18, 19, 31, 34, 35).

The interpretation of signs and symbols depends upon such objective knowledge as is obtainable about the language and the culture of the actor, about the role attributed to him in the culture, and about his personality peculiarities and the criteria by which he makes choices, but this knowledge depends in some measure upon the investigator's subjective knowledge of his own mental processes.

The natural sciences rely ultimately upon observations and experiments, the reproducibility of which depends upon the similarity of sensory experiences of individuals, especially the sense of sight in reading dials, comparing measurements, and observing through telescopes and microscopes, and upon the similarity of their experiences of logical inference, especially in mathematical reasoning. The social sciences, however, depend upon the similarity of other experiences, especially in the realms of feeling, evaluation, and volition. Logical positivists, baffled by the problem of defining operationally, terms which refer to such experiences, question whether they mean anything (25). The methods of cultural anthropology, literary criticism, the historical sciences, and law seek to minimize the dependence upon introspective evidence in the process of interpreting such terms, but this dependence remains greater than in the natural sciences. The courts have said that a state of mind is a fact ascertainable

by evidence as is any other fact, but the evidence for determining motives, intentions, purposes, compulsions, interpretations of situations, and
other states of mind leaves much more room for divergent inference than
does the evidence for more tangible facts. The major task of the social
sciences is not to determine the relation of one state of the world to
another, but to determine the relation of one state of mind to another
and to the state of the world. To this end it is necessary to interpret
language rather than nature (1, 2, 11). Consequently, these sciences
differ at least in degree from the natural sciences (23b).

However, social and political actors intend to deal with situations in
an objective world and the interpretations which control their action are
interpretations of such a world and are influenced by the changes which
take place in it. Thus, while the subjective world, influenced primarily
by culture and personality, is at the center, the objective world of natural
science is also present in the social disciplines. Social science must, therefore, distinguish the subjective sentiments and beliefs by which people
interpret situations, make choices, and act, from the forces and relations
which the observer, after the event, finds most economically accounts for
their action, and which doubtless influenced the interpretations and beliefs of the actors even though unconsciously. The two may differ. For
example, the Polynesians accounted for the occasional departure of groups
of young men in canoes to search for new islands in the Pacific by the
spirit of adventure and love of the sea, while scientists have attributed
such expeditions to population pressure (4). The physicist Heisenberg
has suggested that quantum theory may have a bearing on the problem of
free will through "the recognition of the complementarity between the
situation in which we have to decide something and the situation in
which we study the causes in the behavior of other human beings" (11a).

 It is suggested that the study of international relations may be best
approached through the concept of a field, constituted by the *relations* of
the relevant *entities, forces, sentiments,* and *processes.* These terms have
been explained as follows.

A social entity has a life-history, occupies a definite space at any moment,
and is thought of by analogy to the sensory experience of material things. A
social process is a movement through typical stages from one social situation
to another and is thought of by analogy to the intuitional experience of the
duration of activity. A social force is a condition external to a social entity or a
social process inducing or compelling changes and is thought of by analogy to
the subjective experience of volition or will-power in achieving results. (A
social sentiment is a condition within a social entity stimulated by external or
internal experience and is thought of by analogy to the subjective experience
of emotion.) A social relation is a condition inherent in the co-existence of
many social entities, accounting for social behavior and social changes and is
thought of by analogy to the experience of intellectual analysis in understanding phenomena. These modes of conceiving sociological phenomena may be

compared to the modes of scientific analysis—physicalism, behaviorism, operationalism, (mentalism) and mechanism (1)—and to the modes of legal analysis emphasizing, respectively jural persons, jural procedures, jural interests, (jural intuitions), and jural relations. In the early history of a science (as already noticed) attention has usually been concentrated upon description of the entities or things which the science deals with. Attention has later been shifted to processes and forces which account for the character and distribution of these entities at any time, and which permit of rough prediction and control of their future. The maturity of a science has usually dealt with the analysis of fundamental relations permitting of greater abstraction, of measurement, and of more accurate prediction and control (34).

Concepts of the world as plan, as equilibrium, as organization, and as field, respectively emphasize entities, forces, processes, and relations as subject matters. The concept of the world as plan, however, combines entities with relations, that of the world as equilibrium combines forces with entities and relations, that of the world as organization combines processes with forces, entities and relations, and that of the world as field combines relations with all of the others. The concept of the world as a spiritual community, governed by social sentiments, however inadequate it may be as the foundation for a scientific discipline, exerts an influence which cannot be ignored.

Different men have sought "reality" by use of different formulae. Descartes developed his philosophy from the proposition "I think, therefore I am." The essence of other philosophies may be similarly phrased. I see it, therefore it is (Bacon). It has always been, therefore it always will be (Confucius). I am certain, therefore, it must be (Augustine). I act, therefore I am (Leibnitz). I like it, therefore it is good (Epicurus). I feel, therefore I believe (à Kempis). Men have thought reality was to be tested by the clarity of thought, by the precision or continuity of observation, by the intensity of conviction, by the consciousness of effective action, and by the consciousness of feeling, emotion, or affect. If basic values are discriminated, these respectively locate "reality" as the true, the real, the good, the powerful, and the beautiful. Applying the terminology suggested in Chapter 3 the terms *correct, convincing, persuasive,* and *effective* could be substituted, the last including both the powerful and the beautiful. There is a difference, in the objectivity of these values. Clear thought and precise observation (the *true* and the *real*) can be accurately communicated and reproduced by others under suitable conditions. They may, therefore, provide the bases for disciplines of such objectivity that they can be tested by all who accept logic and observation as suitable tests. Efforts to communicate intense convictions have, on the other hand, conveyed meanings which in practice are uncertain and difficult to reproduce. This has been no less true of the Ten Commandments than of the Universal Declaration of Human Rights. Efforts to communicate intense feelings have led to even more controversial results. The Upani-

Relations of Conceptions of the World, Methods, Subject Matters, and Values in the Discipline of International Relations

Methods of Study / Subject Matter and Values ╲ Conceptions of the World	Field of Relations	Plan of Entities	Equilibrium of Power	Organization of Society	Community of the Spirit
Analysis / Mechanism / Jural Relations	True Relations	Relations	Relations	Relations	Relations
Observation / Physicalism / Jural Persons	Entities	Real Entities	Entities	Entities	
Action / Behaviorism / Jural Interests	Forces		Powerful Forces	Forces	
Evaluation / Operationalism / Jural Procedures	Processes			Good Processes	
Introspection / Mentalism / Jural Intuitions	Sentiments				Beautiful Sentiments

shads, the Apocalypse, and the Imitation of Christ (Thomas à Kempis) carry different meanings to different minds. The *good* and the *beautiful* are, therefore, difficult to communicate and more difficult to reproduce. Science tends to ignore these values, but they are essential aspects of human motivation and the social disciplines must consider them.

The powerful is that which produces its intended effect and is, therefore, by definition communicable. The artist is not powerful unless the observer catches his inspiration. The politician is not powerful unless he captures the votes. The soldier is not powerful unless he wins the battle. Power results from the control of "forces" but the identification of forces depends upon the total situation. Only if a situation remains relatively stable can the forces operating in it be defined in communicable and reproducible terms. The military force of Britain and the "soul force" of Gandhi differ greatly in relative effectiveness according as they are applied in Germany or in India. Power has, therefore, proved less useful as a criterion for scientific verification than has truth or reality, but like goodness and beauty it is a value which cannot be ignored in the present stage of social studies. With the development of a field theory of international relations, the concept of power may be subsumed in the concept of relations. Knowledge may be power. The power of a decision-maker may be a function of the relation among decision-makers in the field and of his understanding of those relations.

It is submitted that the conception of the world as a field can provide the most objective frame of reference for analyzing the entities, processes, forces, and relations involved in international affairs; can best synthesize the conceptions of the world as plan and as equilibrium; and can best indicate the complementarity of these conceptions to those based on the beliefs and activities of the many who view the world as potentially an organization or a spiritual community. Such a field may be made sufficiently complicated to reconcile logic with observation, and both with convictions and sentiments. It can take account of all values, not only the real and the true, but also the powerful, the good, and the beautiful. The diagram on page 538 attempts to relate conceptions of the world, methods of study, the subject matter of study, and values with one another.

There exists no body of empirically established relations which can provide the basis for a field theory of international relations. However, models utilizing the conception of a field may suggest lines of investigation which might eventually make such a theory possible.

It was pointed out in Chapter 31 that the term *field* has been used in two senses—on the one hand, as the actual time-space in which events take place, and on the other, as an analytical system of co-ordinates within which variables may be located in relation to one another. In developing a discipline of international relations both senses of the term may be usefully employed—the first in the geographical approach, and the second in the analytical approach. The following discussion has attempted to abstract the most significant concepts and propositions of the various disciplines discussed in earlier sections of this book and has assumed that these disciplines are related in the manner suggested in the preceding chapter.

THE GEOGRAPHICAL FIELD

The geographical approach locates the people and groups of the world and their characteristics, motivations, actions, institutions, and conditions in actual time and space. It suggests surveys indicating the topics of attention and interest; the direction of attitudes and opinions; the states of tension and unrest; and the policies, laws, and other subjective conditions prevailing among the people at each point of the globe in successive intervals of time. Similarly, changes in objective conditions such as production, trade, technology, population, migration, communication, economy, and polity should be indicated on successive maps in so far as they appear to be relevant to international relations. Such surveys might disclose correlations and suggest hypotheses concerning causal connections among these factors, especially relations between changes in the subjective factors and changes in the objective factors. Social surveys and statistical summaries have appeared in increasing abundance but they have not included many of the most significant factors (24, 26, 32).

In such surveys the importance of political barriers dividing the world into distinct groups would have to be considered. Thus correlations would be made primarily among variables within the same country. Political barriers themselves can be considered from the points of view of (a) their conformity to the "natural" groupings of people and (b) their permeability.

From the first of these points of view, successive maps indicating temporal changes in the geographical extent of systems of communication and transportation, of languages and dialects, of cultures and customs, of religions and ideologies, of producing and trading systems, and of legal and administrative systems might be superimposed to suggest the boundaries between those areas in which many of these factors tend to converge. Studies of nationality suggest that no one of these factors account for national solidarity, nor does the concurrence of many in an area. Such concurrence, however, indicates conditions which permit the realization of national solidarity when active agencies, such as political organizations, patriotic associations, historians, educators, and propagandists have made the public in such an area aware of these conditions, and loyal to symbols, histories, and institutions associated with them (7, 16, 29, 34, 43).

The permeability of existing frontiers can be indicated by mapping the relative obstruction to communication, travel, trade, and invasion across them by natural and artificial barriers, such as mountains, rivers, seas, deserts, fortifications, border patrols, tariff laws, immigration and passport regulations, censorships and prohibitions. Other factors, such as the degree of discontinuity at frontiers of communication and transportation systems; the relative extensiveness of actual communication, trade and travel across frontiers; and the relative abruptness of changes in language, religion, culture, social structure, wealth, and law at frontiers indicate the degree of conformity of existing political boundaries with the "natural" grouping of peoples. All of these factors contribute to the impermeability of iron and other curtains at frontiers (8).

In proportion as the world becomes a more homogeneous field in which national boundaries present less formidable barriers to communication, travel, trade, and migration, and less powerful stimuli to exclusive and hostile attitudes, and in which more abundant transnational communication, travel, trade, and migration moderate the "natural" differences of human groups, the discipline of international relations will be concerned primarily with correlations between the objective and subjective variables mentioned in the first paragraph of this section.

These barriers are, however, today of major importance and hamper the trend in a shrinking world toward a reduction of national differences, consequently factors involved in international relations from the geographic point of view must be divided into two classes—those operating within each of the states and those operating among states. Both types of factors influence the power, the policies, the public opinion, and the attitudes of the leadership of each state, and are the subject matter of the disciplines of international relations, especially of international economics, political geography, diplomatic history, international politics, and the control of foreign relations. These factors are manifested by events and conditions which exist in time and space and can consequently be located on maps or narrated in histories.

The writer has elsewhere sought to define and measure certain changes taking place within a state, such as the tension level, the degree of institutionalization, and the progress of production, population, and education (34, 36, 39); certain aspects of distance between states, technological and strategic, psychic and expectancy, political and social, legal and intellectual (34, 39); and certain processes tending to integrate states and international groups, such as communication and interaction, standardization and acculturation, co-operation and socialization, and organization and administration (22, 34, 37, 38). Karl Deutsch has utilized similar concepts in studying the conditions permitting the integration of nations (7) and security communities (8). The latter are defined operationally as groups, not necessarily politically organized, the participating units of which do not prepare for war against one another, or, more simply, as areas within which there is an expectation of peace. Such a community is distinguished from a political community which is organized to act as a unit to make and maintain internal and external policies. Political integration may or may not increase internal peace and security. Deutsch believes that the historical process of community development is less like that of an incubator (permitting development) than like that of a collective assembly line (implementing plans). He does not consider the possibility that this process (like a conversation) has characteristics of both, synthesizing spontaneous impulses and deliberate purposes by a process of interaction (34). He uses the terms *political integration and amalgamation; psychological identification and assimilation; mutual responsiveness and simple pacification;* and *mutual interdependence and interaction* to describe typical processes which if in proper relation to one another may develop a security community in an area. These appear to be similar, respectively, to the processes which I have described, from the point of view of increasing closeness of groups, as organization, standardization, co-operation, and communication (22, 38), and, from the point of view of increasing separation of groups, as social and political, psychic and expectancy, legal and intellectual, and technological and strategic distances (34, 39). Deutsch discusses the intricate relationships between rates of change in these elements affecting the stability of a security community, and emphasizes the importance of a proper balancing of integration loads with capabilities of the parts. He also suggests indicators for measuring rates of change in these variables.

Measurable changes in factors of this kind do not account directly for political decisions, but they tend to influence such decisions by modifying the sentiments, values, goals, and beliefs in the minds of the decision-makers and of the publics on which decision-makers depend for power or for the implementation of their policies (17, 23, 27, 31). These factors can be dealt with analytically and will be considered in connection with the capabilities and values of governments in the next section.

Obviously many of the significant factors both domestic and international, influencing political decisions, are intangible and difficult to measure or even to describe. Accurate surveys localizing the influence of these factors can be made only if observable and measurable phenomena can be found, so closely correlated with the significant intangible factors, that they can serve as indices. To this end efforts have been made, not only to define significant social and political variables operationally, but also to relate intangible mental dispositions to tangible variables such as physiological types (17, 28), physical conditions (13), economic conditions (15), states of the arts (22), and interactions of all these factors (7, 13).

The object of the study of international relations is not only to understand the factors which account for decisions and actions of governments, but also to facilitate control in order to forward the most generally accepted goals and values. The major problems arise from the diversity of such goals and values among the various nations and governments of the world. Morris and Northrop have suggested that philosophical analysis of the leading ideologies and rational political discussion may lead to synthesis and reconciliation (17, 21). Statesmen have sought to achieve general political agreements on certain goals and values such as those to be found in the United Nations Charter, the Universal Declaration of Human Rights, and other general international instruments. This practical aspect of the study of international relations suggests that a geographical survey should include not only descriptions and statistics of the *factors* significant in international relations and of measurable *indices* disclosing the changes of these variables, but also information concerning the institutions, ideas, procedures, and relations susceptible of human manipulation and the effectiveness of political, administrative, educational, and propaganda activities intended to manipulate these *regulators*.

We may, therefore, conceive of three sets of time series which may be called respectively, *factors*, *indices*, and *regulators*, continuous survey of which would yield both understanding of, and the power to control, international affairs (24). Determination, however, of the most useful series to survey in each of these categories would depend upon a theory of international relations. Such a theory should be elaborated from the psychological point of view and may be represented by a field defined by certain analytical co-ordinates.

THE ANALYTICAL FIELD

The analytical approach to the study of international relations discussed in this section implies that each international organization, national government, association, individual, or other "system of action," or "decision-maker" may be located in a multidimensional field. Such a field may be defined by co-ordinates, each of which measures a political, economic, psychological, sociological, ethical, or other continuum influencing choices, decisions, and actions important for international relations. Much experiment would be necessary to decide what co-ordinates could most usefully be employed. Material factors, relatively easy to measure, such as degree of military strength or weakness, or degree of technical advancement or backwardness, might prove to be indices of important political factors. Moral factors such as degree of reputability or disreputability, or degree of reliability or unreliability are probably important, but difficult to measure and the same is true of intellectual factors such as degree of literacy or of illiteracy, or degree of scientific and philosophical productiveness. Psychic factors, such as degree of satisfaction or dissatisfaction, or degree of anxiety or complacency are undoubtedly important, but not easy to measure. Many other co-ordinates could be suggested.

While recognizing the need of balancing measurability against importance in selecting co-ordinates, in this chapter, I have given primary consideration to importance. Further research is necessary to discover accurately measurable indices parallel to these factors. Only after that is done can the hypotheses discussed be verified.

The field might be defined by combinations of alternatives. Parsons has suggested five alternative sets of values or "pattern variables," all possible combinations of which would define a field or matrix of thirty-two cells within one of which each system of action might be located (23). It seems probable that such subjective values or pattern variables are significant factors in international relations, but estimates of conditions, facilitating or hampering their realization, of the kind suggested by Deutsch (7), are also important. Systems of action are guided by both "wish" and "reality" criteria. Such criteria may, however, be regarded as continuous variables rather than as alternatives. Each decision-maker or system of action, judged by its normal criteria in making decisions, can be located at a positive or negative distance from the origin in the field. This method seems preferable to a matrix model. Political decision-makers seldom think theoretically in terms of this or that but practically in terms of more of this and less of that.

The location of systems of action within a field defined by suitable co-ordinates is, however, complicated by the fact that each system of action has different structural levels which may have different criteria of choice. Thus the individual, as Freud pointed out, is influenced at the biological level by basic drives and wishes (the id), at the social level by values internalized in the character (the super ego), and at the psychological level by the personality co-ordinating wishes and values with realities (the ego). At the action level, the other levels struggle against each other in concrete situations resulting in decision and action (the will) (10). Similarly social and political systems of action are influenced at the psychological level by the attitudes and opinions of the people whom they serve, at the cultural level by the values and beliefs accepted by the culture or nationality within which they function, at the social level by the ideology or law of the society or state which regulates them, and at the political level by the policies and skills of the government whose procedures permit them to act. The relationship between these levels, as well as the homogeneity of each and the adequacy of the decision-making process, influence the efficiency of the system of action.

The state of international relations during a period of time may be defined in terms of the power and the policies of each of the principal governments of the world at each moment, and of the trends of change in both power and policy. A decision-maker's power is measured by his capability and his policy by his values, relative to the particular situation. The peculiar characteristics of the situation including communication discontinuities and barriers can only be discovered by geographical and historical study. General tendencies may, however, be indicated by analyzing the values and capabilities of decision-makers, and these general tendencies become increasingly determinative of choice and action as technology advances and the world shrinks. The underlying dynamism of international relations may, therefore, be described, within a field defined by suitable analytical co-ordinates, by vectors, the location of which indicates the values motivating the policy and the capabilities underlying the power of each important government at a given moment. The length and direction of each vector indicates the rapidity and direction of change. The other levels of each of these political systems of action, their relation to the government, and the relative size of the population participating in each, can also be indicated.

The internal conditions and tendencies of a system of action in respect to tension, skill, reliability, security, satisfaction and expansiveness may be indicated by the location and direction of movement of its vector in the capability field; and those in respect to tolerance, rationality, democracy, individualism, tranquillity, and optimism may be indicated by the location and direction of movement of its vector in the value field. The relations of friendliness or hostility of two systems of action can be indicated by the direction of their vectors toward or away from one another in the value field. If in the latter field the vectors are headed for a large number of different points, the tendency would be toward a stable balance of power, but, if all the vectors are headed toward two remote points of the field, a tendency toward bi-polarization and instability would be indicated. If all of the vectors are headed toward the center of the field, a trend toward general international organization would be indicated, and if they are headed away from the center, a trend toward international anarchy would be indicated. If the tendencies indicated by such a model were interpreted in the light of empirical knowledge of geographical, technological, and demographic conditions in each state and in the world as a whole, and of the trends of change in these conditions, as suggested by the geographical approach, prediction and control of the future of international relations might be facilitated.

What continua can most usefully be employed as co-ordinates for defining this analytical field? The problem is similar to that of determining the factors which account for mental performance, studied by psychologists. C. E. Spearman assumed a single factor, E. L. Thorndike assumed a great number of independent factors, and L. L. Thurstone devised methods for determining the minimum number of factors necessary to account for the results of numerous tests of mental ability. He found that factors concerning the use of words, numbers, and visual images were sufficient to account for the results of certain tests (30). Application of similar methods to a limited body of data suggested that the psychic relations among certain states could be accounted for by four factors—opinions concerning change, ideology, war, and form of government (24, 34). No such analysis is attempted here. A dozen factors are postulated and relations among them suggested from some familiarity with the field, in the hope that eventually measurement of these factors may permit of correlations to determine the degree of their sufficiency, redundancy, and applicability. Karl Pearson's method of multiple correlation and regression or Sewall Wright's method of "path coefficients" might prove applicable (40, 41). Stuart Dodd has applied such methods to test factors postulated for measuring the progress of peoples toward capacity for self-government (9).

A single multidimensional field including both capabilities and values should be envisaged. It will occasionally be convenient to treat these two aspects of the analytical field separately, but with recognition that they are not entirely independent. Values influence capabilities and vice versa. Furthermore the efficiency of the decision-making process in any system of action influences both aspects of the field as well as the rapidity and direction of that system's movement in the field. (See p. 564 and Appendix.)

A scheme is suggested on the diagrams on pages 547-549 with six capability, and six value, dimensions within which systems of action can be located, the rapidity and direction of movement of each depending in considerable measure upon the relation of its four structural levels. This cannot, of course, be represented visually in three-dimensional space but imagination may picture a twelve-dimensional semi-opaque cheese, within which maggots crawl around, the larger ones representing states with the government at the head and the people at the tail. They vaguely perceive each other as they approach, often changing direction in response to primitive instincts and urges, to sophisticated patterns and policies, and to deliberate appraisals of purposes and powers.

Among general factors influencing the capability of a state, internal, international, and mixed factors have been distinguished. The internal factors may be grouped into those influencing the energy, the rigidity, the tensions and the skills of the state, respectively limiting the vigor, the persistence, the direction and the wisdom of the government's political activity. It may be possible to measure changes in the social energy of a state by using data relevant to economic progress, such as population and production; to measure changes in social rigidity or institutionalization of a state by utilizing such variables as the centralization of government and the pervasiveness of law and custom. Changes in social tensions, probably dependent on changes in social energy and social rigidity, may be measured by utilizing data on the intensity of public opinion and private attitude, especially in respect to domestic scapegoats and potential foreign aggressors. Changes in the fourth factor, social skill or intellectual progress, may also be related to social energy and social rigidity and may

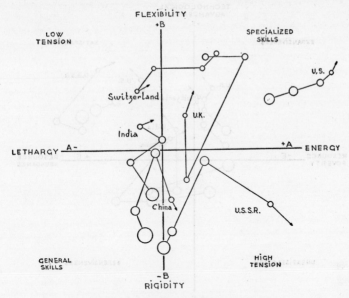

THE CAPABILITY FIELD (a)

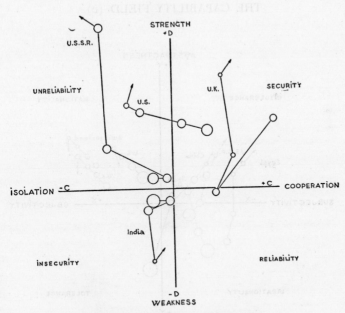

THE CAPABILITY FIELD (b)

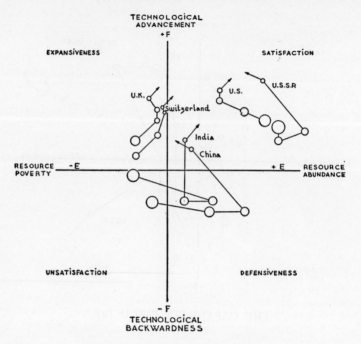

THE CAPABILITY FIELD (c)

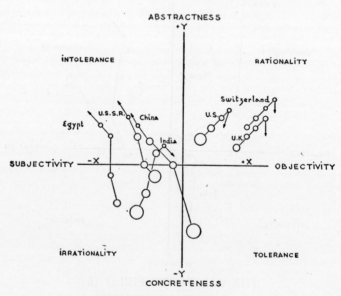

THE VALUE FIELD (a)

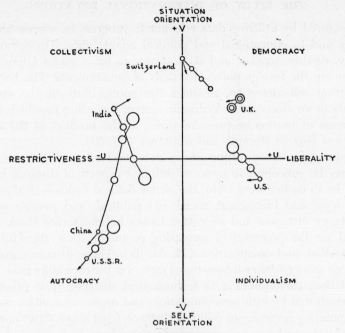

THE VALUE FIELD (b)

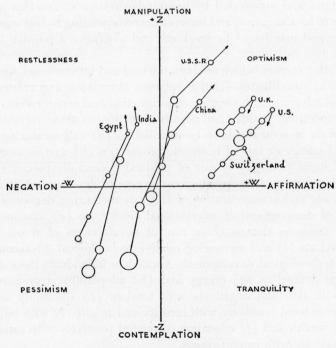

THE VALUE FIELD (c)

be measured by utilizing data relevant to progress in science and technology and to educational and political adaptability. These variables—energy, rigidity, tension, and skill—appear to be of major importance in influencing the foreign-policy decisions of governments. The last factor, permitting self-correction, modifies the applicability of the analogous formula of an electrical or hydraulic system according to which the rate of change of tension or pressure varies as the product of the rates of change of current strength and resistance (36, 39).

Persistent factors operating among states and influencing their capabilities may be conceived in terms of different aspects of distance between them. In an earlier work (34), the writer defined technological and strategic, legal and ideological, social and political, and psychic and war expectancy distances and suggested means for measuring them. Closely related are the processes of increasing communication, standardization, organization, and co-operation (22, 34, 38). These distances and processes can serve to define international factors in the capability field. Degree of isolation, corresponding to technological distance from other states and manifested by little communication; and degree of military weakness corresponding inversely to political distance from other states and manifested by dependence on superorganizations, have been selected as suitable co-ordinates. Unreliability, corresponding to legal distance from other states and manifested by nonstandardization of reaction patterns, appears to be a negative, and insecurity, corresponding to war-expectancy distance and manifested by weakness and aloofness, a positive function of these two variables.

Two other factors, which are both internal and international, have been selected as co-ordinates—relative resource abundance and relative technological advancement. Degrees of satisfaction and expansiveness appear to be respectively positive and negative functions of these variables.

These six co-ordinates have been called an (a) axis measuring degree of social energy or rate of economic progress; a (b) axis measuring degree of social flexibility or rate of political decentralization, a (c) axis measuring degree of co-operativeness or rate of development of international trade and communication, a (d) axis measuring degree of power or rate of development of international rivalry, an (e) axis measuring relative resource abundance or rate of development of resources and skills, and an (f) axis measuring relative technological advancement or rate of technological development. Applied to individuals these six axes might be defined as (a) energy and (b) adaptability correlated positively with skill and negatively with tension; (c) sociability and (d) ability correlated positively with security and negatively with reliability; and (e) wealth and (f) education correlated positively with satisfaction and negatively with expansiveness.

Recent studies of the values influencing civilizations, religions, ideologies and systems of action suggest that three sets of co-ordinates are of basic importance in the value field. They represent, respectively, objective-subjective, concrete-abstract, and manipulative-contemplative continua.

The first or (x) axis locates systems of action according to the degree in which they evaluate the persons and things with which they deal by objective examination of their capacities or roles in relation to the situation or to the interests of the actor; or by application of subjective categories in the mind of the actor. This axis corresponds to Parsons' "achievement-ascription" pattern variable. Systems of action guided by objective criteria are observant, accurate, realistic, practical, and interested in the effectiveness or ineffectiveness of action, in the strength or weakness of persons, and in the expediencies of action in the existing situation. Systems of action guided by subjective criteria are introspective, vague, idealistic, moralistic, and interested in the rightness or wrongness of actions, in the goodness or badness of persons, and in the principles and standards which should guide actions in general.

The (y) axis (concrete-abstract) locates each system of action according to the degree in which it perceives reality by immediate experience or by deduction from abstract concepts. Northrop emphasizes this distinction and believes it marks the fundamental difference between oriental and occidental cultures (21). Parsons' pattern variable defined as "particularism-universalism" is similar. Systems of action guided by concrete criteria are synthetic, intuitive, inductive, aesthetic, and interested in art, history, and immediate experiences. On the other hand, systems of action guided by abstract criteria are analytical, rational, deductive, mathematical. They are interested in abstract propositions of logic and philosophy, and in the correctness or incorrectness of processes of reasoning.

The (z) axis, (manipulative-contemplative) emphasized by Lasswell (14), locates systems of action according to the degree in which they seek to achieve purposes or to expand understanding—to reform or to comprehend—to do or to know. Morris uses the terms *attachment* and *detachment* in the same sense (17). The pattern variable which Parsons denominates "affectivity-affective neutrality," though related, is different. By affectivity he means reflex, impulsive, or spontaneous behavior. But *action* implies some deliberation upon alternatives. An entity which behaves wholly spontaneously is not a *system of action*. Its behaviour is a function of its inherent properties and the environmental stimuli which impinge upon it, and can be entirely explained within a system of geographic co-ordinates. Nor does this criteria correspond to the contrast between active and passive. All systems of action are active in that behavior is internally generated (25). Contemplation is not passivity. Nevertheless there is more of spontaneity in the manipulative than in the contemplative, and the latter may lead to a "passive personality" "sicklied o'er by the pale cast of thought." Systems of action guided by the manipulative criterion are active, creative, constructive, and interested in the adaptation of means to ends. They tend to build their power and to be militant and authoritarian. Systems of action guided by the contemplative criterion are deliberative, analytic, reflective, and interested in relating causes to effects. They tend to be pacifistic, cosmopolitan, and democratic, and to favor stability, and decentralization of power. This distinction seems to correspond to that between Yin and Yang in Chinese thought (31), related to the rhythms of stability and progress, rest and motion, and to the scientific idea of maximizing or minimizing entropy, or expending or conserving energy (25).

Other co-ordinates of importance appear to be a (*u*) axis (restrictive-liberal) locating systems of action according to the degree in which they identify themselves and interpret their relations with others narrowly or broadly. This axis corresponds to Parsons' "specificity-generality" pattern variable. Systems of action guided by a restrictive concept of relations are contractual, suspicious, precise, legalistic and interested in the concrete aspects of relationships. Systems of action guided by a liberal concept of relations are tolerant, expansive, accommodating, broad minded and inclined to identify themselves with other persons and with organizations.

A (*v*) *axis* (self-orientation-situation-orientation) may also be significant, locating systems of action according to the degree in which they guide decisions by self-interest or by consideration of, and reciprocal interest in, others. Such a continuum would correspond to Parsons' pattern variable denominated "self-orientation-collective-orientation." Systems of action oriented by self-interest are competitive, self-assertive, domineering, and, in regard to collective systems of action, nationalistic or imperialistic. On the other hand, systems of action oriented by the situation are co-operative, conciliatory, renunciatory, and, in regard to governments, internationalistic. This axis has often been assumed to be the basic criterion of ethical judgment and has sometimes been considered to define the distinction between *interest* and *principle*, between *realism* and *idealism* or between *egoism* and *altruism* but these terms are all somewhat ambiguous (37).

A (*w*) axis (affirmation-negation) may also be suggested, locating systems of action according as they guide decisions by a positive or negative attitude toward the world. The first is attracted to the world, and tends to be optimistic, idealisic, extroverted. The latter withdraws from the world and tends to be realistic, pessimistic, and introverted. This axis corresponds to Schweitzer's distinction between affirmation and negation (27). It differs from the (*z*) axis of manipulation-contemplation in that it refers to the expectations of the actor from the world rather than to his action upon it.

Each of these axes indicates a continuum, positions near the origin indicating neutrality or balance, and those toward the periphery indicating extremes in one direction or the other. They discriminate the criteria by which systems of action evaluate (x), perceive (y), act upon (z), identify themselves with (u), interest themselves in (v), and entertain expectations from (w) the persons, things, and situations with which they are faced.

THE LOCATION OF PERSONS IN THE ANALYTICAL FIELD

Systems of action are of two kinds—individual and collective. Each of the two billion odd human beings in the world's population is an individual system of action and in theory each could be located in the analytical field by ascertaining the basic capabilities and patterns of value influencing its decision-making. These capabilities and values, it must be recalled, reside in instincts and drives of the biological man, in goals and ideals of the social man, in ideas and concepts of the thinking man, and in expediencies and skills of the active man. Because of the influence on the individual's attitudes, of the culture in which he lives and because of the tendency of cultures, dependent as they are upon abundance of contact and communication, to be localized, persons near together in the value field may also be near together in the geographical field defined by space and time. This relation obviously does not hold in respect to the capability field and even in respect to the value field it may not be the case as commonly as often supposed. Morris suggests that basic value patterns may be more influenced by the physical build of the individual than by his cultural associations (17).

It seems probable that individual attitudes and value criteria which people apply when not under any social or legal compulsion, often differ greatly from the opinions which they express in public. The latter are probably much more influenced by the prevailing culture and ideology establishing the individual's social role than are the former. So far as this is true, it becomes a matter of no small difficulty to locate individuals in the value field unless, indeed, further study supports the correlation which Morris suggests. Even if it were demonstrated that visceral, cerebral and muscular types of bodily build tend respectively to accept *dionysian, buddhistic,* or *promethean* values, it would still be necessary to examine the extent to which conditioning by culture, institutions, ideologies and law, giving different emphases, actually overcome initial tendencies and produce persistent attitudes in the adult conforming to the prevailing cultural and social environment. If one considers the number among his own acquaintances who are easy going, pleasure loving, extroverted, aesthetic *dionysians;* the number who are tense, argumentative, passion-subduing, introverted, ascetic *buddhists;* and the number who are energetic, active, planning, extroverted, ethical *prometheans,* one may question how far this conditioning process goes. How many husbands and wives have such different patterns of evaluation that they seldom understand one another and differ on every family decision? The divorce courts manifest many such situations. It seems probable that location in the value field would bring many people close together who live in areas of the world remote from one another, who profess divergent religions, and who publicly conform to varied conditions of society and law. On the other hand, many people who live in the same town or even belong to the same family might be widely separated in the value field.

It also seems probable that all parts of the analytic field would be populated but with varying density. Near the center of the capability field would be the "average man," and near the center of the value field would be the "well balanced man," Morris's *Maitreyans.* They are at the same time detached observers and contemplators and attached actors and manipulators. They judge people and things by observation of their relations to the situation but utilize deduction from subjective categories developed by individual, group, and human experience to infer properties and characteristics which cannot be directly observed; and they combine aesthetic appreciation of immediate experience with a sense for the reality of constructs deduced from generalizations verified by appropriate methods.

Far out from the center of the capability field would be geniuses and morons and far out from the center of the value field would be extremists and cranks of all kinds. Nearer the center would be the hermits and the ascetics in the subjective-concrete-contemplative area contrasted to the builders and planners in the objective-abstract-manipulative area. The crusaders and revolutionists would be in the subjective-abstract-manipulative area contrasted to the reactionaries and formalists in the objective-concrete-contemplative area. The liberals and the reformers would be in the subjective-concrete-manipulative area contrasted with the conservatives in the objective-abstract-contemplative area. The sentimentalists and sympathizers (bleeding hearts) would be in the subjective-abstract-contemplative area, the gourmets in the objective-concrete-manipulative area. Each of these types could also be located on the (u), (v) and (w) axes.

THE LOCATION OF ORGANIZATIONS IN THE ANALYTICAL FIELD

Each of the millions of collective systems of action might also be located in the field. These include all organizations capable of making decisions which exert important influence upon their members. Organizational decision-making implies that a group accepts some procedures to give form and effectiveness to decisions in its name and accepts some theory of the function and authority of its agents in making and implementing decisions. Such decision-making also implies that the agents and members supposed to be affected by decisions accept some responsibility for observing, or at least considering, the decision. In short, collective decision-making implies some government and some acceptance of organizational roles.

A variety of groups exhibit this capacity of independent decision-making within broader or narrower ranges of situations. Sovereign states make decisions on a wide range of subjects. International organizations, dependent states, cities, villages, political parties, churches, business concerns, and educational institutions make decisions on lesser ranges of subjects and usually with a lesser degree of effectiveness. Cultural, social, and recreational associations and families make decisions independently within an even more restricted range.

As has been noticed the efficiency of a system of action depends not only on the adequacy of the decision-making procedure, but also on the relation in the field of the four levels (psychological, cultural, social, and political) of the system of action and on the homogeneity of each of these levels. If each level centers at the same point in the field and contains no subgroups or individuals at a distant point, it is capable of manifesting a maximum of efficiency, but a minimum of adaptability.

Collective systems of action are of course composed of individuals and the larger ones may also include lesser collective systems of action. There is much interlocking. The same individual may have a role in many collective systems of action. It is also clear that an individual belonging to a collective system of action, apart from his role in that system, may be located in a part of the field distant from the system of action itself. A large collective system of action, such as the United States government, probably located at a point not far from the center in the abstract-objective-manipulative sector, has citizens in every part of the field, but probably a considerable proportion of American citizens are located in its psychological neighborhood. This results from the influence of culture, ideology, and law.

By culture is meant the cumulative growth of techniques, customs, and beliefs, among people in continuous and abundant communication with one another (greatly facilitated by the use of common language and by geographical proximity); transmitted to the rising generation by parents and educational processes; giving an objective character to certain values, processes, and institutions; and conditioning the desires, goals, and personalities of the individuals subjected to it. While the cultural process does not completely shape the choice criteria of individuals, its influence is so great that members of a common culture or nationality are often in close proximity in the value field as well as in the geographical field.

By ideology is here meant a logically organized system of values, goals, and beliefs exerting a certain coercive influence over individuals. Systems of religious doctrine, like Buddhism, Christianity, and Islam; systems of philosophy and of political or economic theory, like communism, capitalism, and fascism; and systems of law, like natural law, international law, Roman law, and common law, are ideologies in this sense. Ideologies are closely related to cultures on the one hand and to collective systems of action on the other. But they should not be confused with either. While an ideology springs from some culture or from a combination of cultures, its major influence may be in a different culture. Buddhism sprang from Indian culture, Christianity from Jewish culture, and Marxism from western European culture, but the major influence of Buddhism was outside of India, of Christianity outside of Palestine, and of Marxism outside of western Europe. Many religions have been organized in churches which give them positive sanctions, and systems of law are usually maintained by governments. But this is not always the case. Buddhism spread without a centralized organization. International law has had considerable influence even though the area of its operation has not been regulated by an effective organization. During much of their histories the ideology of each of the great religions has been maintained by a number of governments often in conflict with one another. Roman law, the common law, and international law have been professed and maintained by many governments.

Ideologies differ from cultures in being more systematically and consciously integrated. Consequently they are more capable of transmission by organized propaganda and educational efforts. They are, however, more abstract, more dependent on the understanding of symbols, less influential in early childhood, and consequently less influential in conditioning the responses and attitudes of individuals. Only if an ideology penetrates into, and is absorbed by, a culture or is enforced by a powerful church, state, or other collective systems of action does it greatly influence the personality of individuals.

Cultures and ideologies are not in themselves systems of action. But like systems of action they can be located in the value field, and they serve to bring individuals and collective systems of action together.

In political literature the terms people, nation, state, and government are often used interchangeably. They have been here used to designate respectively the psychological, cultural, social, and political levels at which collective systems of action function. They refer respectively to the group conceived as communicating individuals, as a culture, as an ideology, and as an organization. By a people is meant a population related by communication and subject to a government. By a nation is meant a people sharing a common body of techniques, customs, beliefs, and aspirations. By a state is meant a people subject to and consenting to a system of law maintained by a government. By a government is meant the organization of persons, officers, procedures, and legal powers by which the state makes and enforces decisions. The government that decides law and policy is always a smaller group than the state which manifests consent to these decisions, and the state is usually a smaller group than the nation which includes all who share in the dominant culture. The nation, however, is always smaller and may be very much smaller than the population subject to the government. With respect to location in the geographic field, these circles would usually be concentric, but in respect to location in the analytic field, their centers may be widely separated especially if great disparities in size manifest undemocratic conditions.

These terms might be applied to any political group or indeed to any collective system of action, but they are applied especially to the relatively large, territorially independent, coercive entities known as sovereign states (34). Some eighty of these entities divide the land surface of the earth, the air above it, and the adjacent waters of the sea as defined by international law. Since it is with these entities that international relations is primarily concerned at the present time, it is with their location and movement in the value field that we are mainly concerned in studying contemporary international relations. It is, however, important to emphasize the distinctions here made between the attitudes of the people, the opinion of the nation, the law of the state, and the policy of the government, and the variations in size of the populations denoted by each, because these different aspects of each sovereign state influence the direction of its movement in the field and its tendency toward opposition or co-operation with other sovereign states.

These four aspects of the state are respectively related to decreasing proportions of its population. The "people" include the entire population, except primitive peoples with a wholly self-subsistent economy, who feel the effects of major policy decisions but exert only a passive influence upon policy through the attitudes which they vaguely manifest as those effects prove to be pleasant or unpleasant. The "nation" includes only those members of the population who are aware of the values implicit in the national culture and character, and who influence those values by their communications with one another. In modern civilization only the literate can participate effectively in the "nation." The "state" includes that portion of the population who by voting or other direct participation in politics influence government policy. This section of the population may be different from that which contributes to the national culture but it is usually smaller. In modern states many literate people are ineligible to vote and many of those eligible fail to vote. The "government" is a much smaller group but it includes, not only the official decision-makers in the legislative, executive, and judicial branches of the government, but also the governing élite comprising those who advise and influence deci-

sion-makers directly and usually personally because of government position, or because of power in party, business, labor, agriculture, church or
other important pressure group within the state. No estimates are available of the proportion of the population in the "people," "nation," "state,"
and "government" of different countries, but these proportions vary
greatly. The "people" usually includes over 90 per cent of the population
if colonial areas are excluded. The "nation" may include from 20 to 60
per cent of the population. The state from 1 to 50 per cent and the
government from .01 to 2 per cent. The character and direction of change
of a state are greatly influenced by the proportion of the population participating at the higher levels. The greater the proportion of the people in
the nation, the state, and the government, the more democratic is the
group in, respectively, the social, the political, and the legal sense.

Levels in the process of foreign-policy making in the United States
have been defined respectively as the passive but affected "general
public," the interested and "attentive public," the "articulate policy and
opinion élites," and the "official policy leadership." They respectively
contribute impulse (id), values (super ego), policy (ego) and decision
(will) in the process of policy-making. Of the 150 million Americans
affected by foreign policy decisions, there can hardly be over 30 million
(20 per cent) in the attentive public, over 1.5 million (1 per cent) in the
articulate public, and over 1.5 thousand (.001 per cent) in the foreign-
policy leadership.

This classification suggested by Gabriel Almond resembles that
here made between "people," "nation," "state," and "government," as
does Plato's distinction among "workers," "soldiers," and "guardians"
(assuming that the workers include both the "people" and the "nation")
exhibiting respectively the virtues of temperance, courage, and wisdom.
His fourth virtue, justice, may be identified with the "nation," including
all active citizens who synthesize values in the culture. The "philosopher-
kings" who combine justice with action synthesize the nation and the
government (1a, 23a).

The identification here suggested, following Plato and Aristotle, of
qualitative aspects of the state with proportions of its population, opens
the way for quantitative comparisons of states according to the relative
size of these proportions roughly indicating degrees of democracy or
autocracy. A more refined analysis should consider also the proportions
of the population from which these classes are recruited. If everyone has
an opportunity to become a governor, the state may be democratic even
though the number of governors is small (14).

Criteria for locating systems of action in the capability field have been
discussed. Statistics concerning standards of living, proportion of the
national income in the central government's budget, proportion of international trade in the total business of the country, political independence

from foreign influence, relative dependence on imported raw materials, proportion of population at various levels of education, and circulation of mass media would be relevant. Rough estimates suggest that the Soviet government would be located in the area characterized by great rigidity, moderate energy, great strength and political independence, great resources, and limited technical advancement. The Soviet people would be nearer the center. The United States government would be located in the area of moderate decentralization, great energy, moderate strength and political independence, great resources and great technical advancement and the people would in respect to some of the co-ordinates be further from the center. Compared with the United States the Soviet Union seems to be under higher tensions, to have less specialized skills, and to be less reliable and secure. In respect to satisfaction and expansiveness, the two countries appear to be similar.

It seems probable that the location of collective systems of action in the value field would present less difficulties than the location of individuals in that field. Governments often have public ideologies, creeds, or constitutions which can assist in locating them. Merriam and Lasswell have distinguished political *credenda, formulae,* and *miranda,* commanding, respectively, belief, observance, and admiration, as indices for locating political systems of action (16a, 38).

International organizations would probably cluster around the center of the value field. Their efforts to synthesize the criteria of all nations and parties militate against extreme positions, but the heterogeneity of their constituencies tends to make them inefficient. On the other hand, special interest associations and parties would probably be far toward the periphery of the field and may be more homogeneous and efficient. Organized churches would be on the subjective side. Those guided by a well organized theology or ideology, like the Catholic church and the Communist party, would be on the abstract side. Those engaged in missionary operations or vigorous propagandas would be on the manipulative side.

National governments would probably tend to be in an intermediate position between international organizations at the center and special interest groups and parties on the periphery. They are less selective in their membership than the latter and consequently, like international organizations, must usually accommodate themselves to a greater variety of pressures from their membership, a circumstance militating against efficiency, especially in the case of democracies.

MOVEMENT IN THE FIELD OF
INTERNATIONAL RELATIONS

General changes in the character of international relations may be interpreted as movements of systems of action in the analytic field and may be attributed to (*a*) general changes in the field, (*b*) to interaction between the capability and the value fields, and (*c*) to interaction between the geographic and the analytical fields.

General changes in the field. The most important general factors which influence both the geographical and the analytical fields appear to have been the accelerating progress of science and technology. In respect to the geographical field this progress has on the one hand continually augmented production, communication, and the interdependence of groups, increasing social energy and tending to shrink and unify the geographical field, and, on the other hand, it has augmented the efficiency of administration, education, and propaganda, enlarging and co-ordinating institutions, increasing rigidities, erecting barriers, developing armament races, and tending to increase material distances between groups and to divide the world into a number of artificial geographical fields.

These opposing tendencies have probably been influential since the history of man began, and have had the general tendency to diminish the differentials in values among human groups and to increase the differentials in their capabilities. As a result the more capable groups have absorbed the less, and huge power aggregations, each seeking to impose its values upon the world, have developed. Since these efforts have never been entirely successful, history has chronicled the advance of civilization through a balance between forces of union and division. Sporadic serious disturbances of this balance have resulted in great oscillations marking the rise and fall of civilizations (31). Periods of progress toward the unity of a civilization have been followed by periods of disorganization with intervals of stability between (34, 39).

In recent times, extraordinary scientific and technological advances, augmenting the abundance of communications and the possibilities of profitable trade, have tended to a synthesis of peoples and cultures. By augmenting the vulnerability of all to destruction, this advance has also tended to a synthesis of states and governments in international organizations, thus moving all peoples, nations, states, and governments toward the center of the value field. National systems of administration, education, and propaganda, however, devoted to developing loyalty to traditional national values and institutions have tended to emphasize the distinctiveness of the principal ideologies and to diminish their ambiguities. National culture and popular attitudes have tended to conform to a particular ideology, and governments have become more determined to preserve the one to which they are committed. These factors have tended to move all systems of action away from the center of the value field. The shrinking of distances, the differentials of capabilities, and the resulting increase in the vigor of the power struggle has tended to the assimilation of nations and governments into two great systems in opposing parts of the value field. These opposing tendencies in both the geographical and the analytical fields have made it increasingly difficult for governments in either one of these opposing systems to conciliate those in the other with the result that anxiety and tensions become ever greater (39).

Some relations between capabilities and values. The relative capabilities of states are continually changing under the influence of science and invention, of internal development, and of international politics. What is the effect of these changes in a state's capability in respect to the six dimensions here suggested, that is, its (a) energy, (b) rigidity, (c) co-operativeness, (d) strength, (e) resources and (f) technical advancement upon its values. Other factors influencing capability, such as tension, skill, reliability, security, satisfaction, and expansiveness, are believed to be functions of these six as indicated on the diagram.

Increase in the energy of a people, roughly measured by the average rate of increase in wealth, tends to move a people toward the manipulative end of the (z) axis. Increasing poverty tends to move a people toward the contemplative end. The distribution of wealth may, however, be very unequal. For a considerable period of time a government may be increasing in wealth and energy while the people are becoming poorer. Thus the attitudes of the people may become more contemplative while the policies of the government become more manipulative. Such opposite movements, likely in a totalitarian state, clearly bode ill for the continuous stability of the system of action.

Rigidity refers to the degree of centralization of authority and may be measured by the proportion of the national income administered by central authority, by the degree of mobility of the people in what Lasswell has called the "safety-income-deference pyramid" (14) or by subjective estimates concerning respect for civil liberties and separations of power. A rigid society has a stratification of castes and classes, is permeated by institutions with fixed values, and is regulated by a vigorous system of law. In a flexible society, on the other hand, government is decentralized geographically and functionally; the attitudes of people, the influence of institutions, and the acceptance of values is in continuous flux; and the law is continually changed by central and local legislative processes. Rigidifying systems of action tend to move toward the subjective end of the (x) axis, and those becoming more flexible to the objective end. Here again governments may differ from cultures. The two may be moving in opposite directions, again rendering the society unstable.

Increasing energy and increasing rigidity, strengthening allegiance to existing values, tends to increase tensions. Inflexible institutions, especially political institutions, and developing economy, especially if coupled with a system of finance augmenting the capacity of the government, tends to an externalization of these tensions and to aggressive policies.

Tensions may, however, arise from causes other than the relation between the economy and the polity. A challenge of new conditions in the material or social environment, threatening the security or prosperity of the people or the government, if beyond the experience of the existing culture or law, may require significant changes in popular attitudes, in national opinions, in the law of the state, and in the policies of the government if a proper response is to be made. If institutions are rigid, such a response is not likely to be made. As Toynbee has pointed out, only rarely have primitive peoples made a suitable response to such challenges and, thereby, produced a "civilization" (31). Only rarely have civilizations been able to adjust themselves to major changes in their conditions. Adjustments to such challenges require a skillful combination of realism in appreciating the nature of the challenge and the requirements of suitable adaptation, and of idealism, in appreciating the potentialities of the system of action to be preserved from nonessentials and excrescences to be modified.

Tension may also arise because government policies and state laws are unadapted to the attitudes of the people and the opinion of the nation. Such conditions, which lead to political revolution are less likely to occur as the development of democracy decreases the disparity between government and people. If not only the government and the state, but also social institutions and traditional opinions become out of harmony with widespread, but hitherto unvoiced attitudes of the people, social revolution is likely, especially if the government is lacking in skill and resources (39).

From whatever cause, increasing tensions within a system of action tends, up to the point of revolution, to a consolidation of existing values by the government, to a displacement of aggressive dispositions upon an external or internal scapegoat, to an aggressive policy, and to a location on the restrictive end of the (u) axis.

Only by the exercise of great skill can a government avoid occasional revolution and war, and a rapid rise of tensions creates conditions unfavorable to the influence of persons with skill. The original mind, capable of solving social problems, becomes suspect with the tendency of both people and government to regress in times of severe crisis to an absolute allegiance to traditional but obsolete values. Such skills are most likely to be used in a system of action near the origin in the (a) (energy), (b) (rigidity) and (y) (abstract-concrete) axes. The sort of skills required involves a combination of techniques arising from specialized abstract thought and of human understanding arising from general concrete experience. A nation of specialists tends to be far out on the abstract end of the (y) axis and to be positively related to high energy and negatively related to social rigidity. A nation of generalists, on the other hand, tends to be far out on the concrete end of the (y) axis and to be negatively related to high energy and positively related to social rigidity. Skill in social and political management is to be found in a culture recognizing both virtues and consequently located near the origin on all these axes (37).

Primitive peoples tend to be at the subjective and concrete ends of the (x) and (y) axes, civilized peoples at the objective and abstract ends. This is because civilization tends to objectivity, abstraction and specialization, to what psychoanalysts call "maturity," modifying the "wish" principle by the "reality" principle, and to division of labor encouraging appreciation of abstract intellectual formulae rather than concrete aesthetic experience. Primitive peoples also tend to be on the low energy and rigid ends of the (a) and (b) axes while civilized peoples tend to be at the opposite ends of these axes. The result is that civilized man has tended to increase his mastery of nature but to decrease his mastery of men. Only if modern culture preserves a supply of generalists, along with the specialists, can political problems be solved. As Northrop and Hsu have pointed out, the aesthetic spirit is less controversial and more conciliatory than the scientific spirit (12, 21).

Movements of governments toward the rigidity, the isolation, and the power ends of the (b), (c), and (d) axes tend to produce autocracy, authoritarianism and a decreasing participation of the people in the state and the government. Movements in the opposite direction tend to produce democracy. The democratic or autocratic organization of a government determines the influence of popular attitudes and public opinion upon the law and policy of the government. Autocratic governments controlling the means of communication tend to decide autonomously upon law and policy and to bring about whatever general consent of the people is necessary by appropriate educational, propaganda, and intimidating methods. Thus the government continually draws the state, the nation, the people to itself, thereby increasing its efficiency and the rigidity of its values. Such a system of action can be represented by a vector with its tail at the location of the people passing through the location of the nation and the state to its head at the location of the government.

In a large state the center of gravity of the people tends to be located near the center of the field in respect to the value co-ordinates because the people usually includes individuals located in all parts of the field. The movement of an autocratic state led by a government which is likely to be further from the center, tends to be away from the center

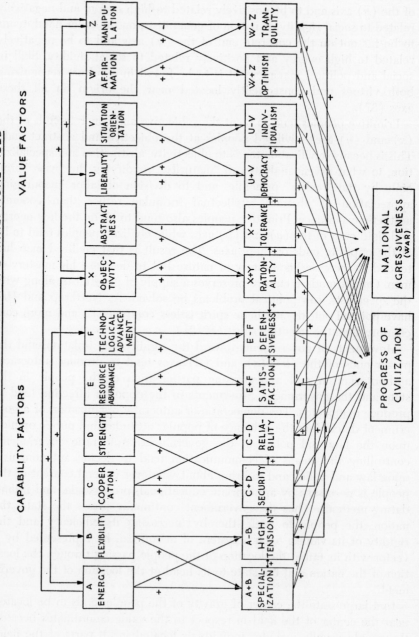

PATHS OF INFLUENCE WITHIN THE ANALYTICAL FIELD

CAPABILITY FACTORS   VALUE FACTORS

A	B	C	D	E	F	X	Y	U	V	W	Z
ENERGY	FLEXIBILITY	COOPERATION	STRENGTH	RESOURCE ABUNDANCE	TECHNOLOGICAL ADVANCEMENT	OBJECTIVITY	ABSTRACTNESS	LIBERALITY	SITUATION ORIENTATION	AFFIRMATION	MANIPULATION

A+B SPECIALIZATION

A−B HIGH TENSION

C+D SECURITY

C−D RELIABILITY

E+F SATISFACTION

E−F DEFENSIVENESS

X+Y RATIONALITY

X−Y TOLERANCE

U+V DEMOCRACY

U−V INDIVIDUALISM

W+Z OPTIMISM

W−Z TRANQUILITY

NATIONAL AGGRESSIVENESS (WAR)

PROGRESS OF CIVILIZATION

toward more and more extreme positions in the value field. In democratic systems of action, on the other hand, popular attitudes control public opinion. This controls the law, which in turn controls the government policy and action. The people continually draw the government toward themselves. Thus, a democratic government tends to move toward the center of the value field. Democratic governments, therefore, in a shrinking world, tend to cluster near the center of the field and to unite in international organizations, while autocratic governments move toward the periphery and become totalitarian parties, seeking to absorb people, nation, and state. A revolution may suddenly change the autocratic or democratic character of a system of action, and such a change may reverse the direction of movement of the system in the field. Since government policies are likely to be more mobile than the attitudes of a large population of individuals, autocratically governed systems of action are likely to move more rapidly in the field than are democratically organized systems of action. "Autocracy," said Fisher Ames, "is a ship which gallantly sails the seas, but someday it strikes a reef and goes down while democracy is a raft which will never sink, but then your feet are always in the water" (33).

Many other influences of changing capabilities upon values could be explored. For example, a positive relation of resource abundance and technological advancement makes for satisfaction and this induces objectivity, tolerance, and affirmation, characteristic of the United States during most of its history. On the other hand, poor resources and technological backwardness make for dissatisfaction which induces subjectivity, intolerance, and negation, characteristic of the Arabs in recent times. A negative relation of these capability factors (i.e., resource abundance and technological backwardness) makes for aggressiveness as in the Soviet Union, while the opposite relations (poor resources and technological advancement) makes for defensive policies, as in the cases of Norway and Switzerland. The diagram on page 564 suggests the direction of influence of many factors affecting international relations. (See also Appendix.)

Some relations between geography and analysis. As already noticed democracies tend to be located near the center of the value field, to promote common goals, and to co-operate with one another, while autocracies tend to move toward the periphery of the field and to pursue divergent policies.

These relations are, however, affected by relations in actual time and space. States so geographically related that each is vulnerable to attack by the other will, because of this decreasing strategic distance, become increasingly hostile if in psychic relations of opposition. If, on the other hand, geographic relations and technological conditions are such that each is relatively invulnerable to attack, psychic relations of opposition are not likely to lead to conflict.

In the case of states tending to co-operate because moving to the same point in the value field, shrinking geographical distance is likely to augment this tendency. Thus, if between two states psychic distances are diminishing more rapidly than strategic distances, peace becomes increasingly probable. But if strategic distances are diminishing more rapidly than psychic distances, war is probable. As states become less cooperative and more armed, they become less reliable and more belligerent. The writer has examined the relations of changes in different aspects of distance elsewhere. The consequences of changes in these different aspects of distance can be indicated by combined consideration of changes in the analytic and the geographic fields (34).

Negotiations of statesmen might be facilitated if the entire field of international relations were so represented that the negotiators could see the relations of the circles and vectors representing their respective peoples, nations, states, and governments located at particular points both in the geographical and analytical fields, and moving in certain directions in the latter. An observer might calculate with less margin of error the probable outcome of such negotiations by the use of such a model.

The five conceptions of the world, discussed in the preceding chapter, may be interpreted as the attribution of a particular character to the analytical field and to the systems of action within it.

If all systems of action were controlled by a well articulated law, maintained by an effective government, at one point in the field, the world would appear to be the plan or idea defined by that system of law. Such a system would imply that the attitudes of all people reflect a common culture, uniting all nations, and manifesting the ideology implicit in the universal law. The nature of the idea would, of course, vary greatly according to the point in the field at which the universal state is located.

If all systems of action were controlled by a small number of governments in relations of general opposition to one another, the vector representing each would head toward a different point in the field; each of the governments would regulate the attitudes, cultures, law, and policies of the people within its domain and the domain of its satellites. None would acknowledge any norms of culture, law, or authority except the criteria which guided its own behavior, and the world would appear as a military equilibrium. The stability of the equilibrium would depend upon the number, the power, the relations, and the alliances of the governments.

If collective systems of action were reduced to unimportance, and all individuals guided their behavior by a universal culture maintained, not by coercive laws but by the internalization of the attitudes of all the people, the world would appear to be a universal community. The location of this universal culture in the field would determine the character of the community. A community dominated by Christian love would probably be in the contemplative, subjective, concrete sector of the value field and would differ greatly from a universal commune, dominated by loyalty to the group, giving to each according to his needs and expecting from each according to his capacity, probably located in the manipulative, objective, abstract sector, from a Buddhistic nirvana of individuals emancipated from all desires in the contemplative, subjective, abstract sector, or from an epicurean community of individuals joyfully satisfying their desires without mutual interference in the manipulative, objective, concrete sector. All would differ from a Maitreyan community of individuals at the center of the field (17).

If both individual and collective systems of action existed in all parts of the field; if in each collective system the attitudes of the people, the culture of the nation, the law of the state, and the policies of the government were near the same point thus militating against movement; and if these points were related to certain universal principles of morals and law maintained by a universal organization of limited competency, to prevent sudden or violent changes and to facilitate continuous and gradual adjustments and accommodations among the various systems of action, the world would appear as an organization. Such an organization would imply a certain equilibrium of power among the major systems of action; a degree of international protection of certain spheres of freedom for individuals and lesser collective systems of action; and a system of law and culture guiding it located near the center of the field.

We may conclude that the world of man, first conceived as a static ideology expressing the origin and destiny of man in fixed symbols revealed by an imperfectly known God, nature, or history, or as a community in which men lived in harmony because they loved one another, has in fact usually resembled an equilibrium resulting from the interplay of forces directed by the government of each of the major groups into which the territory of the world has been divided. As the world shrinks it appears to be becoming an organization designed to maintain the interests of groups and individuals by suitable procedures, by developing certain standards of universal culture, and by enforcing certain rules of universal law. For the scientist, however, the world may be best conceived as a field, a dynamic complex of relations among groups and individuals developing knowledge of which may increase the capacity of man to know his interests and his conditions, and to control his destiny by continually recreating his world in the image best synthesizing the progress and stability of these systems of action as they change under his touch.

REFERENCES

1a. ALMOND, Gabriel, The American People and Foreign Policy (New York, Harcourt, 1950).

1. BLOOMFIELD, Leonard, "Linguistic Aspects of Science," International Encyclopedia of Unified Science, Vol. 1, No. 4 (Chicago, University of Chicago Press, 1939).

2. BLOOMFIELD, Leonard, *Language* (New York, Holt, 1933).
3. BRUNSWIK, Egon, "The Conceptual Framework of Psychology," *International Encyclopedia of Unified Science*, Vol. 1, No. 10 (Chicago, University of Chicago Press, 1952).
4. BUCK, Peter, in *Problems of the Pacific*, Institute of Pacific Relations (Chicago, University of Chicago Press, 1929), pp. 232 ff.
5. BUTTERFIELD, Herbert, *The Origins of Modern Science, 1300-1800* (London, Bell, 1950).
6. CONANT, James B., *Science and Common Sense* (New Haven, Yale University Press, 1951).
7. DEUTSCH, Karl, *Nationalism and Social Communication* (New York, Wiley, 1953).
8. ———, *Political Community at the International Level, Problems of Definition and Measurement* (New York, Doubleday, 1954).
9. DODD, Stuart C., "The Scientific Measurement of Fitness for Self-government," *The Scientific Monthly*, Vol. 78 (February, 1954), pp. 94 ff.
10. FREUD, Anna, *The Ego and the Mechanisms of Defense* (New York, International Universities Press, 1946).
11. HAYEK, F. A., *The Counter Revolution of Science* (Glencoe, Ill., Free Press, 1952), pp. 30, 42.
11a. HEISENBERG, Werner, "The Bearing of Science on Man and His Nature," *Conference on Science and Human Responsibility* (St. Louis, Mo., Washington University, October, 1954).
12. HSU, Francis, *American and Chinese, Two Ways of Life* (New York, Schuman, 1953).
13. HUNTINGTON, Ellsworth, *Mainsprings of Civilization* (New York, Wiley, 1945).
14. LASSWELL, Harold D., *World Politics and Personal Insecurity* (New York, McGraw-Hill, 1935).
15. MARX, Karl, *Capital, A Critical Analysis of Capitalist Production* (London, Swan Sonnenschein, 1902).
16. MERRIAM, Charles E., *The Making of Citizens* (Chicago, University of Chicago Press, 1931).
16a. ———, *Political Power* (New York, McGraw-Hill, 1934).
17. MORRIS, Charles, *Paths of Life, Preface to a World Religion* (New York, Harper, 1942).
18. MYRDAL, Gunnar, *An American Dilemma* (New York. Harper, 1943), 2 vols.
19. ———, "Social Trends in America and Strategic Approaches to the Negro Problem," *Phylon*, Vol. 9, No. 3 (1948), pp. 211 ff.
20. NEUGEBAUER, O., "Babylonian Planetary Theory," *Proceedings, American Philosophical Society*, Vol. 98 (February, 1954), pp. 60 ff.
21. NORTHROP, F. S. C., *The Meeting of the East and West* (New York, Macmillan, 1946).
22. OGBURN, W. F., ed., *Technology and International Relations*, Harris Institute Lectures (Chicago, University of Chicago Press, 1949).
23. PARSONS, Talcott, and SHILS, E. A., eds., *Toward a General Theory of Action* (Cambridge, Harvard University Press, 1951).
23a. PLATO, *The Republic*.
23b. POLANYI, Michael, "On the Introduction of Science into Moral Subjects," *The Cambridge Journal*, Vol. 7, No. 4.

24. Pool, Ithiel de Sola, *Symbols of Nationalism and Internationalism*, Introduction by Quincy Wright, Radir Project (Stanford, Stanford University Press, 1951).

25. Rapaport, Anatol, *Operational Philosophy* (New York, Harper, 1953).

26. Russell Sage Foundation, *A Bibliography of Social Surveys* (New York, Russell Sage Foundation, 1930).

27. Schweitzer, Albert, "Ethics for Twentieth Century Man," *Saturday Review* (June 13, 1953).

28. Sheldon, W. H., "Integration in the Biological and Social Sciences," in *Contributions to the Analysis and Synthesis of Knowledge*, Proceedings, American Academy of Arts and Sciences, in co-operation with Institute for the Unity of Science, Vol. 80 (July, 1951), pp. 31 ff.

29. Sulzbach, Walter, *National Consciousness* (Washington, American Council on Public Affairs, 1943).

30. Thurstone, L. L., *The Vectors of Mind* (Chicago, University of Chicago Press, 1935), p. 170.

31. Toynbee, Arnold J., *A Study of History* (New York, Oxford University Press, 1934), Vol. 1, p. 300.

32. United Nations, Statistical Office, *Statistical Year Book* (New York, United Nations, 1948–).

33. Wright, Quincy, ed., *Public Opinion and World Politics*, Harris Institute Lectures (Chicago, University of Chicago Press, 1933), p. 9.

34. ———, *A Study of War* (Chicago, University of Chicago Press, 1942), pp. 1240-ff, 1254, 1433 ff, 1471.

35. ———, "Method in the Study of War," *World Politics*, Vol. 1 (June, 1949), pp. 243 ff.

36. ———, "Measurement of Variations in International Tensions," in Bryson, Finkelstein, and McIver, eds., *Learning and World Peace*, Eighth Symposium on Science, Philosophy and Religion (New York, Harper, 1948), pp. 54 ff.

37. ———, "Specialization and Universal Values in General International Organization," in *Approaches to Group Understanding*, Sixth Symposium on Science, Philosophy and Religion (New York, Harper, 1947), pp. 207 ff.

38. ———, ed., *The World Community*, Harris Institute Lectures (Chicago, University of Chicago Press, 1948).

39. ———, *Problems of Stability and Progress in International Relations* (Berkeley, University of California Press, 1954).

40. Wright, Sewall, "Correlation and Causation," *Journal of Agricultural Research*, Vol. 20 (Washington, D. C., January 3, 1921), pp. 557 ff.

41. ———, "The Theory of Path Coefficients," *Genetics*, Vol. 7 (May, 1923), pp. 239 ff.

42. ———, "Evolution, Organic," *Encyclopædia Britannica* (1948).

43. Znaniecki, Florian, *Modern Nationalities* (Urbana, University of Illinois Press, 1952).

Searching for unified discipline of int. relations that would be of theoretical + practical value to general people; readers, professionals, + research education

p 582

The Value of a Discipline of International Relations

THE THREE PRECEDING chapters have discussed the conception, sources, and form of a unified discipline of international relations, under the assumption that such a discipline would be of both theoretical and practical value. This chapter will examine the values of such a discipline apart from the intellectual and aesthetic satisfaction it might give as an end in itself. Among possible values might be assistance to general education and public information; assistance to statesmen and politicians in the conduct of international affairs; assistance to experts and advisors in the carrying on of their professional work relating to international affairs; and stimulation of fruitful research. If education is regarded as a process continuing through life, these values may be defined as assistance to general, leadership, professional, and research education. The discipline should serve the elementary, secondary, and college teacher; the journalist and commentator; the ﹡statesman, diplomat, and international official; the lawyer, economist, civil servant, and professional-school teacher; and especially the graduate-school teacher, the scholar, and the research worker in the field. Can the same discipline serve all of these ends?

The educational and research objectives of the discipline of international relations have been discussed in Chapter 7 of this book. It was pointed out that there have been divergencies of opinion on whether the study of international relations is valuable for citizenship and, if it is, what aspects are most valuable and at what stage of education they should be taught. These differences of opinion exist among different countries and usually among different groups in any one country. In the United States there has been considerable difference in emphasis at different periods of recent history with different consequences upon opinion and policy. It was considered that the student, who will become the citizen, should be educated rather than indoctrinated. "He needs to understand the circumstances and conditions which account for these shifts in public opinion and policy and to have criteria for appraising the consequences of founding policy on one or the other opinion under varying circumstances and conditions."

In respect to education for leadership, it was pointed out that the leader "need not, in fact should not, be a professional himself but he should be able to choose among experts" and that it is "particularly important that the education of leaders should be based as broadly as possible in time and space."

In regard to professional education it was pointed out that foreign service examiners "had tended to emphasize general culture and ability rather than specific professional equipment" giving the latter by "in-service" training adapted to the particular activities which the individual will pursue. Nevertheless, persons who had received specialized training in aspects of international relations at universities were in demand for professional services. The special difficulties of reconciling expert standards with policy-making were mentioned.

The unique task of a discipline of international relations is to advance knowledge in the field, but it was pointed out that fruitful research is more likely to be on the periphery of established disciplines than at their centers. "When new ways of looking at things is of the essence, familiarity with the traditional modes of thought may do more harm than good."

These observations are not very encouraging for the utility of a unified discipline of international relations at any level. Let us consider in more detail the function of such a discipline in general education, in practical action, and in scholarly research.

GENERAL EDUCATION

If the task is education for citizenship the content of instruction can hardly be unrelated to the values of the culture and the political situation at the time. It is doubtful whether there is any body of information or any fundamental attitudes equally good for all peoples in a varied world, or equally good for all times in a rapidly changing world. Every people needs to know more about the resources, conditions, values, and policies of its own nation than about others, and about its neighbors more than about distant countries, valuable as a general perspective of world geography and world history may be. Even if attitudes favorable to conciliation and world mindedness are a virtue in a shrinking world, yet general education must be geared to the existing state of opinion or it may achieve results opposite to those expected. In Los Angeles in 1952, for example, after a vigorous discussion in the Board of Education and among the public a handbook concerning UNESCO was barred from the schools in response to prevailing sentiments of nationalism. Following this the American National Commission on UNESCO declared that statements alleging that it was "engaged in supporting the concepts of one world government and one world citizenship" had "no basis in fact," but that the Commission supported "education of peoples to live as citizens of sovereign states in a community of all mankind preserving the values of diverse cultures and the rights and responsibilities of national citizenship" (23). This careful wording adapted the objectives of UNESCO to local sentiments.

In the modern world it is not easy to decide what condition of public opinion is desirable in a given community. Clearly a public opinion is not satisfactory if it is based on the repression of unpleasant facts (escapism), on the universalization of local values (narcissism), on impossible demands (frustration), or on false evaluations of problems or displacement of fears leading to neurotic apathies and anxieties (hysteria). A sound public opinion should be neither aggressive nor supine, neither neglectful of international responsibilities nor meddlesome with affairs of others. It should balance national policy with international law, the national interest with the principle of reciprocity, the value of strength with the value of reputation, the need of domestic defense with the danger of foreign provocation, useful conciliation with unnecessary appeasements. To provide information, education, and interpretation is an art of extraordinary difficulty.

It is clear that a discipline of international relations, if it is to be of broad utility in general education, cannot emphasize concrete information nor can it deal with specific attitudes or opinions on concrete issues. It should rather emphasize the general facts of world geography, the general trends of history, the philosophical analysis of values, and the scientific analysis of international relations. It cannot neglect the varied interpretations which each particular culture and value system is likely to give to its generalizations. Whatever may be the scientific meaning of its content, the presentation of the discipline of international relations would have to be adapted for use in general education in each community.

PRACTICAL ACTION

What might a discipline of international relations contribute to the effectiveness of practice in the field? As has been noted, its contribution to the education of practitioners is problematic. Statesmen, politicians, and other decision-makers need a more general education while experts and advisors need a more specialized education. Writers on statecraft and diplomacy in the seventeenth and eighteenth centuries discussed the professional education needed by persons who aspired to engage in these activities, including therein a general knowledge of history, language, and philosophy, as well as the more practical arts of diplomacy, war, and law, not overlooking the need of good birth, good manners, and proficiency in the polite arts. The persons who engaged in these activities at that time, while they may have often fallen short in some of these requirements, could in a wide sense be called professionals (8). They were given, or at least held, their jobs because of their proficiency, and they were proficient because they had incorporated knowledge of both the techniques and the values of the field in their personalities (25). This knowledge was, therefore, always available in the making of decisions. It is true they had to continue to hold the favor of the monarch who employed them and this was one of the requirements of the art, but so long as they could do that, they had considerable freedom in decision-making (12).

Democratic conditions have tended toward a differentiation of statesmen and experts in the international field. The former often owe their position to the arts of persuading a wide electorate rather than to competence in international relations, and the latter, whether they serve national or international organizations, are usually highly specialized in some geographical area or in some speciality such as international finance, international law, international economics, communications, or public relations. It may be, however, that familiarity with a general discipline of international relations could assist both types of person. A statesman who has even a superficial acquaintance with such a discipline might better focus his general knowledge and experience in a field which presents special problems and requires methods different from those learned in general education or from experience in domestic politics, business, or law. He would also be in a better position to appraise the advice which he receives from experts.

The expert himself, by acquaintance with such a discipline, could better orient his highly specialized knowledge so as to communicate with his colleagues in other specialties and with the decision-maker, whom he advises. He would be more likely to be aware of the need of balancing his specialized analysis of a problem with that of others in arriving at a decision on what to do in the actual situation (1, 9). He would also be less likely to forget that there is much more in the art of deciding wisely than any science can give (18). Diplomacy and mediation are arts rather than sciences (8, 11).

To the liaison men who connect the decision-makers and the experts—the professional foreign service officers, the professional administrators in foreign offices and international organizations, the expert advisers at the elbow of the international and foreign policy-maker, and the mediators and conciliators seeking to bring about agreement in international disputes—such a discipline might prove particularly useful (2).

Apart from the education of persons before assuming practical responsibilities, a general discipline of international relations might contribute much to the day by day conduct of international affairs, whether by national or international officials. Disciplines have been developed to assist in the practical activity of military men, diplomats, colonial administrators, international lawyers, international financiers, international propagandists, and international educators. These activities differ greatly from one another, and specialized disciplines for each are undoubtedly essential, but they share with one another and with all the practical arts and professions, not only the need for skill derived from experience, but the necessity (a) to define situations which have to be dealt with, (b) to obtain relevant information, (c) to formulate objectives, and (d) to make decisions initiating action.

The medical profession, for example, designates these four aspects of cases as diagnosis, etiology, prognosis, and treatment. For physicians the general objective, restoration of health in the patient, is assumed, indeed enjoined by the Hippocratic Oath, and more specific objectives are defined by the prognosis. Military commanders usually define the aspects of the situation with which they deal by formulating strategic objectives, appraising their own and the enemies resources and capabilities, planning operations on the basis of calculated risks, and reaching decisions in respect to orders and time of initiating action. They define the situation in terms of a hierarchy of objectives—political, grand strategic, strategic, and tactical—the latter being formulated in the plan of operations. Lawyers define a case in terms of categories formulated by the law, search for evidence and for rules of law, appraise the probable impact of evidence and arguments on the court, and reach a decision whether to litigate or compromise. Businessmen define a situation in terms of the interests of the persons involved in a pending transaction—managers, stockholders, workers, sellers, buyers; gather information on costs of possible alternatives, available assets, and bargaining margins; appraise the risks or profits of the alternatives; and decide whether to initiate negotiation or to close a deal. Here the general objective of maximizing profits is usually assumed. Specific objectives result from an appraisal of risks and profits.

In all of these activities the decision is usually made by someone whose competence rests less on scientific knowledge than on practice and experience. Physicians do not practice independently until they have had clinical experience as interns. Major military decisions are made by officers of long experience in both staff and line. Both lawyers and judges in responsible positions have usually had experience as office apprentices. Only men who have grown into the business make important business decisions. The wisdom to make decisions appears to come from observing a master or from acting one's self rather than from knowledge of either fact or theory, though the latter may help. The professions are arts more than they are sciences (11, 18, 21).

Are there any peculiarities in the conduct of international relations that differentiate it from other practical arts and justify a special discipline? These peculiarities seem to lie in the lack of clear guides for defining situations; in the inaccessibility of much relevant information; in the variableness of objectives and the uncertainty of values; and in the difficulty of bringing all relevant ideas available to bear at the time of decision. Furthermore there is unusual difficulty in assuring that statesmen will acquire adequate experience before assuming full responsibility and that they will not utilize their discretion for unacceptable ends.

Defining the situation. The medical man knows from the discipline of medicine certain definite diseases and the diagnosis permits him to define cases in terms of this knowledge. The lawyer also has established legal categories with which he can define situations. The commander and businessman deal with less definable situations, but each usually has clear general objectives which assist in defining situations in terms of the obstacles to, or opportunities for, the achievement of these goals. The statesman, on the other hand, often finds himself without established landmarks. He may be faced with a situation presented by an act of aggression, a proposal from another country, a public demand from his own country, and if so the situation may be somewhat defined. He may treat it, by analogy to the lawyer, as a legal case or, by analogy to the general, as an attack on national interest or policy, but he may be uncertain which analogy is most applicable. Furthermore, often a condition of danger or opportunity may have been gradually developing and he may have to consider whether at any moment to treat this as a *situation* and to take the initative himself. The atmosphere which statesmanship may create, can contribute to the definition of the situation (25). Almost every *situation* involves imagination to recognize it as a situation at all to define it as legal, political, economic, psychological, or something else, and even to modify it by an appropriate word or gesture. The term *situation* and *dispute* referred to in the United Nations Charter have provided a basis for wide divergencies of opinion as to their meaning.

Information. The most important information for the decision-maker in international affairs is usually the values and capabilities of the statesmen of other countries. But, as in the case of the military commander, this kind of information is difficult to get. Often methods of espionage have to be used, but the statesman, seeking peace, is more hampered in the use of such methods than is the general. For the statesman, especially if he represents a democracy, the utilization of such methods tends to augment suspicions and hamper negotiations. Information on the values and policies of another state can be gathered from scrutiny of biographies of leaders, from the history of the country, from analysis of prevailing ideologies, and from deductions from the assumed interests of the state. Information on its armaments; resources; production; morale; technical personnel; divisive opinions, parties, and politics; and other elements affecting its capability can also be gathered from general sources. Agencies like the American Office of Strategic Services during World War II (superseded by the Central Intelligence Agency), carefully collecting and piecing together bits of information in these fields, have been increasingly used by all governments.

It has been suggested that systematic publication by an international scientific agency of surveys of opinion and political developments as well as of armaments, industrial production and trade, would, by making relevant information available to all, narrow the range of misinformation and decrease excessive anxieties rising from exaggerated reports (19, 28). When a few great arms manufacturers made and sold arms for profit to all countries, there were dangers, because of the interest of these firms in expanding their markets by creating "war scares," but there was less anxiety about new weapons and secret preparations than in the present period of rigorous secrecy under the control of national governments. So long, however, as international relations is dominated by a spirit of opposition rather than of co-operation, accurate information on some of the most relevant factors will be difficult to obtain. On the whole it appears that absolutistic countries are in a better position than democracies both to conceal information about themselves and to obtain information about the democracies. Anything that can be done to make information in the field more generally available would seem to promote the cause of democracy.

More current, accurate, and public information would probably also promote the cause of peace. So long, however, as peace depends upon the balance of power, precise information which makes projection of the trends of power more accurate, may disclose that time is definitely running against an important participant in the equilibrium, thus encouraging that government to initiate hostilities in the apprehension that its possibility of success will steadily decline. This situation hardly arises in a multilateral equilibrium because diplomatic negotiation to change the alliance system and rectify the balance is then always possible, but where a bipolar situation exists, the state against which time is running may perceive no alternative to initiating hostilities. This paradoxical situation, in which ignorance of the future may be the best assurance of peace, can only be remedied by better and more generally distributed information on the probable consequences of war (22), and by a more stable situation in the world as a result of a more complicated balance of power or a more effective international organization.

Uncertain objectives. It has been said that national statesmen must always serve the national interest (15), but what is the national interest in a particular situation? It can perhaps be assumed that states have a national interest in survival, but it is often doubtful whether it is the authority of the government of the day, the independence of the state, the autonomy of the national culture, or the livelihood of the people, survival of which is threatened. Both the kind of "survival" desired and the means to assure it are in most situations, highly controversial. Does a state by joining a federation abandon its "national interest" in "survival"? Objectives must be formulated in terms more narrow and precise than survival if they are to be useful guides to action. Increase in power, in prosperity, in security, in prestige (sometimes substituting for power), and in reputation (useful in attracting allies), have all been considered national interests and have all on occasion been objectives influencing state policy. Such objectives must, at least in democracies, be interpreted with reference to the domestic situation indicating what the people are interested in. Democratic theory may consider that this defines the national interest, and in any case it influences the timing and methods by which foreign policy objectives can be pursued (25).

The objectives of a national statesman must, therefore, usually be more fluid than those of other decision-makers. No general theory of international ethics or of national interest would prove applicable to all situations. Objectives and values are a resultant of a continually changing situation in domestic and international politics. While the statesmen of international organizations may find their objectives somewhat more precisely formulated in international instruments, a changing situation always leaves a wide margin for interpreting these objectives at any moment.

Complexity of decision-making. The problem of making adequate decisions is complicated in international relations by the complexity of the facts, interests, values, and policy-alternatives often involved. Close co-operation of the decision-maker and his expert advisors is necessary. The decision-maker can seldom have either sufficient facts or sufficient background in his own mind to act wisely without advice. In organizations as large as the modern national government or international organization serious problems of structure and procedure must be solved if the decision-maker is to have appropriate information, analyses, and evaluations before him at the time the decision must be made. If the experts prepare intelligence reports or analyze situations without complete awareness of the way in which the decision-maker envisages the situation these reports are almost certain to be irrelevant, inappropriate, and of little use in making the decision. This is true because the definition of the situation and the formulation of the problem necessarily determine the relevance of information and the appropriate forms of analysis (12).

A general discipline of international relations known to both decision-maker and expert might give such guidance, in the definition of situations and the formulation of problems, that the decision-maker and his staff would immediately see it the same way. In other practical activities, such as law, an accepted discipline has so formalized the subject that complex situations can rapidly be analyzed in terms which all lawyers understand and which indicate the relevance of factual evidence and legal sources. It may be questioned, however, whether in the more flexible conditions of decision-making in international relations such a discipline is possible. The essence of the matter may be the inventiveness of the decision-maker in seeing the situation in a new light which gives relevance to new kinds of information and new forms of analysis. In so far as any discipline would be helpful in this situation it would seem to be that of general administration providing an organization and procedures for maximizing the co-operation of the decision-maker and his staff (2, 9).

Inexperience of decision-makers. In so far as effective action in international relations is an art rather than a science, the responsible decision-maker needs experience more than he needs knowledge. This is not to say that an analysis of the kind which a discipline of international relations might develop would be unimportant. The diplomat should have studied international law and the general should have studied military science, but in both cases long experience under supervision is required before important decisions are made. Can the kind of experience which precedes primary responsibility in the professions be obtained by major decision-makers in national governments and international organizations?

Older writers on international politics attached great importance to the training of princes and diplomats (7, 8). Prime ministers have usually gained experience in lesser cabinet positions. Presidents of the United States have often served as state governors and occasionally in diplomatic or other foreign policy positions. Secretaries-general of international organizations have often served in national governments. Mediators in international disputes have sometimes had experience in mediating industrial disputes (11). Decision-making in international relations is, however, *sui generis*. Experience in analogous situations may not be adequate. The succession of a new prime minister, president, or secretary-general presents peculiar difficulties, not met in other professions or positions of executive responsibility. In his memoirs Winston Churchill expresses regret that he did not go to Washington when Truman succeeded to Roosevelt in the spring of 1945 in order to make the new president aware of the situation of the world in a way which no one could do except a person with direct responsibility for making decisions. "There is no comparison," he wrote, "between reading about events afterward and living through them from hour to hour" (4).

Apart from the difficulty of gaining experience, immediately relevant for statesmanship in international relations, except through actual decision-making, there is some evidence that the skills required for adequate performance in this field demand abilities which are rare. A historian of monarchs finds that few have been able to do the job well (26). A historian of the American presidency finds that only eight of the thirty-two presidents were "great," though nearly all grew with responsibilities of office. The "great" president must be a dignified Chief of State, a good administrator, a good party leader, a good maker of public opinion, and a good decision-maker in the international field. This is an order which no president has completely filled (10, 14).

Among the personal qualifications for international decision-making seem to be skill in combining logical analysis and calculation with judgment in weighing alternatives and balancing considerations. Such skill requires what semanticists have called "predictive behavior" (20). Such behavior is active rather than passive in that it is internally generated. It is also purposive rather than nonpurposive in that it is guided by ideal goals. Furthermore, it is self-corrective or influenced by the "feed-back" in that action is continually modified as the characteristics of, and information about, the goal changes. A pursuit airplane which continually changes its course so as to be always headed toward the target bomber manifests such active, purposive, corrective behavior, while a gunner on the ground shooting at an airplane though active and purposive is not corrective because once the projectile has been fired its flight is determined. Corrective devices may, it is true, be built into guided missiles to a limited extent (3). Predictive behavior goes one step further. The pursuit pilot, instead of keeping his plane headed on the target, calculates what the bomber pilot will probably do and diverts his course so as to intercept the target. Similarly the anti-aircraft gunner may calculate the probable manoeuvres of the invading plane and shoot, not at where the plane is nor where it would be if it continued its present course, but at where it will probably be when the bullet arrives. From such first order prediction it is possible to move to second order prediction by which the pursuer calculates the probable calculations made by the target's pilot in regard to the pursuer's manoeuvres and the probable modification of the expected behavior in view of such calculations. Such predictive behavior may be pushed further as by experienced chess players who calculate each others probable action for a dozen moves ahead (6, 20). This line of thought pursued by makers of calculating machines hardly approaches the complexity of the factors which an experienced statesman unconsciously considers in dealing with an opposing statesman of equal ability.

The process of interaction between persons has been discussed in Chapter 28.

This examination of the skill which responsible officials practicing the art of international relations ought to exercise suggests the great difficulty of formulating methods of analysis which can be learned by formal study and the importance that such officials have experience in action and have minds of unusual sensitivity. The problem is, therefore, to so organize national governments and international organizations that only personalities with the proper experience and qualifications will occupy positions of responsibility (13).

Control of the exercise of discretion. This does not mean that the problems of organizing expert advice before, and efficient implementing agencies after, a decision is made, can be neglected, nor does it mean that the problems of developing policy, goals, legal standards, predictive criteria, and constitutional controls to keep decision-makers within bounds, are unimportant. The decision-maker, however able and experienced, needs assistance to give him facts, ideas, and analyses before he decides, and to make his decision effective afterwards. The more able and experienced the decision-maker, the more danger that he will depart from his role as representative of a group and seek to use the group for his own purposes.

Political, legal, scientific, and constitutional controls, however, not only guide, but also shackle the decision-maker. They produce a government of law rather than of men, but this may not be either practical or desirable unless the field in which the decision is to function is homogeneous in respect to the attitudes, opinions, and values of the systems of action within it. In an extremely heterogeneous field decision-making must operate through controversy, negotiation, and conciliation rather than through legislation, administration, and adjudication.

Jural law artificially defines situations, reduces the number of factors which must be considered in decision-making, and simplifies that task by maintaining certain reliable expectations in regard to the methods which other decision-makers will use in pursuance of purposes. While increasing the advantage of certain skills, it moderates the advantage of skills tending to upset the social order. It, therefore, tends to promote social equality and stability at the expense of social freedom and change. But a considerable consensus is necessary if law is to live (17).

Effective jural law builds certain expectations of the behavior of all persons and organizations into the social system so that each can rely on the others behaving as the law says they must. Just as skillful engineering may build into the aiming mechanism of an anti-aircraft gun an expectation of the behavior of the target plane so that the gunner, while apparently aiming at the target, will in fact be aiming at the point where the target will be when the bullet arrives, so jural law seeks to build into the behavior of each member of the society an expectation that all will observe its norms, As a result, in making decisions within a jural community it is not necessary to embark upon the difficult task of discovering the psychological attitudes, ethical values, or interested calculations of those who might frustrate the decision but only upon the easier task of discovering their legal rights, duties, and powers. Law, however, is not without dangers (8).

To pursue our analogy, once a target pilot becomes aware of what the mechanism of the anti-aircraft gun expected he would do, he can behave differently and escape. So the law provides an opportunity for crooks. By knowing what the law-abiding citizen expects of them they can take advantage of the unwary. Secretary of State Kellogg pointed out that a legal definition of aggression or self-defense might make it "easy for the unscrupulous to mold events" to accord with that definition. Predictions built into a gun are worse than useless if known to the target pilot and predictions built into the law may be worse than useless if not comprehensive and not enforced. The prospect of law enforcement is not good unless the number and power of the voluntarily law-abiding is overwhelming in comparison with the potential law-breakers. This is another way of saying that law can only function in a field in which attitudes, opinions, and values are relatively homogeneous so that its norms can be made to conform to the actual dispositions of most of its subjects.

A balance of stability and progress, therefore, requires that law be confined to those matters on which there is a substantial consensus and which can, therefore, be enforced, and that major decision-makers be so organized that they check one another. Such a combination of government by laws and by men implies that as a minimum the law deals moderately effectively with violence and fraud. If it does not, as Machiavelli perceived, government will be by the men most skillful in organizing power.

This analysis suggests that in the heterogeneous world of today law must leave wide freedom to decision-makers, and that a suitable balance between law and politics is hardly possible in the situation of universal vulnerability to atomic war, unless the apparent consensus of mankind against war can be sanctioned by effective law (28).

Formulae of universal ethics, of universal law, or even of universal science function as controls by the world community as a whole over its member nations, thus making for stability. Principles of international politics, international economics, and international communications, on the other hand, function as guides whereby the nations, in competition, controversy, or conflict with one another make decisions modifying the whole community and making for change or progress. Preservation of the latter element depends upon the skill of statesmen, national and international, in making decisions which forward the goals of the group they represent. It does not seem likely that the art of statesmanship either can or should be eliminated from the practice of international relations. Some uncertainty and risk is the price of progress.

RESEARCH

It seems likely that a unified discipline of international relations may prove more useful for research than for either general education or practical action. Research, it is true, like statesmanship, seeks new ways of looking at situations, but a discipline serving as a logical catalogue of what is known indicates gaps to be filled, hypotheses to be verified, and inconsistencies to be resolved. In doing this it focuses attention and stimulates investigation (29).

In the world of action, an integrated discipline, so far as it served to unite the decision-maker and his advisors on a common definition and analysis of all situations, might strait-jacket them all within rigid categories and stultify inventiveness, but, in the world of thought the situation is very different. Here the individual works alone and not under the pressure of time. A discipline may serve to disclose lacunae and faults to be pondered over and types of data to be sought for, and may even suggest alternative general concepts. It is likely, therefore, to stimulate inventiveness while at the same time curbing erratic ideas. In the natural sciences, as Conant has pointed out, conceptual systems and the disciplines which have developed from them by the process of deduction and verification have contributed to the march of science because they point to weaknesses which invite innovation and at the same time present a structure of reasonable solidity resistant to change and compelling the innovator to defend his position with adequate materials (5). In the same way, advancement of the science of international relations may be the main function of a discipline of the subject.

Such a science may serve, on the one hand, to make men aware of their participation in the universal society and of the direction in which that society is moving, and, on the other, to indicate gaps in knowledge, both theoretical and practical, challenging further research. Both of these services would contribute to peace, if it is assumed that men want to survive and to enjoy life, and that action is most likely to contribute to those ends if based on an accurate estimate of its probable consequences. In this field knowledge is related to both virtue and power. It tends to develop legal and ethical standards and procedures to the limit of their potentialities in a given state of opinion, and to assist politicians in achieving their goals within the limits of those standards and procedures.

REFERENCES

1. BLOUGH, Roy, "The Role of the Economist in Federal Policy Making," *University of Illinois Bulletin*, Vol. 5, No. 28 (November, 1953).

2. BRYSON, Lyman, "Notes on a Theory of Advice," in *Freedom and Authority in Our Time*, Twelfth Symposium on Science, Philosophy and Religion (New York, Harper, 1953), pp. 27 ff.

3. BUSH, Vannevar, *Modern Arms and Free Men* (New York, Simon and Schuster, 1949).

4. CHURCHILL, Winston S., *Triumph and Tragedy* (New York, Houghton Mifflin, 1953).

5. CONANT, James B., *Science and Common Sense* (New Haven, Yale University Press, 1951).

6. DEUTSCH, Karl W., "Game Theory and Politics: Some Problems of Application," *The Canadian Journal of Economics and Political Science*, Vol. 20 (February, 1954), pp. 76 ff.

7. FÉNELON, François, *Télémaque* (1699).

8. HEATLEY, D. P., *Diplomacy and the Study of International Relations* (Oxford, Clarendon Press, 1919).

9. HILSMAN, Roger, Jr., "Intelligence and Policy Making in Foreign Affairs," *World Politics*, Vol. 5 (October, 1952), pp. 1 ff.

10. HYMAN, Sidney, *The American President* (New York, Harper, 1954).

11. JACKSON, Elmore, *Meeting of Minds, A Way to Peace Through Mediation* (New York, McGraw-Hill, 1952).

12. KECSKEMETI, Paul, "The 'Policy Sciences': Aspiration and Outlook," *World Politics*, Vol. 4 (July, 1952), pp. 520 ff.

13. LASSWELL, Harold D., *Politics: Who Gets What, When, How* (New York, McGraw-Hill, 1936).

14. MILTON, George Fort, *The Use of Presidential Power, 1789-1943* (Boston, Little, Brown, 1944).

15. MORGENTHAU, Hans J., *Politics Among Nations*, 2nd ed. (New York, Knopf, 1954).

16. MORRIS, Charles, *Paths of Life* (New York, Harper, 1942).

17. NORTHROP, F. S. C., *The Taming of the Nations* (New York, Macmillan, 1952).

18. POLANYI, Michael, "Skills and Connoisseurship," *Atti del Congresso di Metodologia* (Turin, December, 1952), pp. 381 ff.

19. POOL, Ithiel de Sola, *Symbols of Internationalism* (Stanford, Stanford University Press, 1951).

20. RAPAPORT, Anatol, *Operational Philosophy* (New York, Harper, 1953).

21. RIEZLER, Kurt, "Political Decisions in Modern Society," *Ethics*, Vol. 64 (January, 1954), Part 2.

22. RUSSELL, Bertrand, "The Danger to Mankind," *Bulletin of the Atomic Scientists*, Vol. 10 (January, 1954), p. 8.

23. UNESCO, *News Letter* (Washington, United States National Commission for UNESCO, October 27, 1952).

24. VINER, Jacob, "The Short View and the Long in Economic Policy," *American Economic Review*, Vol. 30, No. 1 (March, 1940).

25. WEBSTER, Sir Charles K., *The Art and Practice of Diplomacy* (London School of Economics and Political Science, 1952).

26. WOODS, Frederick Adams, *The Influence of Monarchs* (New York, Macmillan, 1913).

27. WRIGHT, Quincy, *A Study of War* (Chicago, University of Chicago Press, 1942), pp. 1299 ff.

28. ——, *Problems of Stability and Progress in International Relations* (Berkeley, University of California Press, 1954).

29. ——, "Criteria for Judging the Relevance of Researches on the Problems of Peace" in *Research for Peace*, Essays submitted to the Institute for Social Research, Oslo, Norway (Amsterdam, North Holland Publishing Co., 1954).

Appendix

TABLE 1: *Statistics Used in Locating States in Analytical Field*

Country	Population (10 million) 1	"People" Dependent on National or Internat'l Economy (10 million) 2	"Nation" Literate (10 million) 3	"State" Partici-pants in Nat'l or Internat'l Politics (10 million) 4	"Gov't" Decision-Makers and Major Advisors (10 million) 5	Income per Capita ($) 6	Income per Capita of Literate ($) 7	National Income (billion $) 8	National Gov't Budget (billion $) 9	International Trade per Capita ($) 10	International Letters per Capita ($) 11
World	250	220	2.5	1	.0025	280	2000	25.0	.1	60.0	40.0
China	47	40	2.8	6.6	.047	27	400	11.0	10.0	1.4	.18
India	36	28.8	2.5	5.8	.054	57	500	17.0	1.6	8.3	.4
USSR	20	18	7.8	6	.05	308	700	55.0	50.0	2.6	.1
US	16	15.7	12.8	10.4	.13	1453	1600	228.0	72.0	162.0	4.4
Germany	7	7	5.5	4.9	.049	320	800	22.0	8.0	112.0	3.9
Brazil	5.4	4.8	1.3	.81	.0036	112	600	5.4	1.0	63.0	1.4
UK	5	5	4.0	3.6	.045	773	1100	39.0	14.0	331.0	14.4
Italy	4.7	4.65	2.8	2.35	.028	235	700	11.0	3.3	78.0	5.0
France	4.2	4.2	3.1	2.52	.031	482	800	20.0	11.1	199.0	7.7
Egypt	2	1.9	.14	.2	.0036	100	600	1.9	.76	51.2	2.6
Switzerland	.5	.5	.4	.37	.006	849	1000	4.6	.44	461.0	35.4
Denmark	.4	.4	.32	.32	.004	689	900	2.7	.40	453.0	12.0

Country	12. % of Economy in International Trade	13. Participation in International Organizations	14. Energy Production (10 mil. tons bituminous coal)	15. Energy Production per Capita (tons bit. coal)	16. Energy Resources (10 billion tons bit. coal)	17. Energy Resources per Capita (tons bit. coal)	18. Land Area (10,000 sq. miles)	19. Land Area per Capita (sq. miles)	20. In Primary Education (million)	21. In Secondary Education (million)	22. In Higher Education (million)
World	50	44	165.0	.66	867.0	3468	5816.4	.0210	200.0	37.0	12.0
China	5	37	2.7	.06	215.9	4593	387.4	.0081	37.0	1.1	.2
India	15	44	2.5	.07	9.9	277	117.4	.0032	18.4	5.2	.6
USSR	1	18	14.1	.7	131.4	6568	859.9	.0440	37.0	10.1	1.4
US	11	44	62.1	3.9	251.4	15710	302.2	.0190	22.0	6.5	2.6
Germany	35	28	20.7	2.9	30.8	4900	13.7	.0020	10.3	1.5	2.0
Brazil	56	43	1.0	.2	8.0	1481	328.6	.0055	5.2	.4	.3
UK	43	44	22.6	4.5	17.7	3541	9.5	.0019	5.1	2.3	.2
Italy	33	33	1.1	.24	1.1	241	11.6	.0025	5.6	.5	.7
France	41	44	5.4	1.3	3.3	797	21.3	.0050	5.3	.9	.5
Egypt	51	43	.42	.21	.5	250	38.6	.0190	1.4	.1	.1
Switzerland	54	24	.8	1.6	.8	1600	1.6	.0032	.5	.1	.04
Denmark	66	43	.5	1.25	.5	1250	1.7	.0040	.4	.1	.1

TABLE 2: *Location of the United States in the Analytical Field*

Axes		People	Nation	State	Govern-ment
		23	24	25	26
A	Energy–Lethargy	+10	+12	+15	+16
B	Flexibility–Rigidity	+ 4	+ 5	+ 6	+ 7
C	Co-operation–Isolation	+ 4	+ 1	− 4	− 5
D	Strength–Weakness	+ 6	+ 7	+ 8	+ 9
E	Resource Abundance–Poverty	+10	+ 8	+ 6	+ 6
F	Technological Advancement–Backwardness	+ 5	+ 6	+ 7	+ 8
X	Objectivity–Subjectivity	+ 2	+ 3	+ 4	+ 5
Y	Abstractness–Concreteness	+ 3	+ 4	+ 5	+ 6
U	Liberality–Restrictiveness	+ 5	+ 6	+ 7	+ 8
V	Situation–Self Orientation	+ 1	0	− 1	− 2
W	Affirmation–Negation	+ 8	+ 9	+10	+11
Z	Manipulation–Contemplation	+ 4	+ 5	+ 6	+ 7

TABLE 3: *Location of States on the Capability Axes*

Country	A-AXIS ENERGY–LETHARGY				B-AXIS FLEXIBILITY–RIGIDITY				C-AXIS CO-OPERATION–ISOLATION			
	People (from Col. 6)	*Nation* (from Col. 7)	*State* (from Col. 8)	*Government* (from Col. 9)	*People*	*Nation*	*State*	*Government*	*People* (from Col. 10)	*Nation* (from Col. 11)	*State* (from Cols. 12 and 13)	*Government* (from Cols. 1 and 4)
	27	28	29	30	31	32	33	34	35	36	37	38
World	0	+17	+ .4	− 2	0	+ 9	+12	+13	0	+12.8	+ 9	+13
China	− 1.8	− 3	− .4	+ .5	− 8	− 6	0	− 4	− 2.3	− .4	− 6.4	− 8.4
India	− 1.5	− 2	0	− 1.6	− 4	− 1	+ 1	+ 2	− 2.0	− .4	− 2.6	− 1.9
USSR	+ .14	+ .5	+ 2.7	+10	− 9	− 7	− 1	− 5	− 2.3	+ .43	− 7.6	− 8.4
US	+10.0	+12	+15.0	+16	+ 4	+ 5	+ 6	+ 7	+ 4.0	+ 1.0	− 4.0	− 5
Germany	+ .28	+ 2.5	+ .3	0	+ 2	+ 2	+ 3	− 2	+ 2.0	+ .8	− .15	0
Brazil	− 1.2	0	− .8	− 1.7	− 1	0	+ 4	− 1	+ 1.1	0	+11.0	+ .3
U.K.	+ 3.4	+ 7	+ 1.5	+ 1.5	+ 8	+ 8	+ 3	+ 3	+11.0	+ 4.3	+ 7.0	+ 5.1
Italy	− .31	+ 1	+ .4	− 1.2	+ 3	+ 2	− 4	+ 1	+ .7	+ 1.2	+ .7	− 2.9
France	+ 1.4	+ 2	+ .2	+ .8	+ 4	+ 6	− 5	0	+ 5.6	+ 2.1	+ 6.0	+ .4
Egypt	− 1.3	− 1	− 1.1	− 1.8	− 2	− 3	− 8	− 3	− .3	+ .4	+ 9.0	− 2.7
Switzerland	+ 4.0	+ 4	− .9	− 1.9	+ 8	+ 7	+ 7	+ 5	+16.0	+11.3	+ 2.0	− 3.1
Denmark	+ 2.8	+ 3	− 1.0	− 1.9	+ 7	+ 7	− 7	+ 2	+15.7	+ 3.8	+14.0	+ 7.4

Country	D-AXIS STRENGTH—WEAKNESS				E-AXIS RESOURCE ABUNDANCE—POVERTY				F-AXIS TECHNOLOGICAL ADVANCEMENT—BACKWARDNESS			
	People	*Nation*	*State*	*Government*	*People* (from Cols. 7 and 19)	*Nation* (from Cols. 20, 21 and 22)	*State* (from Cols. 16 and 18)	*Government* (from Cols. 14 and 44)	*People* (from Cols. 2, 21, and 22)	*Nation*	*State*	*Government*
	39	40	41	42	43	44	45	46	47	48	49	50
World	−12	0	− 8.0	−10.0	0	+56.0	+76.0	+30.0	0	+ 7	+ 8	+10
China	0	− .3	+ 6.3	0	− 1.7	+ 4.1	+ 7.6	+ 1.8	− 2.6	− 4	− 4	+ 2
India	− 1	+ .6	− 1.4	− 7.8	− 3.3	+ 4.5	+ 1.3	+ 1.9	− .1	− 3	− 3	+ 3
USSR	+ 1	+ 1.0	+ 3.3	+17.0	+10.4	+10.4	+14.0	+ 4.8	+ 4.7	+ 3	+ 4	+ 9
US	+ 6	+ 7.0	+ 8.0	+ 9.0	+10.0	+ 8.0	+ 6.0	+ 6.0	+ 5.0	+ 6	+ 7	+ 8
Germany	+ 4	− .2	− 5.3	− 3.4	− 3.0	+ 3.2	+ .4	+ 2.2	+ 5.4	+ 4	+ 6	+ 7
Brazil	− 2	− 1.3	0	− 4.0	+ .4	0	+ 3.6	+ .05	− .1	− 1	0	+ 2
U.K.	+ 7	− .4	+ 3.1	+12.0	− 3.0	+ .9	+ .2	+ 1.3	+ 2.8	+ 5	+ 6	+ 7
Italy	+ 3	− 1.3	− 4.6	+ 1.0	− 3.3	+ .6	+ .03	+ .3	+ 1.4	0	+ 4	− 1
France	+ 5	− 1.3	− 3.4	+ 3.3	− 3.2	+ .5	+ .2	+ .05	+ 1.8	+ 2	+ 4	− 1
Egypt	− 4	− 1.4	− 6.1	− 4.5	− 3.1	− .8	+ .3	− .4	− 1.3	− 5	− 4	0
Switzerland	+ 9	− 1.4	− 1.8	+ 3.0	− 3.1	− 1.0	− .1	− .4	+ 1.3	+ 4	+ 6	+ 6
Denmark	+ 8	− 1.4	− 6.4	0	− 3.1	− .9	− .1	− .4	+ 5.0	+ 4	+ 6	+ 5

TABLE 4: Location of States on the Value Axes

Country	X-AXIS OBJECTIVITY—SUBJECTIVITY				Y-AXIS ABSTRACTNESS—CONCRETENESS				U-AXIS LIBERALITY—RESTRICTIVENESS			
	People	Nation	State	Government	People	Nation	State	Government	People	Nation	State	Government
	51	52	53	54	55	56	57	58	59	60	61	62
World	0	0	0	0	0	0	0	0	0	0	0	0
China	+1	0	—4	—5	—7	—1	+2	+4	—5	—6	—7	—8
India	—5	—4	—3	—2	—5	—3	+1	+2	—4	—5	—6	—7
USSR	—3	—4	—5	—6	—1	0	+3	+5	—7	—8	—9	—10
US	+2	+3	+4	+5	+3	+4	+5	+6	+5	+6	+7	+8
Germany	—1	0	+1	+2	+6	+7	+8	+9	—1	—2	—2	—3
Brazil	—6	—5	—5	—4	—3	—2	—1	0	—3	—4	—5	—6
U.K.	+6	+7	+8	+9	+2	+3	+4	+5	+5	+5	+6	+6
Italy	+4	+5	+6	+7	+7	+8	+9	+10	+1	0	—1	—2
France	+5	+6	+7	+8	+8	+9	+10	+11	+2	+1	0	—1
Egypt	—7	—8	—8	—9	—4	—1	+3	+4	—5	—6	—7	—8
Switzerland	+7	+8	+9	+10	+4	+5	+6	+7	+3	+2	+1	0
Denmark	+3	+4	+5	+6	+5	+6	+7	+8	+4	+5	+6	+7

Country	V-AXIS SITUATION—SELF-ORIENTATION				W-AXIS AFFIRMATION—NEGATION				Z-AXIS MANIPULATION—CONTEMPLATION			
	People 63	Nation 64	State 65	Government 66	People 67	Nation 68	State 69	Government 70	People 71	Nation 72	State 73	Government 74
World	0	0	0	0	0	0	0	0	0	0	0	0
China	+4	+2	−2	−8	−3	−2	+1	+4	−7	−2	+5	+8
India	−2	0	+3	+5	−7	−6	−4	−2	−8	−6	+3	+6
USSR	−7	−8	−9	−10	−1	0	+2	+5	−1	+2	+8	+12
US	+1	0	−1	−2	+8	+9	+10	+11	+4	+5	+6	+7
Germany	−1	0	+2	+4	+3	+4	+5	+6	+7	+8	+9	+10
Brazil	−4	−5	−6	−7	−4	−3	−3	−2	−3	−1	+2	+4
U.K.	+5	+5	+6	+6	+6	+7	+8	+9	+5	+6	+7	+8
Italy	+2	+2	+3	+3	+1	0	−1	−2	+6	+6	+7	+7
France	+3	+3	+4	+4	+2	+1	0	−1	+6	+6	+7	+7
Egypt	−5	−3	−1	+1	−8	−7	−5	−3	−5	−3	+1	+5
Switzerland	+7	+8	+9	+10	+5	+6	+7	+8	+1	+2	+3	+4
Denmark	+8	+9	+10	+11	+4	+3	+2	+1	+2	+3	+4	+5

LOCATION OF STATES WITHIN THE ANALYTICAL FIELD

Explanation of Diagrams (pp. 547-549) and Tables (586-593)

The tables present the data from which the diagrams on pp. 547, 548 and
549 were constructed. They give the size (indicated on the diagram by the
relative area of circles) of each of the "peoples," "nations," "states," and
"governments" selected to illustrate a variety of cultural and power conditions;
the various statistical indices utilized in locating these entities on the axes; and
the actual location of each on these axes.

The "populations" (col. 1) are for the year 1953 as given in the *Britannica
Book of the Year*, 1954, "Areas and Populations."

The "people" (col. 2) consists of the population affected by policy decisions
and consequently manifesting attitudes, at least after the event, which have
some influence on subsequent decisions. Under modern conditions the "people"
would include that portion of the entire population dependent upon the national economy, thus excluding primitive and tribal peoples supporting themselves by a subsistence economy in small communities.

The "nation" (col. 3) consists of that portion of the population which is
interested in national cultural values, pays some attention to the bearing of
political decisions upon these values, and, therefore, develops attitudes and
predispositions indirectly affecting public opinion. Under modern conditions,
the "nation" may be roughly measured by the literate population of the state. In
the case of the "world community" however, it consists only of that small proportion of the world's population aware of a developing world culture. This would
include members of associations interested in world citizenship and the United
Nations, and in other international associations which examine cultural and
political problems from a world point of view. The percentages of literacy in
the adult population were estimated from figures in the *Britannica Book of the
Year*, 1954, "Illiteracy," and from the *Encyclopaedia of the Social Sciences*,
"Literacy."

The "state" (col. 4) consists of that portion of the population which is articulate on national political issues through discussion, participation in political
parties, voting, and other direct contributions to the formation of public opinion. While in democratic countries this could be roughly measured by actual
voting (not potential voting or eligibility to vote), in totalitarian countries,
where the voter has no choice, other criteria such as participation in party
activity or civic organizations were considered. While in general the "state"
would be a smaller proportion of the population than the "nation," this may
not be true of countries with a very low literacy rate, such as India and China.
In the case of the "world community" only the estimated portion of the world's
population contributing to "world public opinion" by being articulate in international institutions and associations, was included. In the five great occidental

powers—the United States, the Soviet Union, the United Kingdom, France, and Germany—about 50 per cent, according to the above criteria, appear to be articulate in national affairs. Press surveys indicate that about 33 per cent of political editorials in the leading papers of these countries deal with international affairs, but of this proportion only 7 per cent deal with international symbols or institutions.[1] If it is assumed that this proportion of press attention indicates popular attention, only about one per cent (.50 x .33 x .07) of the population in these countries were "world citizens" in the sense of articulateness concerning world institutions. In the world as a whole, only about 20 per cent of the population appears to be articulate on national affairs compared to 50 per cent in the great western powers, but it seems probable that in the smaller countries and in the less developed countries, the proportion of that group interested in international institutions is enough greater to compensate for this difference. Of this small number of "world citizens," it seems unlikely that more than half identify themselves more with the world community than with their respective states.

The "government" (col. 5) consists of the portion of the population exercising leadership in policy-making for the group. It refers not to the ruling class or elite from which policy-makers are drawn,[2] but to the actually influential, which by virtue of official policy-making positions, official positions advisory to policy-makers, or positions in party or non-governmental pressure groups, actually influence the policy-makers directly. It is difficult to isolate a single criterion for measuring this group. The proportion of the population in the civil service would give a rough indication, but where the government is decentralized a much larger proportion of the civil servants are influential in policy-making. Furthermore, where the government leaves a large sphere for individual initiative in political, economic, religious, or other activites, leadership in these activities outside of the official government exerts a direct influence on policy-making. Finally, the smaller the population, the larger the proportion likely to be influential in policy-making. A certain minimum size of legislative, judicial and administrative decision-makers is necessary to obtain the degree of specialization required under the complex conditions of modern civilization, however small the population may be. Thus in proportion as government is centralized and totalitarian and the population of the state is large, the proportion of leadership to the population may be expected to shrink. The estimates presented in column five give consideration to all these factors. In the case of the "world community," the total number of persons directly engaged in international institutions is less than 10,000 and the number of national government officials and officials in non-governmental organizations directly influencing them cannot be over 15,000. Thus it seems unlikely that over 25,000 or one in 100,000 of the world's population directly influence decisions of world institutions.

---

[1] Quincy Wright, *Problems of Stability and Progress in International Relations* (University of California Press, 1954) p. 222, summarizing Ithiel de Sola Pool, *Symbols of Nationalism and Internationalism* (Stanford University Press, 1951).

[2] See Harold D. Lasswell, Daniel Lerner, and C. Easton Rothwell, *The Comparative Study of Elites* (Stanford University, Stanford University Press, 1952), p. 8.

The location of each of the thirteen "peoples," "nations," "states," and "governments" on each of the twelve axes (cols. 27-74) was determined in the following manner.

The thirteen "peoples" were ranged in rank order according to the author's judgment in respect to each axis by answering the questions given below. The thirteen "nations," "states," and "governments" were similarly arranged. By judging the degree of similarity or difference of adjacent entities on this rank order scale, utilizing statistical indices where available, the latter was converted to a scale of equal-appearing intervals.

To convert these continua to locations on the axis, an average or zero point was judged on each, and the position of the United States on each axis was judged (cols. 25-26). With these two points determined, the position of each of the other thirteen entities on the axis could be established.

Measurement of a group's capabilities and values in international relations assumes that the group makes decisions with some independence. It does not, however, imply complete equality of status. Thus "the world" as organized in the United Nations can be located on the capability axes along with states, sovereign and semi-sovereign, although the location of its "government" is atypical because of its imperfect organization for decision-making.

On each of the axes except the D-axis (strength-weakness) the "world" (treated as a "people" or economic community) was regarded as the average and placed at the zero point. On the D-axis the "world's people" were considered to be the weakest of all the peoples considered. Though potentially larger and stronger than the "people" of any one state, the people of the world are so divided by barriers and are so lacking in attitudes favorable to a world community, that this judgment seemed necessary. On the value axes, the "world" treated as a "nation" or cultural complex, as a "state" or condition of political opinion, and as a "government" or formulator of policy, was also regarded as average and located at the zero point. But on the capability axes, this would obviously not be the case.

In judging the relative position of the "people," "nation," "state," and "government" of a given entity, it was assumed that the nation and state would be located between the people and the government and that the people would be nearer the zero point than the government; but in some cases empirical data or subjective judgments overruled these assumptions.

Statistical indices should of course be utilized to verify or modify judgments based upon this highly subjective method. With respect to many of the axes in the capability field, such indices were readily available and were utilized. Indices based upon measurements of attitudes, opinions, laws and policies might be devised for the value axes; but this would be a complicated process and no such attempt was made.

Statistical indices available through a period of time could be utilized to indicate the rate of change of the location of each "people," "nation," "state," and "government" on each axis, but this was not attempted. The vectors in the diagrams indicating such rates of movement of governments in the analytical field were based on subjective judgments.

The results presented in the tables and diagrams are in large measure based upon the author's subjective judgment, and are, therefore, far from reliable.

They are presented in the hope that they may stimulate others to develop more objective methods and indices.

The questions providing the bases for rank order arrangement in respect to each axis and the statistical indices utilized in some instances are described in the following paragraphs.

A-AXIS (energy-lethargy). *Which entity has the most social energy?* This was measured for the "people" by per capita income (col. 6), for the "nation" by the estimated average income of the literate (col. 7), for the "state" by the total national income (col. 8), and for the "government" by the annual national budget (col. 9). The special significance given to these terms as applied to the "world" has been indicated. The sum of the budgets of the United Nations and the Specialized Agencies was considered the budget of the "world's" government.

B-AXIS (flexibility-rigidity). *Which entity has the greatest capacity to adapt its domestic institutions to new situations?* This was intended to apply to domestic institutions, not to foreign policy. Decentralization, tending to maximize the freedom of individuals, of localities and of functional organizations, was deemed to make for such adaptability of domestic institutions, though it might make for unadaptability of foreign policy. Thus a centralized dictatorship, though tending to be extremely rigid in the sense here used, may have a great deal of flexibility in foreign-policy making. The freedom of the individual may militate against the freedom of the government.

Flexibility was measured for the "people" by the estimated degree of freedom of the individual from arbitrary control of his activities by social custom, public opinion, law, or administration (due process of law and equal protection of laws); for the "nation," by the estimated degree of freedom of the individual to believe, to express himself, to communicate, to associate, to teach and to learn, without censorship of religion, art, ideas, opinions, or associations (freedom of opinion); for the "state," by the estimated degree of constitutional and practical distribution of the functions and activities of government among regional or local agencies with independent powers (geographical decentralization); and for the "government," by the estimated degree of constitutional and practical distribution of the functions and activities of the central government among agencies, officials, or parties with independent powers (functional decentralization). While the "world" was considered average in respect to the "people," in respect to the others it was considered the most flexible.

C-AXIS (co-operation-isolation). *Which entity is most capable of participating in effective international institutions?* Such capability was believed to depend, on the one hand, upon relative necessity to co-operate arising from economic and military inter-dependency, and on the other hand, upon a disposition to co-operate, manifested by attitudes, opinions, acts, and policies. With modern military techniques all states are highly vulnerable to attack. There is little difference in this respect, even though the probability of such attack may vary with relative power or defense capacity measure on the D-axis. The criteria for determining relative necessity to co-operate were, therefore, drawn from the economic field. States do differ greatly in the degree of their dependence upon international trade, or, conversely, the degree of their economic self-sufficiency. It should be noticed that a nonco-operative or isolationist capability is not equivalent to a demand for independence from imperial control. Groups demanding political independence often manifest great co-operativeness internationally. An "imperialist-self-determination" axis would refer to values rather than to capabilities.

Location on the C-axis was measured for the "people" by the amount of international trade per capita (col. 10); for the "nation" by the number of international letters per capita (col. 11) (in the case of the "world" this was based on an estimate of the per capita international correspondence of those sufficiently aware of the world community to be considered "world citizens"); for the "state" by the proportion of international trade in the national economy (or the ratio of international trade per capita to income per capita (col. 12)) multiplied by the degree of actual participation in the United Nations and the Specialized Agencies rated according to relative importance; [3] and for the "government," by an estimate of the relative internationalism of foreign policy added to an estimate of the relative internationalism (free trade) of economic policy.

D-AXIS (military strength-military weakness). *Which is most capable of defending its territory from invasion?* Such capability, so far as it can be measured without reference to the particular geographic relations of the states involved in a conflict, was believed to depend on the morale of the people, the military potential of the nation, the armed forces immediately available to the state, and the military effectiveness of the organization of the government. Capacity to make allies may have major military importance in a long war [4] but it was not considered a factor on this axis. Capacity to make allies is a consequence of capacity to co-operate measured on the C-axis. Many factors enter into each of these elements of military strength or weakness.

The location of the "people" on this axis was actually measured by estimates of their relative spirit of loyalty and patriotism. This spirit may vary rapidly in time. Thus estimates of the degree of "patriotism" or "nationalism" of the people of the principal states in 1954 [5] were very different from estimates made in respect to the same states in the early 1930's.[6] In reference to the "world," the loyalty and patriotism of the "people" referred not to the average degree of loyalty to their own state by each people, but to the degree of "world loyalty" or "internationalism" of the world's people compared with national loyalties, and was rated very low.

For the "nation" military strength was measured by the product of the population and energy available to it (col. 1 x col. 14). Manpower and industrialization were considered the main elements in military potential. Actual energy production (col. 14) rather than energy resources (col. 16) (which figure on the E-axis) was employed on the theory that unexploited energy resources (which average more than 5000 times actual energy production) were not a

[3] U.N. counted ten points, I.L.O., F.A.O., UNESCO, and W.H.O. five points each, the Bank, the Fund, and ICITO, three points each, ICAO, U.P.U., I.T.U., W.M.O., and IMCO, one point each (col. 15).

[4] Quincy Wright, *Problems of Stability and Progress in International Relations*, p. 154, 245.

[5] See Pool, *op. cit.*, p. 55.

[6] See Q. Wright, *A Study of War*, p. 1000.

military potential, since they could not be utilized in a major degree during the course of a war. In respect both to population and energy production, the "world" would theoretically equal that of all the "nations" added together, but since most of this population is identified with the national symbols it seemed more realistic to consider only the small group of persons actively participating in world politics as a military potential for the "world" (col. 4 x col. 14).

For the "state" strength was measured by the product of the estimated effectiveness for defense respectively (1) of geographical position, including fortifications and bases and (2) of mobile armaments in being including land, sea, and air forces. For the world, such effectiveness would depend upon the relation of the factors making for a stable or unstable power equilibrium, and on the effectiveness or ineffectiveness of the system of collective security. From either of these points of view, the "world" is today very weak.

For the "government" strength was measured by the product of the estimated effectiveness respectively of political organization and military organization. Both imply a high degree of centralization; consequently this axis tends to be the converse of the B-axis. Capacity to make rapid and effective group decisions implies considerable institutional rigidity, though too much rigidity may be detrimental.[7] Political organization refers to capacity to mobilize manpower and industry for war and depends to a considerable extent on constitutional and legal structure. Military organization refers to capacity to plan strategy, to move military forces, to co-ordinate information, and to make decisions rapidly. It depends on executive structure, line and staff relations, and skills in strategic planning.[8]

E-AXIS (abundance-poverty of resources). *Which has the most capacity to advance in wealth and power through utilization of natural resources?* This axis refers to *potential* energy, wealth and power, and differs from the A, D, and F axes, which refer to aspects of *actual* energy, wealth, and power.

This was measured for the "people" by the sum of the estimated mechanical energy resources and land area per capita. Precise estimates might consider all resources in detail—agricultural land of various grades, rainfall, minerals, coal, oil, water power, etc.—but, in view of the probable future introduction of new resources such as deserts for sun engines, tides, fissionable materials, etc., such estimates would not long remain more accurate than estimates based on area and mechanical energy resources alone. Estimates of mechanical energy resources made by A. P. Usher were utilized.[9] For the "nation" resource abundance was measured by the school population, counting those in higher education ten times those in secondary, and those in secondary five times those in primary education (cols. 20, 21, 22).[10] This provides an index of the degree of education of the population of the rising generation, and this may be the

---

[7] Quincy Wright, "Freedom and Authority in International Organization" in *Freedom and Authority in Our Time, Twelfth Symposium on Science, Philosophy and Religion* (New York, Harper, 1953), pp. 170 ff.

[8] See Quincy Wright, *A Study of War*, p. 291; *Problems of Stability and Progress in International Relations*, p. 245.

[9] See W. F. Ogburn, editor, *Technology and International Relations* (University of Chicago Press, 1949), p. 69.

[10] See United Nations, *Statistical Yearbook*, 1953.

major resource of the nation's culture. For the "state," potential resources were measured by the sum of the area and the mechanical energy resources (col. 16 and col. 18). While the state's actual energy was measured by the national income (A-axis), its potential energy was believed to depend on its area and mechanical energy resources, setting limits to the growth of its population and wealth. For the "government" resources were confined to those available, measured by the sum of mechanical energy production (col. 14) and skilled population. The latter was estimated in the same manner as the resources of the "nation." While the government's actual wealth is measured by the national budget (A-axis), its potential wealth—assuming the state's area remains constant—would seem to depend on the available skilled population and energy production setting limits to available sources of national income and taxation.

F-AXIS (technological advancement-backwardness). *Which entity is most advanced in quality and quantity of technological skill and equipment?* This was measured for the "people" by estimating the proportion of the population in higher, technical and secondary institutions. Those in secondary education were added to those in higher education giving double weight to the latter. (cols. 21, 22). For the "nation" technological advancement was measured by estimating the favorableness of public opinion and social policy to science and technology. In the case of the "world," this referred only to the population aware of world culture. For the "state," technological advancement was estimated by the degree of actual utilization of advanced technologies in the national economy. In the case of the world, this referred only to the population directly contributing to the development of international organization. For the "government," an estimate of the relative favorableness of official policy to technology, technological education, and economic development was used as a measure of technological advancement. In the case of the "world," this referred to the policy of the United Nations and its Specialized Agencies.

X-AXIS (objectivity-subjectivity in evaluation). *Which entity tends to be most impartial and least prejudiced in judging the values involved in a situation?* Where class or caste distinctions, rigid ideologies, or hysterical feelings are influential, judgment tends to be subjective. Where specialized knowledge of the consequences of action, procedures permitting presentation of all interests, and deliberation in decision making, are utilized, judgments tend to be objective. It was assumed that in democracies, the "government"—representing an average opinion and with better sources of information—tends to be more objective than the people; but that in autocracies, the influence of ideologies upon the government tends to make it more subjective than the people. To locate the "people," on this axis, and on all the value axes, the stated question was asked with respect to private attitudes; to locate the "nation," it was asked with respect to prevailing public opinion; to locate the "state," it was asked with respect to prevailing laws and procedures; and with respect to the "government," it was asked with respect to official policies.

Y-AXIS (abstractness-concreteness in perception). *Which entity tends most to perceive situations by deduction from abstract conceptions and least by immediate sensory experience?* Where rational classifications, typical forms, and generalizations based upon extensive experience direct attention to the "essentials" of a situation, perception tends to be abstract. Where interesting details, unique circumstances, and sensational incidents attract attention, perception tends to be concrete. It was assumed that governments obliged to plan and to act for the future tend to be more abstract in evaluation than people.

U-AXIS (liberality-restrictiveness in identification). *Which entity tends to be most receptive to new interests, goals and purposes and least cautious in protecting itself from innovations?* Where legalistic interpretations, contractual relations, and suspicious attitudes define and protect existing interests, identifications are restrictive. Where abundant associations and mutual confidence continually expand interests, identifications are liberal. It was assumed that established governments, regarding themselves as trustees of popular interests, tend to be more restrictive than the people in identifying themselves with novel interests, but that revolutionary governments are often more liberal than their people in this respect.

V-AXIS (situation oriented-self oriented in interests). *Which entity tends most to define interests by the total situation, giving attention to principles, acknowledging the reciprocal interests of others, rather than to the immediate wants and needs of the self?* Where ideas of the whole, the general good, and broad principles of conduct are influential, interests are situation oriented. Where immediate wishes, historic goals, and internally-generated objectives are influential, interests are self oriented. It was assumed that strong governments tend to be more self oriented than their peoples, and that weak governments, because of their appreciation that it is necessary for their survival, tend to be more situation oriented than their people.

W-AXIS (affirmation-negation in expectations). *Which entity tends to have the most hopeful expectations in facing new situations?* Entities which are welcoming, favorable and extroverted have affirmative expectations; those which are reluctant, suspicious, and aloof, have negative expectations. It was assumed that in conservative, *status quo,* or feeble states, the government tends to be more negative than the people; but in revolutionary, dynamic, and powerful states, the government tends to be more affirmative than the people.

Z-AXIS (manipulation or contemplation in action). *Which entity tends to be most interested in controlling and least interested in fully understanding situations?* Where an entity tends to relate situations to its goals and to act promptly, impulsively and vigorously upon the perception and evaluation of a situation, it is manipulative; where it tends to examine, reflect, and consider the causes and effects involved in a situation, it is contemplative. It was assumed that governments tend to be more manipulative than peoples, because it is more necessary for them to act.

PATHS OF INFLUENCE WITHIN THE ANALYTICAL FIELD

Explanation of Diagram (p. 564)

The diagram on p. 564 suggests the paths and direction of influence of the axes upon one another in the analytical field, with special reference to the influence of each upon the progress of civilization and war (national aggressiveness). The factors making for civilization and for war are in considerable measure the same. Thus energy, specialization, high tension, insecurity, resource poverty, dissatisfaction, expansiveness, manipulativeness, and restlessness make for both. Strength, however, makes for unreliability, which makes for war and against civilization, though it favors security which makes against both. Thus its influence is indeterminate. The influence of co-operativeness and of technological advancement is similarly indeterminate. Objectivity makes for rationality and tolerance, which make for progress and against war. Abstractness makes for rationality and intolerance; thus its influence on civilization and war is indeterminate. Democracy, individualism, and optimism make for progress and against war.

The writer has elsewhere [1] suggested that modern civilization has been measured by the progress of liberalism, humanism, pragmatism, and relativism. In the senses used, these terms appear to be related respectively to individualism, democracy, rationality, and tolerance. But according to this diagram, democracy and individualism, while influenced in the same direction by liberality (U-axis) are influenced in an opposite direction by situation orientation (V-axis). Rationality and tolerance, while influenced in the same direction by objectivity (X-axis) are influenced in an opposite direction by abstractness (Y-axis). Thus, according to this interpretation, the progress of modern civilization, while favored by increasing objectivity in evaluation and liberality in identification, has required a balance of abstract and concrete interpretations of reality [2] and a balance of situation orientation and self orientation in decision-making.[3] If one assumes that balance in all values is desirable for continuous progress of civilization, it may be that modern civilization, influenced overmuch by the standards of science, has erred in neglecting the importance of some subjectivity in evaluation and of some restrictiveness in identification. This unbalance may have contributed to evoking enemies of modern civilization, such as fascism and communism, which over-emphasize these characteristics. Balance on all axes of the value field, which would imply a balance of peacefulness and aggressiveness, may be the key to continued progress in civilization.

This diagram illustrates an hypothesis, analyzing the major factors involved in international relations and the direction of influence exerted by each upon others. This hypothesis cannot be considered valid except in so far as tested by empirical data. No such test has been made. If indices could be found for measuring these factors and for correlating them, the method of "path coefficients" might serve as such a test.[4]

[1] *A Study of War*, pp. 169 ff., 615 ff.
[2] *Op. cit.*, p. 435.
[3] *Op. cit.*, p. 968.
[4] Sewall Wright, "Correlation and Causation," *Journal of Agricultural Research* (Government Printing Office, Washington, D. C.), XX, Jan. 3, 1921, pp. 557 ff; "Theory of Path Coefficients," *Genetics*, VIII, May, 1923, pp. 24 ff.

INDEX

(Bibliographic references are italicized)

Abbaside Caliphs, 382

Absolutism, 4; and centralization, 294; rise of, 175; *see also* Autocracy

Academic freedom, and international education, 322; and research, 78

Academy of Political Science, 26

Acculturation, and communication, 284

Action, and communication, 283; spontaneous and deliberate, 460; *see also* System of action

Acton, Lord, 89, 103, 263, 346, *471*, 785; on history, 84

Actual, type of reality, 11

Adams, Brooks, 89

Adams, Charles Francis, *301*

Adams, Henry, 89, 378, 387

Adams, John, *323*

Adjudication, and diplomacy, 160; procedures of, 454

Adler, Mortimer J., *60*, 419, *495*, *528*

Administration, and organization, 199, 200

Administrative analysis, of international organization, 209

Administrators, on colonies, 192

Age, and area theory of diffusion, 377; of societies, 342

Aggression, crime of, 219; and defense, 142; definition of, 581; and international education, 316; under international law, 229; and leadership types, 430; psychic, 428; legal and sociological meanings, 142, 143; and tension, 430; and war, 148

Aggressiveness, causes of, 98, 603; diagram of causes, 564

Agrarian states, characteristics of, 255

Airplane, influence of, 382; invention of, 371

À Kempis, Thomas, 537, 539

Alexander, Franz, *212*, *434*

Alexander I, Czar, 37

Algeria, 185

Aliens, attitude toward, 427; diplomatic protection of, 182

Alihan, Milla Aissa, *410*, *528*

Alison, Sir Archibald, *366*

Allee, Warder C., *60*, *495*

Allport, Gordon W., *301*

Almond, Gabriel, *80*, *301*, *323*, *410*, 558, 569

Alsop, Joseph, *178*

Alternatives, and continua, 454

Althusius, Johannes, 489

Ambiguity, of communications, 280; in propaganda, 287; sources of, 282, 283; of reality and truth, 9 f., 16 f.; of key terms, ix; of United Nations Charter, 204; value of, 280, 284

American Academy of Arts and Sciences, 481

American Academy of Social and Political Science, 26

American Association for the United Nations, *323*

American Association of University Professors, *323*

American Council on Education, *323*

American Council of Learned Societies, 26

American Economic Association, 26

American Historical Association, *323*

American Philosophical Society, 25

American Political Science Association, 26

American Society of International Law, 26, *324*

Ames, Fisher, on autocracy and democracy, 565

Analysis, methods of, 125, 126; and synthesis, 57, 481, 482, 483

Analytical field, 543 f.; and conceptions of the world, 566; co-ordinates of, 546 f.; description of, 545; diagrams of, 547 f.; location of organizations in, 554 f.; location of persons in, 553 f.; location of states in, 595 f.; movements in, 546; paths of influence in, diagram, 564, 602; statistical tables on, 586, 587

Anarchy, and decentralized communications, 294

Anderson, Frank Maloy, *166*

Angell, Norman, 240, *301*, 322

Angell, Robert, 53, *410*

Angle, Paul, on history, 85

Anglo-American relations, 6

Animals, guided by instinct, 298; societies of, 55

Congress. *See* United States Congress

Conquest, of territory, 345

Conscience, and population type, 360

Consent of states, source of international law, 216

Constitution. *See* United States constitution

Constitutionalism, and foreign policy-making, 170, 175

Contemplation, and manipulation, 114

Content analysis, 272; of communications, 277; sources and evidence, 278; and strategic policies, 279

Contingency, in history, 87; and reality, 11

Control, and influence, 133; national and international, 581; of foreign policy, *see* Foreign policy-making

Cooley, Charles Horton, *302, 410, 426, 427, 434;* on communication, 270

Co-operation, and conflict, 393; between enemies, 162; and organizations, 205, 206, 396; and opposition, 205, 206, 241, 242, 396; and social change, 393

Co-operative research, 57

Copeland, D. B., *302*

Copernicus, 443, 508, 532

Corbett, Percy, *212, 234, 325, 495*

Conwell-Evans, T. P., *212*

Corps Diplomatique, 163

Correlation, methods of, 546

Cortez, Hernando, 33, 188, 190

Corwin, Edward S., 178

Cosmopolitanism, and economic policy, 258; and Marxism, 246; meaning of, 4, 44; and nationalism, 2, 45, 59, 241, 276, 521; weakness of, 466, 467

Costa Rica, 185

Council for Education in World Citizenship, 325

Council on Foreign Relations, New York, 26, 28, 80, 96, *325;* and Study of International Relations, viii

Counts, George S., *322, 325*

Cousins, Norman, *472*

Cowles Commission for Research in Economics, 265

Craig, G. A., *156*

Crandall, Samuel B., *178*

Crane, Ronald S., *302*

Creativity, of man, 12

Credibility, of communications, 286, 291, 292

Criteria, of choice, 454

Criticism, forms of, 277 f.

Croce, Benedetto, *302*

Cromer, Lord, *196*

Crowther, J. G., *387*

Crucé, Emeric, 37, 39

Crusades, 295

Cultural ideals, of states, diagram, 455

Cultural lag, 377

Culture, definition, 555; and education, 286, 311, 314; formation of, 284; and inequality, 184; and location of states in analytical field, 555; material and moral, 369, 370, 373; meaning of, 284; national and world, 274; and personality, 433; and technology, 373; and values, 442; universal, 316; *see also* Universal culture, World culture

Cultures, adaptation to conditions, 315; American and Chinese, 458; capacity to survive, 185; centralization and disintegration of, 468; diffusion of, 284; national, 315, 465; persistence of, 465; progressive and customary, 372; relativism of, 448; static and dynamic, 466, 467; and technological introductions, 372; vulnerability to contacts, 320

Curiosity, and science, 114

Curti, Merle, *302*

Cushman, Robert E., *325*

Custom, and population types, 360; source of international law, 216

Customs unions, 257

Cuvier, Georges, 533

Cybernetics, 57, 116, 270, 449

Cynics, 37

Dahl, Robert A., *179, 410, 472*

Dalton, John, 553

Dampier, Sir W. C., *120*

Dangerfield, Royden, *100, 157, 179, 265*

Dante, 37, 45, 46, 441, 484, 487, 495, 512, 529

Darby, W. Evans, 38, *212*

Darwin, Charles, 45, 113, 241, 342, 393, 443, 489, 518, 533

Darwin, Leonard, *366*

Davidson, Philip, *302*

Davie, Maurice, *366, 411*

Davies, Lord, *212*

Davis, D. H., *349*

Day, Clive, *42, 265*

Day, Edmund E., *325*

Dean, Dorothy Arden, *80*

Death rates, variation of, 353

DeCastro, Josue, *366*

Decatur, Stephen, on loyalty, 21, 66

Decision-makers, experience of, 578; on international relations, 508; location in analytical field, 543; power of, 539